PHILIP'S

COMPACT ATLAS
Britain

Contents

II **Route planning maps** with key to map pages

VIII **Key to road map symbols**

2 **Road maps at 3.3 miles to 1 inch**

289 **Town plans**

- **289** Aberdeen
  - Bath
- **290** Birmingham
- **291** Bristol
- **292** Cardiff
- **293** Cambridge
  - Coventry
- **294** Edinburgh
- **295** Glasgow
- **296** Gloucester
  - Leicester
- **297** Leeds
- **298** Liverpool
- **299** London
- **300** Manchester
- **301** Newcastle
- **302** Nottingham
  - Oxford
- **303** Sheffield
- **304** Swansea
  - York

305 **Index** to road maps of Great Britain

First published in 2006 by
Philip's a division of
Octopus Publishing Group Ltd
2–4 Heron Quays, London E14 4JP
An Hachette Livre UK Company

www.philips-maps.co.uk

Second edition 2007
First impression 2007

Cartography by Philip's
Copyright © 2007 Philip's

Ordnance Survey®

This product includes mapping data licensed from Ordnance Survey®, with the permission of the Controller of Her Majesty's Stationery Office. © Crown copyright 2007. All rights reserved. Licence number 100011710

Data for the speed cameras provided by PocketGPSWorld.com Ltd.

Information for tourist attractions shown on the mapping supplied by VisitBritain.

Information for National Parks, Areas of Outstanding Natural Beauty, National Trails and Country Parks in Wales supplied by the Countryside Council for Wales.

Information for National Parks, Areas of Outstanding Natural Beauty, National Trails and Country Parks in England supplied by the Countryside Agency.

Data for Regional Parks, Long Distance Footpaths and Country Parks in Scotland provided by Scottish Natural Heritage.

Gaelic name forms used in the Western Isles provided by Comhairle nan Eilean.

Data for the National Nature Reserves in England provided by English Nature.

Data for the National Nature Reserves in Wales provided by Countryside Council for Wales. Darparwyd data'n ymwneud â Gwarchodfeydd Natur Cenedlaethol Cymru gan Gyngor Cefn Gwlad Cymru.

Information on the location of National Nature Reserves in Scotland was provided by Scottish Natural Heritage.

Data for National Scenic Areas in Scotland provided by the Scottish Executive Office. Crown copyright material is reproduced with the permission of the Controller of HMSO and the Queen's Printer for Scotland. Licence number C02W0003960.

Printed in Spain by Rotocayfo-Quebecor

About Philip's maps

This atlas contains maps at different scales to get you to your destination as easily and as quickly as possible.

Route planning maps show the whole country at a glance, so you can choose the most direct route, whether on motorways or A-roads. Major road numbers and dual carriageways are all clearly marked.

Road maps at 3.3 miles to 1 inch (Scottish Islands at 6.7 miles to 1 inch) show the road network in detail and mark hundreds of places of interest. The roads are colour coded according to importance. Scenic routes are highlighted and in country areas lanes over 4 metres wide are coloured yellow.

Town plans show the streets in the central area and mark one ways, car parks, stations and important buildings.

Philip's road maps were voted the clearest and most detailed in an independent consumer survey with 442 respondents.

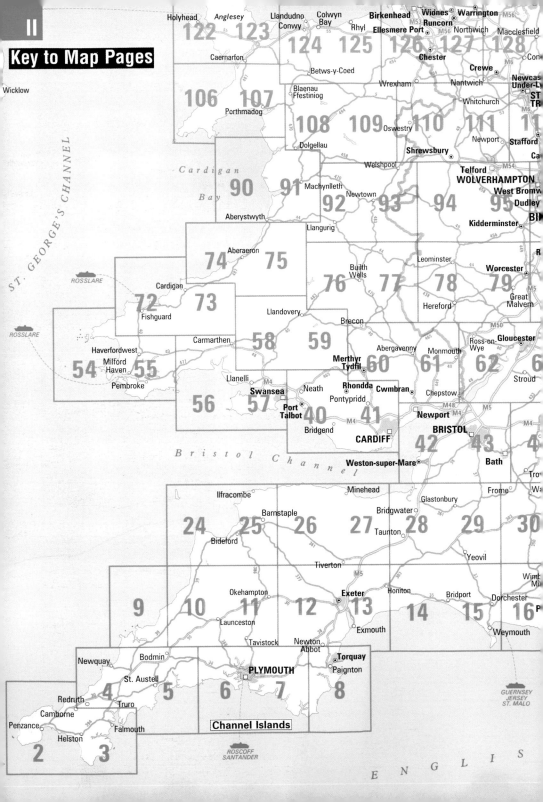

Key to Map Pages

ST. GEORGE'S CHANNEL

ROSSLARE

ROSSLARE

Wicklow

Cardigan Bay

Bristol Channel

B r i s t o l   C h a n n e l

E N G L I S

Holyhead · *Anglesey* · Llandudno · Colwyn Bay · Birkenhead · Widnes · Warrington
Conwy · Rhyl · Runcorn · Northwich · Macclesfield
Ellesmere Port
Chester
Crewe · Newcastle-Under-Lyme
Caernarfon · Betws-y-Coed · Nantwich · ST TR
Wrexham · Whitchurch
Blaenau Ffestiniog
Porthmadog · Dolgellau · Oswestry · Newport · Stafford · Ca
Shrewsbury
Welshpool · Telford · WOLVERHAMPTON
Machynlleth · Newtown · West Brom
Dudley
Aberystwyth · Llangurig · Kidderminster · BI
Leominster · Worcester
Aberaeron · R
Builth Wells · Great Malvern
Cardigan · Llandovery · Hereford
Fishguard · Brecon · Ross-on-Wye · Gloucester
Carmarthen · Abergavenny · Monmouth
Haverfordwest · Stroud
Milford Haven · Llanelli · Merthyr Tydfil · Cwmbran
Pembroke · Swansea · Neath · Rhondda · Chepstow
Port Talbot · Pontypridd · Newport
Bridgend · CARDIFF · BRISTOL
Bath
Weston-super-Mare · Tro · Wa
Minehead · Frome
Ilfracombe · Bridgwater · Glastonbury
Barnstaple · Taunton
Bideford · Yeovil
Tiverton · Wim Mi
Okehampton · Honiton · Bridport · Dorchester
Exeter · Weymouth
Launceston · Exmouth
Tavistock · Newton Abbot · Torquay
Newquay · Bodmin · PLYMOUTH · Paignton
St. Austell
Redruth · Truro · GUERNSEY JERSEY ST. MALO
Camborne · Falmouth
Penzance · Helston
Channel Islands
ROSCOFF SANTANDER

Map page numbers: 122, 123, 124, 125, 126, 127, 128, 106, 107, 108, 109, 110, 111, 90, 91, 92, 93, 94, 95, 74, 75, 76, 77, 78, 79, 72, 73, 58, 59, 60, 61, 62, 54, 55, 56, 57, 40, 41, 42, 43, 24, 25, 26, 27, 28, 29, 30, 9, 10, 11, 12, 13, 14, 15, 16, 2, 3, 4, 5, 6, 7, 8

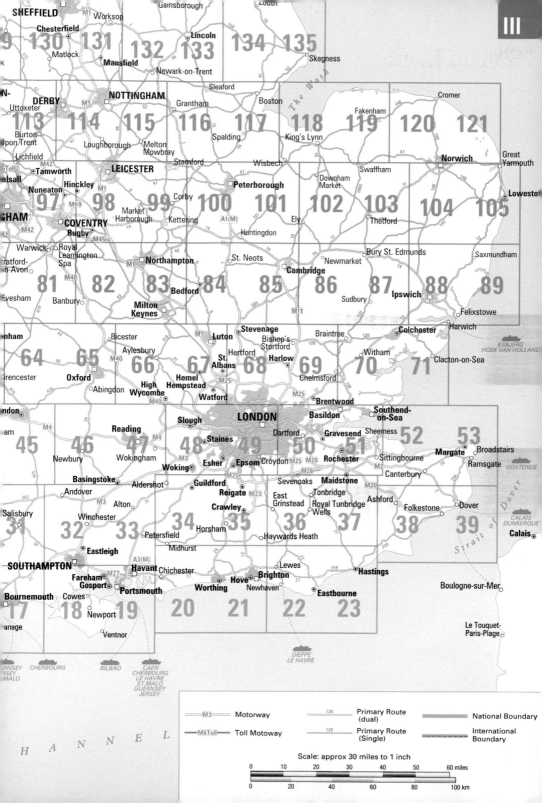

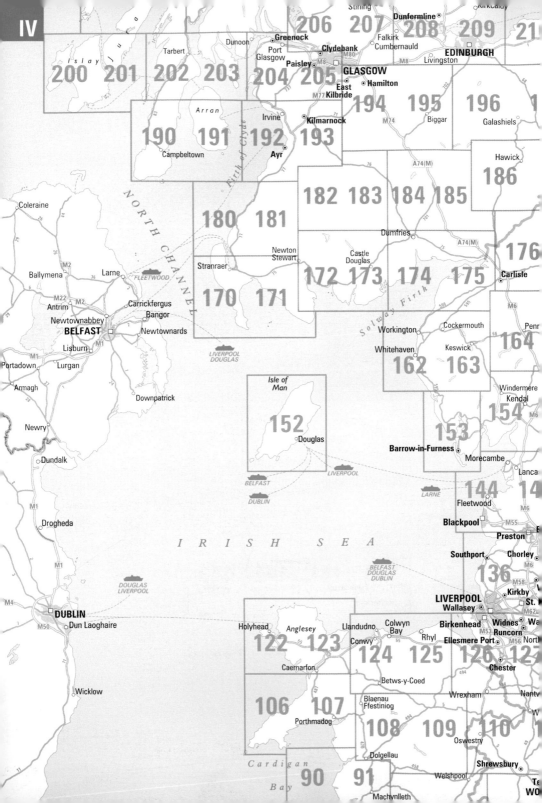

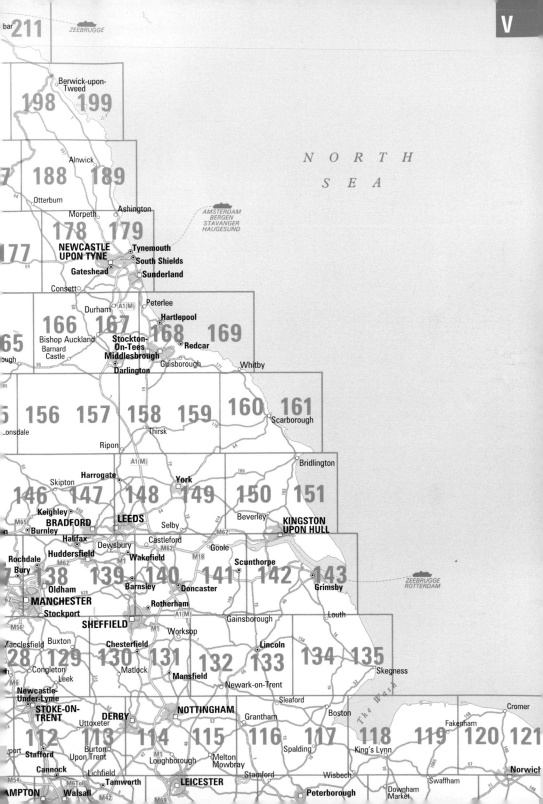

bar **211** *ZEEBRUGGE*

Berwick-upon-Tweed
198   **199**

N O R T H

S E A

Alnwick
7   **188**   **189**

Otterburn

Morpeth   Ashington

AMSTERDAM
BERGEN
STAVANGER
HAUGESUND

178   **179**

NEWCASTLE
UPON TYNE   **Tynemouth**
South Shields
177   **Gateshead**   **Sunderland**

Consett

Durham   A1(M)   Peterlee

Hartlepool
166   **167**   **168**   **169**
Bishop Auckland   **Stockton-**
On-Tees   Redcar
65   Barnard
Castle   **Middlesbrough**
ough   **Darlington**   Guisborough   Whitby

156   **157**   **158**   **159**   **160**   **161**
5   Scarborough
onsdale   Thirsk

Ripon

A1(M)   Bridlington

Harrogate
Skipton   York
146   **147**   **148**   **149**   **150**   **151**
Keighley   Beverley
BRADFORD   **KINGSTON**
M65   Burnley   **LEEDS**   Selby   **UPON HULL**
Halifax   Dewsbury   Castleford
Rochdale   **Huddersfield**   **Wakefield**   Goole
Bury   M62   M18
7   **138**   **139**   **140**   **141**   **142**   **143**
Oldham   **Barnsley**   Scunthorpe   Grimsby
MANCHESTER   **Doncaster**
Stockport   **Rotherham**   *ZEEBRUGGE*
ROTTERDAM
M56   **SHEFFIELD**   Louth
Macclesfield   Buxton   Worksop   Gainsborough
28   **129**   **130**   **131**   **132**   **133**   **134**   **135**
Congleton   Chesterfield   Lincoln
Leek   Matlock   Skegness
Newcastle-   **Mansfield**
Under-Lyme   Newark-on-Trent
STOKE-ON-   Sleaford
TRENT   **NOTTINGHAM**   Grantham   Boston   Cromer
Uttoxeter   **The Wash**
112   **113**   **114**   **115**   **116**   **117**   **118**   **119**   **120**   **121**
Stafford   Burton   Spalding   King's Lynn   Fakenham
port   Upon Trent   Melton   Wisbech   Norwich
Cannock   Lichfield   Loughborough   Mowbray   Stamford   Swaffham
M54   **Tamworth**   **LEICESTER**   Downham
AMPTON   **Walsall**   M42   **Peterborough**   Market

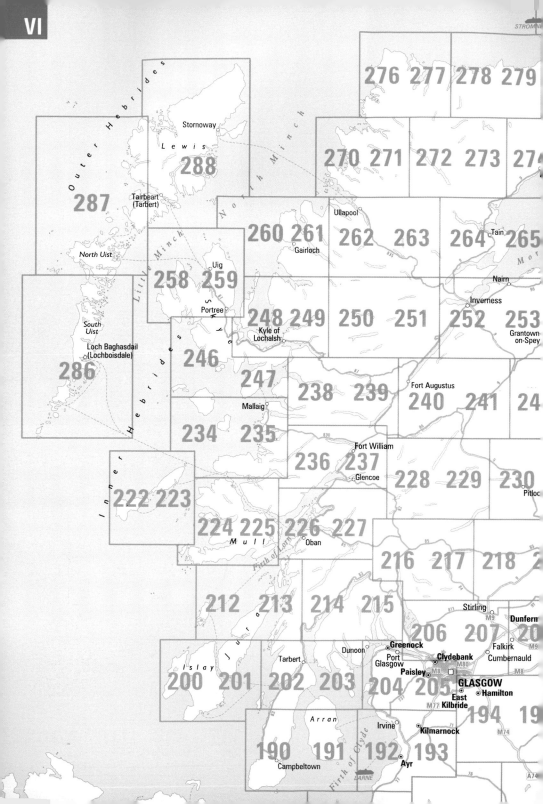

Shetland

284

M a i n l a n d

Lerwick

285

BERGEN
TORSHAVN
SEYDISFJORDUR
(May–Sept)

ABERDEEN
KIRKWALL

Orkney

282

Kirkwall
Mainland

ABERDEEN
LERWICK

Pentland Firth

283

Thurso

Wick

N O R T H

S E A

281

Wick

Pentland Firth

75

rth

66 267 Fraserburgh

gin 268 269

Peterhead

54 255 256 257

Aberdeen KIRKWALL
LERWICK

243 244 245

Stonehaven

31 232 233

Brechin Montrose

Forfar

Dundee

220 221

St. Andrews

ZEEBRUGGE

Kirkcaldy *Firth of Forth*

209 210 211

NBURGH Dunbar
ston

Berwick-upon-
Tweed

196 197 198 199

Galashiels

Hawick Alnwick

186 187 188 189

Road map symbols

Motorway, toll motorway

Motorway junction – full, restricted access

Motorway service area – full, restricted access

Motorway under construction

Primary route – dual, single carriageway

Service area, roundabout, multi-level junction

Numbered junction – full, restricted access

Primary route under construction

Narrow primary route

Primary destination

Derby

A34

A road – dual, single carriageway

A road under construction, narrow A road

B2135

B road – dual, single carriageway

B road under construction, narrow B road

Minor road – over 4 metres, under 4 metres wide

Minor road with restricted access

Distance in miles

Scenic route

Speed camera – single, multiple

Tunnel

Toll, steep gradient – arrow points downhill

National trail – England and Wales

Long distance footpath – Scotland

Railway with station

Level crossing, tunnel

Preserved railway with station

National boundary

County / unitary authority boundary

Car ferry, catamaran

Passenger ferry, catamaran

Hovercraft, freight ferry

CALAIS 1:10

Ferry

Ferry destination, journey time – hrs : mins

Car ferry – river crossing

Principal airport, other airport

Relief

Feet	metres
3000	914
2600	792
2200	671
1800	549
1400	427
1000	305
0	0

Speed Cameras

Fixed camera locations are shown using the ⑳ symbol.

In congested areas the ⑳ symbol is used to show that there are two or more cameras on the road indicated.

Due to the restrictions of scale the camera locations are only approximate and cannot indicate the operating direction of the camera. Mobile camera sites, and cameras located on roads not included on the mapping are not shown. Where two or more cameras are shown on the same road, drivers are warned that this may indicate that a SPEC system is in operation. These cameras use the time taken to drive between the two camera positions to calculate the speed of the vehicle.

Road map symbols

National park

Area of Outstanding Natural Beauty – England and Wales **National Scenic Area** – Scotland
forest park / regional park / national forest

Woodland

Beach

Linear antiquity

Roman road

Hillfort, battlefield – with date

Viewpoint, nature reserve, spot height – in metres

Golf course, youth hostel, sporting venue

Camp site, caravan site, camping and caravan site

Shopping village, park and ride

29 Adjoining page number – road maps

Road map scale 1 : 212 857 or 3·36 miles to 1 inch

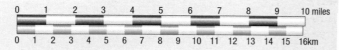

Town plan symbols

Motorway

Primary route –
dual, single carriageway

A road – dual, single carriageway

B road – dual, single carriageway

Minor through road

one-way street

Pedestrian roads

Shopping streets

Railway with station

Tramway with station

Bus or railway station building

Shopping precinct or retail park

Park

Building of public interest

Theatre, cinema

Parking, shopmobility

Underground station

Metro station

Hospital, Police station

Post office

Tourist information

✝ Abbey, cathedral or priory

Ancient monument

Aquarium

Art gallery

Bird collection or aviary

Castle

Church

Country park
England and Wales
Scotland

Farm park

Garden

Historic ship

House

House and garden

Motor racing circuit

Museum

Picnic area

Preserved railway

Race course

Roman antiquity

Safari park

Theme park

Tourist information
i centre open all year
i open seasonally

Zoo

✦ Other place of interest

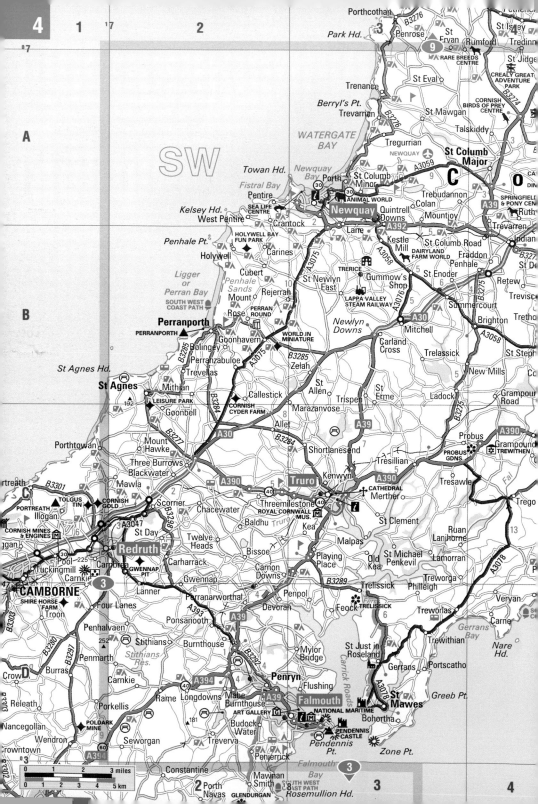

SR SS

SW SX

Fire Beacon Pt.

BOSCASTLE HARBOUR
Trevalga
Bos

CASTLE
Tintagel Hd.
OLD POST OFFICE
TINTAGEL
Bossiney
Tintagel
Treknow
Trewarmett
B3263
308
B3266

Start Pt.
Trebarwith
BRITISH CYCLING MUS.
B3

Treligga
SOUTH WEST COAST PATH
Delabole
Valley Truckle

Helstone

Port Isaac Bay
B3314
B3267

Port Quin Bay
Pentire Pt.
Port Isaac
Port Quin
Port Gaverne
B3267
St Teath
Treveighan
Treveighan

New Polzeath
LONG CROSS
Trelights
Pendoggett
Padstow Bay
Trebetherick
Polzeath
St Endellion
Trelill
A39
Michaelstow
St Br
Gulland Rock
Trelill
Row

Gunver Hd.
St Minver
Trewethern
St Kew
10
10

TREVOSE HEAD
Crugmeer
PRIDEAUX PLACE
Pityme
B3314
Chapel Amble
St Tudy
St Kew
Wet
drbri

Trevone
Rock
St Kew Highway
B3266

TREYARNON BAY
Constantine Bay
St Merryn
Padstow
NATIONAL LOBSTER HATCHERY
Camel
Bodieve
Trevanson
St Mabyn
Dordbridge
Blis

Constantine Bay
Treyarnon
SOUTH WEST COAST PATH
Shop
Little Petherick
Whitecross
Wadebridge
PENCARROW HOUSE
Camel
Helland

Porthcothan
B3276
St Issey
A389
St Breock
Egloshayle
A389
Burlawn

Park Hd.
Penrose
St Ervan
Rumford
Tredinnick
A39
6
Washaway
Bodmin Forest

4
RARE BREEDS CENTRE
St Jidgey
CREALY GREAT ADVENTURE PARK
S REOCK DOWNS MONOLITH
5
2
6
A30
Card

Trenance
St Eval

St Giles
Cripplestyle
Charing Cross
Bickton
Fryde
Hungerford
Stoney Cross
GDNS.
Minstead
KNOWLTON CHURCH
Edmondsham HO.
Edmondsham
North Gorley
Broomy Lodge
Newtown
N E W
6
4
HEAVY HORSE CENTRE
31
Ibsley
South Gorley
A31
FOREST
Knowlton
Verwood
Mockbeggar
Linwood
Emery Down
Lyn
Woodlands
Ringwood Forest
Moyles Court
A31
Clay
Horton
Rockford
REPTILIARY
Chalbury Common
B3081
Blashford
Linford
Burley Lodge
Bank
Mannington
B3072
Three Legged Cross
MOORS VALLEY
Ashley
Picket Post
Burley Street
New Park
NATIONAL
Gaunt's Common
HOLT HEATH
Ashley Heath
St Ives
Ringwood
Moortown
Burley
BURLEY
Bisterne Close
Brockenhurst
Broom Hill
West Moors
ST LEONARDS SERVICES
RAPTOR AND REPTILE CENTRE
Burley
Clapgate
AVON HEATH
St Leonards
Kingston
KINGSTON GREAT COMMON
PARK
Colehill
A31
Bottom
18
Wimborne
Stapehill
Trickett's Cross
THE MATCHAMS EXPERIENCE
Avon
Ripley
Thorney Hill
Wootton
Sway
Minster
Ferndown
Moortown
Bransgore
B3058
Bashley
Marley Mount
Mount Pleasant
Longham
West Parley
BOURNEMOUTH INTERNATIONAL
A338
Hurn
Sopley
Beckley
B3055
Golden Hill
Hordle
Buckla
Parley Cross
ADVENTURE WONDERLAND
Neacroft
Godwinscroft
New Milton
LYMINGTON
Bear Cross
Ensbury
Holdenhurst
Jumpers Green
Winkton
Hinton
SAMMY MILLER'S MOTORCYCLE MUS
Ashley
Everton
B O U R N E M O U T H
Burton
A35
Highcliffe
Old Milton
Downton
Lymore
Talbot Village
Winton
THE RED HOUSE MUS
Somerford
Walkford
B3058
OLE
Newtown
Pokesdown
Purewell
CHRISTCHURCH
Barton on Sea
Branksome
Boscombe
Wick
PRIORY CHURCH
Mudeford
Milford on Sea
Parkstone
Westbourne
ART GALL. AND MUS.
Southbourne
Poole
Lilliput
Branksome Park
Bournemouth
Hengistbury Head
Christchurch Bay
Totland Bay
Canford Cliffs
OCEANARIUM
COMPTON ACRES
BROWNSEA ISLAND
Sandbanks
P O O L E   B A Y
The Needles
THE NEEDLES OLD BATTERY
TOLL
STUDLAND BEACH AND NATURE RESERVE
SZ
Alum Bay
Studland
Bay
STUDLAND AND GODLINGSTON HEATH
Studland
The Foreland
SOUTH WEST COAST PATH
Ulwell
New Swanage
Swanage Bay
18
SWANAGE RAILWAY
Swanage
Peveril Pt.
SWANAGE
DURLSTON
Durlston Head
Tilly Whim Caves
GUERNSEY 2:30
JERSEY 3:45
ST. MALO 5:25
CHERBOURG 2:15
(Apr-Oct)
CHERBOURG 4:15
(May-Sept)
D
4
5
6
7

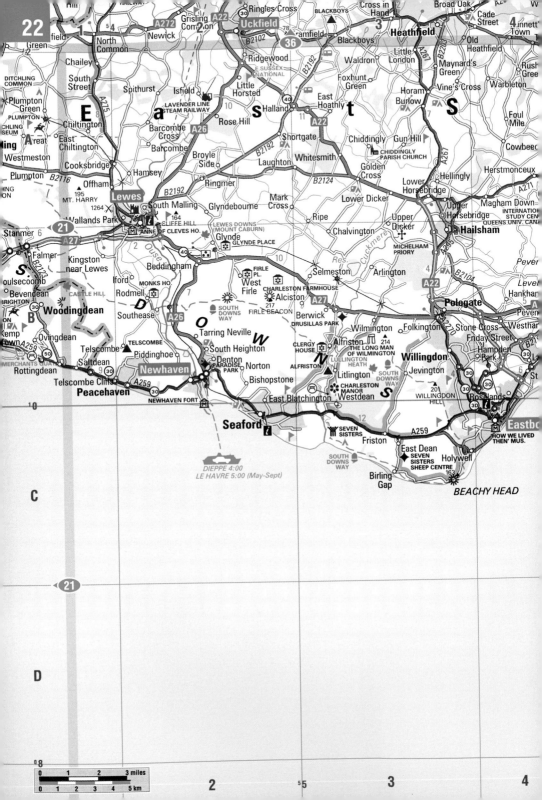

1   ²1   2   3   4

¹5

A

North West
Point

North East
Point

LUNDY MARINE
NATURE RESERVE

142▲

LUNDY

ILFRACOMBE 2:15
BIDEFORD 2:15

South West
Point

Surf
Point

B

BIDE

N   O   R   T   H

C

SS

HARTLAND POINT

Windbury
Pt.

Titchberry

CLOVELLY VI
Clovelly

Hartland Quay

Stoke

Hartland

B3248

Higher Clo

SOUTH WEST
COAST PATH

Philham

THE MILKY W
ADVENTURE F

Milford

Eddistone

ELMSCOTT

Elmscott

Tosberry

Woolfardisworthy

Hartland
Forest

South Hole

Knaps
Longpeak

Welcombe

235▲

Meddon

Woolley

Higher
Sharpnose Pt.

Gooseham

156

Eastcott

Youlstone

Dinworthy

Morwenstow

KILLARNEY SPRINGS
FAMILY LEISURE PARK

D

Lower
Sharpnose Pt.

Shop

A39

Woodford

BROCKLANDS
ADVENTURE
PARK

14

Bradworthy
Cross

Bra

Coombe

Kilkhampton

Alfardisworthy

Stibb

Sold
Cro

¹1

0   1   2   3 miles
0   1   2   3   4   5 km

10

2

3

DUNSDON

4

Poughill

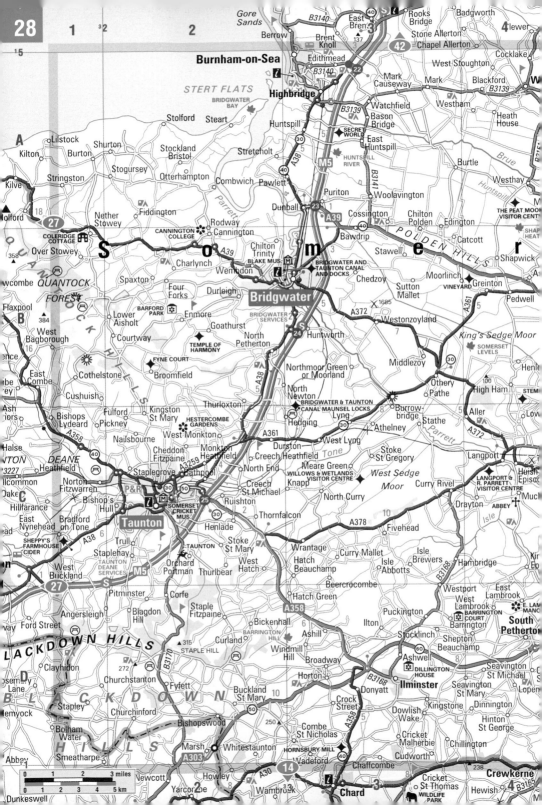

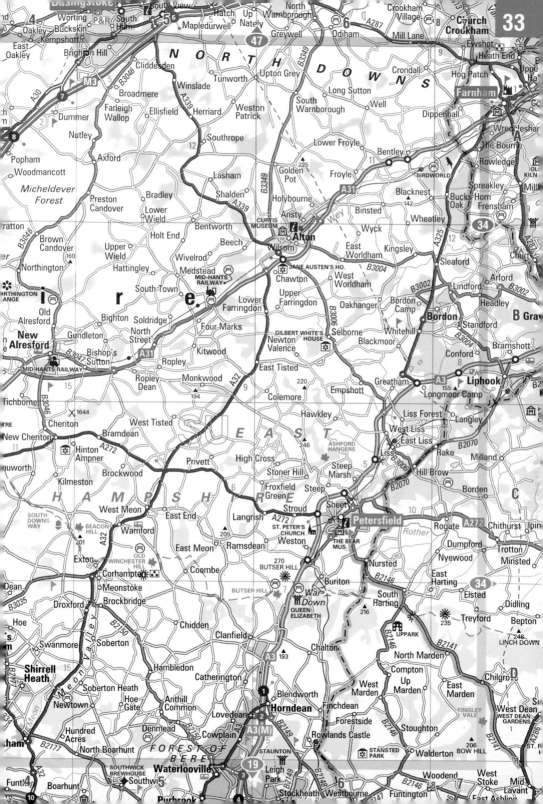

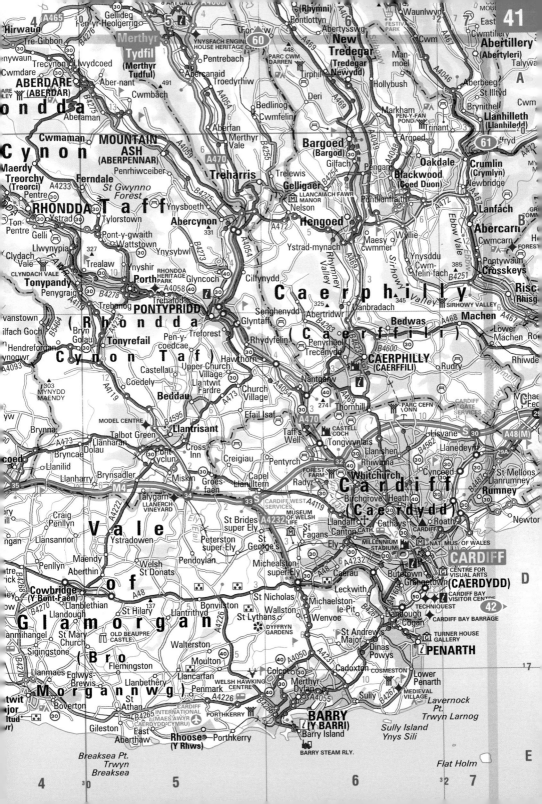

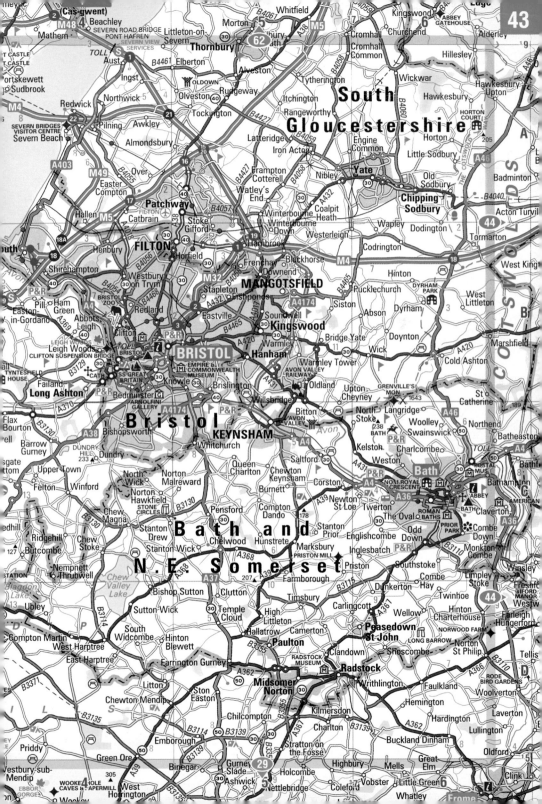

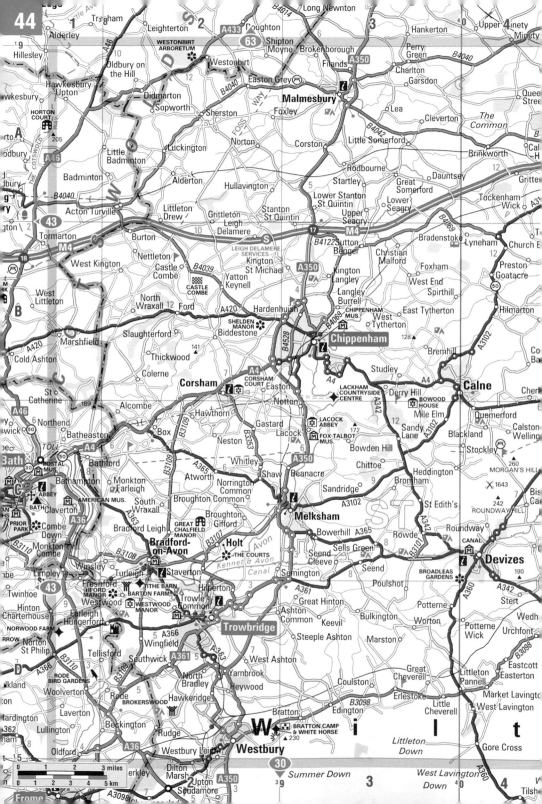

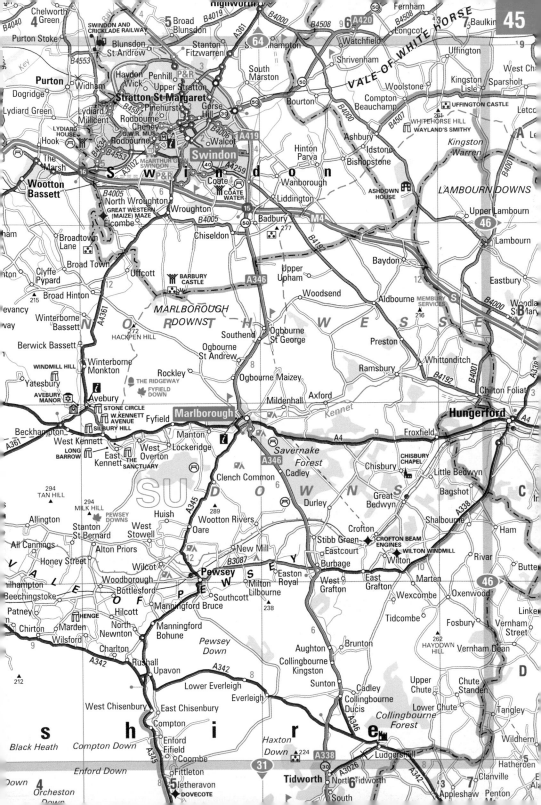

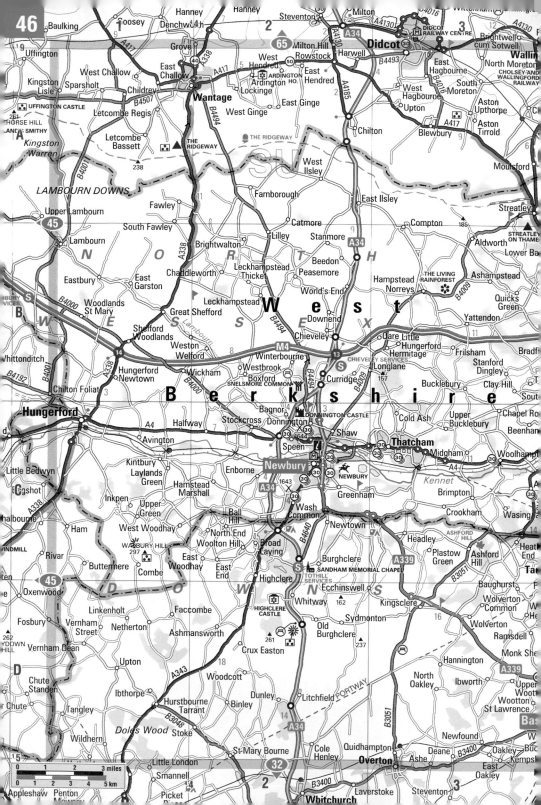

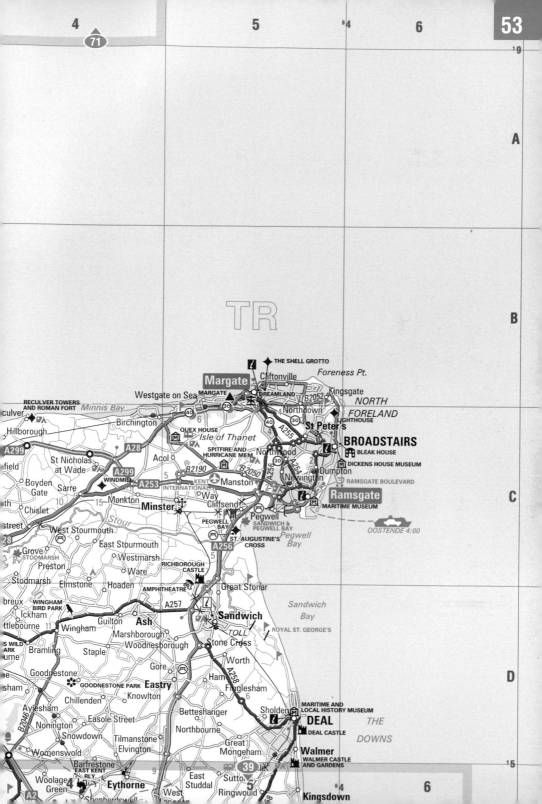

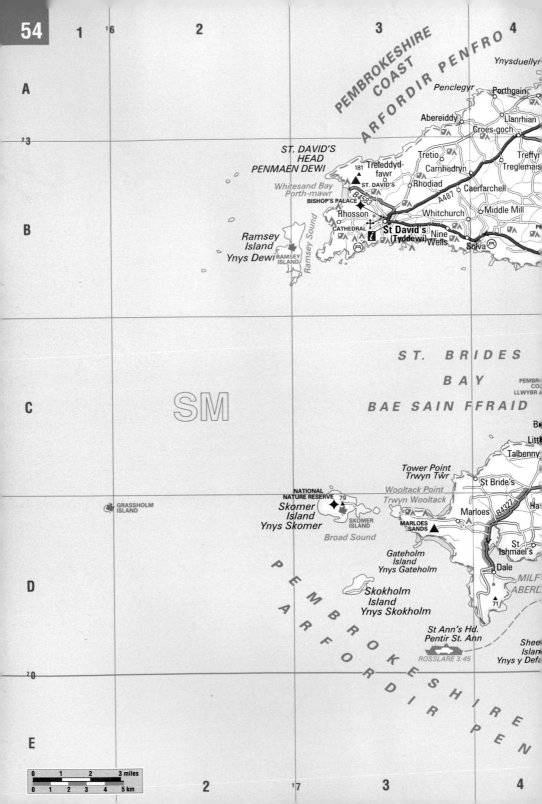

A

B

C

D

E

1   ¹6   2   3   4

²3

PEMBROKESHIRE COAST
ARFORDIR PENFRO

Ynysduellyr

Penclegyr   Porthgain

Abereiddy   Llanrhian

Croes-goch

Tretio   Treffy

ST. DAVID'S
HEAD
PENMAEN DEWI

181 Trefeddyd-
fawr   Carnhedryn   Treglemais

ST. DAVID'S

Whitesand Bay
Porth-mawr   Rhodiad   Caerfarchell

BISHOP'S PALACE   B4583

Rhosson   Whitchurch   Middle Mill

Ramsey
Island
Ynys Dewi   CATHEDRAL   **St David's**
(Tyddewi)   Nine
Wells

RAMSEY
ISLAND   Solva

Ramsey Sound

ST. BRIDES

BAY

PEMBR
CO
LLWYBR A

BAE SAIN FFRAID

B
Litt

SM   Talbenny

Tower Point
Trwyn Twr   St Bride's

NATIONAL
NATURE RESERVE   79   Wooltack Point
Trwyn Wooltack

GRASSHOLM
ISLAND   Skomer
Island
Ynys Skomer   Marloes   B4327   Ha

SKOMER
ISLAND   **MARLOES
SANDS**   St
Ishmael's

Broad Sound   Gateholm
Island
Ynys Gateholm   Dale

MILF
ABERD

Skokholm
Island
Ynys Skokholm   71

St Ann's Hd.
Pentir St. Ann   Shee
Islan
Ynys y Defa

ROSSLARE 3:45

²0

PEMBROKESHIRE   PEN
ARFORDIR

| 0 | 1 | 2 | 3 miles |
| 0 | 1 2 3 4 | 5 km |

2   ¹7   3   4

Llandissilio
Hraeth
Henllan
Amgoed
Dyffryn
73
Meidrim
Merthyr
Tre-vaug
LOVESPOON
Carmarthen
(Caerfyr
Llanfallteg
Clunderwen
Bethesda
B4313
A478
A40
Cwmfelin
Boeth
Langynin
GROVELANDS
Pwll-trap
Sarnau
Bancyfelin
CORS GOCH.
LLANLLWCH
Llanllwch
Llanddewi
Velfrey
145
Whitland
Trevaughan
Backe
A40
Langynog
153
Llangain
St Clears
(Sanclêr)
Afon Tâf
Lampeter
Velfrey
Crinow
Llwyn-y-
brain
Llanddowror
A4066
Morfa
Bach
Afon Ty
rbed
Crinow
B4328
A4077
Llanybri
Tavernspite
Halfpenny
Furze
Llansteffan
CASTLE
Ferryside
Cold
Blow
Princes
Gate
Red Roses
Llandawke
Broadlay
B4314
B4314
178
Llansadurnen
DYLAN THOMAS
BOATHOUSE
Laugharne
Llansaint
Ludchurch
55
ngstone
Llanteg
12
Marros
Brook
Broadway
9
East Marsh
Thomas
Chapel
Stepaside
COLBY WOODLAND
GARDEN
152
Pendine
MUSEUM OF
SPEED
Begelly
ffreyston
Kilgetty
Amroth
Pendine Sands
Traeth Pentywyn
Pemb
Fores
Hill
B4316
PEMBROKESHIRE
COAST
ARFORDIR PENFRO
SN
Williamston
A478
Broadfield
New Hedges
Saundersfoot
CARMARTHEN
PE
OR HOUSE
LIFE PARK
Gumfreston
TUDOR
MERCHANT'S HOUSE
Tenby
(Dinbych-
y-Pysgod)
BAY
B
Ho
Penally
BAE CAERFYRDDIN
ydstep
ANORBIER
Giltar Pt.
Caldey Sound
Caldey
Island
Ynys Bŷr
SS
Rh
Chapel Pt.
Trwyn Capel
Bae Rh
Worms Head
Penrhyn-Gŵyr
C
D

0   1   2   3 miles
0 1 2 3 4 5 km

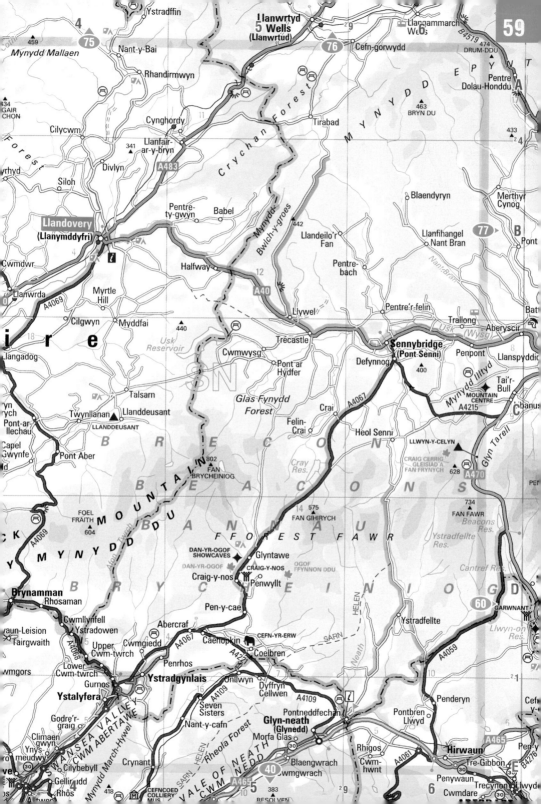

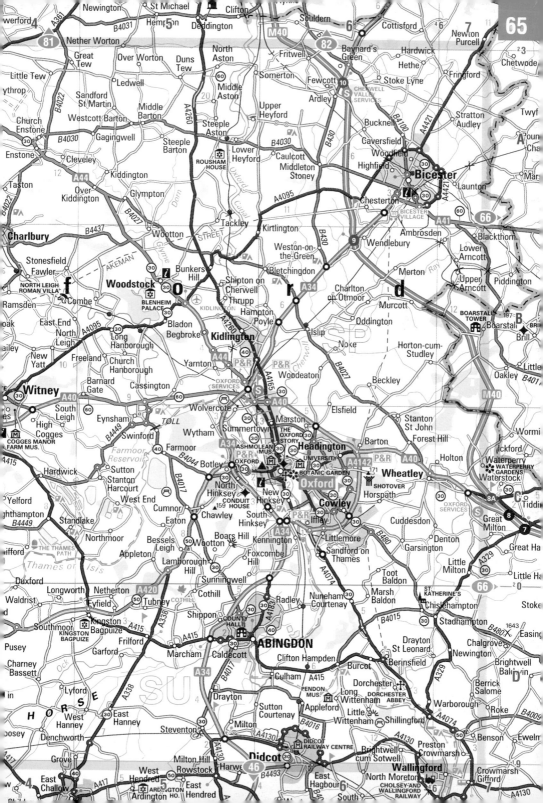

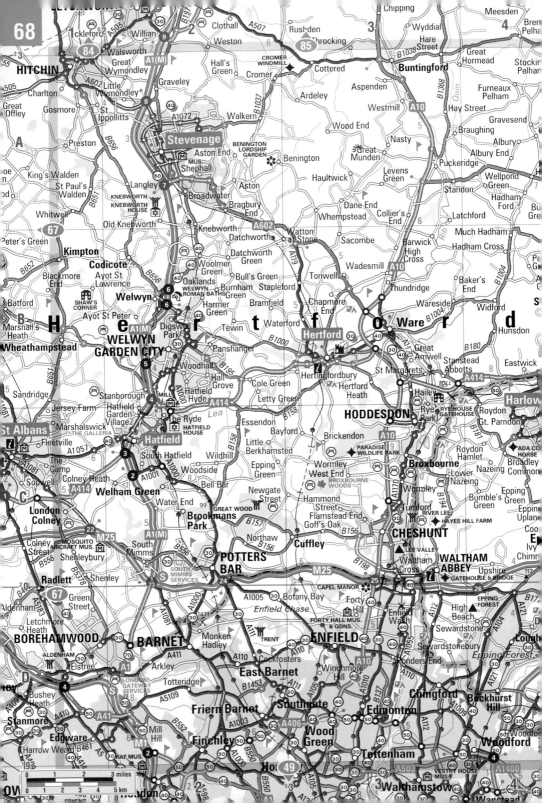

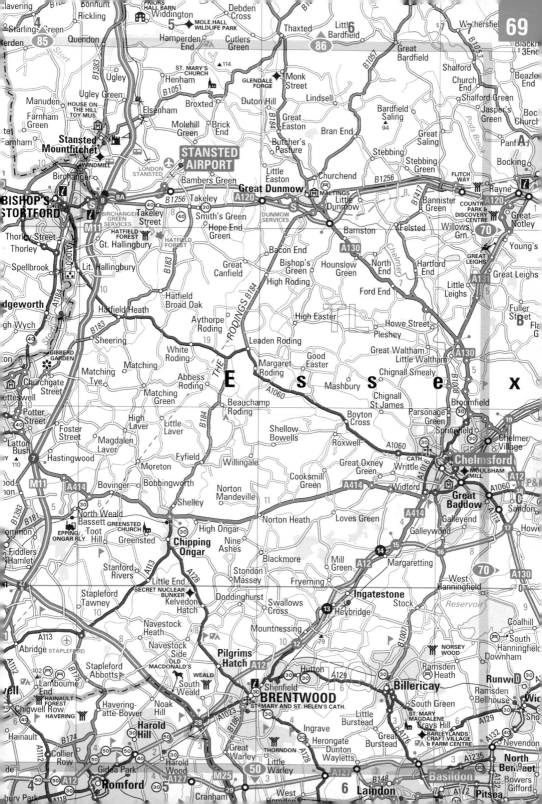

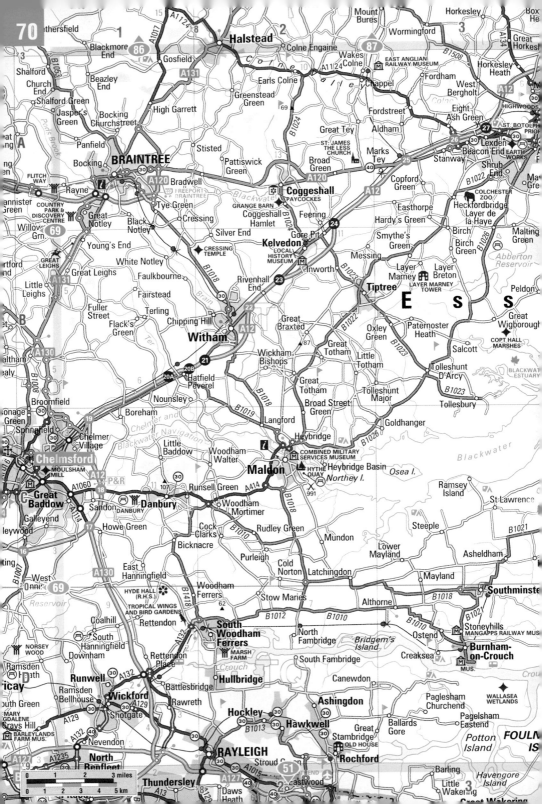

Cross
Langham
Dedham
Lawford
MUNNINGS ART MUSEUM
MISTLEY TOWERS
Mistley
Parkeston
HARWICH REDOUBT
A12
87
A137
B1035
Manningtree
Bradfield
88
Wrabness
Ramsey
Upper Dovercourt
Dovercourt

29
B1029
Ardleigh
Little Bromley
B1035
Bradfield Heath
A120
Wix
Little Oakley

30
Fox Street
Crockleford Heath
A120
Horsley Cross
Horsleycross Street
Stone's Green
Great Oakley

Colchester
Elmstead Market
Great Bromley
Little Bentley
Tendring Green
B1414
Horsey Island
The Naze

A137
Hare Green
Balls Green
BETH CHATTO GDNS
Tendring
Beaumont
HAMFORD WATER
MARITIME MUSEUM

Old Heath
Wivenhoe Cross
Frating Green
A133
Great Bentley
Weeley
Thorpe Green
Thorpe-le-Soken
Kirby-le-Soken

BOURNE MILL
Wivenhoe
40
Aingers Green
Weeley Heath
B1414
B1033
Kirby Cross
Walton-on-the-Naze

Blackheath
Alresford
B1027
Row Heath
B1033
Frinton-on-Sea

Rowhedge
Thorrington
B1029
Little Clacton
Great Holland
HOLLAND HAVEN

Fingringhoe
St Osyth Heath
CLACTON VILLAGE
Holland-on-Sea

Abberton
River Colne
A133
St Osyth's Priory
Great Clacton
B1032

Langenhoe
e
X
Mersea Island
East Mersea
CUDMORE GROVE
St Osyth
B1027
Clacton-on-Sea

Blue Row
COLNE ESTUARY
Point Clear
Jaywick

West Mersea
MERSEA ISLAND MUSEUM
Colne Pt.
Virley Channel

Sales Pt.
ST. PETERS ON THE WALL
well erside
TM

radwell a Sea
DENGIE

am

Ray Sand
Montsale
Deal Hall
Foulness Sand
Foulness Pt.
TR

Courtsend
urchend
M A P L I N   S A N D S

52
53
4
5
6

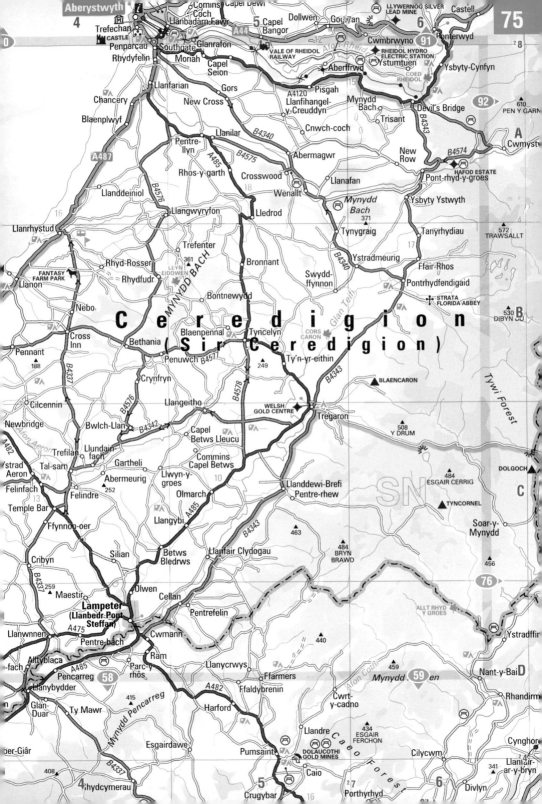

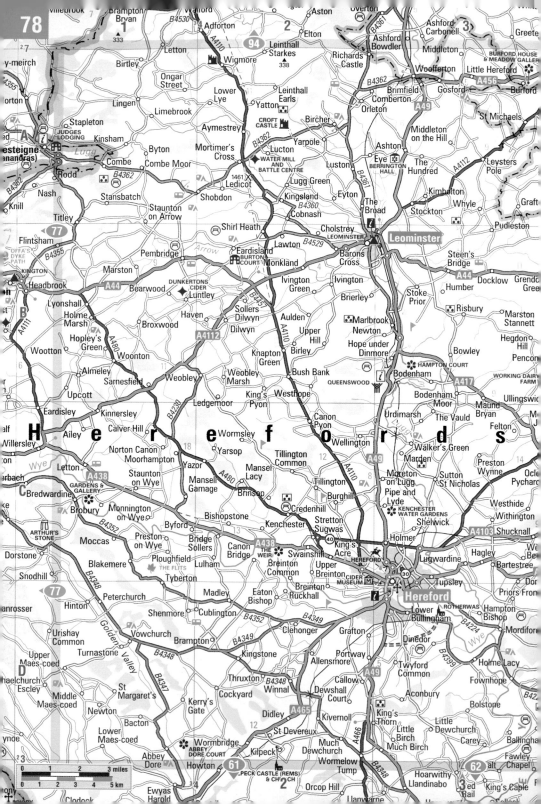

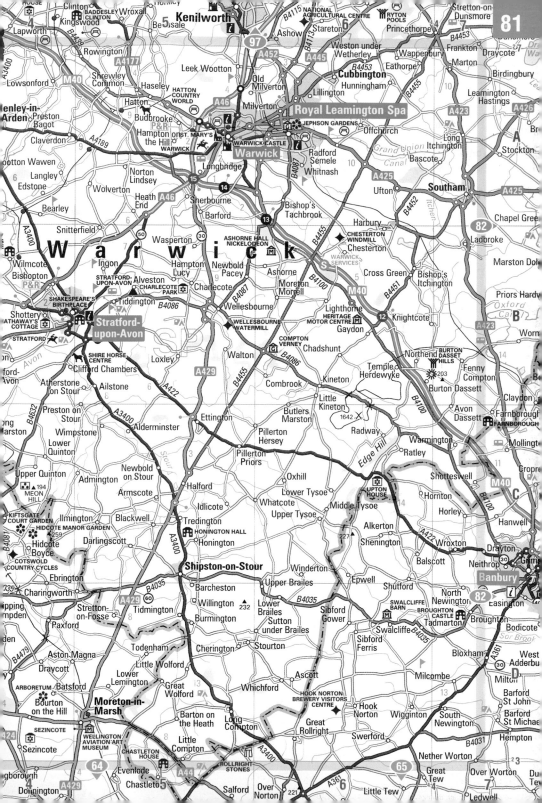

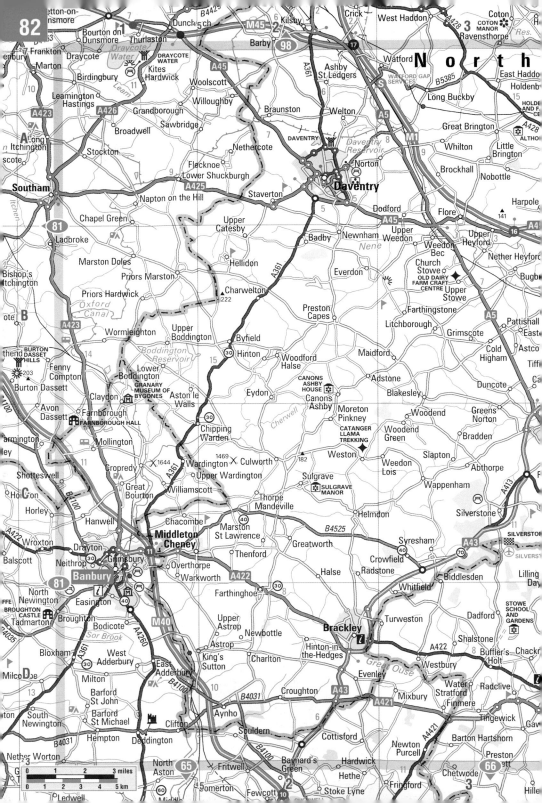

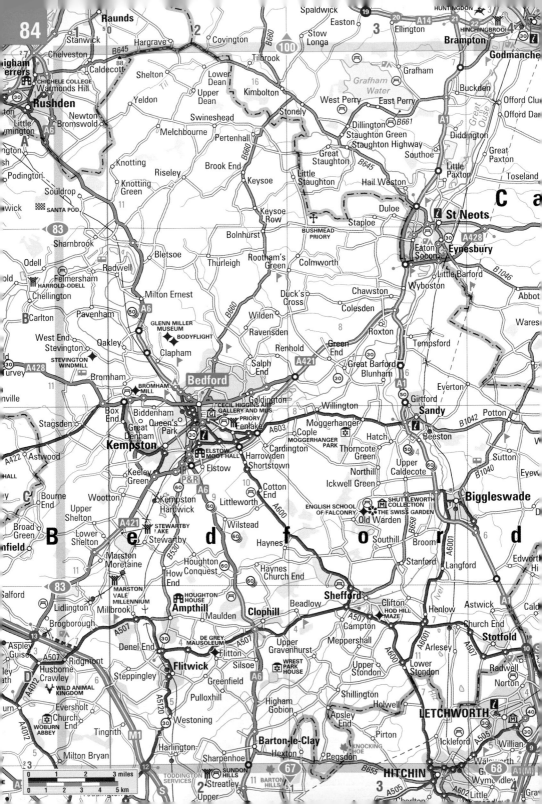

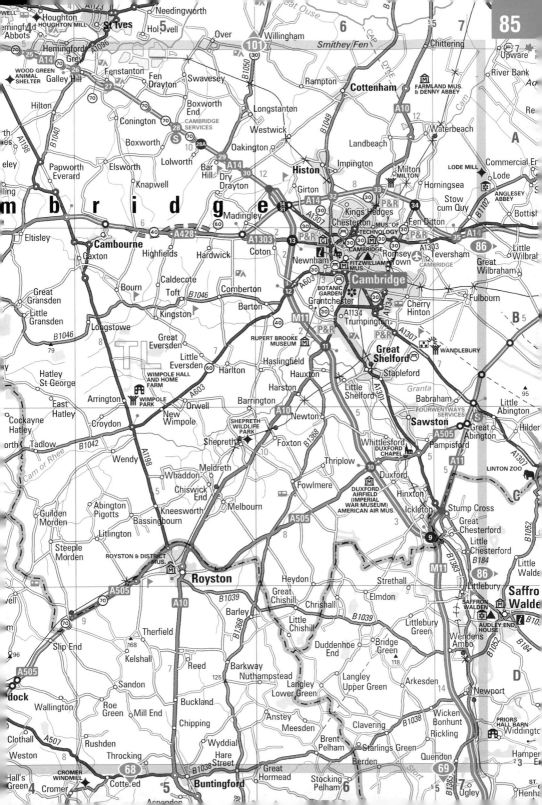

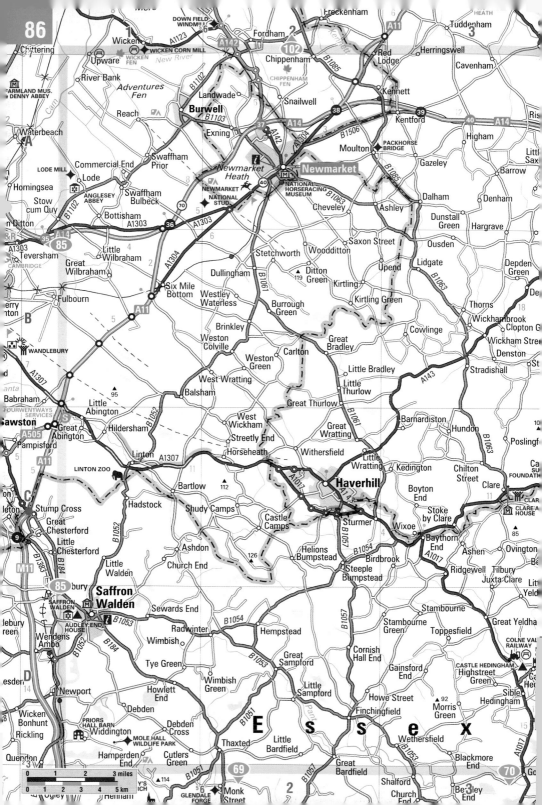

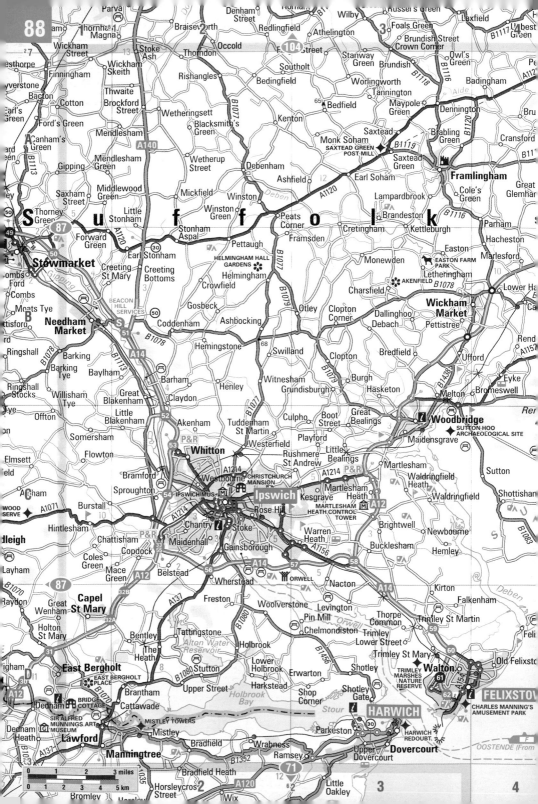

Sibton Green
High Street
4
Dunwich
5
Forest
6
DUNWICH UNDERWATER
EXPLORATION EXHIBITION
7
6 6
7
Hemp Green
Darsham
Dunwich 105
2 7

Sibton
2
WESTLETON HEATH
Yoxford
Middleton Moor
Westleton
B1122
MINSMERE RSPB
NATURE RESERVE

Rotten End
A12
North Green
Middleton
Curlew Green am
Theberton
Eastbridge
B1122
A

Kelsale
LEISTON ABBEY
Benhall Street
B1121
Carlton
B1119
Leiston
Sizewell

Saxmundham
Knodishall
Aldringham

Sternfield
Coldfair Green
B1353

Benhall Green
Friston
B1121
B1069
Thorpeness

Farnham
Gromford
A1094
B1122
6
NORTH WARREN RSPB
NATURE RESERVE
B

SNAPE MALTINGS RIVERSIDE CENTRE
Snape
Aldeburgh

Blaxhall
Iken
High Street
Aldeburgh Bay

Tunstall
Tunstall Forest
B1078
Sudbourne
Alde

TM

Chillesford
ley
B1084
Orford

ORFORD CASTLE
Orford
Orford Ness

Butley High Corner
ORFORDNESS-HAVERGATE

ndrew
Boyton

Stores Corner
Hollesley Bay
C

lesley
lesey

Shingle Street

ESBJERG 20:00
HOEK VAN HOLLAND 6:00

GOTHENBURG 38:30
ROTTERDAM 8:00
2 3

4
5
6
6 6
7

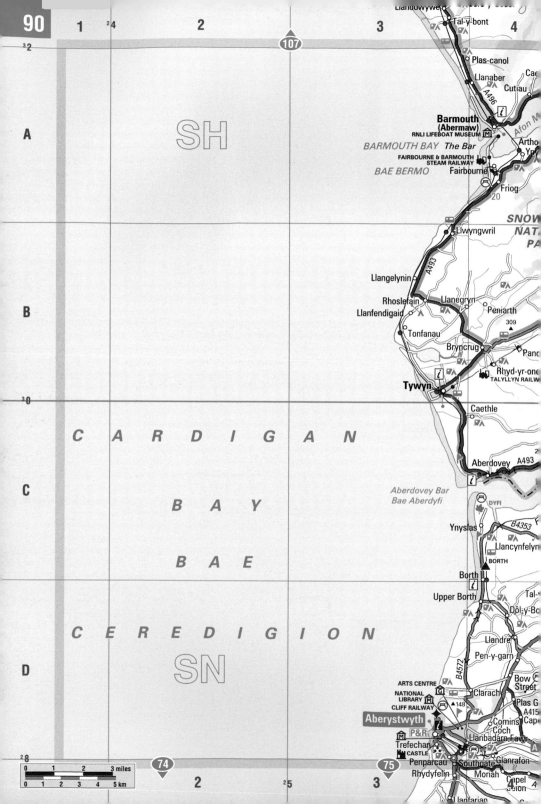

1 ²4 2 3 4

³2

107

SH

Llanddwywe

Tal-y-bont

Plas-canol

Llanaber

Cutiau

Cae

A496

Barmouth
(Abermaw)
RNLI LIFEBOAT MUSEUM

Artho
Yr

BARMOUTH BAY The Bar
FAIRBOURNE & BARMOUTH
STEAM RAILWAY
Bae Bermo

Fairbourne

Friog
20

SNOW
NAT
PA

A

Llwyngwril

A493

Llangelynin

Llanegryn

Peniarth

309

Rhoslefain

Llanfendigaid

B

Tonfanau

Bryncrug

Pand

Rhyd-yr-one
TALYLLYN RAILW

Tywyn

³0

Caethle

C A R D I G A N

Aberdovey A493

Aberdovey Bar
Bae Aberdyfi

DYFI

C

B A Y

Ynyslas

B4353

Llancynfelyn

BORTH

B A E

Borth

Upper Borth

Tal-

Dôl-y-Bo

C E R E D I G I O N

Llandre

Pen-y-garn

B4572

SN

ARTS CENTRE

NATIONAL
LIBRARY
CLIFF RAILWAY

Bow
Street

Clarach

Plas G

A415

Comins
Coch Cape

Aberystwyth

P&R

Llanbadarn Fawr

Trefechan

CASTLE

Penparcau

Glanrafon

Southgate

Rhydyfelin

Moriah

Capel
Seion

Llanfarian

D

²8

0   1   2   3 miles
0 1 2 3 4 5 km

74

2

²5

75

3

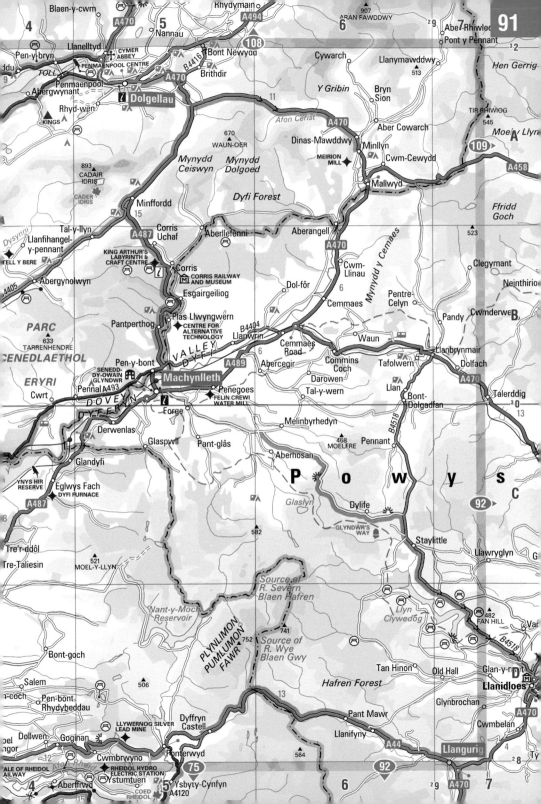

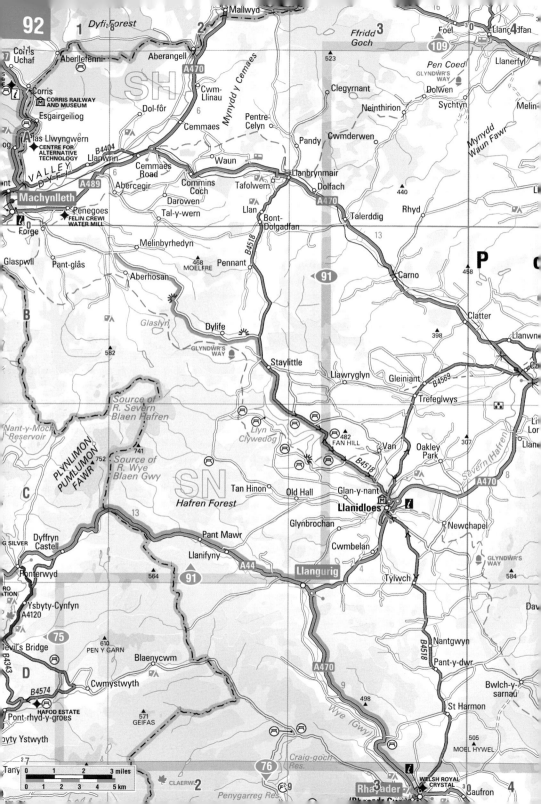

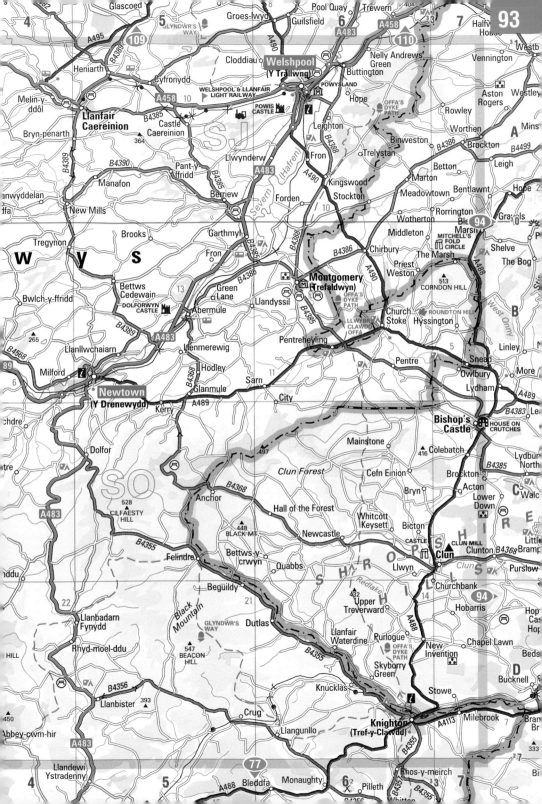

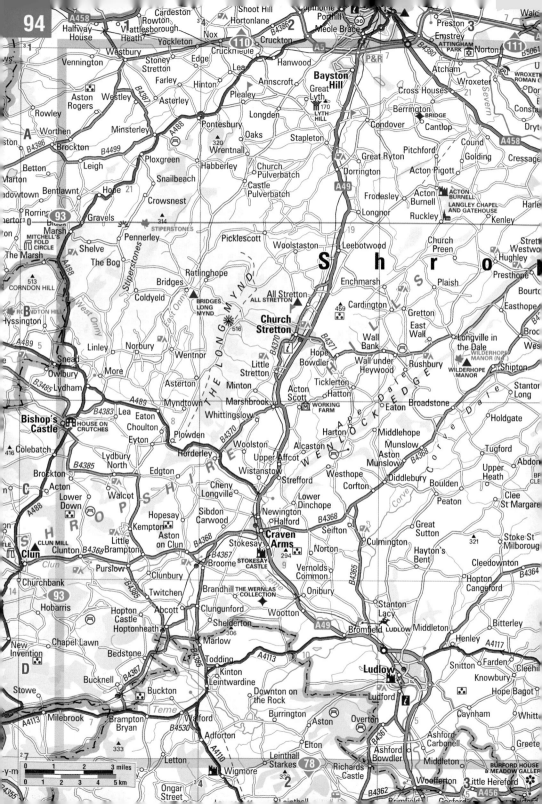

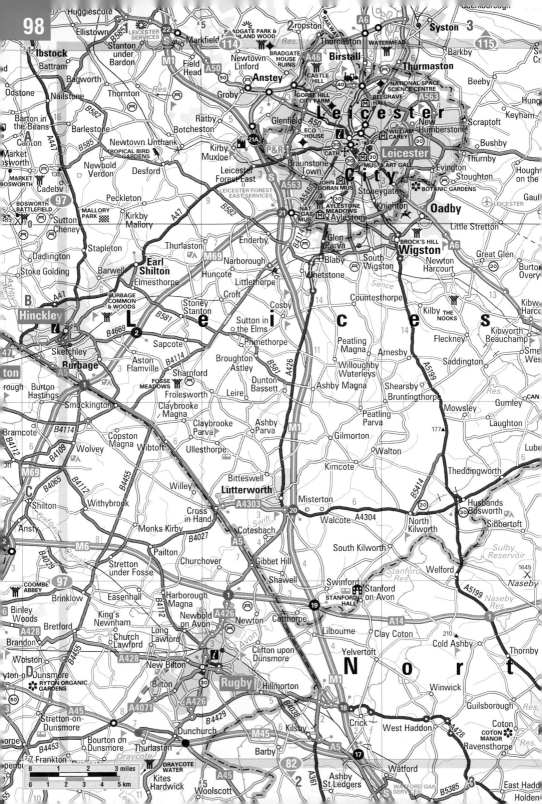

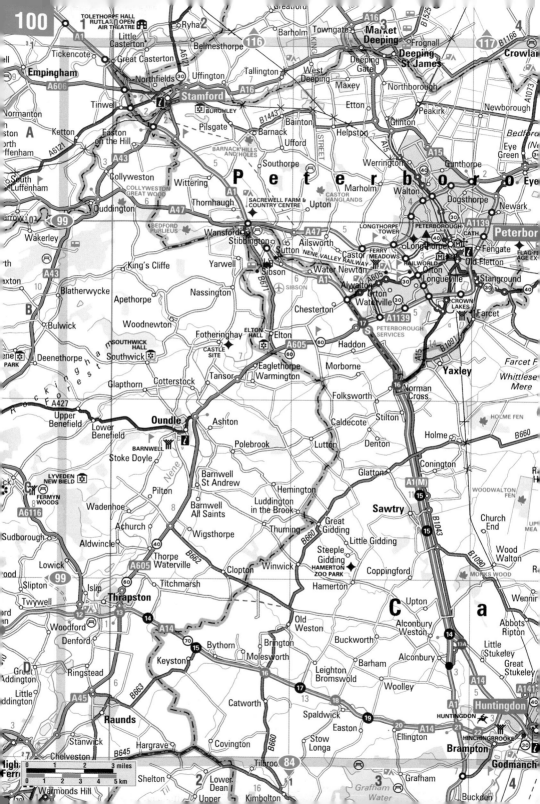

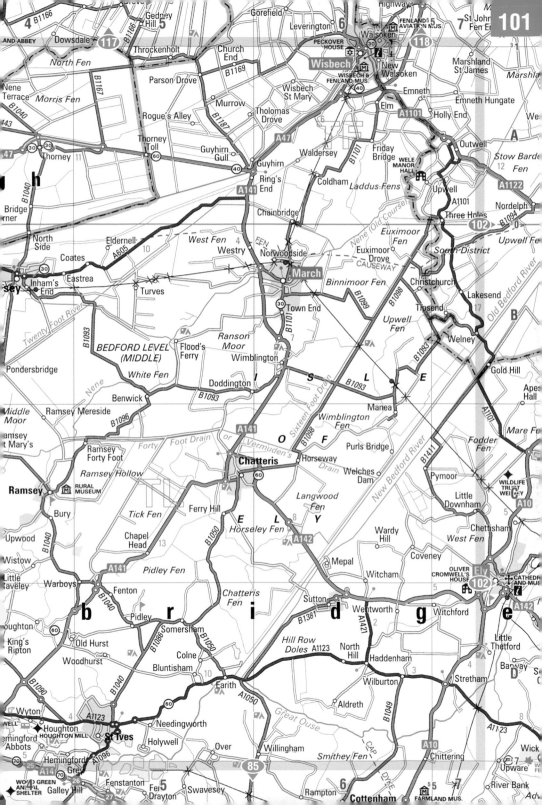

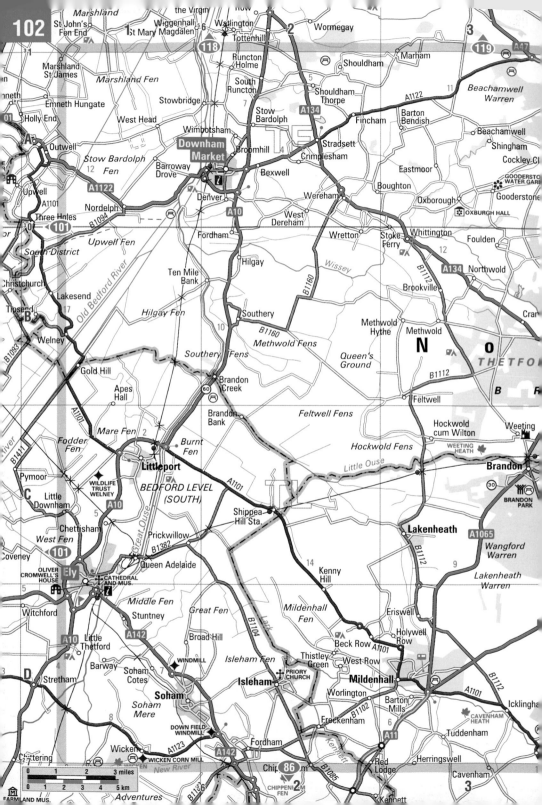

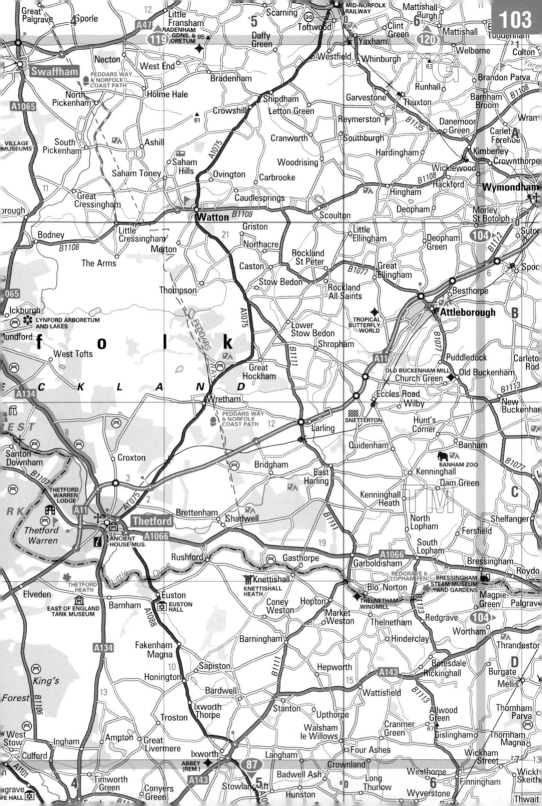

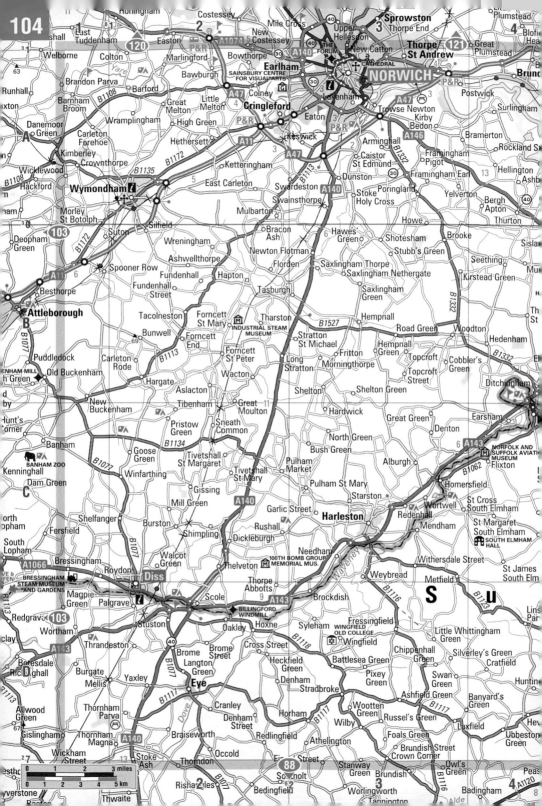

Ynys Llanddwyn

122

C A E R N A R F O

B A Y

B A E

C A E R N A R F O

SH

Gyr
Bryn-yr-eryr

Trefor

564
YR EIFL

A
B
C
D

1   2   2   3

Carreg Ddu
Porth Dinllaen

Morfa Nefyn

Nefyn

B4417   6   Llithfaen

Pistyll
Llwyndyrys

LLEYN HISTORICAL
MARITIME MUSEUM

Edern   Fron

Tan-y-graig   Rhos-fawr

Glanrhyd   Boduan

Rhos-y-llan   CORS
GEIRCH   Llannor

Tudweiliog   BODVEL HALL
ADVENTURE PARK   Efailnewydd

Dinas   Rhyd-y-clafdy   Denio

Porth Golmon   14   Garnfadryn   Pwll

Bryn-mawr   Llaniestyn   B4415   Penrhos   South Be

Pen-y-graig   Llangwnnadl   Rhedyn   7

Penrhyn Mawr   Pen-y-groeslon   Sarn Meyllteyrn   Llanbedrog

Ty-hen   Bryncroes   Botwnnog   Nanhoron   Trwyn Llanbedrog

Methlem   Rhydlios   Mynytho

Rhoshirwaun   Llandegwning

Capel Carmel   304   PLAS-YN-RHIW   Llawr Dref   Llangian   St Tudwal's Road

191   MYNYDD RHIW   Angorfa St Tudwal

Uwchmynydd   B4413   Rhiw   Llanengan   Abersoch

Aberdaron   Llanfaelrhys   Sarn Bach   St Tudwal's Island East
Ynys St Tudwal Dwyrai

Bodermid   Bwlchtocyn   Marchroes

Porth Neigwl or Hell's Mouth   St Tudwal's Island West
Ynys St Tudwal Gorllewin

Pen-y-cil   Cilan Uchaf

Trwyn Cilan

Bardsey Sound
Swnt Enlli

167   Bardsey Island
Ynys Enlli

YNYS ENLLI

Penrhyn Mawr   P E N R H Y N   L L Y N

L L E Y N

L L E Y N

0   1   2   3 miles
0   1   2   3   4   5 km

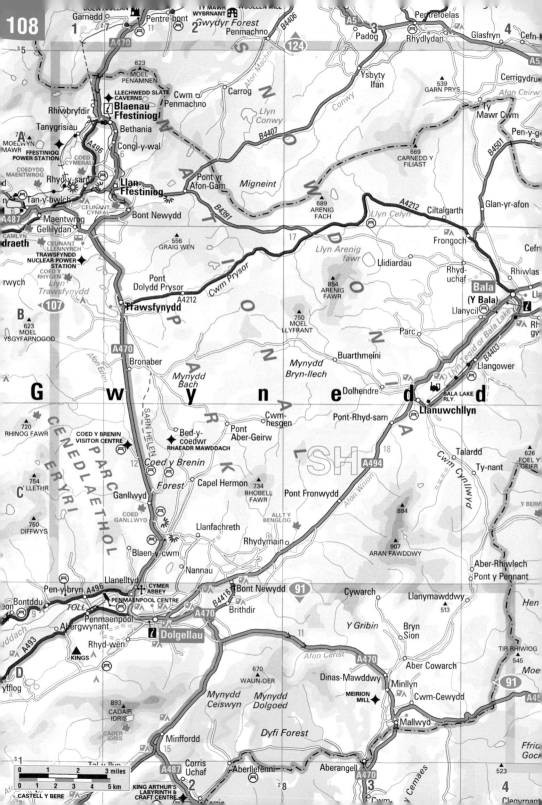

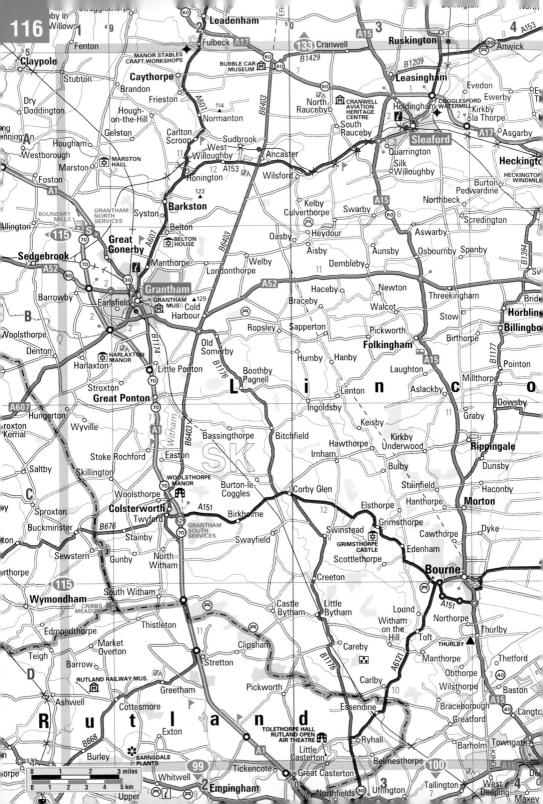

1 **2** **3**

Wrangle Lowgate
Friskney Flats
135

Wrangle
Hurn's End
A52
Leverton Outgate
Leverton Highgate
Leverton Lucasgate

Scrane End

A
Butterwick

BOSTON DEEPS

LYNN DEEPS

T H E   W A S H

OBSERVAT
RESE

Old Hunstanton
Hunstanton
SEA LIFE
SANCTUARY
HUNS

117

B
Holbeach
St Matthew

Heacham
50

Dawsmere

Gedney Marsh
Gedney
Drove End
B1359

Lynn Channel

SNETTISHAM
NATURE
RESERVE
Shepherd's
Port
10

Gedney
Dyke
Lutton

THE WASH

DERSINGHAM BOG
SANDRINGHA

Wolferton

C
Chapelgate
Gedney
Fleet
Gedney
oadgate
A17
Little London
BUTTERFLY &
WILDLIFE PARK
Long Sutton

Guy's
Head

Terrington Marsh

Ongar
Hill

North
Wootton

Castle
Rising
CASTLE
RISING

ROYDON
COMMON

South Wootton

60
Sutton
Crosses
B1390
60
Sutton Bridge

Orange
Row
Clenchwarton
A17
Walpole
Cross Keys
Terrington
St Clement

King's
Lynn
MARITIME
EXHIBITION
GUILDHALL
A1078
Gaywood
A148
A149

West
Lynn
KING'S LYNN
Hardwick
Fairstead
4

117
Tydd St Mary

11
Walpole
St Andrew
Hay
Green
Tilney
High End
Tilney
All Saints

Lezi

Sutton
St James
Tydd
Gote
Four
Gotes
Walpole
Marsh
Walpole
St Peter

2

Fair
Green
Tower En

Tydd St
Giles
Newton
A1101
Ingleborough
St John's
Highway
Terrington
St John
Tilney
St Lawrence
A47
Saddle Bow
West
Winch
A10
North
Runcton
Middleton

B1165
D
St Giles Fen
Fitton
End
West
Walton
12
Walpole
Highway
Wiggenhall
St Germans
West
Winch
Setchey
Blackborou
End

Gorefield
West Walton
Highway
Marshland
Wiggenhall
St Mary
the Virgin
Tottenhill
Row
Wormegay

Leverington
St John's
Fen End
Wiggenhall
St Mary Magdalen
Watlington
A134

PECKOVER
HOUSE
30
Walsoken
FENLAND
AVIATION MUS
101
Runcton
Holme
A10

0   1   2   3 miles
0 1 2 3 4 5 km
New
Walsoken
FENLAND MUS
Marshland
St James
Marshland Fen
102
South

1 **2** **3**

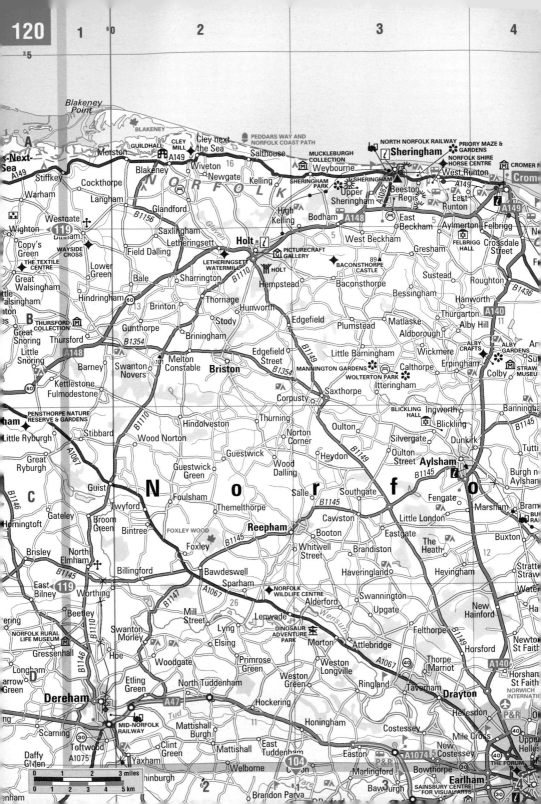

A

The Skerries
Ynysoedd y
Moelrhoniaid

Carmel Head
Pen Carmel

Llanfairynghornwy

Church Bay
Porth Swtan

*Wilfa
Head
Pen Wilfa*

*Cemaes
Bay
Bae
Cemaes*

Cemlyn Bay
Bae Cemlyn

WYLFA POWER STATION
AND OBSERVATION TOWER

Tregele

Cemaes

Llant

Llanfechell

17

Llanfflewyn

Rhydwyn   Llanrhyddlad

Llanbabo

A5025

I S L

A n g l

Ca

DUBLIN 1:49
DUN LAOGHAIRE 1:40

DUBLIN 3:00

B

North Stack   BREAKWATER
HOLYHEAD MOUNTAIN ▲220
South Stack   Llaingoch
ELLINS TOWER RSPB RESERVE
STANDING STONES   PENRHOS FEILW
Goferydd

Holyhead
(Caergybi)

Kingsland

Penrhosfeilw

HOLYHEAD BAY
BAE
CAERGYBI

Llanfaethlu

Llanfwrog

Llanfachraeth

Newlands
Park

A5

4

Valley

LLYNON
WINDMILL
Llanddeusant

Elim

Llantrisant

Pen-llyn
Res.

Llanynghenedl

Bodedern

Carmel

Lle

S i r   Y n

Penrhyn Mawr

Trearddur
Glan-traeth

Four Mile
Bridge

B4545

A55

3

Caergeiliog
2

4

Bryngwran

Trefor

Holy Island
Ynys Gybi

Rhoscolyn

*Cymyran
Bay
Bae Cymyran*

Llanfihangel
yn Nhowyn

Llanfairyneubwll

Capel-
gwyn

Llanfaelog

Bryn Du

Pencarnisiog

Ddrydw

A4080

5

A5

Rhosneigr

C

Llangwyfan-isaf

Aberffraw

Llangadwaladr

Hermon

Bet

Bodorgan

NEWBOROUGH WARREN
AND YNYS LLANDDWYN

*Malltraeth Bay
Bae Malltraeth*

Llanddwyn I.
Ynys Llanddwyn

D

A N G L E S E Y   /   M Ô N

0   1   2   3 miles
0   1   2   3   4   5 km

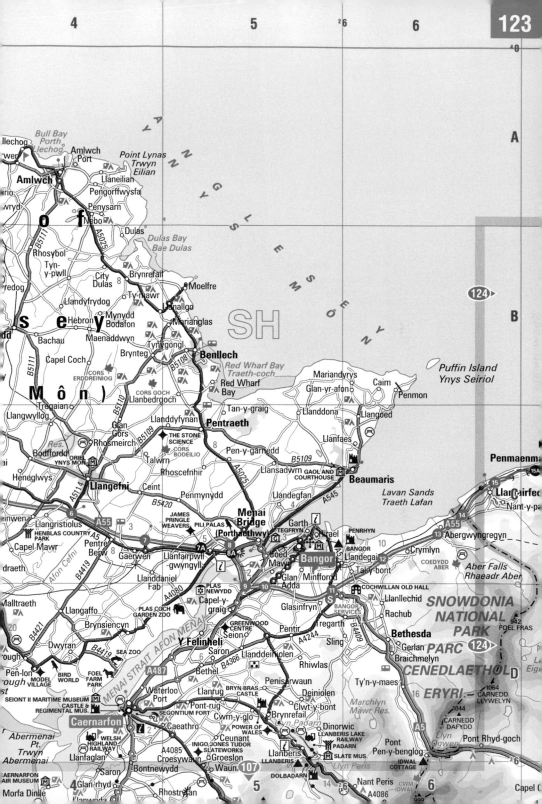

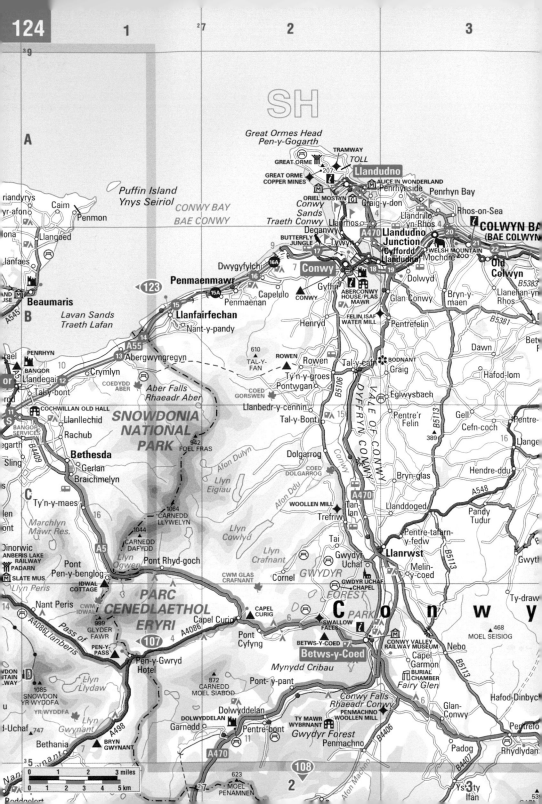

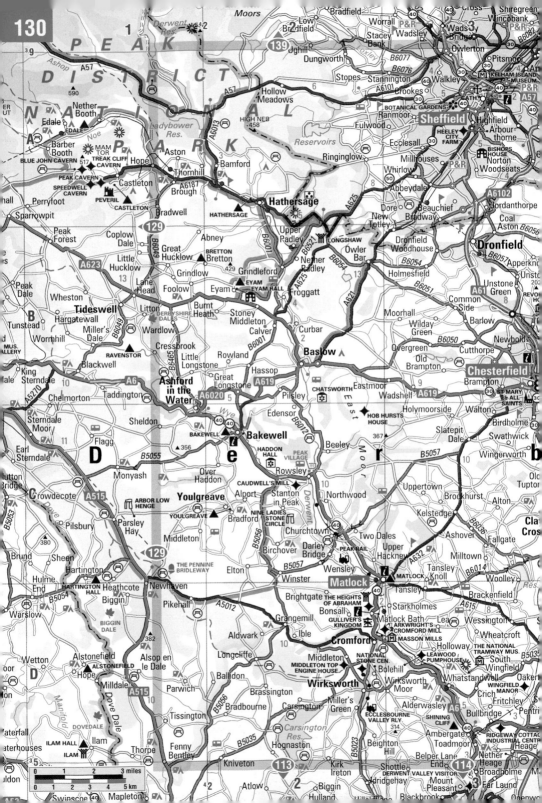

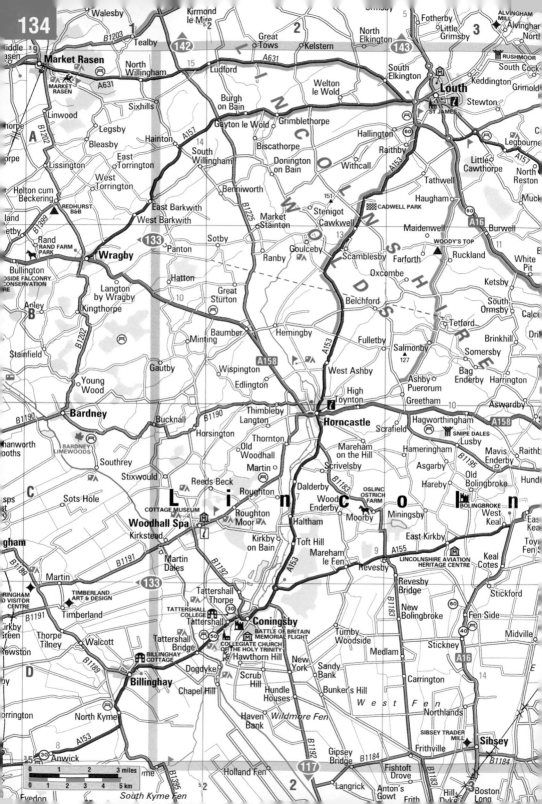

Saltfleetby
St Clements
Saltfleetby
All Saints
143
Saltfleetby
St Peter
A1031
SALTFLEETBY
THEDDLETHORPE
Theddlethorpe
St Helen

A

Great
Carlton
SEAL SANCTUARY
& NATURE CENTRE
Meers
Bridge
Mablethorpe
Gayton
le Marsh
Trusthorpe
Strubby
A1104
Withern
A157
Thorpe
Sutton
on Sea
Maltby
le Marsh
Woodthorpe
Beesby
Sandilands
CLAYTHORPE WATER MILL
AND WILDFOWL GARDENS
Saleby
Hannah
Aby
Markby
ALFORD
WINDMILL
ALFORD
MANOR HOUSE
A1111
Asserby
Huttoft
Rigsby
Alford
Bilsby
B1449
A52

B

TF

A1104
Well
Farlesthorpe
Anderby
ON YOUR MARQUES
Authorpe
Row
Ulceby
Cumberworth
Mumby
Bonthorpe
Helsey
Claxby
17
Willoughby
Hogsthorpe
**Chapel
St Leonards**
Skendleby
Sloothby
A52
A1028
B1196
Partney
HARDY'S ANIMAL FARM
Welton
le Marsh
Addlethorpe
Ingoldmells
Scremby
FANTASY ISLAND
CHILDREN'S PLAYDROME &
THE MILLENNIUM ROLLERCOASTER
Ashby by
Partney
Candlesby
Orby
Orby Marsh
FUNCOAST WORLD
NORTHCOTE HEAVY
HORSE CENTRE
GUNBY HALL
A158
Winthorpe
Seathorne

C

Halton
Holegate
Great
Steeping
Bratoft
**Burgh
le Marsh**
BURGH LE
MARSH WINDMILL
NATURELAND SEAL
SANCTUARY
B1195
Irby in
the Marsh
7
CHURCH
FARM
MUS.
Skegness
Little
Steeping
Firsby
Thorpe
Culvert
Croft
THE LIFEBOAT
STATION
Thorpe
St Peter
A52
Seacroft
Thorpe
Fendykes
**Wainfleet
All Saints**
Croft Marsh
Seacroft
GIBRALTAR POINT
Wainfleet Bank
MAGDALEN
MUSEUM
Wainfleet St Mary
GIBRALTAR
POINT

D

Wainfleet Tofts
Wainfleet
Sand
Friskney
Eaudike
Friskney
Fen
20
Wrangle
Bank
Friskney
Tofts
Friskney Flats
Commonside
40
Wrangle Lowgate
Wrangle
Hurn's End
118
Leverton Outgate
Leverton Highgate

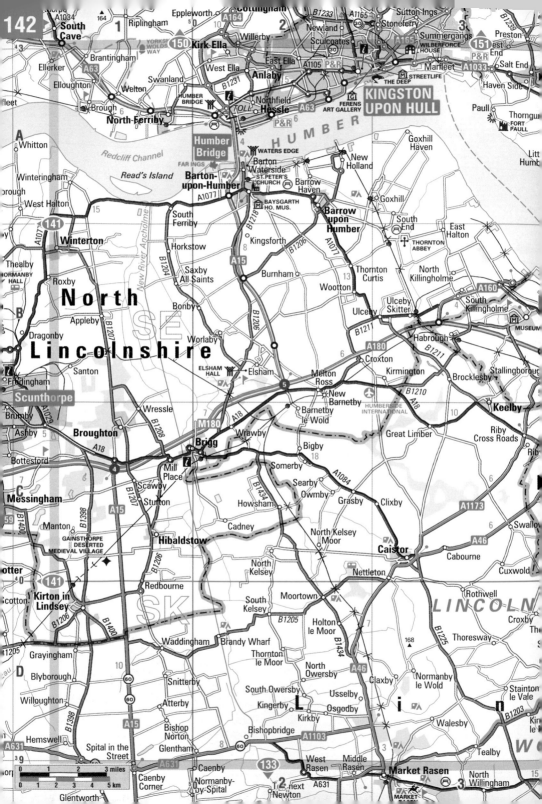

4 **5** **6**

Elstronwick
Tunstall
Burton Pidsea
North End
Roos **151** B1242
Waxholme
Rimswell
Owthorne
Withernsea
Burstwick B1362 Halsham East End
Camerton
Ryehill 18 Keyingham
Ottringham Hollym
Winestead A1033
Patrington 5
Holmpton
B1445
Out Newton
Welwick 6 Weeton
Sunk Island
Skeffling Easington

A

ngham

ROTTERDAM 12:30
ZEEBRUGGE 12:45
Kilnsea

TA

ROTTERDAM
ZEEBRUGGE

SPURN

SPURN HEAD

B

A180 Pyewipe
HOEK VAN HOLLAND 13:00
OOSTENDE 15:00

Healing West Marsh **Grimsby** A180
Great Coates Freshney National Fishing Heritage Centre Old Clee
sby 5 **CLEETHORPES** MOUTH OF THE HUMBER
aceby Nunsthorpe A46 CLEETHORPES COAST LIGHT RAILWAY
Bradley Scartho A1098 CLEETHORPES PLEASURE ISLAND THEME PARK
rth East B1219 **Humberston**
Barnoldby le Beck **Waltham** A16 9 New Waltham
A18 WALTHAM WINDMILL **Holton le Clay**
ncolnshire Brigsley Ashby cum Fenby A1031
Beelsby Waithe Tetney Lock
Hatcliffe B1203 Tetney North Cotes

BREVIK 33:00
CUXHAVEN 22:00
ESBJERG 22:00
GOTHENBURG 26:00
KRISTIANSAND 30:00
ROTTERDAM 11:45
ZEEBRUGGE 14:00

C

East Ravendale 10 Grainsby
Wold Newton B1201 Marshchapel
IRE North Thoresby Eskham
Fulstow Wragholme Grainthorpe
A16 Ludborough LINCOLNSHIRE WOLDS RLY.
Binbrook North Ormsby Utterby Covenham St Bartholomew Conisholme North Somercotes
Skidbrooke North End
A1031 **Saltfleet**
South Somercotes
Covenham St Mary
5 Yarburgh Skidbrooke
Donna Nook

TF

Donna Nook

25

D

c o l n
Fotherby Little Grimsby Alvingham ALVINGHAM MILL North Cockerington Saltfleetby St Clements
DS Great Tows Kelstern North Elkington RUSHMOOR South Cockerington SALTFLEET THEDDLET
A631 **134** South Elkington A16 B1200 **135** Saltfleetby St Peter Theddlethorpe St Helen
ford **4** Welton le Wold **5** Keddington Grimoldby Saltfleetby All Saints
Louth Theddlethorpe

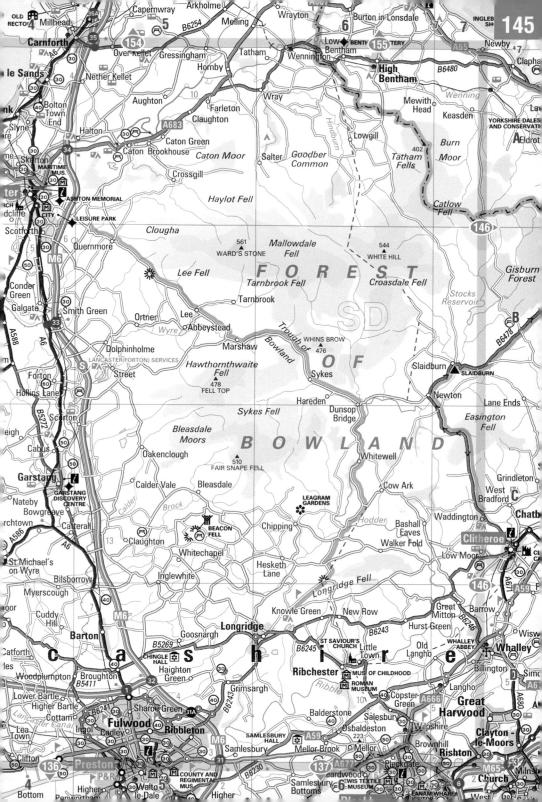

N I D D E R D A L E

Moor
4
Stean Moor
Bouthwaite 5
Dallowgill Moor
Dallow 2
Low Grantley
Winksley 6
Greygarth

Ramsgill

157

Gouthwaite Res.

Grantley

 St Mary's

Studley Roger
STUDLEY ROYAL WATER GDNS
FOUNTAINS ABBEY

Heathfield Moor

Wath

Eavestone

Risplith

Aldfield

t h
i r e
h i r e
Hebden Moor

Pateley Moor

B6265

Sawley

Markington

Grimwith Res.

NIDDERDALE MUSEUM

ssington
UPPER WHARFEDALE MUSEUM

Pateley Bridge

Wilsill

Glasshouses

Brimham Rocks

A

Greenhow Hill

Beverley

Low Laithe

Bishop Thornton

11
B6265

Hebden

STUMP CROSS CAVERNS

New York
Dacre Banks

Summer Bridge

Shaw Mills

Bedlam
12

Thorpe
Burnsall

PARCEVALL HALL GARDENS

Dacre

B6165

Burnt Yates

Ripley
RIPLEY CASTLE

Pockstones Moor

Skyreholme

Padside

Darley Head

Darley

Birstwith

Clint

Hampsthwaite

Killinghall
KNOX
148

Appletreewick

Upper Barden Res.
12

Drebley
449
Barden Fell

West End

Thornthwaite

Kettlesing Bottom

Forest

New Pa

MERCER ART GALLERY

B6161

Barden Scale

BOLTON ABBEY ESTATE

Hill End

Blubberhouses

Kettlesing Head

Moor

Harrogate
B

Lower Barden Res.

Bolton Abbey

Pace Gate

Fewston Res.

Fewston

RHS GARDEN HARLOW CARR

tby
EMBSAY STEAM RAILWAY

Halton East

Hazlewood

BUFFERS

409

Timble

Swinsty Res.

Bland Hill

Beckwithshaw

Harlow Hill
Rossett Green

Draughton

Bolton Bridge

Beamsley

Langbar

Jack Hill

Brackenthwaite

Pannal

A65

SE

Lindley Wood Res.

Lindley Green

North Rigton

A658

Addingham

Middleton

Denton

Askwith

Farnley

Braythorn

Stainburn

Huby

Weeton

Dunkeswick

Cringles

ILKLEY
B6382

Clifton

Weston

Newall

Leathley

Pool

Arthington

Weard

arnhill

Kildwick

Silsden

Ilkley Moor
402

Burley in Wharfedale

Otley
A659

Gastley

Eastburn

ton-in-aven

Steeton

CLIFFE CASTLE

Utley

Riddlesden
EAST RIDDLESDEN HALL

Menston

CHEVIN FOREST

East Carlton

Old Bramhope

Bramhope

Eccup

Keighley

Braithwaite

Knowle Park

Thwaites

East Morton

Hawksworth

Guiseley
3

Eccup Res.

Laycock

se Eye

Exley Head

Micklethwaite

Crossflatts

Yeadon

LEEDS BRADFORD INTERNATIONAL

Cookridge
YORK GATE GARDEN

woodley

Moor Allerton

Oakworth

B6143

Thwaites Brow

ELDWICK BRACKEN HALL COUNTRYSIDE CENTRE

Adel

Dockroyd
BRONTE PARSONAGE MUS.

Lees

Ingrow

1853 GALLERY

Baildon

Esholt

Rawdon

Tinshill

Holt Park

148

Marsh

HAWORTH
PENISTONE HILL

BINGLEY

Harden

Cottingley

Wilsden

Saltaire

A658

A65

Horsforth

Meanwood

B6157

Headingley

Y AND LLEY LWAY

Oxenhope

A629

Cullingworth

Lingbob

B6144

Moorhead

Frizinghall
CARTWRIGHT HALL ART GALLERY

Apperley Bridge

Calverley
BRADFORD IND. MUS.

Bodley

Farsley

KIRKSTALL ABBEY

Bramley

Kirkstall

CITY ART GAL.

Burley

Denholme

Allerton

Heaton

Manningham

SHIPLEY

Eccleshill

Undercliffe
Thornbury

Swinnow Moor

Stanningley

LEEDS INDUSTRIAL MUS.

Denholme Well Heads

COLOUR MUS.

CATH

Armley

Wortley

Holbe

B6141

Thornton

Lidget Green

Bradford

Laisterdyke

Bowling

A647

PUDSEY

A6110

Causeway Foot

Clayton

Great Horton

NAT. MUS. PHOTOGRAPHY

West Bowling

Holme Wood

BOLLING HALL

Tong

New Farnley

2A

Narley Moor Res.

Dean Head Res.

138

Queensbury

Illingworth

Buttershaw

Wibsey

Low Moor

139

Bierley

Drighlington

A58

Churwell

Beeston

erley Wainstalls
4

Buttershaw
5

Shelf

Ambler Thorn

A6036

Wyke

M606

Birkenshaw

A650

Adwalton

M621

A653

MIDDLE AL

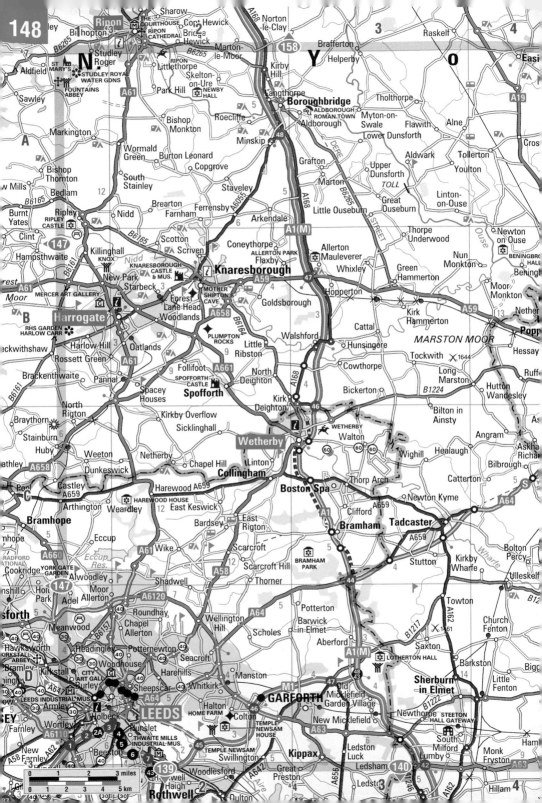

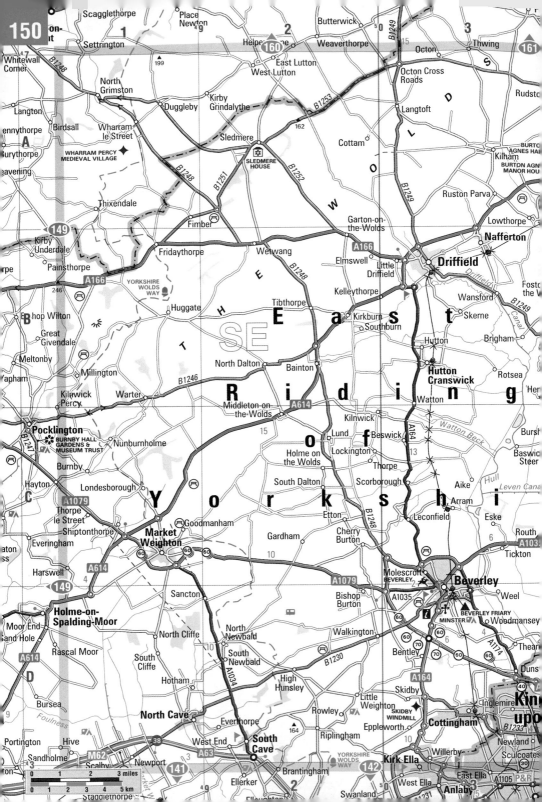

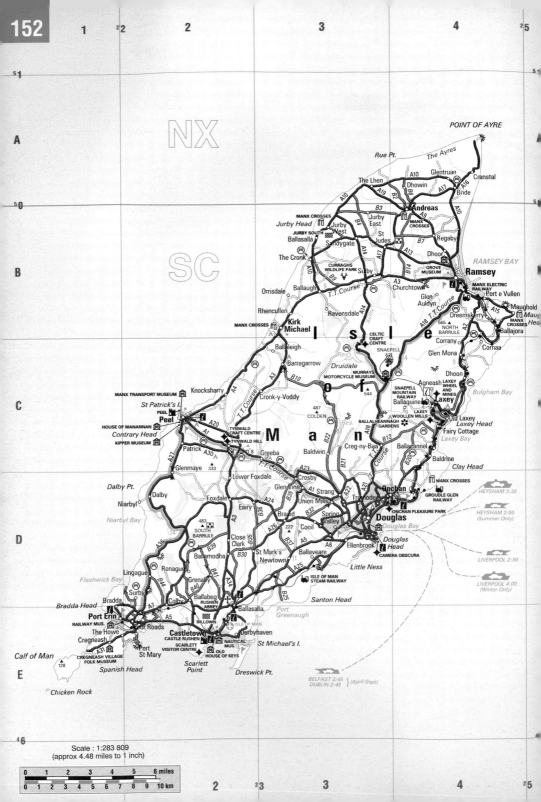

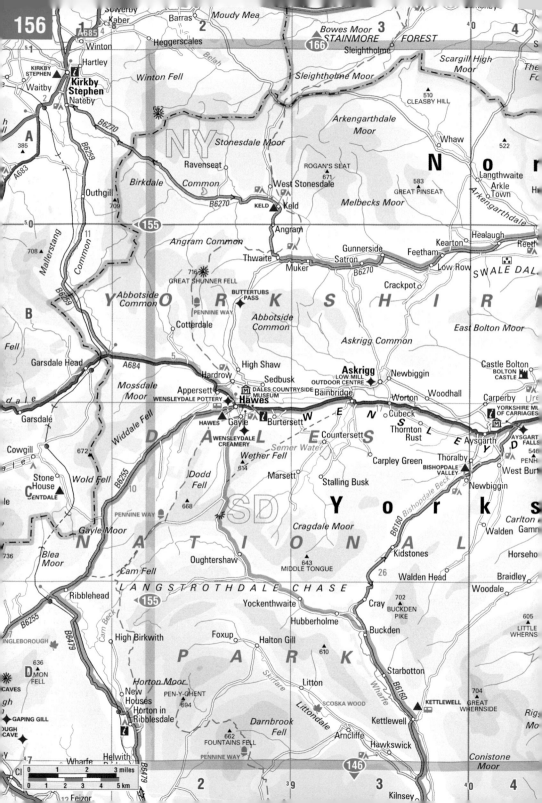

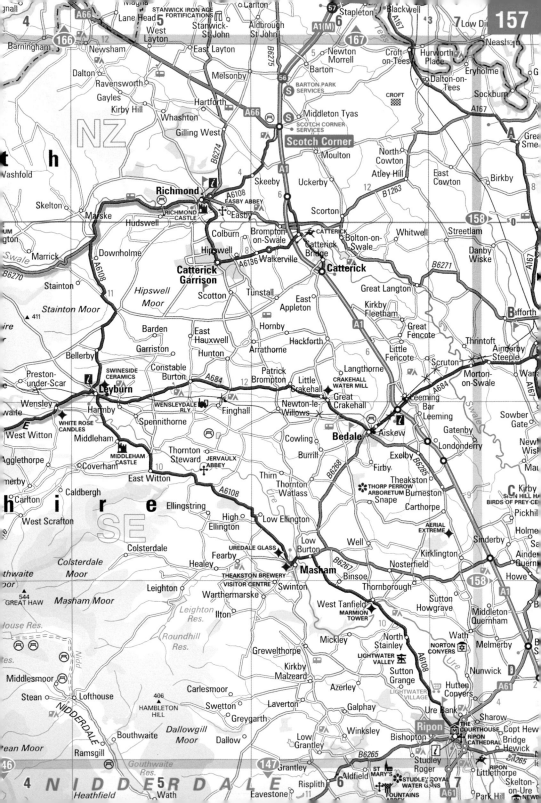

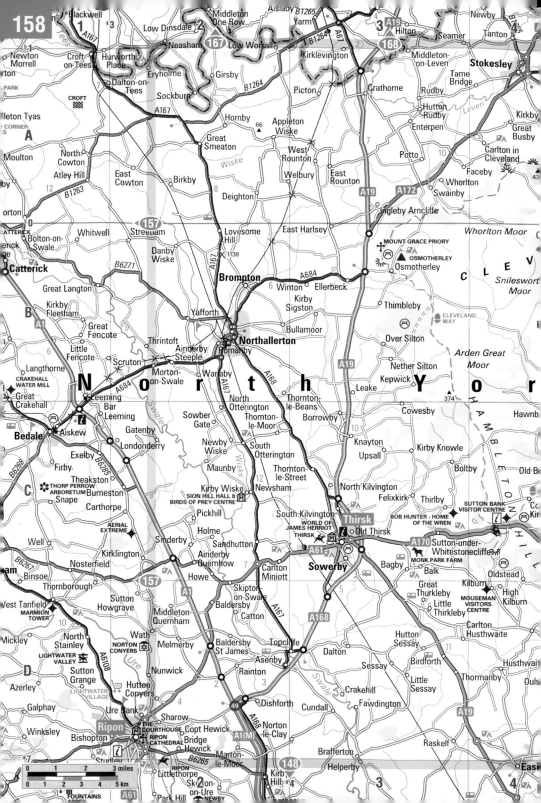

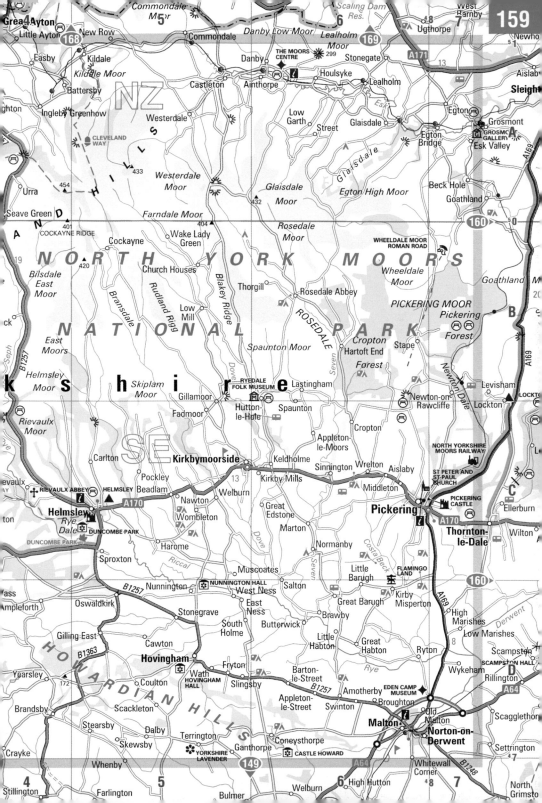

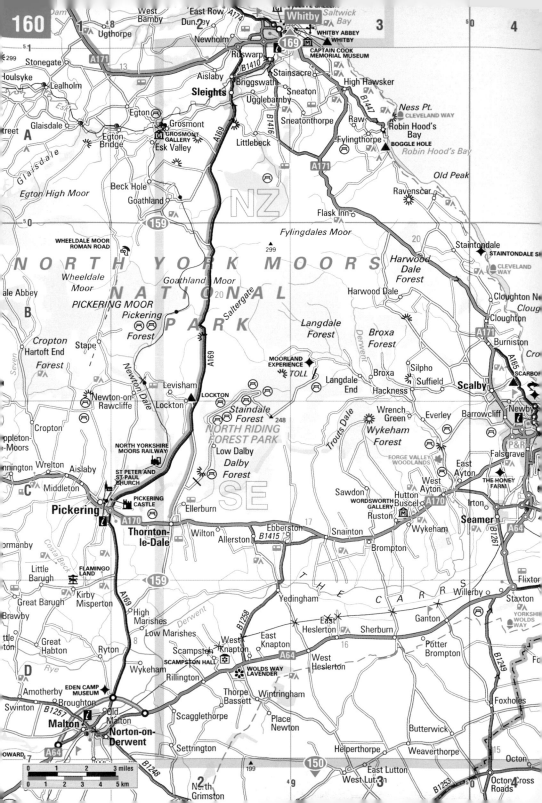

OV

A

50

FARM

ke

B

ess Rocks
D MARINE SANCTUARY
ay

RBOROUGH CASTLE
A MUSEUM
borough
uth Bay

TA

C

Cayton Bay
Yons Nab
CLEVELAND
WAY
A165
bberston
Gristhorpe A1039
Filey Brigg
olkton
Filey
5
Muston
Filey Bay
Primrose Valley
Hunmanby
Moor
Reighton
Sands
Hunmanby
Reighton Gap
Reighton
Speeton
D
10
B1229
Buckton
Bempton
Burton
Fleming
B1255
Grindale
A165
FLAMBOROUGH
HEAD
Flamborough
B1259
150
151
47
B1255
SEWERBY HALL A D GARDENS

B1253
Sewerby
BONDVILLE MODEL VILLAGE

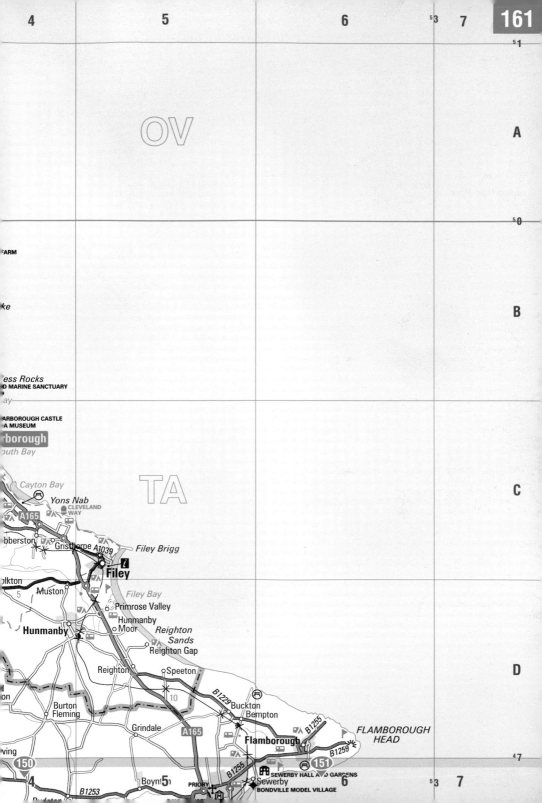

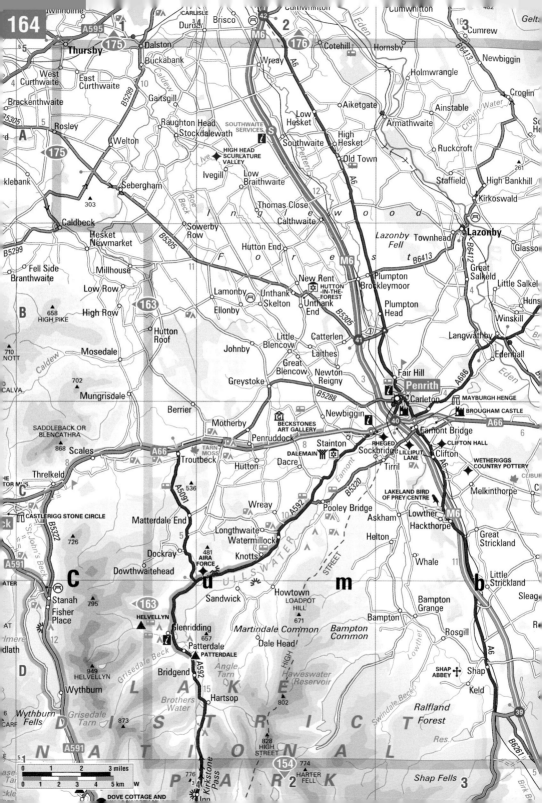

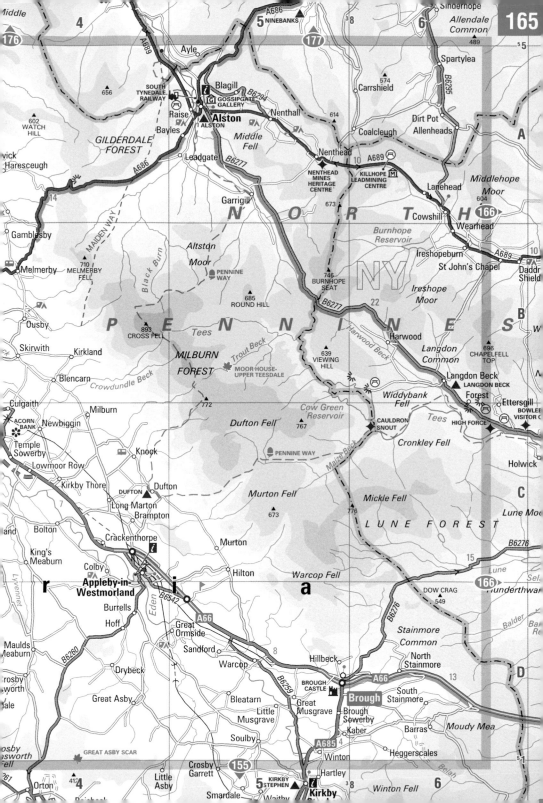

⁵5

A

B

NZ

C

MINIATURE
RAILWAY

**Saltburn-
by-the-Sea**

CHRIS BIRKBECK
INTERNATIONAL RALLY
166   SCHOOL

Brotton   Skinningrove

Carlin
How   Boulby

5   **Loftus**   A174   **Staithes**

North
Skelton   Easington   Port Mulgrave

Kilton
Thorpe   Hinderwell   *Runswick Bay*

d

Lingdale

argrove   Stanghow   Liverton   Roxby   Newton   Runswick   Kettleness
ark   Mulgrave   Bay

Goldsborough

d   9   Moorsholm   Scaling   Ellerby   14   D

A171   B1266   A174   Lythe   Sandsend

Res.   Mickleby   East   THE DRACULA
                  Barnby   EXPERIENCE
           Scaling Dam   West   *Sandsend Wyke*   SUTCLIFFE GALLERY
           Res.   Barnby   East Row
                    Dunsley   **Whitby**   *Saltwick*
Commondale   *Danby Low Moor* / *Lealholm*   *Bay*
               Ugthorpe   WHITBY ABBEY
               Moor   Newholm   **Whitby**
                             CAPTAIN COOK
                             MEMORIAL MUSEUM
159   LE MOORS   *Moor*   **160**   Ruswarp   ⁵1
           CENTRE   299   Stonegate   B1410   Sta acre

Commondale

Danby   Houlsyke   13   A171   Aislaby   High Hawsker
                             Briggswath

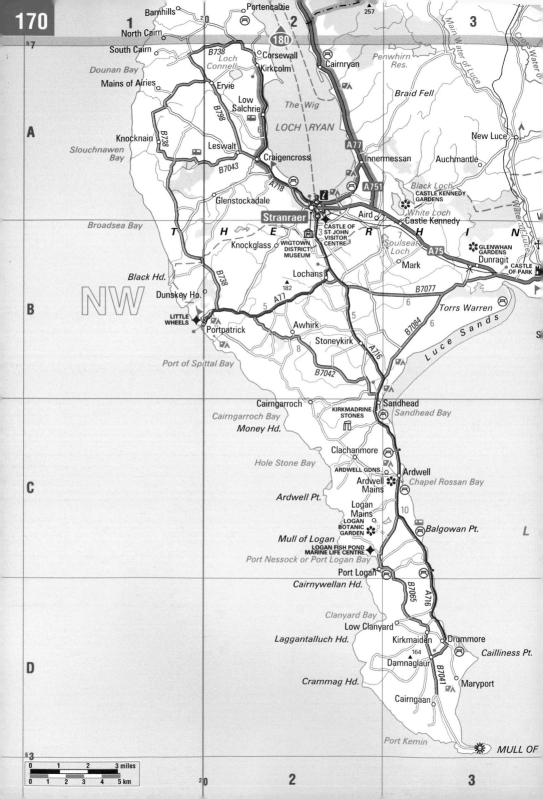

1   **2**   **3**

Barnhills
Portencalzie
North Cairn
257
South Cairn
180
B738
Loch Connell
Corsewall
Dounan Bay
Kirkcolm
Cairnryan
Penwhirn Res.
Mains of Airies
Ervie
Braid Fell
B798
Low Salchrie
The Wig
LOCH RYAN
New Luce

A
Knocknain
B738
Leswalt
Craigencross
A77
Innermessan
Auchmantle
Slouchnawen Bay
B7043
A718
A751
Black Loch
CASTLE KENNEDY GARDENS
Glenstockadale
i
White Loch
THE
Stranraer
Aird
Castle Kennedy
Broadsea Bay
E
R
H
I
N
Knockglass
Castle of St John Visitor Centre
Soulseat Loch
GLENWHAN GARDENS
Wigtown District Museum
Mark
Dunragit
Black Hd.
Lochans
182
B7077
CASTLE OF PARK

B
NW
Dunskey Ho.
B738
A77
5
A716
6
Torrs Warren
LITTLE WHEELS
Portpatrick
Awhirk
5
B7084
6
Luce Sands
Port of Spittal Bay
Stoneykirk
8
B7042
A716

Cairngarroch
Sandhead
Cairngarroch Bay
KIRKMADRINE STONES
Sandhead Bay
Money Hd.
Clachanmore

C
Hole Stone Bay
ARDWELL GDNS.
Ardwell
Chapel Rossan Bay
Ardwell Pt.
Ardwell Mains
Logan Mains
10
Balgowan Pt.
LOGAN BOTANIC GARDEN
L
Mull of Logan
LOGAN FISH POND MARINE LIFE CENTRE
Port Nessock or Port Logan Bay
Port Logan
Cairnywellan Hd.
B7065
A716
Clanyard Bay
Low Clanyard
Laggantalluch Hd.
Kirkmaiden
Drummore

D
Crammag Hd.
164
Damnaglaur
Cailliness Pt.
B7041
Maryport
Cairngaan
Port Kemin
MULL OF

0   1   2   3 miles
0   1   2   3   4   5 km

1   **2**   **3**

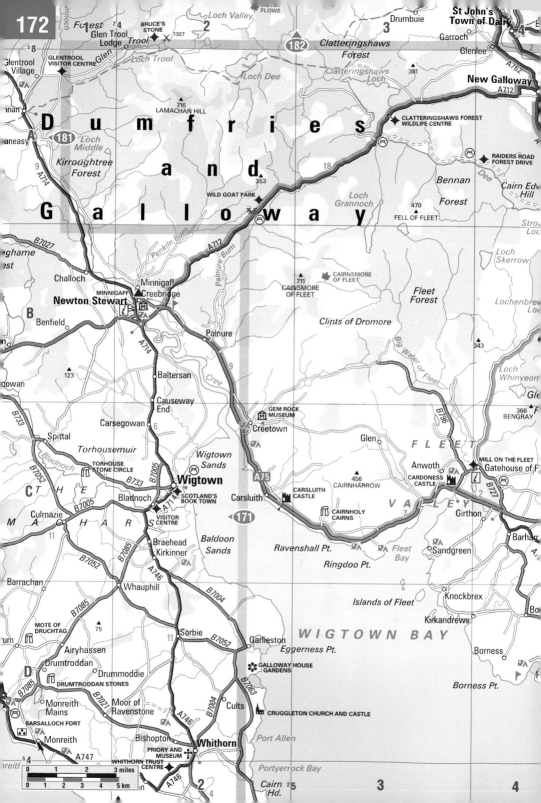

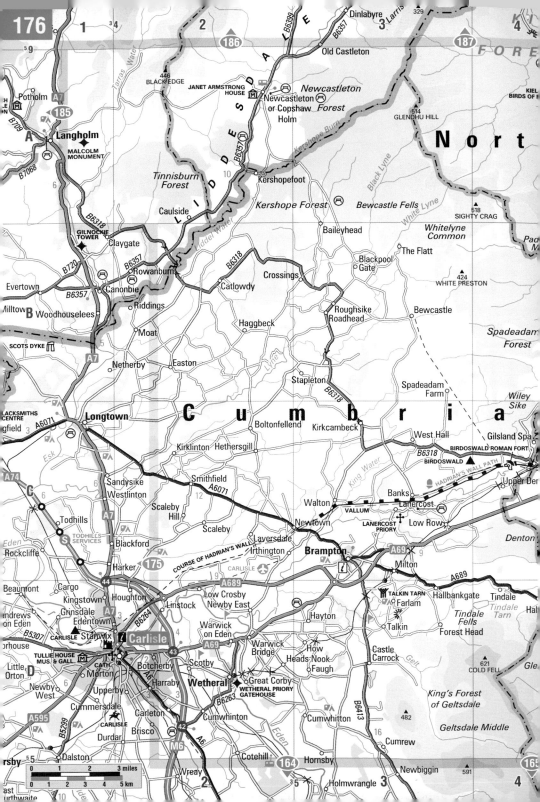

1 3 4 2 3 4

5 9

FORE

B6399 L B6357 Dinlabyre 329 Larris

186 Old Castleton 187

TARRAS WATER L I D D E S D A L E KIEL
446 BIRDS OF F
BLACK EDGE
JANET ARMSTRONG Newcastleton
HOUSE Newcastleton or Copshaw Forest
Holm 514
GLENDHU HILL

A Potholm A7 Kershope Burn **N o r t**

HEN 185 B709

Langholm

MALCOLM Black Lyne
MONUMENT Tinnisburn 10 Kershopefoot White Lyne
Forest
6 B7068 Kershopefoot

Kershope Forest Bewcastle Fells 518
SIGHTY CRAG

B6318 Caulside Whitelyne
GILNOCKIE Baileyhead Common
TOWER Claygate Liddel Water
The Flatt Pad
424 M
B720 B6357 Rowanburn Crossings Blackpool WHITE PRESTON
Gate
Evertown B6357 Canonbie Catlowdy Bewcastle
Milltown **B** Woodhouselees Roughsike Spadeadam
Riddings Roadhead Forest
Moat Haggbeck

SCOTS DYKE 5 Netherby Easton Lyne Spadeadam Wiley
Farm Sike

A7 Stapleton

LACKSMITHS B6318 King Water
CENTRE **C u m b r i a**
gfield A6071 **Longtown**
Boltonfellend Kirkcambeck West Hall Gilsland Spa
Esk BIRDOSWALD ROMAN FORT
A74 Kirklinton Hethersgill B6318 BIRDOSWALD
HADRIAN'S WALL PATH Upper Der
C 6 Sandysike Smithfield Birdoswald
Westlinton A6071 Banks
12 Walton Lanercost Low Row
Todhills Scaleby Newtown VALLUM Denton
TODHILLS Hill LANERCOST
SERVICES Scaleby Laversdale PRIORY Low Row
Eden Blackford Irthington
Rockcliffe Harker COURSE OF HADRIAN'S WALL **Brampton** A69 9
175 CARLISLE Milton
Beaumont Cargo 44 Low Crosby A689
Kingstown Houghton Newby East TALKIN TARN Hallbankgate Tindale
ndrews A7 Linstock Farlam Tindale Tindale
on Eden Grinsdale B6264 Hayton Tarn Ha
B5307 Edentown Warwick Talkin Fells
rhouse CARLISLE Starwix on Eden How Forest Head
TULLIE HOUSE **Carlisle** Warwick Heads Nook Castle
Little MUS. & GALL. CATH Bridge Faugh Carrock 621
Orton Scotby COLD FELL Gle
D Morton Botcherby **Wetheral** Great Corby King's Forest
Newby Harraby WETHERAL PRIORY of Geltsdale
West Upperby GATEHOUSE 482 Geltsdale Middle
Cummersdale B6263 Cumwhitton
A595 Carleton Cumrew
CARLISLE 42 Eden
B5299 Brisco M6 A6 B6413 16 Cumrew
Durdar 164 591
rsby Dalston Wreay Hornsby Newbiggin
ast 10 Holmwrangle 165

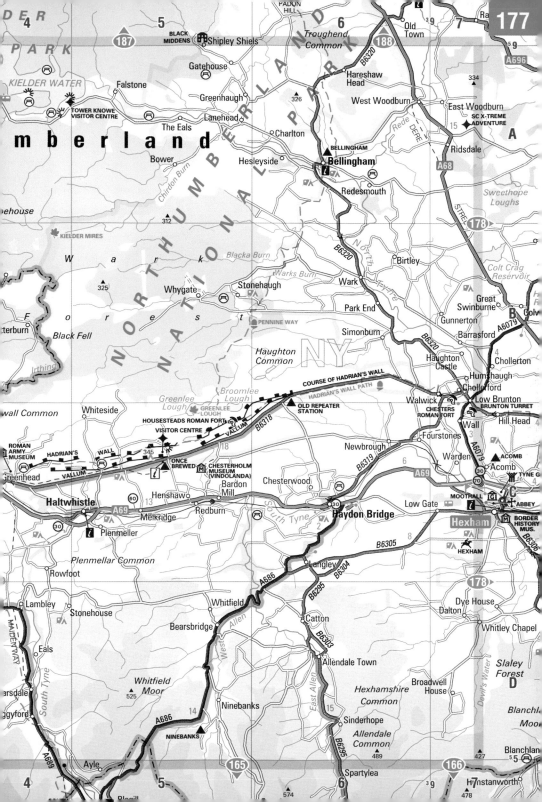

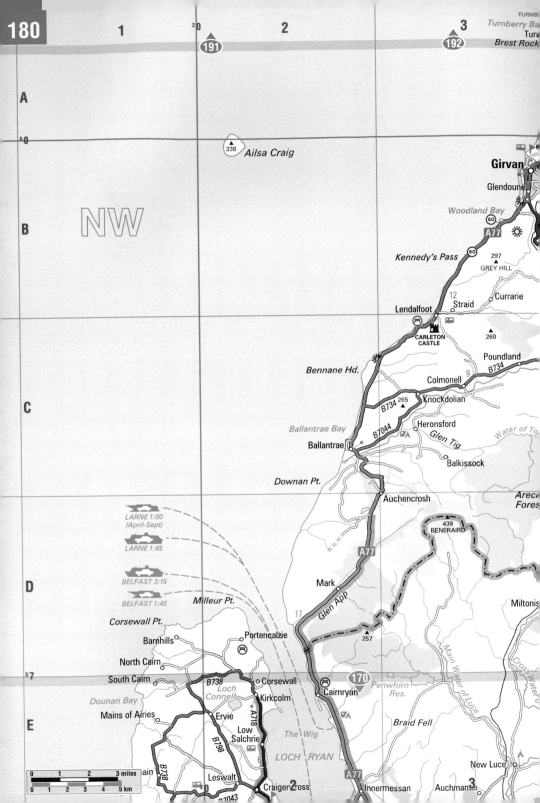

1   2   3

A

B

NW

C

D

E

Ailsa Craig
338

TURNB
Turnberry Ba
191   192   Turn
Brest Rock

Girvan
Glendoune
Woodland Bay
60
A77

Kennedy's Pass   60
297
GREY HILL
Currarie
12
Lendalfoot   Straid
CARLETON
CASTLE   260

Poundland
B734
Colmonell   9
B734 265   Knockdolian
Bennane Hd.   B7044   Heronsford
Ballantrae Bay   Glen Tig
Ballantrae   Balkissock

Downan Pt.

Auchencrosh

Arec
Fores

439
BENERAIRD

LARNE 1:00
(April-Sept)
LARNE 1:45

BELFAST 3:15

Mark
257
Milton

BELFAST 1:45   Milleur Pt.
Glen App
17
Corsewall Pt.
Barnhills
Portencalzie   A77   170   Penwhirn
North Cairn   Res.
South Cairn   Corsewall   Cairnryan
B738
Dounan Bay   Loch   Kirkcolm   Braid Fell
Connell
Mains of Airies   A718
Ervie   Low   The Wig
Salchrie   LOCH RYAN   New Luce
B798
B738   Leswalt   A77
0   1   2   3 miles   Craiger Cross   Innermessan   Auchman
0   1   2   3   4   5 km   B7043   3

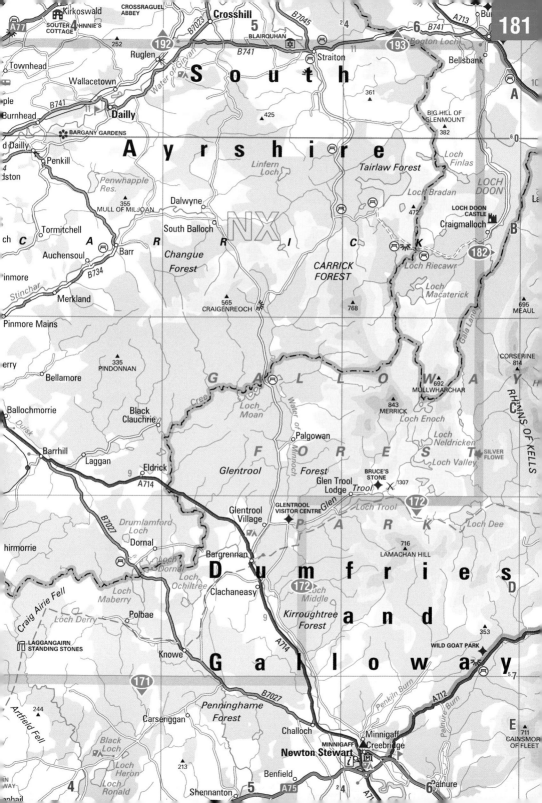

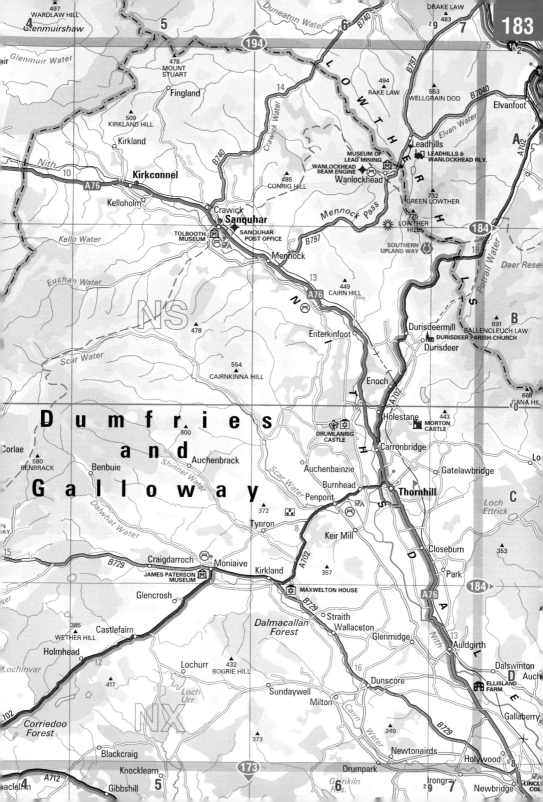

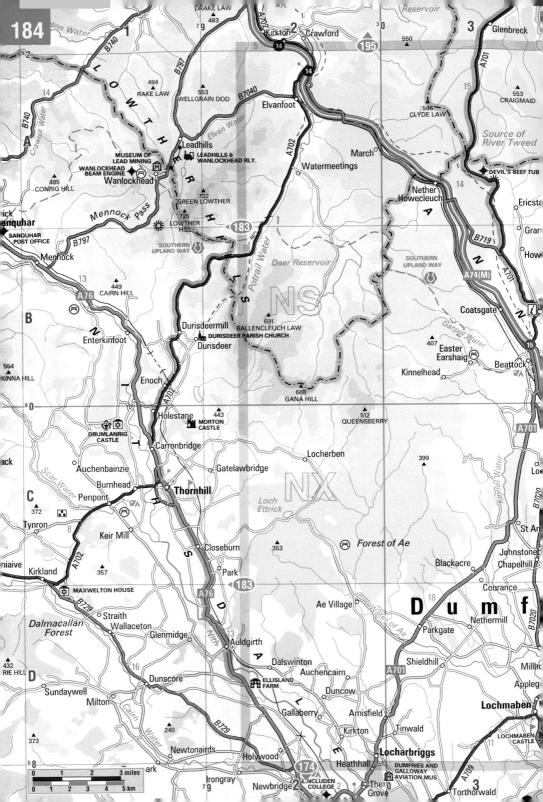

DRAKE LAW
483
Kirkton
14
Crawford
195
Glenbreck
B740
B797
550
LOWTHER
494
RAKE LAW
553
WELLGRAIN DOD
B7040
553
CRAIGMAID
Elvanfoot
546
CLYDE LAW
Leadhills
LEADHILLS & WANLOCKHEAD RLY.
March
Source of River Tweed
MUSEUM OF LEAD MINING
Watermeetings
DEVIL'S BEEF TUB
WANLOCKHEAD BEAM ENGINE
Wanlockhead
Nether Howecleuch
485
CONRIG HILL
732
GREEN LOWTHER
14
ick
anquhar
725
LOWTHER HILL
183
B719
SANQUHAR POST OFFICE
Ericsta
B797
Mennock
SOUTHERN UPLAND WAY
Grar
Mennock Pass
Daer Reservoir
SOUTHERN UPLAND WAY
How
A74(M)
13
449
CAIRN HILL
A76
NS
Coatsgate
B
N
Enterkinfoot
Durisdeermill
691
BALLENCLEUCH LAW
Garpol Water
15
i
554
KINNA HILL
DURISDEER PARISH CHURCH
Durisdeer
407
Easter Earshaig
Beattock
Enoch
Kinnelhead
668
GANA HILL
0
Holestane
443
MORTON CASTLE
512
QUEENSBERRY
399
A701
DRUMLANRIG CASTLE
Carronbridge
Locherben
Auchenbainzie
Gatelawbridge
NX
Burnhead
Penpont
Thornhill
Loch Ettrick
Forest of Ae
Johnstone
Chapelhill
C
372
Tynron
Keir Mill
353
Blackacre
Closeburn
Courance
niaive
Kirkland
A702
357
Park
183
Ae Village
18
D u m f
MAXWELTON HOUSE
B729
Straith
Wallaceton
Parkgate
Nethermill
B720
Dalmacallan Forest
Glenmidge
13
Auldgirth
Shieldhill
Millh
432
RIE HILL
16
Dalswinton
A701
Appleg
D
Dunscore
Auchencairn
Duncow
Sundaywell
Milton
ELLISLAND FARM
Lochmaben
373
240
Gallaberry
Amisfield
Tinwald
LOCHMABEN CASTLE
Newtonairds
Kirkton
11
B729
174
Heathhall
Locharbriggs
Irongray
Holywood
L.NCLUDEN COLLEGE
The Grove
DUMFRIES AND GALLOWAY AVIATION MUS.
A709
Torthorwald
Newbridge
8
3 miles
0   1   2   3   4   5 km

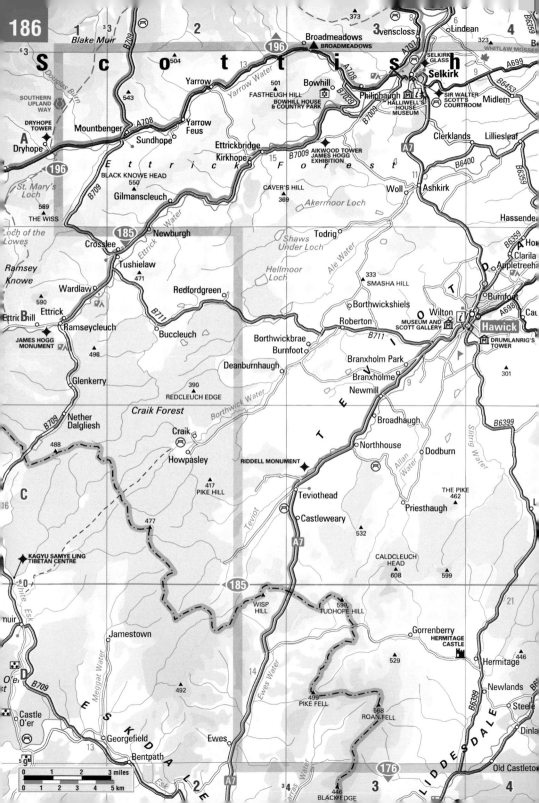

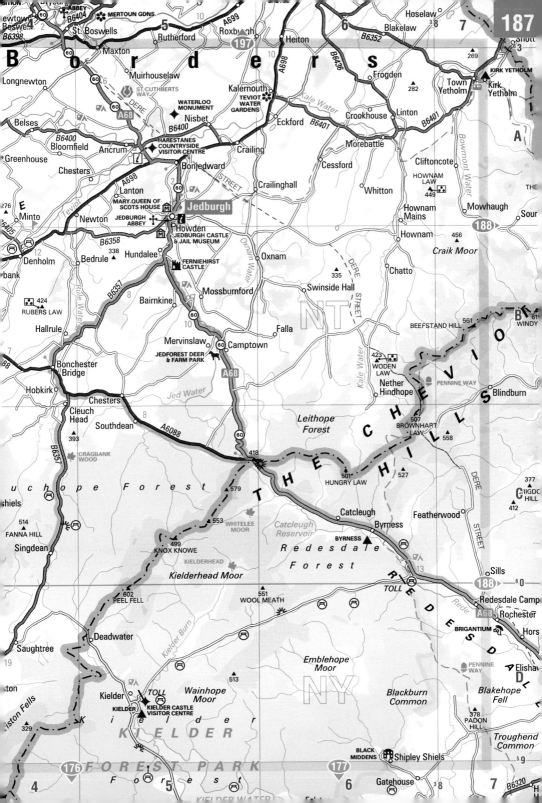

NORTHUMBERLAND COAST

NU

NZ

Seahouses
Bradford
Bellshill
Mousen
B1341
Elford
North Sunderland
Adderstone
Lucker
Warenford
Newham Hall
Newham
Newstead
Swinhoe
Beadnell
Benthall
Beadnell Bay
Rosebrough
Chathill
Ellingham
Preston
Brunton
Brockdam
PRESTON TOWER
High Newton-by-the-Sea
Low Newton-by-the-Sea
Brownside
North Charlton
Doxford
Chiliston Bank
B6347
Embleton
Embleton Bay
West Ditchburn
South Charlton
Rock
Dunstan Steads
Castle Point
DUNSTANBURGH CASTLE
ope
169
B6347
B6346
B6341
Rennington
101
Littlemill
Dunstan
Craster
Howick
Howick Haven
Littlehoughton
ington
Shipley
HULNE ABBEY
250
Denwick
Longhoughton
Boulmer
don Hall
ALNWICK ABBEY
1093
Alnwick
Boulmer Haven
Abberwick
Broome Park
Hawkhill
3
Lemmington Hall
7
B6341
Bilton
Lesbury
Alnmouth
EDLINGHAM CASTLE
250
Alnmouth Bay
lingham
Shilbottle
High Buston
A1068
Low Buston
179
Birling
Newton-on-the-Moor
Eastfield Hall
Warkworth
A697
188
Hazon
Gloster Hill
Amble
Coquet I.
Swarland Estate
Brainshaugh
Guyzance
Hauxley
Swarland
15
Acklington
North Togston
Radcliffe
gframlington
70
Togston
5
Felton
B6345
8
Broomhill
50
DRURIDGE BAY
LONGFRAMLINGTON GARDENS
B6344
West Thirston
East Thirston
South Broomhill
Red Row
Weldon
Eshott
West Chevington
A1068
Druridge Bay
sleyhurst
Helm
9
Widdrington
ngates
Longhorsley
Causey Park Bridge
Stobswood
The Scars
Fenrother
Widdrington Station
Cresswell
Tritlington
Ellington
l a n d
A697
Ulgham
Linton
LYNEMOUTH
Stanton
178
Hebron
Longhirst
B1337
THE SANCTUARY WILDLIFE CENTRE
QUEEN ELIZABETH II
A189
A1068
179
Beacon Pt.
Ashington
Woodhorn
Font

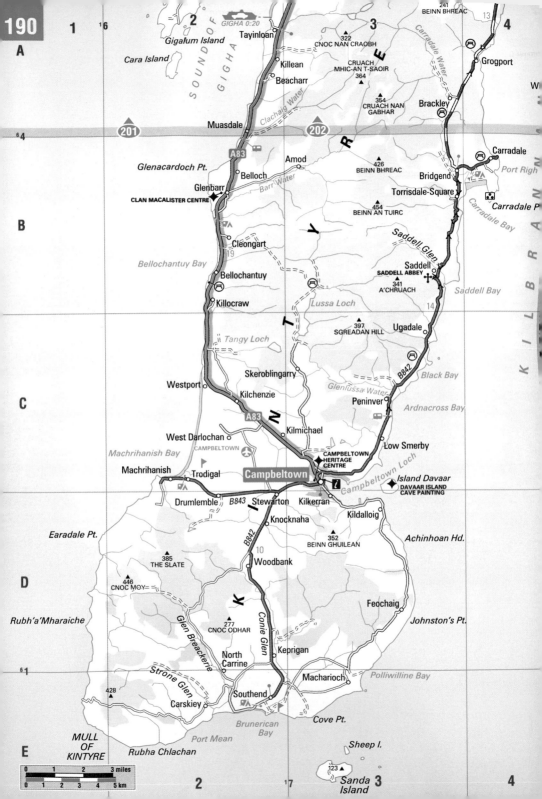

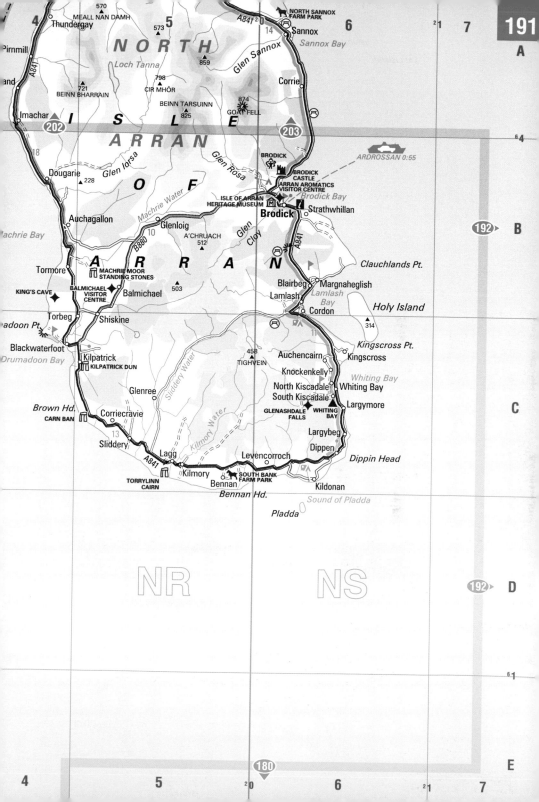

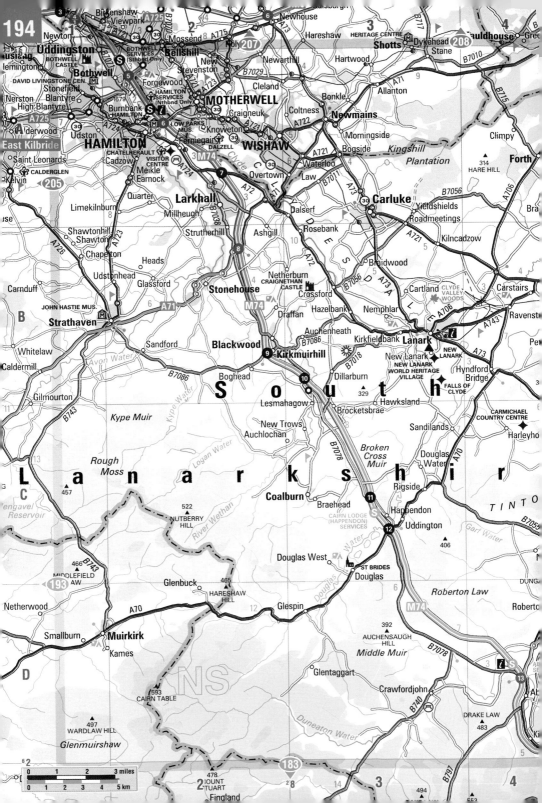

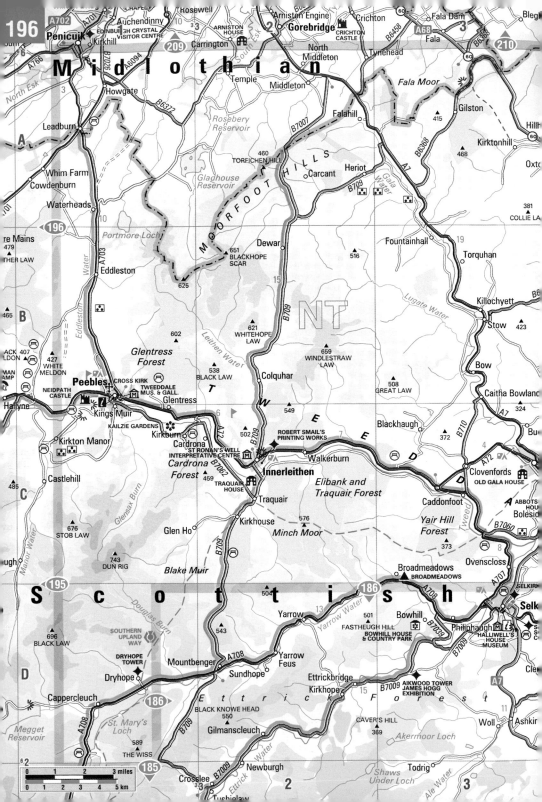

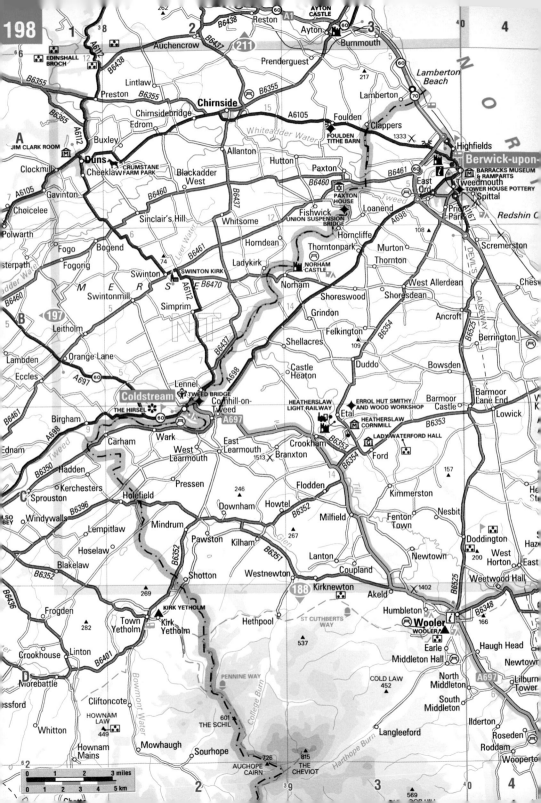

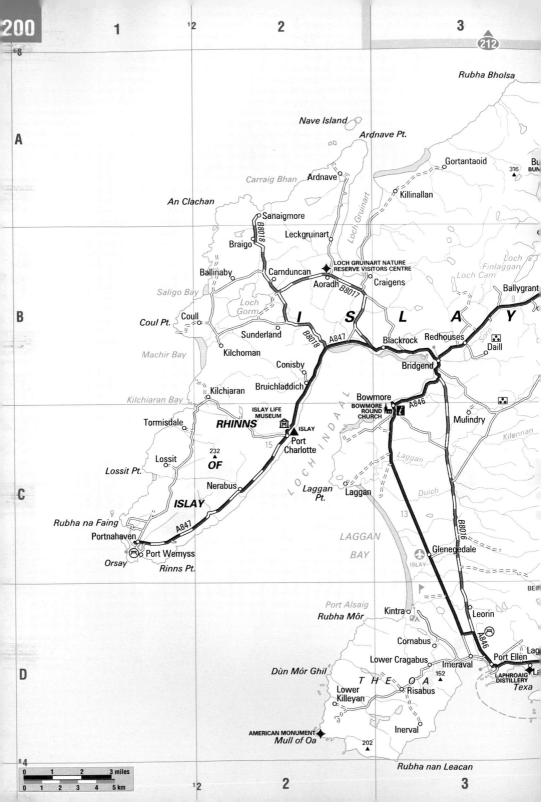

1 12 2 3

8

A

B

C

D

6 4

ISLAY

Rubha Bholsa

Nave Island
Ardnave Pt.

Carraig Bhan
Ardnave
Gortantaoid
316
Bu
BUN

An Clachan
Killinallan

Sanaigmore
Leckgruinart
Braigo
B8018
Loch Gruinart
Loch
Finlaggan
Loch Cam
Ballinaby
Carnduncan
LOCH GRUINART NATURE
RESERVE VISITORS CENTRE
Aoradh
B8017
Craigens
Ballygrant
Saligo Bay
Loch
Gorm
8
Coul Pt.
Coull
I S L A Y
Sunderland
B8018
A847
Blackrock
Redhouses
Machir Bay
Kilchoman
Bridgend
Daill
Conisby
Bruichladdich

Kilchiaran Bay
Kilchiaran
Bowmore
BOWMORE
ROUND
CHURCH
A846
Mulindry
Tormisdale
ISLAY LIFE
MUSEUM
M
ISLAY
Port
Charlotte
Kilennan
RHINNS
15
Lossit
232
OF
LOCHINDAAL
Laggan
Lossit Pt.
Nerabus
Laggan
Pt.
Laggan
Duich
13
ISLAY
Rubha na Faing
A847
B8016
Portnahaven
LAGGAN
Orsay
Port Wemyss
BAY
Glenegedale
Rinns Pt.

Port Alsaig
Rubha Mór
Kintra
Leorin
Dùn Mór Ghil
T H E   O A
Cornabus
A846
Port Ellen
Lag
Lower Cragabus
Imeraval
LAPHROAIG
DISTILLERY
Texa
152
Lower
Killeyan
Risabus
Inerval
AMERICAN MONUMENT
Mull of Oa
202
Rubha nan Leacan

BEIN

0 1 2 3 miles
0 1 2 3 4 5 km

12 2 3

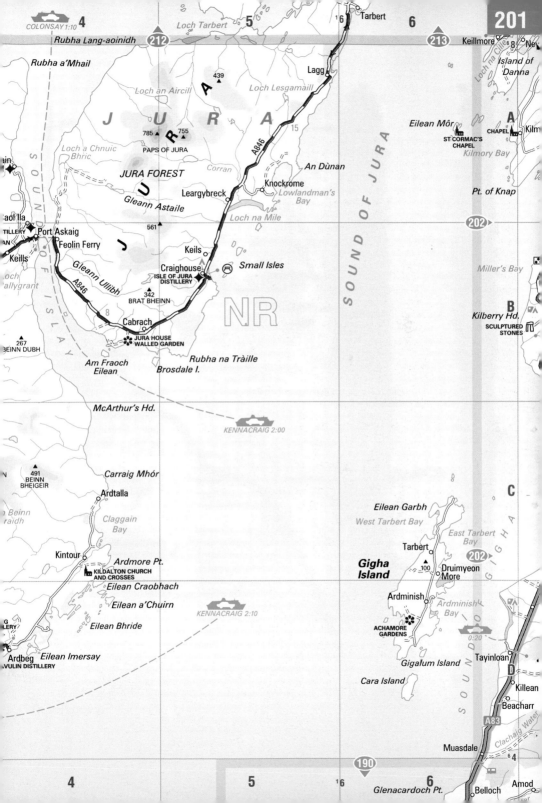

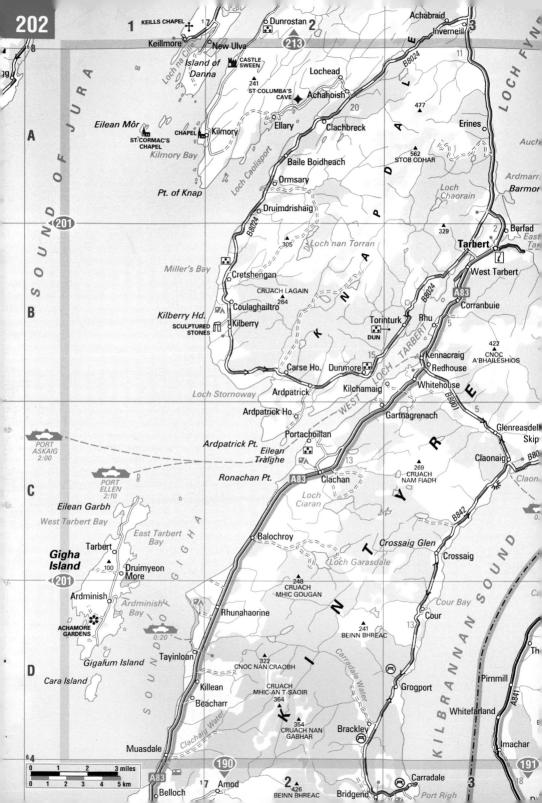

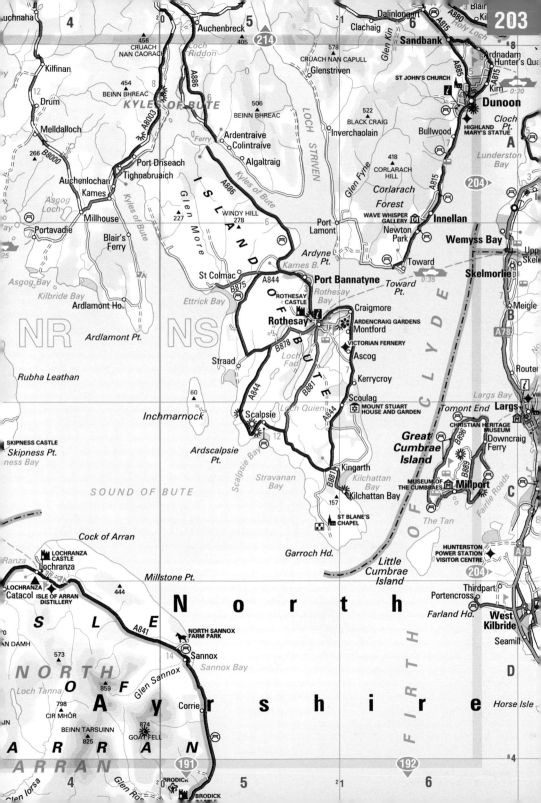

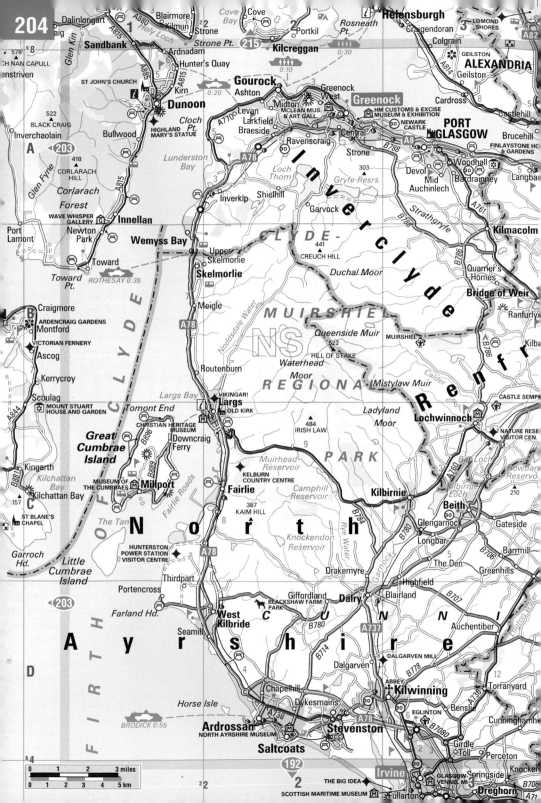

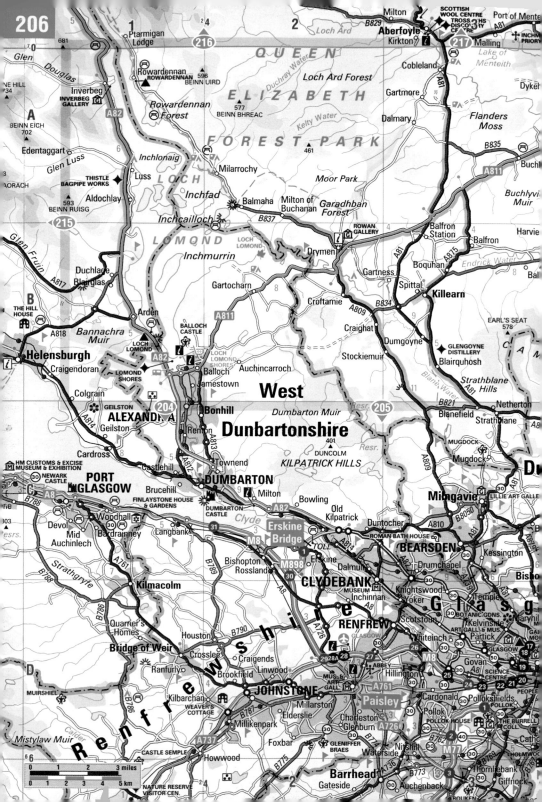

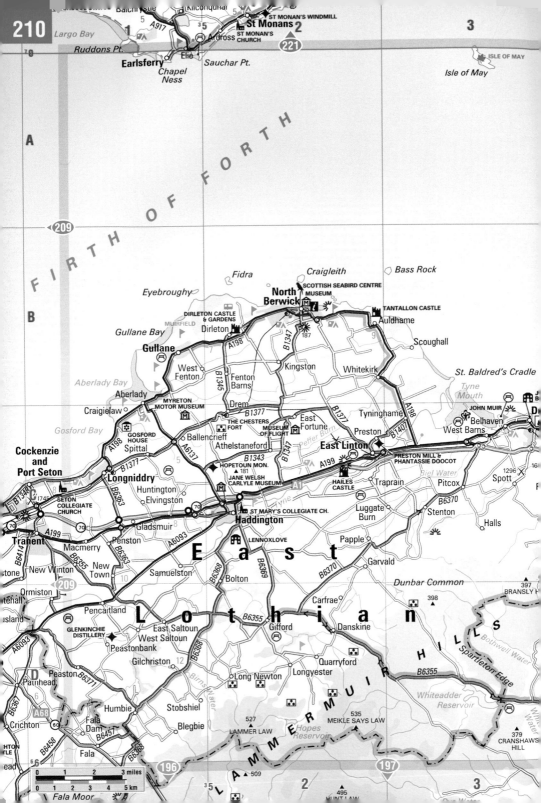

Largo Bay

FIRTH OF FORTH

209

Ruddons Pt.

St Monans
ST MONAN'S WINDMILL
ST MONAN'S CHURCH
221

Earlsferry   Elie   Sauchar Pt.
Chapel
Ness

ISLE OF MAY
Isle of May

A

FIRTH OF FORTH

Fidra   Craigleith   Bass Rock
Eyebroughy
SCOTTISH SEABIRD CENTRE
MUSEUM
North
Berwick
187
TANTALLON CASTLE
Auldhame
DIRLETON CASTLE
& GARDENS
MUIRFIELD
Dirleton
9
Scoughall
St. Baldred's Cradle

B

Gullane Bay
Gullane
A198
West
Fenton
Kingston
Whitekirk
Tyne
Mouth
Aberlady Bay
Fenton
Barns
B1345
JOHN MUIR
D
Aberlady
Drem
B1377
Belhaven
Gosford Bay
Craigielaw
MYRETON
MOTOR MUSEUM
B1377
Tyninghame
West Barns
THE CHESTERS
FORT
East
Fortune
MUSEUM
OF FLIGHT
A198
Cockenzie
and
Port Seton
GOSFORD
HOUSE
Spittal
A198
A6137
Ballencrieff
Athelstaneford
Preston
East Linton
PRESTON MILL &
PHANTASSIE DOOCOT
1296
Spott
B1371
B1343
HOPETOUN MON.
181
A199
HAILES
CASTLE
Traprain
Pitcox
Longniddry
Huntington
Elvingston
JANE WELSH
CARLYLE MUSEUM
Luggate
Burn
B6370
Stenton
Halls
SETON
COLLEGIATE CHURCH
1745
70
Gladsmuir
St MARY'S COLLEGIATE CH.
Haddington
Papple
Biel Water
397
BRANSLY
Tranent
A199
Macmerry
Penston
B6363
A6093
LENNOXLOVE
Garvald
Dunbar Common
New Winton
New
Town
Samuelston
Bolton
B6370
Carfrae
398
Ormiston
Pencaitland
GLENKINCHIE
DISTILLERY
East Saltoun
West Saltoun
Peastonbank
Gilchriston
Danskine
Sparleton Edge
Bothwell Water
B6355
Gifford
Quarryford
Longyester
Whiteadder
Reservoir
Peaston
Panhead
A68
Humbie
Stobshiel
Long Newton
527
LAMMER LAW
535
MEIKLE SAYS LAW
379
CRANSHAWS
HILL
Crichton
Fala
Dam
Blegbie
Hopes
Reservoir
Fala
Fala Moor
196
509
197
495

C

D

East Lothian

LAMMERMUIR HILLS

0   1   2   3 miles
0   1 2 3 4 5 km

4　　　　　5　　³9　　6　　⁷0

A

NT

B

Barns Ness

East Barns
Skateraw

13

herwick
Thorntonloch
60

OCKLAW
HILL
319

DUNGLASS
COLLEGIATE
CHURCH
Reed Pt.
Cove

Cockburnspath
60

hamstocks

Ecclaw

Siccar Pt.

Wheat Stack
FAST CASTLE

ST ABB'S HEAD

St. Abb's Head
KITTIWAKE GALLERY

Lumsdaine

Northfield
St Abbs

A1107
245

Coldingham
Moor

12

B6438

St. Abb's Haven
COLDINGHAM SANDS
COLDINGHAM PRIORY

Coldingham Bay

SOUTHERN
UPLAND WAY

Grantshouse
60

Huxton

Coldingham

EYEMOUTH MUSEUM

T LAW

Nether
Monynut

Houndwood

Eye Water

12

Cairncross

Eyemouth

Abbey
St. Bathans

262

AYTON
CASTLE

A6112

Auchencrow

Reston
60
A1

Ayton
60

A1107

B6355

Burnmouth

nford

197
EDINSHALL
BROCH

B6355

B6438

198

Prenderguest

B6437

Lintlaw

B6438

⁶6

C

D

⁹9

Ayton
60

217

Lamberton
Beach

A   4   B6355   5   ³9   6

MMERMUIR

Ale Water

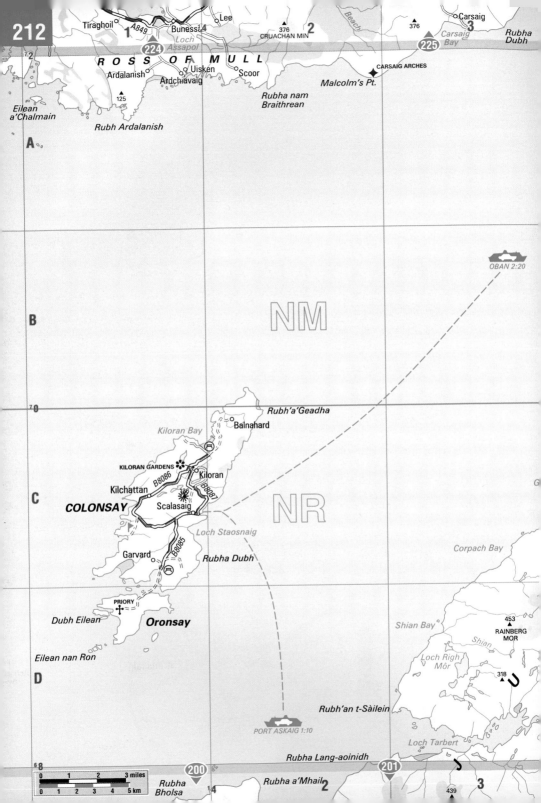

ROSS OF MULL

Tiraghoil 1 A849 Bunessan Lee 2 Carsaig 3

Loch Assapol 224 376 CRUACHAN MIN 376 Carsaig 225 Rubha
Bay Dubh

Ardalanish Uisken Scoor CARSAIG ARCHES
Ardchiavaig Malcolm's Pt.

125 Rubha nam
Braithrean

Eilean
a'Chalmain Rubh Ardalanish

A

NM

OBAN 2:20

B

Rubh'a'Geadha

Kiloran Bay Balnahard

KILORAN GARDENS

B8086 Kiloran

Kilchattan NR

COLONSAY Scalasaig B8087

Loch Staosnaig Corpach Bay

C

B8085

Garvard Rubha Dubh

Shian Bay 453
RAINBERG
PRIORY MÔR
Dubh Eilean Oronsay Shian

Eilean nan Ron Loch Righ 318
Môr

D

Rubh'an t-Sàilein

PORT ASKAIG 1:10 Loch Tarbert

8 Rubha Lang-aoinidh

0 1 2 3 miles
200 201
0 1 2 3 4 5 km Rubha
Bholsa 4 Rubha a'Mhail 2 3

439

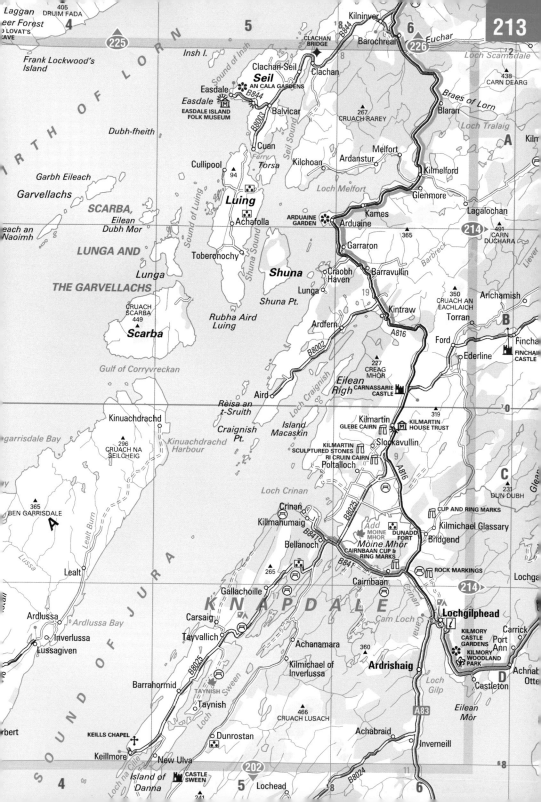

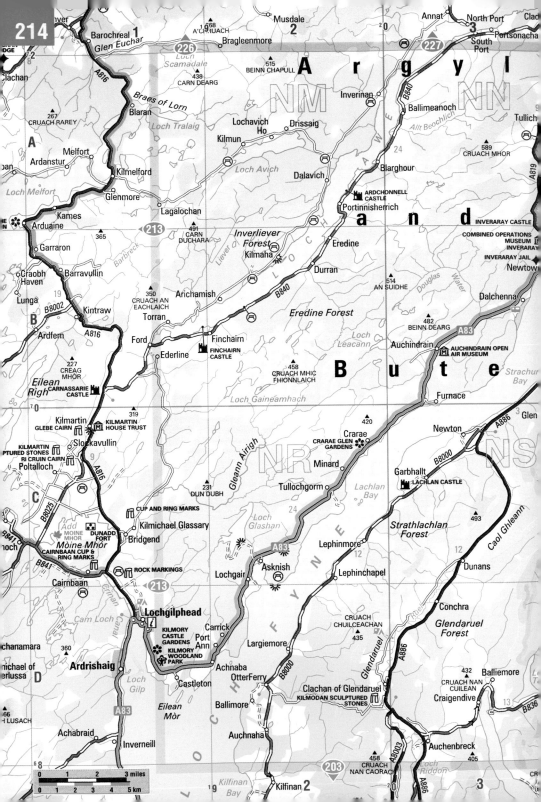

LOCH LOMOND
AND THE
TROSSACHS
NATIONAL
PARK

4 5 6 7

Stronuich Reservoir
Castile

Glen Lochay n e
228
229
MEALL NAN TARMACHAN 1043
1214 BEN LAWERS 6
BEN LAWERS VISITOR CENTRE (N.T.S.)
Lawers
A827
Carie
Ardtalnaig
BEINN BHREAC 714
888

Milton Morenish
Morenish
Ardeonaig
A
Gleann a'Chilleine

FALLS OF LOCHAY AND FISH LIFT
Boreland
MOIRLANICH LONGHOUSE
Finlarig
KILLIN
Killin
BREADALBANE FOLKLORE CENTRE
Achmore
FALLS OF DOCHART
637
879 CREAG UCHDAG

Auchlyne
Ardchyle
Glen Ogle
A827
218
Loch Lednock Reservoir
Glen Lednock
Inverge

GLEN DOCHART
A85
Ledcharrie
11
5
A85
Beich Burn
672 SRON MHOR
13
Invergel
Fur

852
Lochearnhead
Dalveich
LOCH EARN
St Fillans
A85
RIVER
B
Dunira
MELV MONUM

EDINAMPLE FALLS
Edinample
Ardvorlich
Ardtrostan
EARN
Earn
Tullybannocher
EARTHQUAKE HOUS

Braes of Balquhidder
Craigruie
Balquhidder
ROB ROY'S GRAVE
Auchtubh
A84
678
AUCHING WILDLIFE & HIG CATTLE C

lemore
larig
Loch Voil
Loch Doine
Ballimore
Strathyre Forest
Strathyre
985 BEN VORLICH
Forest of Glenartney
Dalchruin
Glen Artney
Tigh-
Auchnashelloch
BEN

771
13
811 BEINN EACH
Ardchullarie More
Keltie Water
Allt Strath a Ghlinne
C
665 UAMH BHEAG

t i r l i n g
687 BEINN BHREAC
820 BENVANE
Loch Lubnaig
Glen Finglas Res.

879 BEN LEDI
Anie
Pass of Leny
Leny Ho.
ROB ROY AND TROSSACHS VISITOR CENTRE
BRACKLINN FALLS
218
RINE
The Trossachs
FALLS OF LENY
Kilmahog
Bochastle
Callander

OSSACHS PIER COMPLEX SIR WALTER SCOTT
Trossachs Hotel
Brig o'Turk
Coilantogle
A821
Braes of Doune

BEN VENUE 727
Loch Achray
Duncraggan
Lendrick Lodge
Loch Venachar
Torrie Forest
Loch Rusky
Drumvaich
Burn of Cambus
D
Doune

THE TROSSACHS
Achray Forest
FOREST PARK VISITOR CENTRE
SCOTTISH WOOL CENTRE
TROSSACHS DISCOVERY CENTRE
Menteith Hills
Port of Menteith
A81
11
B8032
B822
Deanston
BLAIR DRU SAFARI PA

ard
Altskeith
B829
Milton
A821
A822
Aberfoyle
Kirkton
BETH
Loch Ard
PARK
206
Cobleland
INCHMAHOME PRIORY
Malling
Lake of Menteith
A81
Goodie Water
DUNAVERIG FARMLIFE CENTRE
Ruskie A873
Thornhill
207
B826
Blair Drummond
BLAIR DRU

4 5 6 7
Dykehead
Flanders Moss
FLANDERS MO
B8031

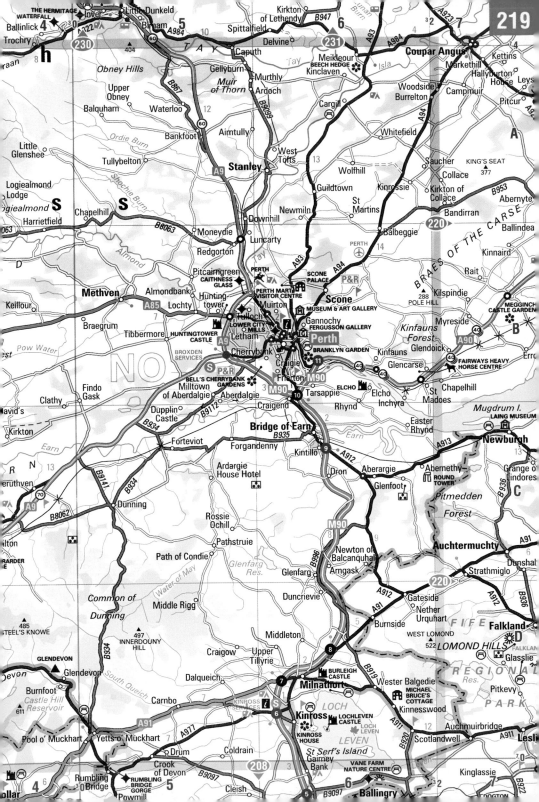

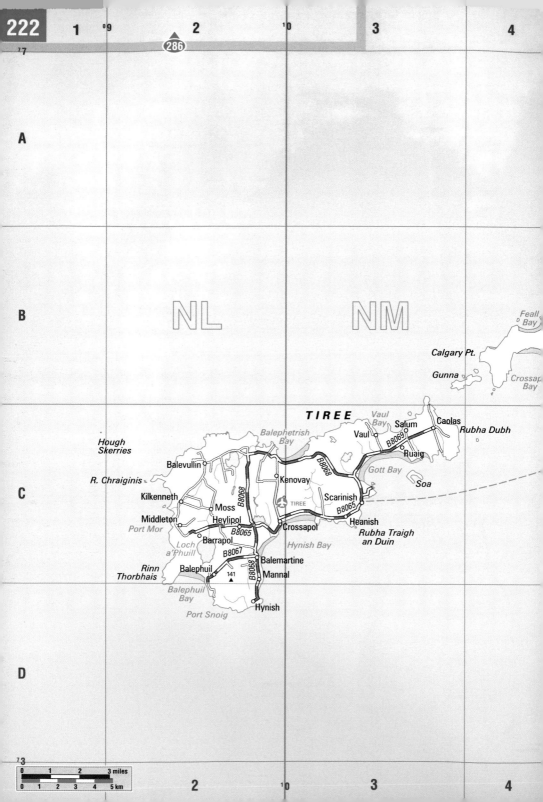

1 ⁰9 **2** ¹0 **3** **4**

⁷7

A

NL **NM**

Feall
Bay

Calgary Pt.

Gunna

Crossap
Bay

B

TIREE

Vaul
Bay

Salum

Caolas

Rubha Dubh

Vaul

B8069

Hough
Skerries

Ruaig

Balevullin

Balephetrish
Bay

Gott Bay

R. Chraiginis

Kenovay

B8068

Soa

C

Kilkenneth

B8068

Scarinish

Moss

TIREE

B8065

Middleton

Heylipol

Heanish

Port Mor

B8065

Crossapol

Rubha Traigh
an Duin

Barrapol

Loch
a'Phuill

B8067

Hynish Bay

Balemartine

Rinn
Thorbhais

Balephuil

141 ▲

Mannal

B8068

Balephuil
Bay

Hynish

Port Snoig

D

⁷3

0   1   2   3 miles
0   1   2   3   4   5 km

2 ¹0 **3** **4**

Sanna Point

Sanna Bay   San

Portuairk

Point of   Achos
Ardnamurchan
ARDNAMURCHAN LIGHTHOUSE

Cairns of Coll

234

Rubha Mor   **A**

Eilean Mor   Orms

Ormsai

Bousd   Sorisdale

An Acairseid

Cliad Bay   B8072

Arnabost   Gallanach

Grishipoll   B8071

Ardmore
Bay

▲ 73

haugh   B8071   **C O L L**

OBAN 2:40   Glengor
Quinish Pt.   *Castle*

Loch
Cliad   ▲ 104

B8070

Arinagour

Rubha   *M i s h n i s h*
an Aird   **MULL LITTLE**

otronald   Acha

Breacacha
Castle   Friesland

Eilean Ornsay

Caliach Pt.   Sunipol

M o r n i s h   Penmore
Mill

THEATRE

Dervaig   Ac

THE OLD BYRE
HERITAGE CEN

Soa   *Loch Breachacha*

0:55

Calgary

Calgary Bay

Ensay   ▲ 342
CARN MOR

Achna

Treshnish Pt.   B8073

Haunn

Rubh a'Chaoil

224

Treshnish Isles   Fladda

Burg   Kilninian

Achleck

23   Fanmore ▲ 390   **C**

L O C H   *T U A T H*   Ballygown

Lunga

Eilean Dioghlum

EAS FORS
WATERFALL

Gometra   Bearnus ▲ 313   *Laggan*
Bay

U l v a

Bac Mor   Ulva House

Little
Colonsay

INCH KENNETH
CHAPEL

Staffa   **STAFFA**   *Inch*
Kenneth   **D**

FINGAL'S CAVE   B

MACKINNON'S CAVE

Erisgeir

519

IONA 0:45
(April-Oct)

BEN NA S

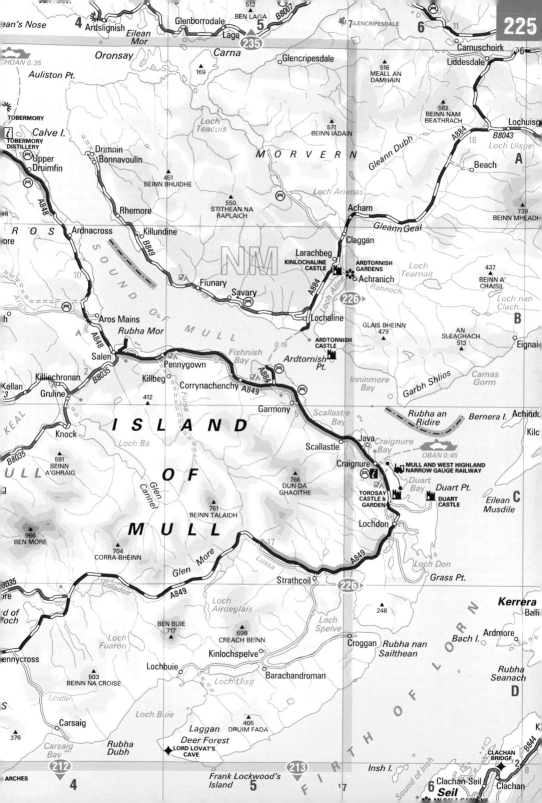

MORVERN

LYNN OF LORN

LORN

BENDERL

NM

FIRTH OF LORN

Oban

Kerrera

Lismore

Seil

Glencripesdale
Glencripesdale
Ardnastang
Strontian
Camuschoirk
Liddesdale
516 MEALL AN DAMHAIN
582 BEINN NAM BEATHRACH
Lochuisge
583 CREACH BHEINN
Kilmalieu
571 BEINN IADAIN
765 FUAR BHEINN
Kingairloch
Camasnacroise
Beach
Loch Uisge
18
Loch a'Choire
Shuna I.
Acharn
Gleann Geal
739 BEINN MHEADHOIN
236
Portnacroish
Port Appin
Larachbeg
Claggan
KINLOCHALINE CASTLE
ARDTORNISH GARDENS
Achranich
437
BEINN A' CHAISIL
Glensanda
Pørt Ramsay
North Shian
Lochaline
Loch Tearnait
Loch nan Clach
Clachan
Eriska
South Shian
SCOTTISH SEA LIFE SANCTUARY
GLAIS BHEINN 479
AN SLEAGHACH 513
Eignaig
Achnacroish
ARDTORNISH CASTLE
Ardtornish Pt.
Baravullin
Ferlochan
Fishnish Bay
Inninmore Bay
Garbh Shlios
Camas Gorm
Rubha an Ridire
Bernera I.
Achinduin
Kilcheran
Kiel Crofts
Benderloch
Ledaig
Garmony
Scallastle Bay
Eilean Dubh
Ardmucknish Bay
A828
Scallastle
Java
Craignure Bay
MULL AND WEST HIGHLAND NARROW GAUGE RAILWAY
Eilean Mor
DUNSTAFFNAGE CASTLE
North Connel
Connel
FALLS OF LORA
Black C
766 DUN DA GHAOITHE
Craignure
Duart Bay
Duart Pt.
DUART CASTLE
Eilean Musdile
0:45
Dunbeg
TOROSAY CASTLE & GARDENS
Lochdon
CASTLEBAY 5:10
COLL 2:40
TIREE 3:40
LOCHBOISDALE 5:15
Ganavan
Dunollie
OBAN/OBAN LODGE
MCCAIG'S TOWER
OBAN DISTILLERY
Strathcoil
225
Loch Don
Grass Pt.
Dunollie
OBAN VISITOR CENTRE
Altnacraig
OBAN RARE BREEDS FAR
248
Balliemore
Glenmachrie
Loch Nell
Loch Spelve
Ardmore
Gallanach
Barran
Croggan
Rubha nan Sailthean
Bach I.
Kilbride
Kilmore
Kilbride
Barachandroman
Rubha Seanach
Am Buth
GLENFEOCHAN HOUSE GARDENS
Loch Feochan
Glen Feochan
405 UIM FADA
Kilninver
A816
Barochreal
Glen Euchar
368 A'CHRUACH
Bragleenmore
CLACHAN BRIDGE
213
B844
Barochreal
Loch Scamadale
214
Insh I.
Clachan-Seil
Clachan
CARN DEARG
AN CALA GARDENS

Strontian
A861
Glen Tarbert
Tarbert
In
635 GARBH BHEINN
B8043
Kilmalieu
Ru
Eilean Balnago

0 1 2 3 miles
0 1 2 3 4 5 km

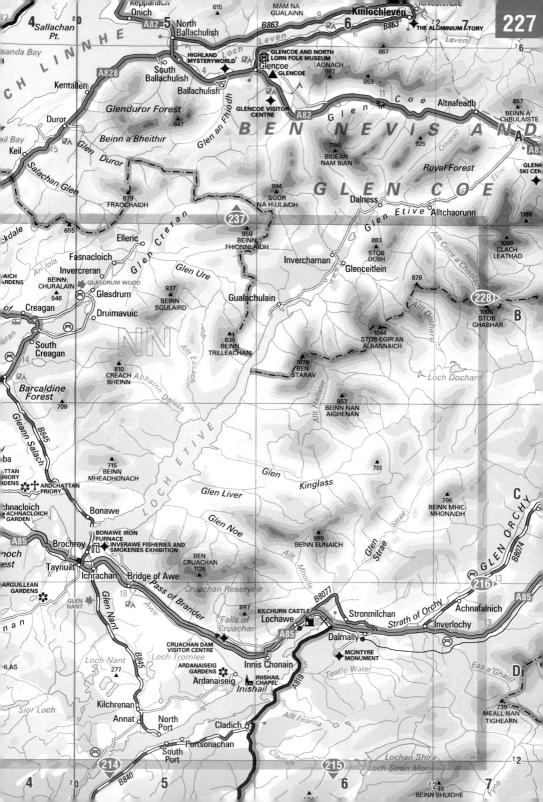

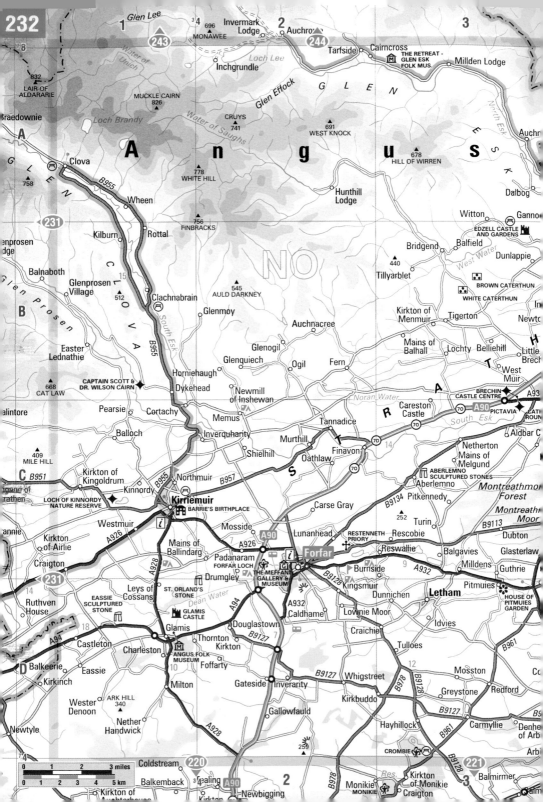

T H E   S M A L L   I S L E S

1

Guirdil Bay

Kilmory Glen

246

Kinloch Glen

CANNA 1:15

3

Rubha na Roinne

A'Bhrideanach

388

Schooner Pt.

571
ORVAL

R   Ù   M

Kinloch

Loch Scresort

RÙM

KINLOCH
CASTLE

Rubha Port
na Caranean

A

Harris

Glen Harris

812
ASKIVAL

1:30

Rubha Sgorr
an t-Snidhe

781
AINSHVAL

1:15

SOUND   OF   RÙM

Bay of Laig

Cleac

Rubha nam
Meirleach

Rubha an
Fhasaidh

Eigg

B

393
AN SGURR

Galr

k

Eilean nan Each

SOUND   OF   EIGG

0:40

Muck

137

Port Mor

C

Sanna Point

223

Sanna Bay

Sanna

Portuairk

Achnaha

Point of
Ardnamurchan
ARDNAMURCHAN LIGHTHOUSE

Achosnich

Cairns of Coll

223

B8007

Rubha Mor

Eilean Mor

D

Bousd

Sorisdale

An Acairseid

Ormsaigmore

Kilc

B8072

Ormsaigbeg

Kilchoan
Bay

Gallanach

C O L L

nab

B071

0   1   2   3 miles
0   1   2   3   4   5 km

224

2

Ardmore Bay

Ardmore P

3

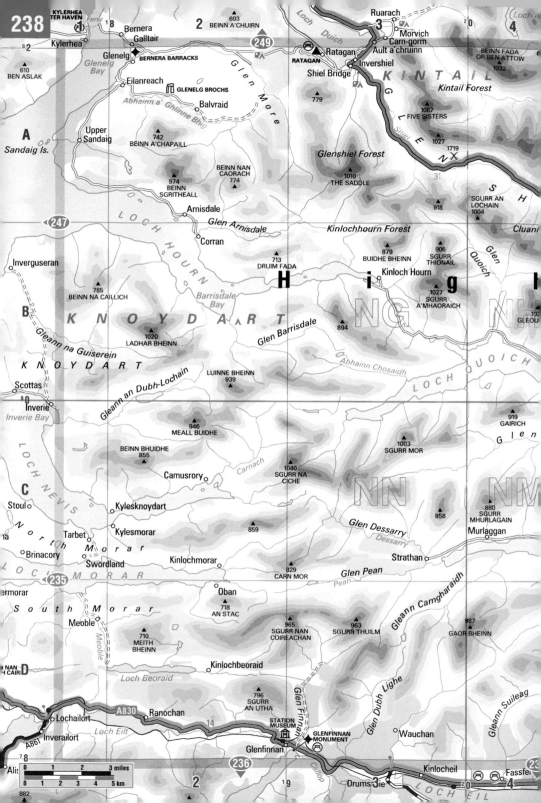

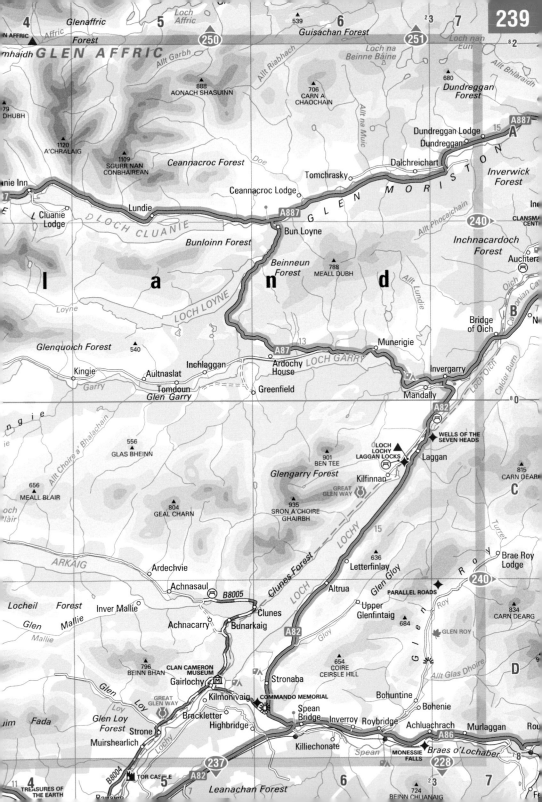

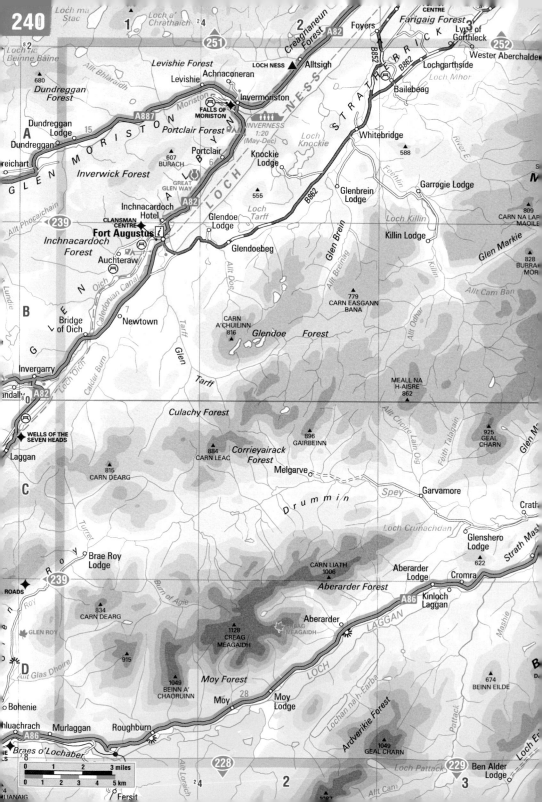

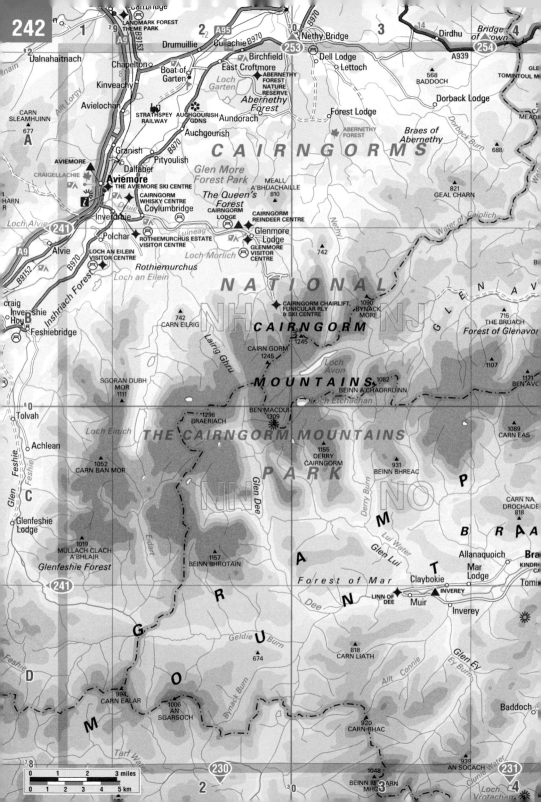

Loch Varkasaig
Loch Bracadale
Harlosh I.
Harlosh
Balmore
Tarner I.
Ullinish
Ose
Bracadale
Coillore
Struan
A863
B885
A863
258
259
Glenmore
Heatherfield
417
Mugeary
A87
Glen Varragill
Varragill
ISLA
Loch Duagrich
488
ABHAL BHEAG

Wiay
Oronsay
Portnalong
Fiskavaig
Fernilea
ARNAVAL
369
TALISKER DISTILLERY
Carbost
Drynoch
Crossal
439
ROINEVAL
B8009
Loch Harport
A863
Drynoch
Rubha nan Clach
Idrigill Point
MACLEOD'S MAIDENS

Gleann Oraid
Talisker Bay
Merkadale
Sligachan Hotel

NG

Talisker
Eynort
Glen Brittle Forest
Grula
459
445
BEINN BHREAC
Loch Eynort
MINGINIS
SGURR NAN GILLEAN
964
SGURR A'GHREADAIDH
973
THE C
GLENBRITTLE
CUILLIN HILLS
Glenbrittle House
Bualintur
992
SGURR ALASDAIR
Loch Coruisk
924
SGURR NAN EAG
Brittle
Glen Brittle
Eynort

Rubh an Dunain
Loch Brittle
Soay Sound
Soay

Mol-chlach

PRI

Canna
Garrisdale Pt.
A'Chill
Canna Harbour
Rubha Shamhnan Insir
Sanday
Sound of Canna
Kilmory
1:15
MALLAIG 2:30
Guirdil Bay
Kilmory Glen
Kinloch Glen
Rubha na Roinne
A'Bhrideanach
388
234
Kinloch
Loch Scresort
571
ORVAL
R U M
KINLOCH CASTLE
Rubha Port na Caranean

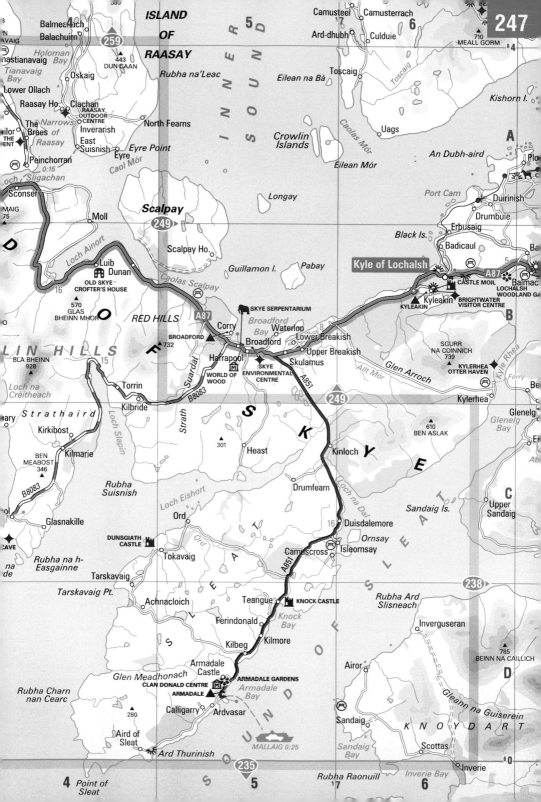

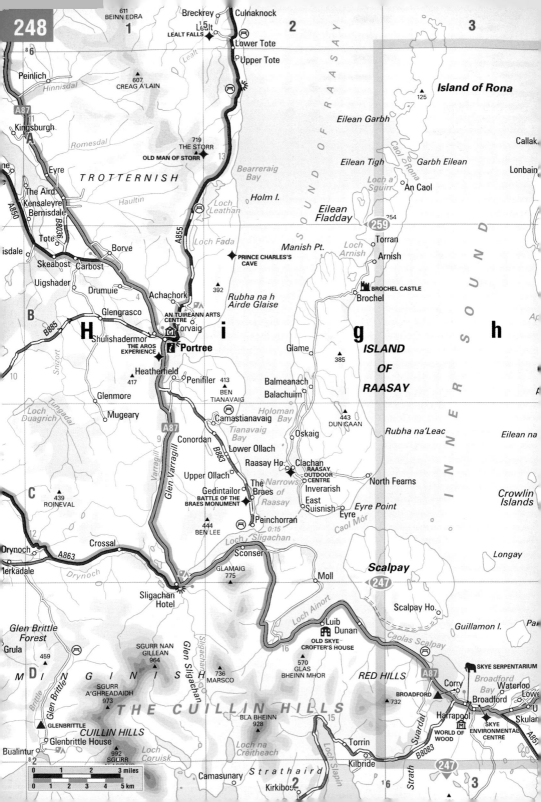

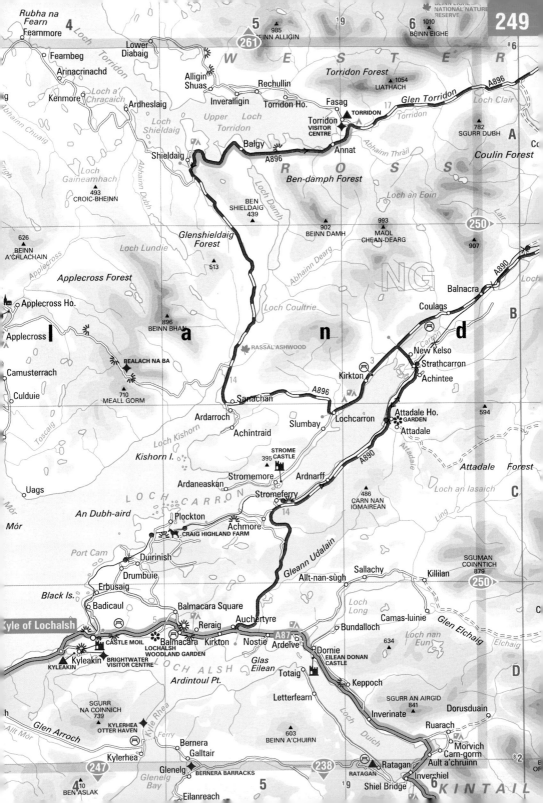

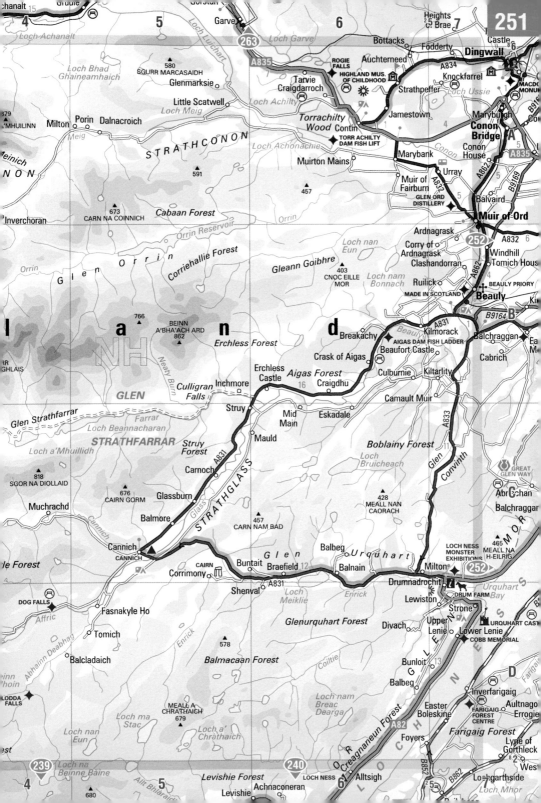

Loch a'chanalt 15 Grudie

Garve
Loch Achanalt
263 A835
Loch Luichart
Loch Garve
Loch Bhad Ghaineamhaich
580
SGURR MARCASAIDH
Glenmarksie
Little Scatwell
Loch Meig
Loch Achilty
ROGIE FALLS
Tarvie
Craigdarroch
HIGHLAND MUS. OF CHILDHOOD
379 'MHUILINN
Milton
Porin Dalnacroich
Meig
STRATHCONON
Contin
TORRACHILY WOOD
TORR ACHILTY DAM FISH LIFT
Loch Achonachie
Muirton Mains
591
INVERCHORAN
673 CARN NA COINNICH
Cabaan Forest
457
Orrin
NON
Orrin Reservoir
Orrin
Glen Orrin
Corriehallie Forest
Gleann Goibhre
403 CNOC EILLE MOR
Loch nan Eun

Heights of Brae 7
Bottacks Fodderty
Auchterneed
A834 Knockfarrel
Strathpeffer
Loch Ussie
Jamestown 4
Conon Bridge A
Maryburgh
Conon House
Marybank
Muir of Fairburn
Urray
GLEN ORD DISTILLERY
Balvaird
Muir of Ord
252 A832
Ardnagrask
Corry of Ardnagrask
Clashandorran
Ruilick
Loch nam Bonnach
MADE IN SCOTLAND
Windhill
Tomich House
BEAULY PRIORY
Beauly B
B9164
Eas

Dingwall
Castle 6
MACDO MONU
1

l
a
n
d
NH
766
BEINN A'BHA'ACH ARD 862
Erchless Forest
GHLAIS
Neaty Burn
GLEN
Culligran Falls
Inchmore
Struy
Erchless Castle
Aigas Forest 16
Craigdhu
Mid Main
Eskadale
Camault Muir

Breakachy
Crask of Aigas
AIGAS DAM FISH LADDER
Beaufort Castle
Culburnie
Kiltarlity
Kilmorack
Balchraggan
Cabrich

Glen Strathfarrar
Farrar
Loch Beannacharan
STRATHFARRAR
Struy Forest
Mauld
Carnoch
818 SGOR NA DIOLLAID
Loch a'Mhuillidh
676 CAIRN GORM
Glassburn
Balmore
Muchrachd
Cannich
CANNICH
CAIRN
Corrimony
457 CARN NAM BAD
Buntait
Braefield 12
Shenval
A831
Loch Meiklie

Boblainy Forest
Loch Bruicheach
Glen Convinth
A833
428 MEALL NAN CAORACH
Glen Urquhart
Balbeg
Balnain
Milton
Drumnadrochit
Lewiston
A831
Enrick
LOCH NESS MONSTER EXHIBITIONS
252
465 MEALL NA H-EILRIG
DRUM FARM
Strone

GREAT GLEN WAY
Abriachan
Balchraggar
C

le Forest
DOG FALLS
Affric
Fasnakyle Ho
Tomich
Balcladaich
'hoin
LODDA FALLS
Abhainn Deabhag
Loch nan Eun
Loch ma Stac
MEALL A' CHRATHAICH 679
Loch a' Chrathaich
578
Balmacaan Forest
Glenurquhart Forest
Coiltie
Divach
Upper Lenie
Lower Lenie
COBB MEMORIAL
Bunloit 13
Balbeg
Loch nam Breac Dearga
Foyers
Easter Boleskine

URQUHART CAST
Strone
G L E N
M O R
Inverfarigaig
FARIGAIG FOREST CENTRE
Farigaig Forest
Aultnago Errogie
Lyne of Gorthleck
West
D

239
Loch na Beinne Baine
680
Levishie Forest
Levishie
Achnaconeran
240
LOCH NESS 6
Alltsig
A82
Creagnaneun Forest
B862
B852
Loch Mhor
garthside
4
5
6

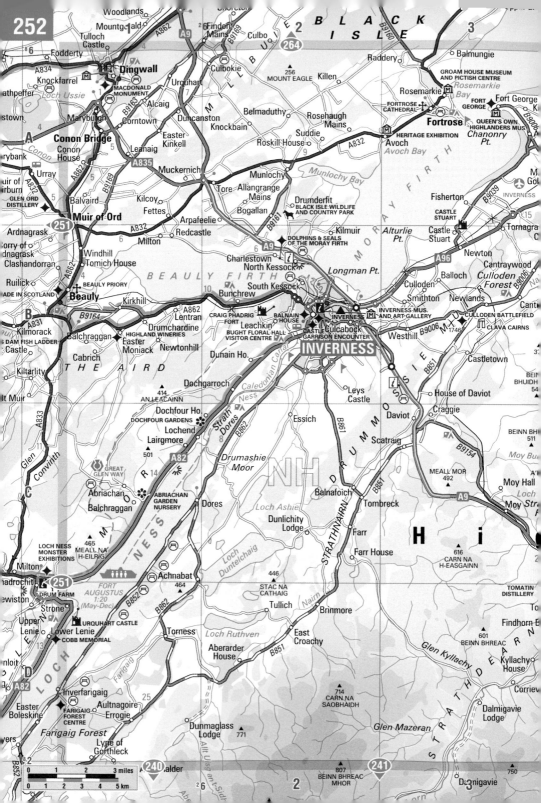

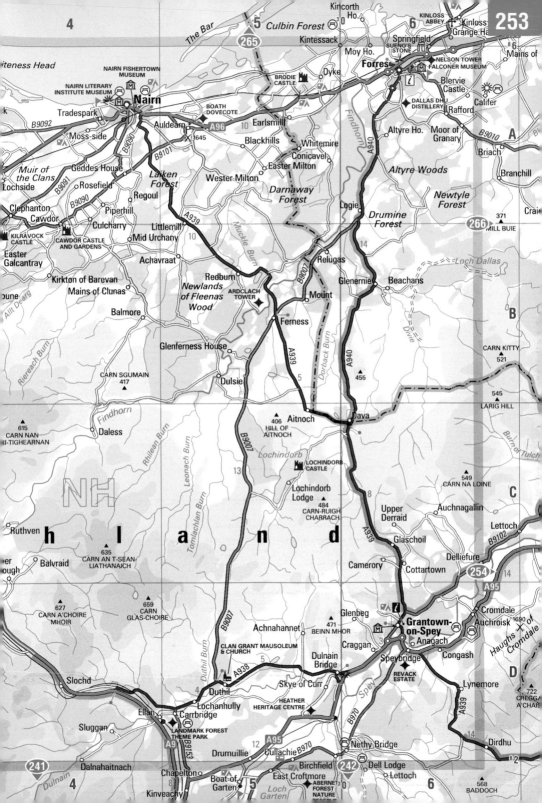

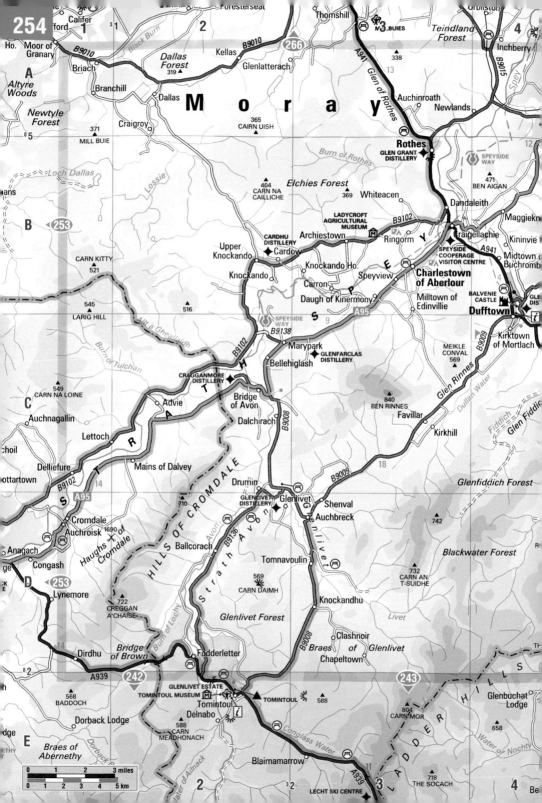

Moray

Orbliston
Teindland Forest
Inchberry

Califer
Ho.
Moor of Granary
ford
B9010
Black Burn
Dallas Forest
319
Kellas
B9010
266
Thomshill
BUIES
N3
A941
Glen of Rothes
338
13
Spey
B9015

Briach
Branchill
Dallas
Glenlatterach
Auchinroath
Newlands

Altyre Woods
Newtyle Forest
Craigroy
Mill Buie
371
365
Cairn Uish
404
Carn na Cailliche
369
Whiteacen
Dandaleith
Maggiekno
Ben Aigan
471
Speyside Way
12

253
Carn Kitty
521
Loch Dallas
Lossie
Mill a' Gheallaidh
Elchies Forest
Ladycroft Agricultural Museum
Archiestown
Ringorm
B9102
Craigellachie
Kininvie
Midtown
Buchromb
Speyside Cooperage Visitor Centre
A941
Cardhu Distillery
Upper Knockando
Cardow
Knockando Ho.
Speyview
Charlestown of Aberlour
Balvenie Castle
Gle Dis
Larig Hill
545
516
Knockando
Carron
Daugh of Kinermony
Milltown of Edinvillie
Dufftown
Kirktown of Mortlach
Speyside Way
B9138
Marypark
9
A95
Meikle Conval
569
Burn of Tulchan
Bellehiglash
Glenfarclas Distillery
Glen Rinnes
Glen Fiddi
Carn na Loine
549
Cragganmore Distillery
Bridge of Avon
Ben Rinnes
840
Favillar
Dullan Water
Auchnagallin
Advie
Dalchirach
B9008
Kirkhill
Fiddich
Lettoch
18
Delliefure
B9102
Mains of Dalvey
Glenfiddich Forest
ottartown
A95
14
Drumin
B9009
S
Cromdale
Auchroisk
1690
Glenlivet Distillery
Glenlivet
Shenval
Auchbreck
742
Blackwater Forest
Anagach
Congash
Haughs of Cromdale
710
Ballcorach
B9136
Strath Avon
Tomnavoulin
Carn an T-Suidhe
732
253
Lynemore
Creggan A'Chaise
722
Carn Daimh
569
Knockandhu
Livet
Glenlivet Forest
Dirdhu
Bridge of Brown
Fodderletter
Clashnoir
Braes of Glenlivet
Chapeltown
B9008
A939
242
Glenlivet Estate
Tomintoul Museum
Tomintoul
588
243
Glenbuchat Lodge
Baddoch
568
Dorback Lodge
Delnabo
Carn Meadhonach
588
804
Carn Mor
658
Braes of Abernethy
Blairnamarrow
Conglass Water
The Socach
718
Lecht Ski Centre
A939
11

0	1	2	3 miles
0	1	2	3	4	5 km

HILLS OF CROMDALE

LADDER HILLS

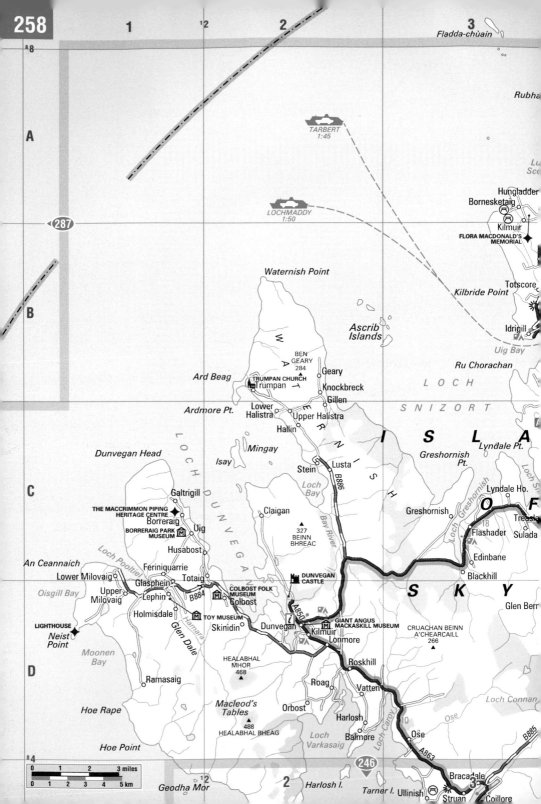

1 ¹2 2 3

Fladda-chùain

A

287

B

Rubha

Hungladder
Bornesketaig
Kilmuir
FLORA MACDONALD'S MEMORIAL

Totscore

Kilbride Point

Idrigill

Uig Bay

Waternish Point

Ascrib Islands

BEN GEARY 284

Geary

Ard Beag

TRUMPAN CHURCH
Trumpan

Knockbreck

Gillen

Ardmore Pt.

Lower Halistra

Upper Halistra

Ru Chorachan

LOCH

SNIZORT

Hallin

Dunvegan Head

Mingay

Isay

Stein

Lusta

Loch Bay

B886

ISLA

Lyndale Pt.

Greshornish Pt.

Lyndale Ho.

C

Galtrigill

THE MACCRIMMON PIPING HERITAGE CENTRE
Borreraig
BORRERAIG PARK MUSEUM
Uig

Claigan

327 BEINN BHREAC

Greshornish

Loch Greshornish

18
Flashader

Treasla

Sulada

O

F

An Ceannaich

Husabost

Feriniquarrie

Lower Milovaig

Glasphein

Totaig

B884

Edinbane

Blackhill

Glen Berr

Loch Pooltiel

Upper Milovaig

Lephin

COLBOST FOLK MUSEUM
Colbost

DUNVEGAN CASTLE

SKY

Oisgill Bay

Holmisdale

TOY MUSEUM

Skinidin

Dunvegan

Kilmuir

Lonmore

GIANT ANGUS MACKASKILL MUSEUM

Y

Glen Berr

LIGHTHOUSE
Neist Point

Moonen Bay

HEALABHAL MHOR 468

Ramasaig

CRUACHAN BEINN A'CHEARCAILL 266

Glen Berr

D

Roskhill

Roag

Vatten

Loch Connan

Hoe Rape

Macleod's Tables

Orbost

Harlosh

Loch Caroy

Ose

10

Balmore
Ose

Loch Varkasaig

Ose

B885

488 HEALABHAL BHEAG

Hoe Point

A863

Bracadale

246

3

0 1 2 3 miles
0 1 2 3 4 5 km

Geodha Mor

¹2

2

Harlosh I.

Tarner I. Ullinish

Struan

Coillore

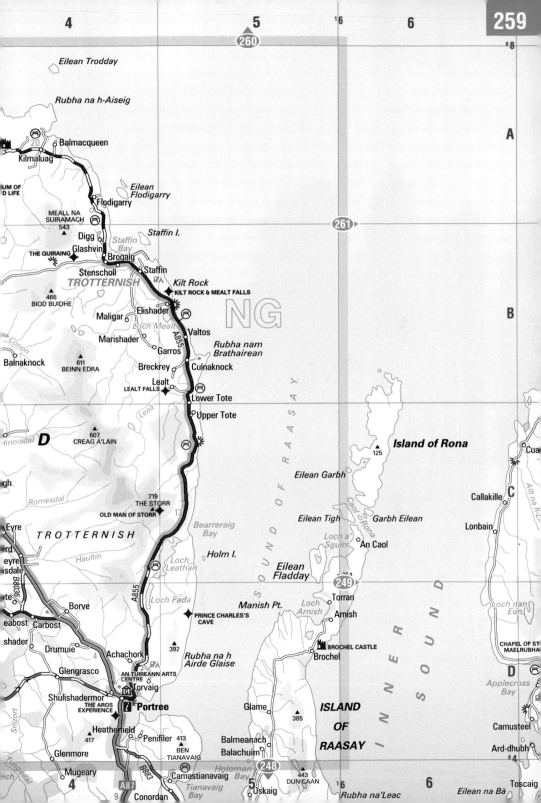

4   **5**   6   6

260

Eilean Trodday

Rubha na h-Aiseig

A

20
Balmacqueen
Kilmaluag

UM OF
D LIFE

Eilean Flodigarry
Flodigarry

MEALL NA
SUIRAMACH
543

Digg   Staffin I.
Glashvin   Staffin
THE QUIRAING   Brogaig   Bay
Stenscholl   Staffin

261

TROTTERNISH

Kilt Rock
KILT ROCK & MEALT FALLS

NG

466
BIOD BUIDHE
Maligar   Elishader
Loch Mealt

Balnaknock   Marishader   Valtos

Conon   Garros   Rubha nam
Brathairean

B

611
BEINN EDRA
Breckrey   Culnaknock

Lealt
LEALT FALLS   Lower Tote

A855

Lealt   Upper Tote

innisdale   607
CREAG A'LAIN
D

S   125
O   **Island of Rona**
U
N
D

Romesdal

Eilean Garbh

gh   **O**
F

Callakille   **C**
Lonbain

Eyre   719
ird   THE STORR
eyre
isdale   OLD MAN OF STORR   13

R
A   Eilean Tigh   Garbh Eilean
A
S   An Caol
A
Y

Bearreraig
Bay

Holm I.

Loch
Leathan

T R O T T E R N I S H

Haultin

Eilean
Fladday

249

B8036

te
eabost   Borve
Carbost   A855
shader
Drumuie   Loch Fada

Manish Pt.   Loch
Arnish   Torran
Arnish

392   Rubha na h
Achachork   Airde Glaise

BROCHEL CASTLE
Brochel

I
N
N
E
R

CHAPEL OF ST
MAELRUBHA

D

Applecross
Bay

Glengrasco   AN TUIREANN ARTS
CENTRE
Shulishadermor   Torvaig
THE AROS
EXPERIENCE   **Portree**

Heatherfield
417   Penifiler   413
Glenmore   BEN
TIANAVAIG

Glame   **ISLAND**
OF
RAASAY
Balmeanach
Balachuirn

385

S
O
U
N
D

Camusteel
Ard-dhubh

4   4

Mugeary   B883   **4**
A87
9   Conordan

Camastianavaig   Holoman   **5**
Tianavaig   **248**
Bay   Oskaig

443
DUN CAAN

Rubha na'Leac   **6**
Eilean na Bà   Toscaig

1   ⁵5   2   3

Garbh Eilean

Eilean Mhuire

Eilean an Tighe

Na h-Eileanan Mòra
(Shiant Islands)

◀ 288

A

288

B

NG

259

Eilean Trodday

Rubha Hunish

Rubha na h-Aiseig

C

DUNTULM CASTLE
20
Balmacqueen
Duntulm
Kilmaluag

MUSEUM OF ISLAND LIFE

Eilean Flodigarry

Flodigarry

MEALL NA SUIRAMACH
▲543
Digg
Glashvin   *Staffin I.*

◀ 259

Kilvaxter
Balgown   THE QUIRAING   Brogaig

Linicro
TROTTERNISH   Stenscholl   ▲ Staffin

Staffin Bay

A855
▲466
BIOD BUIDHE   Maligar   Elishader   **Kilt Rock**
KILT ROCK & MEALT FALLS

D

▣ **Uig**   Marishader   *Loch Mealt*   Valtos

▲ **UIG**   *Conon*   Garros   *Rubha nam Brathairean*

Balnaknock   ▲611
BEINN EDRA   Breckrey   Culnaknock

Earlish   **Island of Rona**

Lealt
LEALT FALLS

Lealt   Lower Tote

Upper Tote

0   1   2   3 miles
0   1   2   3   4   5 km

⁸6

Hinnisdal   607
CREAG A'LAIN   ⁵5   2   3

A855

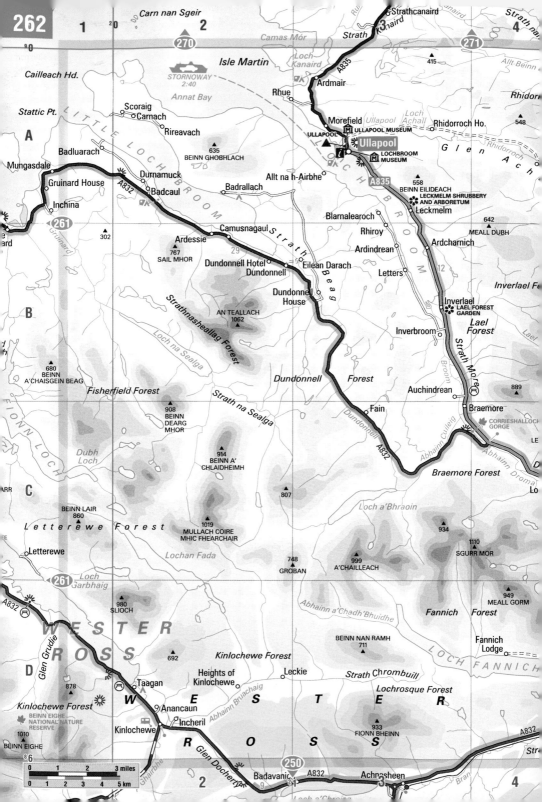

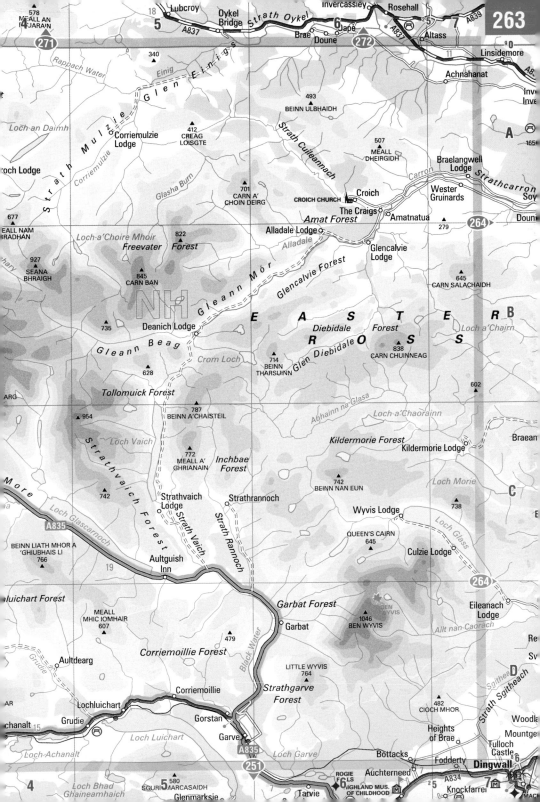

Backlies
A9
4 DUNROBIN CASTLE
MUSEUM & GARDENS
Golspie
274

i

ton

CH
EET
ittleferry

urpenny

Embo

mbo Street

WITCHES STONE
OLD POST OFFICE
VISITOR CENTRE
noch

CH FIRTH

NH

NJ

A

*Whiteness
Sands*

B

Tarbat Ness
TARBAT NESS LIGHTHOUSE
Wilkhaven

TARBAT DISCOVERY
CENTRE
Bindal
Portmahomack
Rockfield

Inver
Arboll
Balnagall
Lochslin
Tarrel

*Loch
Eye*
Rhynie
Fearn Station
B9165
Geanies House

Hill of Fearn
Fearn
B9166
FEARN
ABBEY
Hilton of Cadboll
Loans of Tullich
Balintore
SHANDWICK STONE
Shandwick

C

Ankerville
Chapelhill

Pitcalnie
Port an Righ

Nigg
t Canisp
203
King's Cave
bruaich

Castlecraig
266

Burghead

erry
OUSE
Sutors of Cromarty

BURGHEAD BAY

D

Findhorn
Lower
Hempriggs
Miltonhill

*Findhorn
Bay*

KINLOSS
ABBEY
Kinloss
Grange Hall
A96

Kincorth
Ho.
The Bar
Culbin Forest
Kintessack

Springfield
SUENO'S
STONE
Moy Ho.
253
NELSON TOWER
ALCONER MUSEUM

Forres

Mains

Whiteness Head
4
5
BRODIE
CASTLE
Dyke
i
Blervie

MORAY FIRTH

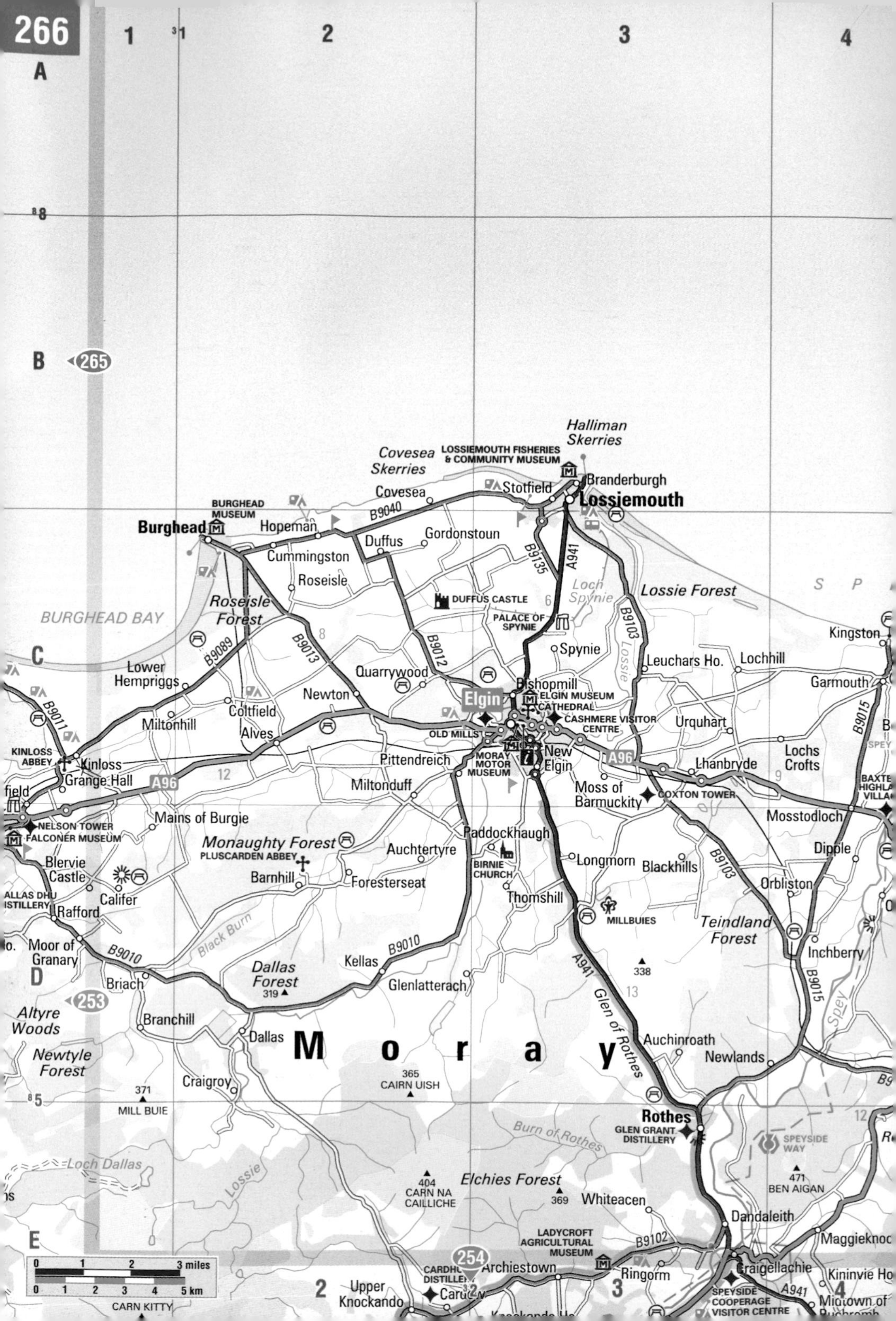

A

B ◁265

C

D

E

1   1   2   3   4

BURGHEAD BAY

Covesea
Skerries

Halliman
Skerries

LOSSIEMOUTH FISHERIES
& COMMUNITY MUSEUM

Branderburgh

Lossiemouth

Stotfield

Covesea

BURGHEAD
MUSEUM

Burghead
Hopeman

B9040

Duffus   Gordonstoun

Cummingston

Roseisle

Roseisle
Forest

B9013

DUFFUS CASTLE

PALACE OF
SPYNIE

Loch
Spynie

Lossie Forest

Kingston

B9012

Spynie

Leuchars Ho.   Lochhill

Garmouth

Lower
Hempriggs

B9089

Quarrywood

Newton

Elgin

Bishopmill
ELGIN MUSEUM
CATHEDRAL

CASHMERE VISITOR
CENTRE

Urquhart

Lochs
Crofts

B9015

SPEY

B9011

Coltfield

Alves

Miltonhill

OLD MILLS

New
Elgin

A96

Lhanbryde

BAXTE
HIGHLA
VILLA

KINLOSS
ABBEY

Kinloss

Grange Hall

A96

Pittendreich

Miltonduff

MORAY
MOTOR
MUSEUM

Moss of
Barmuckity

COXTON TOWER

Mosstodloch

field

NELSON TOWER
FALCONER MUSEUM

Mains of Burgie

Paddockhaugh

Longmorn   Blackhills

B9103

Dipple

Blervie
Castle

Monaughty Forest

PLUSCARDEN ABBEY

Auchtertyre

BIRNIE
CHURCH

Orbliston

ALLAS DHU
ISTILLERY

Rafford

Barnhill

Califer

Foresterseat

Thomshill

MILLBUIES

Teindland
Forest

Inchberry

No.   Moor of
Granary

B9010

Black Burn

Dallas
Forest
319 ▲

Kellas

B9010

Glenlatterach

338 ▲

13

B9015

Bg

Briach

Branchill

Dallas

M   o   r   a   y

A941

Glen of Rothes

Auchinroath

Newlands

Altyre
Woods

253

Newtyle
Forest

Craigroy

371
MILL BUIE

365
CAIRN UISH

Burn of Rothes

Rothes

GLEN GRANT
DISTILLERY

SPEYSIDE
WAY

471 ▲
BEN AIGAN

12

Loch Dallas

Lossie

404 ▲
CARN NA
CAILLICHE

369 ▲   Whiteacen

Elchies Forest

LADYCROFT
AGRICULTURAL
MUSEUM

B9102

Dandaleith

Maggieknoc

0   1   2   3 miles
0   1   2   3   4   5 km

CARN KITTY

CARDH
DISTILLE

254

Archiestown

Ringorm

Upper
Knockando

Car

2   3

SPEYSIDE
COOPERAGE
VISITOR CENTRE

A941

raigellachie

Kininvie Ho

Midown of

4

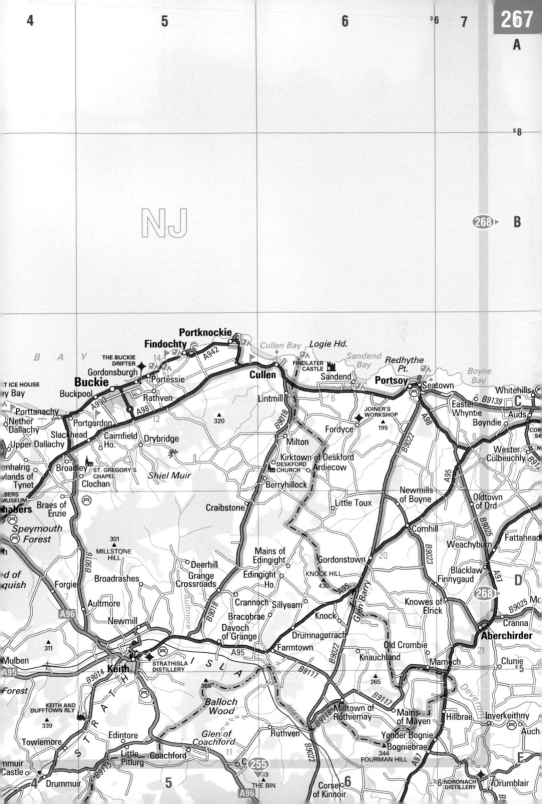

4   5   6   ³6   7

A

⁸8

268▶ B

NJ

Portknockie
Findochty   *Cullen Bay*   *Logie Hd.*
B A Y   THE BUCKIE DRIFTER   14   A942
Gordonsburgh   *Sandend Bay*   *Redhythe Pt.*   *Boyne Bay*
Buckie   Portessie   **Cullen**   FINDLATER CASTLE   Sandend   **Portsoy**   Seatown
Buckpool   Rathven   Lintmill   6   Whitehills
T ICE HOUSE   A990   A98   JOINER'S WORKSHOP   Easter   B9139   C
y Bay   Porttanachy   12   Fordyce   199   Whyntie   Auds
Nether   Portgordon   320   Boyndie
Dallachy   Slackhead   Cairnfield Ho.   Drybridge   Milton   A98   8
Upper Dallachy   Kirktown of Deskford   A95   Wester   Culbeuchly
enhalrig   Broadley   DESKFORD CHURCH   Ardiecow
lands of   ST. GREGORY'S CHAPEL   *Shiel Muir*   Berryhillock   Newmills of Boyne   Oldtown of Ord
Tyne   Clochan
BERS   Little Toux   Cornhill   Weachyburn   Fattahead
MUSEUM   Craibstone   B9025
habers   Braes of Enzie   Gordonstown   20   Blacklaw   D
Speymouth Forest   301   Mains of Edinight   KNOCK HILL   Finnygaud
h   MILLSTONE HILL   Deerhill   Edingight Ho.   430   Knowes of Elrick   268   A97   Cranna
d of   Grange Crossroads   Crannoch   Knock   B9025   **Aberchirder**
quish   Forgie   B9016   Broadrashes   Sillyearn   *Glen Barry*   Old Crombie   21
7   Aultmore   Bracobrae   Drumnagorrach   Knauchland   Clunie
A96   Newmill   Davoch of Grange   Farmtown   Marnoch   5
Mulben   311   A95   265   Hillbrae   Inverkeithny
A95   STRATHISLA DISTILLERY   B9117   *Deveron*   Auch
Forest   **Keith**   366   Milltown of Rothiemay   Mains of Mayen
B9014   KEITH AND DUFFTOWN RLY   *Balloch Wood*   B9117   Yonder Bognie   Bogniebrae
339   *Glen of Coachford*   Ruthven   344   FOURMAN HILL
Towiemore   Edintore   Little   B9022   NDRONACH DISTILLERY   E
muir   Pitlurg   Coachford   11   255   Corse   ³6   Drumblair
Castle   4   Drummuir   5   ·13   THE BIN   of Kinnoir   6
A96

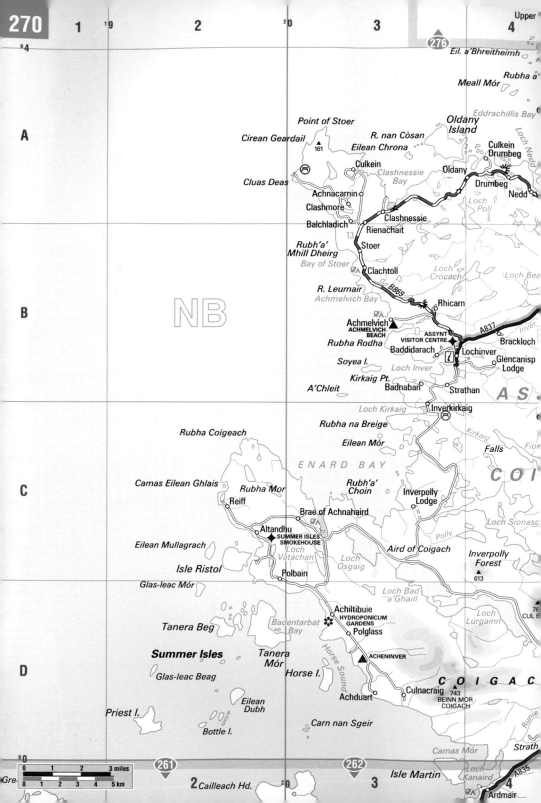

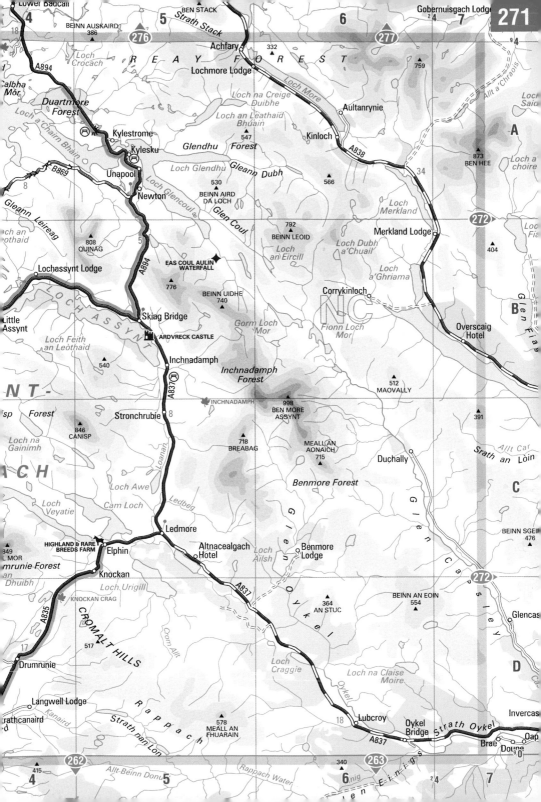

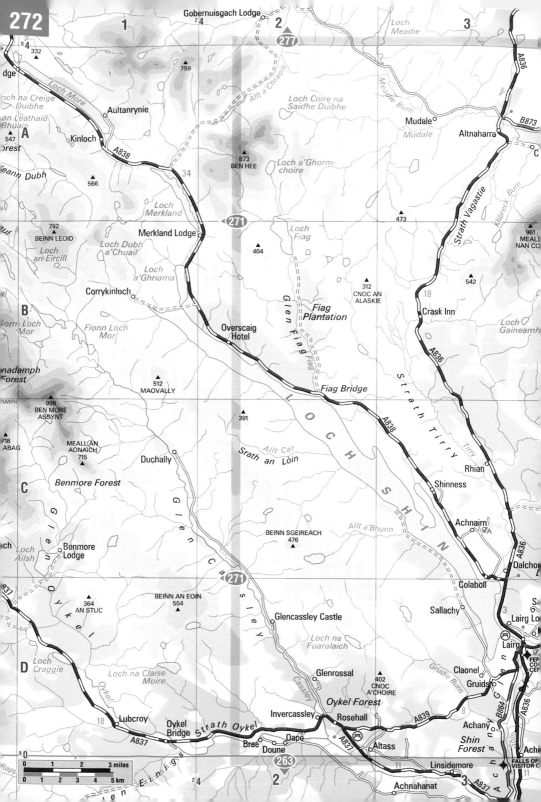

1

Gobernuisgach Lodge

2 4

2

277

Loch Meadie

3

9 4
▲ 332

Loch na Creige
Duibhe

759

Loch More

Loch Coire na
Saidhe Duibhe

an Leathaid
Bhuain

Aultanrynie

Mudale

A838

B873

547
▲
A

Kinloch

A838

34

▲ 873
BEN HEE

Loch a'Ghorm-
choire

Mudale

Altnaharra

C

rest

566
▲

Loch
Merkland

271

473
▲

Loch
Fiag

Strath Vagastie

Kilbreck Burn

792
▲
BEINN LEOID

Merkland Lodge

404
▲

312
CNOC AN
ALASKIE

542
▲

961
MEALL
NAN CO

Loch
an Eircill

Loch
Dubh
a'Chuail

Loch
a'Ghriama

Corrykinloch

B

orm Loch
Mor

Fionn Loch
Mor

Overscaig
Hotel

Glen Fiag Fiag

Fiag
Plantation

18

Crask Inn

Loch
Gaineamh

A836

adamph
Forest

512
MAOVALLY

L

Fiag Bridge

Strath Tirry

AMPH

998
BEN MORE
ASSYNT

391
▲

O

C
H

A838

718
ABAG

MEALL AN
AONAICH
715

Duchally

Srath an Lòin

Allt Car

S
H

Allt a'Bhunn

Rhian

Shinness

C

Benmore Forest

Glen

BEINN SGEIREACH
476
▲

Achnairn

I
N

Glen Oykel

Benmore
Lodge

Cassley

271

Dalcho

Loch
Ailsh

364
AN STUC

BEINN AN EOIN
554
▲

Glencassley Castle

Colaboll

Lairg Lo

Loch na
Fuaralaich

Sallachy

Lairg

D

Loch
Craggie

Loch na Claise
Moire

Glenrossal

402
CNOC
A'CHOIRE

Grudie Burn

A839

Claonel

FEF
CO
CEN

Oykel

Oykel Forest

Gruids

Lubcroy

18

Oykel
Bridge

Strath Oykel

Invercassley

Rosehall

A837

8

Achany

B864

A836

Brae

Oape

A837

Altass

Shin
Forest

Achi

Doune

Linsidemore

FALLS OF
VISITOR

263

2

Achnahanat

A837

9 0

0   1   2   3 miles
0 1 2 3 4 5 km

2 4

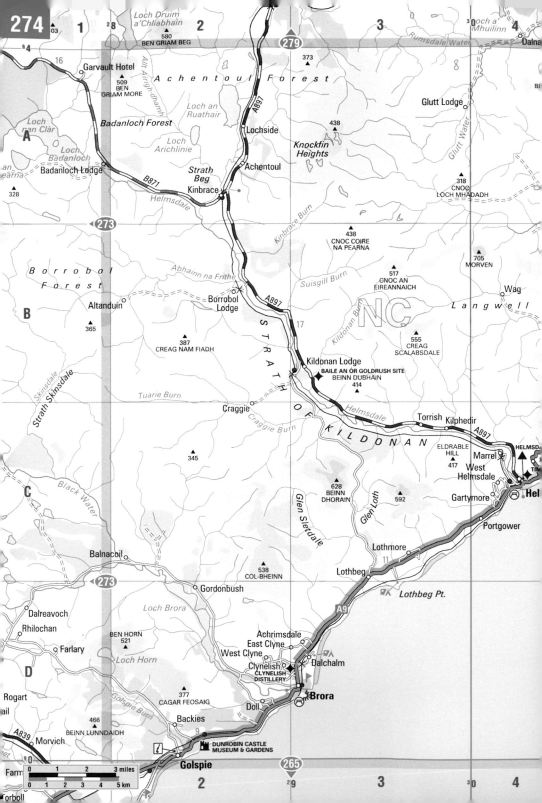

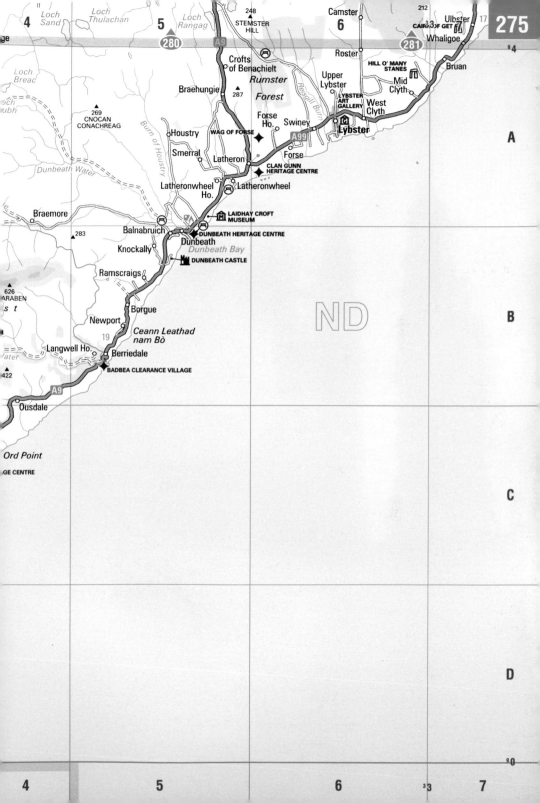

4 Loch Sand

Loch Thulachan

Loch Rangag

5

280

A9

248 STEMSTER HILL

Camster **6**

212

Ulbster

CAIRN OF GET

Whaligoe

281

17

⁹4

Crofts of Benachielt

Roster

HILL O' MANY STANES

Bruan

Braehungie

287

Rumster Forest

Upper Lybster

Mid Clyth

Forse Ho.

LYBSTER ART GALLERY

West Clyth

Houstry

269 CNOCAN CONACHREAG

WAG OF FORSE

Swiney

Lybster

A

Smerral

Latheron

Forse

Dunbeath Water

Burn of Houstry

Latheronwheel Ho.

Latheronwheel

CLAN GUNN HERITAGE CENTRE

Reisgill Burn

A99

Braemore

LAIDHAY CROFT MUSEUM

283

Balnabruich

Knockally

DUNBEATH HERITAGE CENTRE

Dunbeath

Dunbeath Bay

ND

B

Ramscraigs

DUNBEATH CASTLE

626 ARABEN *s t*

Borgue

Newport

19

Ceann Leathad nam Bò

Langwell Ho.

Berriedale

Water

422

BADBEA CLEARANCE VILLAGE

A9

Ousdale

Ord Point

GE CENTRE

C

D

⁹0

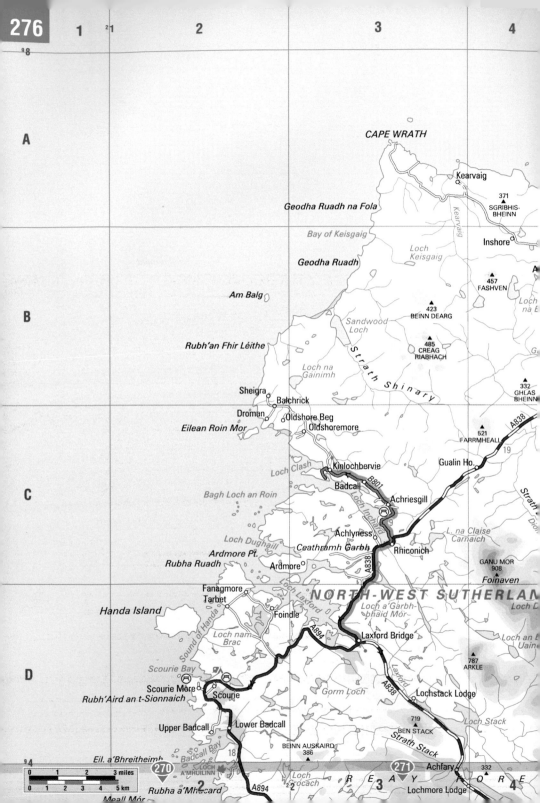

CAPE WRATH

Kearvaig

371
SGRIBHIS-
BHEINN

Inshore

Geodha Ruadh na Fola

Bay of Keisgaig

Loch
Keisgaig

Geodha Ruadh

457
FASHVEN

Am Balg

Strath Shinary

423
BEINN DEARG

Sandwood
Loch

Rubh'an Fhir Léithe

485
CREAG
RIABHACH

Loch na
Gàinimh

332
GHLAS BHEINN

Sheigra

Balchrick

A838

Droman
Oldshore Beg
Oldshoremore

Eilean Roin Mor

521
FARRMHEALL

19

Kinlochbervie

Gualin Ho.

Strath Din

Loch Clash

B801

Badcall

Achriesgill

Bagh Loch an Roin

Loch Inchard

9

Loch Dughaill

Achlyness

L. na Claise
Carnaich

Ardmore Pt.
Rubha Ruadh

Ceathramh Garbh

Rhiconich

GANU MOR
908

Ardmore

A838

Foinaven

Fanagmore
Tarbet

NORTH-WEST SUTHERLAN

Loch a'Garbh-
bhaid Mór

Loch

Handa Island

Foindle

Loch Laxford

Loch an
Uaine

Sound of Handa

Loch nam
Brac

A894

Laxford Bridge

Scourie Bay

787
ARKLE

Scourie More
Rubh'Aird an t-Sionnaich

Scourie

A838

Gorm Loch

Laxford

Lochstack Lodge

Loch Stack

719
BEN STACK

Upper Badcall

Lower Badcall

BEINN AUSKAIRD
386

Strath Stack

332

18

270

Eil. a'Bhreitheimh

LOCH
A'MHUILINN

271

Achfary

Rubha a'Mhacard

A894

Loch
Crocach

R E A Y

F O R E

Lochmore Lodge

Meall Mór

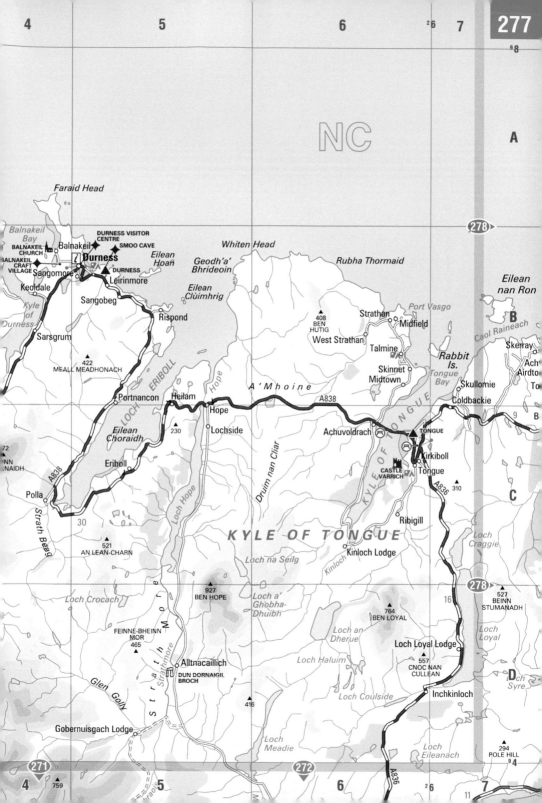

NC

Faraid Head

Balnakeil
Bay
BALNAKEIL
CHURCH
BALNAKEIL
CRAFT
VILLAGE
Sangomore
Keoldale

DURNESS VISITOR
CENTRE
Balnakeil
Durness
DURNESS
Leirinmore
Sangobeg
Rispond
Sarsgrum

SMOO CAVE

Eilean
Hoan

Whiten Head

Geodh'a'
Bhrideoin

Eilean
Clùimhrig

Rubha Thormaid

Port Vasgo

Strathan
Midfield

408
BEN
HUTIG
West Strathan

Talmine

Skinnet
Midtown

Eilean
nan Ron

Caol Raineach

Skerray
Ach
Airdto
To

Skullomie
Coldbackie

Rabbit
Is.
Tongue
Bay

422
MEALL MEADHONACH

Portnancon
Heilam
Hope
230
Lochside
Eilean
Choraidh
Eriboll

A'Mhoine
A838

Achuvoldrach
Tongue
Kirkiboll
Tongue
CASTLE
VARRICH

NN
NAIDH

Polla

30

521
AN LEAN-CHARN

Loch Crocach

FEINNE-BHEINN
MOR
465

927
BEN HOPE

Alltnacaillich
DUN DORNAIGIL
BROCH

Glen Golly

Gobernuisgach Lodge

KYLE OF TONGUE

Ribigill

Kinloch Lodge

Loch na Seilg

Loch a'
Ghobha-
Dhuibh

Loch an
Dherue

Loch Haluim

416

Loch Coulside

Loch
Meadie

Loch
Eileanach

764
BEN LOYAL

Loch Loyal Lodge

557
CNOC NAN
CULLEAN

Inchkinloch

Loch
Craggie

527
BEINN
STUMANADH

Loch
Loyal

294
POLE HILL

ch
Syre

759

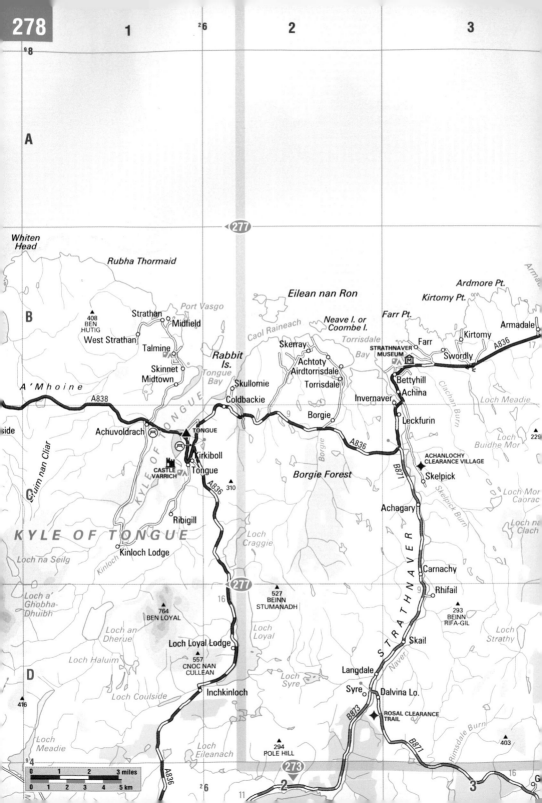

1 ²6 2 3

⁹8

A

277

Whiten
Head

Rubha Thormaid

Port Vasgo

Eilean nan Ron

Ardmore Pt.

Kirtomy Pt.

B

408
BEN
HUTIG

Strathan

Midfield

Caol Raineach

Neave I. or
Coombe I.

Farr Pt.

Torrisdale
Bay

STRATHNAVER
MUSEUM

Farr

Kirtomy

Armadale

West Strathan

Talmine

Skerray

Achtoty

Swordly

17

Rabbit
Is.

Skinnet
Midtown

Tongue
Bay

Airdtorrisdale

Torrisdale

Bettyhill

Achina

A836

A'Mhoine

A838

Skullomie

Coldbackie

Borgie

Invernaver

Loch Meadie

Achuvoldrach

Tongue

9

Leckfurin

Loch
Buidhe Mor

229

Càim nan Cliar

Kirkiboll

Tongue

Borgie

A836

ACHANLOCHY
CLEARANCE VILLAGE

C

CASTLE
VARRICH

Borgie Forest

B871

Skelpick

Skelpick Burn

Loch Mor
Caorac

310

Achagary

Loch na Seilg

Ribigill

Loch
Craggie

Loch na'
Clach

KYLE OF TONGUE

Kinloch Lodge

Carnachy

Loch a'
Ghobha-
Dhuibh

277

527
BEINN
STUMANADH

16

9

Rhifail

293
BEINN
RIFA-GIL

Loch
Strathy

Loch an
Dheru e

764
BEN LOYAL

Loch
Loyal

Skail

D

416

557
CNOC NAN
CULLEAN

Loch
Syre

Langdale

Syre

Dalvina Lo.

STRATHNAVER

Naver

Loch Halium

Loch Loyal Lodge

Inchkinloch

Loch Coulside

Loch
Meadie

Loch
Eileanach

294
POLE HILL

B873

ROSAL CLEARANCE
TRAIL

B871

403

⁹4

0   1   2   3 miles
0   1   2   3   4   5 km

A836

273

²6

11

2

3

16

G

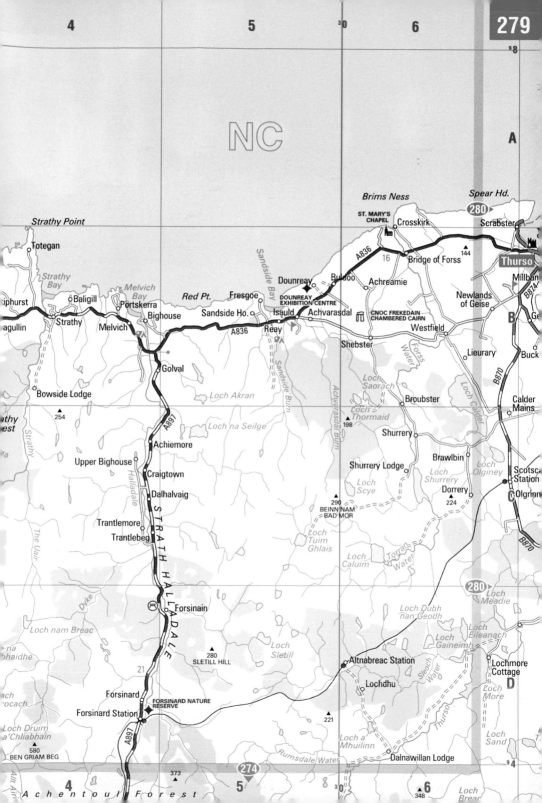

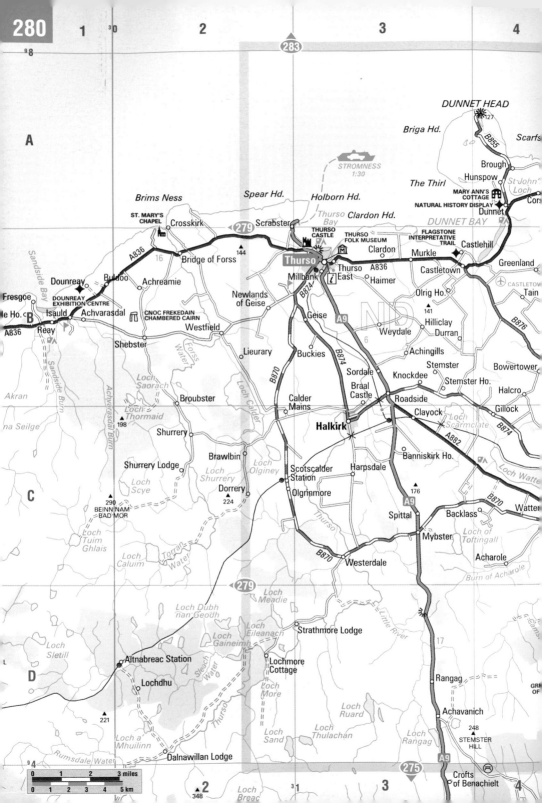

⁹8

Langaton Point
Nethertown
Red Head
ST. MARGARETS HOPE 1:00
BURWICK 0:45 (May-Sept)
Muckle Skerry
Pentland Skerries

Island of Stroma
53
Mell Head
Uppertown

Men of Mey
St John's Pt.
East Mey
CASTLE OF MEY
Mey
Gills
A836
Kirkstyle
Canisbay
Huna
JOHN O'GROATS
John o' Groats
DUNCANSBY HEAD
Stacks of Duncansby

A

⁹rock
⁴kstack

Boars of Duncansby
Gills Bay

A99

124
Brabster
Tofts
Skirza
Skirza Head
Freswick
Freswick Bay

B

Gill Burn
Lochend
Slickly
easter
den
Alterwall
Lyth
rock Ho.
LYTH ARTS CENTRE
Sortat
Howe
Nybster
16
A99
Ness Head
BUCHOLLY CASTLE
NORTHLANDS VIKING CENTRE
Auckengill
Brough Head

ND

Keiss
Mireland
KEISS CASTLE

Kirk
Burn of Lyth
Loch of Wester
Myrelandhorn
SINCLAIR'S
BAY

C

of Watten
Killimster
B876
Reiss
Winless
60
B874
Ackergill
CASTLE SINCLAIR
CASTLE GIRNIGOE
Noss Head
Sealky Head
Staxigoe
WICK
WICK HERITAGE CENTRE
Papigoe
Broadhaven

B870
⁴ilbster
ath
A882
Stirkoke Ho.
Milton
Wick
Wick Bay
Newton
Old Wick
South Hd.
CASTLE OF OLD WICK
Gote O'Tram

Whiterow
Tannach
Loch Hempriggs
Hempriggs House
Helman Hd.

D

141
HILL OF OLICLETT
A99
Gansclet
Thrumster
Sarclet
Sarclet Hd.

Loch of Yarrows
212
Ulbster
17
CAIRN OF GET
Whaligoe

⁹4

HILL O' MANY STANES
275
4
Bruan
Mid
⁵ 5 6 ³5 7

⁹rock

283

283

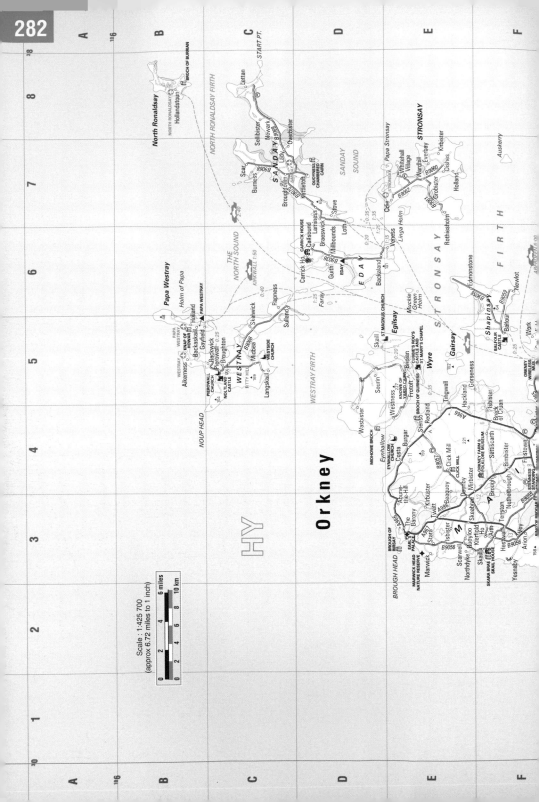

Scale : 1:425 700
(approx 6.72 miles to 1 inch)

0   2   4   6 miles
0   2   4   6   8   10 km

Orkney

HY

North Ronaldsay

NORTH RONALDSAY
Hollandstoun
BROCH OF BURRIAN

START PT.

Lettan

NORTH RONALDSAY FIRTH

THE
NORTH SOUND

2:40

Scar
Burnes's
Sellibister
Newark
Overbister
Lady
Kettletoft
Broughton
SANDAY
B9069
B9068
Kirbister

Stove
QUOYNESS
CHAMBERED
CAIRN

Braeswick
Lammass
Loth

SANDAY
SOUND

Papa Stronsay
STRONSAY

Whitehall
Village
Evertaw
Kirbister
B9060
Wardhill
Grobister
Holland
Distles

Odie
STRONSAY

B9062

Rothiesholm

Auskerry

Papa Westray

Holm of Papa

PAPA WESTRAY
Gayfield
Holland
Backaskaill

KNAP OF
HOWAR
PAPA
WESTRAY

Skelwick
Rapness

CARRICK HOUSE
Carrick Ho.
Calfsound
B9063
Braeswick
Guth

EDAY

Backaland

Veness

Linga Holm

Muckle
Green
Holm

STRONSAY

FIRTH

Edmonstone

B9059

Newlot

ABERDEEN 8:00

Shapinsay

Aikerness
Midbea
Broughton
Sulland

Rackwick

WESTSIDE
CHURCH

WESTRAY

Langskaill

PIEROWALL
CHURCH

NOLTLAND
CASTLE

FITTY HILL
169

Faray

ST MAGNUS CHURCH

Egilsay

CUBBIE ROO'S
CASTLE AND
ST MARY'S CHAPEL

Wyre

Gairsay

BALFOUR
CASTLE
Balfour

Work

ORKNEY
WIRELESS
MUS.

Skaill
Bridan
Westness
Frotoft
Hackland
Tingwall
Isbister
Corseness
Brock
of Gurness

NOUP HEAD

WESTRAY FIRTH

Washbister

MIDHOWE BROCH

Eynhallow
Costa
Burgar

EYNHALLOW
CHURCH

KNOWE OF
GURNESS

BROCH OF GURNESS

Sourin

WESTNESS

Stenso

Redland

Evie

Settiscarth

BROUGH HEAD

BROUGH OF
BIRSAY

EARL'S
PALACE

MARWICK HEAD
NATURE RESERVE

Marwick

The
Brony
Aikerness
B9056

Twatt
Isbister
Dounby
CLICK MILL
Click Mill
Mirbister

Kirbister
Beaquoy
Skeabrae
Binscarth

B9057

ORKNEY FARM &
FOLKLORE MUSEUM

Brough
Netherbrough
Finstown

Scanwick

Northdyke
Quoyloo
Skaill
Kierfield
Tenston

SKAIL
HOUSE

SKARA BRAE

Yesnaby

Arion

B9056

STENNESS
STANDING
STONES

B9055

RING OF BROGAR

Aith
Stenness

Hestwall

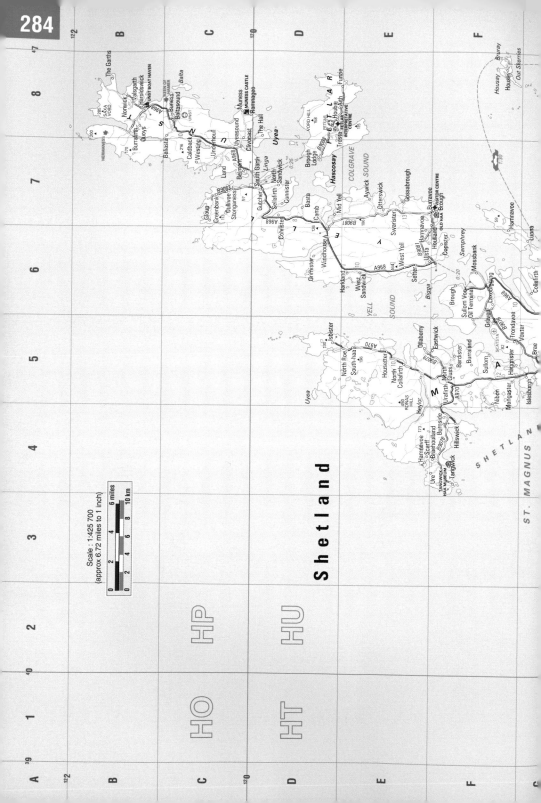

Scale : 1:425 700
(approx 6.72 miles to 1 inch)

6 miles

10 km

Shetland

ST. MAGNUS

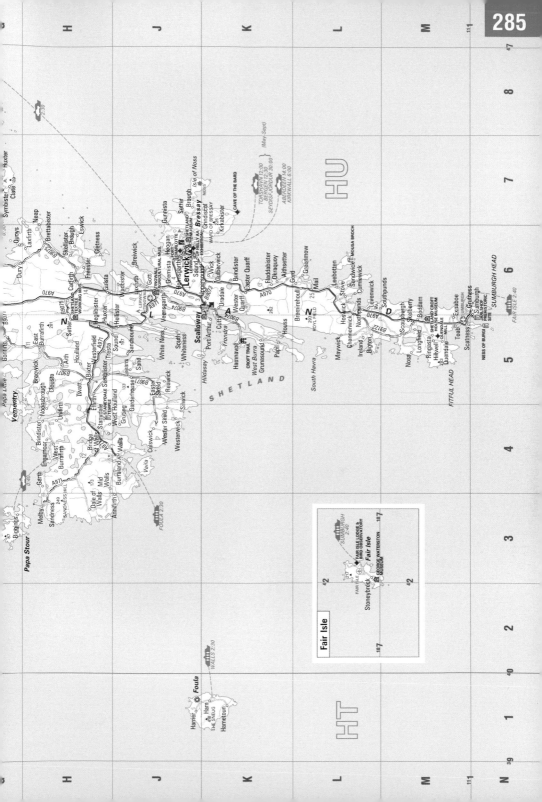

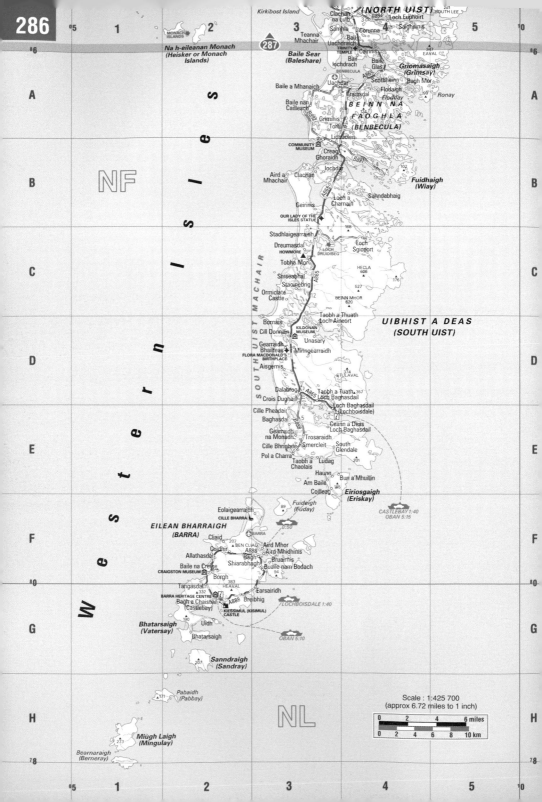

Kirkibost Island

(NORTH UIST) SOUTH LEE

Clachan na Luib
Samhla
Corunna
Ceannis
Baile Iochdrach
TRINITY TEMPLE
EAVAL

Teanna Mhachair
Baile Sear (Baleshare)
Bail' Uachdrach
Ballivanich

Na h-eileanan Monach (Heisker or Monach Islands)

MONACH ISLANDS

287

Baile a Mhanaich
Baile Glas
Griomasaigh (Grimsay)
Bagh Mor
Scolpaig
Flodday
Ronay

BENBECULA

Baile nan Cailleach
Gramsdal
Griminis
Tofum
BEINN NA FAOGHLA (BENBECULA)

Lìonacleit

COMMUNITY MUSEUM
Creag Ghoraidh
Iochdar
Loch Euphoirt
Saighdinis

NF

Aird a Mhachair
Clachan
Sanndabhaig
Fuidhaigh (Wiay)

Geirinis
Loch a Charnain

OUR LADY OF THE ISLES STATUE
Stadhlaigearraidh
Loch Sgioport

Dreumasdal
HOWMORE
Loch DRUIDIBEG

Tobha Mor
HECLA 606

Shìseabhal
Staoinebrig
BEINN MHOR 620

Ormiclate Castle

Taobh a Thuath
Loch Aineort

Bornais
KILDONAN MUSEUM
UIBHIST A DEAS (SOUTH UIST)

Cill Donnain
Unasary

Gearraidh Bhailteas
FLORA MACDONALD'S BIRTHPLACE
Mìnngearraidh

Aisgernis

Dalabrog
Taobh a Tuath
Loch Baghasdail
Crois Dughaill
Loch Baghasdail (Lochboisdale)

Cille Pheadair
Ceann a Deas
Loch Baghasdail
Baghasdal

Gearraidh na Monadh
Trosaraidh
Smercleit
South Glendale

Cille Bhrighde
Pol a Charra
Taobh a Chaolais
Ludag

Hauun
Bun a'Mhuillin

S O U T H   U I S T   M A C H A I R

Am Baile
Coilleag

Eiriosgaigh (Eriskay)

CASTLEBAY 1:40
OBAN 5:15

Fuidheigh (Fuday)

Eolaigearraidh
CILLE BHARRA
EILEAN BHARRAIGH (BARRA)

Cliaid
BARRA
Aird Mhor

Cuidhir
BEN CLIAG
Aird Mhidhinis
A888
Bruairnis

Allathasdal
Bagh a
Buaile nam Bodach

Baile na Creige
Shiarabhagh

CRAIGSTON MUSEUM
Borgh
HEAVAL

Tangasdal
A888
Earsairidh

BARRA HERITAGE CENTRE
Bagh a Chaisteil (Castlebay)
Breibhig
LOCHBOISDALE 1:40

KIESSIMUL (KISIMUL) CASTLE

Bhatarsaigh (Vatersay)
Uidh
OBAN 5:10

Bhatarsaigh

Sanndraigh (Sandray)

Pabaidh (Pabbay)

NL

Miùgh Laigh (Mingulay)

Bearnaraigh (Berneray)

W e s t e r n   I s l e s

Scale : 1:425 700
(approx 6.72 miles to 1 inch)

0   2   4   6 miles
0 2 4 6 8 10 km

berdeen

erdeen ⤢ C2
erdeen College
(Gallowgate Centre) . A2
ademy, The B1
ert Basin. B1
t Gallery B1
ts Centre 🏛 A2
ck Wynd B2
rry St A2
ackfriars St. B1
n-Accord Centre . . . B2
n-Accord St B1
dge St B2
ad St B2
s Station C3
r Ferry Terminal C3
stlegate B3
thedral ✝ B1
ntral Library B1
llege St C2
mmerce St B3
mmercial Quay C3
nstitution St A3
wn St C1
nburn Rd B1
st North St A3
h Market C3
lleria, The C1
llowgate A2
orge St A1
lden Sq B1
rdon's College. A1
ild St C2
Majesty's
heatre 🎭 B1
spital H B1
ormation Ctr 🛈 B2

Jamieson Quay C3
John St A1
Justice St B3
King St. A3
Lemon Tree, The A2
Loch St A1
Maberly St. A1
Marischal College 🏛 . . A2
Maritime Museum &
Provost Ross's
House 🏛 B2
Mercat Cross ✦ B3
Market B2
Market St C2/C3
Music Hall 🏛 C1
Park St A3
Police Station 🏛 B2
Post Office 🏛 B2/B3
Provost Skene's
House 🏛 B2
Queen St B2
Regent Quay B3
St Andrew St A1
St Andrew's
Cathedral ✝ B3
St Nicholas Centre . . . B2
St Nicholas St B2
School Hill B1
Spring Garden. A1
Town House 🏛 B2
Trinity Centre C2
Trinity Quay B3
Union St B2/C1
Union Terr B1
Upper Dock. C3
Upper Kirkgate B2
Virginia St B3
West North St A2
Windmill Brae C1

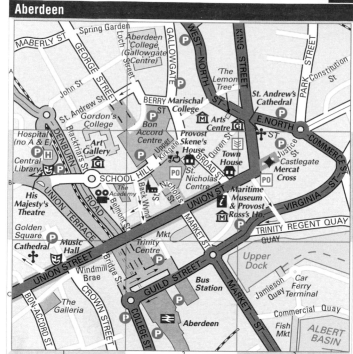

th

ua Theatre of
lass 🏛 A2
sembly Rooms and
useum of
ostume 🏛 A2
n St C2
ton St B2
h Abbey ✝ B2
h City College C2
h Rugby Club. C2
h Spa Station ⤢ C3
nnett St A2
ad Quay C2
ad St A2
ck St A1
lding of Bath 🏛 A2
s Station C3
arlotte St B1
eap St B2
cus Mews A1
n St C2
cket Ground C3
orge St A2
at Pulteney St B3
en Park C1
en Park Rd. C1
ve St. A3
ldhall B2
rietta Gdns A3
rietta Mews A3
rietta Park A3
rietta Rd A3
rietta St A3
ary St C3
ormation Ctr 🛈 B3
nes St West B1
e Austen
entre 🏛 B2
ary B2

Lower Bristol Rd C1
Manvers St C3
Midland Bridge Rd . . . B1
Milk St C2
Milsom St B2
Monmouth Pl. B1
Monmouth St B2
New King St B1
No. 1 Royal
Crescent 🏛 A1
Norfolk Bldgs B1
North Parade Rd B3
Paragon. A2
Police Station 🏛 C3
Post Office 🏛 . B1/B2/C2
Postal Museum 🏛 . . . B2
Pulteney Bridge ✦ . . . B3
Queen Sq B2
Recreation Ground . . . B3
Rivers St A2
Roman Baths &
Pump Room 🏛 B2
Royal Ave A1
Royal Cr. A1
Royal Victoria Park . . . A1
St John's Rd A3
Southgate C2
South Pde C3
Sports & Leisure
Centre B3
Spring Gdns C3
Stall St. B2
Theatre Royal 🎭 B2
Thermae Bath Spa ✦ . C2
Union St B2
Victoria Art Gallery 🏛 . B3
Walcot St. A2/B2
Westgate Bldgs B2
Westgate St. B2
William Herschel
Museum 🏛 B1

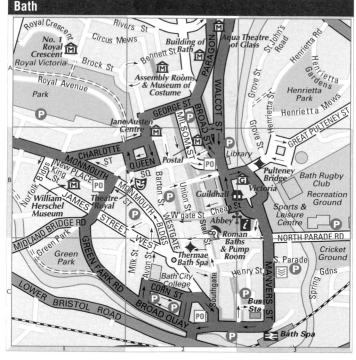

Birmingham

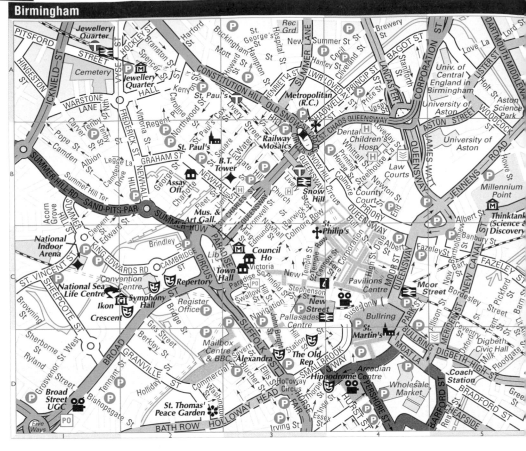

Birmingham

Acorn Gr B1
Albert St B5/C4
Albion St B1
Alexandra Theatre ♥ . . D3
Allison St C5
Arcadian Centre D4
Assay Office ⌂ B2
Aston Science Park A5
Aston St B5
BT Tower ✦ B3
Bagot St A4
Banbury St C5
Barford St D5
Barn St C5
Bartholomew St C5
Barwick St B3
Bath Row D2
Berkley St D2
Bishopsgate St D1
Blucher St D3
Bordesley St C5
Bradford St D5
Branston St A2
Brewery St A4
Bridge St C2
Brindley Dr. C2
Broad St C2/D1
Broad Street UGC ♥ . . D1
Browning St C1
Buckingham St A3
Bull Ring C4
Bullring D4
Bull St C4
Cambridge St C2
Camden Dr B1
Camden St B1
Cannon St C3
Caroline St A2

Carver St B1
Cecil St A4
Cemetery A1
Charlotte St B2
Cheapside D5
Children's Hospital Ⓗ . . . B4
Church St B3
Clement St C1
Cleveland St A4
Coach Station D5
Colmore Circus B4
Colmore Row C3
Commercial St. D2
Constitution Hill A3
Convention Centre C2
Corporation St. A4/B4/C4
County Court B4
Coventry St D5
Cox St A2
Crescent Theatre ♥ C2
Cromwell St B3
Dale End C4
Dartmouth Middleway . . . A5
Dental Hospital Ⓗ B4
Digbeth Civic Hall D5
Digbeth High St D5
Edmund St C3
Edward St C1
Ellis St D3
Essex St D3
Fazeley St C5
Five Ways D1
Fleet St B2
Floodgate St D5
Fore St C4
Frederick St B2
Gas St D2
George St B2
Graham St B2

Granville St D2
Great Charles St B3
Green St D5
Grosvenor St West D1
Hall St A2
Hampton St A3
Hanley St A4
Harford St A3
Henrietta St A3
High St C4
Hill St C3/D3
Hingeston St A1
Hippodrome
  Theatre ♥ D4
Hockley St A2
Holliday St D1
Holloway Circus D3
Holloway Head D3
Holt St A5
Horse Fair D3
Hospital St A3
Howard St A3
Howe St B5
Hurst St D4
Icknield St A1
Ikon Gallery ⌂ C2
Information Ctr ⓘ C3
Inge St D3
Irving St D3
James Watt
  Queensway B4
Jennens Rd B5
Jewellery Quarter ⇌ . A1
Jewellery Quarter
  Museum ⌂ A2
John Bright St D3
Kenyon St A2
King Edwards Rd C1
Lancaster St A4
Law Courts B4

Legge La B1
Library C2
Lionel St B3
Lister St A5
Little Ann St D5
Livery St B3
Lord St A5
Love La A5
Loveday St A4
Lower Loveday St A4
Ludgate Hill B3
Mailbox Centre & BBC . . . D2
Margaret St C3
Meriden St C5
Metropolitan (R.C.) ✝ . B3
Milk St D5
Millennium Point B5
Moat La D4
Moor Street ⇌ C4
Moor St Queensway C4
Mott St A3
Museum & Art
  Gallery ⌂ C3
National Indoor
  Arena ✦ C1
National Sea Life
  Centre C1
Navigation St C3
New Bartholomew St C5
New Canal St C5
New St C3
New Street ⇌ C3
New Summer St A3
Newhall Hill B2
Newhall St B2/C3
Newton St B4
Northwood St A3
Old Snow Hill A3
Oxford St D5
Pallasades Centre C3

Paradise Circus C2
Paradise St C3
Park St C4
Pavilions Centre C4
Pershore St D4
Pickford St C5
Pinfold St C3
Pitsford St A1
Police Station Ⓢ B4/D5
Pope St B1
Post Office ⌂ C3/D1
Price St A4
Princip St A4
Printing House St B4
Priory Queensway B4
Rea St D5
Regent Pl. B2
Register Office C2
Repertory Theatre ♥ C2
Ryland St D1
St Chads Circus B3
St Chads Queensway B4
St George's St A3
St Martin's ⛪ D4
St Paul's ⛪ B2
St Paul's Metro station ⇌ . B2
St Paul's Sq B2
St Philip's ✝ C3
St Thomas' Peace
  Garden ✿ D2
St Vincent St C1
Sand Pits Pde B1
Severn St D3
Shadwell St A4
Sheepcote St C1
Sherborne St D1

Smallbrook
  Queensway . . . .
Snow Hill ⇌ . . . .
Snow Hill Queensway . . .
Spencer St . . . .
Staniforth St . . . .
Station St . . . .
Steelhouse La . . . .
Stephenson St . . . .
Suffolk St . . . .
Summer Hill Rd . . . .
Summer Hill St . . . .
Summer Hill Terr . . . . . .
Summer La . . . .
Summer Row . . . .
Swallow St . . . .
Symphony Hall ♥ . . . . . .
Temple Row . . . .
Temple St . . . .
Tenby St . . . .
Tenby St North . . . .
Tennant St . . . .
Thinktank (Science
  & Discovery) . . . .
Thorpe St . . . .
Town Hall ⌂ . . . .
Trent St . . . .
University of Central
  England . . . .
University of Aston A5
Vesey St . . . .
Victoria Sq. . . . .
Vittoria St . . . .
Vyse St . . . .
Warstone La . . . .
Washington St . . . .
Water St . . . .
Whittall St . . . .
Wholesale Market . . . . . .
Woodcock St . . . .

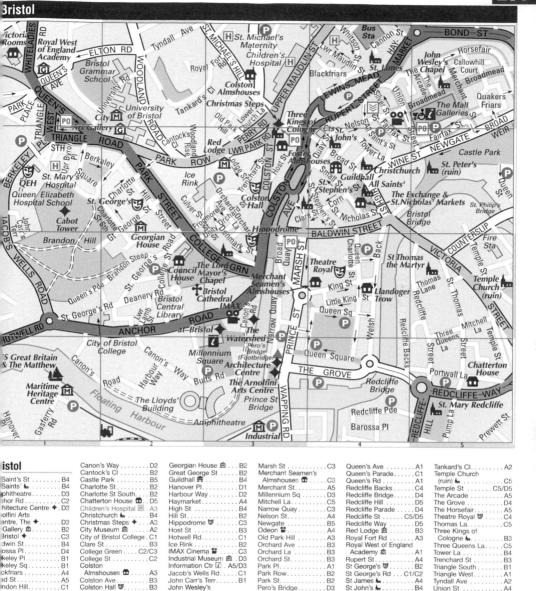

istol

Saint's St B4
Saints' ┗ B4
phitheatre D3
hor Rd C2
hitecture Centre ✦ . D3
olfini Arts
entre, The ✦ D3
Gallery ⋒ B2
Bristol ✦ C3
dwin St B4
ossa Pl D4
keley Pl B1
keley Sq B1
ckfriars A4
ad St A5
ndon Hill C1
ndon Steep C2
stol Bridge B5
stol Cathedral
E) ✝ C2
stol Central Library . C2
toi Grammar
hool A2
ad Quay C3
ad St B4
ad Weir A5
admead A5
Station A4
ts Rd D3
ot Tower ✦ B1
owhill Ct A5
non St A4
on's Rd C3/D1

Canon's Way D2
Cantock's Cl B2
Castle Park B5
Charlotte St B2
Charlotte St South . . . B2
Chatterton St D5
Children's Hospital Ⓗ . A3
Christchurch ┗ B4
Christmas Steps ✦ . . A3
City Museum ⋒ A2
City of Bristol College . C1
Clare St B3
College Green . . . C2/C3
College St C2
Colston
  Almshouses ⋒ B3
Colston Ave B3
Colston Hall ⋓ B3
Colston St B3
Corn St B4
Council House C2
Countership C5
Courts C5
Culver St C2
Deanery Rd C2
Denmark St B3
Elton Rd A1/A2
Exchange and St Nicholas
  Mkts, The ⋒ B4
Fairfax St B4/B5
Fire Station C5
Floating Harbour . . . D2
Foster Almshouses ⋒ B3
Frogmore St B2
Gasferry Rd D1

Georgian House ⋒ . . B2
Great George St B2
Guildhall ⋒ B4
Hanover Pl D1
Harbour Way D2
Haymarket A4
High St B4
Hill St B2
Hippodrome ⋓ C3
Host St B3
Hotwell Rd C1
Ice Rink B2
IMAX Cinema ⋈ C3
Industrial Museum ⋒ . D3
Information Ctr ⓘ . A5/D3
Jacob's Wells Rd C1
John Carr's Terr B1
John Wesley's
  Chapel ┗ A5
King St C4
Lewins Mead A4
Little King St C4
Llandoger Trow ⋒ . . C4
Lloyds' Building, The . . D2
Lodge St B3
Lord Mayor's
  Chapel, The ┗ C3
Lower Church La A3
Lower Lamb St C2
Lower Maudlin St A4
Lower Park Rd B3
Mall Galleries
  Shopping Ctr, The . . A5
Maritime Heritage
  Centre ⋒ D1

Marsh St C3
Merchant Seamen's
  Almshouses ⋒ C3
Merchant St A5
Millennium Sq D3
Mitchell La C5
Narrow Quay C3
Nelson St A4
Newgate B5
Odeon ⋓ B4
Old Park Hill A3
Orchard Ave B3
Orchard La B3
Orchard St B3
Park Pl A1
Park Row B2
Park St B2
Pero's Bridge D3
Perry Rd B3
Police Sta ⬛ A4
Post Office
  . . . . A1/A5/B3/C3
Portwall La D5
Prewett St D5
Prince St C3/D3
Prince St Bridge D3
Pump La D5
QEH Theatre ⋓ B1
Quakers Friars A5
Quay St B4
Queen Charlotte St . . C4
Queen Elizabeth
  Hospital School B1
Queen Sq C4/D4
Queen St B5

Queen's Ave A1
Queen's Parade C1
Queen's Rd A2
Redcliffe Backs C4
Redcliffe Bridge C4
Redcliffe Hill D5
Redcliffe Parade D5
Redcliffe St C5/D5
Redcliffe Way D5
Red Lodge ⋒ B3
Royal Fort Rd A3
Royal West of England
  Academy ⋒ A1
Rupert St A4
St George's ⋓ B2
St George's Rd . . . C1/C2
St James ┗ A4
St John's ┗ B4
St Mary Redcliffe ┗ . . D5
St Mary's Hospital Ⓗ . B1
St Michael's Hill A3
St Michael's Maternity
  Hospital Ⓗ A3
St Nicholas St B4
St Peter's (ruin) ┗ . . . B4
St Philip's Bridge B5
St Stephen's ┗ B4
St Stephen's St B4
St Thomas St C5
St Thomas the
  Martyr ┗ C5
Silver St A4
Small St B4
SS Great Britain and
  The Matthew ⋓ D1

Tankard's Cl A2
Temple Church
  (ruin) ┗ C5
Temple St C5/D5
The Arcade A5
The Grove D4
The Horsefair A5
Theatre Royal ⋓ . . . C4
Thomas La C5
Three Queens La C5
Tower La B4
Trenchard St B3
Triangle South B1
Triangle West A1
Tyndall Ave A2
Union St A4
Unity St B3
University of Bristol . . A2
University Rd A2
Upper Maudlin St . . . A3
Upper Byron Pl B1
Victoria Rooms ⋒ . . . A1
Victoria St C5
Wapping Rd D3
Watershed, The ✦ . . . C3
Welsh Back C4
Whiteladies Rd A1
Whitson St A4
Wine St B4
Woodland Rise B2
Woodland Rd A2
YHA ▲ D3

Cardiff / Caerdydd

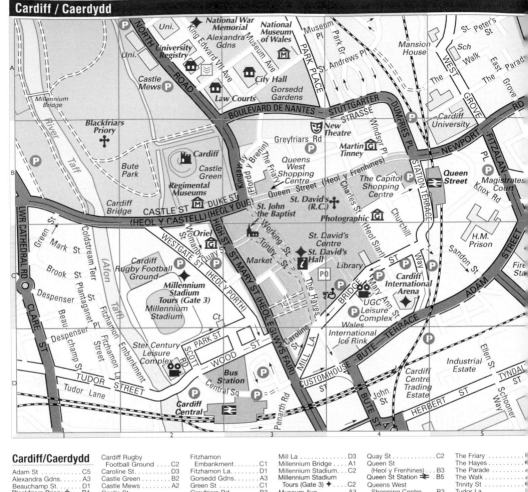

Cardiff/Caerdydd

Adam St C5
Alexandra Gdns A3
Beauchamp St. D1
Blackfriars Priory ✝ . . B1
Boulevard De
 Nantes. A3
Bridge St C4
Brook St C1
Bus Station D3
Bute Park. B2
Bute St D4
Bute Terr D4
Capitol Shopping
 Centre, The B4
Cardiff Bridge B1
Cardiff Castle ⚏ B2
Cardiff Central
 Station ⇌ D3
Cardiff Centre
 Trading Estate D4
Cardiff International
 Arena ✦ C4

Cardiff Rugby
 Football Ground . . . C2
Caroline St. D3
Castle Green B2
Castle Mews A2
Castle St
 (Heol y Castell) . . . B2
Central Sq. D2
Charles St B4
Churchill Way C4
City Hall ⚏ A3
Clare St D1
Coldstream Terr. C1
Court C2
Customhouse St D3
Despenser Place D1
Despenser St. C1
Duke St (Heol y Dug). . . B3
Dumfries Pl B2
East Grove. A5
Ellen St D5
Fire Station C5
Fitzalan Place B5

Fitzhamon
 Embankment C1
Fitzhamon La. D1
Gorsedd Gdns A3
Green St C1
Greyfriars Rd B3
H.M. Prison C5
Herbert St D5
High St C2
Information Ctr ℹ . . . C3
John St D4
King Edward VII Ave . . . A2
Kingsway
 (Ffordd y Brenin) . . . B2
Knox Rd B5
Law Courts ⚏ A2
Library C4
Lower Cathedral Rd . . . C1
Magistrates Court B5
Mansion House A5
Mark St C1
Market C2
Martin Tinney ⚏ B4
Mary Ann St C4

Mill La D3
Millennium Bridge A1
Millennium Stadium. . . . C2
Millennium Stadium
 Tours (Gate 3) ✦ . . . C2
Museum Ave A3
Museum Place A3
National Museum
 of Wales ⚏ A3
National War
 Memorial ✦ A2
New Theatre ⚏ B3
Newport Rd B5
North Rd A2
Oriel ⚏ C2
Park Grove A4
Park Place A3
Park St. D2
Penarth Rd D2
Photographic
 Library ⚏ B4
Plantaganet St. C1
Police Station ▦ C3
Post Office ▣ C3

Quay St C2
Queen St
 (Heol y Frenhines) . . B3
Queen St Station ⇌ . B5
Queens West
 Shopping Centre. . . . B3
Regimental
 Museums ⚏ B2
St Andrews Place . . . A4
St David's ✝ B4
St David's Centre C3
St David's Hall ✦ . . . C3
St John The
 Baptist ⅃. C3
St Mary St
 (Heol Eglwys Fair) . . C3
St Peter's St A5
Sandon St C5
Schooner Way D5
Scott Rd D2
Station Terr B4
Ster Century Leisure
 Complex ⚏ D2
Stuttgarter Strasse . . . A4

The Friary . . . .
The Hayes . . . .
The Parade . . . .
The Walk . . . .
Trinity St . . . .
Tudor La . . . .
Tudor St. . . . .
Tyndall St. . . . .
Tyndall Street
 Industrial Estate . . . .
UGC Leisure
 Complex ⚏ . . . .
Cardiff University . . . A2/
University Registry ⚏ . .
Wales International
 Ice Rink . . . .
West Gr . . . .
Westgate St
 (Heol y Porth) . . . . .
Windsor Place . . . .
Womanby St . . . .
Wood St. . . . .
Working St. . . . .

ambridge

|C 🏛️ A2
chaeology &
  nthropology 🏛️ B2
s Theatre 🎭 B1
cks, The B1
ne't St B1
s Station A2
tt Green A3
ambridge Contemporary
  rt Gallery A2
rist's (Coll) A2
rist's Pieces A3
are (Coll) B1
arendon St B3
rpus Christi (Coll) . . B2
rwin (Coll) C1
wning St B3
rl St B3
n St A2
mmanuel (Coll) B3
manuel Rd A2
manuel St B2
r St A3
zwilliam
  useum 🏛️ C2
tzwilliam St C2
nville & Caius (Coll) . A1
nville Place C3
ildhall 🏛️ B2
bson St A2
ormation Ctr ℹ️ . . . B2
sus La A3
sus Terr A3
g St B2
g's (Coll) B1
g's College
  hapel ⛪ B1
g's Parade B1
n Yard Centre B2
le St Mary's La C1

Maid's Causeway A3
Malcolm St A2
Market Hill B2
Market St. B2
Mathematical Bridge . . B1
Mill La C1
New Square A3
Newnham Rd. C1
Orchard St. A3
Park Terr B3
Parker St B3
Parker's Piece C3
Parkside. B3
Pembroke (Coll) C2
Pembroke St B2
Peterhouse (Coll) . . . C1
Petty Cury B2
Post Office 🅿️ . . A1/B2/C2
Queens' (Coll) B1
Queen's La B1
Regent St C3
Regent Terr C3
Round Church, The 🛐. A2
St Andrew's St. B2
St Benet's 🛐. B2
St Catharine's (Coll). . B1
St John's (Coll) A1
St Mary's 🛐. B1
Scott Polar Institute
  & Museum 🏛️ C3
Sedgwick Museum 🏛️. B2
Sidney St. A2
Sidney Sussex (Coll) . . A2
Silver St. C1
Tennis Court Rd. C2
Trinity (Coll) A1
Trinity Hall (Coll). . . . A1
Trinity St A1
Trumpington St C2
Victoria St B3
Westcott House (Coll) . A2
Whipple 🏛️ B2
Willow Walk. A3
Zoology 🏛️. B2

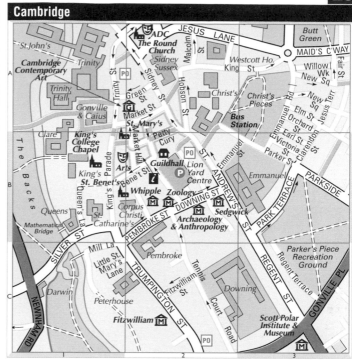

ventry

oots La A1
Faculty B3
hs B3
grade 🎭 A1
hop Burges St A2
nd's Hospital 🏛️ . . B1
adgate B2
s Station A3
nal Basin ✦ C2
eylesmore Manor
ouse 🏛️ C2
rist Church
pire ✦ C2
y Walls & Gates ✦ . A2
rporation St B1
uncil House B2
ventry Cathedral ✝️ . B3
ventry Transport
useum 🏛️ A2
x St A3/B3
ft Rd B3
fax St A3
d's Hospital 🏛️ . . . C2
rs Rd C2
yfriars Green ✦ . . . C1
yfriars Rd C1
es St A2
bert Art Gallery &
useum 🏛️ B3
tford St. B2
h St B2
St B1
y Trinity 🛐. B2
ormation Ctr ℹ️ . . . B2
dan Well B3
y Godiva Statue ✦ . B2
nb St A2
rary B1

Little Park St C2
Magistrates & Crown
  Courts B3
Manor House Dr C2
Market B1
Martyr's Memorial ✦ . . C2
Middleborough Rd. . . . A1
Millennium Place ✦. . . A2
Much Park St C3
New Union. C2
Parkside. C3
Police HQ 🅿️ C2
Post Office 🅿️ B2
Precinct, The B2
Primrose Hill St A3
Priory Gardens &
  Visitor Centre B2
Priory St. B3
Ringway (Hill Cross) . . A1
Ringway (Queens) . . . C1
Ringway (St Johns) . . . C3
Ringway (St Nicholas) . A2
Ringway (St Patricks) . C2
Ringway (Swanswell). . A3
St John St C3
St John The
  Baptist 🛐. B1
Skydome B1
Spon St B1
Sports Centre B3
Swanswell Pool A3
Sydney Stringer
  School. A3
Technology Park C3
Toy Museum 🏛️ C3
Trinity St B2
University. B3
Upper Hill St A1
Upper Well St A1
White St. A3

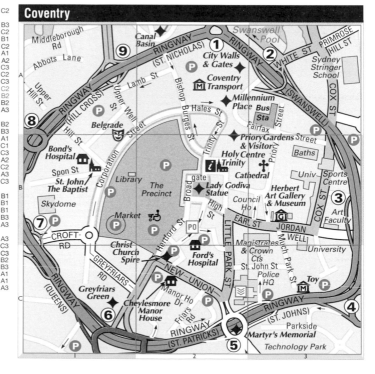

Edinburgh

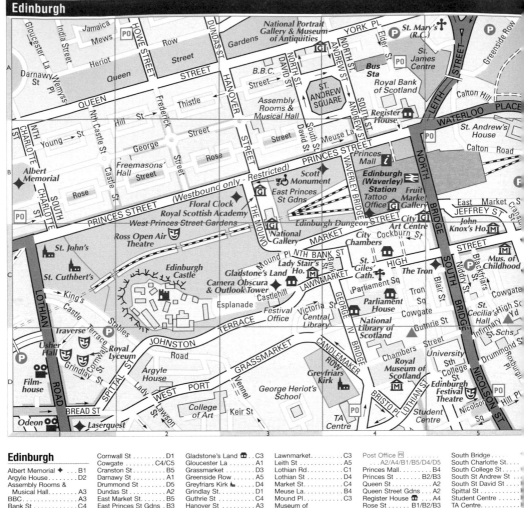

Edinburgh

Albert Memorial ✦ . . . B1
Argyle House D2
Assembly Rooms &
  Musical Hall A3
BBC A3
Bank St C4
Blackfriars St C5
Blair St C5
Bread St D1
Bristo Pl D4
Bus Station A4
Calton Hill A5
Calton Rd B5
Camera Obscura &
  Outlook Tower ✦ . . C3
Candlemaker Row C4
Castle St B1
Castle Terr C1
Castlehill C3
Central Library C4
Chambers St D4
City Art Centre ⌂ B4
City Chambers ⌂ C4
Cockburn St C4
College of Art D2

Cornwall St D1
Cowgate C4/C5
Cranston St B5
Darnawy St A1
Drummond St D5
Dundas St A2
East Market St B5
East Princes St Gdns . B3
Edinburgh
  (Waverley) ⇌ B4
Edinburgh Castle ⛫ . . C2
Edinburgh
  Dungeon ✦ B4
Edinburgh Festival
  Theatre ☕ D5
Esplanade C3
Festival Office C3
Filmhouse ☕ D1
Floral Clock ✦ B3
Frederick St A2
Freemasons' Hall B2
Fruit Market ⌂ B4
George Heriot's
  School D3
George IV Bridge C4
George St B2

Gladstone's Land ⌂ . . C3
Gloucester La A1
Grassmarket D3
Greyfriars Kirk ⛪ D4
Grindlay St D1
Guthrie St C4
Hanover St A3
Heriot Row A1/A2
High School Yard C5
High St C4
Hill Pl D5
Hill St B2
Howe St A2
India St A1
Infirmary St D5
Jamaica Mews A1
Jeffrey St B5
John Knox's
  House ⌂ C5
Johnston Terr C1
Keir St D3
King's Stables Rd . C1/D2
Lady Lawson St D2
Lady Stair's House ⌂ . C3
Laserquest ✦ D1

Lawnmarket C3
Leith St A5
Lothian Rd C1
Lothian St D4
Market St B4
Meuse La B4
Mound Pl C3
Museum of
  Childhood ⌂ C5
National Gallery ⌂ . . . C3
National Library of
  Scotland ⌂ C4
National Portrait
  Gallery & Museum
  of Antiquities ⌂ . . . A3
Nicolson Sq D5
Nicolson St D5
Niddry St C5
North Bridge B4
North Bank St C3
North Castle St B1
North Charlotte St B1
North St Andrew St . . . A4
North St David St A3
Odeon ☕ D1
Parliament House ⌂ . . C4
Parliament Sq C4

Post Office ⊡ . . . .
  . . . A2/A4/B1/B5/D4/D5
Princes Mall B4
Princes St B2/B3
Queen St A2
Queen Street Gdns . . . A2
Register House ⌂ . . . A4
Ross Open
  Air Theatre ☕ C2
Roxburgh Pl D5
Royal Bank
  of Scotland A4
Royal Lyceum ☕ D1
Royal Museum
  of Scotland ⌂ D4
Royal Scottish
  Academy ⌂ B3
St Andrew Sq A4
St Andrew's House . . . B5
St Cecilia's Hall C5
St Cuthbert's ⛪ C1
St Giles' † C4
St James Centre A4
St John's ⛪ C1
St Mary's † (R.C.) . . . A5
Scott Monument ✦ . . B4

South Bridge . . . . .
South Charlotte St . .
South College St . . .
South St Andrew St .
South St David St . .
Spittal St . . . .
Student Centre . . . .
TA Centre . . . .
Tattoo Office . . . . .
The Mound . . . . . .
Thistle St A2/
Traverse Theatre ☕ .
Tron Sq . . . .
Tron, The ✦ . . . . . .
University . . . .
Usher Hall ☕ . . . . .
Vennel . . . .
Victoria St . . . .
Waterloo Pl . . . . . .
Waverley Bridge . . .
Wemyss Pl . . . .
West Port . . . .
West Princes
  Street Gdns . . . . .
York Pl . . . .
Young St . . . .
Youth Hostel ▲ . . . C5/

Glasgow

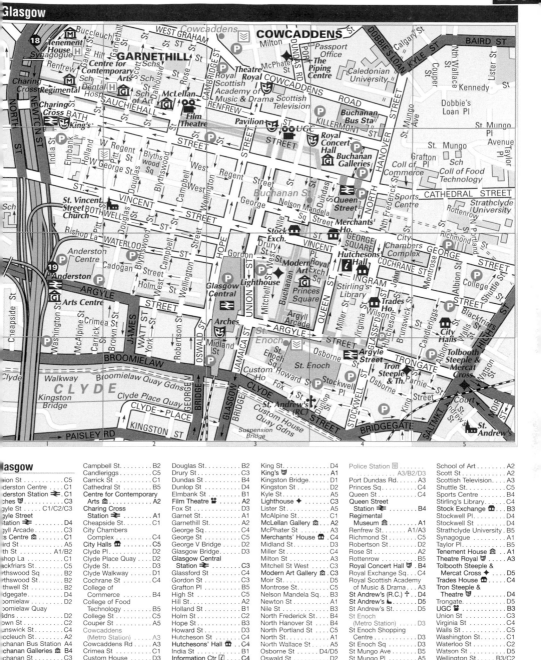

...ion St C5
...derston Centre . . . C1
...derston Station ⇌ . C1
...ches ⇌ C3
...gyle St C1/C2/C3
...gyle Street
...station ⇌ D4
...gyll Arcade C4
...s Centre 🏛 C4
...rd St A1/B2
...ith St C5
...ackfriars St C5
...rthswood Sq B2
...rthswood St B2
...thwell St B2
...idgegate D4
...oomielaw D2
...oomielaw Quay
...dns D2
...own St D2
...unswick St C3
...ccleuch St A2
...chanan Bus Station A4
...chanan Galleries 🏛 B4
...chanan St C3
...chanan St
...(Metro Station) . . . B3
...dogan St B2
...ledonian University . A4
...lgary St A5
...mbridge St A3

Campbell St B2
Candleriggs C5
Carrick St C1
Cathedral St C5
Centre for Contemporary
  Arts 🏛 A2
Charing Cross
  Station ⇌ A1
Cheapside St C1
City Chambers
  Complex C4
City Halls 🏛 C5
Clyde Pl D2
Clyde Place Quay . . . D2
Clyde St D2
Clyde Walkway D1
Cochrane St C4
College of
  Commerce B4
College of Food
  Technology B5
College St C5
Couper St A5
Cowcaddens
  (Metro Station) . . . A3
Cowcaddens Rd . . . A3
Crimea St C1
Custom House D3
Custom House
  Quay Gdns D3
Dalhousie St A2
Dental Hospital 🏥 . . A2
Dobbie's Loan A4
Dobbie's Loan Pl . . . A5

Douglas St B2
Drury St C3
Dundas St B4
Dunlop St D4
Elmbank St B1
Film Theatre 🎬 . . . A2
Fox St D3
Garnet St A1
Garnethill St A2
George Sq C4
George St C5
George V Bridge . . . D2
Glasgow Bridge . . . D3
Glasgow Central
  Station ⇌ C3
Glassford St C4
Gordon St C3
Grafton Pl B5
High St C5
Hill St A2
Holland St B1
Holm St C2
Hope St B3
Howard St D3
Hutcheson St C4
Hutchesons' Hall 🏛 . C4
India St B1
Information Ctr ℹ . . C4
Ingram St C4/C5
Jamaica St D3
James Watt St C2
John St C4
Kennedy St A5
Killermont St B4

King St D4
King's 🎭 A1
Kingston Bridge . . . D1
Kingston St D2
Kyle St A5
Lister St A5
Lighthouse ✦ C3
Lister St A5
McAlpine St C1
McLellan Gallery 🏛 . A1
McPhater St A3
Merchants' House 🏛 C4
Midland St D3
Miller St C4
Milton St A3
Mitchell St West . . . C3
Modern Art Gallery 🏛 C4
Moir St D5
Montrose St C4
Nelson Mandela Sq. . B3
Newton St A1
Nile St B3
North Frederick St . . B4
North Hanover St . . . B4
North Portland St . . . C5
North St A1
North Wallace St . . . A5
Osborne St D4/D5
Oswald St D2
Paisley Rd D1
Parnie St D5
Passport Office A4
Pavilion Theatre 🎭 . A3
Piping Centre, The ✦ . A3
Pitt St B2

Police Station 👮 . . . . .
. . . . A3/B2/D3
Port Dundas Rd A3
Princes Sq C4
Queen St C4
Queen Street
  Station ⇌ B4
Regimental
  Museum 🏛 A1
Renfrew St A1/A3
Richmond St C5
Robertson St D2
Rose St A1
Rottenrow B5
Royal Concert Hall 🎵 B4
Royal Exchange Sq. . C4
Royal Scottish Academy
  of Music & Drama. . A3
St Andrew's (R.C.) ✝ . D4
St Andrew's ⚓ D5
St Andrew's St D5
St Enoch
  (Metro Station) . . . D3
St Enoch Shopping
  Centre D3
St Enoch Sq D3
St Mungo Ave A5
St Mungo Pl A5
St Vincent Pl B2
St Vincent St B2
St Vincent Street
  Church ⚓ B2
Saltmarket D5
Sauchiehall St . . . A2/B3

School of Art A2
Scott St A2
Scottish Television . . A3
Shuttle St C5
Sports Centre B4
Stirling's Library . . . C4
Stock Exchange 🏛 . . B3
Stockwell Pl D4
Stockwell St D4
Strathclyde University . B5
Synagogue A1
Taylor Pl B5
Tenement House 🏛 . A1
Theatre Royal 🎭 . . . A3
Tolbooth Steeple &
  Mercat Cross ✦ . . . D5
Trades House 🏛 . . . C4
Tron Steeple &
  Theatre 🎭 D4
Trongate D5
Union St C3
Virginia St C4
Walls St C5
Washington St C1
Waterloo St C2
Watson St D5
Wellington St B2
West George St. . B2/B3
West Graham St . . . A2
West Regent St . . B2/B3
Wilson St C4
York St West C2

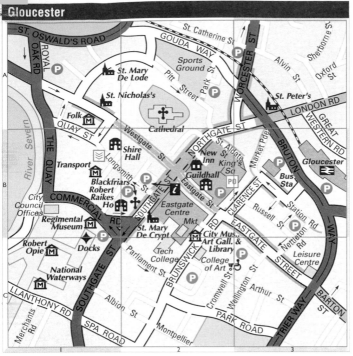

Gloucester

Leicester

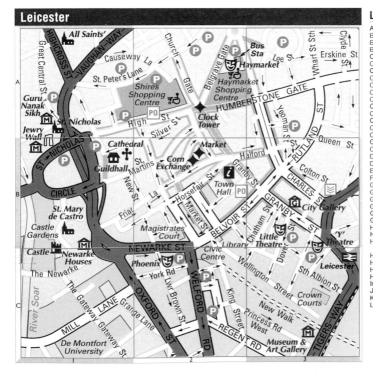

Leeds

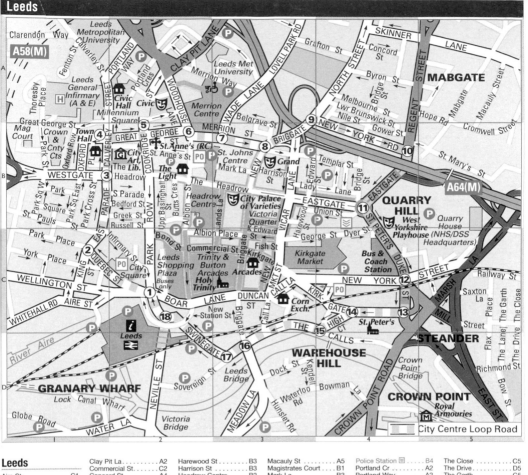

Leeds

Aire St C1
Albion Place C2
Albion St B2
Arcades 🏛 C3
Bedford St B2
Belgrave St A3
Boar La C2
Bond St C2
Bow St D5
Bowman La D4
Bridge St A4/B4
Briggate C3
Bus & Coach Station . . C4
Butts Cres B2
Byron St A4
Call La C3
Calverley St A1/B1
City Art Gallery &
Library 🏛 B2
City Palace of
Varieties 🎭 B3
City Sq. C2
Civic Theatre 🎭 A2
Civic Hall 🏛 A2
Clarendon Way A1

Clay Pit La A2
Commercial St. C2
Concord St A4
Cookridge St B2
Corn Exchange 🏛 . . . C3
Cromwell St. B5
Crown & County
Courts B1
Crown Point Bridge . . . D4
Crown Point Rd. D4
Dock St D3
Duke St C4
Duncan St C3
Dyer St B4
East St D5
Eastgate B4
Edward St B3
Fenton St. A1
Fish St C3
Flax Place C5
George St B3
Globe Rd D1
Gower St B4
Grafton St A4
Grand Theatre 🎭 B3
Great George St . . B1/B2
Greek St B2

Harewood St B3
Harrison St B3
Headrow Centre B2
High Court C4
Holy Trinity ⛪ C3
Hope Rd A5
Hunslet Rd. D3
Infirmary St C2
King Edward St C3
Kendell St D3
King St. C1
Kirkgate C3/C4
Kirkgate Market C3
Lady La B3/B4
Lands La B3
Leeds Bridge D3
Leeds General
Infirmary (A&E) 🏥 . . . A1
Leeds Metropolitan
University A1/A3
Leeds Shopping
Plaza C2
Leeds Station 🚉 D2
Light, The 🏛 B2
Lovell Park Rd A3
Lower Brunswick St . . . A4
Mabgate A5

Macauly St A5
Magistrates Court B1
Mark La B3
Marsh La C5
Meadow La D3
Melbourne St. A4
Merrion Centre A2
Merrion St B3
Merrion Way A2
Mill St C5
Millennium Sq A2
Neville St D2
New Briggate B3
New Market St C3
New Station St C2
New York Rd B4
New York St C4
Nile St A4
North St A4
Oxford Place B1
Oxford Row B1
Park Cross St B1
Park Place C1
Park Row C2
Park Sq B1
Park Sq East B1
Park Sq West B1
Park St B1

Police Station 🏛 B4
Portland Cr A2
Portland Way A2
Post Office 🏤 . B2/C2/C4
Quarry House (NHS/DSS
Headquarters) B5
Quebec St C1
Railway St C5
Regent St A4
Richmond St D5
Royal Armouries
Museum 🏛 D5
Russell St B2
St Anne's
Cathedral (RC) ✝. . . B2
St Anne's St. B2
St Johns Centre B3
St Mary's St. B5
St Pauls St B1
St Peter's B4
St Peter's ⛪. C4
Saxton La C5
Skinner La A4/A5
South Parade B1
Sovereign St D2
Swinegate D2
Templar St B4
The Calls D4

The Close C5
The Drive D5
The Garth D5
The Headrow B2/B3
The Lane D5
Thoresby Place A1
Town Hall 🏛 B1
Trinity & Burton
Arcades C2
Union St B4
Upper Basinghall St . . B3
Vicar La B3
Victoria Bridge D2
Victoria Quarter B3
Wade La A3
Water La D1
Waterloo Rd D3
Wellington St C1
West Yorkshire
Playhouse 🎭 B4
Westgate B1
Whitehall Rd C1
Woodhouse La A1
York Place C1

Liverpool

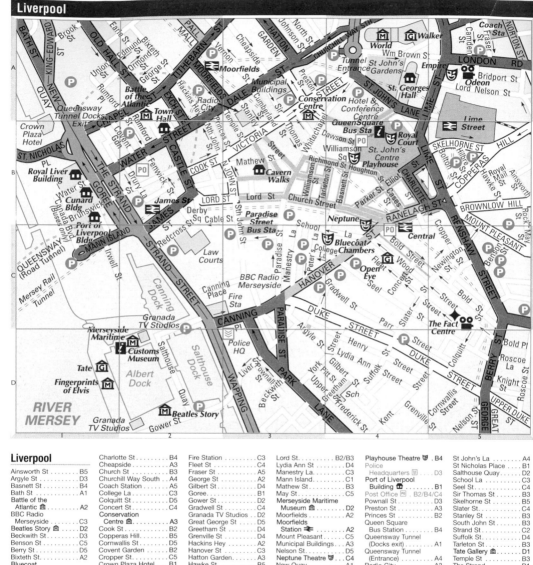

Liverpool

Ainsworth St B5
Argyle St D3
Basnett St B4
Bath St A1
Battle of the
  Atlantic 🏛 A2
BBC Radio
  Merseyside C3
Beatles Story 🏛 . . . D2
Beckwith St D3
Benson St C5
Berry St D5
Bixteth St A2
Bluecoat
  Chambers 🎭 C4
Bold Place D5
Bold St C4/C5
Bolton St B5
Bridport St A5
Brook St A1
Brownlow Hill B5
Brunswick St B1
Cable St B2
Camden St A5
Canada Blvd B1
Canning Place C3
Cases St B4
Castle St B2
Cavern Walks 🏛 . . . B3
Central Station 🚊 . . . C4
Chapel St A2

Charlotte St B4
Cheapside A3
Church St B3
Churchill Way South . A4
Coach Station A5
College La C3
Colquitt St D5
Concert St C4
Conservation
  Centre 🏛 A3
Cook St B2
Copperas Hill B5
Cornwallis St D5
Covent Garden B2
Cropper St C5
Crown Plaza Hotel. . . . A1
Cumberland St A3
Cunard Building 🏛 . . B1
Customs Museum 🏛 . D2
Dale St. A3
Dawson St B4
Derby St B2
Drury La. B2
Duke St C3/D4/D5
Earle St A1
Edmund St A2
Elliot St B4
Empire Theatre 🎭 . . A5
Exchange St East A2
Fact Centre, The ✦🎬 . C5
Fenwick St B2
Fingerprints
  of Elvis 🏛 D1

Fire Station C3
Fleet St C4
Fraser St A5
George St A4
Gilbert St D4
Goree. B1
Gower St D2
Gradwell St C4
Granada TV Studios . . D2
Great George St D5
Greetham St D4
Grenville St D4
Hackins Hey A2
Hanover St C3
Hatton Garden. A3
Hawke St B5
Henry St C4
Hilbre St. B5
Houghton St B4
Information Ctr 🛈 . B4/D2
Irwell St C1
James St B2
James St Station 🚊 . B2
Johnson St A3
Kent St D4
King Edward St A1
Knight St D5
Law Courts C3
Lime St A5/B5
Lime St Station 🚊. . . B5
Liver St C2
London Rd. A5
Lord Nelson St A5

Lord St. B2/B3
Lydia Ann St D4
Manesty La. C3
Mann Island. C1
Mathew St B3
May St. C5
Merseyside Maritime
  Museum 🏛 D2
Moorfields A2
Moorfields
  Station 🚊 A2
Mount Pleasant C5
Municipal Buildings . . A3
Nelson St. D5
Neptune Theatre 🎭 . . C4
New Quay A1
Newington St C5
North John St B2/B3
North St. A3
Norton St. A5
Odeon 🎬. A5
Old Hall St A1
Open Eye Gallery 🏛 . C4
Ormond St. A2
Pall Mall A2
Paradise St C3
Paradise St
  Bus Station C3
Park La D3
Parker St B4
Parr St D4
Peter's La C3
Pitt St D4

Playhouse Theatre 🎭 . B4
Police
  Headquarters 🏛 . . . D3
Port of Liverpool
  Building 🏛 B1
Post Office . B2/B4/C4
Pownall St D3
Preston St A3
Princes St B2
Queen Square
  Bus Station B4
Queensway Tunnel
  (Docks exit) A1
Queensway Tunnel
  (Entrance) A4
Radio City A3
Ranelagh St. B4
Redcross St C2
Renshaw St C5
Richmond St B4
Rock St B5
Roscoe La D5
Roscoe St D5
Royal Court
  Theatre 🎭 B4
Royal Liver
  Building 🏛 B1
Royal Mail St B5
Rumford Place A1
Rumford St B2
St Georges Hall 🏛 . . A4
St John's Centre B4
St John's Gdns A4

St John's La A4
St Nicholas Place . . . B1
Salthouse Quay. D2
School La C3
Seel St C4
Sir Thomas St B3
Skelhorne St B5
Slater St C4
Stanley St B3
South John St B3
Strand St C2
Suffolk St. D4
Tarleton St B3
Tate Gallery 🏛 D1
Temple St B3
The Strand. B1
Titheburn St. A2
Town Hall 🏛 B2
Union St A1
Upper Duke St. D5
Upper Frederick St . . . D4
Vernon St. A3
Victoria St B3
Walker Art Gallery 🏛 . A4
Wapping D3
Water St B1/B2
Whitechapel. B4
Williamson Sq B4
Williamson St. B3
William Brown St A4
Wood St. C4
World Museum 🏛 . . . A4
York St D4

London

Congestion Charging Zone

London

Abbey St C5
Albany St A2
Albert Embankment D4
Aldersgate St A4
Aldwych B3
Amwell St A3
Apsley House &
  Wellington
  Museum ⋒ C1
Baker St B1
Banqueting
  House ⋒ C3
Barbican ✦ ⋒ B4
Bath St A5
Beech St B4
Belgrave Pl C1
Belgrave Rd D2
Berkeley Sq C2
Bermondsey St C5
BFI London Imax ≋ C3
Birdcage Walk C2
Bishopsgate B5
Black Prince Rd D3
Blackfriars ≋ B4
Blackfriars Bridge . .C4
Blackfriars Rd C4
Borough High St . . .C5
Borough Rd C4
Brill Pl A2
B.A. London Eye ✦ .C3
British Library ⋒ . . .A2
British Museum ⋒ . .B3
B.T. Tower ✦ ⋒ . . .B2
Brompton Rd C1
Brook Dr D4
Buckingham Gate . .C2
Buckingham
  Palace ⋒ C2
Buckingham Palace
  . . . . .D2
Cabinet War
  Rooms ⋒ C3

Cannon St ≋ B5
Carter La ▲ B4
Central St A4
Chancery La B3
Charing Cross ≋ . .C3
Charing Cross Rd . .B3
Charterhouse St . . .B4
Cheapside B4
Chelsea Bridge Rd D1
Chelsea Royal
  Hospital ⋒ D1
Chester Rd A1
Chiswell St B5
City Hall ⋒ C5
City Rd A4/A5
City Thameslink ≋ B4
Clerkenwell Rd A4
Cleveland St B2
Commercial St A5
Conduit St B2
Constitution Hill . . .C2
Cuming
  Museum ⋒ D4
Curzon St C2
Davies St B1
Dickens House ⋒ . .A3
Doughty St A3
Downing Street ✦ . .C3
Drury La B3
Dunton Rd D5
East Rd A5
East St D5
Eastcheap. B5
Ebury Br Rd D1
Eccleston St D1
Edgware Rd B1
Elephant &
  Castle ≋ D4
Euston ≋ A2
Euston Rd A2
Eversholt St A2
Falmouth Rd D4
Farringdon ≋ A4

Farringdon Rd A3
Fenchurch St ≋ . . .B5
Fleet St B4
Flood St D1
George St B1
Gloucester Pl B1
Golden La A4
Goswell Rd A4
Gower St A2
Grange Rd D5
Gray's Inn Rd A3
Great Dover St D5
Great Eastern St. . . .A5
Great Portland St . .A2
Great St Helen's ≋ .B5
Great Smith St D3
Great Suffolk St . . .C4
Great Tower St B5
Green Park C2
Gresham St B4
Grosvenor Pl C1
Grosvenor Rd D2
Grosvenor St B2
Guilford St A3
Guy's Hospital ⋒ . .C5
Hackney Rd A5
Hampstead Rd A2
Harley St B1
Haymarket C2
Hayward Gallery ⋒ .C3
High Holborn B3
Hyde Park C1
HMS Belfast ⋒ C5
Holborn Viaduct . . .B4
Horseferry Rd D2
Houndsditch B5
Houses of
  Parliament ⋒ C3
Hyde Park C1
Imperial War
  Museum ⋒ D4
Information
  Ctr ⓩ C2/C3
Inner Circle A1
Jermyn St C2

Judd St A3
Kennington La .D3/D4
Kennington
  Park Rd D4
Kennington Rd D4
King's Cross ≋ A3
King's Cross
  Thameslink ≋ . . .A3
King's Rd D1
Kingsland Rd A5
Kingsway B3
Knightsbridge C1
Lamb's Conduit St .A3
Lambeth Bridge . . .D3
Lambeth Palace ⋒ .D3
Lambeth Palace RdC3
Lambeth Rd D3
Lambeth Walk D3
Leadenhall St B5
Lever St A4
Liverpool St ≋ B5
Lombard St B5
London
  Aquarium ⋒⋯ . . .C3
London Bridge C5
London Dungeon ⋒C5
London Mosque ✦ .A1
London Rd D4
London Wall . .B4/B5
London Zoo ⋒ A1
Long Acre B3
Long La A4
Long La C5
Ludgate Hill B4
Lupus St D2
Lower Thames St. . .B5
Madame
  Tussaud's ⋒ A1
Mansell St B5
Marylebone ≋ A1
Marylebone High StB1
Middlesex St
  (Petticoat La) . . .B5

Midland Rd A3
Millbank D3
Millennium Bridge .B4
Minories B5
Monument, The ✦ .B5
Moorgate ≋ B5
Mortimer St B2
Mount St C1
Museum of
  London ⋒ B4
National Army
  Museum ⋒ D1
National Gallery ⋒ .C3
National Theatre ⋓ .C3
New Bond St B2
New Bridge St B4
New Cavendish St . .B2
New Kent Rd D5
New Oxford St B3
New Scotland
  Yard ⋒ C2
Newgate St B4
Newington Butts . . .D4
Newman St. B2
North Audley St . . .B1
Old Bond St B2
Old Curiosity
  Shop ✦ B3
Old Kent Rd D5
Old St ≋ A4/A5
Open Air Theatre ⋓ .A1
Ossulston St A2
Outer Circle A1
Oval Cricket
  Ground, The. D3
Oxford St B2
Oxford St ▲ B2
Pall Mall C2
Park La C1
Park Rd A1
Parliament Sq C3
Penton Pl D4
Pentonville Rd A3

Petty France C2
Piccadilly C2
Pimlico Rd D1
Pittield St A5
Police Station ⋒ . . .A3/
  . . .B1/B2/B3/B4/B5/
  . . .C2/C3/D1/D3/D5
Pont St C1
Portland St B2
Post Office ⋒ . A2/A3/
  A4/B2/B3/C2/C3/C4
Queen Elizabeth and
  Royal Festival
  Halls ✦ C3
Queen Mary's
  Gardens ✦ A1
Queen Victoria St. .B4
Queen's Gallery ⋒ .C2
Queen's Sq. A3
Regency St D2
Regent St B2
Regent's Park A2
Robert St A2
Rochester Row D2
Rodney Rd D5
Rosebery Ave A3
Royal Academy ⋒ . .B2
Royal College of
  Physicians A2
Royal Hospital Rd . .D1
Russell Sq A3
St. Bartholomew's
  Hospital ⋒ B4
St. George's Cath
  (R.C.) ✦ D4
St. George's Rd D4
St. George's Rd D2
St. James's
  Palace ⋒ C2
St. James's Park . . .C2
St. James's St C2
St. John St A4
St. Pancras ≋ A3
St. Pancras ▲ A3

St. Paul's
  Cathedral ✝ B4
St. Thomas St C5
St. Thomas'
  Hospital ⋒ C3
Seymour Pl B1
Seymour St. B1
Shaftesbury Ave . . .B2
Shepherdess Walk .A4
Skinner St A4
Sloane Ave D1
Sloane Sq D1
Sloane St D1
Soane's
  Museum ⋒. B3
Somerset House ⋒ B3
South Audley St . . .C1
South Carriage Dr .C1
Southwark Bridge . .C4
Southwark
  Bridge Rd. C4
Southwark
  Cathedral ✝ C5
Southwark St C4
Stamford St C4
Stanhope St A2
Sutherland St D2
Tabernacle St A5
Tate Britain ⋒ D3
Tate Modern ⋒ C4
Tavistock Pl A3
Temple ⊖ B3
The Cut C4
The Mall C2
The Strand B3
Theobalds Rd B3
Threadneedle St . . .B5
Thurloe St D1
Tooley St C5
Torrington Pl A2
Tottenham
  Court Rd A2
Tower Bridge ✦ . . .C5
Tower Bridge Rd . . .C5

Tower of London ⋒ C5
Trafalgar Sq C3
Transport
  Museum ⋒ B3
Tyers St D3
Union St C4
University College
  Hospital ⋒ A2
Upper Thames St . .B4
Upper Woburn Pl . .A2
Vauxhall ≋ D3
Vauxhall Bridge . . .D3
Vauxhall Bridge Rd D2
Victoria ≋ D2
Victoria Coach
  Station D1
Victoria Embankment
  . . . . .B3/C3
Victoria St C2
Wallace
  Collection ⋒ B1
Walworth Rd D4
Wardour St B2
Warwick Way D2
Waterloo Bridge . . .B3
Waterloo East ≋ . . .C4
Waterloo
  International ≋ . . .C4
Waterloo Rd C4
Wesley's House ⋒ .A5
Westminster
  Abbey ✝ C3
Westminster
  Bridge B4
Westminster
  Cathedral (R.C) ✝ D2
Weston St C5
Whitehall C3
Wigmore St B1
Worship St A5
York Rd C3

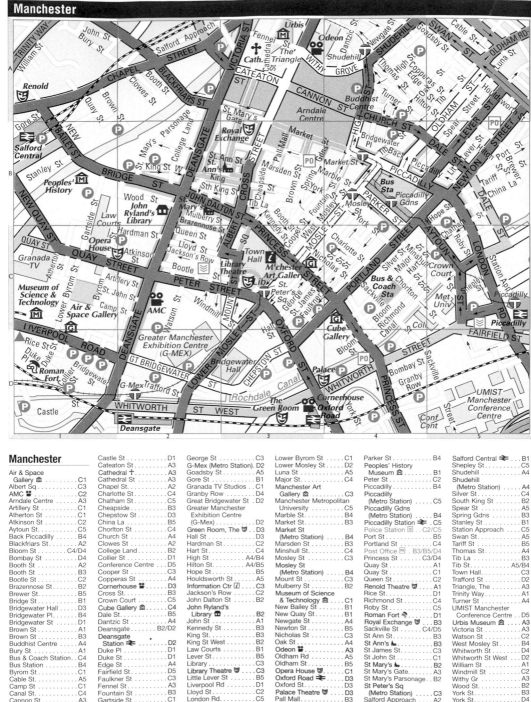

Manchester

Air & Space
Gallery 📷 C1
Albert Sq C3
AMC 📷 C2
Arndale Centre A3
Artillery St C1
Atherton St C1
Atkinson St C2
Aytoun St C5
Back Piccadilly B4
Blackfriars St A2
Bloom St C4/D4
Bombay St D4
Booth St A2
Booth St B3
Bootle St C2
Brazennose St B2
Brewer St B5
Bridge St B1
Bridgewater Hall D3
Bridgewater Pl B4
Bridgewater St D1
Brown St A1
Brown St B3
Buddhist Centre A4
Bury St A1
Bus & Coach Station C4
Bus Station B4
Byrom St C1
Cable St A5
Camp St C1
Canal St C4
Cannon St A3

Castle St D1
Cateaton St A3
Cathedral † A3
Cathedral St A3
Chapel St A2
Charlotte St C4
Chatham St C5
Cheapside B3
Chepstow St D3
China La B5
Chorlton St C4
Church St A4
Clowes St A2
College Land B2
Collier St D1
Conference Centre D5
Cooper St C3
Copperas St A4
Cornerhouse 📷 D3
Cross St B3
Crown Court C5
Dale St B5
Dantzic St A4
Deansgate B2/D2
Deansgate
Station ⇌ D2
Duke Pl D1
Duke St D1
Edge St A4
Fairfield St D5
Faulkner St C3
Fennel St A3
Fountain St B3
Gartside St C1

George St C3
G-Mex (Metro Station) . . D2
Goadsby St A5
Gore St B1
Granada TV Studios C1
Granby Row D4
Great Bridgewater St D2
Greater Manchester
Exhibition Centre
(G-Mex) D2
Green Room, The 📷 D3
Hall St D3
Hardman St B2
Hart St C4
High St A4/B4
Hilton St A4/B5
Hope St B5
Houldsworth St A5
Information Ctr ℹ A4
Jackson's Row C2
John Dalton St B2
John Ryland's
Library 📷 B2
John St A1
Kennedy St C3
King St B3
King St West B2
Law Courts B2
Lever St B5
Library C3
Library Theatre 📷 C3
Little Lever St B5
Liverpool Rd D1
Lloyd St C2
London Rd C5

Lower Byrom St C1
Lower Mosley St D2
Luna St A5
Major St C4
Manchester Art
Gallery 📷 C3
Manchester Metropolitan
University C5
Marble St B4
Market St B3
Market St
(Metro Station) B4
Marsden St B3
Minshull St C4
Mosley St C3
Mosley St
(Metro Station) B4
Mount St C3
Mulberry St B2
Museum of Science
& Technology 📷 C1
New Bailey St B1
New Quay St B1
Newgate St A4
Newton St B5
Nicholas St C3
Oak St A4
Odeon 📷 A3
Oldham Rd A5
Oldham St B5
Opera House 📷 C1
Oxford Road ⇌ D3
Oxford St D3
Palace Theatre 📷 D3
Pall Mall B3

Parker St B4
Peoples' History
Museum 📷 B1
Peter St C2
Piccadilly B4
Piccadilly
(Metro Station) C5
Piccadilly Gdns B4
Piccadilly Station ⇌ B4
Police Station 🚓 . . . C2/C5
Port St B5
Portland St C4
Post Office 🏤 . . B3/B5/D4
Princess St C3/D4
Quay St A1
Quay St C1
Queen St B2
Renold Theatre 📷 A1
Rice St D1
Richmond St C4
Roby St C5
Roman Fort 🏛 D1
Royal Exchange 📷 B3
Sackville St C4/D5
St Ann St B3
St Ann's ⛪ B3
St James St C3
St John St C1
St Mary's ⛪ B2
St Mary's Gate A3
St Mary's Parsonage B2
St Peter's Sq
(Metro Station) C3
Salford Approach A2

Salford Central ⇌ B1
Shepley St C5
Shudehill A4
Shudehill
(Metro Station) A4
Silver St C4
South King St B2
Spear St A5
Spring Gdns B3
Stanley St B1
Station Approach C5
Swan St A5
Tariff St B5
Thomas St A4
Tib La B3
Tib St A5/B4
Town Hall C3
Trafford St D2
Triangle, The A3
Trinity Way A1
Turner St A4
UMIST Manchester
Conference Centre D5
Urbis Museum 📷 A3
Victoria St A3
Watson St C2
West Mosley St B4
Whitworth St D4
Whitworth St West D2
William St A1
Windmill St C2
Withy Gr A3
Wood St B2
York St B3
York St C4

Newcastle upon Tyne

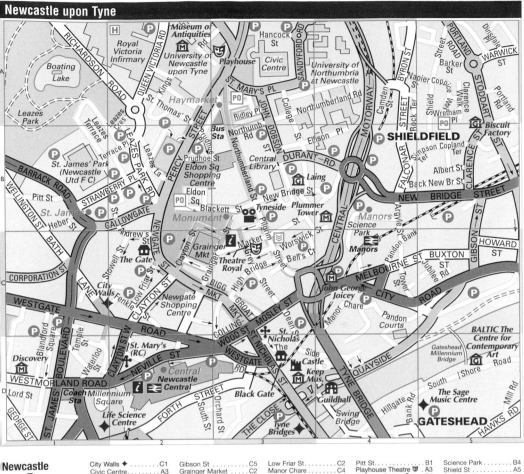

Newcastle upon Tyne

Albert St B5
Argyle St B4
Back New Bridge St . . B5
BALTIC The Centre for
  Contemporary Art 🏛. D5
Bank Rd D4
Barker St A5
Barrack Rd B1
Bath La C1
Bigg Market C3
Biscuit Factory 🏛 . . . B5
Black Gate 🏛 D3
Blackett St B2
Blandford Sq D1
Boating Lake A1
Bus Station A3
Buxton St C5
Byron St A4
Camden St A4
Castle 🏛 D3
Central (metro station). D2
Central Library B3
Central Motorway B4
City Rd C4/C5

City Walls ✦ C1
Civic Centre A3
Clarence St B5
Clarence Walk A5
Clayton St C2
Clayton St West C2
Coach Station D1
College St A3
Collingwood St C3
Copland Terr A5
Coppice Way A5
Corporation St. C1
Courts C4
Dean St C3
Dinsdale Pl A5
Discovery Museum 🏛. D1
Durant Rd B3
Eldon Sq B2
Eldon Sq Shopping
  Centre B2
Ellison Pl A4
Falconar St B4
Fenkle St C2
Forth St D2
Gallowgate B2
Gate, The 🏛 C2
Gateshead Millennium
  Bridge ✦ D5
George St D1

Gibson St C5
Grainger Market C2
Grainger St C2
Grey St C3
Groat Market C3
Guildhall 🏛 D4
Hancock St A3
Hawks Rd D5
Haymarket
  (metro station) A3
Heber St B1
High Bridge C3
Hillgate D4
Howard St C5
Information Ctr ℹ . C3/D2
John Dobson St A3
John George
  Joicey Museum 🏛 . . C4
Jubilee Rd C5
Keep Museum 🏛 D3
Kings Rd A2
Laing Gallery 🏛 B3
Leazes Cr A2
Leazes La B2
Leazes Park A1
Leazes Park Rd B2
Leazes Terr B1
Life Science Centre ✦ D2
Lord St D1

Low Friar St C2
Manor Chare C4
Manors
  (metro station) B4
Manors Station ⇌ . . . C4
Market St C3
Melbourne St C4
Mill Rd D5
Millennium Sq D1
Monument
  (metro station) B3
Mosley St C3
Museum of
  Antiquities 🏛 A2
Napier St A4
Neville St D2
New Bridge St . . . B3/B5
Newcastle Central
  Station ⇌ D2
Newgate Shopping
  Centre C2
Newgate St C2
Northumberland Rd. . . A3
Northumberland St . . . B3
Orchard St D3
Pandon Bank C4
Pandon C4
Percy St B2
Pilgrim St B3

Pitt St B1
Playhouse Theatre 🎭 . A3
Plummer Tower 🏛. . . B4
Police Station 🏛 B3
Portland Rd A5
Post Office . . . A3/A5/B2
Prudhoe Pl. B2
Prudhoe St B2
Quayside D4
Queen Victoria Rd . . . A2
Richardson Rd A1
Ridley Pl A3
Rock Terr A4
Royal Victoria
  Infirmary 🏥 A2
Sage Music
  Centre, The ✦. D5
St James
  (metro station) B1
St James' Blvd D1
St James' Park
  (Newcastle Utd FC). . B1
St Mary's (RC) ✝ D2
St Mary's Place A2
St Nicholas ✝ C3
St Thomas' St A2
Sandyford Rd A3

Science Park B4
Shield St A5
Simpson Terr B5
South Shore Rd. D5
South St D2
Stoddart St A5
Stowell St C2
Strawberry Pl B1
Swing Bridge. D4
Temple St D1
Terrace Pl B1
The Close D3
The Side D3
Theatre Royal 🎭 C3
Tower St C4
Tyne Bridge D4
Tyne Bridges ✦ D3
Tyneside 🎭 B3
University of Newcastle
  upon Tyne A3
University of Northumbria
  at Newcastle A4
Warwick St A5
Waterloo St D1
Wellington St B1
Westgate Rd C1/D3
Westmorland Rd D1
Worswick St C3
Wretham Pl A5

Nottingham

Oxford

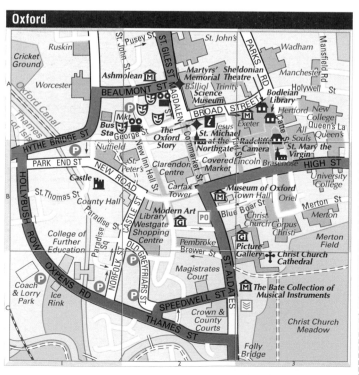

Sheffield

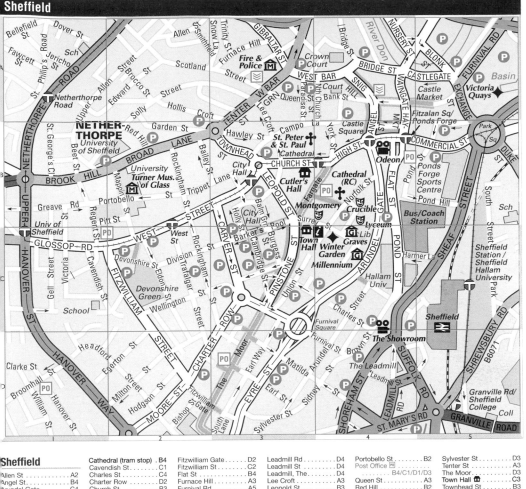

Sheffield

Allen St A2
Angel St. B4
Arundel Gate C4
Arundel St D4
Bailey St B2
Balm Green B3
Bank St A4
Barker's Pool C3
Beet St B1
Bellefield St A1
Bishop St. D2
Blonk St A5
Bridge St A4
Broad La B2
Brocco St A2
Brook Hill B1
Broomhall St D1
Brown St D4
Burgess St C3
Bus/Coach Station . . . B5
Cambridge St C3
Campo La B3
Carver St C3
Castle Square
    (tram stop) B4
Castlegate A5
Cathedral (RC) ✝ B4

Cathedral (tram stop) . B4
Cavendish St C1
Charles St C4
Charter Row C3
Church St B3
City Hall (tram stop) . . B3
City Hall B3
Clarke St D1
Commercial St B5
Court A4
Crown Court A4
Cutler's Hall 🏛 B3
Devonshire Green C2
Devonshire St C2
Division St C2
Dover St A1
Duke St B5
Earl St D3
Earl Way D3
Edward St A2
Egerton St D1
Eldon St C2
Exchange St A5
Eyre St D3
Fargate B3
Fawcett St A1
Fire & Police 🏛 A3
Fitzalan Sq / Ponds
    Forge (tram stop) . . B4

Fitzwilliam Gate D2
Fitzwilliam St C2
Flat St B4
Furnace Hill A3
Furnival Rd A5
Furnival Sq C4
Furnival St D4
Garden St B2
Gell St C1
Gibraltar St A3
Glossop Rd C1
Granville Rd D5
Granville Rd / Sheffield
    College (tram stop) . D5
Graves Gallery
    & Museum 🏛 C4
Greave Rd B1
Hallam University C4
Hanover St D1
Hanover Way D1
Harmer La C5
Hawley St B3
Haymarket A4
Headford St D1
High St B4
Hodgson St D2
Hollis Croft A3
Holly St B3
Information Ctr 🅸 C4
Jericho St A1

Leadmill Rd D4
Leadmill St D4
Leadmill, The D4
Lee Croft A3
Leopold St B3
Library C4
Lyceum Theatre 🎭 . . . B2
Mappin St C2
Matilda St D3
Millennium
    Galleries 🏛 C4
Milton St D2
Montgomery 🎭 B4
Moore St D2
Netherthorpe Rd B1
Netherthorpe Rd
    (tram stop) A1
Norfolk St B4
North Church St A4
Nursery St A4
Odeon 🎬 B4
Paradise St A3
Park Sq B5
Pinstone St C3
Pitt St B1
Police Station 🚓 . . . A3/A4
Pond Hill B5
Pond St B4/C4
Ponds Forge
    Sports Centre B5

Portobello St B2
Post Office 🅿 . . . .
    . . . . B4/C1/D1/D3
Queen St C5
Red Hill B2
Regent St B1
Rockingham St B2/C2
St George's Cl B1
St Mary's Rd D4
St Peter & St Paul
    Cathedral ✝ B3
St Philip's Rd A1
Scotland St A2
Sheaf St C5
Sheffield Station ≠ . . . C5
Sheffield Station /
    Sheffield Hallam Uni.
    (tram stop) C5
Shoreham St D4
Showroom, The 🎬 . . . D4
Shrewsbury Rd D5
Sidney St D3
Smithfield A2
Snig Hill A4
Snow La A3
Solly St A2
South La D3
South Street Park B5
Suffolk Rd D5
Surrey St B3

Sylvester St D3
Tenter St A3
The Moor D3
Town Hall 🏛 C3
Townhead St B3
Trafalgar St C2
Trinity St A3
Trippet La B2
Turner Museum
    of Glass B2
Union St C3
University of Sheffield . C1
University of Sheffield
    (tram stop). C1
Upper Allen St A1
Upper Hanover St C1
Victoria Quays ✦ A5
Victoria St C1
Waingate A4
Wellington St C2
West Bar A3
West Bar Green A3
West St C2
West St (tram stop) . . . C2
William St D1
Winter Garden ✦ C4
York St B4

Swansea / Abertawe

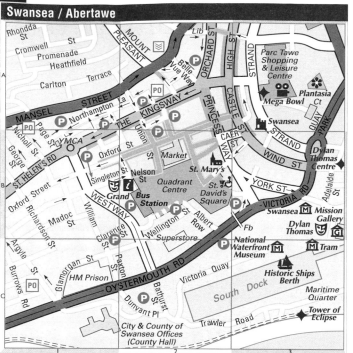

Swansea/ Abertawe

Adelaide St B3
Albert Row B2
Argyle St C1
Bathurst St C2
Belle Vue Way B2
Burrows Rd C1
Bus Station B2
Caer St B2
Carlton Terr A1
Castle St A3
City & County of
  Swansea Offices
  (County Hall) C1
Clarence St B1
Court A3
Cromwell St. A1
Dunvant Pl C2
Dylan Thomas
  Centre ◆ B3
Dylan Thomas
  Theatre ♥ B2
George St B1
Glamorgan St C1
Grand Theatre ♥ A1
Heathfield A1
High St A2
Historic Ships
  Berth ⚓ C3
HM Prison C1
Information Ctr ⓘ B2
Library A2
Madoc St. B1
Mansel St A1
Maritime Quarter C3
Market B2
Mega Bowl ◆ 🎳 A3
Mission Gallery 🏛 B3
Mount Pleasant A2

National Waterfront
  Museum 🏛 C3
Nelson St B2
Nicholl St B1
Northampton La A1
Orchard St A2
Oxford St B1
Oystermouth Rd C2
Page St A1
Parc Tawe Shopping &
  Leisure Centre. A3
Paxton St C1
Plantasia ✿ A3
Police Station 🏢 A2
Post Office 🏤 . A1/A2/C1
Princess Way A2
Promenade A1
Quadrant Centre B2
Quay Park A3
Rhondda St A1
Richardson St B1
St David's Sq. B1
St Helen's Rd B1
St Mary's ⛪ B2
Singleton St B1
Strand A3/B3
Swansea Castle ⚔ . . . A3
Swansea Museum 🏛 . . B3
The Kingsway A2
Tower of Eclipse ◆ . . . C3
Tram Station 🚊 C3
Trawler Rd C2
Union St B2
Victoria Quay C2
Victoria Rd. B3
Wellington St B1
Westway B1
William St B1
Wind St B3
YMCA B1
York St B3

York

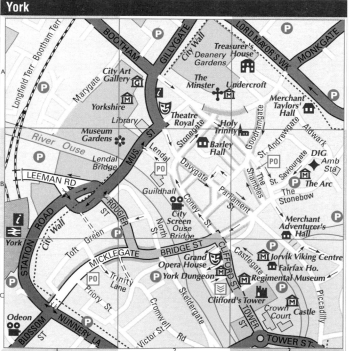

York

Aldwark B3
Ambulance Station . . . B3
Arc Museum, The 🏛 . . B3
Barley Hall 🏛 B2
Blossom St C1
Bootham A1
Bootham Terr. A1
Bridge St C2
Castle Museum 🏛 . . . C3
Castlegate C3
City Art Gallery 🏛 . . . A2
City Wall A2/B1
Clifford St C2
Clifford's Tower 🏰 . . . C3
Coney St B2
Cromwell Rd C2
Crown Court C3
Davygate B2
Deanery Gdns A2
DIG ◆ B3
Fairfax House 🏛 C3
Gillygate A2
Goodramgate B3
Grand Opera
  House ♥ C2
Guildhall. B2
Holy Trinity ⛪ B3
Information Ctr ⓘ . A2/B1
Jorvik Viking
  Centre 🏛 C3
Leeman Rd B1
Lendal B2
Lendal Bridge B1
Library A2
Longfield Terr. A1
Lord Mayor's Walk . . . A3
Marygate A1

Merchant Adventurer's
  Hall 🏛 B3
Merchant Taylors'
  Hall 🏛 A3
Micklegate. C1
Minster, The ✝ A2
Monkgate A3
Museum Gdns ✿ B2
Museum St B2
North St B2
Nunnery La C1
Odeon 🎬 C1
Ouse Bridge B2
Parliament St. B3
Piccadilly C3
Police Station 🏢 C2
Post Office 🏤 . B2/B3/C1
Priory St. C1
Regimental
  Museum 🏛 B3
Rougier St B1
St Andrewgate. B3
St Saviourgate. B3
Skeldergate C2
Station Rd C1
Stonegate B2
The Shambles B3
The Stonebow B3
Theatre Royal ♥ A2
Toft Green C1
Tower St C3
Treasurer's House 🏛 . A3
Trinity La C1
Undercroft Mus 🏛 . . . A2
Victor St. C2
York City Screen 🎦 . . B2
York Dungeon 🏛 C2
York Station �station . . B1
Yorkshire Museum 🏛 . A2

Abbreviations used in the index

Aberdeen	**Aberdeen City**	Invclyd	**Inverclyde**
Aberds	**Aberdeenshire**	Jersey	**Jersey**
Ald	**Alderney**	Kent	**Kent**
Anglesey	**Isle of Anglesey**	Lancs	**Lancashire**
Angus	**Angus**	Leicester	**City of Leicester**
Argyll	**Argyll and Bute**	Leics	**Leicestershire**
Bath	**Bath and North East**	Lincs	**Lincolnshire**
	Somerset	London	**Greater London**
Beds	**Bedfordshire**	Luton	**Luton**
Bl Gwent	**Blaenau Gwent**	M Keynes	**Milton Keynes**
Blkburn	**Blackburn with**	M Tydf	**Merthyr Tydfil**
	Darwen	M'bro	**Middlesbrough**
Blkpool	**Blackpool**	Medway	**Medway**
Bmouth	**Bournemouth**	Mers	**Merseyside**
Borders	**Scottish Borders**	Midloth	**Midlothian**
Brack	**Bracknell**	Mon	**Monmouthshire**
Bridgend	**Bridgend**	Moray	**Moray**
Brighton	**City of Brighton and**	N Ayrs	**North Ayrshire**
	Hove	N Lincs	**North Lincolnshire**
Bristol	**City and County of**	N Lnrk	**North Lanarkshire**
	Bristol	N Som	**North Somerset**
Bucks	**Buckinghamshire**	N Yorks	**North Yorkshire**
Caerph	**Caerphilly**	NE Lincs	**North East**
Cambs	**Cambridgeshire**		**Lincolnshire**
Cardiff	**Cardiff**	Neath	**Neath Port Talbot**
Carms	**Carmarthenshire**	Newport	**City and County of**
Ceredig	**Ceredigion**		**Newport**
Ches	**Cheshire**	Norf	**Norfolk**
Clack	**Clackmannanshire**	Northants	**Northamptonshire**
Conwy	**Conwy**	Northumb	**Northumberland**
Corn	**Cornwall**	Nottingham	**City of Nottingham**
Cumb	**Cumbria**	Notts	**Nottinghamshire**
Darl	**Darlington**	Orkney	**Orkney**
Denb	**Denbighshire**	Oxon	**Oxfordshire**
Derby	**City of Derby**	P'boro	**Peterborough**
Derbys	**Derbyshire**	Pembs	**Pembrokeshire**
Devon	**Devon**	Perth	**Perth and Kinross**
Dorset	**Dorset**	Plym	**Plymouth**
Dumfries	**Dumfries and**	Poole	**Poole**
	Galloway	Powys	**Powys**
Dundee	**Dundee City**	Ptsmth	**Portsmouth**
Durham	**Durham**	Reading	**Reading**
E Ayrs	**East Ayrshire**	Redcar	**Redcar and**
E Dunb	**East Dunbartonshire**		**Cleveland**
E Loth	**East Lothian**	Renfs	**Renfrewshire**
E Renf	**East Renfrewshire**	Rhondda	**Rhondda Cynon Taff**
E Sus	**East Sussex**	Rutland	**Rutland**
E Yorks	**East Riding of**	S Ayrs	**South Ayrshire**
	Yorkshire	S Glos	**South**
Edin	**City of Edinburgh**		**Gloucestershire**
Essex	**Essex**	S Lnrk	**South Lanarkshire**
Falk	**Falkirk**	S Yorks	**South Yorkshire**
Fife	**Fife**	Scilly	**Scilly**
Flint	**Flintshire**	Shetland	**Shetland**
Glasgow	**City of Glasgow**	Shrops	**Shropshire**
Glos	**Gloucestershire**	Slough	**Slough**
Gtr Man	**Greater Manchester**	Som	**Somerset**
Guern	**Guernsey**	Soton	**Southampton**
Gwyn	**Gwynedd**	Staffs	**Staffordshire**
Halton	**Halton**	Sthend	**Southend-on-Sea**
Hants	**Hampshire**	Stirl	**Stirling**
Hereford	**Herefordshire**	Stockton	**Stockton-on-Tees**
Herts	**Hertfordshire**	Stoke	**Stoke-on-Trent**
Highld	**Highland**	Suff	**Suffolk**
Hrtlpl	**Hartlepool**	Sur	**Surrey**
Hull	**Hull**	Swansea	**Swansea**
I o M	**Isle of Man**	T & W	**Tyne and Wear**
I o W	**Isle of Wight**	Telford	**Telford and Wrekin**

Thamesdown	**Thamesdown**	W Sus	**West Sussex**
Thurrock	**Thurrock**	W Yorks	**West Yorkshire**
Torbay	**Torbay**	Warks	**Warwickshire**
Torf	**Torfaen**	Warr	**Warrington**
V Glam	**The Vale of**	Wilts	**Wiltshire**
	Glamorgan	Windsor	**Windsor and**
W Berks	**West Berkshire**		**Maidenhead**
W Dunb	**West**	Wokingham	**Wokingham**
	Dunbartonshire	Worcs	**Worcestershire**
W Isles	**Western Isles**	Wrex	**Wrexham**
W Loth	**West Lothian**	York	**City of York**
W Mid	**West Midlands**		

A

Ab Kettleby Leics 115 C5
Ab Lench Worcs 80 B3
Abbas Combe Som 29 C7
Abberley Worcs 79 A5
Abberton Essex 71 B4
Abberton Worcs 80 B2
Abberwick Northumb 189 B4
Abbess Roding Essex 69 B5
Abbey Devon 27 D6
Abbey-cwm-hir Powys 93 D4
Abbey Dore Hereford 78 D1
Abbey Field Essex 70 A3
Abbey Hulton Stoke 112 A3
Abbey St Bathans
  Borders 211 D4
Abbey Town Cumb 175 C4
Abbey Village Lancs 137 A5
Abbey Wood London 50 B1
Abbeydale S Yorks 130 A3
Abbeystead Lancs 145 B5
Abbots Bickington Devon 25 D4
Abbots Bromley Staffs 113 C4
Abbots Langley Herts 67 C5
Abbots Leigh N Som 43 B4
Abbots Morton Worcs 80 B3
Abbots Ripton Cambs 100 D4
Abbots Salford Warks 80 B3
Abbotsbury Dorset 15 C5
Abbotsbury Sub Tropical
  Gardens Dorset 15 C5
Abbotsham Devon 25 C5
Abbotskerswell Devon 8 A2
Abbotsley Cambs 84 B4
Abbotswood Hants 32 C2
Abbotts Ann Hants 32 A2
Abcott Shrops 94 D1
Abdon Shrops 94 C3
Aber Ceredig 74 D3
Aber-Arad Carms 73 C6
Aber-banc Ceredig 73 B6
Aber Cowarch Gwyn 91 A6
Aber-Giâr Carms 58 A2
Aber-gwynfi Neath 40 B3
Aber-Hirnant Gwyn 109 B4
Aber-Rhiwlech Gwyn 108 C4
Aber-Village Powys 60 A3
Aberaeron Ceredig 74 B3
Aberaman Rhondda 41 A5
Aberangell Gwyn 91 A6
Aberarder Highld 240 D2
Aberarder House Highld 252 D2
Aberarder Lodge Highld 240 D3
Aberargie Perth 219 C6
Aberarth Ceredig 74 B3
Aberavon Neath 40 B2
Aberbeeg Bl Gwent 41 A7
Abercanaid M Tydf 41 A5
Abercarn Caerph 41 B7
Abercastle Pembs 55 A4
Abercegir Powys 91 B6
Aberchirder Aberds 268 D1
Aberconwy House,
  Conwy Conwy 124 B2
Abercraf Powys 59 D5
Abercrombie Fife 221 D5
Abercych Pembs 73 B5
Abercynafon Powys 60 B2
Abercynon Rhondda 41 B5
Aberdalgie Perth 219 B5
Aberdâr = Aberdare
  Rhondda 41 A4
Aberdare = Aberdâr
  Rhondda 41 A4
Aberdaron Gwyn 106 D1
Aberdaugleddau =
  Milford Haven Pembs 55 D5
Aberdeen Aberdeen 245 B6
Aberdeen Airport
  Aberdeen 245 A5
Aberdesach Gwyn 107 A4
Aberdour Fife 209 B4
Aberdovey Gwyn 90 C4
Aberdulais Neath 40 A2
Aberedw Powys 77 C4
Abereiddy Pembs 54 A3
Abererch Gwyn 106 C3
Aberfan M Tydf 41 A5
Aberfeldy Perth 230 D2
Aberffraw Anglesey 122 D3

Aberffrwd Ceredig 75 A5
Aberford W Yorks 148 D3
Aberfoyle Stirl 217 D5
Abergavenny = Y Fenni
  Mon 61 B4
Abergele Conwy 125 B4
Abergorlech Carms 58 B2
Abergwaun = Fishguard
  Pembs 72 C2
Abergwesyn Powys 76 B2
Abergwili Carms 58 C1
Abergwynant Gwyn 91 A4
Abergwyngregyn Gwyn 123 C6
Abergynolwyn Gwyn 91 B4
Aberhonddu = Brecon
  Powys 60 A2
Aberhosan Powys 91 C6
Aberkenfig Bridgend 40 C3
Aberlady E Loth 210 B1
Aberlemno Angus 232 C3
Aberllefenni Gwyn 91 B5
Abermagwr Ceredig 75 A5
Abermaw = Barmouth
  Gwyn 90 A4
Abermeurig Ceredig 75 C4
Abermule Powys 93 B5
Abernant Powys 109 C6
Abernant Carms 73 D6
Abernethy Perth 219 C6
Abernyte Perth 220 A2
Aberpennar = Mountain
  Ash Rhondda 41 B5
Aberporth Ceredig 73 A5
Abersoch Gwyn 106 D3
Abersychan Torf 61 C4
Abertawe = Swansea
  Swansea 57 C6
Aberteifi = Cardigan
  Ceredig 73 B4
Aberthin V Glam 41 D5
Abertillery = Abertyleri
  Bl Gwent 41 A7
Abertridwr Caerph 41 C6
Abertridwr Powys 109 D5
Abertyleri = Abertillery
  Bl Gwent 41 A7
Abertysswg Caerph 60 C3
Aberuthven Perth 219 C4
Aberyscir Powys 60 A1
Aberystwyth Ceredig 90 D3
Abhainn Suidhe W Isles 287 D5
Abingdon Oxon 65 D5
Abinger Common Sur 35 B4
Abinger Hammer Sur 34 B3
Abington S Lnrk 194 D4
Abington Pigotts Cambs 85 C5
Ablington Glos 64 C2
Ablington Wilts 31 A5
Abney Derbys 130 B1
Aboyne Aberds 244 C2
Abram Gtr Man 137 C5
Abriachan Highld 252 C1
Abridge Essex 69 D4
Abronhill N Lnrk 207 C5
Abson S Glos 43 B6
Abthorpe Northants 82 C3
Abune-the-Hill Orkney 282 E3
Aby Lincs 135 B4
Acaster Malbis York 149 C4
Acaster Selby N Yorks 149 C4
Accrington Lancs 137 A6
Acha Argyll 223 B4
Acha Mor W Isles 288 E4
Achabraid Argyll 213 D6
Achachork Argyll 259 D4
Achafolla Argyll 213 A5
Achagary Highld 278 C3
Achahoish Argyll 202 A2
Achalader Perth 231 D5
Achallader Argyll 228 D2
Ach'an Todhair Highld 237 B4
Achanalt Highld 263 D4
Achanamara Argyll 213 D5
Achandunie Highld 264 C2
Achany Highld 272 D3
Achaphubuil Highld 237 B4
Acharacle Highld 235 D5
Acharn Highld 236 D1
Acharn Perth 229 D6
Acharole Highld 280 C4
Achath Aberds 245 A4
Achavanich Highld 280 D3
Achavraat Highld 253 B5
Achddu Carms 57 B4
Achduart Highld 270 D3
Achentoul Highld 274 A2
Achfary Highld 271 A5

Achgarve Highld 261 A5
Achiemore Highld 277 B4
Achiemore Highld 279 C4
A'Chill Highld 246 D1
Achiltibuie Highld 270 D3
Achina Highld 278 B3
Achinduich Highld 272 D3
Achinduin Argyll 226 C3
Achingills Highld 280 B3
Achintee Highld 237 B5
Achintee Highld 249 B6
Achintraid Highld 249 C5
Achlean Highld 241 C6
Achleck Argyll 224 B3
Achluachrach Highld 239 D6
Achlyness Highld 276 C3
Achmelvich Highld 270 B3
Achmore Highld 249 C5
Achmore Stirl 217 A5
Achnaba Argyll 226 C4
Achnaba Argyll 214 D2
Achnabat Highld 252 C1
Achnacarnin Highld 270 A3
Achnacarry Highld 239 D5
Achnacloich Argyll 227 C4
Achnacloich Highld 247 D4
Achnaconeran Highld 240 A2
Achnacraig Argyll 224 B3
Achnacroish Argyll 226 B3
Achnadrish Argyll 224 A3
Achnafalnich Argyll 227 D7
Achnagarron Highld 264 D2
Achnaha Highld 234 D3
Achnahanat Highld 263 A7
Achnahannet Highld 253 D5
Achnairn Highld 272 C3
Achnaluachrach Highld 273 D4
Achnasaul Highld 239 D5
Achnasheen Highld 250 A3
Achosnich Highld 234 D3
Achranich Highld 226 B2
Achreamie Highld 279 B6
Achriabhach Highld 237 C5
Achriesgill Highld 276 C3
Achrimsdale Highld 274 D3
Achtoty Highld 278 B2
Achurch Northants 100 C2
Achuvoldrach Highld 277 C6
Achvaich Highld 264 A3
Achvarasdal Highld 279 B5
Ackergill Highld 281 C5
Acklam M'bro 168 D2
Acklam N Yorks 149 A6
Ackleton Shrops 95 B5
Acklington Northumb 189 C5
Ackton W Yorks 140 A2
Ackworth Moor Top
  W Yorks 140 B2
Acle Norf 121 D6
Acock's Green W Mid 96 C4
Acol Kent 53 C5
Acomb Northumb 178 C1
Acomb York 149 B4
Aconbury Hereford 78 D3
Acre Lancs 137 A6
Acre Street W Sus 19 B6
Acrefair Wrex 110 A1
Acton Ches 127 D6
Acton Dorset 16 D3
Acton London 49 A5
Acton Shrops 93 C7
Acton Suff 87 C4
Acton Wrex 126 D3
Acton Beauchamp
  Hereford 79 B4
Acton Bridge Ches 127 B5
Acton Burnell Shrops 94 A3
Acton Green Hereford 79 B4
Acton Pigott Shrops 94 A3
Acton Round Shrops 95 B4
Acton Scott Shrops 94 C2
Acton Trussell Staffs 112 D3
Acton Turville S Glos 44 A2
Adbaston Staffs 111 C6
Adber Dorset 29 C5
Adderley Shrops 111 A5
Adderstone Northumb 199 C5
Addiewell W Loth 208 D2
Addingham W Yorks 147 C4
Addington Bucks 66 A2
Addington Kent 37 A4
Addington London 49 C6
Addinston Borders 197 A4
Addiscombe London 49 C6
Addlestone Sur 48 C3
Addlethorpe Lincs 135 C5
Adel W Yorks 148 D1

Adeney Telford 111 D6
Adfa Powys 93 A4
Adforton Hereford 94 D2
Adisham Kent 53 D4
Adlestrop Glos 64 A3
Adlingfleet E Yorks 141 A6
Adlington Lancs 137 B5
Admaston Staffs 112 C4
Admaston Telford 111 D5
Admington Warks 81 C5
Adstock Bucks 83 D4
Adstone Northants 82 B2
Adversane W Sus 34 D3
Advie Highld 254 C2
Adwalton W Yorks 139 A5
Adwell Oxon 66 D1
Adwick le Street S Yorks 140 C3
Adwick upon Dearne
  S Yorks 140 C2
Adziel Aberds 269 D4
Ae Village Dumfries 184 D2
Affleck Aberds 256 D3
Affpuddle Dorset 16 B2
Affric Lodge Highld 250 D3
Afon-wen Flint 125 B6
Afton I o W 18 C2
Agglethorpe N Yorks 157 C4
Agneash I o M 152 C4
Aigburth Mers 126 A3
Aiginis W Isles 288 D5
Aike E Yorks 150 C3
Aikerness Orkney 282 B5
Aikers Orkney 283 H5
Aiketgate Cumb 164 A2
Aikton Cumb 175 C5
Ailey Hereford 78 C1
Ailstone Warks 81 B5
Ailsworth P'boro 100 B3
Ainderby Quernhow
  N Yorks 158 C2
Ainderby Steeple N Yorks 158 B2
Aingers Green Essex 71 A5
Ainsdale Mers 136 B2
Ainsdale-on-Sea Mers 136 B2
Ainstable Cumb 164 A3
Ainsworth Gtr Man 137 B6
Ainthorpe N Yorks 159 A6
Aintree Mers 136 D2
Aintree Racecourse Mers 136 D2
Aird Argyll 213 B5
Aird Dumfries 170 A2
Aird W Isles 288 D6
Aird a Mhachair W Isles 286 B3
Aird a'Mhulaidh W Isles 288 F2
Aird Asaig W Isles 288 G2
Aird Dhail W Isles 288 A5
Aird Mhidhinis W Isles 286 F3
Aird Mhighe W Isles 288 H2
Aird Mhighe W Isles 287 F5
Aird Mhor W Isles 286 F3
Aird of Sleat Highld 247 D4
Aird Thunga W Isles 288 D5
Aird Uig W Isles 287 A5
Airdens Highld 264 A2
Airdrie N Lnrk 207 D5
Airdtorrisdale Highld 278 B2
Airidh a Bhruaich W Isles 288 F3
Airieland Dumfries 173 C5
Airmyn E Yorks 141 A5
Airntully Perth 219 A5
Airor Highld 247 D6
Airth Falk 208 B1
Airton N Yorks 146 B3
Airyhassen Dumfries 171 C5
Aisby Lincs 141 D6
Aisby Lincs 116 B3
Aisgernis W Isles 286 D3
Aiskew N Yorks 157 C6
Aislaby N Yorks 159 C6
Aislaby N Yorks 160 A2
Aislaby Stockton 168 D2
Aisthorpe Lincs 133 A4
Aith Orkney 282 F3
Aith Shetland 285 H5
Aith Shetland 284 D8
Aithsetter Shetland 285 K6
Aitkenhead S Ayrs 192 E3
Aitnoch Highld 253 C5
Akeld Northumb 188 A2
Akeley Bucks 83 D4
Akenham Suff 88 C2
Albaston Corn 11 D5
Albourne W Sus 21 A5

Albrighton Shrops 110 D3
Albrighton Shrops 95 A6
Alburgh Norf 104 C3
Albury Herts 68 A4
Albury Sur 34 B3
Albury End Herts 68 A4
Alby Hill Norf 120 B3
Alcaig Highld 252 A1
Alcaston Shrops 94 C2
Alcester Warks 80 B3
Alciston E Sus 22 B3
Alcombe Som 27 A4
Alcombe Wilts 44 C2
Alconbury Cambs 100 D3
Alconbury Weston Cambs 100 D3
Aldbar Castle Angus 232 C3
Aldborough Norf 120 B3
Aldborough N Yorks 148 A3
Aldbourne Wilts 45 B6
Aldbrough E Yorks 151 D5
Aldbrough St John
  N Yorks 167 D5
Aldbury Herts 67 B4
Aldcliffe Lancs 145 A4
Aldclune Perth 230 B3
Aldeburgh Suff 89 B5
Aldeby Norf 105 B5
Aldenham Herts 67 D6
Alderbury Wilts 31 C5
Aldercar Derbys 114 A2
Alderford Norf 120 D3
Alderholt Dorset 31 D5
Alderley Glos 62 D3
Alderley Edge Ches 128 B3
Aldermaston W Berks 46 C3
Aldermaston Wharf
  W Berks 47 C4
Alderminster Warks 81 C5
Alderney Airport Ald 7
Alder's End Hereford 79 C4
Aldersey Green Ches 127 D4
Aldershot Hants 34 A1
Alderton Glos 80 D3
Alderton Northants 83 C4
Alderton Shrops 110 C3
Alderton Suff 88 C4
Alderton Wilts 44 A2
Alderwasley Derbys 130 D3
Aldfield N Yorks 147 A6
Aldford Ches 127 D4
Aldham Essex 70 A3
Aldham Suff 87 C6
Aldie Highld 264 B3
Aldingbourne W Sus 20 B2
Aldingham Cumb 154 D1
Aldington Kent 38 B2
Aldington Worcs 80 C3
Aldington Frith Kent 38 B2
Aldochlay Argyll 206 A1
Aldreth Cambs 101 D6
Aldridge W Mid 96 A3
Aldringham Suff 89 A5
Aldsworth Glos 64 B2
Aldunie Moray 255 D4
Aldwark Derbys 130 D2
Aldwark N Yorks 148 A3
Aldwick W Sus 20 C2
Aldwincle Northants 100 C2
Aldworth W Berks 46 B3
Alexandria W Dunb 206 C1
Alfardisworthy Devon 24 D3
Alfington Devon 13 B6
Alfold Sur 34 C3
Alfold Bars W Sus 34 C3
Alfold Crossways Sur 34 C3
Alford Aberds 244 A2
Alford Lincs 135 B4
Alford Som 29 B6
Alfreton Derbys 131 D4
Alfrick Worcs 79 B5
Alfrick Pound Worcs 79 B5
Alfriston E Sus 22 B3
Algaltraig Argyll 203 A5
Algarkirk Lincs 117 B5
Alhampton Som 29 B6
Aline Lodge W Isles 288 F2
Alisary Highld 235 C6
Alkborough N Lincs 141 A6
Alkerton Oxon 81 C6
Alkham Kent 39 A4
Alkington Shrops 111 B4
Alkmonton Derbys 113 B5
Alladale Lodge Highld 263 B6
All Cannings Wilts 45 C4
All Saints Church,
  Godshill I o W 18 C4
All Saints South Elmham
  Suff 104 C4
All Stretton Shrops 94 B2

Alladale Lodge Highld 263 B6
Allaleigh Devon 8 B2
Allanaquoich Aberds 242 C4
Allangrange Mains Highld 252 A2
Allanton Borders 198 A2
Allanton N Lnrk 194 A3
Allathasdal W Isles 286 F2
Allendale Town Northumb 177 D6
Allenheads Northumb 165 A6
Allens Green Herts 69 B4
Allensford Durham 178 D2
Allensmore Hereford 78 D2
Allenton Derby 114 B1
Aller Som 28 C4
Allerby Cumb 162 A3
Allerford Som 27 A4
Allerston N Yorks 160 C2
Allerthorpe E Yorks 149 C6
Allerton Mers 127 A4
Allerton W Yorks 147 D5
Allerton Bywater W Yorks 140 A2
Allerton Mauleverer
  N Yorks 148 B3
Allesley W Mid 97 C6
Allestree Derby 114 B1
Allet Corn 4 C2
Allexton Leics 99 A5
Allgreave Ches 129 C4
Allhallows Medway 51 B5
Allhallows-on-Sea
  Medway 51 B5
Alligin Shuas Highld 249 A5
Allimore Green Staffs 112 D2
Allington Lincs 115 A6
Allington Wilts 31 B6
Allington Wilts 45 C4
Allithwaite Cumb 154 D2
Alloa Clack 208 A1
Allonby Cumb 174 D3
Alloway S Ayrs 192 D3
Allt Carms 57 B5
Allt na h-Airbhe Highld 262 A3
Allt-nan-sùgh Highld 249 D6
Alltchaorunn Highld 237 D5
Alltforgan Powys 109 C4
Alltmawr Powys 77 C4
Alltnacaillich Highld 277 D5
Alltsigh Highld 240 A2
Alltwalis Carms 58 B1
Alltwen Neath 40 A2
Alltyblaca Ceredig 75 D4
Allwood Green Suff 103 D6
Almeley Hereford 78 B1
Almer Dorset 16 B3
Almholme S Yorks 140 C3
Almington Staffs 111 B6
Alminstone Cross Devon 24 C4
Almondbank Perth 219 B5
Almondbury W Yorks 139 B4
Almondsbury S Glos 43 A5
Alne N Yorks 148 A3
Alness Highld 264 D2
Alnham Northumb 188 B2
Alnmouth Northumb 189 B5
Alnwick Northumb 189 B4
Alperton London 49 A4
Alphamstone Essex 87 D4
Alpheton Suff 87 B4
Alphington Devon 13 B4
Alport Derbys 130 C2
Alpraham Ches 127 D5
Alresford Essex 71 A4
Alrewas Staffs 113 D5
Alsager Ches 128 D2
Alsagers Bank Staffs 112 A2
Alsop en le Dale Derbys 129 D6
Alston Cumb 165 A5
Alston Devon 14 A3
Alstone Glos 80 D2
Alstonefield Staffs 129 D6
Alswear Devon 26 C2
Altandhu Highld 270 C2
Altanduin Highld 274 B2
Altarnun Corn 10 C3
Altass Highld 272 D2
Aiterwall Highld 281 B4
Altham Lancs 146 D1
Althorne Essex 70 D3
Althorp House, Great
  Brington Northants 82 A3
Althorpe N Lincs 141 C6
Alticry Dumfries 171 B4
Altnabreac Station Highld 279 D6
Altnacealgach Hotel
  Highld 271 C5
Altnacraig Argyll 226 D3
Altnafeadh Highld 237 D6
Altnaharra Highld 272 A3

Altofts W Yorks 139 A6
Alton Derbys 130 C3
Alton Hants 33 B6
Alton Staffs 113 A4
Alton Pancras Dorset 15 A7
Alton Priors Wilts 45 C5
Alton Towers Staffs 113 A4
Altrincham Gtr Man 128 A2
Altrua Highld 239 D6
Altskeith Stirl 217 D4
Altyre Ho. Moray 253 A6
Alva Clack 208 A1
Alvanley Ches 127 B4
Alvaston Derby 114 B1
Alvechurch Worcs 96 D3
Alvecote Warks 97 A5
Alvediston Wilts 30 C3
Alveley Shrops 95 C5
Alverdiscott Devon 25 C6
Alverstoke Hants 19 B5
Alverstone I o W 19 C4
Alverton Notts 115 A5
Alves Moray 266 C2
Alvescot Oxon 64 C3
Alveston S Glos 43 A5
Alveston Warks 81 B5
Alvie Highld 241 B6
Alvingham Lincs 143 D5
Alvington Glos 62 C2
Alwalton Cambs 100 B3
Alweston Dorset 29 D6
Alwinton Northumb 188 C2
Alwoodley W Yorks 148 C1
Alyth Perth 231 D6
Am Baile W Isles 286 E3
Am Buth Argyll 226 D3
Amatnatua Highld 263 A6
Amber Hill Lincs 117 A5
Ambergate Derbys 130 D3
Amberley Glos 63 C4
Amberley W Sus 20 A3
Amble Northumb 189 C5
Amblecote W Mid 96 C1
Ambleside Cumb 154 A2
Ambrosden Oxon 65 B7
Amcotts N Lincs 141 B6
American Air Museum,
  Duxford Cambs 85 C6
Amersham Bucks 67 D4
Amerton Working Farm,
  Stowe-by-Chartley
  Staffs 112 C3
Amesbury Wilts 31 A5
Amington Staffs 97 A5
Amisfield Dumfries 184 D2
Amlwch Anglesey 123 A4
Amlwch Port Anglesey 123 A4
Ammanford = Rhydaman
  Carms 57 A6
Amod Argyll 190 B3
Amotherby N Yorks 159 D6
Ampfield Hants 32 C3
Ampleforth N Yorks 159 D4
Ampney Crucis Glos 63 C6
Ampney St Mary Glos 64 C1
Ampney St Peter Glos 64 C1
Amport Hants 32 A1
Ampthill Beds 84 D2
Ampton Suff 103 D4
Amroth Pembs 56 B1
Amulree Perth 218 A3
An Caol Highld 248 A3
An Cnoc W Isles 288 D5
An Gleann Ur W Isles 288 D5
An t-Ob = Leverburgh
  W Isles 287 F5
Anagach Highld 253 D6
Anaheilt Highld 236 C2
Anancaun Highld 262 D2
Ancaster Lincs 116 A2
Anchor Shrops 93 C5
Anchorsholme Blkpool 144 C3
Ancroft Northumb 198 B3
Ancrum Borders 187 A5
Anderby Lincs 135 B5
Anderson Dorset 16 B2
Anderton Ches 127 B6
Andover Hants 32 A2
Andover Down Hants 32 A2
Andoversford Glos 63 B6
Andreas I o M 152 B4
Anfield Mers 136 D2
Angersleigh Som 28 D1
Angle Pembs 55 D4
Angmering W Sus 20 B3
Angram N Yorks 148 C4

Angram N Yorks 156 B2
Anie Stirl 217 C5
Ankerville Highld 265 C4
Anlaby E Yorks 142 A2
Anmer Norf 119 C4
Anna Valley Hants 32 A2
Annan Dumfries 175 B4
Annat Argyll 227 D5
Annat Highld 249 A5
Annbank S Ayrs 193 C4
Anne Hathaway's
  Cottage, Stratford-
  upon-Avon Warks 81 B4
Annesley Notts 131 D5
Annesley Woodhouse
  Notts 131 D4
Annfield Plain Durham 178 D3
Annifirth Shetland 285 J3
Annitsford T & W 179 B4
Annscroft Shrops 94 A2
Ansdell Lancs 136 A2
Ansford Som 29 B6
Ansley Warks 97 B5
Anslow Staffs 113 C6
Anslow Gate Staffs 113 C5
Anstey Herts 85 D6
Anstey Leics 98 A2
Anstruther Easter Fife 221 D5
Anstruther Wester Fife 221 D5
Ansty Hants 33 A6
Ansty Warks 97 C6
Ansty Wilts 30 C3
Ansty W Sus 35 D5
Anthill Common Hants 33 D5
Anthorn Cumb 175 C4
Antingham Norf 121 B4
Anton's Gowt Lincs 117 A5
Antonshill Falk 208 B1
Antony Corn 6 B3
Anwick Lincs 133 D6
Anwoth Dumfries 172 C3
Aoradh Argyll 200 B2
Apes Hall Cambs 102 B1
Apethorpe Northants 100 B2
Apeton Staffs 112 D2
Apley Lincs 133 B6
Apperknowle Derbys 130 B3
Apperley Glos 63 A4
Apperley Bridge W Yorks 147 D5
Appersett N Yorks 156 B2
Appin Argyll 226 B4
Appin House Argyll 226 B4
Appleby N Lincs 142 B1
Appleby-in-Westmorland
  Cumb 165 C4
Appleby Magna Leics 97 A6
Appleby Parva Leics 97 A6
Applecross Highld 249 B4
Applecross Ho. Highld 249 B4
Appledore Devon 25 B5
Appledore Devon 27 D5
Appledore Kent 38 C1
Appledore Heath Kent 38 B1
Appleford Oxon 65 D6
Applegarthtown Dumfries 185 D4
Appleshaw Hants 32 A2
Applethwaite Cumb 163 B5
Appleton Halton 127 A5
Appleton Oxon 65 C5
Appleton-le-Moors
  N Yorks 159 C6
Appleton-le-Street
  N Yorks 159 D6
Appleton Roebuck
  N Yorks 149 C4
Appleton Thorn Warr 127 A6
Appleton Wiske N Yorks 158 A2
Appletreehall Borders 186 B4
Appletreewick N Yorks 147 A4
Appley Som 27 C5
Appley Bridge Lancs 136 C4
Apse Heath I o W 19 C4
Apsley End Beds 84 D3
Apuldram W Sus 20 B1
Aquhythe Aberds 245 A4
Arabella Highld 265 C4
Arbeadie Aberds 244 C3
Arbeia Roman Fort and
  Museum T & W 179 C5
Arberth = Narberth Pembs 55 C7
Arbirlot Angus 233 D4
Arboll Highld 265 B4
Arborfield Wokingham 47 C5
Arborfield Cross
  Wokingham 47 C5
Arborfield Garrison
  Wokingham 47 C5
Arbour-thorne S Yorks 130 A3

Arbroath Angus 233 D4
Arbuthnott Aberds 233 A5
Archiestown Moray 254 B3
Arclid Ches 128 C2
Ard-dhubh Highld 249 B4
Ardachu Highld 273 D4
Ardalanish Argyll 224 E2
Ardanaiseig Argyll 227 D5
Ardaneaskan Highld 249 C5
Ardanstur Argyll 213 A6
Ardargie House Hotel
  Perth 219 C5
Ardarroch Highld 249 C5
Ardbeg Argyll 201 C5
Ardbeg Argyll 215 D4
Ardbeg Distillery, Port
  Ellen Argyll 201 D4
Ardcharnich Highld 262 B3
Ardchiavaig Argyll 224 E2
Ardchullarie More Stirl 217 C5
Ardchyle Stirl 217 B5
Arddleen Powys 110 D1
Ardechvie Highld 239 C5
Ardeley Herts 68 A3
Ardelve Highld 249 D5
Arden Argyll 206 B1
Ardens Grafton Warks 80 B4
Ardentinny Argyll 215 D4
Ardentraive Argyll 203 A5
Ardeonaig Stirl 217 A6
Ardersier Highld 252 A3
Ardessie Highld 262 B2
Ardfern Argyll 213 B6
Ardgartan Argyll 215 B5
Ardgay Highld 264 A1
Ardgour Highld 237 C4
Ardheslaig Highld 249 A4
Ardiecow Moray 267 C6
Ardindrean Highld 262 B3
Ardingly W Sus 35 D6
Ardington Oxon 46 A2
Ardlair Aberds 255 D6
Ardlamont Ho. Argyll 203 B4
Ardleigh Essex 71 A4
Ardler Perth 231 D6
Ardley Oxon 65 A6
Ardlui Argyll 215 A6
Ardlussa Argyll 213 D4
Ardmair Highld 262 A3
Ardmay Argyll 215 B5
Ardminish Argyll 202 D1
Ardmolich Highld 235 C6
Ardmore Argyll 226 D2
Ardmore Highld 276 C3
Ardmore Highld 264 B3
Ardnacross Argyll 225 B4
Ardnadam Argyll 203 A6
Ardnagrask Highld 251 B7
Ardnarff Highld 249 C5
Ardnastang Highld 236 C2
Ardnave Argyll 200 A2
Ardno Argyll 215 B4
Ardo Aberds 256 C3
Ardo Ho. Aberds 257 D4
Ardoch Perth 219 A5
Ardochy House Highld 239 B6
Ardoyne Aberds 256 D1
Ardpatrick Argyll 202 B2
Ardpatrick Ho. Argyll 215 D5
Ardpeaton Argyll 215 D5
Ardrishaig Argyll 213 D6
Ardross Fife 221 D5
Ardross Highld 264 C2
Ardross Castle Highld 264 C2
Ardrossan N Ayrs 204 D2
Ardshealach Highld 235 D5
Ardsley S Yorks 140 C1
Ardslignish Highld 235 D4
Ardtalla Argyll 201 C4
Ardtalnaig Perth 218 A2
Ardtoe Highld 235 C5
Ardtrostan Perth 217 B6
Arduaine Argyll 213 A5
Ardullie Highld 264 D1
Ardvasar Highld 247 D5
Ardverikie Highld 240 C3
Ardwell Dumfries 170 C3
Ardwell Mains Dumfries 170 C3
Ardwick Gtr Man 138 D1
Areley Kings Worcs 95 D6
Arford Hants 34 C1
Argoed Caerph 41 B6
Argoed Mill Powys 76 A3
Argyll & Sutherland
  Highlanders Museum
  (See Stirling Castle)
  Stirl 207 A5

All – Ash 307

Arichamish Argyll 214 B2
Arichastlich Argyll 216 A2
Aridhglas Argyll 224 D2
Arileod Argyll 223 B4
Arinacrinachd Highld 249 A4
Arinagour Argyll 223 B5
Arion Orkney 282 F3
Arisaig Highld 235 B5
Ariundle Highld 236 C2
Arkendale N Yorks 148 A2
Arkesden Essex 85 D6
Arkholme Lancs 155 D4
Arkle Town N Yorks 156 A4
Arkley London 68 D2
Arksey S Yorks 140 C3
Arkwright Town Derbys 131 B4
Arle Glos 63 A5
Arlecdon Cumb 162 C3
Arlesey Beds 84 D3
Arleston Telford 111 D5
Arley Ches 128 A1
Arlingham Glos 62 B3
Arlington Devon 25 A7
Arlington E Sus 22 B3
Arlington Glos 64 C2
Arlington Court Devon 25 A7
Armadale Highld 278 B3
Armadale W Loth 208 D2
Armadale Castle Highld 247 D5
Armathwaite Cumb 164 A3
Arminghall Norf 104 A3
Armitage Staffs 113 D4
Armley W Yorks 148 D1
Armscote Warks 81 C5
Armthorpe S Yorks 140 C4
Arnabost Argyll 223 B5
Arncliffe N Yorks 156 D3
Arncroach Fife 221 D5
Arne Dorset 16 C3
Arnesby Leics 98 B3
Arngask Perth 219 C6
Arnisdale Highld 238 A2
Arnish Highld 248 B2
Arniston Engine Midloth 209 D6
Arnol W Isles 288 C4
Arnold E Yorks 151 C4
Arnold Notts 114 A3
Arnolfini Gallery Bristol 43 B4
Arnprior Stirl 207 A4
Arnside Cumb 154 D3
Aros Mains Argyll 225 B4
Arowry Wrex 110 B3
Arpafeelie Highld 252 A2
Arrad Foot Cumb 154 C2
Arram E Yorks 150 C3
Arrathorne N Yorks 157 B6
Arreton I o W 18 C4
Arrington Cambs 85 B5
Arrivain Argyll 216 A2
Arrochar Argyll 215 B5
Arrow Warks 80 B3
Arthington W Yorks 147 C6
Arthingworth Northants 99 C4
Arthog Gwyn 90 A4
Arthrath Aberds 257 C4
Arthurstone Perth 231 D6
Artrochie Aberds 257 C5
Arundel W Sus 20 B3
Arundel Castle W Sus 20 B3
Aryhoulan Highld 237 C4
Asby Cumb 162 B3
Ascog Argyll 203 B6
Ascot Windsor 48 C2
Ascot Racecourse Windsor 48 C2
Ascott Warks 81 D6
Ascott-under-Wychwood
  Oxon 64 B4
Asenby N Yorks 158 D2
Asfordby Leics 115 D5
Asfordby Hill Leics 115 D5
Asgarby Lincs 116 A4
Asgarby Lincs 134 C3
Ash Kent 50 C2
Ash Kent 53 D4
Ash Som 29 C4
Ash Sur 34 A1
Ash Bullayne Devon 12 A2
Ash Green Warks 97 C6
Ash Magna Shrops 111 B4
Ash Mill Devon 26 C2
Ash Priors Som 27 C6
Ash Street Suff 87 C6
Ash Thomas Devon 27 D5
Ash Vale Sur 34 A1

Ashampstead *W Berks* 46 B3
Ashbocking *Suff* 88 B2
Ashbourne *Derbys* 113 A5
Ashbrittle *Som* 27 C5
Ashburton *Devon* 7 A6
Ashbury *Devon* 11 B6
Ashbury *Oxon* 45 A6
Ashby *N Lincs* 141 C7
Ashby by Partney *Lincs* 135 C4
Ashby cum Fenby *NE Lincs* 143 C4
Ashby de la Launde *Lincs* 133 D5
Ashby-de-la-Zouch *Leics* 114 D1
Ashby Folville *Leics* 115 D5
Ashby Magna *Leics* 98 B2
Ashby Parva *Leics* 98 C2
Ashby Puerorum *Lincs* 134 B3
Ashby St Ledgers *Northants* 82 A2
Ashby St Mary *Norf* 104 A4
Ashchurch *Glos* 80 D2
Ashcombe *Devon* 13 D4
Ashcott *Som* 28 B4
Ashdon *Essex* 86 C1
Ashe *Hants* 32 A4
Asheldham *Essex* 70 C3
Ashen *Essex* 86 C3
Ashendon *Bucks* 66 B2
Ashfield *Carms* 58 C3
Ashfield *Stirl* 218 D2
Ashfield *Suff* 88 A3
Ashfield Green *Suff* 104 D3
Ashfold Crossways *W Sus* 35 D5
Ashford *Devon* 25 B6
Ashford *Hants* 31 D5
Ashford *Kent* 38 A2
Ashford *Sur* 48 B3
Ashford Bowdler *Shrops* 94 D3
Ashford Carbonell *Shrops* 94 D3
Ashford Hill *Hants* 46 C3
Ashford in the Water *Derbys* 130 C1
Ashgill *S Lnrk* 194 B2
Ashill *Devon* 27 D5
Ashill *Norf* 103 A4
Ashill *Som* 28 D3
Ashingdon *Essex* 70 D2
Ashington *Som* 29 C5
Ashington *W Sus* 21 A4
Ashintully Castle *Perth* 231 B5
Ashkirk *Borders* 186 A3
Ashlett *Hants* 18 A3
Ashleworth *Glos* 63 A4
Ashley *Cambs* 86 A2
Ashley *Ches* 128 A2
Ashley *Devon* 26 D1
Ashley *Dorset* 17 A5
Ashley *Glos* 63 D5
Ashley *Hants* 17 B6
Ashley *Hants* 32 B2
Ashley *Northants* 99 B4
Ashley *Staffs* 111 B6
Ashley Green *Bucks* 67 C4
Ashley Heath *Dorset* 17 A5
Ashley Heath *Staffs* 111 B6
Ashmanhaugh *Norf* 121 C5
Ashmansworth *Hants* 46 D2
Ashmansworthy *Devon* 24 D4
Ashmore *Dorset* 30 D3
Ashorne *Warks* 81 B6
Ashover *Derbys* 130 C3
Ashow *Warks* 97 D6
Ashprington *Devon* 8 B2
Ashreigney *Devon* 26 D1
Ashtead *Sur* 35 A4
Ashton *Ches* 127 C5
Ashton *Corn* 3 C4
Ashton *Hants* 33 D4
Ashton *Hereford* 78 A3
Ashton *Invclyd* 204 A2
Ashton *Northants* 83 C4
Ashton *Northants* 100 C2
Ashton Common *Wilts* 44 D2
Ashton-In-Makerfield *Gtr Man* 137 D4
Ashton Keynes *Wilts* 63 D6
Ashton under Hill *Worcs* 80 D2
Ashton-under-Lyne *Gtr Man* 138 D2
Ashton upon Mersey *Gtr Man* 137 D6
Ashurst *Hants* 32 D2
Ashurst *Kent* 36 C3

Ashurst *W Sus* 21 A4
Ashurstwood *W Sus* 36 C2
Ashwater *Devon* 11 B4
Ashwell *Herts* 85 D4
Ashwell *Rutland* 115 D6
Ashwell *Som* 28 D3
Ashwellthorpe *Norf* 104 B2
Ashwick *Som* 29 A6
Ashwicken *Norf* 119 D4
Ashybank *Borders* 186 B4
Askam in Furness *Cumb* 153 C3
Askern *S Yorks* 140 B3
Askerswell *Dorset* 15 B5
Askett *Bucks* 66 C3
Askham *Cumb* 164 C3
Askham *Notts* 132 B2
Askham Bryan *York* 149 C4
Askham Richard *York* 148 C4
Asknish *Argyll* 214 C2
Askrigg *N Yorks* 156 B3
Askwith *N Yorks* 147 C5
Aslackby *Lincs* 116 B3
Aslacton *Norf* 104 B2
Aslockton *Notts* 115 B5
Asloun *Aberds* 244 A2
Aspatria *Cumb* 174 D4
Aspenden *Herts* 68 A3
Asperton *Lincs* 117 B5
Aspley Guise *Beds* 83 D6
Aspley Heath *Beds* 83 D6
Aspull *Gtr Man* 137 C5
Asselby *E Yorks* 141 A5
Asserby *Lincs* 135 B4
Assington *Suff* 87 D5
Assynt Ho. *Highld* 264 D1
Astbury *Ches* 128 C3
Astcote *Northants* 82 B3
Asterley *Shrops* 94 A1
Asterton *Shrops* 94 B1
Asthall *Oxon* 64 B3
Asthall Leigh *Oxon* 64 B4
Astley *Shrops* 111 D4
Astley *Warks* 97 C6
Astley *Worcs* 79 A5
Astley Abbotts *Shrops* 95 B5
Astley Bridge *Gtr Man* 137 B6
Astley Cross *Worcs* 79 A6
Astley Green *Gtr Man* 137 D6
Aston *Ches* 111 A5
Aston *Ches* 127 B5
Aston *Derbys* 130 A1
Aston *Hereford* 94 D2
Aston *Herts* 68 A2
Aston *Oxon* 64 C4
Aston *Shrops* 111 C4
Aston *Staffs* 111 A6
Aston *S Yorks* 131 A4
Aston *Telford* 95 A4
Aston *W Mid* 96 C3
Aston *Wokingham* 47 A5
Aston Abbotts *Bucks* 66 A3
Aston Botterell *Shrops* 95 C4
Aston-By-Stone *Staffs* 112 B3
Aston Cantlow *Warks* 80 B4
Aston Clinton *Bucks* 66 B3
Aston Crews *Hereford* 62 A2
Aston Cross *Glos* 80 D2
Aston End *Herts* 68 A2
Aston Eyre *Shrops* 95 B4
Aston Fields *Worcs* 80 A2
Aston Flamville *Leics* 98 B1
Aston Ingham *Hereford* 62 A2
Aston juxta Mondrum *Ches* 127 D6
Aston le Walls *Northants* 82 B1
Aston Magna *Glos* 81 D4
Aston Munslow *Shrops* 94 C3
Aston on Clun *Shrops* 94 C1
Aston-on-Trent *Derbys* 114 C2
Aston Rogers *Shrops* 94 A1
Aston Rowant *Oxon* 66 D2
Aston Sandford *Bucks* 66 C2
Aston Somerville *Worcs* 80 D3
Aston Subedge *Glos* 80 C4
Aston Tirrold *Oxon* 46 A3
Aston Upthorpe *Oxon* 46 A3
Astrop *Northants* 82 D2
Astwick *Beds* 84 D4
Astwood *M Keynes* 83 C6
Astwood *Worcs* 79 B6
Astwood Bank *Worcs* 80 A3
Aswarby *Lincs* 116 B3
Aswardby *Lincs* 134 B3
Atch Lench *Worcs* 80 B3
Atcham *Shrops* 94 A3
Athelhampton *Dorset* 16 B1
Athelington *Suff* 104 D3

Athelney *Som* 28 C3
Athelstaneford *E Loth* 210 C2
Atherington *Devon* 25 C6
Atherstone *Warks* 97 B6
Atherstone on Stour *Warks* 81 B5
Atherton *Gtr Man* 137 C5
Atley Hill *N Yorks* 157 A6
Atlow *Derbys* 113 A6
Attadale *Highld* 249 C6
Attadale Ho. *Highld* 249 C6
Attenborough *Notts* 114 B3
Atterby *Lincs* 142 D1
Attercliffe *S Yorks* 130 A3
Attleborough *Norf* 103 B6
Attleborough *Warks* 97 B6
Attlebridge *Norf* 120 D3
Atwick *E Yorks* 151 B4
Atworth *Wilts* 44 C2
Auburn *Lincs* 133 C4
Auchagallon *N Ayrs* 191 B4
Auchallater *Aberds* 243 D4
Aucharnie *Aberds* 256 B1
Auchattie *Aberds* 244 C3
Auchavan *Angus* 231 B5
Auchbreck *Moray* 254 D3
Auchenback *E Renf* 205 C5
Auchenbainzie *Dumfries* 183 C6
Auchenblae *Aberds* 233 A5
Auchenbrack *Dumfries* 183 C5
Auchenbreck *Argyll* 214 D3
Auchencairn *Dumfries* 173 C5
Auchencairn *Dumfries* 184 D2
Auchencairn *N Ayrs* 191 C6
Auchencrosh *S Ayrs* 180 D3
Auchencrow *Borders* 211 D5
Auchendinny *Midloth* 209 D5
Auchengray *S Lnrk* 195 A4
Auchenhalrig *Moray* 267 C4
Auchenheath *S Lnrk* 194 B3
Auchenlochan *Argyll* 203 A4
Auchenmalg *Dumfries* 171 B4
Auchensoul *S Ayrs* 181 B4
Auchentiber *N Ayrs* 204 D3
Auchertyre *Highld* 249 D5
Auchgourish *Highld* 242 A2
Auchincarroch *W Dunb* 206 B2
Auchindrain *Highld* 214 B3
Auchindrean *Highld* 262 B3
Auchininna *Aberds* 256 B1
Auchinleck *E Ayrs* 193 C5
Auchinloch *N Lnrk* 205 A6
Auchinroath *Moray* 266 D3
Auchintoul *Aberds* 244 A2
Auchiries *Aberds* 257 C5
Auchlee *Aberds* 245 C5
Auchleven *Aberds* 256 D1
Auchlochan *S Lnrk* 194 C3
Auchlossan *Aberds* 244 B2
Auchlunies *Aberds* 245 C5
Auchlyne *Stirl* 217 B5
Auchmacoy *Aberds* 257 C4
Auchmair *Moray* 255 D4
Auchmantle *Dumfries* 170 A3
Auchmillan *E Ayrs* 193 C5
Auchmithie *Angus* 233 D4
Auchmuirbridge *Fife* 220 D2
Auchmull *Angus* 232 A3
Auchnacree *Angus* 232 B2
Auchnagallin *Highld* 253 C6
Auchnagatt *Aberds* 257 B4
Aucholzie *Aberds* 243 C6
Auchrannie *Angus* 231 C6
Auchroisk *Highld* 253 D6
Auchronie *Angus* 244 D1
Auchterarder *Perth* 218 C4
Auchteraw *Highld* 240 B1
Auchterderran *Fife* 209 A5
Auchterhouse *Angus* 220 A3
Auchtermuchty *Fife* 220 C2
Auchterneed *Highld* 251 A6
Auchtertool *Fife* 209 A5
Auchtertyre *Moray* 266 D2
Auchtubh *Stirl* 217 B5
Auckengill *Highld* 281 B5
Auckley *S Yorks* 140 C4
Audenshaw *Gtr Man* 138 D2
Audlem *Ches* 111 A5
Audley *Staffs* 128 D2
Audley End *Essex* 87 D4
Audley End House *Essex* 86 D1
Auds *Aberds* 268 C1
Aughton *E Yorks* 149 D6
Aughton *Lancs* 136 C2
Aughton *Lancs* 145 A5

Aughton *S Yorks* 131 A4
Aughton *Wilts* 45 D6
Aughton Park *Lancs* 136 C3
Auldearn *Highld* 253 A5
Aulden *Hereford* 78 B2
Auldhame *E Loth* 210 B2
Auldhouse *S Lnrk* 205 C6
Ault a'chruinn *Highld* 249 D6
Aultanrynie *Highld* 271 A6
Aultbea *Highld* 261 B5
Aultdearg *Highld* 263 D4
Aultgrishan *Highld* 261 B4
Aultibea *Highld* 274 B4
Aultiphurst *Highld* 279 B4
Aultmore *Moray* 267 D5
Aultnagoire *Highld* 252 D1
Aultnamain Inn *Highld* 264 B2
Aultnaslat *Highld* 239 B5
Aulton *Aberds* 255 D7
Aundorach *Highld* 242 A2
Aunsby *Lincs* 116 B3
Auquhorthies *Aberds* 256 D3
Aust *S Glos* 43 A4
Austendike *Lincs* 117 C5
Austerfield *S Yorks* 141 D4
Austrey *Warks* 97 A5
Austwick *N Yorks* 146 A1
Authorpe *Lincs* 135 A4
Authorpe Row *Lincs* 135 B5
Avebury *Wilts* 45 C5
Aveley *Thurrock* 50 A2
Avening *Glos* 63 D4
Averham *Notts* 132 D2
Aveton Gifford *Devon* 7 C5
Avielochan *Highld* 242 A2
Aviemore *Highld* 242 A1
Avington *Hants* 32 B4
Avington *W Berks* 46 C1
Avoch *Highld* 252 A3
Avon *Hants* 17 B5
Avon Dassett *Warks* 81 C7
Avonbridge *Falk* 208 C2
Avonmouth *Bristol* 43 B4
Avonwick *Devon* 7 B6
Awbridge *Hants* 32 C2
Awhirk *Dumfries* 170 B2
Awkley *S Glos* 43 A4
Awliscombe *Devon* 13 A6
Awre *Glos* 62 C3
Awsworth *Notts* 114 A2
Axbridge *Som* 42 D3
Axford *Hants* 33 A5
Axford *Wilts* 45 C6
Axminster *Devon* 14 B2
Axmouth *Devon* 14 B2
Axton *Flint* 125 A6
Aycliff *Kent* 39 A5
Aycliffe *Durham* 167 C5
Aydon *Northumb* 178 C2
Aylburton *Glos* 62 C2
Ayle *Northumb* 165 A5
Aylesbeare *Devon* 13 B5
Aylesbury *Bucks* 66 B3
Aylesby *NE Lincs* 143 C4
Aylesford *Kent* 37 A5
Aylesham *Kent* 53 D4
Aylestone *Leicester* 98 A2
Aylmerton *Norf* 120 B3
Aylsham *Norf* 120 C3
Aylton *Hereford* 79 D4
Aymestrey *Hereford* 78 A2
Aynho *Northants* 82 D2
Ayot St Lawrence *Herts* 68 B1
Ayot St Peter *Herts* 68 B2
Ayr *S Ayrs* 192 C3
Ayr Racecourse *S Ayrs* 192 C3
Aysgarth *N Yorks* 156 C4
Ayside *Cumb* 154 C2
Ayston *Rutland* 99 A5
Aythorpe Roding *Essex* 69 B5
Ayton *Borders* 211 D6
Aywick *Shetland* 284 E7
Azerley *N Yorks* 157 D6

B

Babbacombe *Torbay* 8 A3
Babbinswood *Shrops* 110 B2
Babcary *Som* 29 C5
Babel *Carms* 59 B5
Babell *Flint* 125 B6
Babraham *Cambs* 85 B7
Babworth *Notts* 132 A1
Bac *W Isles* 288 C5
Bachau *Anglesey* 123 B4

Back of Keppoch *Highld* 235 B5
Back Rogerton *E Ayrs* 193 C5
Backaland *Orkney* 282 D6
Backaskaill *Orkney* 282 B5
Backbarrow *Cumb* 154 C2
Backe *Carms* 56 A2
Backfolds *Aberds* 269 D5
Backford *Ches* 127 B4
Backford Cross *Ches* 126 B3
Backhill *Aberds* 256 C2
Backhill *Aberds* 257 C5
Backhill of Clackriach *Aberds* 257 B4
Backhill of Fortree *Aberds* 257 B4
Backhill of Trustach *Aberds* 244 C3
Backies *Highld* 274 D2
Backlass *Highld* 280 C4
Backwell *N Som* 42 C3
Backworth *T & W* 179 B5
Bacon End *Essex* 69 B6
Baconsthorpe *Norf* 120 B3
Bacton *Hereford* 78 D1
Bacton *Norf* 121 B5
Bacton *Suff* 87 A6
Bacton Green *Suff* 87 A6
Bacup *Lancs* 138 A1
Badachro *Highld* 261 C4
Badanloch Lodge *Highld* 273 A5
Badavanich *Highld* 250 A3
Badbury *Swindon* 45 A5
Badby *Northants* 82 B2
Badcall *Highld* 276 C3
Badcaul *Highld* 262 A2
Baddeley Green *Stoke* 129 D4
Baddesley Clinton *Warks* 97 D5
Baddesley Clinton Hall *Warks* 97 D5
Baddesley Ensor *Warks* 97 B5
Baddidarach *Highld* 270 B3
Baddoch *Aberds* 242 D4
Baddock *Highld* 252 A3
Badenscoth *Aberds* 256 C2
Badenyon *Aberds* 243 A6
Badger *Shrops* 95 B5
Badger's Mount *Kent* 50 C1
Badgeworth *Glos* 63 B5
Badgworth *Som* 42 D2
Badicaul *Highld* 249 D4
Badingham *Suff* 88 A4
Badlesmere *Kent* 52 D2
Badlipster *Highld* 280 D4
Badluarach *Highld* 262 A1
Badminton *S Glos* 44 A2
Badnaban *Highld* 270 B3
Badninish *Highld* 264 A3
Badrallach *Highld* 262 A2
Badsey *Worcs* 80 C3
Badshot Lea *Sur* 34 B1
Badsworth *W Yorks* 140 B2
Badwell Ash *Suff* 87 A5
Bae Colwyn = Colwyn Bay *Conwy* 124 B3
Bag Enderby *Lincs* 134 B3
Bagby *N Yorks* 158 C3
Bagendon *Glos* 63 C6
Bagh a Chaisteil = Castlebay *W Isles* 286 G2
Bagh Mor *W Isles* 286 A4
Bagh Shiarabhagh *W Isles* 286 F3
Baghasdal *W Isles* 286 E3
Bagillt *Flint* 126 B2
Baginton *Warks* 97 D6
Baglan *Neath* 40 B2
Bagley *Shrops* 110 C3
Bagnall *Staffs* 129 D4
Bagnor *W Berks* 46 C2
Bagshot *Sur* 48 C2
Bagshot *Wilts* 45 C7
Bagthorpe *Norf* 119 B4
Bagthorpe *Notts* 131 D4
Bagworth *Leics* 98 A1
Bagwy Llydiart *Hereford* 61 A6
Bail Ard Bhuirgh *W Isles* 288 B5
Bail Uachdraich *W Isles* 287 H3
Baildon *W Yorks* 147 D5
Baile *W Isles* 287 F4
Baile a Mhanaich *W Isles* 286 A3
Baile Ailein *W Isles* 288 E3
Baile an Truiseil *W Isles* 288 B4
Baile Boidheach *Argyll* 202 A2
Baile Glas *W Isles* 286 A4
Baile Mhartainn *W Isles* 287 G2
Baile Mhic Phail *W Isles* 287 G3
Baile Mor *Argyll* 224 D1

Baile Mor W Isles 287 H2
Baile na Creige W Isles 286 F2
Baile nan Cailleach W Isles 286 A3
Baile Raghaill W Isles 287 G2
Bailebeag Highld 240 A3
Baileyhead Cumb 176 B3
Bailiesward Aberds 255 C5
Baillieston Glasgow 205 B6
Bail'lochdrach W Isles 286 A4
Bail'Ur Tholastaidh W Isles 288 C6
Bainbridge N Yorks 156 B3
Bainsford Falk 208 B1
Bainshole Aberds 255 C7
Bainton E Yorks 150 B2
Bainton P'boro 100 A2
Bairnkine Borders 187 B5
Baker Street Thurrock 50 A3
Baker's End Herts 68 B3
Bakewell Derbys 130 C2
Bala = Y Bala Gwyn 108 B4
Balachuirn Highld 248 B2
Balavil Highld 241 B5
Balbeg Highld 251 D6
Balbeg Highld 251 C6
Balbeggie Perth 219 B6
Balbithan Aberds 245 A4
Balbithan Ho. Aberds 245 A5
Balblair Highld 264 D3
Balblair Highld 264 A1
Balby S Yorks 140 C3
Balchladich Highld 270 A3
Balchraggan Highld 252 C1
Balchraggan Highld 252 B1
Balchrick Highld 276 C2
Balchrystie Fife 221 D4
Balcladaich Highld 251 D4
Balcombe W Sus 35 C6
Balcombe Lane W Sus 35 C6
Balcomie Fife 221 C6
Balcurvie Fife 220 D3
Baldersby N Yorks 158 D2
Baldersby St James N Yorks 158 D2
Balderstone Lancs 145 D6
Balderton Ches 126 C3
Balderton Notts 132 D3
Baldhu Corn 4 C2
Baldinnie Fife 220 C4
Baldock Herts 84 D4
Baldovie Dundee 221 A4
Baldrine I o M 152 C4
Baldslow E Sus 23 A5
Baldwin I o M 152 C3
Baldwinholme Cumb 175 C6
Baldwin's Gate Staffs 112 A1
Bale Norf 120 B2
Balearn Aberds 269 D5
Balemartine Argyll 222 C2
Balephuil Argyll 222 C2
Balerno Edin 209 D4
Balevullin Argyll 222 C2
Balfield Angus 232 B3
Balfour Orkney 282 F5
Balfron Stirl 206 B3
Balfron Station Stirl 206 B3
Balgaveny Aberds 256 B1
Balgavies Angus 232 C3
Balgonar Fife 208 A3
Balgove Aberds 256 C3
Balgowan Highld 241 C4
Balgown Highld 258 B3
Balgrochan E Dunb 205 A6
Balgy Highld 249 A5
Balhaldie Stirl 218 D3
Balhalgardy Aberds 256 D2
Balham London 49 B5
Balhary Perth 231 D6
Baliasta Shetland 284 C8
Baligill Highld 279 B4
Balintore Angus 231 C6
Balintore Highld 265 C4
Balintraid Highld 264 C3
Balk N Yorks 158 C3
Balkeerie Angus 232 D1
Balkemback Angus 220 A3
Balkholme E Yorks 141 A5
Balkissock S Ayrs 180 C3
Ball Shrops 110 C2
Ball Haye Green Staffs 129 D4
Ball Hill Hants 46 C2
Ballabeg I o M 152 D2
Ballacannel I o M 152 C4
Ballachulish Highld 237 D4
Ballajora I o M 152 B4
Ballaleigh I o M 152 C3
Ballamodha I o M 152 D2
Ballantrae S Ayrs 180 C2
Ballaquine I o M 152 C4
Ballards Gore Essex 70 D3
Ballasalla I o M 152 B3
Ballasalla I o M 152 D2
Ballater Aberds 243 C6
Ballaugh I o M 152 B3
Ballaveare I o M 152 D3
Ballcorach Moray 254 D2
Ballechin Perth 230 C3
Balleigh Highld 264 B3
Ballencrieff E Loth 210 C1
Ballentoul Perth 230 B2
Ballidon Derbys 130 D2
Balliemore Argyll 214 D3
Balliemore Argyll 226 D3
Ballikinrain Stirl 206 B3
Ballimeanoch Argyll 214 A3
Ballimore Argyll 214 D2
Ballimore Stirl 217 C5
Ballinaby Argyll 200 B2
Ballindean Perth 220 B2
Ballingdon Suff 87 C4
Ballinger Common Bucks 67 C4
Ballingham Hereford 78 D3
Ballingry Fife 209 A4
Ballinlick Perth 230 D3
Ballinluig Perth 230 C3
Ballintuim Perth 231 C5
Balloch Angus 232 C1
Balloch Highld 252 B3
Balloch N Lnrk 207 C5
Balloch W Dunb 206 B1
Ballochan Aberds 244 C2
Ballochford Moray 255 C4
Ballochmorrie S Ayrs 181 C4
Balls Cross W Sus 34 D2
Balls Green Essex 71 A4
Ballygown Argyll 224 B3
Ballygrant Argyll 200 B3
Ballyhaugh Argyll 223 B4
Balmacara Highld 249 D5
Balmacara Square Highld 249 D5
Balmaclellan Dumfries 173 A4
Balmacneil Perth 230 C3
Balmacqueen Highld 259 A4
Balmae Dumfries 173 D4
Balmaha Stirl 206 A2
Balmalcolm Fife 220 D3
Balmeanach Highld 248 B2
Balmedie Aberds 245 A6
Balmer Heath Shrops 110 B3
Balmerino Fife 220 B3
Balmerlawn Hants 18 A2
Balmichael N Ayrs 191 B5
Balmirmer Angus 221 A5
Balmoral Castle and Gardens Aberds 243 C5
Balmore Highld 258 D2
Balmore Highld 251 C5
Balmore Highld 253 B4
Balmore Perth 230 C3
Balmule Fife 209 B5
Balmullo Fife 220 B4
Balmungie Highld 252 A3
Balnaboth Angus 231 B7
Balnabruaich Highld 264 D3
Balnabruich Highld 275 B5
Balnacoil Highld 274 C2
Balnacra Highld 250 B1
Balnafoich Highld 252 C2
Balnagall Highld 265 B4
Balnaguard Perth 230 C3
Balnahard Argyll 212 C2
Balnahard Argyll 224 C3
Balnain Highld 251 C6
Balnakeil Highld 277 B4
Balnaknock Highld 259 B4
Balnapaling Highld 264 D3
Balne N Yorks 140 B3
Balochroy Argyll 202 C2
Balone Fife 221 C4
Balornock Glasgow 205 B6
Balquharn Perth 219 A5
Balquhidder Stirl 217 B5
Balsall W Mid 97 D5
Balsall Common W Mid 97 D5
Balsall Heath W Mid 96 C3
Balscott Oxon 81 C6
Balsham Cambs 86 B1
Baltasound Shetland 284 C8
Balterley Staffs 128 D2
Baltersan Dumfries 171 A6
Balthangie Aberds 268 D3
Baltonsborough Som 29 B5
Balvaird Highld 252 A1
Balvicar Argyll 213 A5
Balvraid Highld 238 A2
Balvraid Highld 253 C4
Bamber Bridge Lancs 137 A4
Bambers Green Essex 69 A5
Bamburgh Northumb 199 C5
Bamburgh Castle Northumb 199 C5
Bamff Perth 231 C6
Bamford Derbys 130 A2
Bamford Gtr Man 138 B1
Bampton Cumb 164 D3
Bampton Devon 27 C4
Bampton Oxon 64 C4
Bampton Grange Cumb 164 D3
Banavie Highld 237 B5
Banbury Oxon 82 C1
Bancffosfelen Carms 57 A4
Banchory Aberds 244 C3
Banchory-Devenick Aberds 245 B6
Bancycapel Carms 57 A4
Bancyfelin Carms 56 A3
Bancyffordd Carms 73 C7
Bandirran Perth 220 A2
Banff Aberds 268 C1
Bangor Gwyn 123 C5
Bangor-is-y-coed Wrex 110 A2
Bangor on Dee Racecourse Wrex 110 A2
Banham Norf 103 C6
Banham Zoo, Diss Norf 103 C6
Bank Hants 18 A1
Bank Newton N Yorks 146 B3
Bank Street Worcs 79 A4
Bankend Dumfries 174 B3
Bankfoot Perth 219 A5
Bankglen E Ayrs 182 A4
Bankhead Aberdeen 245 A5
Bankhead Aberds 244 B3
Banknock Falk 207 C5
Banks Cumb 176 C3
Banks Lancs 136 A2
Bankshill Dumfries 185 D4
Banningham Norf 120 C4
Banniskirk Ho. Highld 280 C3
Bannister Green Essex 69 A6
Bannockburn Stirl 207 A6
Banstead Sur 35 A5
Bantham Devon 7 C5
Banton N Lnrk 207 C5
Banwell N Som 42 D2
Banyard's Green Suff 104 D3
Bapchild Kent 51 C6
Bar Hill Cambs 85 A5
Barabhas W Isles 288 C4
Barabhas Iarach W Isles 288 C4
Barabhas Uarach W Isles 288 B4
Barachandroman Argyll 225 D5
Barassie S Ayrs 192 B3
Baravullin Argyll 226 C3
Barbaraville Highld 264 C3
Barber Booth Derbys 129 A6
Barbieston S Ayrs 182 A2
Barbon Cumb 155 C5
Barbridge Ches 127 D6
Barbrook Devon 26 A2
Barby Northants 98 D2
Barcaldine Argyll 227 B4
Barcaldine Sea Life Centre Argyll 226 B4
Barcheston Warks 81 D5
Barcombe E Sus 22 A2
Barcombe Cross E Sus 22 A2
Barden N Yorks 157 B5
Barden Scale N Yorks 147 B4
Bardennoch Dumfries 182 C3
Bardfield Saling Essex 69 A6
Bardister Shetland 284 F5
Bardney Lincs 133 C6
Bardon Leics 114 D2
Bardon Mill Northumb 177 C5
Bardowie E Dunb 205 A5
Bardrainney Invclyd 204 A3
Bardsea Cumb 154 D2
Bardsey W Yorks 148 C2
Bardwell Suff 103 D5
Bare Lancs 145 A4
Barfad Argyll 202 B3
Barford Norf 104 A2
Barford Warks 81 A5
Barford St John Oxon 82 D1
Barford St Martin Wilts 31 B4
Barford St Michael Oxon 82 D1
Barfrestone Kent 53 D4
Bargod = Bargoed Caerph 41 B6
Bargoed = Bargod Caerph 41 B6
Bargrennan Dumfries 181 D5
Barham Cambs 100 D3
Barham Kent 53 D4
Barham Suff 88 B2
Barharrow Dumfries 172 C4
Barhill Dumfries 173 B6
Barholm Lincs 116 D3
Barkby Leics 98 A3
Barkestone-le-Vale Leics 115 B5
Barkham Wokingham 47 C5
Barking London 50 A1
Barking Suff 87 B6
Barking Tye Suff 87 B6
Barkingside London 50 A1
Barkisland W Yorks 138 B3
Barkston Lincs 116 A2
Barkston N Yorks 148 D3
Barkway Herts 85 D5
Barlaston Staffs 112 B2
Barlavington W Sus 20 A2
Barlborough Derbys 131 B4
Barlby N Yorks 149 D5
Barlestone Leics 98 A1
Barley Herts 85 D5
Barley Lancs 146 C2
Barley Mow T & W 179 D4
Barleythorpe Rutland 99 A5
Barling Essex 51 A6
Barlow Derbys 130 B3
Barlow N Yorks 140 A4
Barlow T & W 178 C3
Barmby Moor E Yorks 149 C6
Barmby on the Marsh E Yorks 141 A4
Barmer Norf 119 B5
Barmoor Castle Northumb 198 C3
Barmoor Lane End Northumb 198 C4
Barmouth = Abermaw Gwyn 90 A4
Barmpton Darl 167 D6
Barmston E Yorks 151 B4
Barnack P'boro 100 A2
Barnacle Warks 97 C6
Barnard Castle Durham 166 D3
Barnard Gate Oxon 65 B5
Barnardiston Suff 86 C3
Barnbarroch Dumfries 173 C6
Barnburgh S Yorks 140 C2
Barnby Suff 105 C5
Barnby Dun S Yorks 140 C4
Barnby in the Willows Notts 132 D3
Barnby Moor Notts 131 A6
Barnes Street Kent 36 B4
Barnet London 68 D2
Barnetby le Wold N Lincs 142 C2
Barney Norf 120 B1
Barnham Suff 103 D4
Barnham W Sus 20 B2
Barnham Broom Norf 104 A1
Barnhead Angus 233 C4
Barnhill Ches 127 D4
Barnhill Dundee 221 A4
Barnhill Moray 266 D2
Barnhills Dumfries 180 D1
Barningham Durham 166 D3
Barningham Suff 103 D5
Barnoldby le Beck NE Lincs 143 C4
Barnoldswick Lancs 146 C2
Barns Green W Sus 35 D4
Barnsley Glos 64 C1
Barnsley S Yorks 139 C6
Barnstaple Devon 25 B6
Barnston Essex 69 B6
Barnston Mers 126 A2
Barnstone Notts 115 B5
Barnt Green Worcs 96 D3
Barnton Ches 127 B6
Barnton Edin 209 C4
Barnwell All Saints Northants 100 C2
Barnwell St Andrew Northants 100 C2
Barnwood Glos 63 B4
Barochreal Argyll 226 D3
Barons Cross Hereford 78 B2
Barr S Ayrs 181 B4
Barra Airport W Isles 286 F2
Barra Castle Aberds 256 D2
Barrachan Dumfries 171 C5
Barrack Aberds 256 B3
Barraglom W Isles 288 D2
Barrahormid Argyll 213 D5
Barran Argyll 226 D3
Barrapol Argyll 222 C2
Barras Aberds 245 D5
Barras Cumb 165 D6
Barrasford Northumb 177 B7
Barravullin Argyll 213 B6
Barregarrow I o M 152 C3
Barrhead E Renf 205 C4
Barrhill S Ayrs 181 C4
Barrington Cambs 85 C5
Barrington Som 28 D3
Barripper Corn 3 B4
Barrmill N Ayrs 204 C3
Barrock Highld 281 A4
Barrock Ho. Highld 281 B4
Barrow Lancs 146 D1
Barrow Rutland 116 D1
Barrow Suff 86 A3
Barrow Green Kent 51 C6
Barrow Gurney N Som 43 C4
Barrow Haven N Lincs 142 A2
Barrow-in-Furness Cumb 153 D3
Barrow Island Cumb 153 D2
Barrow Nook Lancs 136 C3
Barrow Street Wilts 30 B2
Barrow upon Humber N Lincs 142 A2
Barrow upon Soar Leics 114 D3
Barrow upon Trent Derbys 114 C1
Barroway Drove Norf 102 A1
Barrowburn Northumb 188 B1
Barrowby Lincs 116 B1
Barrowcliff N Yorks 160 C4
Barrowden Rutland 99 A6
Barrowford Lancs 146 D2
Barrows Green Ches 128 D1
Barrows Green Cumb 154 C4
Barrow's Green Mers 127 A5
Barry Angus 221 A5
Barry = Y Barri V Glam 41 E6
Barry Island V Glam 41 E6
Barsby Leics 115 D4
Barsham Suff 105 C4
Barston W Mid 97 D5
Bartestree Hereford 78 C3
Barthol Chapel Aberds 256 C3
Barthomley Ches 128 D2
Bartley Hants 32 D2
Bartley Green W Mid 96 C3
Bartlow Cambs 86 C1
Barton Cambs 85 B6
Barton Ches 127 D4
Barton Glos 64 A2
Barton Lancs 136 C2
Barton Lancs 145 D5
Barton N Yorks 157 A6
Barton Oxon 65 C6
Barton Torbay 8 A3
Barton Warks 80 B4
Barton Bendish Norf 102 A3
Barton Hartshorn Bucks 82 D3
Barton in Fabis Notts 114 B3
Barton in the Beans Leics 97 A6
Barton-le-Clay Beds 84 D2
Barton-le-Street N Yorks 159 D6
Barton-le-Willows N Yorks 149 A6
Barton Mills Suff 102 D3
Barton on Sea Hants 17 B6
Barton on the Heath Warks 81 D5
Barton St David Som 29 B5
Barton Seagrave Northants 99 D5
Barton Stacey Hants 32 A3
Barton Turf Norf 121 C5
Barton-under-Needwood Staffs 113 D5
Barton-upon-Humber N Lincs 142 A2
Barton Waterside N Lincs 142 A2
Barugh S Yorks 139 C6
Barway Cambs 102 D1
Barwell Leics 98 B1
Barwick Herts 68 B3
Barwick Som 29 D5
Barwick in Elmet W Yorks 148 D2
Baschurch Shrops 110 C3
Bascote Warks 81 A7
Basford Green Staffs 129 D4
Bashall Eaves Lancs 145 C6
Bashley Hants 17 B6
Basildon Essex 51 A4
Basingstoke Hants 47 D4
Baslow Derbys 130 B2
Bason Bridge Som 28 A3

Bassaleg Newport 42 A1
Bassenthwaite Cumb 163 A5
Bassett Soton 32 D3
Bassingbourn Cambs 85 C5
Bassingfield Notts 115 B4
Bassingham Lincs 133 C4
Bassingthorpe Lincs 116 C2
Basta Shetland 284 D7
Baston Lincs 116 C4
Bastwick Norf 121 D6
Baswick Steer E Yorks 150 C3
Batchworth Heath Herts 67 D5
Batcombe Dorset 15 A6
Batcombe Som 29 B6
Bate Heath Ches 128 B1
Bateman's, Burwash E Sus 37 D4
Batford Herts 67 B6
Bath Bath 43 C6
Bath Abbey Bath 43 C6
Bath Racecourse Bath 43 C6
Bathampton Bath 44 C1
Bathealton Som 27 C5
Batheaston Bath 44 C1
Bathford Bath 44 C1
Bathgate W Loth 208 D2
Bathley Notts 132 D2
Bathpool Corn 10 D3
Bathpool Som 28 C2
Bathville W Loth 208 D2
Batley W Yorks 139 A5
Batsford Glos 81 D4
Battersby N Yorks 159 A4
Battersea London 49 B5
Battisborough Cross Devon 7 C4
Battisford Suff 87 B6
Battisford Tye Suff 87 B6
Battle E Sus 23 A5
Battle Powys 76 D4
Battle Abbey E Sus 23 A5
Battledown Glos 63 A5
Battlefield Shrops 111 D4
Battlesbridge Essex 70 D1
Battlesden Beds 67 A4
Battlesea Green Suff 104 D3
Battleton Som 27 C4
Battram Leics 98 A1
Battramsley Hants 18 B2
Baughton Worcs 80 C1
Baughurst Hants 46 D3
Baulking Oxon 64 D4
Baumber Lincs 134 B2
Baunton Glos 63 C6
Baverstock Wilts 31 B4
Bawburgh Norf 104 A2
Bawdeswell Norf 120 C2
Bawdrip Som 28 B3
Bawdsey Suff 88 C4
Bawtry S Yorks 141 D4
Baxenden Lancs 137 A6
Baxterley Warks 97 B5
Baybridge Hants 32 C4
Baycliff Cumb 154 D1
Baydon Wilts 45 B6
Bayford Herts 68 C3
Bayford Som 30 C1
Bayles Cumb 165 A5
Baylham Suff 88 B2
Baynard's Green Oxon 65 A6
Bayston Hill Shrops 94 A2
Baythorn End Essex 86 C3
Bayton Worcs 95 D4
Beach Highld 236 D3
Beachampton Bucks 83 D4
Beachamwell Norf 102 A3
Beachans Moray 253 B6
Beacharr Argyll 202 D1
Beachborough Kent 38 B3
Beachley Glos 62 D1
Beacon Devon 14 A1
Beacon End Essex 70 A3
Beacon Hill Sur 34 C1
Beacon's Bottom Bucks 66 D2
Beaconsfield Bucks 67 E4
Beacrabhaic W Isles 288 H2
Beadlam N Yorks 159 C5
Beadlow Beds 84 D3
Beadnell Northumb 189 A5
Beaford Devon 25 D6
Beal Northumb 199 B4
Beal N Yorks 140 A3
Beale Park, Goring W Berks 47 B3
Beamhurst Staffs 113 B4
Beaminster Dorset 15 A4

Beamish Durham 179 D4
Beamish Open Air Museum, Stanley Durham 179 D4
Beamsley N Yorks 147 B4
Bean Kent 50 B2
Beanacre Wilts 44 C3
Beanley Northumb 188 B3
Beaquoy Orkney 282 E4
Bear Cross Bmouth 17 B4
Beardwood Blkburn 137 A5
Beare Green Sur 35 B4
Bearley Warks 81 A4
Bearnus Argyll 224 B2
Bearpark Durham 167 A5
Bearsbridge Northumb 177 D5
Bearsden E Dunb 205 A5
Bearsted Kent 37 A5
Bearstone Shrops 111 B6
Bearwood Hereford 78 B1
Bearwood Poole 17 B4
Bearwood W Mid 96 C3
Beattock Dumfries 184 B3
Beauchamp Roding Essex 69 B5
Beauchief S Yorks 130 A3
Beaufort Bl Gwent 60 B3
Beaufort Castle Highld 251 B7
Beaulieu Hants 18 A2
Beauly Highld 252 B1
Beaumaris Anglesey 123 C6
Beaumaris Castle Anglesey 123 C6
Beaumont Cumb 175 C6
Beaumont Essex 71 A5
Beaumont Hill Darl 167 D5
Beausale Warks 97 D5
Beaworthy Devon 11 B5
Beazley End Essex 70 A1
Bebington Mers 126 A3
Bebside Northumb 179 A4
Beccles Suff 105 B5
Becconsall Lancs 136 A3
Beck Foot Cumb 155 B5
Beck Hole N Yorks 159 A7
Beck Row Suff 102 D2
Beck Side Cumb 153 B3
Beckbury Shrops 95 A5
Beckenham London 49 C6
Beckermet Cumb 162 D3
Beckfoot Cumb 163 D4
Beckfoot Cumb 174 D3
Beckford Worcs 80 D2
Beckham Wilts 45 C4
Beckingham Lincs 132 D3
Beckingham Notts 141 E5
Beckington Som 44 D2
Beckley E Sus 37 D6
Beckley Hants 17 B6
Beckley Oxon 65 B6
Beckton London 50 A1
Beckwithshaw N Yorks 147 B6
Becontree London 50 A1
Bed-y-coedwr Gwyn 108 C2
Bedale N Yorks 157 C6
Bedburn Durham 166 B4
Bedchester Dorset 30 D2
Beddau Rhondda 41 C5
Beddgelert Gwyn 107 B5
Beddingham E Sus 22 B2
Beddington London 49 C6
Bedfield Suff 88 A3
Bedford Beds 84 B2
Bedgebury Pinetum Kent 37 C5
Bedham W Sus 34 D3
Bedhampton Hants 19 A6
Bedingfield Suff 88 A2
Bedlam N Yorks 147 A6
Bedlington Northumb 179 A4
Bedlington Station Northumb 179 A4
Bedlinog M Tydf 41 A5
Bedminster Bristol 43 B4
Bedmond Herts 67 C5
Bednall Staffs 112 D3
Bedrule Borders 187 B5
Bedstone Shrops 94 D1
Bedwas Caerph 41 C6
Bedworth Warks 97 C6
Bedworth Heath Warks 97 C6
Beeby Leics 98 A3
Beech Hants 33 B5
Beech Staffs 112 B2
Beech Hill Gtr Man 137 C4
Beech Hill W Berks 47 C4
Beechingstoke Wilts 45 D4
Beedon W Berks 46 B2

Beeford E Yorks 151 B4
Beeley Derbys 130 C2
Beelsby NE Lincs 143 C4
Beenham W Berks 46 C3
Beeny Corn 10 B2
Beer Devon 14 C2
Beer Hackett Dorset 29 D6
Beercrocombe Som 28 C3
Beesands Devon 8 C2
Beesby Lincs 135 A4
Beeson Devon 8 C2
Beeston Beds 84 C3
Beeston Ches 127 D5
Beeston Norf 119 D6
Beeston Notts 114 B3
Beeston W Yorks 148 D1
Beeston Castle Ches 127 D5
Beeston Regis Norf 120 A3
Beeswing Dumfries 173 B6
Beetham Cumb 154 D3
Beetley Norf 119 D6
Begbroke Oxon 65 B5
Begelly Pembs 55 D7
Beggar's Bush Powys 77 A6
Beguildy Powys 93 D5
Beighton Norf 105 A4
Beighton S Yorks 131 A4
Beighton Hill Derbys 130 D2
Beith N Ayrs 204 C3
Bekesbourne Kent 52 D3
Bekonscot Model Village, Beaconsfield Bucks 67 D4
Belaugh Norf 121 D4
Belbroughton Worcs 96 D2
Belchamp Otten Essex 87 C4
Belchamp St Paul Essex 86 C3
Belchamp Walter Essex 87 C4
Belchford Lincs 134 B2
Belford Northumb 199 C5
Belhaven E Loth 210 C3
Belhelvie Aberds 245 A6
Belhinnie Aberds 255 D5
Bell Bar Herts 68 C2
Bell Busk N Yorks 146 B3
Bell End Worcs 96 D2
Bell o'th'Hill Ches 111 A4
Bellabeg Aberds 243 A6
Bellamore S Ayrs 181 C4
Bellanoch Argyll 213 C5
Bellaty Angus 231 C6
Belleau Lincs 135 B4
Bellehiglash Moray 254 C2
Bellerby N Yorks 157 B5
Bellever Devon 12 D1
Belliehill Angus 232 B3
Bellingdon Bucks 67 C4
Bellingham Northumb 177 A6
Belloch Argyll 190 B2
Bellochantuy Argyll 190 B2
Bells Yew Green E Sus 36 C4
Bellsbank E Ayrs 182 B2
Bellshill N Lnrk 207 D5
Bellshill Northumb 199 C5
Bellspool Borders 195 C6
Bellsquarry W Loth 208 D3
Belmaduthy Highld 252 A2
Belmesthorpe Rutland 116 D3
Belmont Blkburn 137 B5
Belmont London 49 C5
Belmont S Ayrs 192 C3
Belmont Shetland 284 C7
Belnacraig Aberds 243 A6
Belowda Corn 5 A4
Belper Derbys 114 A1
Belper Lane End Derbys 114 A1
Belsay Northumb 178 B3
Belsay Hall Northumb 178 B2
Belses Borders 187 A4
Belsford Devon 7 B6
Belstead Suff 88 C2
Belston S Ayrs 192 C3
Belstone Devon 11 B7
Belthorn Lancs 137 A6
Beltinge Kent 52 C3
Belton Leics 114 C2
Belton Lincs 116 B2
Belton N Lincs 141 C5
Belton Norf 105 A5
Belton House, Grantham Lincs 116 B2
Belton in Rutland Rutland 99 A5
Beltring Kent 37 B4
Belts of Collonach Aberds 244 C3
Belvedere London 50 B1
Belvoir Leics 115 B6

Belvoir Leics 115 B6
Bembridge I o W 19 C5
Bemersyde Borders 197 C4
Bemerton Wilts 31 B5
Bempton E Yorks 161 D5
Ben Alder Lodge Highld 229 A4
Ben Armine Lodge Highld 273 C5
Ben Casgro W Isles 288 E5
Benacre Suff 105 C6
Benbecula Airport W Isles 286 A3
Benbuie Dumfries 183 C5
Benderloch Argyll 226 C4
Bendronaig Lodge Highld 250 C2
Benenden Kent 37 C6
Benfield Dumfries 171 A5
Bengate Norf 121 C5
Bengeworth Worcs 80 C3
Benhall Green Suff 89 A4
Benhall Street Suff 89 A4
Benholm Aberds 233 B6
Beningbrough N Yorks 148 B4
Beningbrough Hall N Yorks 148 B4
Benington Herts 68 A2
Benington Lincs 117 A6
Benllech Anglesey 123 B5
Benmore Argyll 215 D4
Benmore Stirl 216 B4
Benmore Lodge Highld 271 C6
Bennacott Corn 10 B3
Bennan N Ayrs 191 C5
Benniworth Lincs 134 A2
Benover Kent 37 B5
Bensham T & W 179 C4
Benslie N Ayrs 204 D3
Benson Oxon 65 D7
Bent Aberds 233 A4
Bent Gate Lancs 137 A6
Benthall Northumb 189 A5
Benthall Shrops 95 A4
Bentham Glos 63 B5
Benthoul Aberdeen 245 B5
Bentlawnt Shrops 94 A1
Bentley Hants 33 A6
Bentley Suff 88 D2
Bentley S Yorks 140 C3
Bentley Warks 97 B5
Bentley Worcs 80 A2
Bentley Heath W Mid 97 D4
Benton Devon 26 B1
Bentpath Dumfries 185 C6
Bents W Loth 208 D2
Bentworth Hants 33 A5
Benvie Dundee 220 A3
Benwick Cambs 101 B5
Beoley Worcs 80 A3
Beoraidbeg Highld 235 A5
Bepton W Sus 20 A1
Berden Essex 69 A4
Bere Alston Devon 6 A3
Bere Ferrers Devon 6 A3
Bere Regis Dorset 16 B2
Berepper Corn 3 C4
Bergh Apton Norf 104 A4
Berinsfield Oxon 65 D6
Berkeley Glos 62 D2
Berkhamsted Herts 67 C4
Berkley Som 30 A2
Berkswell W Mid 97 D5
Bermondsey London 49 B6
Bernera Highld 249 D5
Bernice Argyll 215 C4
Bernisdale Highld 259 C4
Berrick Salome Oxon 65 D7
Berriedale Highld 275 B5
Berrier Cumb 164 C1
Berriew Powys 93 A5
Berrington Shrops 94 A3
Berrington Worcs 78 A3
Berrow Som 42 D2
Berrow Green Worcs 79 B5
Berry Down Cross Devon 25 A6
Berry Hill Glos 62 B1
Berry Hill Pembs 72 B3
Berry Pomeroy Devon 8 A2
Berryhillock Moray 267 C6
Berrynarbor Devon 25 A6
Bersham Wrex 110 A2
Berstane Orkney 282 F5
Berwick E Sus 22 B3
Berwick Bassett Wilts 45 B4
Berwick Hill Northumb 178 B3
Berwick St James Wilts 31 B4
Berwick St John Wilts 30 C3
Berwick St Leonard Wilts 30 B3

Berwick-upon-Tweed Northumb 198 A3
Bescar Lancs 136 B2
Besford Worcs 80 C2
Bessacarr S Yorks 140 C4
Bessels Leigh Oxon 65 C5
Bessingby E Yorks 151 A4
Bessingham Norf 120 B3
Besthorpe Norf 103 B6
Besthorpe Notts 132 C3
Bestwood Nottingham 114 A3
Bestwood Village Notts 114 A3
Beswick E Yorks 150 C3
Betchworth Sur 35 B5
Beth Shalom Holocaust Centre, Laxton Notts 132 C2
Bethania Ceredig 75 B4
Bethania Gwyn 107 A6
Bethania Gwyn 108 A2
Bethel Anglesey 122 C3
Bethel Gwyn 123 D5
Bethel Gwyn 109 B4
Bethersden Kent 38 A1
Bethesda Gwyn 123 D6
Bethesda Pembs 55 C6
Bethlehem Carms 58 C3
Bethnal Green London 49 A6
Betley Staffs 111 A6
Betsham Kent 50 B3
Betteshanger Kent 53 D5
Bettiscombe Dorset 14 B3
Bettisfield Wrex 110 B3
Betton Shrops 93 A7
Betton Shrops 111 B5
Bettws Bridgend 40 C4
Bettws Newport 61 B4
Bettws Newport 61 D4
Bettws Cedewain Powys 93 B5
Bettws Gwerfil Goch Denb 109 A5
Bettws Ifan Ceredig 73 B6
Bettws Newydd Mon 61 C5
Bettws-y-crwyn Shrops 93 C6
Bettyhill Highld 278 B3
Betws Carms 57 A6
Betws Bledrws Ceredig 75 C4
Betws-Garmon Gwyn 107 A5
Betws-y-Coed Conwy 124 D2
Betws-y-Rhos Conwy 125 B4
Beulah Ceredig 73 B5
Beulah Powys 76 B3
Bevendean Brighton 21 B6
Bevercotes Notts 132 B1
Beverley E Yorks 150 D3
Beverley Minster E Yorks 150 D3
Beverley Racecourse E Yorks 150 C3
Beverston Glos 63 D4
Bevington Glos 62 D2
Bewaldeth Cumb 163 A5
Bewcastle Cumb 176 B3
Bewdley Worcs 95 D5
Bewerley N Yorks 147 A5
Bewholme E Yorks 151 B4
Bexhill E Sus 23 B5
Bexley London 50 B1
Bexleyheath London 50 B1
Bexwell Norf 102 A2
Beyton Suff 87 A5
Bhaltos W Isles 287 A5
Bhatarsaigh W Isles 286 G2
Bibury Glos 64 C2
Bicester Oxon 65 A6
Bickenhall Som 28 D2
Bickenhill W Mid 97 C4
Bicker Lincs 117 B5
Bickershaw Gtr Man 137 C5
Bickerstaffe Lancs 136 C3
Bickerton Ches 127 D5
Bickerton N Yorks 148 B3
Bickington Devon 12 D2
Bickington Devon 25 B6
Bickleigh Devon 13 A4
Bickleigh Devon 7 A4
Bickleton Devon 25 B6
Bickley London 49 C7
Bickley Moss Ches 111 A4
Bicknacre Essex 70 C1
Bicknoller Som 27 B6
Bicknor Kent 37 A6
Bickton Hants 31 D5
Bicton Shrops 110 D3
Bicton Shrops 93 C6
Bicton Park Gardens Devon 13 C5
Bidborough Kent 36 B3

Biddenden Kent 37 C6
Biddenham Beds 84 C2
Biddestone Wilts 44 B2
Biddisham Som 42 D2
Biddlesden Bucks 82 C3
Biddlestone Northumb 188 C2
Biddulph Staffs 128 D3
Biddulph Moor Staffs 129 D4
Bideford Devon 25 C5
Bidford-on-Avon Warks 80 B4
Bidston Mers 136 D1
Bielby E Yorks 149 C6
Bieldside Aberdeen 245 B5
Bierley I o W 18 D4
Bierley W Yorks 147 D5
Bierton Bucks 66 B3
Big Pit National Mining Museum, Blaenavon Torf 60 C4
Big Sand Highld 261 C4
Bigbury Devon 7 C5
Bigbury on Sea Devon 7 C5
Bigby Lincs 142 C2
Biggar Cumb 153 D2
Biggar S Lnrk 195 C5
Biggin Derbys 129 D6
Biggin Derbys 113 A6
Biggin N Yorks 148 D4
Biggin Hill London 36 A2
Biggings Shetland 285 G3
Biggleswade Beds 84 C3
Bighouse Highld 279 B4
Bighton Hants 33 B5
Bignor W Sus 20 A2
Bigton Shetland 285 L5
Bilberry Corn 5 A5
Bilborough Nottingham 114 A3
Bilbrook Som 27 A5
Bilbrough N Yorks 148 C4
Bilbster Highld 281 C4
Bildershaw Durham 167 C5
Bildeston Suff 87 C5
Billericay Essex 69 D6
Billesdon Leics 99 A4
Billesley Warks 80 B4
Billingborough Lincs 116 B4
Billinge Mers 136 C4
Billingford Norf 120 C2
Billingham Stockton 168 C2
Billinghay Lincs 133 D6
Billingley S Yorks 140 C2
Billingshurst W Sus 34 D3
Billingsley Shrops 95 C5
Billington Beds 67 A4
Billington Lancs 145 D7
Billockby Norf 121 D6
Billown Motor Racing Circuit I o M 152 E2
Billy Row Durham 167 B4
Bilsborrow Lancs 145 D5
Bilsby Lincs 135 B4
Bilsham W Sus 20 B2
Bilsington Kent 38 B2
Bilson Green Glos 62 B2
Bilsthorpe Notts 131 C6
Bilsthorpe Moor Notts 131 D6
Bilston Midloth 209 D5
Bilston W Mid 96 B2
Bilstone Leics 97 A6
Bilting Kent 38 A2
Bilton E Yorks 151 D4
Bilton Northumb 189 B5
Bilton Warks 98 D1
Bilton in Ainsty N Yorks 148 C3
Bimbister Orkney 282 F4
Binbrook Lincs 143 D4
Binchester Blocks Durham 167 B5
Bincombe Dorset 15 C6
Bindal Highld 265 B5
Binegar Som 29 A6
Binfield Brack 47 B6
Binfield Heath Oxon 47 B5
Bingfield Northumb 178 B1
Bingham Notts 115 B5
Bingley W Yorks 147 D5
Bings Heath Shrops 111 D4
Binham Norf 120 B1
Binley Hants 46 D2
Binley W Mid 97 D6
Binley Woods Warks 97 D6
Binniehill Falk 207 C6
Binsoe N Yorks 157 D6
Binstead I o W 19 B4
Binsted Hants 33 A6
Binton Warks 80 B4
Bintree Norf 120 C2
Binweston Shrops 93 A7
Birch Essex 70 B3
Birch Gtr Man 138 C1
Birch Green Essex 70 B3
Birch Heath Ches 127 C5
Birch Hill Ches 127 B5
Birch Vale Derbys 129 A5
Bircham Newton Norf 119 B4
Bircham Tofts Norf 119 B4
Birchanger Essex 69 A5
Birchencliffe W Yorks 139 B4
Bircher Hereford 78 A2
Birchfield Highld 253 D5
Birchgrove Cardiff 41 D6
Birchgrove Swansea 40 B2
Birchington Kent 53 C4
Birchmoor Warks 97 A5
Birchover Derbys 130 C2
Birchwood Lincs 133 C4
Birchwood Warr 137 D5
Bircotes Notts 140 D4
Birdbrook Essex 86 C3
Birdforth N Yorks 158 D3
Birdham W Sus 20 C1
Birdholme Derbys 130 C3
Birdingbury Warks 82 A1
Birdland Park, Bourton-on-the-Water Glos 64 A2
Birdlip Glos 63 B5
Birds Edge W Yorks 139 C5
Birdsall N Yorks 149 A7
Birdsgreen Shrops 95 C5
Birdsmoor Gate Dorset 14 A3
Birdston E Dunb 205 A6
Birdwell S Yorks 139 C6
Birdwood Glos 62 B3
Birgham Borders 198 C1
Birkby N Yorks 158 A2
Birkdale Mers 136 B2
Birkenhead Mers 126 A3
Birkenhills Aberds 256 B2
Birkenshaw N Lnrk 207 D4
Birkenshaw W Yorks 139 A5
Birkhall Aberds 243 C6
Birkhill Angus 220 A3
Birkhill Dumfries 185 A5
Birkholme Lincs 116 C2
Birkin N Yorks 140 A3
Birley Hereford 78 B2
Birling Kent 50 C3
Birling Northumb 189 C5
Birling Gap E Sus 22 C3
Birlingham Worcs 80 C2
Birmingham W Mid 96 C3
Birmingham Botanical Gardens W Mid 96 C3
Birmingham International Airport W Mid 97 C4
Birmingham Museum and Art Gallery W Mid 96 C3
Birmingham Museum of Science and Technology W Mid 96 C3
Birnam Perth 230 D4
Birse Aberds 244 C2
Birsemore Aberds 244 C2
Birstall Leics 98 A2
Birstall W Yorks 139 A5
Birstwith N Yorks 147 B6
Birthorpe Lincs 116 B4
Birtley Hereford 78 A1
Birtley Northumb 177 B6
Birtley T & W 179 D4
Birts Street Worcs 79 D5
Bisbrooke Rutland 99 B5
Biscathorpe Lincs 134 A2
Biscot Luton 67 A5
Bish Mill Devon 26 C2
Bisham Windsor 47 A6
Bishampton Worcs 80 B2
Bishop Auckland Durham 167 C5
Bishop Burton E Yorks 150 D2
Bishop Middleham Durham 167 B6
Bishop Monkton N Yorks 148 A2
Bishop Norton Lincs 142 D1
Bishop Sutton Bath 43 D4
Bishop Thornton N Yorks 147 A6
Bishop Wilton E Yorks 149 B6
Bishopbridge Lincs 142 D2
Bishopbriggs E Dunb 205 B6
Bishopmill Moray 266 C3
Bishops Cannings Wilts 44 C4
Bishop's Castle Shrops 93 C7
Bishop's Caundle Dorset 29 D6
Bishop's Cleeve Glos 63 A5
Bishops Frome Hereford 79 C4
Bishop's Green Essex 69 B6
Bishop's Hull Som 28 C2
Bishop's Itchington Warks 81 B6
Bishops Lydeard Som 27 C6
Bishops Nympton Devon 26 C2
Bishop's Offley Staffs 112 C1
Bishop's Stortford Herts 69 A4
Bishop's Sutton Hants 33 B5
Bishop's Tachbrook Warks 81 A6
Bishops Tawton Devon 25 B6
Bishop's Waltham Hants 33 D4
Bishop's Wood Staffs 95 A6
Bishopsbourne Kent 52 D3
Bishopsteignton Devon 13 D4
Bishopstoke Hants 32 D3
Bishopston Swansea 57 D5
Bishopstone Bucks 66 B3
Bishopstone E Sus 22 B2
Bishopstone Hereford 78 C2
Bishopstone Swindon 45 A6
Bishopstone Wilts 31 C4
Bishopstrow Wilts 30 A2
Bishopswood Som 28 D2
Bishopsworth Bristol 43 C4
Bishopthorpe York 149 C4
Bishopton Darl 167 C6
Bishopton Dumfries 171 C6
Bishopton N Yorks 157 D7
Bishopton Renfs 205 A4
Bishopton Warks 81 B4
Bishton Newport 42 A2
Bisley Glos 63 C5
Bisley Sur 34 A2
Bispham Blkpool 144 C3
Bispham Green Lancs 136 B3
Bissoe Corn 4 C2
Bisterne Close Hants 17 A6
Bitchfield Lincs 116 C2
Bittadon Devon 25 A6
Bittaford Devon 7 B5
Bittering Norf 119 D6
Bitterley Shrops 94 D3
Bitterne Soton 32 D3
Bitteswell Leics 98 C2
Bitton S Glos 43 C5
Bix Oxon 47 A5
Bixter Shetland 285 H5
Blaby Leics 98 B2
Black Bourton Oxon 64 C3
Black Callerton T & W 178 C3
Black Clauchrie S Ayrs 181 C4
Black Corries Lodge Highld 228 C1
Black Crofts Argyll 226 C4
Black Dog Devon 12 A3
Black Heddon Northumb 178 B2
Black Lane Gtr Man 137 C6
Black Marsh Shrops 94 B1
Black Mount Argyll 228 D1
Black Notley Essex 70 A1
Black Pill Swansea 57 C6
Black Tar Pembs 55 D5
Black Torrington Devon 11 A5
Blackacre Dumfries 184 C3
Blackadder West Borders 198 A2
Blackawton Devon 8 B2
Blackborough Devon 13 A5
Blackborough End Norf 118 D3
Blackboys E Sus 36 D3
Blackbrook Derbys 114 A1
Blackbrook Mers 136 D4
Blackbrook Staffs 111 B6
Blackburn Aberds 255 C6
Blackburn Aberds 245 A5
Blackburn Blkburn 137 A5
Blackburn W Loth 208 D2
Blackcraig Dumfries 183 D5
Blackden Heath Ches 128 B2
Blackdog Aberds 245 A6
Blackfell T & W 179 D4
Blackfield Hants 18 A3
Blackford Cumb 175 B6
Blackford Perth 218 D3
Blackford Som 28 A4
Blackford Som 29 C6
Blackfordby Leics 114 D1
Blackgang I o W 18 D3
Blackgang Chine Fantasy I o W 18 D3
Blackhall Colliery Durham 168 B2
Blackhall Mill T & W 178 D3
Blackhall Rocks Durham 168 B2
Blackham E Sus 36 C2
Blackhaugh Borders 196 C3
Blackheath Essex 71 A4
Blackheath Suff 105 D5
Blackheath Sur 34 B3
Blackheath W Mid 96 C2
Blackhill Aberds 257 B5
Blackhill Aberds 269 D5
Blackhill Highld 258 C3
Blackhills Highld 253 A5
Blackhills Moray 266 D3
Blackhorse S Glos 43 B5
Blackland Wilts 44 C4
Blacklaw Aberds 268 D1
Blackley Gtr Man 138 C1
Blacklunans Perth 231 B5
Blackmill Bridgend 40 C4
Blackmoor Hants 33 B6
Blackmoor Gate Devon 26 A1
Blackmore Essex 69 C6
Blackmore End Essex 86 D3
Blackmore End Herts 67 B6
Blackness Falk 208 C3
Blacknest Hants 33 A6
Blacko Lancs 146 C2
Blackpool Blkpool 144 D3
Blackpool Devon 8 C2
Blackpool Pembs 55 C6
Blackpool Airport Lancs 144 D3
Blackpool Gate Cumb 176 B3
Blackpool Pleasure Beach Blkpool 144 D3
Blackpool Sea Life Centre Blkpool 144 D3
Blackpool Tower Blkpool 144 D3
Blackpool Zoo Park Blkpool 144 D3
Blackridge W Loth 208 D1
Blackrock Argyll 200 B3
Blackrock Mon 60 B4
Blackrod Gtr Man 137 B5
Blackshaw Dumfries 174 B3
Blackshaw Head W Yorks 138 A2
Blacksmith's Green Suff 88 A2
Blackstone W Sus 21 A5
Blackthorn Oxon 65 B7
Blackthorpe Suff 87 A5
Blacktoft E Yorks 141 A6
Blacktop Aberdeen 245 B5
Blacktown Newport 42 A1
Blackwall Tunnel London 49 A6
Blackwater Corn 4 C2
Blackwater Hants 34 A1
Blackwater I o W 18 C4
Blackwaterfoot N Ayrs 191 C4
Blackwell Darl 167 D5
Blackwell Derbys 129 B6
Blackwell Derbys 131 D4
Blackwell Warks 81 C5
Blackwell Worcs 96 D2
Blackwell W Sus 36 C1
Blackwood S Lnrk 194 B2
Blackwood = Coed Duon Caerph 41 B6
Blackwood Hill Staffs 129 D4
Blacon Ches 126 C3
Bladnoch Dumfries 171 B6
Bladon Oxon 65 B5
Blaen-gwynfi Neath 40 B3
Blaen-waun Carms 73 D5
Blaen-y-coed Carms 73 D6
Blaen-y-Cwm Denb 109 B5
Blaen-y-cwm Gwyn 108 C2
Blaen-y-cwm Powys 109 C5
Blaenannerch Ceredig 73 B5
Blaenau Ffestiniog Gwyn 108 A2
Blaenavon Torf 61 C4
Blaencelyn Ceredig 73 A6
Blaendyryn Powys 59 B6
Blaenffos Pembs 73 C4
Blaengarw Bridgend 40 B4
Blaengwrach Neath 59 E5
Blaenpennal Ceredig 75 B5
Blaenplwyf Ceredig 75 A4
Blaenporth Ceredig 73 B5
Blaenrhondda Rhondda 40 A4
Blaenycwm Ceredig 92 D2
Blagdon N Som 43 D4
Blagdon Torbay 8 A2
Blagdon Hill Som 28 D2
Blagill Cumb 165 A5
Blaguegate Lancs 136 C3
Blaich Highld 237 B4
Blain Highld 235 D5
Blaina Bl Gwent 60 C4
Blair Atholl Perth 230 B2
Blair Castle, Blair Atholl Perth 230 B2
Blair Drummond Stirl 207 A5
Blair Drummond Safari Park, Dunblane Stirl 207 A5
Blairbeg N Ayrs 191 B6
Blairdaff Aberds 244 A3
Blairglas Argyll 206 B1
Blairgowrie Perth 231 D5
Blairhall Fife 208 B3
Blairingone Perth 208 A2
Blairland N Ayrs 204 D3
Blairlogie Stirl 207 A6
Blairlomond Argyll 215 C4
Blairmore Argyll 215 D4
Blairnamarrow Moray 243 A5
Blairquhosh Stirl 206 B3
Blair's Ferry Argyll 203 B4
Blairskaith E Dunb 205 A5
Blaisdon Glos 62 B3
Blakebrook Worcs 95 D6
Blakedown Worcs 96 D1
Blakelaw Borders 197 C6
Blakeley Staffs 95 B6
Blakeley Lane Staffs 112 A3
Blakemere Hereford 78 C1
Blakeney Glos 62 C2
Blakeney Norf 120 A2
Blakeney Point NNR Norf 120 A2
Blakenhall Ches 111 A6
Blakenhall W Mid 96 B2
Blakeshall Worcs 95 C6
Blakesley Northants 82 B3
Blanchland Northumb 178 D1
Bland Hill N Yorks 147 B6
Blandford Forum Dorset 16 A2
Blandford St Mary Dorset 16 A2
Blanefield Stirl 205 A5
Blankney Lincs 133 C5
Blantyre S Lnrk 194 A1
Blar a'Chaorainn Highld 237 C5
Blaran Argyll 214 A1
Blarghour Argyll 214 A2
Blarmachfoldach Highld 237 C4
Blarnalearoch Highld 262 A3
Blashford Hants 17 A5
Blaston Leics 99 B5
Blatherwycke Northants 99 B6
Blawith Cumb 154 C1
Blaxhall Suff 89 B4
Blaxton S Yorks 141 C4
Blaydon T & W 178 C3
Bleadon N Som 42 D2
Bleak Hey Nook Gtr Man 138 C3
Blean Kent 52 C3
Bleasby Lincs 133 A6
Bleasby Notts 115 A5
Bleasdale Lancs 145 C5
Bleatarn Cumb 165 D5
Blebocraigs Fife 220 C4
Bleddfa Powys 77 A6
Bledington Glos 64 A3
Bledlow Bucks 66 C2
Bledlow Ridge Bucks 66 D2
Blegbie E Loth 210 D1
Blencarn Cumb 165 B4
Blencogo Cumb 175 D4
Blendworth Hants 33 D6
Blenheim Palace, Woodstock Oxon 65 B5
Blenheim Park Norf 119 B5
Blennerhasset Cumb 175 D4
Blervie Castle Moray 253 A6
Bletchingdon Oxon 65 B6
Bletchingley Sur 35 A6
Bletchley M Keynes 83 D5
Bletchley Shrops 111 B5
Bletherston Pembs 55 B6
Bletsoe Beds 84 B2
Blewbury Oxon 46 A3
Blickling Norf 120 C3
Blickling Hall, Aylsham Norf 120 C3
Blidworth Notts 131 D5
Blindburn Northumb 188 B1
Blindcrake Cumb 163 A4
Blindley Heath Sur 35 B6
Blisland Corn 10 D2
Bliss Gate Worcs 95 D5
Blissford Hants 31 D5
Blisworth Northants 83 B4
Blithbury Staffs 113 C4
Blitterlees Cumb 174 C4
Blockley Glos 81 D4
Blofield Norf 104 A4
Blofield Heath Norf 121 D5
Blo'Norton Norf 103 D6
Bloomfield Borders 187 A4
Blore Staffs 113 A5

Blount's Green Staffs 113 B4
Blowick Mers 136 B2
Bloxham Oxon 82 D1
Bloxholm Lincs 133 D5
Bloxwich W Mid 96 A2
Bloxworth Dorset 16 B2
Blubberhouses N Yorks 147 B5
Blue Anchor Som 27 A5
Blue Anchor Swansea 57 C5
Blue Planet Aquarium
 Ches 127 B4
Blue Row Essex 71 B4
Blundeston Suff 105 B6
Blunham Beds 84 B3
Blunsdon St Andrew
 Swindon 45 A5
Bluntington Worcs 96 D1
Bluntisham Cambs 101 D5
Blunts Corn 6 A2
Blyborough Lincs 142 D1
Blyford Suff 105 D5
Blymhill Staffs 112 D2
Blyth Notts 131 A6
Blyth Northumb 179 A5
Blyth Bridge Borders 195 B6
Blythburgh Suff 105 D5
Blythe Borders 197 B4
Blythe Bridge Staffs 112 A3
Blyton Lincs 141 D6
Boarhills Fife 221 C5
Boarhunt Hants 19 A5
Boars Head Gtr Man 137 C4
Boars Hill Oxon 65 C5
Boarshead E Sus 36 C3
Boarstall Bucks 66 B1
Boasley Cross Devon 11 B5
Boat of Garten Highld 242 A2
Boath Highld 264 C1
Bobbing Kent 51 C5
Bobbington Staffs 95 B6
Bobbingworth Essex 69 C5
Bocaddon Corn 5 B6
Bochastle Stirl 217 D6
Bocking Essex 70 A1
Bocking Churchstreet
 Essex 70 A1
Boddam Aberds 257 B6
Boddam Shetland 285 M5
Boddington Glos 63 A4
Bodedern Anglesey 122 B3
Bodelwyddan Denb 125 B5
Bodenham Hereford 78 B3
Bodenham Wilts 31 C5
Bodenham Arboretum
 and Earth Centre Worcs 95 C6
Bodenham Moor Hereford 78 B3
Bodermid Gwyn 106 D1
Bodewryd Anglesey 122 A3
Bodfari Denb 125 B5
Bodffordd Anglesey 123 C4
Bodham Norf 120 A3
Bodiam E Sus 37 D5
Bodiam Castle E Sus 37 D5
Bodicote Oxon 82 D1
Bodieve Corn 9 D5
Bodinnick Corn 5 B6
Bodle Street Green E Sus 23 A4
Bodmin Corn 5 A5
Bodnant Garden, Colwyn
 Bay Conwy 124 B3
Bodney Norf 103 B4
Bodorgan Anglesey 122 C3
Bodsham Kent 38 A3
Boduan Gwyn 106 C3
Bodymoor Heath Warks 97 B4
Bogallan Highld 252 A2
Bogbrae Aberds 257 C5
Bogend Borders 198 B1
Bogend S Ayrs 192 B3
Boghall W Loth 208 D2
Boghead S Lnrk 194 B2
Bogmoor Moray 267 C4
Bogniebrae Aberds 255 B6
Bognor Regis W Sus 20 C2
Bograxie Aberds 256 E2
Bogside N Lnrk 194 A3
Bogton Aberds 268 D1
Bogue Dumfries 182 D4
Bohenie Highld 239 D6
Bohortha Corn 4 D3
Bohuntine Highld 239 D6
Boirseam W Isles 287 F5
Bojewyan Corn 2 B1
Bolam Durham 167 C4

Bolam Northumb 178 A2
Bolberry Devon 7 D5
Bold Heath Mers 127 A5
Boldon T & W 179 C5
Boldon Colliery T & W 179 C5
Boldre Hants 18 B2
Boldron Durham 166 D3
Bole Notts 132 A2
Bolehill Derbys 130 D2
Boleside Borders 196 C3
Bolham Devon 27 D4
Bolham Water Devon 27 D6
Bolingey Corn 4 B2
Bollington Ches 129 B4
Bollington Cross Ches 129 B4
Bolney W Sus 35 D5
Bolnhurst Beds 84 B2
Bolshan Angus 233 C4
Bolsover Derbys 131 B4
Bolsterstone S Yorks 139 D5
Bolstone Hereford 78 D3
Boltby N Yorks 158 C3
Bolter End Bucks 66 D2
Bolton Cumb 165 C4
Bolton E Loth 210 C2
Bolton E Yorks 149 B6
Bolton Gtr Man 137 C6
Bolton Northumb 189 B4
Bolton Abbey N Yorks 147 B4
Bolton Abbey, Skipton
 N Yorks 147 B4
Bolton Bridge N Yorks 147 B4
Bolton-by-Bowland
 Lancs 146 C1
Bolton Castle, Leyburn
 N Yorks 156 B4
Bolton le Sands Lancs 145 A4
Bolton Low Houses Cumb 175 D5
Bolton-on-Swale N Yorks 157 B6
Bolton Percy N Yorks 148 C4
Bolton Town End Lancs 145 A4
Bolton upon Dearne
 S Yorks 140 C2
Boltonfellend Cumb 176 C2
Boltongate Cumb 175 D5
Bolventor Corn 10 D2
Bomere Heath Shrops 110 D3
Bon-y-maen Swansea 57 C6
Bonar Bridge Highld 264 A2
Bonawe Argyll 227 C5
Bonby N Lincs 142 B2
Boncath Pembs 73 C5
Bonchester Bridge
 Borders 187 B4
Bonchurch I o W 19 D4
Bondleigh Devon 12 A1
Bonehill Devon 12 D2
Bonehill Staffs 97 A4
Bo'ness Falk 208 B2
Bonhill W Dunb 206 C1
Boningale Shrops 95 A6
Bonjedward Borders 187 A5
Bonkle N Lnrk 194 A3
Bonnavoulin Highld 225 A4
Bonnington Edin 208 D4
Bonnington Kent 38 B2
Bonnybank Fife 220 D3
Bonnybridge Falk 207 B6
Bonnykelly Aberds 268 D3
Bonnyrigg and Lasswade
 Midloth 209 D6
Bonnyton Aberds 256 C1
Bonnyton Angus 220 A3
Bonnyton Angus 233 C4
Bonsall Derbys 130 D2
Bonskeid House Perth 230 B2
Bont Mon 61 B5
Bont-Dolgadfan Powys 91 B6
Bont-goch Ceredig 91 D4
Bont-newydd Conwy 125 B5
Bont Newydd Gwyn 108 A2
Bont Newydd Gwyn 108 C2
Bontddu Gwyn 91 A4
Bonthorpe Lincs 135 B4
Bontnewydd Ceredig 75 B5
Bontnewydd Gwyn 107 A4
Bontuchel Denb 125 D5
Bonvilston V Glam 41 D5
Booker Bucks 66 D3
Boon Borders 197 B4
Boosbeck Redcar 169 D4
Boot Cumb 163 D4
Boot Street Suff 88 C3
Booth W Yorks 138 A3
Booth Wood W Yorks 138 B3
Boothby Graffoe Lincs 133 D4
Boothby Pagnell Lincs 116 B2

Boothen Stoke 112 A2
Boothferry E Yorks 141 A5
Boothville Northants 83 A4
Bootle Cumb 153 B2
Bootle Mers 136 D2
Booton Norf 120 C3
Boquhan Stirl 206 B3
Boraston Shrops 95 D4
Borden Kent 51 C5
Borden W Sus 34 D1
Bordley N Yorks 146 A3
Bordon Hants 33 B7
Bordon Camp Hants 33 B6
Boreham Essex 70 C1
Boreham Wilts 30 A2
Boreham Street E Sus 23 A4
Borehamwood Herts 68 D1
Boreland Dumfries 185 C4
Boreland Stirl 217 A5
Borgh W Isles 286 F2
Borgh W Isles 287 F4
Borghastan W Isles 288 C3
Borgie Highld 278 C2
Borgue Dumfries 172 D4
Borgue Highld 275 B5
Borley Essex 87 C4
Bornais W Isles 286 D3
Bornesketaig Highld 258 A3
Borness Dumfries 172 D4
Borough Green Kent 36 A4
Boroughbridge N Yorks 148 A2
Borras Head Wrex 126 D3
Borreraig Highld 258 C1
Borrobol Lodge Highld 274 B2
Borrowash Derbys 114 B2
Borrowby N Yorks 158 C3
Borrowdale Cumb 163 C5
Borrowfield Aberds 245 C5
Borth Ceredig 90 C4
Borth-y-Gest Gwyn 107 C5
Borthwickbrae Borders 186 B3
Borthwickshiels Borders 186 B3
Borve Highld 259 D4
Borve Lodge W Isles 287 E5
Borwick Lancs 154 D4
Bosavern Corn 2 B1
Bosbury Hereford 79 C4
Boscastle Corn 10 B2
Boscombe Bmouth 17 B5
Boscombe Wilts 31 B6
Boscoppa Corn 5 B5
Bosham W Sus 19 A7
Bosherston Pembs 55 E5
Boskenna Corn 2 C2
Bosley Ches 129 C4
Bossall N Yorks 149 A6
Bossiney Corn 9 C6
Bossingham Kent 38 A3
Bossington Som 26 A3
Bostock Green Ches 127 C6
Boston Lincs 117 A6
Boston Long Hedges
 Lincs 117 A6
Boston Spa W Yorks 148 C3
Boston West Lincs 117 A5
Boswinger Corn 5 C4
Botallack Corn 2 B1
Botany Bay London 68 D2
Botcherby Cumb 175 C7
Botcheston Leics 98 A1
Botesdale Suff 103 D6
Bothal Northumb 179 A4
Bothamsall Notts 131 B6
Bothel Cumb 163 A4
Bothenhampton Dorset 15 B4
Bothwell S Lnrk 194 A2
Botley Bucks 67 C4
Botley Hants 32 D4
Botley Oxon 65 C5
Botolph Claydon Bucks 66 A2
Botolphs W Sus 21 B4
Bottacks Highld 263 D6
Bottesford Leics 115 B6
Bottesford N Lincs 141 C6
Bottisham Cambs 86 A1
Bottlesford Wilts 45 D5
Bottom Boat W Yorks 139 A6
Bottom House Staffs 129 D5
Bottom of Hutton Lancs 136 A3
Bottom o'th'Moor
 Gtr Man 137 B5
Bottomcraig Fife 220 B3
Botusfleming Corn 6 A3
Botwnnog Gwyn 106 C2
Bough Beech Kent 36 B2
Boughrood Powys 77 D5
Boughspring Glos 62 D1

Boughton Norf 102 A2
Boughton Notts 131 C6
Boughton Northants 83 A4
Boughton Aluph Kent 38 A2
Boughton Lees Kent 38 A2
Boughton Malherbe Kent 37 B6
Boughton Monchelsea
 Kent 37 A5
Boughton Street Kent 52 D2
Boulby Redcar 169 D5
Boulden Shrops 94 C3
Boulmer Northumb 189 B5
Boulston Pembs 55 C5
Boultenstone Aberds 243 A7
Boultham Lincs 133 C4
Bourn Cambs 85 B5
Bourne Lincs 116 C3
Bourne End Beds 83 C6
Bourne End Bucks 48 A1
Bourne End Herts 67 C5
Bournemouth Bmouth 17 B4
Bournemouth
 International Airport
 Dorset 17 B5
Bournes Green Glos 63 C5
Bournes Green Sthend 51 A6
Bournheath Worcs 96 D2
Bournmoor Durham 179 D5
Bournville W Mid 96 C3
Bourton Dorset 30 B1
Bourton N Som 42 C2
Bourton Oxon 45 A6
Bourton Shrops 94 B3
Bourton on Dunsmore
 Warks 98 D1
Bourton on the Hill Glos 81 D4
Bourton-on-the-Water
 Glos 64 A2
Bousd Argyll 223 A5
Boustead Hill Cumb 175 C5
Bouth Cumb 154 C2
Bouthwaite N Yorks 157 D5
Boveney Bucks 48 B2
Boverton V Glam 41 E4
Bovey Tracey Devon 12 D3
Bovingdon Herts 67 C5
Bovingdon Green Bucks 47 A6
Bovingdon Green Herts 67 C5
Bovinger Essex 69 C5
Bovington Camp Dorset 16 C2
Bow Borders 196 B3
Bow Devon 12 A2
Bow Orkney 283 H4
Bow Brickhill M Keynes 83 D6
Bow of Fife Fife 220 C3
Bow Street Ceredig 90 D4
Bowbank Durham 166 C2
Bowburn Durham 167 B6
Bowcombe I o W 18 C3
Bowd Devon 13 B6
Bowden Borders 197 C4
Bowden Devon 8 C2
Bowden Hill Wilts 44 C3
Bowderdale Cumb 155 A5
Bowdon Gtr Man 128 A2
Bower Northumb 177 A5
Bower Hinton Som 29 D4
Bowerchalke Wilts 31 C4
Bowerhill Wilts 44 C3
Bowermadden Highld 280 B4
Bowers Gifford Essex 51 A4
Bowershall Fife 208 A3
Bowertower Highld 280 B4
Bowes Durham 166 D2
Bowgreave Lancs 145 C4
Bowgreen Gtr Man 128 A2
Bowhill Borders 186 A3
Bowhouse Dumfries 174 B3
Bowland Bridge Cumb 154 C3
Bowley Hereford 78 B3
Bowlhead Green Sur 34 C2
Bowling W Dunb 205 A4
Bowling W Yorks 147 D5
Bowling Bank Wrex 110 A2
Bowling Green Worcs 79 B6
Bowmanstead Cumb 154 B2
Bowmore Argyll 200 C3
Bowness-on-Solway
 Cumb 175 B5
Bowness-on-
 Windermere Cumb 154 B3
Bowood House and
 Gardens, Calne Wilts 44 C3
Bowsden Northumb 198 B3
Bowside Lodge Highld 279 B4
Bowston Cumb 154 B3
Bowthorpe Norf 104 A2

Box Glos 63 C4
Box Wilts 44 C2
Box End Beds 84 C2
Boxbush Glos 62 B3
Boxford Suff 87 C5
Boxford W Berks 46 B2
Boxgrove W Sus 20 B2
Boxley Kent 37 A5
Boxmoor Herts 67 C5
Boxted Essex 87 D6
Boxted Suff 87 B4
Boxted Cross Essex 87 D6
Boxted Heath Essex 87 D6
Boxworth Cambs 85 A5
Boxworth End Cambs 85 A5
Boyden Gate Kent 53 C4
Boylestone Derbys 113 B5
Boyndie Aberds 268 C1
Boynton E Yorks 151 A4
Boysack Angus 233 D4
Boyton Corn 10 B4
Boyton Suff 89 C4
Boyton Wilts 30 B3
Boyton Cross Essex 69 C6
Boyton End Suff 86 C3
Bozeat Northants 83 B6
Braaid I o M 152 D3
Braal Castle Highld 280 B3
Brabling Green Suff 88 A3
Brabourne Kent 38 A2
Brabourne Lees Kent 38 A2
Brabster Highld 281 B5
Bracadale Highld 246 A2
Bracara Highld 235 A6
Braceborough Lincs 116 D3
Bracebridge Lincs 133 C4
Bracebridge Heath Lincs 133 C4
Bracebridge Low Fields
 Lincs 133 C4
Braceby Lincs 116 B3
Bracewell Lancs 146 C2
Brackenfield Derbys 130 D3
Brackenthwaite Cumb 175 D5
Brackenthwaite N Yorks 148 B1
Bracklesham W Sus 19 B7
Brackletter Highld 239 D5
Brackley Argyll 202 D2
Brackley Northants 82 D2
Brackloch Highld 270 B4
Bracknell Brack 47 C6
Braco Perth 218 D3
Bracobrae Moray 267 D6
Bracon Ash Norf 104 B2
Bracorina Highld 235 A6
Bradbourne Derbys 130 D2
Bradbury Durham 167 C6
Bradda I o M 152 E1
Bradden Northants 82 C3
Braddock Corn 5 A6
Bradeley Stoke 128 D3
Bradenham Bucks 66 D3
Bradenham Norf 103 A5
Bradenstoke Wilts 44 B4
Bradfield Essex 88 D2
Bradfield Norf 121 B4
Bradfield W Berks 47 B4
Bradfield Combust Suff 87 B4
Bradfield Green Ches 128 D1
Bradfield Heath Essex 71 A5
Bradfield St Clare Suff 87 B4
Bradfield St George Suff 87 A4
Bradford Corn 10 D2
Bradford Derbys 130 C2
Bradford Devon 11 A5
Bradford Northumb 199 C5
Bradford W Yorks 147 D5
Bradford Abbas Dorset 29 D5
Bradford Cathedral
 W Yorks 147 D5
Bradford Industrial
 Museum W Yorks 147 D5
Bradford Leigh Wilts 44 C2
Bradford-on-Avon Wilts 44 C2
Bradford on Tone Som 28 C1
Bradford Peverell Dorset 15 B6
Brading I o W 19 C5
Bradley Derbys 113 A6
Bradley Hants 33 A5
Bradley NE Lincs 143 C4
Bradley Staffs 112 D2
Bradley W Mid 96 B2
Bradley Green Worcs 80 A2
Bradley in the Moors
 Staffs 113 A4
Bradlow Hereford 79 D5
Bradmore Notts 114 B3

Bradmore W Mid 96 B1
Bradninch Devon 13 A5
Bradnop Staffs 129 D5
Bradpole Dorset 15 B4
Bradshaw Gtr Man 137 B6
Bradshaw W Yorks 138 B3
Bradstone Devon 11 C4
Bradwall Green Ches 128 C2
Bradway S Yorks 130 A3
Bradwell Derbys 129 A6
Bradwell Essex 70 A2
Bradwell M Keynes 83 D5
Bradwell Norf 105 A6
Bradwell Staffs 112 A2
Bradwell Grove Oxon 64 C3
Bradwell on Sea Essex 71 C4
Bradwell Waterside Essex 70 C3
Bradworthy Devon 24 D4
Bradworthy Cross Devon 24 D4
Brae Dumfries 173 A6
Brae Highld 261 B5
Brae Highld 272 D2
Brae Shetland 284 G5
Brae of Achnahaird Highld 270 C3
Brae Roy Lodge Highld 240 C1
Braeantra Highld 264 C1
Braedownie Angus 231 A6
Braefield Highld 251 C6
Braegrum Perth 219 B5
Braehead Dumfries 171 B6
Braehead Orkney 283 G6
Braehead Orkney 282 C5
Braehead S Lnrk 194 C3
Braehead S Lnrk 195 A4
Braehead of Lunan Angus 233 C4
Braehoulland Shetland 284 F4
Braehungie Highld 275 A5
Braelangwell Lodge Highld 263 A7
Braemar Aberds 243 C4
Braemore Highld 275 A4
Braemore Highld 262 C3
Braes of Enzie Moray 267 D4
Braeside Invclyd 204 A2
Braeswick Orkney 282 D7
Braewick Shetland 285 H5
Brafferton Darl 167 C5
Brafferton N Yorks 158 D3
Brafield-on-the-Green Northants 83 B5
Bragar W Isles 288 C3
Bragbury End Herts 68 A2
Bragleenmore Argyll 226 D4
Braichmelyn Gwyn 123 D6
Braid Edin 209 D5
Braides Lancs 144 B4
Braidley N Yorks 156 C4
Braidwood S Lnrk 194 B3
Braigo Argyll 200 B2
Brailsford Derbys 113 A6
Brainshaugh Northumb 189 C5
Braintree Essex 70 A1
Braiseworth Suff 104 D2
Braishfield Hants 32 C2
Braithwaite Cumb 163 B5
Braithwaite S Yorks 140 B4
Braithwaite W Yorks 147 C4
Braithwell S Yorks 140 D3
Bramber W Sus 21 A4
Bramcote Notts 114 B3
Bramcote Warks 97 C7
Bramdean Hants 33 C5
Bramerton Norf 104 A3
Bramfield Herts 68 B2
Bramfield Suff 105 D4
Bramford Suff 88 C2
Bramhall Gtr Man 128 A3
Bramham W Yorks 148 C3
Bramhope W Yorks 147 C6
Bramley Hants 47 D4
Bramley Sur 34 B3
Bramley S Yorks 140 D2
Bramley W Yorks 147 D6
Bramling Kent 53 D4
Brampford Speke Devon 13 B4
Brampton Cambs 100 D4
Brampton Cumb 165 C4
Brampton Cumb 176 C3
Brampton Derbys 130 B3
Brampton Hereford 78 D2
Brampton Lincs 132 B3
Brampton Norf 120 C4
Brampton Suff 105 C5
Brampton S Yorks 140 C2
Brampton Abbotts Hereford 62 A2
Brampton Ash Northants 99 C4
Brampton Bryan Hereford 94 D1
Brampton en le Morthen S Yorks 131 A4
Bramshall Staffs 113 B4
Bramshaw Hants 31 D6
Bramshill Hants 47 C5
Bramshott Hants 34 C1
Bran End Essex 69 A6
Branault Highld 235 D4
Brancaster Norf 119 A4
Brancaster Staithe Norf 119 A4
Brancepeth Durham 167 B5
Branch End Northumb 178 C2
Branchill Moray 266 D1
Brand Green Glos 62 A3
Branderburgh Moray 266 B3
Brandesburton E Yorks 151 C4
Brandeston Suff 88 A3
Brandhill Shrops 94 D2
Brandis Corner Devon 11 A5
Brandiston Norf 120 C3
Brandon Durham 167 B5
Brandon Lincs 116 A2
Brandon Northumb 188 B3
Brandon Suff 102 C3
Brandon Warks 97 D7
Brandon Bank Norf 102 C2
Brandon Creek Norf 102 B2
Brandon Parva Norf 104 A1
Brands Hatch Motor Racing Circuit Kent 50 C2
Brandsby N Yorks 159 D4
Brandy Wharf Lincs 142 D2
Brane Corn 2 C2
Branksome Poole 17 B4
Branksome Park Poole 17 B4
Bransby Lincs 132 B3
Branscombe Devon 14 C1
Bransford Worcs 79 B5
Bransgore Hants 17 B5
Branshill Clack 208 A1
Bransholme Hull 151 D4
Branson's Cross Worcs 96 D3
Branston Leics 115 C6
Branston Lincs 133 C5
Branston Staffs 113 C6
Branston Booths Lincs 133 C5
Branstone I o W 19 C4
Bransty Cumb 162 C2
Brant Broughton Lincs 133 D4
Brantham Suff 88 D2
Branthwaite Cumb 162 B3
Branthwaite Cumb 163 A5
Brantingham E Yorks 142 A1
Branton Northumb 188 B3
Branton S Yorks 140 C4
Branxholm Park Borders 186 B3
Branxholme Borders 186 B3
Branxton Northumb 198 C2
Brassey Green Ches 127 C5
Brassington Derbys 130 D2
Brasted Kent 36 A2
Brasted Chart Kent 36 A2
Brathens Aberds 244 C3
Bratoft Lincs 135 C4
Brattleby Lincs 133 A4
Bratton Telford 111 D5
Bratton Wilts 44 D3
Bratton Clovelly Devon 11 B5
Bratton Fleming Devon 26 B1
Bratton Seymour Som 29 C6
Braughing Herts 68 A3
Braunston Northants 82 A2
Braunston-in-Rutland Rutland 99 A5
Braunstone Town Leics 98 A2
Braunton Devon 25 B5
Brawby N Yorks 159 D6
Brawl Highld 279 B4
Brawlbin Highld 279 C6
Bray Windsor 48 B2
Bray Shop Corn 10 D4
Bray Wick Windsor 48 B1
Braybrooke Northants 99 C4
Braye Ald 7
Brayford Devon 26 B1
Braystones Cumb 162 D3
Braythorn N Yorks 147 C6
Brayton N Yorks 149 D5
Brazacott Corn 10 B3
Breach Kent 51 C5
Breachacha Castle Argyll 223 B4
Breachwood Green Herts 67 A6
Breacleit W Isles 288 D2
Breaden Heath Shrops 110 B3
Breadsall Derbys 114 B1
Breadstone Glos 62 C3
Breage Corn 3 C4
Breakachy Highld 251 B6
Bream Glos 62 C2
Breamore Hants 31 D5
Brean Som 42 D1
Breanais W Isles 287 B4
Brearton N Yorks 148 A2
Breascleit W Isles 288 D3
Breaston Derbys 114 B2
Brechfa Carms 58 B2
Brechin Angus 232 B3
Breck of Cruan Orkney 282 F4
Breckan Orkney 283 G3
Breckrey Highld 259 B5
Brecon = Aberhonddu Powys 60 A2
Brecon Beacons Mountain Centre Powys 60 A1
Bredbury Gtr Man 138 D2
Brede E Sus 23 A6
Bredenbury Hereford 79 B4
Bredfield Suff 88 B3
Bredgar Kent 51 C5
Bredhurst Kent 51 C4
Bredicot Worcs 80 B2
Bredon Worcs 80 D2
Bredon's Norton Worcs 80 D2
Bredwardine Hereford 78 C1
Breedon on the Hill Leics 114 C2
Breibhig W Isles 286 G2
Breibhig W Isles 288 D5
Breich W Loth 208 D2
Breightmet Gtr Man 137 C6
Breighton E Yorks 149 D6
Breinton Hereford 78 D2
Breinton Common Hereford 78 C2
Breiwick Shetland 285 J6
Bremhill Wilts 44 B3
Bremirehoull Shetland 285 L6
Brenchley Kent 37 B4
Brendon Devon 26 A2
Brenkley T & W 179 B4
Brent Eleigh Suff 87 C5
Brent Knoll Som 42 D2
Brent Pelham Herts 85 D6
Brentford London 49 B4
Brentingby Leics 115 D5
Brentwood Essex 69 D5
Brenzett Kent 38 C2
Brereton Staffs 113 D4
Brereton Green Ches 128 C2
Brereton Heath Ches 128 C3
Bressingham Norf 104 C1
Bretby Derbys 113 C6
Bretford Warks 98 D1
Bretforton Worcs 80 C3
Bretherdale Head Cumb 155 A4
Bretherton Lancs 136 A3
Brettabister Shetland 285 H6
Brettenham Norf 103 C5
Brettenham Suff 87 B5
Bretton Derbys 130 B2
Bretton Flint 126 C3
Brewer Street Sur 35 A6
Brewlands Bridge Angus 231 B5
Brewood Staffs 96 A1
Briach Moray 266 D1
Briants Puddle Dorset 16 B2
Brick End Essex 69 A5
Brickendon Herts 68 C3
Bricket Wood Herts 67 C6
Bricklehampton Worcs 80 C2
Bride I o M 152 A4
Bridekirk Cumb 163 A4
Bridell Pembs 73 B4
Bridestowe Devon 11 C6
Brideswell Aberds 255 C6
Bridford Devon 12 C3
Bridfordmills Devon 12 C3
Bridge Kent 52 D3
Bridge End Lincs 116 B4
Bridge Green Essex 85 D6
Bridge Hewick N Yorks 158 D2
Bridge of Alford Aberds 244 A2
Bridge of Allan Stirl 207 A5
Bridge of Avon Moray 254 C2
Bridge of Awe Argyll 227 D5
Bridge of Balgie Perth 229 D4
Bridge of Cally Perth 231 C5
Bridge of Canny Aberds 244 C3
Bridge of Craigisla Angus 231 C6
Bridge of Dee Dumfries 173 C5
Bridge of Don Aberdeen 245 A6
Bridge of Dun Angus 233 C4
Bridge of Dye Aberds 244 D3
Bridge of Earn Perth 219 C6
Bridge of Ericht Perth 229 C4
Bridge of Feugh Aberds 245 C4
Bridge of Forss Highld 279 B6
Bridge of Gairn Aberds 243 C6
Bridge of Gaur Perth 229 C4
Bridge of Muchalls Aberds 245 C5
Bridge of Oich Highld 240 B1
Bridge of Orchy Argyll 216 A2
Bridge of Waith Orkney 282 F3
Bridge of Walls Shetland 285 H4
Bridge of Weir Renfs 204 B3
Bridge Sollers Hereford 78 C2
Bridge Street Suff 87 C4
Bridge Trafford Ches 127 B4
Bridge Yate S Glos 43 B5
Bridgefoot Angus 220 A3
Bridgefoot Cumb 162 B3
Bridgehampton Som 29 C5
Bridgehill Durham 178 D2
Bridgemary Hants 19 A4
Bridgemont Derbys 129 A5
Bridgend Aberds 255 C6
Bridgend Aberds 244 A2
Bridgend Angus 232 B3
Bridgend Argyll 214 C1
Bridgend Argyll 200 B3
Bridgend Argyll 190 B3
Bridgend Cumb 164 D1
Bridgend Fife 220 C3
Bridgend Moray 255 C4
Bridgend N Lnrk 207 C4
Bridgend Pembs 73 B4
Bridgend W Loth 208 C3
Bridgend = Pen-y-bont ar Ogwr Bridgend 40 D4
Bridgend of Lintrathen Angus 231 C6
Bridgerule Devon 10 A3
Bridges Shrops 94 B1
Bridgeton Glasgow 205 B6
Bridgetown Corn 10 C4
Bridgetown Som 27 B4
Bridgham Norf 103 C5
Bridgnorth Shrops 95 B5
Bridgnorth Cliff Railway Shrops 95 B5
Bridgtown Staffs 96 A2
Bridgwater Som 28 B3
Bridlington E Yorks 151 A4
Bridport Dorset 15 B4
Bridstow Hereford 62 A1
Brierfield Lancs 146 D2
Brierley Glos 62 B2
Brierley Hereford 78 B2
Brierley S Yorks 140 B2
Brierley Hill W Mid 96 C2
Briery Hill Bl Gwent 60 C3
Brig o'Turk Stirl 217 D5
Brigg N Lincs 142 C2
Briggswath N Yorks 160 A2
Brigham Cumb 162 A3
Brigham E Yorks 150 B3
Brighouse W Yorks 139 A4
Brighstone I o W 18 C3
Brightgate Derbys 130 D2
Brighthampton Oxon 65 C4
Brightling E Sus 37 D4
Brightlingsea Essex 71 B4
Brighton Brighton 21 B6
Brighton Corn 4 B4
Brighton Hill Hants 33 A5
Brighton Museum and Art Gallery Brighton 21 B6
Brighton Racecourse Brighton 21 B6
Brighton Sea Life Centre Brighton 21 B6
Brightons Falk 208 C2
Brightwalton W Berks 46 B2
Brightwell Suff 88 C3
Brightwell Baldwin Oxon 66 D1
Brightwell cum Sotwell Oxon 65 D6
Brignall Durham 166 D3
Brigsley NE Lincs 143 C4
Brigsteer Cumb 154 C3
Brigstock Northants 99 C6
Brill Bucks 66 B1
Brilley Hereford 77 C6
Brimaston Pembs 55 B5
Brimfield Hereford 78 A3
Brimington Derbys 131 B4
Brimley Devon 12 D2
Brimpsfield Glos 63 B5
Brimpton W Berks 46 C3
Brims Orkney 283 K3
Brimscombe Glos 63 C4
Brimstage Mers 126 A3
Brinacory Highld 235 A6
Brind E Yorks 149 D6
Brindister Shetland 285 H4
Brindister Shetland 285 K6
Brindle Lancs 137 A5
Brindley Ford Staffs 128 D3
Brineton Staffs 112 D2
Bringhurst Leics 99 B5
Brington Cambs 100 D2
Brinian Orkney 282 E5
Briningham Norf 120 B2
Brinkhill Lincs 134 B3
Brinkley Cambs 86 B2
Brinklow Warks 98 D1
Brinkworth Wilts 44 A4
Brinmore Highld 252 D2
Brinscall Lancs 137 A5
Brinsea N Som 42 C3
Brinsley Notts 114 A2
Brinsop Hereford 78 C2
Brinsworth S Yorks 131 A4
Brinton Norf 120 B2
Brisco Cumb 175 C7
Brisley Norf 119 C6
Brislington Bristol 43 B5
Bristol Bristol 43 B4
Bristol City Museum and Art Gallery Bristol 43 B4
Bristol International Airport N Som 43 C4
Bristol Zoo Bristol 43 B4
Briston Norf 120 B2
Britannia Lancs 138 A1
Britford Wilts 31 C5
Brithdir Gwyn 91 A5
British Legion Village Kent 37 A5
British Museum London 49 A5
Briton Ferry Neath 40 B2
Britwell Salome Oxon 66 D1
Brixham Torbay 8 B3
Brixton Devon 7 B4
Brixton London 49 B6
Brixton Deverill Wilts 30 B2
Brixworth Northants 99 D4
Brize Norton Oxon 64 C4
Broad Blunsdon Swindon 64 D2
Broad Campden Glos 81 D4
Broad Chalke Wilts 31 C4
Broad Green Beds 83 C6
Broad Green Essex 70 A2
Broad Green Worcs 79 B5
Broad Haven Pembs 55 C4
Broad Heath Worcs 79 A4
Broad Hill Cambs 102 D1
Broad Hinton Wilts 45 B5
Broad Laying Hants 46 C2
Broad Marston Worcs 80 C4
Broad Oak Carms 58 C2
Broad Oak Cumb 153 A2
Broad Oak Dorset 14 B4
Broad Oak Dorset 30 D1
Broad Oak E Sus 23 A6
Broad Oak E Sus 36 D4
Broad Oak Hereford 61 A6
Broad Oak Mers 136 D4
Broad Street Kent 37 A6
Broad Street Green Essex 70 C2
Broad Town Wilts 45 B4
Broadbottom Gtr Man 138 D2
Broadbridge W Sus 19 A7
Broadbridge Heath W Sus 35 C4
Broadclyst Devon 13 B4
Broadfield Gtr Man 138 B1
Broadfield Lancs 136 A4
Broadfield Pembs 56 B1
Broadfield W Sus 35 C5
Broadford Highld 247 B5
Broadford Bridge W Sus 34 D3
Broadhaugh Borders 186 C3
Broadhaven Highld 281 C5
Broadheath Gtr Man 128 A2
Broadhembury Devon 13 A6
Broadhempston Devon 8 A2
Broadholme Derbys 114 A1
Broadholme Lincs 132 B3
Broadland Row E Sus 23 A6
Broadlay Carms 56 B3
Broadley Lancs 138 B1
Broadley Moray 267 C4
Broadley Common Essex 68 C4
Broadmayne Dorset 16 C1

Broadmeadows Borders 196 C3
Broadmere Hants 33 A5
Broadmoor Pembs 55 D6
Broadoak Kent 52 C3
Broadrashes Moray 267 D5
Broadsea Aberds 269 C4
Broadstairs Kent 53 C5
Broadstone Poole 17 B4
Broadstone Shrops 94 C3
Broadtown Lane Wilts 45 B4
Broadview Gardens,
  Hadlow Kent 36 B4
Broadwas Worcs 79 B5
Broadwater Herts 68 A2
Broadwater W Sus 21 B4
Broadway Carms 56 B2
Broadway Pembs 55 C4
Broadway Som 28 D3
Broadway Suff 105 D4
Broadway Worcs 80 D3
Broadwell Glos 64 A3
Broadwell Glos 62 B1
Broadwell Oxon 64 C3
Broadwell Warks 82 A1
Broadwell House
  Northumb 177 D7
Broadwey Dorset 15 C6
Broadwindsor Dorset 14 A4
Broadwood Kelly Devon 11 A7
Broadwoodwidger Devon 11 C5
Brobury Hereford 78 C1
Brochel Highld 248 B2
Brochloch Dumfries 182 C3
Brochroy Argyll 227 C5
Brockamin Worcs 79 B5
Brockbridge Hants 33 D5
Brockdam Northumb 189 A4
Brockdish Norf 104 D3
Brockenhurst Hants 18 A2
Brocketsbrae S Lnrk 194 C3
Brockford Street Suff 88 A2
Brockhall Northants 82 A3
Brockham Sur 35 B4
Brockhampton Glos 63 A6
Brockhampton Hereford 78 D3
Brockhole - National
  Park Visitor Centre,
  Windermere Cumb 154 A2
Brockholes W Yorks 139 B4
Brockhurst Derbys 130 C3
Brockhurst Hants 19 A5
Brocklebank Cumb 175 D6
Brocklesby Lincs 142 B3
Brockley N Som 42 C3
Brockley Green Suff 87 B4
Brockleymoor Cumb 164 B2
Brockton Shrops 94 C1
Brockton Shrops 94 B3
Brockton Shrops 93 A7
Brockton Shrops 95 A5
Brockton Telford 111 D6
Brockweir Glos 62 C1
Brockwood Hants 33 C5
Brockworth Glos 63 B4
Brocton Staffs 112 D3
Brodick N Ayrs 191 B6
Brodick Castle N Ayrs 191 B6
Brodsworth S Yorks 140 C3
Brogaig Highld 259 B4
Brogborough Beds 83 D6
Broken Cross Ches 128 B3
Broken Cross Ches 128 B3
Brokenborough Wilts 44 A3
Bromborough Mers 126 A3
Brome Suff 104 D2
Brome Street Suff 104 D2
Bromeswell Suff 88 B4
Bromfield Cumb 175 D4
Bromfield Shrops 94 D2
Bromham Beds 84 B2
Bromham Wilts 44 C3
Bromley London 49 C7
Bromley W Mid 96 C2
Bromley Common London 49 C7
Bromley Green Kent 38 B1
Brompton Medway 51 C4
Brompton N Yorks 158 B2
Brompton N Yorks 160 C3
Brompton-on-Swale
  N Yorks 157 B6
Brompton Ralph Som 27 B5
Brompton Regis Som 27 B4
Bromsash Hereford 62 A2
Bromsberrow Heath Glos 79 D5

Bromsgrove Worcs 96 D2
Bromyard Hereford 79 B4
Bromyard Downs Hereford 79 B4
Bronaber Gwyn 108 B2
Brongest Ceredig 73 B6
Bronington Wrex 110 B3
Bronllys Powys 77 D5
Bronnant Ceredig 75 B5
Bronte Parsonage
  Museum, Keighley
  W Yorks 147 D4
Bronwydd Arms Carms 73 D7
Bronydd Powys 77 C6
Brongarth Shrops 110 B1
Brook Carms 56 B2
Brook Hants 32 D1
Brook Hants 32 C2
Brook I o W 18 C2
Brook Kent 38 A2
Brook Sur 34 C2
Brook Sur 34 B3
Brook End Beds 84 A2
Brook Hill Hants 31 D6
Brook Street Kent 36 B3
Brook Street Kent 38 B1
Brook Street W Sus 35 D6
Brooke Norf 104 B3
Brooke Rutland 99 A5
Brookenby Lincs 143 D4
Brookend Glos 62 D1
Brookfield Renfs 205 B4
Brookhouse Lancs 145 A5
Brookhouse Green Ches 128 C3
Brookland Kent 38 C1
Brooklands Dumfries 173 A6
Brooklands Gtr Man 137 D6
Brooklands Shrops 111 A4
Brookmans Park Herts 68 C2
Brooks Powys 93 B5
Brooks Green W Sus 35 D4
Brookthorpe Glos 63 B4
Brookville Norf 102 B3
Brookwood Sur 34 A2
Broom Beds 84 C3
Broom S Yorks 140 D2
Broom Warks 80 B3
Broom Worcs 96 D2
Broom Green Norf 120 C1
Broom Hill Dorset 17 A4
Broome Norf 105 B4
Broome Shrops 94 C2
Broome Park Northumb 189 B4
Broomedge Warr 128 A2
Broomer's Corner W Sus 35 D4
Broomfield Aberds 257 C4
Broomfield Essex 69 B7
Broomfield Kent 37 A6
Broomfield Kent 52 C3
Broomfield Som 28 B2
Broomfleet E Yorks 141 A6
Broomhall Ches 111 A5
Broomhall Windsor 48 C2
Broomhaugh Northumb 178 C2
Broomhill Norf 102 A2
Broomhill Northumb 189 C5
Broomhill S Yorks 140 C2
Broomholm Norf 121 B5
Broomley Northumb 178 C2
Broompark Durham 167 A5
Broom's Green Hereford 79 D5
Broomy Lodge Hants 31 D6
Brora Highld 274 D3
Broseley Shrops 95 A4
Brotherhouse Bar Lincs 117 D5
Brotherstone Borders 197 C5
Brothertoft Lincs 117 A5
Brotherton N Yorks 140 A2
Brotton Redcar 169 D4
Broubster Highld 279 B6
Brough Cumb 165 D5
Brough Derbys 130 A1
Brough E Yorks 142 A1
Brough Highld 280 A4
Brough Notts 132 D3
Brough Orkney 282 F4
Brough Shetland 284 F6
Brough Shetland 284 G7
Brough Shetland 284 F7
Brough Shetland 285 J7
Brough Shetland 285 H6
Brough Lodge Shetland 284 D7
Brough Sowerby Cumb 165 D5
Broughall Shrops 111 A4
Broughton Borders 195 C6
Broughton Cambs 101 D4
Broughton Flint 126 C3
Broughton Hants 32 B2

Broughton Lancs 145 D5
Broughton M Keynes 83 C5
Broughton N Lincs 142 C1
Broughton Northants 99 D5
Broughton N Yorks 146 B3
Broughton N Yorks 159 D6
Broughton Orkney 282 C5
Broughton Oxon 81 D7
Broughton V Glam 40 D4
Broughton Astley Leics 98 B2
Broughton Beck Cumb 154 C1
Broughton Common Wilts 44 C2
Broughton Gifford Wilts 44 C2
Broughton Hackett Worcs 80 B2
Broughton in Furness
  Cumb 153 B3
Broughton Mills Cumb 153 A3
Broughton Moor Cumb 162 A3
Broughton Park Gtr Man 138 C1
Broughton Poggs Oxon 64 C3
Broughtown Orkney 282 C7
Broughty Ferry Dundee 221 A4
Browhouses Dumfries 175 B5
Browland Shetland 285 H4
Brown Candover Hants 33 B4
Brown Edge Lancs 136 B2
Brown Edge Staffs 129 D4
Brown Heath Ches 127 C4
Brownhill Aberds 256 D5
Brownhill Aberds 256 B1
Brownhill Blkburn 145 D6
Brownhill Shrops 110 C3
Brownhills Fife 221 C5
Brownhills W Mid 96 A3
Brownlow Ches 128 C3
Brownlow Heath Ches 128 C3
Brownmuir Aberds 233 A5
Brown's End Glos 79 D5
Brownshill Glos 63 C4
Brownston Devon 7 B6
Brownyside Northumb 189 A4
Broxa N Yorks 160 B3
Broxbourne Herts 68 C3
Broxburn E Loth 210 C3
Broxburn W Loth 208 C3
Broxholme Lincs 133 B4
Broxted Essex 69 A5
Broxton Ches 127 D4
Broxwood Hereford 78 B1
Broyle Side E Sus 22 A2
Brù W Isles 288 C4
Bruairnis W Isles 286 F3
Bruan Highld 275 A7
Bruar Lodge Perth 230 A2
Brucehill W Dunb 206 C1
Bruera Ches 127 C4
Bruern Abbey Oxon 64 A3
Bruichladdich Argyll 200 B2
Bruisyard Suff 88 A4
Brundy N Lincs 141 C6
Brund Staffs 129 C6
Brundall Norf 104 A4
Brundish Suff 88 A3
Brundish Street Suff 104 D3
Brunery Highld 235 C6
Brunshaw Lancs 146 D2
Brunswick Village T & W 179 B4
Bruntcliffe W Yorks 139 A5
Bruntingthorpe Leics 98 B3
Brunton Fife 220 B3
Brunton Northumb 189 A5
Brunton Wilts 45 D6
Brushford Devon 12 A1
Brushford Som 27 C4
Bryan's Green Worcs —
Bryanston Dorset 16 A2
Brydekirk Dumfries 175 A4
Bryher Scilly 2 E3
Brymbo Wrex 126 D2
Brympton Som 29 D5
Bryn Carms 57 B5
Bryn Gtr Man 137 C4
Bryn Neath 40 B3
Bryn Shrops 93 C6
Bryn-coch Neath 40 B2
Bryn Du Anglesey 122 C3
Bryn Gates Gtr Man 137 C4
Bryn-glas Conwy 124 C3
Bryn Golau Rhondda 41 C4
Bryn-Iwan Carms 73 C6
Bryn-mawr Gwyn 106 C2
Bryn-nantllech Conwy 125 C4
Bryn-penarth Powys 93 A5
Bryn Rhyd-yr-Arian
  Conwy 125 C4
Bryn Saith Marchog
  Denb 125 D5

Bryn Sion Gwyn 91 A6
Bryn-y-gwenin Mon 61 B5
Bryn-y-maen Conwy 124 B3
Bryn-yr-eryr Gwyn 106 B3
Brynamman Carms 59 D4
Brynberian Pembs 72 C4
Brynbryddan Neath 40 B2
Brynbuga = Usk Mon 61 C5
Bryncae Rhondda 41 C4
Bryncethin Bridgend 40 C4
Bryncir Gwyn 107 B4
Bryncroes Gwyn 106 C2
Bryncrug Gwyn 90 B4
Bryneglwys Denb 109 A6
Brynford Flint 126 B1
Bryngwran Anglesey 122 C3
Bryngwyn Ceredig 73 B5
Bryngwyn Mon 61 C5
Bryngwyn Powys 77 C5
Brynhenllan Pembs 72 C3
Brynhoffnant Ceredig 73 A6
Brynithel Bl Gwent 41 A7
Brynmawr Bl Gwent 60 B3
Brynmenyn Bridgend 40 C4
Brynmill Swansea 57 C6
Brynna Rhondda 41 C4
Brynrefail Anglesey 123 B4
Brynrefail Gwyn 123 D5
Brynsadler Rhondda 41 C5
Brynsiencyn Anglesey 123 D4
Brynteg Anglesey 123 B4
Brynteg Ceredig 58 A1
Buaile nam Bodach
  W Isles 286 F3
Bualintur Highld 246 B3
Buarthmeini Gwyn 108 B3
Bubbenhall Warks 97 D6
Bubwith E Yorks 149 D6
Buccleuch Borders 185 A6
Buchanty Perth 218 B4
Buchlyvie Stirl 206 A3
Buckabank Cumb 164 A1
Buckden Cambs 84 A3
Buckden N Yorks 156 D3
Buckenham Norf 105 A4
Buckerell Devon 13 A6
Buckfast Devon 7 A6
Buckfast Abbey,
  Buckfastleigh Devon 7 A6
Buckfastleigh Devon 7 A6
Buckhaven Fife 209 A6
Buckholm Borders 196 C3
Buckholt Mon 61 B7
Buckhorn Weston Dorset 30 C1
Buckhurst Hill Essex 68 D4
Buckie Moray 267 C5
Buckies Highld 280 B3
Buckingham Bucks 82 D3
Buckingham Palace
  London 49 B5
Buckland Bucks 66 B3
Buckland Devon 7 C5
Buckland Glos 80 D3
Buckland Herts 85 D5
Buckland Kent 39 A5
Buckland Oxon 64 D4
Buckland Sur 35 A5
Buckland Abbey Devon 6 A3
Buckland Brewer Devon 25 C5
Buckland Common Bucks 67 C4
Buckland Dinham Som 43 D6
Buckland Filleigh Devon 11 A5
Buckland in the Moor
  Devon 12 D2
Buckland Monachorum
  Devon 6 A3
Buckland Newton Dorset 15 A6
Buckland St Mary Som 28 D2
Bucklebury W Berks 46 B3
Bucklegate Lincs 117 B6
Bucklerheads Angus 221 A4
Bucklers Hard Hants 18 B3
Bucklesham Suff 88 C3
Buckley = Bwcle Flint 126 C2
Bucklow Hill Ches 128 A2
Buckminster Leics 116 C1
Bucknall Lincs 133 C6
Bucknall Stoke 112 A3
Bucknell Oxon 65 A6
Bucknell Shrops 94 D1
Buckpool Moray 267 C5
Buck's Cross Devon 24 C4
Bucks Green W Sus 34 C3
Buck's Hill Herts 67 C5
Bucks Horn Oak Hants 33 A7
Buck's Mills Devon 25 C4

Bucksburn Aberdeen 245 B5
Buckskin Hants 47 D4
Buckton E Yorks 161 D5
Buckton Hereford 94 D1
Buckton Northumb 199 C4
Buckworth Cambs 100 D3
Budbrooke Warks 81 A5
Budby Notts 131 C6
Budd's Titson Corn 10 A3
Bude Corn 10 A3
Budlake Devon 13 B4
Budle Northumb 199 C5
Budleigh Salterton Devon 13 C5
Budock Water Corn 4 D2
Buerton Ches 111 A5
Buffler's Holt Bucks 82 D3
Bugbrooke Northants 82 B3
Buglawton Ches 128 C3
Bugle Corn 5 B5
Bugley Wilts 30 A2
Bugthorpe E Yorks 149 B6
Buildwas Shrops 95 A4
Builth Road Powys 76 B4
Builth Wells = Llanfair-
  ym-Muallt Powys 76 B4
Buirgh W Isles 287 E5
Bulby Lincs 116 C3
Bulcote Notts 115 A4
Buldoo Highld 279 B5
Bulford Wilts 31 A5
Bulford Camp Wilts 31 A5
Bulkeley Ches 127 D5
Bulkington Warks 97 C6
Bulkington Wilts 44 D3
Bulkworthy Devon 25 D4
Bull Hill Hants 18 B2
Bullamoor N Yorks 158 B2
Bullbridge Derbys 130 D3
Bullbrook Brack 48 C1
Bulley Glos 62 B3
Bullgill Cumb 162 A3
Bullington Hants 32 A3
Bullington Lincs 133 B5
Bull's Green Herts 68 B2
Bullwood Argyll 203 A6
Bulmer Essex 87 C4
Bulmer N Yorks 149 A5
Bulmer Tye Essex 87 D4
Bulphan Thurrock 50 A3
Bulverhythe E Sus 23 B5
Bulwark Aberds 257 B4
Bulwell Nottingham 114 A3
Bulwick Northants 99 B6
Bumble's Green Essex 68 C4
Bun Abhainn Eadarra
  W Isles 288 G2
Bun a'Mhuillin W Isles 286 E3
Bun Loyne Highld 239 B6
Bunacaimb Highld 235 B5
Bunarkaig Highld 239 D5
Bunbury Ches 127 D5
Bunbury Heath Ches 127 D5
Bunchrew Highld 252 B2
Bundalloch Highld 249 D5
Buness Shetland 284 C8
Bunessan Argyll 224 D2
Bungay Suff 104 C4
Bunker's Hill Lincs 133 B4
Bunker's Hill Lincs 134 D2
Bunkers Hill Oxon 65 B5
Bunloit Highld 251 D7
Bunnahabhain Argyll 201 A4
Bunny Notts 114 C3
Buntait Highld 251 C5
Buntingford Herts 68 A3
Bunwell Norf 104 B2
Burbage Derbys 129 B5
Burbage Leics 98 B1
Burbage Wilts 45 C6
Burchett's Green Windsor 47 A6
Burcombe Wilts 31 B4
Burcot Oxon 65 D6
Burcott Bucks 66 A3
Burdon T & W 179 D5
Bures Suff 87 D5
Bures Green Suff 87 D5
Burford Ches 127 D6
Burford Oxon 64 B3
Burford Shrops 78 A3
Burg Argyll 224 B2
Burgar Orkney 282 E4
Burgate Hants 31 D5
Burgate Suff 104 D1
Burgess Hill W Sus 21 A6
Burgh Suff 88 B3
Burgh-by-Sands Cumb 175 C6
Burgh Castle Norf 105 A5

Burgh Heath Sur 35 A5
Burgh le Marsh Lincs 135 C5
Burgh Muir Aberds 256 D2
Burgh next Aylsham Norf 120 C4
Burgh on Bain Lincs 134 A2
Burgh St Margaret Norf 121 D6
Burgh St Peter Norf 105 B5
Burghclere Hants 46 C2
Burghead Moray 266 C2
Burghfield W Berks 47 C4
Burghfield Common
  W Berks 47 C4
Burghfield Hill W Berks 47 C4
Burghill Hereford 78 C2
Burghwallis S Yorks 140 B3
Burham Kent 51 C4
Buriton Hants 33 C6
Burland Ches 127 D6
Burlawn Corn 9 D5
Burleigh Brack 48 C1
Burlescombe Devon 27 D5
Burleston Dorset 16 B1
Burley Hants 17 A6
Burley Rutland 116 D1
Burley W Yorks 148 D1
Burley Gate Hereford 78 C3
Burley in Wharfedale
  W Yorks 147 C5
Burley Lodge Hants 17 A6
Burley Street Hants 17 A6
Burleydam Ches 111 A5
Burlingjobb Powys 77 B6
Burlow E Sus 22 A3
Burlton Shrops 110 C3
Burmarsh Kent 38 B2
Burmington Warks 81 D5
Burn N Yorks 140 A3
Burn of Cambus Stirl 218 D2
Burnaston Derbys 113 B6
Burnbank S Lnrk 194 A2
Burnby E Yorks 150 C1
Burncross S Yorks 139 D6
Burneside Cumb 154 B4
Burness Orkney 282 C7
Burneston N Yorks 157 C7
Burnett Bath 43 C5
Burnfoot Borders 186 B3
Burnfoot Borders 186 B4
Burnfoot E Ayrs 182 B2
Burnfoot Perth 219 D4
Burnham Bucks 48 A2
Burnham N Lincs 142 B2
Burnham Deepdale Norf 119 A5
Burnham Green Herts 68 B2
Burnham Market Norf 119 A5
Burnham Norton Norf 119 A5
Burnham-on-Crouch
  Essex 70 D3
Burnham-on-Sea Som 28 A3
Burnham Overy Staithe
  Norf 119 A5
Burnham Overy Town
  Norf 119 A5
Burnham Thorpe Norf 119 A5
Burnhead Dumfries 183 C6
Burnhead S Ayrs 181 A5
Burnhervie Aberds 245 A4
Burnhill Green Staffs 95 A5
Burnhope Durham 167 A4
Burnhouse N Ayrs 204 C3
Burniston N Yorks 160 B4
Burnlee W Yorks 139 C4
Burnley Lancs 146 D2
Burnley Lane Lancs 146 D2
Burnmouth Borders 211 D6
Burnopfield Durham 178 D3
Burnsall N Yorks 147 A4
Burnside Angus 232 C3
Burnside E Ayrs 182 A3
Burnside Fife 219 D6
Burnside Shetland 284 F4
Burnside S Lnrk 205 B6
Burnside W Loth 208 C3
Burnside of Duntrune
  Angus 220 A4
Burnswark Dumfries 175 A4
Burnt Heath Derbys 130 B2
Burnt Houses Durham 166 C4
Burnt Yates N Yorks 147 A6
Burntcommon Sur 34 A3
Burnthouse Corn 3 C6
Burntisland Fife 209 B5
Burnton E Ayrs 182 B2
Burntwood Staffs 96 A3
Burnwynd Edin 208 D4
Burpham Sur 34 A3
Burpham W Sus 20 B3

Burradon Northumb 188 C2
Burradon T & W 179 B4
Burrafirth Shetland 284 B8
Burraland Shetland 284 F5
Burraland Shetland 285 J4
Burras Corn 3 B4
Burravoe Shetland 284 G5
Burravoe Shetland 284 F7
Burray Village Orkney 283 H5
Burrells Cumb 165 D4
Burrelton Perth 220 A2
Burridge Devon 25 B6
Burridge Hants 32 D4
Burrill N Yorks 157 C6
Burringham N Lincs 141 C6
Burrington Devon 26 D1
Burrington Hereford 94 D2
Burrington N Som 42 D3
Burrough Green Cambs 86 B2
Burrough on the Hill
  Leics 115 D5
Burrow-bridge Som 28 C3
Burrowhill Sur 48 C2
Burry Swansea 57 C4
Burry Green Swansea 57 C4
Burry Port = Porth
  Tywyn Carms 57 B4
Burscough Lancs 136 B3
Burscough Bridge Lancs 136 B3
Bursea E Yorks 149 D7
Burshill E Yorks 150 C3
Bursledon Hants 18 A3
Burslem Stoke 112 A2
Burstall Suff 88 C1
Burstock Dorset 14 A4
Burston Norf 104 C2
Burston Staffs 112 B3
Burstow Sur 35 B6
Burstwick E Yorks 143 A4
Burtersett N Yorks 156 C2
Burtle Som 28 A3
Burton Ches 126 B3
Burton Ches 127 C5
Burton Dorset 17 B5
Burton Lincs 133 B4
Burton Northumb 199 C5
Burton Pembs 55 D5
Burton Som 28 A1
Burton Wilts 44 B2
Burton Agnes E Yorks 151 A4
Burton Bradstock Dorset 15 C4
Burton Dassett Warks 81 B6
Burton Fleming E Yorks 161 D4
Burton Green W Mid 97 D5
Burton Green Wrex 126 D3
Burton Hastings Warks 97 B7
Burton-in-Kendal Cumb 154 D4
Burton in Lonsdale
  N Yorks 155 D5
Burton Joyce Notts 115 A4
Burton Latimer Northants 99 D6
Burton Lazars Leics 115 D5
Burton-le-Coggles Lincs 116 C2
Burton Leonard N Yorks 148 A2
Burton on the Wolds
  Leics 114 C3
Burton Overy Leics 98 B3
Burton Pedwardine Lincs 116 A4
Burton Pidsea E Yorks 151 D5
Burton Salmon N Yorks 140 A2
Burton Stather N Lincs 141 B6
Burton upon Stather
  N Lincs 141 B6
Burton upon Trent Staffs 113 C6
Burtonwood Warr 137 D4
Burwardsley Ches 127 D5
Burwarton Shrops 95 C4
Burwash E Sus 37 D4
Burwash Common E Sus 36 D4
Burwash Weald E Sus 36 D4
Burwell Cambs 86 A1
Burwell Lincs 134 B3
Burwen Anglesey 123 A4
Burwick Orkney 283 K5
Bury Cambs 101 C4
Bury Gtr Man 137 B7
Bury Som 27 C4
Bury W Sus 20 A3
Bury Green Herts 68 A4
Bury St Edmunds Suff 87 A4
Burythorpe N Yorks 149 A6
Busby E Renf 205 C5
Buscot Oxon 64 D3
Bush Bank Hereford 78 B2
Bush Crathie Aberds 243 C5
Bush Green Norf 104 C3
Bushbury W Mid 96 A2

Bushby Leics 98 A3
Bushey Herts 67 D6
Bushey Heath Herts 67 D6
Bushley Worcs 80 D1
Bushton Wilts 45 B4
Buslingthorpe Lincs 133 A5
Busta Shetland 284 G5
Butcher's Cross E Sus 36 D3
Butcher's Pasture Essex 69 A6
Butcombe N Som 43 C4
Butetown Cardiff 41 D6
Butleigh Som 29 B5
Butleigh Wootton Som 29 B5
Butler's Cross Bucks 66 C3
Butler's End Warks 97 C5
Butley Suff 89 B4
Butley High Corner Suff 89 C4
Butt Green Ches 127 D6
Butterburn Cumb 177 B4
Buttercrambe N Yorks 149 B6
Butterknowle Durham 166 C4
Butterleigh Devon 13 A4
Buttermere Cumb 163 C4
Buttermere Wilts 46 C1
Buttershaw W Yorks 139 A4
Butterstone Perth 231 D4
Butterton Staffs 129 D5
Butterwick Durham 167 C6
Butterwick Lincs 117 A6
Butterwick N Yorks 159 D6
Butterwick N Yorks 160 D3
Buttington Powys 93 A6
Buttonoak Shrops 95 D5
Butt's Green Hants 32 C2
Buttsash Hants 18 A3
Buxhall Suff 87 B6
Buxhall Fen Street Suff 87 B6
Buxley Borders 198 A2
Buxted E Sus 36 D2
Buxton Derbys 129 B5
Buxton Norf 120 C4
Buxworth Derbys 129 A5
Bwcle = Buckley Flint 126 C2
Bwlch Powys 60 A3
Bwlch-Llan Ceredig 75 C4
Bwlch-y-cibau Powys 109 D6
Bwlch-y-fadfa Ceredig 74 D3
Bwlch-y-ffridd Powys 93 B4
Bwlch-y-sarnau Powys 92 D4
Bwlchgwyn Wrex 126 D2
Bwlchnewydd Carms 73 D6
Bwlchtocyn Gwyn 106 D3
Bwlchyddar Powys 109 C6
Bwlchygroes Pembs 73 C5
Byermoor T & W 178 D3
Byers Green Durham 167 B5
Byfield Northants 82 B2
Byfleet Sur 48 C3
Byford Hereford 78 C1
Bygrave Herts 85 D4
Byker T & W 179 C4
Bylchau Conwy 125 C4
Byley Ches 128 C2
Bynea Carms 57 C5
Byrness Northumb 187 C6
Bythorn Cambs 100 D2
Byton Hereford 78 A1
Byworth W Sus 34 D2

C

Cabharstadh W Isles 288 E4
Cablea Perth 218 A4
Cabourne Lincs 142 C3
Cabrach Argyll 201 B4
Cabrach Moray 255 D4
Cabrich Highld 252 B1
Cabus Lancs 145 C4
Cackle Street E Sus 36 D2
Cadbury Devon 13 A4
Cadbury Barton Devon 26 D1
Cadbury World,
  Bournville W Mid 96 C3
Cadder E Dunb 205 A6
Caddington Beds 67 B5
Caddonfoot Borders 196 C3
Cade Street E Sus 36 D4
Cadeby Leics 97 A7
Cadeby S Yorks 140 C3
Cadeleigh Devon 13 A4
Cadgwith Corn 3 D5
Cadham Fife 220 D2
Cadishead Gtr Man 137 D6
Cadle Swansea 57 C6
Cadley Lancs 145 D5
Cadley Wilts 45 D6

Cadley Wilts 45 C6
Cadmore End Bucks 66 D2
Cadnam Hants 32 D1
Cadney N Lincs 142 C2
Cadole Flint 126 C2
Cadoxton V Glam 41 E6
Cadoxton-Juxta-Neath
  Neath 40 B2
Cadshaw Blkburn 137 B6
Cadwell Park Motor
  Racing Circuit Lincs 134 A2
Cadzow S Lnrk 194 A2
Caeathro Gwyn 123 D4
Caehopkin Powys 59 D5
Caenby Lincs 133 A5
Caenby Corner Lincs 133 A4
Cae'r-bryn Carms 57 A5
Caer Llan Mon 61 C6
Caerau Bridgend 40 B3
Caerau Cardiff 41 D6
Caerdeon Gwyn 90 A4
Caerdydd = Cardiff Cardiff 41 D6
Caerfarchell Pembs 54 B3
Caerffili = Caerphilly
  Caerph 41 C6
Caerfyrddin =
  Carmarthen Carms 73 D7
Caergeiliog Anglesey 122 C3
Caergwrle Flint 126 D3
Caergybi = Holyhead
  Anglesey 122 B2
Caerleon = Caerllion
  Newport 61 D5
Caerllion = Caerleon
  Newport 61 D5
Caernarfon Gwyn 123 D4
Caernarfon Castle Gwyn 123 D4
Caerphilly = Caerffili
  Caerph 41 C6
Caersws Powys 92 B4
Caerwedros Ceredig 73 A6
Caerwent Mon 61 D6
Caerwych Gwyn 107 C6
Caerwys Flint 125 B6
Caethle Gwyn 90 C4
Caim Anglesey 123 B6
Caio Carms 58 B3
Cairinis W Isles 287 H3
Cairisiadar W Isles 287 A5
Cairminis W Isles 287 F5
Cairnbaan Argyll 213 C6
Cairnbanno Ho. Aberds 256 B3
Cairnborrow Aberds 255 B5
Cairnbrogie Aberds 256 D3
Cairnbulg Castle Aberds 269 C5
Cairncross Angus 232 A2
Cairncross Borders 211 D5
Cairndow Argyll 215 A4
Cairness Aberds 269 C5
Cairneyhill Fife 208 B3
Cairnfield Ho. Moray 267 C5
Cairngaan Dumfries 170 D3
Cairngarroch Dumfries 170 C2
Cairnhill Aberds 256 C1
Cairnie Aberds 255 B5
Cairnie Aberds 245 B5
Cairnorrie Aberds 256 B3
Cairnpark Aberds 245 A5
Cairnryan Dumfries 170 A2
Cairnton Orkney 283 G4
Caister-on-Sea Norf 121 D7
Caistor Lincs 142 C3
Caistor St Edmund Norf 104 A3
Caistron Northumb 188 C2
Caitha Bowland Borders 196 B3
Caithness Glass, Perth
  Perth 219 B5
Calais Street Suff 87 D5
Calanais W Isles 288 D3
Calbost W Isles 288 F5
Calbourne I o W 18 C3
Calceby Lincs 134 B3
Calcot Row W Berks 47 B4
Calcott Kent 52 C3
Caldback Shetland 284 C8
Caldbeck Cumb 163 A6
Caldbergh N Yorks 157 C4
Caldecote Cambs 85 B5
Caldecote Cambs 100 C3
Caldecote Herts 84 D4
Caldecote Northants 82 B3
Caldecott Northants 84 A1
Caldecott Oxon 65 D5
Caldecott Rutland 99 B5
Calder Bridge Cumb 162 D3
Calder Hall Cumb 162 D3
Calder Mains Highld 280 C2

Calder Vale Lancs 145 C5
Calderbank N Lnrk 207 D5
Calderbrook Gtr Man 138 B2
Caldercruix N Lnrk 207 D6
Calderwood S Lnrk 205 C6
Caldhame Angus 232 D2
Caldicot Mon 42 A3
Caldwell Derbys 113 D6
Caldwell N Yorks 167 D4
Caldy Mers 126 A2
Caledrhydiau Ceredig 74 C3
Calfsound Orkney 282 D6
Califer Moray 266 D1
California Falk 208 C2
California Norf 121 D7
Calke Derbys 114 C1
Callakille Highld 248 A3
Callaly Northumb 188 C3
Callander Stirl 217 D6
Callaughton Shrops 95 B4
Callestick Corn 4 B2
Calligarry Highld 247 D5
Callington Corn 6 A2
Callow Hereford 78 D2
Callow End Worcs 79 C6
Callow Hill Wilts 44 A4
Callow Hill Worcs 95 D5
Callows Grave Worcs 78 A3
Calmore Hants 32 D2
Calmsden Glos 63 C6
Calne Wilts 44 B4
Calow Derbys 131 B4
Calshot Hants 18 A3
Calstock Corn 6 A3
Calstone Wellington Wilts 44 C4
Calthorpe Norf 120 B3
Calthwaite Cumb 164 A2
Calton N Yorks 146 B3
Calton Staffs 129 D6
Calveley Ches 127 D5
Calver Derbys 130 B2
Calver Hill Hereford 78 C1
Calverhall Shrops 111 B5
Calverleigh Devon 27 D4
Calverley W Yorks 147 D6
Calvert Bucks 66 A1
Calverton M Keynes 83 D4
Calverton Notts 115 A4
Calvine Perth 230 B2
Calvo Cumb 174 C4
Cam Glos 62 D3
Camas-luinie Highld 249 D6
Camasnacroise Highld 236 D2
Camastianavaig Highld 247 A4
Camasunary Highld 247 C4
Camault Muir Highld 251 B7
Camb Shetland 284 D7
Camber E Sus 38 D1
Camberley Sur 47 C6
Camberwell London 49 B6
Camblesforth N Yorks 141 A4
Cambo Northumb 178 A2
Cambois Northumb 179 A5
Camborne Corn 3 A4
Cambourne Cambs 85 B5
Cambridge Cambs 85 B6
Cambridge Glos 62 C3
Cambridge Airport Cambs 85 B6
Cambridge Town Sthend 51 A6
Cambus Clack 207 A6
Cambusavie Farm Highld 264 A3
Cambusbarron Stirl 207 A5
Cambuskenneth Stirl 207 A6
Cambuslang S Lnrk 205 B6
Cambusmore Lodge
  Highld 264 A3
Camden London 49 A5
Camelford Corn 10 C2
Camelot Theme Park,
  Chorley Lancs 136 B4
Camelsdale W Sus 34 C1
Camerory Highld 253 C6
Camer's Green Worcs 79 D5
Camerton Bath 43 D5
Camerton Cumb 162 A3
Camerton E Yorks 143 A4
Camghouran Perth 229 C4
Cammachmore Aberds 245 C6
Cammeringham Lincs 133 A4
Camore Highld 264 A3
Camp Hill Warks 97 B6
Campbeltown Argyll 190 C3

Campbeltown Airport Argyll 190 C2
Camperdown T & W 179 B4
Campmuir Perth 220 A2
Campsall S Yorks 140 B3
Campsey Ash Suff 88 B4
Campton Beds 84 D3
Camptown Borders 187 B5
Camrose Pembs 55 B5
Camserney Perth 230 D2
Camster Highld 281 D4
Camuschoirk Highld 235 D6
Camuscross Highld 247 C5
Camusnagaul Highld 237 B4
Camusnagaul Highld 262 B2
Camusrory Highld 238 C2
Camusteel Highld 249 B4
Camusterrach Highld 249 B4
Camusvrachan Perth 229 D5
Canada Hants 32 D1
Canadia E Sus 23 A5
Canal Side S Yorks 141 B4
Candacraig Ho. Aberds 243 A6
Candlesby Lincs 135 C4
Candy Mill S Lnrk 195 B5
Cane End Oxon 47 B4
Canewdon Essex 70 D2
Canford Bottom Dorset 17 A4
Canford Cliffs Poole 17 C4
Canford Magna Poole 17 B4
Canham's Green Suff 87 A6
Canholes Derbys 129 B5
Canisbay Highld 281 A5
Cann Dorset 30 C2
Cann Common Dorset 30 C2
Cannard's Grave Som 29 A6
Cannich Highld 251 C5
Cannington Som 28 B2
Cannock Staffs 96 A2
Cannock Wood Staffs 112 D4
Canon Bridge Hereford 78 C2
Canon Frome Hereford 79 C4
Canon Pyon Hereford 78 C2
Canonbie Dumfries 175 A6
Canons Ashby Northants 82 B2
Canonstown Corn 2 B3
Canterbury Kent 52 D3
Canterbury Cathedral Kent 52 D3
Canterbury Tales Kent 52 D3
Cantley Norf 105 A4
Cantley S Yorks 140 C4
Cantlop Shrops 94 A3
Canton Cardiff 41 D6
Cantraybruich Highld 252 B3
Cantraydoune Highld 252 B3
Cantraywood Highld 252 B3
Cantsfield Lancs 155 D5
Canvey Island Essex 51 A4
Canwick Lincs 133 C4
Canworthy Water Corn 10 B3
Caol Highld 237 B5
Caol Ila Argyll 201 A4
Caolas Argyll 222 C3
Caolas Scalpaigh W Isles 288 H3
Caolas Stocinis W Isles 288 H2
Capel Sur 35 B4
Capel Bangor Ceredig 91 D4
Capel Betws Lleucu Ceredig 75 C5
Capel Carmel Gwyn 106 D1
Capel Coch Anglesey 123 B4
Capel Curig Conwy 124 D2
Capel Cynon Ceredig 73 B6
Capel Dewi Ceredig 58 A1
Capel Dewi Ceredig 90 D4
Capel Dewi Carms 58 C1
Capel Garmon Conwy 124 D3
Capel Gwyn Carms 58 C1
Capel Gwynfe Carms 59 C4
Capel Hendre Carms 57 A5
Capel Hermon Gwyn 108 C2
Capel Isaac Carms 58 C2
Capel Iwan Carms 73 C5
Capel le Ferne Kent 39 B4
Capel Llanilltern Cardiff 41 C5
Capel Mawr Anglesey 123 C4
Capel St Andrew Suff 89 C4
Capel St Mary Suff 88 D1
Capel Seion Ceredig 75 A5
Capel Tygwydd Ceredig 73 B5
Capel Uchaf Gwyn 107 B4
Capel-y-graig Gwyn 123 D5
Capelulo Conwy 124 B2

Capenhurst Ches 126 B3
Capernwray Lancs 154 D4
Capheaton Northumb 178 A2
Cappercleuch Borders 196 D1
Capplegill Dumfries 185 B4
Capton Devon 8 B2
Caputh Perth 219 A5
Car Colston Notts 115 A5
Carbis Bay Corn 2 B3
Carbost Highld 246 A2
Carbost Highld 259 D4
Carbrook S Yorks 130 A3
Carbrooke Norf 103 A5
Carburton Notts 131 B6
Carcant Borders 196 A2
Carcary Angus 233 C4
Carclaze Corn 5 B5
Carcroft S Yorks 140 B3
Cardenden Fife 209 A5
Cardeston Shrops 110 D2
Cardiff = Caerdydd Cardiff 41 D6
Cardiff Bay Barrage Cardiff 41 D6
Cardiff Castle Cardiff 41 D6
Cardiff International Airport V Glam 41 E5
Cardigan = Aberteifi Ceredig 73 B4
Cardington Beds 84 C2
Cardington Shrops 94 B3
Cardinham Corn 5 A6
Cardonald Glasgow 205 B5
Cardow Moray 254 B2
Cardrona Borders 196 C2
Cardross Argyll 206 C1
Cardurnock Cumb 175 C4
Careby Lincs 116 D3
Careston Castle Angus 232 C3
Carew Pembs 55 D6
Carew Cheriton Pembs 55 D6
Carew Newton Pembs 55 D6
Carey Hereford 78 D3
Carfrae E Loth 210 D2
Cargenbridge Dumfries 174 A2
Cargill Perth 219 A6
Cargo Cumb 175 C6
Cargreen Corn 6 A3
Carham Northumb 198 C2
Carhampton Som 27 A5
Carharrack Corn 4 C2
Carie Perth 217 A6
Carie Perth 229 C5
Carines Corn 4 B2
Carisbrooke I o W 18 C3
Carisbrooke Castle I o W 18 C3
Cark Cumb 154 D2
Carlabhagh W Isles 288 C3
Carland Cross Corn 4 B3
Carlby Lincs 116 D3
Carlecotes S Yorks 139 C4
Carlesmoor N Yorks 157 D5
Carleton Cumb 164 C3
Carleton Cumb 176 D2
Carleton Lancs 144 D3
Carleton N Yorks 146 C3
Carleton Forehoe Norf 104 A1
Carleton Rode Norf 104 B2
Carlin How Redcar 169 D5
Carlingcott Bath 43 D5
Carlisle Cumb 175 C7
Carlisle Airport Cumb 176 C2
Carlisle Cathedral Cumb 175 C6
Carlisle Racecourse Cumb 175 C6
Carlops Borders 195 A6
Carlton Beds 83 B6
Carlton Cambs 86 B2
Carlton Leics 97 A6
Carlton Notts 115 A4
Carlton N Yorks 159 C5
Carlton N Yorks 140 A4
Carlton N Yorks 157 C4
Carlton N Yorks 167 D4
Carlton Stockton 167 C6
Carlton Suff 89 A4
Carlton S Yorks 139 B6
Carlton W Yorks 139 A6
Carlton Colville Suff 105 C6
Carlton Curlieu Leics 98 B3
Carlton Husthwaite N Yorks 158 D3
Carlton in Cleveland N Yorks 158 A4
Carlton in Lindrick Notts 131 A5
Carlton le Moorland Lincs 133 D4
Carlton Miniott N Yorks 158 C2
Carlton on Trent Notts 132 C2

Carlton Scroop Lincs 116 A2
Carluke S Lnrk 194 A3
Carmarthen = Caerfyrddin Carms 73 D7
Carmel Anglesey 122 B3
Carmel Carms 57 A5
Carmel Flint 125 B6
Carmel Guern 6
Carmel Gwyn 107 A4
Carmont Aberds 245 D5
Carmunnock Glasgow 205 C6
Carmyle Glasgow 205 B6
Carmyllie Angus 232 D3
Carn-gorm Highld 249 D6
Carnaby E Yorks 151 A4
Carnach Highld 262 A2
Carnach Highld 250 D2
Carnach W Isles 288 H3
Carnachy Highld 278 C3
Càrnais W Isles 287 A5
Carnbee Fife 221 D5
Carnbo Perth 219 D5
Carnbrea Corn 3 A4
Carnduff S Lnrk 205 D6
Carnduncan Argyll 200 B2
Carne Corn 4 D4
Carnforth Lancs 154 D3
Carnhedryn Pembs 54 B4
Carnhell Green Corn 3 B4
Carnkie Corn 4 D2
Carnkie Corn 3 B4
Carno Powys 92 B3
Carnoch Highld 251 C5
Carnoch Highld 251 A4
Carnock Fife 208 B3
Carnon Downs Corn 4 C2
Carnousie Aberds 268 D1
Carnoustie Angus 221 A5
Carnwath S Lnrk 195 B4
Carnyorth Corn 2 B1
Carperby N Yorks 156 C4
Carpley Green N Yorks 156 C3
Carr S Yorks 140 D3
Carr Hill T & W 179 C4
Carradale Argyll 190 B4
Carragraich W Isles 288 H2
Carrbridge Highld 253 D5
Carrefour Selous Jersey 6
Carreg-wen Pembs 73 B5
Carreglefn Anglesey 122 B3
Carrick Argyll 214 D2
Carrick Fife 220 B4
Carrick Castle Argyll 215 C4
Carrick Ho. Orkney 282 D6
Carriden Falk 208 B3
Carrington Gtr Man 137 D6
Carrington Lincs 134 D3
Carrington Midloth 209 D6
Carrog Conwy 108 A2
Carrog Denb 109 A6
Carron Falk 208 B1
Carron Moray 254 B3
Carron Bridge N Lnrk 207 B5
Carronbridge Dumfries 183 C6
Carrshield Northumb 165 A6
Carrutherstown Dumfries 174 A4
Carrville Durham 167 A6
Carsaig Argyll 225 D4
Carsaig Argyll 213 D5
Carscreugh Dumfries 171 B4
Carse Gray Angus 232 C2
Carse Ho. Argyll 202 B2
Carsegowan Dumfries 171 B6
Carseriggan Dumfries 171 A5
Carsethorn Dumfries 174 C2
Carshalton London 49 C5
Carsington Derbys 130 D2
Carskiey Argyll 190 E2
Carsluith Dumfries 171 B6
Carsphairn Dumfries 182 C3
Carstairs S Lnrk 194 B4
Carstairs Junction S Lnrk 195 B4
Carswell Marsh Oxon 64 D4
Carter's Clay Hants 32 C2
Carterton Oxon 64 C3
Carterway Heads Northumb 178 D2
Carthew Corn 5 B5
Carthorpe N Yorks 157 C7
Cartington Northumb 188 C3
Cartland S Lnrk 194 B3
Cartmel Cumb 154 D2
Cartmel Fell Cumb 154 C3
Cartmel Racecourse Cumb 154 D2
Carway Carms 57 B4
Cary Fitzpaine Som 29 C5

Cas-gwent = Chepstow Mon 62 D1
Cascob Powys 77 A6
Cashlie Perth 228 D3
Cashmere Visitor Centre, Elgin Moray 266 C3
Cashmoor Dorset 30 D3
Casnewydd = Newport Newport 42 A2
Cassey Compton Glos 63 B6
Cassington Oxon 65 B5
Cassop Durham 167 B6
Castell Denb 125 C6
Castell Coch Cardiff 41 C6
Castell-Howell Ceredig 74 D3
Castell-Nedd = Neath Neath 40 B2
Castell Newydd Emlyn = Newcastle Emlyn Carms 73 B6
Castell-y-bwch Torf 61 D4
Castellau Rhondda 41 C5
Casterton Cumb 155 D5
Castle Acre Norf 119 D5
Castle Ashby Northants 83 B5
Castle Bolton N Yorks 156 B4
Castle Bromwich W Mid 96 C4
Castle Bytham Lincs 116 D2
Castle Caereinion Powys 93 A5
Castle Camps Cambs 86 C2
Castle Carrock Cumb 176 D3
Castle Cary Som 29 B6
Castle Combe Wilts 44 B2
Castle Combe Motor Racing Circuit Wilts 44 B2
Castle Donington Leics 114 C2
Castle Douglas Dumfries 173 B5
Castle Drogo, Exeter Devon 12 B2
Castle Eaton Swindon 64 D2
Castle Eden Durham 168 B2
Castle Forbes Aberds 244 A3
Castle Frome Hereford 79 C4
Castle Green Sur 48 C2
Castle Gresley Derbys 113 D6
Castle Heaton Northumb 198 B3
Castle Hedingham Essex 86 D3
Castle Hill Kent 37 B4
Castle Howard, Malton N Yorks 159 D6
Castle Huntly Perth 220 B3
Castle Kennedy Dumfries 170 B3
Castle O'er Dumfries 185 C5
Castle Pulverbatch Shrops 94 A2
Castle Rising Norf 118 C3
Castle Stuart Highld 252 B3
Castlebay = Bagh a Chaisteil W Isles 286 G2
Castlebythe Pembs 55 B6
Castlecary N Lnrk 207 C5
Castlecraig Highld 265 D4
Castlefairn Dumfries 183 D5
Castleford W Yorks 140 A2
Castlehill Borders 195 C7
Castlehill Highld 280 B3
Castlehill W Dunb 206 C1
Castlemaddy Dumfries 182 D3
Castlemartin Pembs 55 E5
Castlemilk Dumfries 174 A4
Castlemilk Glasgow 205 C6
Castlemorris Pembs 55 A5
Castlemorton Worcs 79 D5
Castleside Durham 166 A3
Castlethorpe M Keynes 83 C5
Castleton Angus 232 D1
Castleton Argyll 214 D1
Castleton Derbys 129 A6
Castleton Gtr Man 138 B1
Castleton Newport 42 A1
Castleton N Yorks 159 A5
Castletown Ches 127 D4
Castletown Highld 280 B3
Castletown Highld 252 B3
Castletown I o M 152 E2
Castletown T & W 179 D5
Castleweary Borders 186 C3
Castley N Yorks 147 C6
Caston Norf 103 B5
Castor P'boro 100 B3
Catacol N Ayrs 203 D4
Catbrain S Glos 43 A4
Catbrook Mon 61 C7
Catchall Corn 2 C2
Catchems Corner W Mid 97 D5
Catchgate Durham 178 D3
Catcliffe S Yorks 131 A4
Catcott Som 28 B3

Caterham Sur 35 A6
Catfield Norf 121 C5
Catfirth Shetland 285 H6
Catford London 49 B6
Catforth Lancs 145 D4
Cathays Cardiff 41 D6
Cathcart Glasgow 205 B5
Cathedine Powys 60 A3
Catherington Hants 33 D5
Catherton Shrops 95 D4
Catlodge Highld 241 C4
Catlowdy Cumb 176 B2
Catmore W Berks 46 A2
Caton Lancs 145 A5
Caton Green Lancs 145 A5
Catrine E Ayrs 193 C5
Cat's Ash Newport 61 D5
Catsfield E Sus 23 A5
Catshill Worcs 96 D2
Cattal N Yorks 148 B3
Cattawade Suff 88 D2
Catterall Lancs 145 C4
Catterick N Yorks 157 B6
Catterick Bridge N Yorks 157 B6
Catterick Garrison N Yorks 157 B5
Catterlen Cumb 164 B2
Catterline Aberds 233 A6
Catterton N Yorks 148 C4
Catthorpe Leics 98 D2
Cattistock Dorset 15 B5
Catton Northumb 177 D6
Catton N Yorks 158 D2
Catwick E Yorks 151 C4
Catworth Cambs 100 D2
Caudlesprings Norf 103 A5
Caudwell's Mill, Matlock Derbys 130 C2
Caulcott Oxon 65 A6
Cauldcots Angus 233 D4
Cauldhame Stirl 207 A4
Cauldmill Borders 186 B4
Cauldon Staffs 113 A4
Caulkerbush Dumfries 174 C2
Caulside Dumfries 176 A2
Caunsall Worcs 95 C6
Caunton Notts 132 D2
Causeway End Dumfries 171 A6
Causeway Foot W Yorks 147 D4
Causeway-head Stirl 207 A5
Causewayend S Lnrk 195 C5
Causewayhead Cumb 174 C4
Causey Park Bridge Northumb 189 D4
Causeyend Aberds 245 A6
Cautley Cumb 155 B5
Cavendish Suff 87 C4
Cavendish Bridge Leics 114 C2
Cavenham Suff 86 A3
Caversfield Oxon 65 A6
Caversham Reading 47 B5
Caverswall Staffs 112 A3
Cavil E Yorks 149 D6
Cawdor Highld 253 B4
Cawdor Castle and Gardens Highld 253 B4
Cawkwell Lincs 134 B2
Cawood N Yorks 149 D4
Cawsand Corn 6 B3
Cawston Norf 120 C3
Cawthorne S Yorks 139 C5
Cawthorpe Lincs 116 C3
Cawton N Yorks 159 D5
Caxton Cambs 85 B5
Caynham Shrops 94 D3
Caythorpe Lincs 116 A2
Caythorpe Notts 115 A4
Cayton N Yorks 161 C4
Ceann a Bhaigh W Isles 287 H2
Ceann a Deas Loch Baghasdail W Isles 286 E3
Ceann Shiphoirt W Isles 288 F3
Ceann Tarabhaigh W Isles 288 F3
Ceannacroc Lodge Highld 239 A6
Cearsiadair W Isles 288 E4
Cefn Berain Conwy 125 C4
Cefn-brith Conwy 125 D4
Cefn Canol Powys 110 B1
Cefn-coch Conwy 124 C3
Cefn Coch Powys 109 C6
Cefn-coed-y-cymmer M Tydf 60 C2
Cefn Cribwr Bridgend 40 C3
Cefn Cross Bridgend 40 C3

Cefn-ddwysarn Gwyn	109	B4
Cefn Einion Shrops	93	C6
Cefn-gorwydd Powys	76	C3
Cefn-mawr Wrex	110	A1
Cefn-y-bedd Flint	126	D3
Cefn-y-pant Carms	73	D4
Cefneithin Carms	57	A5
Cei-bach Ceredig	73	A7
Ceinewydd = New Quay Ceredig	73	A6
Ceint Anglesey	123	C4
Cellan Ceredig	75	D5
Cellarhead Staffs	112	A3
Cemaes Anglesey	122	A3
Cemmaes Powys	91	B6
Cemmaes Road Powys	91	B6
Cenarth Carms	73	B5
Cenin Gwyn	107	B4
Central Invclyd	204	A2
Ceos W Isles	288	G4
Ceres Fife	220	C4
Cerne Abbas Dorset	15	A6
Cerney Wick Glos	63	D6
Cerrigceinwen Anglesey	123	C4
Cerrigydrudion Conwy	109	A4
Cessford Borders	187	A6
Ceunant Gwyn	123	D5
Chaceley Glos	79	D6
Chacewater Corn	4	C2
Chackmore Bucks	82	D3
Chacombe Northants	82	C1
Chad Valley W Mid	96	C3
Chadderton Gtr Man	138	C2
Chadderton Fold Gtr Man	138	C1
Chaddesden Derby	114	B1
Chaddesley Corbett Worcs	96	D1
Chaddleworth W Berks	46	B2
Chadlington Oxon	64	A4
Chadshunt Warks	81	B6
Chadwell Leics	115	C5
Chadwell St Mary Thurrock	50	B3
Chadwick End W Mid	97	D5
Chadwick Green Mers	136	D4
Chaffcombe Som	28	D3
Chagford Devon	12	C2
Chailey E Sus	22	A1
Chain Bridge Lincs	117	A6
Chainbridge Cambs	101	A6
Chainhurst Kent	37	B5
Chalbury Dorset	17	A4
Chalbury Common Dorset	17	A4
Chaldon Sur	35	A6
Chaldon Herring Dorset	16	C1
Chale I o W	18	D3
Chale Green I o W	18	D3
Chalfont Common Bucks	67	D5
Chalfont St Giles Bucks	67	D4
Chalfont St Peter Bucks	67	D5
Chalford Glos	63	C4
Chalgrove Oxon	66	D1
Chalk Kent	50	B3
Challacombe Devon	26	A1
Challoch Dumfries	171	A5
Challock Kent	52	D2
Chalton Beds	67	A5
Chalton Hants	33	D6
Chalvington E Sus	22	B3
Chancery Ceredig	75	A4
Chandler's Ford Hants	32	C3
Channel Tunnel Kent	38	B3
Channerwick Shetland	285	L6
Chantry Som	29	A7
Chantry Suff	88	C2
Chapel Fife	209	A5
Chapel Allerton Som	42	D3
Chapel Allerton W Yorks	148	D2
Chapel Amble Corn	9	D5
Chapel Brampton Northants	83	A4
Chapel Chorlton Staffs	112	B2
Chapel-en-le-Frith Derbys	129	A5
Chapel End Warks	97	B6
Chapel Green Warks	97	C5
Chapel Green Warks	82	A1
Chapel Haddlesey N Yorks	140	A3
Chapel Head Cambs	101	C5
Chapel Hill Aberds	257	C5
Chapel Hill Lincs	134	D2
Chapel Hill Mon	62	D1
Chapel Hill N Yorks	148	C2
Chapel Lawn Shrops	93	D7
Chapel-le-Dale N Yorks	155	D6
Chapel Milton Derbys	129	A5
Chapel of Garioch Aberds	256	D2
Chapel Row W Berks	46	C3
Chapel St Leonards Lincs	135	B5
Chapel Stile Cumb	154	A2
Chapelgate Lincs	117	C7
Chapelhall N Lnrk	207	D5
Chapelhill Dumfries	184	D3
Chapelhill Highld	265	C4
Chapelhill N Ayrs	204	D2
Chapelhill Perth	220	B2
Chapelhill Perth	219	A5
Chapelknowe Dumfries	175	A6
Chapelton Angus	233	D4
Chapelton Devon	25	C6
Chapelton Highld	242	A2
Chapelton S Lnrk	194	B1
Chapeltown Blkburn	137	B6
Chapeltown Moray	254	D3
Chapeltown S Yorks	139	D6
Chapmans Well Devon	11	B4
Chapmanslade Wilts	30	A2
Chapmore End Herts	68	B3
Chappel Essex	70	A2
Chard Som	14	A3
Chardstock Devon	14	A3
Charfield S Glos	62	D3
Charford Worcs	80	A2
Charing Kent	38	A1
Charing Cross Dorset	31	D5
Charing Heath Kent	38	A1
Charingworth Glos	81	D5
Charlbury Oxon	65	B4
Charlcombe Bath	43	C6
Charlecote Warks	81	B5
Charlecote Park, Wellesbourne Warks	81	B5
Charles Devon	26	B1
Charles Manning's Amusement Park, Felixstowe Suff	88	D3
Charles Tye Suff	87	B6
Charlesfield Dumfries	175	B4
Charleston Angus	232	D1
Charleston Renfs	205	B4
Charlestown Aberdeen	245	B6
Charlestown Corn	5	B5
Charlestown Derbys	138	D3
Charlestown Dorset	15	D6
Charlestown Fife	208	B3
Charlestown Gtr Man	137	C7
Charlestown Highld	252	B2
Charlestown Highld	261	C5
Charlestown W Yorks	138	A2
Charlestown of Aberlour Moray	254	B3
Charlesworth Derbys	138	D3
Charleton Devon	7	C6
Charlton London	49	B7
Charlton Hants	32	A2
Charlton Herts	68	A1
Charlton Northants	82	D2
Charlton Northumb	177	A6
Charlton Som	43	D5
Charlton Telford	111	D4
Charlton Wilts	30	C3
Charlton Wilts	45	D5
Charlton Wilts	44	A3
Charlton Worcs	80	C3
Charlton W Sus	20	A1
Charlton Abbots Glos	63	A6
Charlton Adam Som	29	C5
Charlton-All-Saints Wilts	31	C5
Charlton Down Dorset	15	B6
Charlton Horethorne Som	29	C6
Charlton Kings Glos	63	A5
Charlton Mackerell Som	29	C5
Charlton Marshall Dorset	16	A2
Charlton Musgrove Som	29	C7
Charlton on Otmoor Oxon	65	B6
Charltons Redcar	168	D4
Charlwood Sur	35	B5
Charlynch Som	28	B2
Charminster Dorset	15	B6
Charmouth Dorset	14	B3
Charndon Bucks	66	A1
Charney Bassett Oxon	65	D4
Charnock Richard Lancs	137	B4
Charsfield Suff	88	B3
Chart Corner Kent	37	A5
Chart Sutton Kent	37	B6
Charter Alley Hants	46	D3
Charterhouse Som	42	D3
Charterville Allotments Oxon	64	B4
Chartham Kent	52	D3
Chartham Hatch Kent	52	D3
Chartridge Bucks	67	C4
Chartwell, Westerham Kent	36	A2
Charvil Wokingham	47	B5
Charwelton Northants	82	B2
Chasetown Staffs	96	A3
Chastleton Oxon	64	A3
Chasty Devon	10	A4
Chatburn Lancs	146	C1
Chatcull Staffs	112	B1
Chatham Medway	51	C4
Chathill Northumb	189	A4
Chatsworth, Bakewell Derbys	130	B2
Chattenden Medway	51	B4
Chatteris Cambs	101	C5
Chattisham Suff	88	C1
Chatto Borders	187	B6
Chatton Northumb	188	A3
Chawleigh Devon	26	D2
Chawley Oxon	65	C5
Chawston Beds	84	B3
Chawton Hants	33	B6
Cheadle Gtr Man	128	A3
Cheadle Staffs	112	A4
Cheadle Heath Gtr Man	128	A3
Cheadle Hulme Gtr Man	128	A3
Cheam London	49	C5
Cheapside Sur	34	A3
Chearsley Bucks	66	B2
Chebsey Staffs	112	C2
Checkendon Oxon	47	A4
Checkley Ches	111	A6
Checkley Hereford	78	D3
Checkley Staffs	112	B4
Chedburgh Suff	86	B3
Cheddar Som	42	D3
Cheddar Showcaves and Gorge Som	42	D3
Cheddington Bucks	67	B4
Cheddleton Staffs	129	D4
Cheddon Fitzpaine Som	28	C2
Chedglow Wilts	63	D5
Chedgrave Norf	105	B4
Chedington Dorset	15	A4
Chediston Suff	105	D4
Chedworth Glos	63	B6
Chedworth Roman Villa Glos	63	B6
Chedzoy Som	28	B3
Cheeklaw Borders	198	A1
Cheeseman's Green Kent	38	B2
Cheglinch Devon	25	A6
Cheldon Devon	26	D2
Chelford Ches	128	B3
Chell Heath Stoke	128	D3
Chellaston Derby	114	B1
Chellington Beds	83	B6
Chelmarsh Shrops	95	C5
Chelmer Village Essex	70	C1
Chelmondiston Suff	88	D3
Chelmorton Derbys	129	C6
Chelmsford Essex	69	C7
Chelsea London	49	B5
Chelsfield London	50	C1
Chelsworth Suff	87	C5
Cheltenham Glos	63	A5
Cheltenham Racecourse Glos	63	A5
Chelveston Northants	84	A1
Chelvey N Som	42	C3
Chelwood Bath	43	C5
Chelwood Common E Sus	36	D2
Chelwood Gate E Sus	36	D2
Chelworth Wilts	63	D5
Chelworth Green Wilts	64	D1
Chemistry Shrops	111	A4
Chenies Bucks	67	D5
Cheny Longville Shrops	94	C2
Chepstow = Cas-gwent Mon	62	D1
Chepstow Racecourse Mon	62	D1
Chequerfield W Yorks	140	A2
Cherhill Wilts	44	B4
Cherington Glos	63	D5
Cherington Warks	81	D5
Cheriton Devon	26	A2
Cheriton Hants	33	C4
Cheriton Kent	38	B3
Cheriton Swansea	57	C4
Cheriton Bishop Devon	12	B2
Cheriton Fitzpaine Devon	12	A3
Cheriton or Stackpole Elidor Pembs	55	E5
Cherrington Telford	111	C5
Cherry Burton E Yorks	150	C2
Cherry Hinton Cambs	85	B6
Cherry Orchard Worcs	79	B6
Cherry Willingham Lincs	133	B5
Cherrybank Perth	219	B6
Chertsey Sur	48	C3
Cheselbourne Dorset	16	B1
Chesham Bucks	67	C4
Chesham Bois Bucks	67	D4
Cheshire Candle Workshops, Burwardsley Ches	127	D5
Cheshunt Herts	68	C3
Cheslyn Hay Staffs	96	A2
Chessington London	49	C4
Chessington World of Adventures London	49	C4
Chester Ches	127	C4
Chester Cathedral Ches	126	C3
Chester-Le-Street Durham	179	D4
Chester Moor Durham	167	A5
Chester Racecourse Ches	126	C3
Chester Zoo Ches	127	B4
Chesterblade Som	29	A6
Chesterfield Derbys	130	B3
Chesters Borders	187	B5
Chesters Borders	187	A5
Chesters Roman Fort Northumb	177	B7
Chesterton Cambs	100	B3
Chesterton Cambs	85	A6
Chesterton Glos	63	C6
Chesterton Oxon	65	A6
Chesterton Shrops	95	B5
Chesterton Staffs	112	A2
Chesterton Warks	81	B6
Chesterwood Northumb	177	C6
Chestfield Kent	52	C3
Cheston Devon	7	B5
Cheswardine Shrops	111	C6
Cheswick Northumb	198	B4
Chetnole Dorset	15	A6
Chettiscombe Devon	27	D4
Chettisham Cambs	102	C1
Chettle Dorset	30	D3
Chetton Shrops	95	B4
Chetwode Bucks	66	A1
Chetwynd Aston Telford	111	D6
Cheveley Cambs	86	A2
Chevening Kent	36	A2
Chevington Suff	86	B3
Chevithorne Devon	27	D4
Chew Magna Bath	43	C4
Chew Stoke Bath	43	C4
Chewton Keynsham Bath	43	C5
Chewton Mendip Som	43	D4
Chicheley M Keynes	83	C6
Chichester W Sus	20	B1
Chichester Cathedral W Sus	20	B1
Chickerell Dorset	15	C6
Chicklade Wilts	30	B3
Chicksgrove Wilts	30	B3
Chidden Hants	33	D5
Chiddingfold Sur	34	C2
Chiddingly E Sus	22	A3
Chiddingstone Kent	36	B2
Chiddingstone Causeway Kent	36	B3
Chiddingstone Hoath Kent	36	B2
Chideock Dorset	14	B4
Chidham W Sus	19	A6
Chidswell W Yorks	139	A5
Chieveley W Berks	46	B2
Chignall St James Essex	69	C6
Chignall Smealy Essex	69	B6
Chigwell Essex	68	D4
Chigwell Row Essex	69	D4
Chilbolton Hants	32	B2
Chilcomb Hants	32	C4
Chilcombe Dorset	15	B5
Chilcompton Som	43	D5
Chilcote Leics	113	D6
Child Okeford Dorset	30	D2
Childer Thornton Ches	126	B3
Childrey Oxon	46	A1
Child's Ercall Shrops	111	C5
Childswickham Worcs	80	D3
Childwall Mers	127	A4
Childwick Green Herts	67	B6
Chilfrome Dorset	15	B5
Chilgrove W Sus	20	A1
Chilham Kent	52	D2
Chilhampton Wilts	31	B4
Chilla Devon	11	A5
Chillaton Devon	11	C5
Chillenden Kent	53	D4
Chillerton I o W	18	C3
Chillesford Suff	89	B4
Chillingham Northumb	188	A3
Chillington Devon	8	C1
Chillington Som	28	D3
Chilmark Wilts	30	B3
Chilson Oxon	64	B4
Chilsworthy Corn	11	D5
Chilsworthy Devon	10	A4
Chilthorne Domer Som	29	D5
Chiltington E Sus	22	A1
Chilton Bucks	66	B1
Chilton Durham	167	C5
Chilton Oxon	46	A2
Chilton Cantelo Som	29	C5
Chilton Foliat Wilts	45	B7
Chilton Lane Durham	167	B6
Chilton Polden Som	28	B3
Chilton Street Suff	86	C3
Chilton Trinity Som	28	B2
Chilvers Coton Warks	97	B6
Chilwell Notts	114	B3
Chilworth Hants	32	D3
Chilworth Sur	34	B3
Chimney Oxon	65	C4
Chineham Hants	47	D4
Chingford London	68	D3
Chinley Derbys	129	A5
Chinley Head Derbys	129	A5
Chinnor Oxon	66	C2
Chipnall Shrops	111	B6
Chippenhall Green Suff	104	D3
Chippenham Cambs	86	A2
Chippenham Wilts	44	B3
Chipperfield Herts	67	C5
Chipping Herts	85	D5
Chipping Lancs	145	C6
Chipping Campden Glos	81	D4
Chipping Hill Essex	70	B2
Chipping Norton Oxon	64	A4
Chipping Ongar Essex	69	C5
Chipping Sodbury S Glos	43	A6
Chipping Warden Northants	82	C1
Chipstable Som	27	C5
Chipstead Kent	36	A2
Chipstead Sur	35	A5
Chirbury Shrops	93	B6
Chirk = Y Waun Wrex	110	B1
Chirk Bank Shrops	110	B1
Chirk Castle Wrex	110	B1
Chirmorrie S Ayrs	181	D4
Chirnside Borders	198	A2
Chirnsidebridge Borders	198	A2
Chirton Wilts	45	D4
Chisbury Wilts	45	C6
Chiselborough Som	29	D4
Chiseldon Swindon	45	B5
Chiserley W Yorks	138	A3
Chislehampton Oxon	65	D6
Chislehurst London	50	B1
Chislet Kent	53	C4
Chiswell Green Herts	67	C6
Chiswick London	49	B5
Chiswick End Cambs	85	C5
Chisworth Derbys	138	D2
Chithurst W Sus	34	D1
Chittering Cambs	101	D6
Chitterne Wilts	30	A3
Chittlehamholt Devon	26	C1
Chittlehampton Devon	26	C1
Chittoe Wilts	44	C3
Chivenor Devon	25	B6
Chobham Sur	48	C2
Choicelee Borders	197	A6
Cholderton Wilts	31	A6
Cholesbury Bucks	67	C4
Chollerford Northumb	177	B7
Chollerton Northumb	178	B1
Cholmondeston Ches	127	C6
Cholsey Oxon	46	A3
Cholstrey Hereford	78	B2
Chop Gate N Yorks	159	B4
Choppington Northumb	179	A4
Chopwell T & W	178	D3
Chorley Ches	127	D5
Chorley Lancs	137	B4
Chorley Shrops	95	C4
Chorley Staffs	113	D4
Chorleywood Herts	67	D5
Chorlton cum Hardy Gtr Man	137	D7
Chorlton Lane Ches	110	A3
Choulton Shrops	94	C1
Chowdene T & W	179	D4
Chowley Ches	127	D4
Crishall Essex	85	D6

Christ Church Oxford Oxon 65 C6	Churton Ches 127 D4	Clark's Green Sur 35 C4	Cleveley Oxon 65 A4	Clun Shrops 93 C7
Christchurch Cambs 101 B6	Churwell W Yorks 139 A5	Clarkston E Renf 205 C5	Cleveleys Lancs 144 C3	Clunbury Shrops 94 C1
Christchurch Dorset 17 B5	Chute Standen Wilts 45 D7	Clashandorran Highld 251 B7	Cleverton Wilts 44 A3	Clunderwen Carms 55 C7
Christchurch Glos 62 B1	Chwilog Gwyn 107 C4	Clashcoig Highld 264 A2	Clevis Bridgend 40 D3	Clune Highld 252 D3
Christchurch Newport 42 A2	Chyandour Corn 2 B2	Clashindarroch Aberds 255 C5	Clewer Som 42 D3	Clunes Highld 239 D6
Christchurch Priory Dorset 17 B5	Cilan Uchaf Gwyn 106 D2	Clashmore Highld 270 A3	Cley next the Sea Norf 120 A2	Clungunford Shrops 94 D1
Christian Malford Wilts 44 B3	Cilcain Flint 126 C1	Clashmore Highld 264 B3	Cliaid W Isles 286 F2	Clunie Aberds 268 D1
Christleton Ches 127 C4	Cilcennin Ceredig 75 B4	Clashnessie Highld 270 A3	Cliasmol W Isles 287 D5	Clunie Perth 231 D5
Christmas Common Oxon 66 D2	Cilfor Gwyn 107 C6	Clashnoir Moray 254 D3	Cliburn Cumb 164 C3	Clunton Shrops 94 C1
Christon N Som 42 D2	Cilfrew Neath 40 A2	Clate Shetland 285 G7	Click Mill Orkney 282 E4	Cluny Fife 209 A5
Christon Bank Northumb 189 A5	Cilfynydd Rhondda 41 B5	Clathy Perth 219 C4	Cliddesden Hants 33 A5	Cluny Castle Highld 241 C4
Christow Devon 12 C3	Cilgerran Pembs 73 B4	Clatt Aberds 255 D6	Cliff End E Sus 23 A6	Clutton Bath 43 D5
Chryston N Lnrk 207 C4	Cilgwyn Carms 59 C4	Clatter Powys 92 B3	Cliffburn Angus 233 D4	Clutton Ches 127 D4
Chudleigh Devon 12 D3	Cilgwyn Gwyn 107 A4	Clatterford I o W 18 C3	Cliffe Medway 51 B4	Clwt-grugoer Conwy 125 C4
Chudleigh Knighton Devon 12 D3	Cilgwyn Pembs 72 C3	Clatterin Bridge Aberds 233 A4	Cliffe N Yorks 149 D5	Clwt-y-bont Gwyn 123 D5
Chulmleigh Devon 26 D1	Ciliau Aeron Ceredig 74 C3	Clatworthy Som 27 B5	Cliffe Woods Medway 51 B4	Clydach Mon 60 B4
Chunal Derbys 138 D3	Cill Donnain W Isles 286 D3	Claughton Lancs 145 C5	Clifford Hereford 77 C6	Clydach Swansea 40 A1
Church Lancs 137 A6	Cille Bhrighde W Isles 286 E3	Claughton Lancs 145 A5	Clifford W Yorks 148 C3	Clydach Vale Rhondda 41 B4
Church Aston Telford 111 D6	Cille Pheadair W Isles 286 E3	Claughton Mers 126 A3	Clifford Chambers Warks 81 B4	Clydebank W Dunb 205 A4
Church Brampton Northants 83 A4	Cilmery Powys 76 B4	Claverdon Warks 81 A4	Clifford's Mesne Glos 62 A3	Clydey Pembs 73 C5
Church Broughton Derbys 113 B6	Cilsan Carms 58 C2	Claverham N Som 42 C3	Cliffsend Kent 53 C5	Clyffe Pypard Wilts 45 B4
Church Crookham Hants 47 D6	Ciltalgarth Gwyn 108 A3	Clavering Essex 85 D6	Clifton Beds 84 D3	Clynder Argyll 215 D5
Church Eaton Staffs 112 D2	Cilwendeg Pembs 73 C5	Claverley Shrops 95 B5	Clifton Bristol 43 B4	Clyne Neath 40 A3
Church End Beds 67 A4	Cilybebyll Neath 40 A2	Claverton Bath 44 C1	Clifton Cumb 164 C3	Clynelish Highld 274 D2
Church End Beds 84 D3	Cilycwm Carms 59 B4	Clawdd-newydd Denb 125 D5	Clifton Derbys 113 A5	Clynnog-fawr Gwyn 107 A4
Church End Beds 84 D1	Cimla Neath 40 B2	Clawthorpe Cumb 154 D4	Clifton Lancs 145 D4	Clyro Powys 77 C6
Church End Cambs 100 C4	Cinderford Glos 62 B2	Clawton Devon 11 B4	Clifton Nottingham 114 B3	Clyst Honiton Devon 13 B4
Church End Cambs 101 A5	Cippyn Pembs 72 B4	Claxby Lincs 142 D3	Clifton Northumb 179 A4	Clyst Hydon Devon 13 A5
Church End E Yorks 150 B3	Circebost W Isles 288 D2	Claxby Lincs 135 B4	Clifton N Yorks 147 C5	Clyst St George Devon 13 C4
Church End Essex 86 C1	Cirencester Glos 63 C6	Claxton Norf 104 A4	Clifton Oxon 82 D1	Clyst St Lawrence Devon 13 A5
Church End Essex 69 A7	Ciribhig W Isles 288 C2	Claxton N Yorks 149 A5	Clifton Stirl 216 A3	Clyst St Mary Devon 13 B4
Church End Hants 47 D4	City Powys 93 C6	Clay Common Suff 105 C5	Clifton S Yorks 140 D3	Cnoc Amhlaigh W Isles 288 D6
Church End Lincs 117 B5	City Dulas Anglesey 123 B4	Clay Coton Northants 98 D2	Clifton Worcs 79 C6	Cnwch-coch Ceredig 75 A5
Church End Warks 97 B5	City of London =	Clay Cross Derbys 130 C3	Clifton York 149 B4	Coachford Aberds 255 B5
Church End Warks 97 B5	London, City of London 49 A6	Clay Hill W Berks 46 B3	Clifton Campville Staffs 113 D6	Coad's Green Corn 10 D3
Church End Wilts 44 B4	Clachaig Argyll 215 D4	Clay Lake Lincs 117 C5	Clifton Green Gtr Man 137 C6	Coal Aston Derbys 130 B3
Church Enstone Oxon 65 A4	Clachan Argyll 202 C2	Claybokie Aberds 242 D3	Clifton Hampden Oxon 65 D6	Coalbrookdale Telford 95 A4
Church Fenton N Yorks 148 D4	Clachan Argyll 213 A5	Claybrooke Magna Leics 98 C1	Clifton Reynes M Keynes 83 B6	Coalbrookvale Bl Gwent 60 C3
Church Green Devon 14 B1	Clachan Argyll 226 B3	Claybrooke Parva Leics 98 C1	Clifton upon Dunsmore	Coalburn S Lnrk 194 C3
Church Green Norf 103 B6	Clachan Argyll 215 A4	Claydon Oxon 82 B1	Warks 98 D2	Coalburns T & W 178 C3
Church Gresley Derbys 113 D6	Clachan Highld 248 C2	Claydon Suff 88 B2	Clifton upon Teme Worcs 79 A5	Coalcleugh Northumb 165 A6
Church Hanborough Oxon 65 B5	Clachan W Isles 286 B3	Claygate Dumfries 175 A6	Cliftoncote Borders 187 A7	Coaley Glos 62 C3
Church Hill Ches 127 C6	Clachan na Luib W Isles 287 H3	Claygate Kent 37 B5	Cliftonville Kent 53 B5	Coalhall E Ayrs 182 A2
Church Houses N Yorks 159 B5	Clachan of Campsie E Dunb 205 A6	Claygate Sur 49 C4	Climaen gwyn Neath 59 E4	Coalhill Essex 70 D1
Church Knowle Dorset 16 C3	Clachan of Glendaruel Argyll 214 D2	Claygate Cross Kent 36 A4	Climping W Sus 20 B3	Coalpit Heath S Glos 43 A5
Church Laneham Notts 132 B3	Clachan-Seil Argyll 213 A5	Clayhanger Devon 27 C5	Climpy S Lnrk 194 A4	Coalport Telford 95 A4
Church Langton Leics 99 B4	Clachan Strachur Argyll 214 B3	Clayhanger W Mid 96 A3	Clink Som 30 A1	Coalsnaughton Clack 208 A2
Church Lawford Warks 98 D1	Clachaneasy Dumfries 181 D5	Clayhidon Devon 27 D6	Clint N Yorks 147 B6	Coaltown of Balgonie Fife 209 A5
Church Lawton Ches 128 D3	Clachanmore Dumfries 170 C2	Clayhill E Sus 37 D6	Clint Green Norf 120 D2	Coaltown of Wemyss Fife 209 A6
Church Leigh Staffs 112 B4	Clachbreck Argyll 202 A2	Clayhill Hants 18 A2	Clintmains Borders 197 C5	Coalville Leics 114 D2
Church Lench Worcs 80 B3	Clachnabrain Angus 232 B1	Clayock Highld 280 C3	Cliobh W Isles 287 A5	Coalway Glos 62 B1
Church Mayfield Staffs 113 A5	Clachtoll Highld 270 B3	Claypole Lincs 115 A6	Clippesby Norf 121 D6	Coat Som 29 C4
Church Minshull Ches 127 C6	Clackmannan Clack 208 A2	Clayton Staffs 112 A2	Clipsham Rutland 116 D2	Coatbridge N Lnrk 207 D5
Church Norton W Sus 20 C1	Clacton-on-Sea Essex 71 B5	Clayton S Yorks 140 C2	Clipston Northants 99 C4	Coatdyke N Lnrk 207 D5
Church Preen Shrops 94 B3	Cladach Chireboist W Isles 287 H2	Clayton Sus 21 A5	Clipstone Notts 131 C5	Coate Swindon 45 A5
Church Pulverbatch Shrops 94 A2	Claddach-knockline W Isles 287 H2	Clayton W Sus 147 D5	Clitheroe Lancs 146 C1	Coate Wilts 44 C4
Church Stoke Powys 93 B6	Cladich Argyll 227 D5	Clayton Green Lancs 137 A4	Cliuthar W Isles 288 H2	Coates Cambs 101 B5
Church Stowe Northants 82 B3	Claggan Highld 225 B5	Clayton-le-Moors Lancs 146 D1	Clive Shrops 111 C4	Coates Glos 63 C5
Church Street Kent 51 B4	Claggan Highld 237 B5	Clayton-le-Woods Lancs 137 A4	Clivocast Shetland 284 C8	Coates Lancs 146 C2
Church Stretton Shrops 94 B2	Claigan Highld 258 C2	Clayton West W Yorks 139 B5	Clixby Lincs 142 C3	Coates Notts 132 A3
Church Town N Lincs 141 C5	Claines Worcs 79 B6	Clayworth Notts 132 A2	Clocaenog Denb 125 D5	Coates W Sus 20 A2
Church Town Sur 35 A6	Clandown Bath 43 D5	Cleadale Highld 234 B3	Clochan Moray 267 C5	Coatham Redcar 168 C3
Church Village Rhondda 41 C5	Clanfield Hants 33 D5	Cleadon T & W 179 C5	Clock Face Mers 136 D4	Coatham Mundeville Darl 167 C5
Church Warsop Notts 131 C5	Clanfield Oxon 64 C3	Clearbrook Devon 7 A4	Clockmill Borders 197 A6	Coatsgate Dumfries 184 B3
Churcham Glos 62 B3	Clanville Hants 32 A2	Clearwell Glos 62 C1	Cloddiau Powys 93 A6	Cobbaton Devon 25 C7
Churchbank Shrops 93 D7	Claonaig Argyll 202 C3	Cleasby N Yorks 167 D5	Clodock Hereford 61 A5	Cobbler's Green Norf 104 B3
Churchbridge Staffs 96 A2	Claonel Highld 272 D3	Cleat Orkney 283 K5	Clola Aberds 257 B5	Coberley Glos 63 B5
Churchdown Glos 63 B4	Clap Hill Kent 38 B2	Cleatlam Durham 166 D4	Clophill Beds 84 D2	Cobham Kent 50 C3
Churchend Essex 69 A6	Clapgate Dorset 17 A4	Cleator Cumb 162 C3	Clopton Northants 100 C2	Cobham Sur 48 C4
Churchend Essex 71 D4	Clapgate Herts 68 A4	Cleator Moor Cumb 162 C3	Clopton Suff 88 B3	Cobholm Island Norf 105 A6
Churchend S Glos 62 D3	Clapham Beds 84 B2	Clebrig Highld 272 A3	Clopton Corner Suff 88 B3	Cobleland Stirl 206 A3
Churchfield W Mid 96 B3	Clapham London 49 B5	Cleckheaton W Yorks 139 A4	Clopton Green Suff 86 B3	Cobnash Hereford 78 A2
Churchgate Street Essex 69 B4	Clapham N Yorks 146 A1	Clee St Margaret Shrops 94 C3	Close Clark I o M 152 D2	Coburty Aberds 269 C4
Churchill Devon 25 A6	Clapham W Sus 20 B3	Cleedownton Shrops 94 C3	Closeburn Dumfries 183 C6	Cock Bank Wrex 110 A2
Churchill Devon 14 A3	Clappers Borders 198 A3	Cleehill Shrops 94 D3	Closworth Som 29 D5	Cock Bridge Aberds 243 B5
Churchill N Som 42 D3	Clappersgate Cumb 154 A2	Cleethorpes NE Lincs 143 C5	Clothall Herts 85 D4	Cock Clarks Essex 70 C2
Churchill Oxon 64 A3	Clapton Som 14 A4	Cleeton St Mary Shrops 95 D4	Clotton Ches 127 C5	Cockayne N Yorks 159 B5
Churchill Worcs 96 D1	Clapton-in-Gordano N Som 42 B3	Cleeve N Som 42 C3	Clough Foot W Yorks 138 A2	Cockayne Hatley Cambs 85 C4
Churchill Worcs 80 B2	Clapton-on-the-Hill Glos 64 B2	Cleeve Hill Glos 63 A5	Cloughton N Yorks 160 B4	Cockburnspath Borders 211 C4
Churchinford Som 28 D2	Clapworthy Devon 26 C1	Cleeve Prior Worcs 80 C3	Cloughton Newlands N Yorks 160 B4	Cockenzie and Port Seton E Loth 209 C7
Churchover Warks 98 C2	Clara Vale T & W 178 C3	Clegyrnant Powys 91 B7	Clousta Shetland 285 H5	Cockerham Lancs 145 B4
Churchstanton Som 28 D1	Clarach Ceredig 90 D4	Clehonger Hereford 78 D2	Clouston Orkney 282 F3	Cockermouth Cumb 163 A4
Churchstow Devon 7 C6	Clarbeston Pembs 55 B6	Cleish Perth 208 A3	Clova Aberds 255 D5	Cockernhoe Green Herts 67 A6
Churchtown Derbys 130 C2	Clarbeston Road Pembs 55 B6	Cleland N Lnrk 194 A3	Clova Angus 232 A1	Cockfield Durham 166 C4
Churchtown I o M 152 B4	Clarborough Notts 132 A2	Clench Common Wilts 45 C5	Clove Lodge Durham 166 D2	Cockfield Suff 87 B5
Churchtown Lancs 145 C4	Clardon Highld 280 B3	Clenchwarton Norf 118 C2	Clovelly Devon 24 C4	Cockfosters London 68 D2
Churchtown Mers 136 B2	Clare Suff 86 C3	Clent Worcs 96 D2	Clovelly Village Devon 24 C4	Cocking W Sus 20 A1
Churnsike Lodge Northumb 177 B4	Clarebrand Dumfries 173 B5	Cleobury Mortimer Shrops 95 D4	Clovenfords Borders 196 C3	Cockington Torbay 8 B2
Churston Ferrers Torbay 8 B3	Claremont Landscape Garden, Esher Sur 48 C4	Cleobury North Shrops 95 C4	Clovenstone Aberds 245 A4	Cocklake Som 28 A4
Churt Sur 34 C1	Clarencefield Dumfries 174 B3	Cleongart Argyll 190 B2	Clovullin Highld 237 C4	Cockley Beck Cumb 163 D5
	Clarilaw Borders 186 B4	Clephanton Highld 253 A4	Clow Bridge Lancs 137 A7	Cockley Cley Norf 102 A3
		Clerklands Borders 186 A4	Clowne Derbys 131 B4	Cockshutt Shrops 110 C3
		Clestrain Orkney 283 G4	Clows Top Worcs 95 D5	Cockthorpe Norf 120 A1
		Cleuch Head Borders 187 B4	Cloy Wrex 110 A2	Cockwood Devon 13 C4
		Cleughbrae Dumfries 174 A3	Cluanie Inn Highld 239 A4	Cockyard Hereford 78 D2
		Clevancy Wilts 45 B4	Cluanie Lodge Highld 239 A4	
		Clevedon N Som 42 B3		

Codda Corn 10 D2
Coddenham Suff 88 B2
Coddington Ches 127 D4
Coddington Hereford 79 C5
Coddington Notts 132 D3
Codford St Mary Wilts 30 B3
Codford St Peter Wilts 30 B3
Codicote Herts 68 B2
Codmore Hill W Sus 34 D3
Codnor Derbys 114 A2
Codrington S Glos 43 B6
Codsall Staffs 95 A6
Codsall Wood Staffs 95 A6
Coed Duon = Blackwood Caerph 41 B6
Coed Mawr Gwyn 123 C5
Coed Morgan Mon 61 B5
Coed-Talon Flint 126 D2
Coed-y-bryn Ceredig 73 B6
Coed-y-paen Mon 61 D5
Coed-yr-ynys Powys 60 A3
Coed Ystumgwern Gwyn 107 D5
Coedely Rhondda 41 C5
Coedkernew Newport 42 A1
Coedpoeth Wrex 126 D2
Coedway Powys 110 D2
Coelbren Powys 59 D5
Coffinswell Devon 8 A2
Cofton Hackett Worcs 96 D3
Cogan V Glam 41 D6
Cogenhoe Northants 83 A5
Cogges Oxon 65 C4
Coggeshall Essex 70 A2
Coggeshall Hamlet Essex 70 A2
Coggins Mill E Sus 36 D3
Coig Peighinnean W Isles 288 A6
Coig Peighinnean Bhuirgh W Isles 288 B5
Coignafearn Lodge Highld 241 A4
Coilacriech Aberds 243 C6
Coilantogle Stirl 217 D5
Coilleag W Isles 286 E3
Coillore Highld 246 A2
Coity Bridgend 40 C4
Col W Isles 288 C5
Col Uarach W Isles 288 D5
Colaboll Highld 272 C3
Colan Corn 4 A3
Colaton Raleigh Devon 13 C5
Colbost Highld 258 D2
Colburn N Yorks 157 B5
Colby Cumb 165 C4
Colby I o M 152 D2
Colby Norf 120 B4
Colchester Essex 71 A4
Colchester Zoo Essex 70 A3
Colcot V Glam 41 E6
Cold Ash W Berks 46 C3
Cold Ashby Northants 98 D3
Cold Ashton S Glos 43 B6
Cold Aston Glos 64 B2
Cold Blow Pembs 55 C7
Cold Brayfield M Keynes 83 B6
Cold Hanworth Lincs 133 A5
Cold Harbour Lincs 116 B2
Cold Hatton Telford 111 C5
Cold Hesledon Durham 168 A2
Cold Higham Northants 82 B3
Cold Kirby N Yorks 158 C4
Cold Newton Leics 99 A4
Cold Northcott Corn 10 C3
Cold Norton Essex 70 C2
Cold Overton Leics 115 D6
Coldbackie Highld 277 C7
Coldbeck Cumb 155 A6
Coldblow London 50 B2
Coldean Brighton 21 B6
Coldeast Devon 12 D3
Colden W Yorks 138 A2
Colden Common Hants 32 C3
Coldfair Green Suff 89 A5
Coldham Cambs 101 A6
Coldharbour Glos 62 C1
Coldharbour Kent 36 A3
Coldharbour Sur 35 B4
Coldingham Borders 211 D6
Coldrain Perth 219 D5
Coldred Kent 39 A4
Coldridge Devon 12 A1
Coldstream Angus 220 A3
Coldstream Borders 198 C2
Coldwaltham W Sus 20 A3
Coldwells Aberds 257 B6
Coldwells Croft Aberds 255 D6
Coldyeld Shrops 94 B1
Cole Som 29 B6
Cole Green Herts 68 B2
Cole Henley Hants 46 D2
Colebatch Shrops 93 C7
Colebrook Devon 13 A5
Colebrooke Devon 12 B2
Coleby Lincs 133 C4
Coleby N Lincs 141 B6
Coleford Devon 12 A2
Coleford Glos 62 B1
Coleford Som 29 A6
Colehill Dorset 17 A4
Coleman's Hatch E Sus 36 C2
Colemere Shrops 110 B3
Colemore Hants 33 B6
Coleorton Leics 114 D2
Colerne Wilts 44 B2
Cole's Green Suff 88 A3
Coles Green Suff 88 C1
Colesbourne Glos 63 B5
Colesden Beds 84 B3
Coleshill Bucks 67 D4
Coleshill Oxon 64 D3
Coleshill Warks 97 C5
Colestocks Devon 13 A5
Colgate W Sus 35 C5
Colgrain Argyll 206 B1
Colinsburgh Fife 221 D4
Colinton Edin 209 D5
Colintraive Argyll 203 A5
Colkirk Norf 119 C6
Collace Perth 220 A2
Collafirth Shetland 284 G6
Collaton St Mary Torbay 8 B2
College Milton S Lnrk 205 C6
Collessie Fife 220 C2
Collier Row London 69 D5
Collier Street Kent 37 B5
Collier's End Herts 68 A3
Collier's Green Kent 37 C5
Colliery Row T & W 167 A6
Collieston Aberds 257 D5
Collin Dumfries 174 A3
Collingbourne Ducis Wilts 45 D6
Collingbourne Kingston Wilts 45 D6
Collingham Notts 132 C3
Collingham W Yorks 148 C2
Collington Hereford 79 A4
Collingtree Northants 83 B4
Collins Green Warr 137 D4
Colliston Angus 233 D4
Collycroft Warks 97 C6
Collynie Aberds 256 C3
Collyweston Northants 100 A1
Colmonell S Ayrs 180 C3
Colmworth Beds 84 B3
Coln Rogers Glos 64 C1
Coln St Aldwyn's Glos 64 C2
Coln St Dennis Glos 64 B1
Colnabaichin Aberds 243 B5
Colnbrook Slough 48 B3
Colne Cambs 101 D5
Colne Lancs 146 C2
Colne Edge Lancs 146 C2
Colne Engaine Essex 87 D4
Colney Norf 104 A2
Colney Heath Herts 68 C2
Colney Street Herts 67 C6
Colpy Aberds 256 C1
Colquhar Borders 196 B2
Colsterdale N Yorks 157 C5
Colsterworth Lincs 116 C2
Colston Bassett Notts 115 B4
Coltfield Moray 266 C2
Colthouse Cumb 154 B2
Coltishall Norf 121 D4
Coltness N Lnrk 194 A3
Colton Cumb 154 C2
Colton Norf 104 A2
Colton N Yorks 148 C4
Colton Staffs 113 C4
Colton W Yorks 148 D2
Colva Powys 77 B6
Colvend Dumfries 173 C6
Colvister Shetland 284 D7
Colwall Green Hereford 79 C5
Colwall Stone Hereford 79 C5
Colwell Northumb 178 B1
Colwich Staffs 112 C4
Colwick Notts 115 A4
Colwinston V Glam 40 D4
Colworth W Sus 20 B2
Colwyn Bay = Bae Colwyn Conwy 124 B3
Colyford Devon 14 B2
Colyton Devon 14 B2
Combe Hereford 78 A1
Combe Oxon 65 B5
Combe W Berks 46 C1
Combe Common Sur 34 C2
Combe Down Bath 43 C6
Combe Florey Som 27 B6
Combe Hay Bath 43 D6
Combe Martin Devon 25 A6
Combe Moor Hereford 78 A1
Combe Raleigh Devon 13 A6
Combe St Nicholas Som 28 D3
Combeinteignhead Devon 13 D4
Comberbach Ches 127 B6
Comberton Cambs 85 B5
Comberton Hereford 78 A2
Combpyne Devon 14 B2
Combridge Staffs 113 B4
Combrook Warks 81 B6
Combs Derbys 129 B5
Combs Suff 87 B6
Combs Ford Suff 87 B6
Combwich Som 28 A2
Comers Aberds 244 B3
Comins Coch Ceredig 90 D4
Commercial End Cambs 86 A1
Commins Capel Betws Ceredig 75 C5
Commins Coch Powys 91 B6
Common Edge Blkpool 144 D3
Common Side Derbys 130 B3
Commondale N Yorks 169 D4
Commonmoor Corn 6 A1
Commonside Ches 127 B5
Compstall Gtr Man 138 D2
Compton Devon 8 A2
Compton Hants 32 C3
Compton Sur 34 B1
Compton Sur 34 B2
Compton W Berks 46 B3
Compton Wilts 45 D5
Compton W Sus 33 D6
Compton Abbas Dorset 30 D2
Compton Abdale Glos 63 B6
Compton Acres Poole 17 C4
Compton Bassett Wilts 44 B4
Compton Beauchamp Oxon 45 A6
Compton Bishop Som 42 D2
Compton Chamberlayne Wilts 31 C4
Compton Dando Bath 43 C5
Compton Dundon Som 29 B4
Compton Martin Bath 43 D4
Compton Pauncefoot Som 29 C6
Compton Valence Dorset 15 B5
Comrie Fife 208 B3
Comrie Perth 218 B2
Conaglen House Highld 237 C4
Conchra Argyll 214 D3
Concraigie Perth 231 D5
Conder Green Lancs 145 B4
Conderton Worcs 80 D2
Condicote Glos 64 A2
Condorrat N Lnrk 207 C5
Condover Shrops 94 A2
Coney Weston Suff 103 D5
Coneyhurst W Sus 35 D4
Coneysthorpe N Yorks 159 D6
Coneythorpe N Yorks 148 B2
Conford Hants 33 B7
Congash Highld 253 D6
Congdon's Shop Corn 10 D3
Congerstone Leics 97 A6
Congham Norf 119 C4
Congl-y-wal Gwyn 108 A2
Congleton Ches 128 C3
Congresbury N Som 42 C3
Congreve Staffs 112 D3
Conicavel Moray 253 A5
Coningsby Lincs 134 D2
Conington Cambs 100 C3
Conington Cambs 85 A5
Conisbrough S Yorks 140 D3
Conisby Argyll 200 B2
Conisholme Lincs 143 D6
Coniston Cumb 154 B2
Coniston E Yorks 151 D4
Coniston Cold N Yorks 146 B3
Conistone N Yorks 146 A3
Connah's Quay Flint 126 C2
Connel Argyll 226 C4
Connel Park E Ayrs 182 A4
Connor Downs Corn 2 B3
Conon Bridge Highld 252 A1
Conon House Highld 252 A1
Cononley N Yorks 146 C3
Conordan Highld 247 A4
Consall Staffs 112 A3
Consett Durham 178 D3
Constable Burton N Yorks 157 B5
Constantine Corn 3 C5
Constantine Bay Corn 9 D4
Contin Highld 251 A6
Contlaw Aberdeen 245 B5
Conwy Conwy 124 B2
Conwy Castle Conwy 124 B2
Conyer Kent 51 C6
Conyers Green Suff 87 A4
Cooden E Sus 23 B5
Cooil I o M 152 D3
Cookbury Devon 11 A5
Cookham Windsor 48 A1
Cookham Dean Windsor 47 A6
Cookham Rise Windsor 48 A1
Cookhill Worcs 80 B3
Cookley Suff 104 D4
Cookley Worcs 95 C6
Cookley Green Oxon 66 D1
Cookney Aberds 245 C5
Cookridge W Yorks 147 C6
Cooksbridge E Sus 22 A2
Cooksmill Green Essex 69 C6
Coolham W Sus 35 D4
Cooling Medway 51 B4
Coombe Corn 24 D3
Coombe Corn 4 B4
Coombe Hants 33 C5
Coombe Wilts 45 D5
Coombe Bissett Wilts 31 C5
Coombe Hill Glos 63 A4
Coombe Keynes Dorset 16 C2
Coombes W Sus 21 B4
Coopersale Common Essex 69 C4
Cootham W Sus 20 A3
Copdock Suff 88 C2
Copford Green Essex 70 A3
Copgrove N Yorks 148 A2
Copister Shetland 284 F6
Cople Beds 84 C3
Copley Durham 166 C3
Coplow Dale Derbys 129 B6
Copmanthorpe York 149 C4
Coppathorne Corn 10 A3
Coppenhall Staffs 112 D3
Coppenhall Moss Ches 128 D2
Copperhouse Corn 2 B3
Coppingford Cambs 100 C3
Copplestone Devon 12 A2
Coppull Lancs 137 B4
Coppull Moor Lancs 137 B4
Copsale W Sus 35 D4
Copshaw Holm = Newcastleton Borders 176 A2
Copster Green Lancs 145 D6
Copston Magna Warks 98 C1
Copt Heath W Mid 97 D4
Copt Hewick N Yorks 158 D2
Copt Oak Leics 114 D2
Copthorne Shrops 110 D3
Copthorne W Sus 35 C6
Copy's Green Norf 119 B6
Copythorne Hants 32 D2
Corbets Tey London 50 A2
Corbridge Northumb 178 C1
Corby Northants 99 C5
Corby Glen Lincs 116 C2
Cordon N Ayrs 191 B6
Coreley Shrops 95 D4
Cores End Bucks 48 A2
Corfe Som 28 D2
Corfe Castle Dorset 16 C3
Corfe Castle Dorset 16 C3
Corfe Mullen Dorset 16 B3
Corfton Shrops 94 C2
Corgarff Aberds 243 B5
Corhampton Hants 33 C5
Corlae Dumfries 183 C4
Corley Warks 97 C6
Corley Ash Warks 97 C5
Corley Moor Warks 97 C5
Cornaa I o M 152 C4
Cornabus Argyll 200 D3
Cornel Conwy 124 C2
Corner Row Lancs 144 D4
Corney Cumb 153 A2
Cornforth Durham 167 B6
Cornhill Aberds 267 D6
Cornhill-on-Tweed Northumb 198 C2
Cornholme W Yorks 138 A2
Cornish Cyder Farm, Truro Corn 4 B2
Cornish Hall End Essex 86 D2
Cornquoy Orkney 283 H6
Cornsay Durham 166 A4
Cornsay Colliery Durham 167 A4
Corntown Highld 252 A1
Corntown V Glam 40 D4
Cornwell Oxon 64 A3
Cornwood Devon 7 B5
Cornworthy Devon 8 B2
Corpach Highld 237 B4
Corpusty Norf 120 B3
Corran Highld 237 C4
Corran Highld 238 B2
Corranbuie Argyll 202 B3
Corrany I o M 152 C4
Corrie N Ayrs 203 D5
Corrie Common Dumfries 185 D5
Corriecravie N Ayrs 191 C5
Corriemoillie Highld 263 D5
Corriemulzie Lodge Highld 263 A5
Corrievarkie Lodge Perth 229 A4
Corrievorrie Highld 252 D3
Corrimony Highld 251 C5
Corringham Lincs 141 D6
Corringham Thurrock 51 A4
Corris Gwyn 91 B5
Corris Uchaf Gwyn 91 B5
Corrour Shooting Lodge Highld 228 B3
Corrow Argyll 215 B4
Corry Highld 247 B5
Corry of Ardnagrask Highld 251 B7
Corrykinloch Highld 271 B6
Corrymuckloch Perth 218 A3
Corrynachenchy Argyll 225 B5
Cors-y-Gedol Gwyn 107 D5
Corsback Highld 280 A4
Corscombe Dorset 15 A5
Corse Aberds 255 B7
Corse Glos 62 A3
Corse Lawn Worcs 79 D6
Corse of Kinnoir Aberds 255 B6
Corsewall Dumfries 170 A2
Corsham Wilts 44 B2
Corsindae Aberds 244 B3
Corsley Wilts 30 A2
Corsley Heath Wilts 30 A2
Corsock Dumfries 173 A5
Corston Bath 43 C5
Corston Wilts 44 A3
Corstorphine Edin 209 C4
Cortachy Angus 232 C1
Corton Suff 105 B6
Corton Wilts 30 A3
Corton Denham Som 29 C6
Coruanan Lodge Highld 237 C4
Corunna W Isles 287 H3
Corwen Denb 109 A5
Coryton Devon 11 C5
Coryton Thurrock 51 A4
Cosby Leics 98 B2
Coseley W Mid 96 B2
Cosgrove Northants 83 C4
Cosham Ptsmth 19 A5
Cosheston Pembs 55 D6
Cossall Notts 114 A2
Cossington Leics 115 D4
Cossington Som 28 A3
Costa Orkney 282 E4
Costessey Norf 120 D3
Costock Notts 114 C3
Coston Leics 115 C6
Cote Oxon 64 C4
Cotebrook Ches 127 C5
Cotehele House Corn 6 A3
Cotehill Cumb 176 D2
Cotes Cumb 154 C3
Cotes Leics 114 C3
Cotes Staffs 112 B2
Cotesbach Leics 98 C2
Cotgrave Notts 115 B4
Cothall Aberds 245 A5
Cotham Notts 115 A5
Cothelstone Som 28 B1
Cotherstone Durham 166 D3
Cothill Oxon 65 D5
Cotleigh Devon 14 A2
Cotmanhay Derbys 114 A2
Cotmaton Devon 13 C6
Coton Cambs 85 B6
Coton Northants 98 D3
Coton Staffs 112 C2
Coton Staffs 112 B3
Coton Clanford Staffs 112 C2

Coton Hill Shrops 110 D3
Coton Hill Staffs 112 B3
Coton in the Elms Derbys 113 D6
Cotswold Wild Life Park,
Burford Oxon 64 C3
Cott Devon 8 A1
Cottam E Yorks 150 A2
Cottam Lancs 145 D5
Cottam Notts 132 B3
Cottartown Highld 253 C6
Cottenham Cambs 85 A6
Cotterdale N Yorks 156 B2
Cottered Herts 68 A3
Cotteridge W Mid 96 D3
Cotterstock Northants 100 B2
Cottesbrooke Northants 99 D4
Cottesmore Rutland 116 D2
Cotteylands Devon 27 D4
Cottingham E Yorks 150 D3
Cottingham Northants 99 B5
Cottingley W Yorks 147 D5
Cottisford Oxon 82 D2
Cotton Staffs 113 A4
Cotton Suff 87 A6
Cotton End Beds 84 C2
Cottown Aberds 255 D6
Cottown Aberds 245 A4
Cottown Aberds 256 B3
Cotwalton Staffs 112 B3
Couch's Mill Corn 5 B6
Coughton Hereford 62 A1
Coughton Warks 80 A3
Coulaghailtro Argyll 202 B2
Coulags Highld 249 B6
Coulby Newham M'bro 168 D3
Coulderton Cumb 162 D2
Coulin Highld 250 A2
Coull Aberds 244 B2
Coull Argyll 200 B2
Coulport Argyll 215 D5
Coulsdon London 35 A5
Coulston Wilts 44 D3
Coulter S Lnrk 195 C5
Coulton N Yorks 159 D5
Cound Shrops 94 A3
Coundon Durham 167 C5
Coundon W Mid 97 C6
Coundon Grange Durham 167 C5
Countersett N Yorks 156 C3
Countess Wilts 31 A5
Countess Wear Devon 13 C4
Countesthorpe Leics 98 B2
Countisbury Devon 26 A2
County Oak W Sus 35 C5
Coup Green Lancs 137 A4
Coupar Angus Perth 231 D6
Coupland Northumb 198 C3
Cour Argyll 202 D3
Courance Dumfries 184 C3
Court-at-Street Kent 38 B2
Court Henry Carms 58 C2
Courteenhall Northants 83 B4
Courtsend Essex 71 D4
Courtway Som 28 B2
Cousland Midloth 209 D6
Cousley Wood E Sus 37 C4
Cove Argyll 215 D5
Cove Borders 211 C4
Cove Devon 27 D4
Cove Hants 34 A1
Cove Highld 261 A5
Cove Bay Aberdeen 245 B6
Cove Bottom Suff 105 D5
Covehithe Suff 105 C6
Coven Staffs 96 A2
Coveney Cambs 101 C6
Covenham St
Bartholomew Lincs 143 D5
Covenham St Mary Lincs 143 D5
Coventry W Mid 97 D6
Coventry Airport Warks 97 D6
Coventry Cathedral W Mid 97 D6
Coverack Corn 3 D5
Coverham N Yorks 157 C5
Covesea Moray 266 B2
Covington Cambs 100 D2
Covington S Lnrk 195 C4
Cow Ark Lancs 145 C6
Cowan Bridge Lancs 155 D5
Cowbeech E Sus 22 A4
Cowbit Lincs 117 D5
Cowbridge Lincs 117 A6
Cowbridge Som 27 A4
Cowbridge = Y
Bont-Faen V Glam 41 D4

Cowdale Derbys 129 B5
Cowden Kent 36 B2
Cowdenbeath Fife 209 A4
Cowdenburn Borders 195 A7
Cowers Lane Derbys 113 A7
Cowes I o W 18 B3
Cowesby N Yorks 158 C3
Cowfold W Sus 35 D5
Cowgill Cumb 155 C6
Cowie Aberds 245 D5
Cowie Stirl 207 B6
Cowley Devon 13 B4
Cowley Glos 63 B5
Cowley London 48 A3
Cowley Oxon 65 C6
Cowleymoor Devon 27 D4
Cowling Lancs 137 B4
Cowling N Yorks 146 C3
Cowling N Yorks 157 C6
Cowlinge Suff 86 B3
Cowpe Lancs 138 A1
Cowpen Northumb 179 A4
Cowpen Bewley Stockton 168 C2
Cowplain Hants 33 D5
Cowshill Durham 165 A6
Cowslip Green N Som 42 C3
Cowstrandburn Fife 208 A3
Cowthorpe N Yorks 148 B3
Cox Common Suff 105 C4
Cox Green Windsor 48 B1
Cox Moor Notts 131 D5
Coxbank Ches 111 A5
Coxbench Derbys 114 A1
Coxford Norf 119 C5
Coxford Soton 32 D2
Coxheath Kent 37 A5
Coxhill Kent 39 A4
Coxhoe Durham 167 B6
Coxley Som 29 A5
Coxwold N Yorks 158 D4
Coychurch Bridgend 40 D4
Coylton S Ayrs 193 C4
Coylumbridge Highld 242 A2
Coynach Aberds 244 B1
Coynachie Aberds 255 C5
Coytrahen Bridgend 40 C3
Crabadon Devon 7 B6
Crabbs Cross Worcs 80 A3
Crabtree W Sus 35 D5
Crackenthorpe Cumb 165 C4
Crackington Haven Corn 10 B2
Crackley Warks 97 D5
Crackleybank Shrops 111 D6
Crackpot N Yorks 156 B3
Cracoe N Yorks 146 A3
Craddock Devon 27 D5
Cradhlastadh W Isles 287 A5
Cradley Hereford 79 C5
Cradley Heath W Mid 96 C2
Crafthole Corn 6 B2
Cragg Vale W Yorks 138 A3
Craggan Highld 253 D6
Craggie Highld 274 C2
Craggie Highld 252 C3
Craghead Durham 179 D4
Crai Powys 59 C5
Craibstone Moray 267 D5
Craichie Angus 232 D3
Craig Dumfries 173 A4
Craig Dumfries 173 B4
Craig Highld 250 B2
Craig Castle Aberds 255 D5
Craig-cefn-parc Swansea 40 A1
Craig Penllyn V Glam 41 D4
Craig-y-don Conwy 124 A2
Craig-y-nos Powys 59 D5
Craiganor Lodge Perth 229 C5
Craigdam Aberds 256 C3
Craigdarroch Dumfries 183 C5
Craigdarroch Highld 251 A6
Craigdhu Highld 251 B6
Craigearn Aberds 245 A4
Craigellachie Moray 254 B3
Craigencross Dumfries 170 A2
Craigend Perth 219 B6
Craigend Stirl 207 B5
Craigendive Argyll 214 D3
Craigendoran Argyll 215 D6
Craigends Renfs 205 B4
Craigens Argyll 182 A3
Craigens E Ayrs 182 A3
Craighat Stirl 206 B2
Craighead Fife 221 D6
Craighlaw Mains
Dumfries 171 A5
Craighouse Argyll 201 B5
Craigie Aberds 245 A6

Craigie Dundee 220 A4
Craigie Perth 219 B6
Craigie Perth 231 D5
Craigie S Ayrs 193 B4
Craigiefield Orkney 282 F5
Craigielaw E Loth 210 C1
Craiglockhart Edin 209 C5
Craigmalloch E Ayrs 182 C2
Craigmaud Aberds 268 D3
Craigmillar Edin 209 C5
Craigmore Argyll 203 B6
Craignant Shrops 110 B1
Craigneuk N Lnrk 194 A2
Craigneuk N Lnrk 207 D5
Craignure Argyll 225 C6
Craigo Angus 233 B4
Craigow Perth 219 D5
Craigrothie Fife 220 C3
Craigroy Moray 266 D2
Craigruie Stirl 217 B4
Craigston Castle Aberds 268 D2
Craigton Aberdeen 245 B5
Craigton Angus 232 C1
Craigton Angus 221 A5
Craigton Highld 264 A2
Craigtown Highld 279 C4
Craik Borders 185 B6
Crail Fife 221 D6
Crailing Borders 187 A5
Crailinghall Borders 187 A5
Craiselound N Lincs 141 D5
Crakehill N Yorks 158 D3
Crakemarsh Staffs 113 B4
Crambe N Yorks 149 A6
Cramlington Northumb 179 B4
Cramond Edin 209 C4
Cramond Bridge Edin 209 C4
Cranage Ches 128 C2
Cranberry Staffs 112 B2
Cranborne Dorset 31 D4
Cranbourne Brack 48 B2
Cranbrook Kent 37 C5
Cranbrook Common Kent 37 C5
Crane Moor S Yorks 139 C6
Crane's Corner Norf 119 D6
Cranfield Beds 83 C6
Cranford London 48 B4
Cranford St Andrew
Northants 99 D6
Cranford St John
Northants 99 D6
Cranham Glos 63 B4
Cranham London 50 A2
Crank Mers 136 D4
Crank Wood Gtr Man 137 C5
Cranleigh Sur 34 C3
Cranley Suff 104 D2
Cranmer Green Suff 103 D6
Cranmore I o W 18 C2
Cranna Aberds 268 D1
Crannich Argyll 225 B4
Crannoch Moray 267 D5
Cranoe Leics 99 B4
Cransford Suff 88 A4
Cranshaws Borders 210 D3
Cranstal I o M 152 A4
Crantock Corn 4 A2
Cranwell Lincs 116 A3
Cranwich Norf 102 B3
Cranworth Norf 103 A5
Craobh Haven Argyll 213 B5
Crapstone Devon 7 A4
Crarae Argyll 214 C2
Crask Inn Highld 272 B3
Crask of Aigas Highld 251 B6
Craskins Aberds 244 B2
Craster Northumb 189 B5
Craswall Hereford 77 D6
Cratfield Suff 104 D4
Crathes Aberds 245 C4
Crathes Castle and
Gardens Aberds 245 C4
Crathie Aberds 243 C5
Crathie Highld 240 C3
Crathorne N Yorks 158 A3
Craven Arms Shrops 94 C2
Crawcrook T & W 178 C3
Crawford Lancs 136 C3
Crawford S Lnrk 195 A4
Crawfordjohn S Lnrk 194 D3
Crawick Dumfries 183 A5
Crawley Hants 32 B3
Crawley Oxon 64 B4
Crawley W Sus 35 C5
Crawley Down W Sus 35 C6
Crawleyside Durham 166 A2
Crawshawbooth Lancs 137 A7

Crawton Aberds 233 A6
Cray N Yorks 156 D3
Cray Perth 231 B5
Crayford London 50 B2
Crayke N Yorks 159 D4
Crays Hill Essex 69 D7
Cray's Pond Oxon 47 A4
Creacombe Devon 26 D3
Creag Ghoraidh W Isles 286 B3
Creagan Argyll 227 B4
Creaguaineach Lodge
Highld 228 B2
Creaksea Essex 70 D3
Creaton Northants 99 D4
Creca Dumfries 175 A5
Credenhill Hereford 78 C2
Crediton Devon 12 A3
Creebridge Dumfries 171 A6
Creech Heathfield Som 28 C2
Creech St Michael Som 28 C2
Creed Corn 4 C4
Creekmouth London 50 A1
Creeting Bottoms Suff 88 B2
Creeting St Mary Suff 88 B1
Creeton Lincs 116 C3
Creetown Dumfries 171 B6
Creg-ny-Baa I o M 152 C3
Creggans Argyll 214 B3
Cregneash I o M 152 E1
Cregrina Powys 77 B5
Creich Fife 220 B3
Creigiau Cardiff 41 C5
Cremyll Corn 6 B3
Creslow Bucks 66 A3
Cressage Shrops 94 A3
Cressbrook Derbys 129 B6
Cresselly Pembs 55 D6
Cressing Essex 70 A1
Cresswell Northumb 189 D5
Cresswell Staffs 112 B3
Cresswell Quay Pembs 55 D6
Creswell Derbys 131 B5
Cretingham Suff 88 A3
Cretshengan Argyll 202 B2
Crewe Ches 128 D2
Crewe Ches 127 D4
Crewgreen Powys 110 D2
Crewkerne Som 14 A4
Crewton Derby 114 B1
Crianlarich Stirl 216 B3
Cribyn Ceredig 75 C4
Criccieth Gwyn 107 C4
Crich Derbys 130 D3
Crichie Aberds 257 B4
Crichton Midloth 209 D6
Crick Mon 61 D6
Crick Northants 98 D2
Crickadarn Powys 77 C4
Cricket Malherbie Som 28 D3
Cricket St Thomas Som 14 A3
Crickheath Shrops 110 C1
Crickhowell Powys 60 B4
Cricklade Wilts 64 D2
Cricklewood London 49 A5
Cridling Stubbs N Yorks 140 A3
Crieff Perth 218 B3
Crieff Visitors' Centre
Perth 218 B3
Criggion Powys 110 D1
Crigglestone W Yorks 139 B6
Crimond Aberds 269 D5
Crimonmogate Aberds 269 D5
Crimplesham Norf 102 A2
Crinan Argyll 213 C5
Cringleford Norf 104 A2
Cringles W Yorks 147 C4
Crinow Pembs 56 A1
Cripplesease Corn 2 B3
Cripplestyle Dorset 31 D4
Cripp's Corner E Sus 37 D5
Croasdale Cumb 162 C3
Crock Street Som 28 D3
Crockenhill Kent 50 C2
Crockernwell Devon 12 B2
Crockerton Wilts 30 A2
Crocketford or Ninemile
Bar Dumfries 173 A6
Crockey Hill York 149 C5
Crockham Hill Kent 36 A2
Crockleford Heath Essex 71 A4
Crockness Orkney 283 H4
Croes-goch Pembs 54 A4
Croes-lan Ceredig 73 B6
Croes-y-mwyalch Torf 61 D5
Croeserw Neath 40 B3
Croesor Gwyn 107 B6
Croesyceiliog Carms 57 A4
Croesyceiliog Torf 61 D5

Croesywaun Gwyn 107 A5
Croft Leics 98 B2
Croft Lincs 135 C5
Croft Pembs 73 B4
Croft Warr 137 D5
Croft Motor Racing
Circuit N Yorks 157 A6
Croftamie Stirl 206 B2
Croftmalloch W Loth 208 D2
Crofton Wilts 45 C6
Crofton W Yorks 140 B1
Crofts of Benachielt
Highld 275 A5
Crofts of Haddo Aberds 256 C3
Crofts of Inverthernie
Aberds 256 B2
Crofts of Meikle Ardo
Aberds 256 B3
Crofty Swansea 57 C5
Croggan Argyll 225 D6
Croglin Cumb 164 A3
Croich Highld 263 A6
Crois Dughaill W Isles 286 D3
Cromarty Highld 264 D3
Cromblet Aberds 256 C2
Cromdale Highld 253 D6
Cromer Herts 68 A2
Cromer Norf 120 A4
Cromford Derbys 130 D2
Cromhall S Glos 62 D2
Cromhall Common S Glos 43 A5
Cromor W Isles 288 E5
Cromra Highld 240 C3
Cromwell Notts 132 C2
Cronberry E Ayrs 193 C6
Crondall Hants 33 A6
Cronk-y-Voddy I o M 152 C3
Cronton Mers 127 A4
Crook Cumb 154 B3
Crook Durham 167 B4
Crook of Devon Perth 219 D5
Crookedholm E Ayrs 193 B4
Crookes S Yorks 130 A3
Crookham Northumb 198 C3
Crookham W Berks 46 C3
Crookham Village Hants 47 D5
Crookhaugh Borders 195 D5
Crookhouse Borders 187 A6
Crooklands Cumb 154 C4
Croome Park, Pershore
Worcs 80 C1
Cropredy Oxon 82 C1
Cropston Leics 114 D3
Cropthorne Worcs 80 C2
Cropton N Yorks 159 C6
Cropwell Bishop Notts 115 B4
Cropwell Butler Notts 115 B4
Cros W Isles 288 A6
Crosbost W Isles 288 E4
Crosby Cumb 162 A3
Crosby I o M 152 D3
Crosby N Lincs 141 B6
Crosby Garrett Cumb 155 A6
Crosby Ravensworth
Cumb 165 D4
Crosby Villa Cumb 162 A3
Croscombe Som 29 A5
Cross Som 42 D3
Cross Ash Mon 61 B6
Cross-at-Hand Kent 37 B5
Cross Green Devon 11 C4
Cross Green Suff 87 B5
Cross Green Suff 87 B4
Cross Green Warks 81 B6
Cross Hands Carms 57 A5
Cross-hands Carms 73 D4
Cross Hands Pembs 55 C6
Cross Hill Derbys 114 A2
Cross Houses Shrops 94 A3
Cross in Hand E Sus 36 D3
Cross in Hand Leics 98 C2
Cross Inn Ceredig 73 A6
Cross Inn Ceredig 75 B4
Cross Inn Rhondda 41 C5
Cross Keys Kent 36 A3
Cross Lane Head Shrops 95 B5
Cross Lanes Corn 3 C4
Cross Lanes N Yorks 148 A4
Cross Lanes Wrex 110 A2
Cross Oak Powys 60 A3
Cross of Jackston Aberds 256 C2
Cross o'th'hands Derbys 113 A6
Cross Street Suff 104 D2
Crossaig Argyll 202 C3
Crossal Highld 246 A3
Crossapol Argyll 222 C2

Crossburn Falk	207	C6
Crossbush W Sus	20	B3
Crosscanonby Cumb	162	A3
Crossdale Street Norf	120	B4
Crossens Mers	136	B2
Crossflatts W Yorks	147	C5
Crossford Fife	208	B3
Crossford S Lnrk	194	B3
Crossgate Lincs	117	C5
Crossgatehall E Loth	209	D6
Crossgates Fife	208	B4
Crossgates Powys	77	A4
Crossgill Lancs	145	A5
Crosshill E Ayrs	193	C4
Crosshill Fife	209	A4
Crosshill S Ayrs	192	E3
Crosshouse E Ayrs	192	B3
Crossings Cumb	176	B3
Crosskeys Caerph	41	B7
Crosskirk Highld	279	A6
Crosslanes Shrops	110	D2
Crosslee Borders	185	A6
Crosslee Renfs	205	B4
Crossmichael Dumfries	173	B5
Crossmoor Lancs	144	D4
Crossroads Aberds	245	C4
Crossroads E Ayrs	193	B4
Crossway Hereford	79	D4
Crossway Mon	61	B6
Crossway Powys	77	B4
Crossway Green Worcs	79	A6
Crossways Dorset	16	C1
Crosswell Pembs	72	C4
Crosswood Ceredig	75	A5
Crosthwaite Cumb	154	B3
Croston Lancs	136	B3
Crostwick Norf	121	D4
Crostwight Norf	121	C5
Crothair W Isles	288	D2
Crouch Kent	36	A4
Crouch Hill Dorset	29	D7
Crouch House Green Kent	36	B2
Croucheston Wilts	31	C4
Croughton Northants	82	D2
Crovie Aberds	268	C3
Crow Edge S Yorks	139	C4
Crow Hill Hereford	62	A2
Crowan Corn	3	B4
Crowborough E Sus	36	C3
Crowcombe Som	27	B6
Crowdecote Derbys	129	C6
Crowden Derbys	138	D3
Crowell Oxon	66	D2
Crowfield Northants	82	C3
Crowfield Suff	88	B2
Crowhurst E Sus	23	A5
Crowhurst Sur	36	B1
Crowhurst Lane End Sur	36	B1
Crowland Lincs	117	D5
Crowlas Corn	2	B3
Crowle N Lincs	141	B5
Crowle Worcs	80	B2
Crowmarsh Gifford Oxon	47	A4
Crown Corner Suff	104	D3
Crownhill Plym	6	B3
Crownland Suff	103	E6
Crownthorpe Norf	104	A1
Crowntown Corn	3	B4
Crows-an-wra Corn	2	C1
Crowshill Norf	103	A5
Crowsnest Shrops	94	A1
Crowthorne Brack	47	C6
Crowton Ches	127	B5
Croxall Staffs	113	D5
Croxby Lincs	142	D3
Croxdale Durham	167	B5
Croxden Staffs	113	B4
Croxley Green Herts	67	D5
Croxton Cambs	84	A4
Croxton N Lincs	142	B2
Croxton Norf	103	C4
Croxton Staffs	112	B1
Croxton Kerrial Leics	115	C6
Croxtonbank Staffs	112	B1
Croy Highld	252	B3
Croy N Lnrk	207	C5
Croyde Devon	25	B5
Croydon Cambs	85	C5
Croydon London	49	C6
Crubenmore Lodge Highld	241	C4
Cruckmeole Shrops	94	A2
Cruckton Shrops	110	D3
Cruden Bay Aberds	257	C5
Crudgington Telford	111	D5
Crudwell Wilts	63	D5
Crug Powys	93	D5

Crugmeer Corn	9	D5
Crugybar Carms	58	B3
Crulabhig W Isles	288	D2
Crumlin = Crymlyn Caerph	41	B7
Crumpsall Gtr Man	138	C1
Crundale Kent	38	A2
Crundale Pembs	55	C5
Cruwys Morchard Devon	26	D3
Crux Easton Hants	46	D2
Crwbin Carms	57	A4
Crya Orkney	283	G4
Cryers Hill Bucks	66	D3
Crymlyn Gwyn	123	C6
Crymlyn = Crumlin Caerph	41	B7
Crymych Pembs	73	C4
Crynant Neath	40	A2
Crynfryn Ceredig	75	B4
Crystal Palace National Sports Centre London	49	B6
Cuaig Highld	249	A4
Cuan Argyll	213	A5
Cubbington Warks	81	A6
Cubeck N Yorks	156	C3
Cubert Corn	4	B2
Cubley S Yorks	139	C5
Cubley Common Derbys	113	B5
Cublington Bucks	66	A3
Cublington Hereford	78	D2
Cuckfield W Sus	35	D6
Cucklington Som	29	C7
Cuckney Notts	131	B5
Cuckoo Hill Notts	141	D5
Cuddesdon Oxon	65	C7
Cuddington Bucks	66	B2
Cuddington Ches	127	B6
Cuddington Heath Ches	110	A3
Cuddy Hill Lancs	145	D4
Cudham London	36	A2
Cudliptown Devon	11	D6
Cudworth Som	28	D3
Cudworth S Yorks	140	C1
Cuffley Herts	68	C3
Cuiashader W Isles	288	B6
Cuidhir W Isles	286	F2
Cuidhtinis W Isles	287	F5
Culbo Highld	264	D2
Culbokie Highld	252	A2
Culburnie Highld	251	B6
Culcabock Highld	252	B2
Culcairn Highld	264	D2
Culcharry Highld	253	A4
Culcheth Warr	137	D5
Culdrain Aberds	255	C6
Culduie Highld	249	B4
Culford Suff	103	D4
Culgaith Cumb	165	C4
Culham Oxon	65	D6
Culkein Highld	270	A3
Culkein Drumbeg Highld	270	A4
Culkerton Glos	63	D5
Cullachie Highld	253	D5
Cullen Moray	267	C6
Cullercoats T & W	179	B5
Cullicudden Highld	264	D2
Cullingworth W Yorks	147	D4
Cullipool Argyll	213	A5
Cullivoe Shetland	284	C7
Culloch Perth	218	C2
Culloden Highld	252	B3
Culloden Battlefield, Inverness Highld	252	B3
Cullompton Devon	13	A5
Culmaily Highld	265	A4
Culmazie Dumfries	171	B5
Culmstock Devon	27	D6
Culnacraig Highld	270	D3
Culnaknock Highld	259	B5
Culpho Suff	88	C3
Culrain Highld	264	A1
Culross Fife	208	B2
Culroy S Ayrs	192	D3
Culsh Aberds	256	B3
Culsh Aberds	243	C6
Culshabbin Dumfries	171	B5
Culswick Shetland	285	J4
Cultercullen Aberds	257	D4
Cults Aberdeen	245	B5
Cults Aberds	255	C6
Cults Dumfries	171	C6
Culverstone Green Kent	50	C3
Culverthorpe Lincs	116	A3
Culworth Northants	82	C2
Culzean Castle, Maybole S Ayrs	192	E2
Culzie Lodge Highld	263	C7
Cumbernauld N Lnrk	207	C5

Cumbernauld Village N Lnrk	207	C5
Cumberworth Lincs	135	B5
Cuminestown Aberds	268	D3
Cumlewick Shetland	285	L6
Cummersdale Cumb	175	C6
Cummertrees Dumfries	174	B4
Cummingston Moray	266	C2
Cumnock E Ayrs	193	C5
Cumnor Oxon	65	C5
Cumrew Cumb	176	D3
Cumwhinton Cumb	176	D2
Cumwhitton Cumb	176	D3
Cundall N Yorks	158	D3
Cunninghamhead N Ayrs	204	D3
Cunnister Shetland	284	D7
Cupar Fife	220	C3
Cupar Muir Fife	220	C3
Cupernham Hants	32	C2
Curbar Derbys	130	B2
Curbridge Hants	32	D4
Curbridge Oxon	64	C4
Curdridge Hants	32	D4
Curdworth Warks	97	B4
Curland Som	28	D2
Curlew Green Suff	89	A4
Currarie S Ayrs	180	B3
Curridge W Berks	46	B2
Currie Edin	209	D4
Curry Mallet Som	28	C3
Curry Rivel Som	28	C3
Curtisden Green Kent	37	B5
Curtisknowle Devon	7	B6
Cury Corn	3	C4
Cushnie Aberds	268	C2
Cushuish Som	28	B1
Cusop Hereford	77	C6
Cutcloy Dumfries	171	D6
Cutcombe Som	27	B4
Cutgate Gtr Man	138	B1
Cutiau Gwyn	90	A4
Cutlers Green Essex	86	D1
Cutnall Green Worcs	80	A1
Cutsdean Glos	80	D3
Cutthorpe Derbys	130	B3
Cutts Shetland	285	K6
Cutty Sark, Greenwich London	49	B6
Cuxham Oxon	66	D1
Cuxton Medway	51	C4
Cuxwold Lincs	142	C3
Cwm Bl Gwent	60	C3
Cwm Denb	125	B5
Cwm Swansea	40	B1
Cwm-byr Carms	58	B3
Cwm-Cewydd Gwyn	91	A6
Cwm-cou Ceredig	73	B5
Cwm-Dulais Swansea	57	B6
Cwm-felin-fach Caerph	41	B6
Cwm Ffrwd-oer Torf	61	C4
Cwm-hesgen Gwyn	108	C2
Cwm-hwnt Rhondda	59	E6
Cwm Irfon Powys	76	C2
Cwm-Llinau Powys	91	B6
Cwm-mawr Carms	57	A5
Cwm-parc Rhondda	40	B4
Cwm Penmachno Conwy	108	A2
Cwm-y-glo Carms	57	A5
Cwm-y-glo Gwyn	123	D5
Cwmafan Neath	40	B2
Cwmaman Rhondda	41	B5
Cwmann Carms	75	D4
Cwmavon Torf	61	C4
Cwmbach Carms	73	D5
Cwmbach Carms	57	B4
Cwmbach Powys	76	B4
Cwmbach Powys	77	D5
Cwmbâch Rhondda	41	A5
Cwmbelan Powys	92	C3
Cwmbran = Cwmbrân Torf	61	D4
Cwmbrân = Cwmbran Torf	61	D4
Cwmbrwyno Ceredig	91	D5
Cwmcarn Caerph	41	B7
Cwmcarvan Mon	61	C6
Cwmcych Pembs	73	C5
Cwmdare Rhondda	41	A4
Cwmderwen Powys	92	A3
Cwmdu Carms	58	B3
Cwmdu Powys	60	A3
Cwmdu Swansea	57	C6
Cwmduad Carms	73	C6
Cwmdwr Carms	59	B4
Cwmfelin Bridgend	40	C3
Cwmfelin M Tydf	41	A5
Cwmfelin Boeth Carms	56	A1

Cwmfelin Mynach Carms	73	D5
Cwmffrwd Carms	57	A4
Cwmgiedd Powys	59	D4
Cwmgors Neath	59	D4
Cwmgwili Carms	57	A5
Cwmgwrach Neath	40	A3
Cwmhiraeth Carms	73	C6
Cwmifor Carms	58	C3
Cwmisfael Carms	57	A4
Cwmllynfell Neath	59	D4
Cwmorgan Carms	73	C5
Cwmpengraig Carms	73	C6
Cwmrhos Powys	60	A3
Cwmsychpant Ceredig	74	D3
Cwmtillery Bl Gwent	60	C4
Cwmwysg Powys	59	C5
Cwmyoy Mon	61	A4
Cwmystwyth Ceredig	92	D1
Cwrt Gwyn	91	B4
Cwrt-newydd Ceredig	74	D3
Cwrt-y-cadno Carms	58	A3
Cwrt-y-gollen Powys	60	B4
Cydweli = Kidwelly Carms	57	B4
Cyffordd Llandudno = Llandudno Junction Conwy	124	B2
Cyffylliog Denb	125	D5
Cyfronydd Powys	93	A5
Cymer Neath	40	B3
Cyncoed Cardiff	41	C6
Cynghordy Carms	59	A5
Cynheidre Carms	57	B4
Cynwyd Denb	109	A5
Cynwyl Elfed Carms	73	D6
Cywarch Gwyn	91	A6

Cro – Dar 321

Dalmadilly Aberds	245	A4
Dalmally Argyll	227	D6
Dalmarnock Glasgow	205	B6
Dalmary Stirl	206	A3
Dalmellington E Ayrs	182	B2
Dalmeny Edin	208	C4
Dalmigavie Highld	241	A5
Dalmigavie Lodge Highld	252	D3
Dalmore Highld	264	D2
Dalmuir W Dunb	205	A4
Dalnabreck Highld	235	D5
Dalnacardoch Lodge Perth	229	A6
Dalnacroich Highld	251	A5
Dalnaglar Castle Perth	231	B5
Dalnahaitnach Highld	253	D4
Dalnaspidal Lodge Perth	229	A5
Dalnavaid Perth	230	B4
Dalnavie Highld	264	C2
Dalnawillan Lodge Highld	279	D6
Dalness Highld	237	D5
Dalnessie Highld	273	C4
Dalqueich Perth	219	D5
Dalreavoch Highld	273	D5
Dalry N Ayrs	204	D2
Dalrymple E Ayrs	192	D3
Dalserf S Lnrk	194	A3
Dalston Cumb	175	C6
Dalswinton Dumfries	184	D2
Dalton Dumfries	174	A4
Dalton Lancs	136	C3
Dalton Northumb	177	D7
Dalton Northumb	178	B3
Dalton N Yorks	158	D3
Dalton N Yorks	157	A5
Dalton S Yorks	140	D2
Dalton-in-Furness Cumb	153	C3
Dalton-le-Dale Durham	168	A2
Dalton-on-Tees N Yorks	157	A6
Dalton Piercy Hrtlpl	168	B2
Dalveich Stirl	217	B6
Dalvina Lodge Highld	278	D2
Dalwhinnie Highld	241	D4
Dalwood Devon	14	A2
Dalwyne S Ayrs	181	B5
Dam Green Norf	103	C6
Dam Side Lancs	144	C4
Damerham Hants	31	D5
Damgate Norf	105	A5
Damnaglaur Dumfries	170	D3
Damside Borders	195	B6
Danbury Essex	70	C1
Danby N Yorks	159	A6
Danby Wiske N Yorks	158	B2
Dandaleith Moray	254	B3
Danderhall Midloth	209	D6
Dane End Herts	68	A3
Danebridge Ches	129	C4
Danehill E Sus	36	D2
Danemoor Green Norf	103	A6
Danesford Shrops	95	B5
Daneshill Hants	47	D4
Dangerous Corner Lancs	136	B4
Danskine E Loth	210	D2
Darcy Lever Gtr Man	137	C6
Darenth Kent	50	B2
Daresbury Halton	127	A5
Darfield S Yorks	140	C2
Darfoulds Notts	131	B5
Dargate Kent	52	C2
Darite Corn	6	A1
Darlaston W Mid	96	B2
Darley N Yorks	147	B6
Darley Bridge Derbys	130	C2
Darley Head N Yorks	147	B5
Darley Moor Motor Racing Circuit Derbys	113	A5
Darlingscott Warks	81	C5
Darlington Darl	167	D5
Darliston Shrops	111	B4
Darlton Notts	132	B2
Darnall S Yorks	130	A3
Darnick Borders	197	C4
Darowen Powys	91	B6
Darra Aberds	256	B2
Darracott Devon	25	B5
Darras Hall Northumb	178	B3
Darrington W Yorks	140	A2
Darsham Suff	89	A5
Dartford Kent	50	B2
Dartford Crossing Kent	50	B2
Dartington Devon	8	A1
Dartington Cider Press Centre Devon	8	A1

D

Dacre Cumb	164	C2
Dacre N Yorks	147	A5
Dacre Banks N Yorks	147	A5
Daddry Shield Durham	166	B1
Dadford Bucks	82	D3
Dadlington Leics	97	B7
Dafarn Faig Gwyn	107	B4
Dafen Carms	57	B5
Daffy Green Norf	103	A5
Dagenham London	50	A1
Daglingworth Glos	63	C5
Dagnall Bucks	67	B4
Dail Beag W Isles	288	C3
Dail bho Dheas W Isles	288	A5
Dail bho Thuath W Isles	288	A5
Dail Mor W Isles	288	C3
Daill Argyll	200	B3
Dailly S Ayrs	181	A4
Dairsie or Osnaburgh Fife	220	C4
Daisy Hill Gtr Man	137	C5
Dalabrog W Isles	286	D3
Dalavich Argyll	214	A2
Dalbeattie Dumfries	173	B6
Dalblair E Ayrs	182	A4
Dalbog Angus	232	A3
Dalbury Derbys	113	B6
Dalby I o M	152	D2
Dalby N Yorks	159	D5
Dalchalloch Perth	229	B6
Dalchalm Highld	274	D3
Dalchenna Argyll	214	B3
Dalchirach Moray	254	C2
Dalchork Highld	272	C3
Dalchreichart Highld	239	A6
Dalchruin Perth	218	C2
Dalderby Lincs	134	C2
Dale Pembs	54	D4
Dale Abbey Derbys	114	B2
Dale Head Cumb	164	D2
Dale of Walls Shetland	285	H3
Dalelia Highld	235	D6
Daless Highld	253	C4
Dalfaber Highld	242	A2
Dalgarven N Ayrs	204	D2
Dalgety Bay Fife	209	B4
Dalginross Perth	218	B2
Dalguise Perth	230	D3
Dalhalvaig Highld	279	C4
Dalham Suff	86	A3
Dalinlongart Argyll	215	D4
Dalkeith Midloth	209	D6
Dallam Warr	137	D4
Dallas Moray	266	D2
Dalleagles E Ayrs	182	A3
Dallinghoo Suff	88	B3
Dallington E Sus	23	A4
Dallington Northants	83	A4
Dallow N Yorks	157	D5

Dartington Crystal Devon 25 D5
Dartmeet Devon 12 D1
Dartmouth Devon 8 B2
Darton S Yorks 139 C6
Darvel E Ayrs 193 B5
Darwell Hole E Sus 23 A4
Darwen Blkburn 137 A5
Datchet Windsor 48 B2
Datchworth Herts 68 B2
Datchworth Green Herts 68 B2
Daubhill Gtr Man 137 C6
Daugh of Kinermony Moray 254 B3
Dauntsey Wilts 44 A3
Dava Moray 253 C6
Davenham Ches 127 B6
Davenport Green Ches 128 B3
Daventry Northants 82 A2
David's Well Powys 93 D4
Davidson's Mains Edin 209 C5
Davidstow Corn 10 C2
Davington Dumfries 185 B5
Daviot Aberds 256 D2
Daviot Highld 252 C3
Davoch of Grange Moray 267 D5
Davyhulme Gtr Man 137 D6
Dawley Telford 95 A4
Dawlish Devon 13 D4
Dawlish Warren Devon 13 D4
Dawn Conwy 124 B3
Daws Heath Essex 51 A5
Daw's House Corn 10 C4
Dawsmere Lincs 118 B1
Dayhills Staffs 112 B3
Daylesford Glos 64 A3
Ddôl-Cownwy Powys 109 D5
Ddrydwy Anglesey 122 C3
Deadwater Northumb 187 D5
Deaf Hill Durham 167 B6
Deal Kent 53 D5
Deal Hall Essex 71 D4
Dean Cumb 162 B3
Dean Devon 7 A6
Dean Devon 25 A6
Dean Dorset 30 D3
Dean Hants 33 D4
Dean Som 29 A6
Dean Prior Devon 7 A6
Dean Row Ches 128 A3
Deanburnhaugh Borders 186 B3
Deane Gtr Man 137 C5
Deane Hants 46 D3
Deanich Lodge Highld 263 B5
Deanland Dorset 30 D3
Deans W Loth 208 D3
Deanscales Cumb 162 B3
Deanshanger Northants 83 D4
Deanston Stirl 218 D2
Dearham Cumb 162 A3
Debach Suff 88 B3
Debden Essex 86 D1
Debden Essex 68 D4
Debden Cross Essex 86 D1
Debenham Suff 88 A2
Dechmont W Loth 208 C3
Deddington Oxon 82 D1
Dedham Essex 87 D6
Dedham Heath Essex 87 D6
Deebank Aberds 244 C3
Deene Northants 99 B6
Deenethorpe Northants 99 B6
Deep Sea World, North Queensferry Fife 208 B4
Deepcar S Yorks 139 D5
Deepcut Sur 34 A2
Deepdale Cumb 155 C6
Deeping Gate Lincs 100 A3
Deeping St James Lincs 100 A3
Deeping St Nicholas Lincs 117 D5
Deerhill Moray 267 D5
Deerhurst Glos 63 A4
Deerness Orkney 283 G6
Defford Worcs 80 C2
Defynnog Powys 59 C6
Deganwy Conwy 124 B2
Deighton N Yorks 158 A2
Deighton W Yorks 139 B4
Deighton York 149 C5
Deiniolen Gwyn 123 D5
Delabole Corn 9 C6
Delamere Ches 127 C5
Delfrigs Aberds 257 D4
Dell Lodge Highld 242 A3

Delliefure Highld 254 C1
Delnabo Moray 243 A4
Delnadamph Aberds 243 B5
Delph Gtr Man 138 C2
Delves Durham 166 A4
Delvine Perth 231 D5
Dembleby Lincs 116 B3
Denaby Main S Yorks 140 D2
Denbigh = Dinbych Denb 125 C5
Denbury Devon 8 A2
Denby Derbys 114 A1
Denby Dale W Yorks 139 C5
Denchworth Oxon 65 D4
Dendron Cumb 153 C3
Denel End Beds 84 D2
Denend Aberds 255 C7
Denford Northants 100 D1
Dengie Essex 70 C3
Denham Bucks 48 A3
Denham Suff 86 A3
Denham Suff 104 D2
Denham Green Bucks 48 A3
Denham Street Suff 104 D2
Denhead Aberds 269 D4
Denhead Fife 221 C4
Denhead of Arbilot Angus 232 D3
Denhead of Gray Dundee 220 A3
Denholm Borders 187 B4
Denholme W Yorks 147 D4
Denholme Clough W Yorks 147 D4
Denio Gwyn 106 C3
Denmead Hants 33 D5
Denmore Aberdeen 245 A6
Denmoss Aberds 256 B1
Dennington Suff 88 A3
Denny Falk 207 B6
Denny Lodge Hants 18 A2
Dennyloanhead Falk 207 B6
Denshaw Gtr Man 138 B2
Denside Aberds 245 C5
Densole Kent 39 A4
Denston Suff 86 B3
Denstone Staffs 113 A5
Dent Cumb 155 C6
Denton Cambs 100 C3
Denton Darl 167 D5
Denton E Sus 22 B2
Denton Gtr Man 138 D2
Denton Kent 39 A4
Denton Lincs 115 B6
Denton Norf 104 C3
Denton Northants 83 B5
Denton N Yorks 147 C5
Denton Oxon 65 C6
Denton's Green Mers 136 D3
Denver Norf 102 A2
Denwick Northumb 189 B5
Deopham Norf 103 A6
Deopham Green Norf 103 B6
Depden Suff 86 B3
Depden Green Suff 86 B3
Deptford London 49 B6
Deptford Wilts 31 B4
Derby Derby 114 B1
Derbyhaven I o M 152 E2
Dereham Norf 120 D1
Deri Caerph 41 A6
Derril Devon 10 A4
Derringstone Kent 39 A4
Derrington Staffs 112 C2
Derriton Devon 10 A4
Derry Hill Wilts 44 B3
Derryguaig Argyll 224 C3
Derrythorpe N Lincs 141 C6
Dersingham Norf 118 B3
Dervaig Argyll 224 A3
Derwen Denb 125 D5
Derwenlas Powys 91 C5
Desborough Northants 99 C5
Desford Leics 98 A1
Detchant Northumb 199 C4
Detling Kent 37 A5
Deuddwr Powys 110 D1
Devil's Bridge Ceredig 75 A6
Devauden Mon 61 D6
Devizes Wilts 44 C4
Devol Inv clyd 204 A3
Devon & Exeter Racecourse Devon 13 C4
Devonport Plym 6 B3
Devonside Clack 208 A2
Devoran Corn 4 D2
Dewar Borders 196 B2
Dewlish Dorset 16 B1
Dewsbury W Yorks 139 A5

Dewsbury Moor W Yorks 139 A5
Dewshall Court Hereford 78 D2
Dhoon I o M 152 C4
Dhoor I o M 152 B4
Dhowin I o M 152 A4
Dial Post W Sus 21 A4
Dibden Hants 18 A3
Dibden Purlieu Hants 18 A3
Dickleburgh Norf 104 C2
Didbrook Glos 80 D3
Didcot Oxon 46 A3
Diddington Cambs 84 A3
Diddlebury Shrops 94 C3
Didley Hereford 78 D2
Didling W Sus 20 A1
Didmarton Glos 44 A2
Didsbury Gtr Man 138 D1
Didworthy Devon 7 A5
Digby Lincs 133 D5
Digg Highld 259 B4
Diggerland, Cullompton Devon 13 A5
Diggerland, Langley Park Durham 167 A5
Diggle Gtr Man 138 C3
Digmoor Lancs 136 C3
Digswell Park Herts 68 B2
Dihewyd Ceredig 74 C3
Dilham Norf 121 C5
Dilhorne Staffs 112 A3
Dillarburn S Lnrk 194 B3
Dillington Cambs 84 A3
Dilston Northumb 178 C1
Dilton Marsh Wilts 30 A2
Dilwyn Hereford 78 B2
Dinas Carms 73 C5
Dinas Gwyn 106 C2
Dinas Cross Pembs 72 C3
Dinas Dinlle Gwyn 107 A4
Dinas-Mawddwy Gwyn 91 A6
Dinas Powys V Glam 41 D6
Dinbych = Denbigh Denb 125 C5
Dinbych-y-Pysgod = Tenby Pembs 56 B1
Dinder Som 29 A5
Dinedor Hereford 78 D3
Dingestow Mon 61 B6
Dingle Mers 126 A3
Dingleden Kent 37 C6
Dingley Northants 99 C4
Dingwall Highld 252 A1
Dinlabyre Borders 186 D4
Dinmael Conwy 109 A5
Dinnet Aberds 244 C1
Dinnington Som 28 D4
Dinnington S Yorks 131 A5
Dinnington T & W 179 B4
Dinorwic Gwyn 123 D5
Dinton Bucks 66 B2
Dinton Wilts 31 B4
Dinwoodie Mains Dumfries 185 C4
Dinworthy Devon 24 D4
Dippen N Ayrs 191 C6
Dippenhall Sur 33 A7
Dipple Moray 266 D4
Dipple S Ayrs 181 A4
Diptford Devon 7 B6
Dipton Durham 178 D3
Dirdhu Highld 254 D1
Dirleton E Loth 210 B2
Dirt Pot Northumb 165 A6
Discoed Powys 77 A6
Discovery Point Dundee 220 B4
Diseworth Leics 114 C2
Dishes Orkney 282 E7
Dishforth N Yorks 158 D2
Disley Ches 129 A4
Diss Norf 104 D2
Disserth Powys 76 B4
Distington Cumb 162 B3
Ditcham W Sus 33 C6
Ditcheat Som 29 B6
Ditchingham Norf 104 B4
Ditchling E Sus 21 A6
Ditherington Shrops 111 D4
Dittisham Devon 8 B2
Ditton Halton 127 A4
Ditton Kent 37 A5
Ditton Green Cambs 86 B2
Ditton Priors Shrops 95 C4
Divach Highld 251 D6
Divlyn Carms 59 B4
Dixton Glos 80 D2
Dixton Mon 61 B7
Dobcross Gtr Man 138 C2
Dobwalls Corn 5 A7

Doc Penfro = Pembroke
Dock Pembs 55 D5
Doccombe Devon 12 C2
Dochfour Ho. Highld 252 C2
Dochgarroch Highld 252 B2
Docking Norf 119 B4
Docklow Hereford 78 B3
Dockray Cumb 164 C1
Dockroyd W Yorks 147 D4
Dodburn Borders 186 C3
Doddinghurst Essex 69 D5
Doddington Cambs 101 B5
Doddington Kent 51 D6
Doddington Lincs 133 B4
Doddington Northumb 198 C3
Doddington Shrops 95 D4
Doddiscombsleigh Devon 12 C3
Dodford Northants 82 A3
Dodford Worcs 96 D2
Dodington S Glos 43 A6
Dodleston Ches 126 C3
Dods Leigh Staffs 112 B4
Dodworth S Yorks 139 C6
Dodworth Shrops 94 C3
Doe Green Warr 127 A5
Doe Lea Derbys 131 C4
Dog Village Devon 13 B4
Dogdyke Lincs 134 D2
Dogmersfield Hants 47 D5
Dogridge Wilts 45 A4
Dogsthorpe P'boro 100 A3
Dol-fôr Powys 91 B6
Dôl-y-Bont Ceredig 90 D4
Dol-y-cannau Powys 77 C6
Dolanog Powys 109 D5
Dolau Powys 77 A5
Dolau Rhondda 41 C4
Dolbenmaen Gwyn 107 B5
Dolfach Powys 91 B7
Dolfor Powys 93 C5
Dolgarrog Conwy 124 C2
Dolgellau Gwyn 91 A5
Dolgran Carms 58 B1
Dolhendre Gwyn 108 B3
Doll Highld 274 D2
Dollar Clack 208 A2
Dolley Green Powys 77 A6
Dollwen Ceredig 91 D4
Dolphin Flint 126 B1
Dolphinholme Lancs 145 B5
Dolphinton S Lnrk 195 B6
Dolton Devon 25 D6
Dolwen Conwy 124 B3
Dolwen Powys 92 A3
Dolwyd Conwy 124 B3
Dolwyddelan Conwy 124 D2
Dolyhir Powys 77 B6
Doncaster S Yorks 140 C3
Doncaster Racecourse S Yorks 140 C4
Dones Green Ches 127 B6
Donhead St Andrew Wilts 30 C3
Donhead St Mary Wilts 30 C3
Donibristle Fife 209 B4
Donington Lincs 117 B5
Donington on Bain Lincs 134 A2
Donington Park Motor Racing Circuit Leics 114 C2
Donington South Ing Lincs 117 B5
Donisthorpe Leics 113 D7
Donkey Town Sur 48 C2
Donnington Glos 64 A2
Donnington Hereford 79 D5
Donnington Shrops 94 A3
Donnington Telford 111 D6
Donnington W Berks 46 C2
Donnington W Sus 20 B1
Donnington Wood Telford 111 D6
Donyatt Som 28 D3
Doonfoot S Ayrs 192 D3
Dorback Lodge Highld 242 A3
Dorchester Dorset 15 B6
Dorchester Abbey, Wallingford Oxon 65 D6
Dordon Warks 97 A5
Dore S Yorks 130 A3
Dores Highld 252 C1
Dorking Sur 35 B4
Dormansland Sur 36 B2
Dormanstown Redcar 168 C3
Dormington Hereford 78 C3
Dormston Worcs 80 B2
Dornal S Ayrs 181 D4
Dorney Bucks 48 B2
Dornie Highld 249 D5

Dornoch Highld 264 B...
Dornock Dumfries 175 B...
Dorrery Highld 279 C...
Dorridge W Mid 97 D...
Dorrington Lincs 133 D...
Dorrington Shrops 94 A...
Dorsington Warks 80 C...
Dorstone Hereford 77 C...
Dorton Bucks 66 B...
Dorusduain Highld 250 D...
Dosthill Staffs 97 B...
Dottery Dorset 15 B...
Doublebois Corn 5 A...
Dougarie N Ayrs 191 B...
Doughton Glos 63 D...
Douglas I o M 152 D...
Douglas S Lnrk 194 C...
Douglas & Angus Dundee 220 A...
Douglas Water S Lnrk 194 C...
Douglas West S Lnrk 194 C...
Douglastown Angus 232 D...
Doulting Som 29 A...
Dounby Orkney 282 E...
Doune Highld 272 D...
Doune Stirl 218 D...
Doune Park Aberds 268 C...
Douneside Aberds 244 B...
Dounie Highld 264 A...
Dounreay Highld 279 B...
Dousland Devon 7 A...
Dovaston Shrops 110 C...
Dove Cottage and Wordsworth Museum Cumb 154 A...
Dove Holes Derbys 129 B...
Dovenby Cumb 162 A...
Dover Kent 39 A...
Dover Castle Kent 39 A...
Dovercourt Essex 88 C...
Doverdale Worcs 79 A...
Doveridge Derbys 113 B...
Doversgreen Sur 35 B...
Dowally Perth 230 D...
Dowbridge Lancs 144 D...
Dowdeswell Glos 63 B...
Dowlais M Tydf 60 C...
Dowland Devon 25 D...
Dowlish Wake Som 28 D...
Down Ampney Glos 64 D...
Down Hatherley Glos 63 A...
Down St Mary Devon 12 A...
Down Thomas Devon 7 B...
Downcraig Ferry N Ayrs 204 C...
Downderry Corn 6 B...
Downe London 50 C...
Downend I o W 18 C...
Downend S Glos 43 B...
Downend W Berks 46 B...
Downfield Dundee 220 A...
Downgate Corn 11 D...
Downham Essex 70 D...
Downham Lancs 146 C...
Downham Northumb 198 C...
Downham Market Norf 102 A...
Downhead Som 29 A...
Downhill Perth 219 A...
Downhill T & W 179 D...
Downholland Cross Lancs 136 C...
Downholme N Yorks 157 B...
Downies Aberds 245 C...
Downley Bucks 66 B...
Downside Som 29 A...
Downside Sur 35 ...
Downton Hants 17 ...
Downton Wilts 31 C...
Downton on the Rock Hereford 94 D...
Dowsby Lincs 116 ...
Dowsdale Lincs 117 ...
Dowthwaitehead Cumb 163 ...
Doxey Staffs 112 ...
Doxford Northumb 189 ...
Doxford Park T & W 179 D...
Doynton S Glos 43 B...
Draffan S Lnrk 194 ...
Dragonby N Lincs 141 ...
Drakeland Corner Devon 7 B...
Drakemyre N Ayrs 204 C...
Drake's Broughton Worcs 80 C...
Drakes Cross Worcs 96 D...
Drakewalls Corn 11 D...
Draughton Northants 99 D...
Draughton N Yorks 146 B...
Drax N Yorks 141 A...
Draycote Warks 98 D...
Draycott Derbys 114 B...
Draycott Glos 81 D...

Draycott Som 42 D3
Draycott in the Clay Staffs 113 C5
Draycott in the Moors Staffs 112 A3
Drayton Devon 26 D2
Drayton Leics 99 B5
Drayton Lincs 117 B5
Drayton Norf 120 D3
Drayton Oxon 82 C1
Drayton Oxon 65 D5
Drayton Ptsmth 19 A5
Drayton Som 28 C4
Drayton Worcs 96 D2
Drayton Bassett Staffs 97 A4
Drayton Beauchamp Bucks 67 B4
Drayton Manor Park, Tamworth Staffs 97 A4
Drayton Parslow Bucks 66 A3
Drayton St Leonard Oxon 65 D6
Dre-fach Ceredig 75 D4
Dre-fach Carms 57 A6
Dreamland Theme Park, Margate Kent 53 B5
Drebley N Yorks 147 B4
Dreemskerry I o M 152 B4
Dreenhill Pembs 55 C5
Drefach Carms 73 C6
Drefach Carms 57 A5
Drefelin Carms 73 C6
Dreghorn N Ayrs 192 B3
Drellingore Kent 39 A4
Drem E Loth 210 C2
Dresden Stoke 112 A3
Dreumasdal W Isles 286 C3
Drewsteignton Devon 12 B2
Driby Lincs 134 B3
Driffield E Yorks 150 B3
Driffield Glos 63 D6
Drigg Cumb 153 A1
Drighlington W Yorks 139 A5
Drimnin Highld 225 A4
Drimpton Dorset 14 A4
Drimsynie Argyll 215 B4
Drinisiadar W Isles 288 H2
Drinkstone Suff 87 A5
Drinkstone Green Suff 87 A5
Drishaig Argyll 215 A4
Drissaig Argyll 214 A2
Drochil Borders 195 B6
Drointon Staffs 112 C4
Droitwich Spa Worcs 80 A1
Droman Highld 276 C2
Dron Perth 219 C6
Dronfield Derbys 130 B3
Dronfield Woodhouse Derbys 130 B3
Drongan E Ayrs 182 A2
Dronley Angus 220 A3
Droxford Hants 33 D5
Droylsden Gtr Man 138 D2
Druid Denb 109 A5
Druidston Pembs 55 C4
Druimarbin Highld 237 B4
Druimavuic Argyll 227 B5
Druimdrishaig Argyll 202 A2
Druimindarroch Highld 235 B5
Druimyeon More Argyll 202 C1
Drum Argyll 203 A4
Drum Perth 219 D5
Drumbeg Highld 270 A4
Drumblade Aberds 255 B6
Drumblair Aberds 256 B1
Drumbuie Dumfries 182 D3
Drumbuie Highld 249 C4
Drumburgh Cumb 175 C5
Drumburn Dumfries 174 B2
Drumchapel Glasgow 205 A5
Drumchardine Highld 252 B1
Drumchork Highld 261 B5
Drumclog S Lnrk 193 B6
Drumderfit Highld 252 A2
Drumeldrie Fife 220 D4
Drumelzier Borders 195 C6
Drumfearn Highld 247 C5
Drumgask Highld 241 C4
Drumgley Angus 232 C2
Drumguish Highld 241 C5
Drumin Moray 254 C2
Drumlasie Aberds 244 B3
Drumlemble Argyll 190 D2
Drumligair Aberds 245 A6
Drumlithie Aberds 245 D4
Drummoddie Dumfries 171 C5
Drummond Highld 264 D2
Drummore Dumfries 170 D3
Drummuir Moray 255 B4

Drummuir Castle Moray 255 B4
Drumnadrochit Highld 251 D7
Drumnagorrach Moray 267 D6
Drumoak Aberds 245 C4
Drumpark Dumfries 183 D6
Drumphail Dumfries 171 A4
Drumrash Dumfries 173 A4
Drumrunie Highld 271 D4
Drums Aberds 257 D4
Drumsallie Highld 236 B3
Drumstinchall Dumfries 173 C6
Drumsturdy Angus 221 A4
Drumtochty Castle Aberds 244 E3
Drumtroddan Dumfries 171 C5
Drumuie Highld 259 D4
Drumuillie Highld 253 D5
Drumvaich Stirl 217 D6
Drumwhindle Aberds 257 C4
Drunkendub Angus 233 D4
Drury Flint 126 C2
Drury Square Norf 119 D6
Drusillas Park, Polegate E Sus 22 B3
Dry Drayton Cambs 85 A5
Drybeck Cumb 165 D4
Drybridge Moray 267 C5
Drybridge N Ayrs 192 B3
Drybrook Glos 62 B2
Dryburgh Borders 197 C4
Dryhope Borders 196 D1
Drylaw Edin 209 C5
Drym Corn 3 B4
Drymen Stirl 206 B2
Drymuir Aberds 257 B4
Drynoch Highld 246 A3
Dryslwyn Carms 58 C2
Dryton Shrops 94 A3
Dubford Aberds 268 C3
Dubton Angus 232 C3
Duchally Highld 271 C6
Duchlage Argyll 206 B1
Duck Corner Suff 89 C4
Duckington Ches 127 D4
Ducklington Oxon 65 C4
Duckmanton Derbys 131 B4
Duck's Cross Beds 84 B3
Duddenhoe End Essex 85 D6
Duddingston Edin 209 C5
Duddington Northants 100 A1
Duddleswell E Sus 36 D2
Duddo Northumb 198 B3
Duddon Ches 127 C5
Duddon Bridge Cumb 153 B3
Dudleston Shrops 110 B2
Dudleston Heath Shrops 110 B2
Dudley W Mid 179 B4
Dudley T & W 179 B4
Dudley Port W Mid 96 B2
Dudley Zoological Gardens W Mid 96 B2
Duffield Derbys 114 A1
Duffryn Newport 42 A1
Duffryn Neath 40 B3
Dufftown Moray 254 C4
Duffus Moray 266 C2
Dufton Cumb 165 C4
Duggleby N Yorks 150 A1
Duirinish Highld 249 C4
Duisdalemore Highld 247 C6
Duisky Highld 237 B4
Dukestown Bl Gwent 60 B3
Dukinfield Gtr Man 138 D2
Dulas Anglesey 123 B4
Dulcote Som 29 A5
Dulford Devon 13 A5
Dull Perth 230 D2
Dullatur N Lnrk 207 C5
Dullingham Cambs 86 B2
Dulnain Bridge Highld 253 D5
Duloe Beds 84 A3
Duloe Corn 6 B1
Dulsie Highld 253 B5
Dulverton Som 27 C4
Dulwich London 49 B6
Dumbarton W Dunb 205 A4
Dumbleton Glos 80 D3
Dumcrieff Dumfries 185 B4
Dumfries Dumfries 174 A2
Dumgoyne Stirl 206 B3
Dummer Hants 33 A4
Dumpford W Sus 34 D1
Dumpton Kent 53 C5
Dun Angus 233 C4
Dun Charlabhaigh W Isles 288 C2

Dunain Ho. Highld 252 B2
Dunalastair Perth 229 C6
Dunan Argyll 214 C3
Dunball Som 28 A3
Dunbar E Loth 210 C3
Dunbeath Highld 275 B5
Dunbeg Argyll 226 C3
Dunblane Stirl 218 D2
Dunbog Fife 220 C2
Duncanston Aberds 255 D6
Duncanston Highld 252 A1
Dunchurch Warks 98 D1
Duncote Northants 82 B3
Duncow Dumfries 184 D2
Duncraggan Stirl 217 D5
Duncrievie Perth 219 D6
Duncton W Sus 20 A2
Dundas Ho. Orkney 283 K5
Dundee Dundee 220 A4
Dundee Airport Dundee 220 B3
Dundeugh Dumfries 182 D3
Dundon Som 29 B4
Dundonald S Ayrs 192 B3
Dundonnell Highld 262 B2
Dundonnell Hotel Highld 262 B2
Dundonnell House Highld 262 B3
Dundraw Cumb 175 D5
Dundreggan Highld 239 A7
Dundreggan Lodge Highld 240 A1
Dundrennan Dumfries 173 D5
Dundry N Som 43 C4
Dunecht Aberds 245 B4
Dunfermline Fife 208 B3
Dunfield Glos 64 D2
Dunford Bridge S Yorks 139 C4
Dungworth S Yorks 130 A2
Dunham Notts 132 B3
Dunham Massey Gtr Man 128 A2
Dunham-on-the-Hill Ches 127 B4
Dunham Town Gtr Man 128 A2
Dunhampton Worcs 79 A6
Dunholme Lincs 133 B5
Dunino Fife 221 C5
Dunipace Falk 207 B6
Dunira Perth 218 B2
Dunkeld Perth 230 D4
Dunkerton Bath 43 D6
Dunkeswell Devon 13 A6
Dunkeswick N Yorks 148 C2
Dunkirk Kent 52 D2
Dunkirk Norf 120 C4
Dunk's Green Kent 36 A4
Dunlappie Angus 232 B3
Dunley Hants 46 D2
Dunley Worcs 79 A5
Dunlichity Lodge Highld 252 C2
Dunlop E Ayrs 205 D4
Dunmaglass Lodge Highld 252 D1
Dunmore Argyll 202 B2
Dunmore Falk 208 B1
Dunnet Highld 280 A4
Dunnichen Angus 232 D3
Dunninald Angus 233 C5
Dunning Perth 219 C5
Dunnington E Yorks 151 B4
Dunnington Warks 80 B3
Dunnington York 149 B5
Dunnockshaw Lancs 137 A7
Dunollie Argyll 226 C3
Dunoon Argyll 203 A6
Dunragit Dumfries 170 B3
Dunrobin Castle Museum & Gardens Highld 274 D2
Dunrostan Argyll 213 D5
Duns Borders 198 A1
Duns Tew Oxon 65 A5
Dunsby Lincs 116 C4
Dunscore Dumfries 183 D6
Dunscroft S Yorks 141 C4
Dunsdale Redcar 168 D4
Dunsden Green Oxon 47 B5
Dunsfold Sur 34 C3
Dunsford Devon 12 C3
Dunshalt Fife 220 C2
Dunshillock Aberds 257 B4
Dunskey Ho. Dumfries 170 B2
Dunsley N Yorks 169 D6
Dunsmore Bucks 66 C3
Dunsop Bridge Lancs 145 B6
Dunstable Beds 67 A5
Dunstall Staffs 113 C5
Dunstall Common Worcs 80 C1
Dunstall Green Suff 86 A3

Dunstan Northumb 189 B5
Dunstan Steads Northumb 189 A5
Dunster Som 27 A4
Dunster Castle, Minehead Som 27 A4
Dunston Lincs 133 C5
Dunston Norf 104 A3
Dunston Staffs 112 D3
Dunston T & W 179 C4
Dunsville S Yorks 140 C4
Dunswell E Yorks 150 D3
Dunsyre S Lnrk 195 B5
Dunterton Devon 11 D4
Duntisbourne Abbots Glos 63 C5
Duntisbourne Leer Glos 63 C5
Duntisbourne Rouse Glos 63 C5
Duntish Dorset 15 A6
Duntocher W Dunb 205 A4
Dunton Beds 84 C4
Dunton Bucks 66 A3
Dunton Norf 119 B5
Dunton Bassett Leics 98 B2
Dunton Green Kent 36 A3
Dunton Wayletts Essex 69 D6
Duntulm Highld 259 A4
Dunure S Ayrs 192 D2
Dunvant Swansea 57 C5
Dunvegan Highld 258 D2
Dunvegan Castle Highld 258 C2
Dunwich Suff 105 D5
Dunwood Staffs 129 D4
Dupplin Castle Perth 219 C5
Durdar Cumb 175 C7
Durgates E Sus 36 C4
Durham Durham 167 A5
Durham Cathedral Durham 167 A5
Durham Tees Valley Airport Stockton 167 D6
Durisdeer Dumfries 183 B6
Durisdeermill Dumfries 183 B6
Durkar W Yorks 139 B6
Durleigh Som 28 B2
Durley Hants 32 D4
Durley Wilts 45 C6
Durnamuck Highld 262 A2
Durness Highld 277 B5
Durno Aberds 256 D2
Duror Highld 236 D3
Durran Argyll 214 B2
Durran Highld 280 B3
Durrington Wilts 31 A5
Durrington W Sus 21 B4
Dursley Glos 62 D3
Durston Som 28 C2
Durweston Dorset 16 A2
Dury Shetland 285 G6
Duston Northants 83 A4
Duthil Highld 253 D5
Dutlas Powys 93 D6
Duton Hill Essex 69 A6
Dutson Corn 10 C4
Dutton Ches 127 B5
Duxford Cambs 85 C6
Duxford Oxon 65 D4
Duxford Airfield (Imperial War Museum), Sawston Cambs 85 C6
Dwygyfylchi Conwy 124 B2
Dwyran Anglesey 123 D4
Dyce Aberdeen 245 A5
Dye House Northumb 178 D1
Dyffryn Bridgend 40 B3
Dyffryn Carms 73 D6
Dyffryn Pembs 72 C2
Dyffryn Ardudwy Gwyn 107 D5
Dyffryn Castell Ceredig 91 D5
Dyffryn Ceidrych Carms 59 C4
Dyffryn Cellwen Neath 59 E4
Dyke Lincs 116 C4
Dyke Moray 253 A5
Dykehead Angus 232 B1
Dykehead N Lnrk 207 E6
Dykehead Stirl 206 A3
Dykelands Aberds 233 B5
Dykends Angus 231 C6
Dykeside Aberds 256 B2
Dykesmains N Ayrs 204 D2
Dylife Powys 91 C6
Dymchurch Kent 38 C2
Dymock Glos 79 D5
Dyrham S Glos 43 B6
Dyrham Park S Glos 43 B6
Dysart Fife 209 A6
Dyserth Denb 125 B5

E

Eachwick Northumb 178 B3
Eadar Dha Fhadhail W Isles 287 A5
Eagland Hill Lancs 144 C4
Eagle Lincs 132 C5
Eagle Barnsdale Lincs 132 C3
Eagle Moor Lincs 132 C3
Eaglescliffe Stockton 168 D2
Eaglesfield Cumb 162 B3
Eaglesfield Dumfries 175 A5
Eaglesham E Renf 205 C5
Eaglethorpe Northants 100 B2
Eairy I o M 152 D2
Eakley Lanes M Keynes 83 B5
Eakring Notts 132 C1
Ealand Lincs 141 B5
Ealing London 49 A4
Eals Northumb 177 D4
Eamont Bridge Cumb 164 C3
Earby Lancs 146 C3
Earcroft Blkburn 137 A5
Eardington Shrops 95 B5
Eardisland Hereford 78 B2
Eardisley Hereford 77 C7
Eardiston Shrops 110 C2
Eardiston Worcs 79 A4
Earith Cambs 101 D5
Earl Shilton Leics 98 B1
Earl Soham Suff 88 A3
Earl Sterndale Derbys 129 C5
Earl Stonham Suff 88 B2
Earle Northumb 188 A2
Earley Wokingham 47 B5
Earlham Norf 104 A3
Earlish Highld 258 B3
Earls Barton Northants 83 A5
Earls Colne Essex 70 A2
Earl's Croome Worcs 79 C6
Earl's Green Suff 87 A6
Earlsdon W Mid 97 D6
Earlsferry Fife 221 E4
Earlsfield Lincs 116 B2
Earlsford Aberds 256 C3
Earlsheaton W Yorks 139 A5
Earlsmill Moray 253 A5
Earlston Borders 197 C4
Earlston E Ayrs 193 B4
Earlswood Mon 61 D6
Earlswood Sur 35 B5
Earlswood Warks 96 D4
Earnley W Sus 19 B7
Earsairidh W Isles 286 G3
Earsdon T & W 179 B5
Earsham Norf 104 C4
Earswick York 149 B5
Eartham W Sus 20 B2
Easby N Yorks 159 A4
Easby N Yorks 157 A5
Easdale Argyll 213 A5
Easebourne W Sus 34 D1
Easenhall Warks 98 D1
Eashing Sur 34 B2
Easington Bucks 66 B1
Easington Durham 168 A2
Easington E Yorks 143 B5
Easington Northumb 199 C5
Easington Oxon 82 D1
Easington Oxon 66 D1
Easington Redcar 169 D5
Easington Colliery Durham 168 A2
Easington Lane T & W 167 A6
Easingwold N Yorks 148 A4
Easole Street Kent 53 D4
Eassie Angus 232 D1
East Aberthaw V Glam 41 E5
East Adderbury Oxon 82 D1
East Allington Devon 7 C6
East Anstey Devon 26 C3
East Appleton N Yorks 157 B6
East Ardsley W Yorks 139 A6
East Ashling W Sus 19 A7
East Auchronie Aberds 245 B5
East Ayton N Yorks 160 C3
East Bank Bl Gwent 60 C4
East Barming Kent 37 A5
East Barnby N Yorks 169 D6
East Barnet London 68 D2
East Barns E Loth 211 C4
East Barsham Norf 119 B6
East Beckham Norf 120 B3

East Bedfont London 48 B3
East Bergholt Suff 87 D6
East Bilney Norf 119 D6
East Blatchington E Sus 22 B2
East Boldre Hants 18 A2
East Brent Som 42 D2
East Bridgford Notts 115 A4
East Buckland Devon 26 B1
East Budleigh Devon 13 C5
East Burrafirth Shetland 285 H5
East Burton Dorset 16 C2
East Butsfield Durham 166 A4
East Butterwick N Lincs 141 C6
East Cairnbeg Aberds 233 A5
East Calder W Loth 208 D3
East Carleton Norf 104 A2
East Carlton Northants 99 C5
East Carlton W Yorks 147 C6
East Chaldon Dorset 16 C1
East Challow Oxon 46 A1
East Chiltington E Sus 21 A6
East Chinnock Som 29 D4
East Chisenbury Wilts 45 D5
East Clandon Sur 34 A3
East Claydon Bucks 66 A2
East Clyne Highld 274 D2
East Coker Som 29 D5
East Combe Som 27 B6
East Common N Yorks 149 D5
East Compton Som 29 A6
East Cottingwith E Yorks 149 C6
East Cowes I o W 18 B4
East Cowick E Yorks 141 A4
East Cowton N Yorks 157 A7
East Cramlington Northumb 179 B4
East Cranmore Som 29 A6
East Creech Dorset 16 C3
East Croachy Highld 252 D2
East Croftmore Highld 242 A2
East Curthwaite Cumb 164 A1
East Dean E Sus 22 C3
East Dean Hants 31 C6
East Dean W Sus 20 A2
East Down Devon 25 A7
East Drayton Notts 132 B2
East Ella Hull 142 A2
East End Dorset 16 B3
East End E Yorks 143 A4
East End Hants 18 B2
East End Hants 33 C5
East End Hants 46 C2
East End Herts 69 A4
East End Kent 37 C6
East End N Som 42 B3
East End Oxon 65 B4
East Farleigh Kent 37 A5
East Farndon Northants 99 C4
East Ferry Lincs 141 D6
East Fortune E Loth 210 C2
East Garston W Berks 46 B1
East Ginge Oxon 46 A2
East Goscote Leics 115 D4
East Grafton Wilts 45 C6
East Grimstead Wilts 31 C6
East Grinstead W Sus 36 C1
East Guldeford E Sus 38 C1
East Haddon Northants 82 A3
East Hagbourne Oxon 46 A3
East Halton N Lincs 142 B3
East Ham London 50 A1
East Hanney Oxon 65 D5
East Hanningfield Essex 70 C1
East Hardwick W Yorks 140 B2
East Harling Norf 103 C5
East Harlsey N Yorks 158 B3
East Harnham Wilts 31 C5
East Harptree Bath 43 D4
East Hartford Northumb 179 B4
East Harting W Sus 33 D6
East Hatley Cambs 85 B4
East Hauxwell N Yorks 157 B5
East Haven Angus 221 A5
East Heckington Lincs 117 A4
East Hedleyhope Durham 167 A4
East Hendred Oxon 46 A2
East Herrington T & W 179 D5
East Heslerton N Yorks 160 D3
East Hoathly E Sus 22 A3
East Horrington Som 29 A5
East Horsley Sur 34 A3
East Horton Northumb 198 C4
East Huntspill Som 28 A3
East Hyde Beds 67 B6

East Ilkerton Devon 26 A2
East Ilsley W Berks 46 A2
East Keal Lincs 134 C3
East Kennett Wilts 45 C5
East Keswick W Yorks 148 C2
East Kilbride S Lnrk 205 C6
East Kirkby Lincs 134 C3
East Knapton N Yorks 160 D2
East Knighton Dorset 16 C2
East Knoyle Wilts 30 B2
East Kyloe Northumb 199 C4
East Lambrook Som 28 D4
East Lamington Highld 264 C3
East Langdon Kent 39 A5
East Langton Leics 99 B4
East Langwell Highld 273 D5
East Lavant W Sus 20 B1
East Lavington W Sus 20 A2
East Layton N Yorks 157 A5
East Leake Notts 114 C3
East Learmonth Northumb 198 C2
East Leigh Devon 12 A1
East Lexham Norf 119 D5
East Lilburn Northumb 188 A3
East Linton E Loth 210 C2
East Liss Hants 33 C6
East Looe Corn 6 B1
East Lound N Lincs 141 D5
East Lulworth Dorset 16 C2
East Lutton N Yorks 150 A2
East Lydford Som 29 B5
East Mains Aberds 244 C3
East Malling Kent 37 A5
East March Angus 220 A4
East Marden W Sus 33 D7
East Markham Notts 132 B2
East Marton N Yorks 146 B3
East Meon Hants 33 C5
East Mere Devon 27 D4
East Mersea Essex 71 B4
East Mey Highld 281 A5
East Molesey Sur 49 C4
East Morden Dorset 16 B3
East Morton W Yorks 147 C4
East Ness N Yorks 159 D5
East Newton E Yorks 151 D5
East Norton Leics 99 A4
East Nynehead Som 27 C6
East Oakley Hants 46 D3
East Ogwell Devon 12 D3
East Orchard Dorset 30 D2
East Ord Northumb 198 A3
East Panson Devon 11 B4
East Peckham Kent 37 B4
East Pennard Som 29 B5
East Perry Cambs 84 A3
East Portlemouth Devon 7 D6
East Prawle Devon 8 D1
East Preston W Sus 20 B3
East Putford Devon 25 D4
East Quantoxhead Som 27 A6
East Rainton T & W 167 A6
East Ravendale NE Lincs 143 D4
East Raynham Norf 119 C5
East Rhidorroch Lodge Highld 262 A4
East Rigton W Yorks 148 C2
East Rounton N Yorks 158 A3
East Row N Yorks 169 D6
East Rudham Norf 119 C5
East Runton Norf 120 A3
East Ruston Norf 121 C5
East Saltoun E Loth 210 D1
East Sleekburn Northumb 179 A4
East Somerton Norf 121 D6
East Stockwith Lincs 141 D5
East Stoke Dorset 16 C2
East Stoke Notts 115 A5
East Stour Dorset 30 C2
East Stourmouth Kent 53 C4
East Stowford Devon 26 C1
East Stratton Hants 32 B4
East Studdal Kent 39 A5
East Suisnish Highld 248 C2
East Taphouse Corn 5 A6
East-the-Water Devon 25 C5
East Thirston Northumb 189 D4
East Tilbury Thurrock 50 B3
East Tisted Hants 33 B6
East Torrington Lincs 133 A6
East Tuddenham Norf 120 D2
East Tytherley Hants 32 C1
East Tytherton Wilts 44 B3
East Village Devon 12 A3
East Wall Shrops 94 B3
East Walton Norf 119 D4
East Wellow Hants 32 C2

East Wemyss Fife 209 A6
East Whitburn W Loth 208 D2
East Williamston Pembs 55 D6
East Winch Norf 118 D3
East Winterslow Wilts 31 B6
East Wittering W Sus 19 B6
East Witton N Yorks 157 C5
East Woodburn Northumb 177 A7
East Woodhay Hants 46 C2
East Worldham Hants 33 B6
East Worlington Devon 26 D2
East Worthing W Sus 21 B4
Eastbourne E Sus 22 C4
Eastbridge Suff 89 A5
Eastburn W Yorks 147 C4
Eastbury Herts 67 D5
Eastbury W Berks 46 B1
Eastby N Yorks 147 B4
Eastchurch Kent 52 B1
Eastcombe Glos 63 C4
Eastcote London 48 A4
Eastcote Northants 82 B3
Eastcote W Mid 97 D4
Eastcott Corn 24 D3
Eastcott Wilts 44 D4
Eastcourt Wilts 63 D5
Eastcourt Wilts 45 C6
Easter Ardross Highld 264 C2
Easter Balmoral Aberds 243 C5
Easter Boleskine Highld 251 D7
Easter Compton S Glos 43 A4
Easter Cringate Stirl 207 B5
Easter Davoch Aberds 244 B1
Easter Earshaig Dumfries 184 B3
Easter Fearn Highld 264 B2
Easter Galcantray Highld 253 B4
Easter Howgate Midloth 209 D5
Easter Howlaws Borders 197 B6
Easter Kinkell Highld 252 A1
Easter Lednathie Angus 232 B1
Easter Milton Highld 253 A5
Easter Moniack Highld 252 B1
Easter Ord Aberds 245 B5
Easter Quarff Shetland 285 K6
Easter Rhynd Perth 219 C6
Easter Row Stirl 207 A5
Easter Silverford Aberds 268 C2
Easter Skeld Shetland 285 J5
Easter Whyntie Aberds 267 C7
Eastergate W Sus 20 B2
Easterhouse Glasgow 207 D4
Eastern Green W Mid 97 C5
Easterton Wilts 44 D4
Eastertown Som 42 D2
Eastertown of Auchleuchries Aberds 257 C5
Eastfield N Lnrk 208 D1
Eastfield N Yorks 160 C4
Eastfield Hall Northumb 189 C5
Eastgate Durham 166 B2
Eastgate Norf 120 C3
Eastham Mers 126 A3
Eastham Ferry Mers 126 A3
Easthampstead Brack 47 C6
Eastheath Wokingham 47 C6
Easthope Shrops 94 B3
Easthorpe Essex 70 A3
Easthorpe Leics 115 B6
Easthorpe Notts 132 D2
Easthouses Midloth 209 D6
Eastington Devon 12 A2
Eastington Glos 62 C3
Eastington Glos 64 B2
Eastleach Martin Glos 64 C3
Eastleach Turville Glos 64 C2
Eastleigh Devon 25 C5
Eastleigh Hants 32 D3
Eastling Kent 51 D6
Eastmoor Derbys 130 B3
Eastmoor Norf 102 A3
Eastney Ptsmth 19 B5
Eastnor Hereford 79 D5
Eastoft N Lincs 141 B6
Eastoke Hants 19 B6
Easton Cambs 100 D3
Easton Cumb 175 C5
Easton Cumb 176 B2
Easton Devon 12 C2
Easton Dorset 15 D6
Easton Hants 32 B4
Easton Lincs 116 C2
Easton Norf 120 D3
Easton Som 29 A5
Easton Suff 88 B3
Easton Wilts 44 B2
Easton Grey Wilts 44 A2
Easton-in-Gordano N Som 43 B4

Easton Maudit Northants 83 B5
Easton on the Hill Northants 100 A2
Easton Royal Wilts 45 C6
Eastpark Dumfries 174 B3
Eastrea Cambs 101 B4
Eastriggs Dumfries 175 B5
Eastrington E Yorks 141 A5
Eastry Kent 53 D5
Eastville Bristol 43 B5
Eastville Lincs 135 D4
Eastwell Leics 115 C5
Eastwick Herts 68 B4
Eastwick Shetland 284 F5
Eastwood Notts 114 A2
Eastwood Sthend 51 A5
Eastwood W Yorks 138 A2
Eathorpe Warks 81 A6
Eaton Ches 127 C5
Eaton Ches 128 C3
Eaton Leics 115 C5
Eaton Norf 104 A3
Eaton Notts 132 B2
Eaton Oxon 65 C5
Eaton Shrops 94 C1
Eaton Shrops 94 C3
Eaton Bishop Hereford 78 D2
Eaton Bray Beds 67 A4
Eaton Constantine Shrops 94 A3
Eaton Green Beds 67 A4
Eaton Hastings Oxon 64 D3
Eaton on Tern Shrops 111 C5
Eaton Socon Cambs 84 B3
Eavestone N Yorks 147 A6
Ebberston N Yorks 160 C2
Ebbesbourne Wake Wilts 30 C3
Ebbw Vale = Glyn Ebwy Bl Gwent 60 C3
Ebchester Durham 178 D3
Ebford Devon 13 C4
Ebley Glos 63 C4
Ebnal Ches 110 A3
Ebrington Glos 81 D4
Ecchinswell Hants 46 D2
Ecclaw Borders 211 D4
Ecclefechan Dumfries 175 A4
Eccles Borders 197 B6
Eccles Gtr Man 137 D6
Eccles Kent 51 C4
Eccles on Sea Norf 121 C6
Eccles Road Norf 103 B6
Ecclesall S Yorks 130 A3
Ecclesfield S Yorks 139 D6
Ecclesgreig Aberds 233 B5
Eccleshall Staffs 112 C2
Eccleshill W Yorks 147 D5
Ecclesmachan W Loth 208 C3
Eccleston Ches 127 C4
Eccleston Lancs 136 B4
Eccleston Mers 136 D3
Eccleston Park Mers 136 D3
Eccup W Yorks 148 C1
Echt Aberds 245 B4
Eckford Borders 187 A6
Eckington Derbys 131 B4
Eckington Worcs 80 C2
Ecton Northants 83 A5
Edale Derbys 129 A6
Edburton W Sus 21 A5
Edderside Cumb 174 D3
Edderton Highld 264 B3
Eddistone Devon 24 C3
Eddleston Borders 196 B1
Eden Camp Museum, Malton N Yorks 159 D6
Eden Park London 49 C6
Edenbridge Kent 36 B2
Edenfield Lancs 137 B6
Edenhall Cumb 164 B3
Edenham Lincs 116 C3
Edensor Derbys 130 C2
Edentaggart Argyll 215 C6
Edenthorpe S Yorks 140 C4
Edentown Cumb 175 C6
Ederline Argyll 214 B1
Edern Gwyn 106 C2
Edgarley Som 29 B5
Edgbaston W Mid 96 C3
Edgcott Bucks 66 A1
Edgcott Som 26 B3
Edge Shrops 94 A1
Edge End Glos 62 B1
Edge Green Ches 127 D4
Edge Hill Mers 136 D2
Edgebolton Shrops 111 C4
Edgefield Norf 120 B2
Edgefield Street Norf 120 B2

Edgeside Lancs 138 A1
Edgeworth Glos 63 C5
Edgmond Telford 111 D6
Edgmond Marsh Telford 111 C6
Edgton Shrops 94 C1
Edgware London 68 D2
Edgworth Blkburn 137 B6
Edinample Stirl 217 B5
Edinbane Highld 258 C3
Edinburgh Edin 209 C5
Edinburgh Airport Edin 209 C4
Edinburgh Castle Edin 209 C5
Edinburgh Crystal Visitor Centre, Penicuik Midloth 209 D5
Edinburgh Zoo Edin 209 C5
Edingale Staffs 113 D6
Edingight Ho. Moray 267 D6
Edingley Notts 131 D6
Edingthorpe Norf 121 B5
Edingthorpe Green Norf 121 B5
Edington Som 28 B3
Edington Wilts 44 D3
Edintore Moray 255 B5
Edith Weston Rutland 99 A6
Edithmead Som 28 A3
Edlesborough Bucks 67 B4
Edlingham Northumb 189 C4
Edlington Lincs 134 B2
Edmondsham Dorset 31 D5
Edmondsley Durham 167 A5
Edmondthorpe Leics 115 D6
Edmonstone Orkney 282 E6
Edmonton London 68 D3
Edmundbyers Durham 178 D2
Ednam Borders 197 C6
Ednaston Derbys 113 A6
Edradynate Perth 230 C3
Edrom Borders 198 A2
Edstaston Shrops 111 B4
Edstone Warks 81 A4
Edvin Loach Hereford 79 B4
Edwalton Notts 114 B3
Edwardstone Suff 87 C5
Edwinsford Carms 58 B3
Edwinstowe Notts 131 C6
Edworth Beds 84 C4
Edwyn Ralph Hereford 79 B4
Edzell Angus 232 B3
Efail Isaf Rhondda 41 C5
Efailnewydd Gwyn 106 C3
Efailwen Carms 72 D4
Efenechtyd Denb 125 D6
Effingham Sur 35 A4
Effirth Shetland 285 H5
Efford Devon 12 A3
Egdon Worcs 80 B2
Egerton Gtr Man 137 B6
Egerton Kent 37 B7
Egerton Forstal Kent 37 B7
Eggborough N Yorks 140 A3
Eggbuckland Plym 7 B4
Eggington Beds 67 A4
Egginton Derbys 113 C6
Egglescliffe Stockton 168 D2
Eggleston Durham 166 C2
Egham Sur 48 B3
Egleton Rutland 99 A5
Eglingham Northumb 189 B4
Egloshayle Corn 9 D5
Egloskerry Corn 10 C3
Eglwys-Brewis V Glam 41 E5
Eglwys Cross Wrex 110 A3
Eglwys Fach Ceredig 91 C4
Eglwysbach Conwy 124 B3
Eglwyswen Pembs 73 C3
Eglwyswrw Pembs 72 C3
Egmanton Notts 132 C2
Egremont Cumb 162 C3
Egremont Mers 136 D2
Egton N Yorks 159 A6
Egton Bridge N Yorks 159 A6
Eight Ash Green Essex 70 A3
Eignaig Highld 226 B3
Eil Highld 241 A5
Eilanreach Highld 238 A2
Eilean Darach Highld 262 B3
Eileanach Lodge Highld 264 D1
Einacleite W Isles 288 E2
Eisgean W Isles 288 F4
Eisingrug Gwyn 107 C5
Elan Village Powys 76 A3
Elberton S Glos 43 A4
Elburton Plym 7 B4
Elcho Perth 219 B6
Elcombe Swindon 45 A4
Eldernell Cambs 101 B5

Eldersfield Worcs 79 D6
Elderslie Renfs 205 B4
Eldon Ayrs 167 C5
Eldrick S Ayrs 181 C4
Eldroth N Yorks 146 A1
Eldwick W Yorks 147 C5
Elfhowe Cumb 154 B3
Elford Northumb 199 C5
Elford Staffs 113 D5
Elgin Moray 266 C3
Elgol Highld 247 C6
Elham Kent 38 A3
Elie Fife 221 D4
Elim Anglesey 122 B3
Eling Hants 32 D2
Elishader Highld 259 B5
Elishaw Northumb 188 D1
Elkesley Notts 132 B1
Elkstone Glos 63 B5
Ellan Highld 253 D4
Elland W Yorks 139 A4
Ellary Argyll 202 A2
Ellastone Staffs 113 A5
Ellemford Borders 211 D4
Ellenbrook I o M 152 D3
Ellenhall Staffs 112 C2
Ellen's Green Sur 34 C3
Ellerbeck N Yorks 158 B3
Ellerburn N Yorks 160 C2
Ellerby N Yorks 169 D5
Ellerdine Heath Telford 111 C5
Ellerhayes Devon 13 A4
Elleric Argyll 227 B5
Ellerker E Yorks 141 A7
Ellerton E Yorks 149 D6
Ellerton Shrops 111 C6
Ellesborough Bucks 66 C3
Ellesmere Shrops 110 B3
Ellesmere Port Ches 127 B4
Ellingham Norf 105 B4
Ellingham Northumb 189 A4
Ellingstring N Yorks 157 C5
Ellington Cambs 100 D3
Ellington Northumb 189 D5
Elliot Angus 221 A6
Ellisfield Hants 33 A5
Ellistown Leics 114 D2
Ellon Aberds 257 C4
Ellonby Cumb 164 B2
Ellough Suff 105 C5
Elloughton E Yorks 142 A1
Ellwood Glos 62 C1
Elm Cambs 101 A6
Elm Hill Dorset 30 C2
Elm Park London 50 A2
Elmbridge Worcs 80 A2
Elmdon Essex 85 D6
Elmdon W Mid 97 C4
Elmdon Heath W Mid 97 C4
Elmers End London 49 C6
Elmesthorpe Leics 98 B1
Elmfield I o W 19 B5
Elmhurst Staffs 113 D5
Elmley Castle Worcs 80 C2
Elmley Lovett Worcs 79 A6
Elmore Glos 62 B3
Elmore Back Glos 62 B3
Elmscott Devon 24 C3
Elmsett Suff 87 C6
Elmstead Market Essex 71 A4
Elmsted Kent 38 A3
Elmstone Kent 53 C4
Elmstone Hardwicke Glos 63 A5
Elmswell E Yorks 150 B2
Elmswell Suff 87 A5
Elmton Derbys 131 B5
Elphin Highld 271 C5
Elphinstone E Loth 209 C6
Elrick Aberds 245 B5
Elrig Dumfries 171 C5
Elsdon Northumb 188 D2
Elsecar S Yorks 140 D1
Elsenham Essex 69 A5
Elsfield Oxon 65 B6
Elsham N Lincs 142 B2
Elsing Norf 120 D2
Elslack N Yorks 146 C3
Elson Shrops 110 B2
Elsrickle S Lnrk 195 B5
Elstead Sur 34 B2
Elsted W Sus 33 D7
Elsthorpe Lincs 116 C3
Elstob Durham 167 C6
Elston Notts 115 A5
Elston Wilts 31 A4
Elstone Devon 26 D1
Elstow Beds 84 C2

Elstree Herts 68 D1
Elstronwick E Yorks 151 D5
Elswick Lancs 144 D4
Elsworth Cambs 85 A5
Elterwater Cumb 154 A2
Eltham London 50 B1
Eltisley Cambs 85 B4
Elton Cambs 100 B2
Elton Ches 127 B4
Elton Derbys 130 C2
Elton Glos 62 B3
Elton Hereford 94 D2
Elton Notts 115 B5
Elton Stockton 168 D2
Elton Green Ches 127 B4
Elvanfoot S Lnrk 184 A2
Elvaston Derbys 114 B2
Elveden Suff 103 D4
Elvingston E Loth 210 C1
Elvington Kent 53 D4
Elvington York 149 C5
Elwick Hrtlpl 168 B2
Elwick Northumb 199 C5
Elworth Ches 128 C2
Elworthy Som 27 B5
Ely Cambs 102 C1
Ely Cardiff 41 D6
Ely Cathedral and
  Museum Cambs 102 C1
Emberton M Keynes 83 C5
Embleton Cumb 163 B4
Embleton Northumb 189 A5
Embo Highld 265 A4
Embo Street Highld 265 A4
Emborough Som 43 D5
Embsay N Yorks 147 B4
Emery Down Hants 18 A1
Emley W Yorks 139 B5
Emmbrook Wokingham 47 C5
Emmer Green Reading 47 B5
Emmington Oxon 66 C2
Emneth Norf 101 A6
Emneth Hungate Norf 101 A7
Empingham Rutland 99 A6
Empshott Hants 33 B6
Emstrey Shrops 111 D4
Emsworth Hants 19 A6
Enborne W Berks 46 C2
Enchmarsh Shrops 94 B3
Enderby Leics 98 B2
Endmoor Cumb 154 C4
Endon Staffs 129 D4
Endon Bank Staffs 129 D4
Enfield London 68 D3
Enfield Wash London 68 D3
Enford Wilts 45 D5
Engamoor Shetland 285 H4
Engine Common S Glos 43 A5
Englefield W Berks 47 B4
Englefield Green Sur 48 B2
Englesea-brook Ches 128 D2
English Bicknor Glos 62 B1
English Frankton Shrops 110 C3
Englishcombe Bath 43 C6
Enham Alamein Hants 32 A2
Enmore Som 28 B2
Ennerdale Bridge Cumb 162 C3
Enoch Dumfries 183 B6
Enochdhu Perth 231 B4
Ensay Argyll 224 B2
Ensbury Bmouth 17 B4
Ensdon Shrops 110 D3
Ensis Devon 25 C6
Enstone Oxon 65 A4
Enterkinfoot Dumfries 183 B6
Enterpen N Yorks 158 A3
Enville Staffs 95 C6
Eolaigearraidh W Isles 286 F3
Eorabus Argyll 224 D2
Eòropaidh W Isles 288 A6
Epperstone Notts 115 A4
Epping Essex 69 C4
Epping Green Essex 68 C4
Epping Green Herts 68 C2
Epping Upland Essex 68 C4
Eppleby N Yorks 167 D4
Eppleworth E Yorks 150 D3
Epsom Sur 49 C5
Epsom Racecourse Sur 35 A5
Epwell Oxon 81 C6
Epworth N Lincs 141 C5
Epworth Turbary N Lincs 141 C5
Erbistock Wrex 110 A2
Erbusaig Highld 249 D4
Erchless Castle Highld 251 B6
Erddig Wrex 110 A2
Erdington W Mid 96 B4

Eredine Argyll 214 B2
Eriboll Highld 277 C5
Ericstane Dumfries 184 A3
Eridge Green E Sus 36 C3
Erines Argyll 202 A2
Eriswell Suff 102 D3
Erith London 50 B2
Erlestoke Wilts 44 D3
Ermine Lincs 133 B4
Ermington Devon 7 B5
Erpingham Norf 120 B3
Errogie Highld 252 D1
Errol Perth 220 B2
Erskine Renfs 205 A4
Erskine Bridge Renfs 205 A4
Ervie Dumfries 170 A2
Erwarton Suff 88 D3
Erwood Powys 77 C4
Eryholme N Yorks 157 A7
Eryrys Denb 126 D2
Escomb Durham 167 C4
Escrick N Yorks 149 C5
Esgairdawe Carms 58 A3
Esgairgeiliog Powys 91 B5
Esh Durham 167 A4
Esh Winning Durham 167 A4
Esher Sur 48 C4
Esholt W Yorks 147 C5
Eshott Northumb 189 D5
Eshton N Yorks 146 B3
Eskadale Highld 251 C6
Eskbank Midloth 209 D6
Eskdale Green Cumb 163 D4
Eskdalemuir Dumfries 185 C5
Eske E Yorks 150 C3
Eskham Lincs 143 D5
Esprick Lancs 144 D4
Essendine Rutland 116 D3
Essendon Herts 68 C2
Essich Highld 252 C2
Essington Staffs 96 A2
Esslemont Aberds 257 D4
Eston Redcar 168 D3
Eswick Shetland 285 H6
Etal Northumb 198 C3
Etchilhampton Wilts 44 C4
Etchingham E Sus 37 D5
Etchinghill Kent 38 B3
Etchinghill Staffs 112 D4
Ethie Castle Angus 233 D4
Ethie Mains Angus 233 D4
Etling Green Norf 120 D2
Eton Windsor 48 B2
Eton Wick Windsor 48 B2
Etteridge Highld 241 C4
Ettersgill Durham 166 C1
Ettingshall W Mid 96 B2
Ettington Warks 81 C5
Etton E Yorks 150 C2
Etton P'boro 100 A3
Ettrick Borders 185 A5
Ettrickbridge Borders 186 A2
Ettrickhill Borders 185 A5
Etwall Derbys 113 B6
Eureka!, Halifax W Yorks 138 A3
Euston Suff 103 D4
Euximoor Drove Cambs 101 B6
Euxton Lancs 137 B4
Evanstown Bridgend 41 C4
Evanton Highld 264 D2
Evedon Lincs 116 A3
Evelix Highld 264 A3
Evenjobb Powys 77 A6
Evenley Northants 82 D2
Evenlode Glos 64 A3
Evenwood Durham 167 C4
Evenwood Gate Durham 167 C4
Everbay Orkney 282 E7
Evercreech Som 29 B6
Everdon Northants 82 B2
Everingham E Yorks 149 C7
Everleigh Wilts 45 D6
Everley N Yorks 160 C3
Eversholt Beds 84 D1
Evershot Dorset 15 A5
Eversley Hants 47 C5
Eversley Cross Hants 47 C5
Everthorpe E Yorks 150 D2
Everton Beds 84 B4
Everton Hants 18 B1
Everton Mers 136 D2
Everton Notts 141 D4
Evertown Dumfries 175 A6
Evesbatch Hereford 79 C4
Evesham Worcs 80 C3
Evington Leicester 98 A3

Ewden Village S Yorks 139 D5
Ewell Sur 49 C5
Ewell Minnis Kent 39 A4
Ewelme Oxon 66 D1
Ewen Glos 63 D6
Ewenny V Glam 40 D4
Ewerby Lincs 116 A4
Ewerby Thorpe Lincs 116 A4
Ewes Dumfries 185 C6
Ewesley Northumb 188 D3
Ewhurst Sur 34 B3
Ewhurst Green E Sus 37 D5
Ewhurst Green Sur 34 C3
Ewloe Flint 126 C3
Ewloe Green Flint 126 C2
Ewood Blkburn 137 A5
Eworthy Devon 11 B5
Ewshot Hants 33 A7
Ewyas Harold Hereford 61 A5
Exbourne Devon 11 A7
Exbury Hants 18 B3
Exbury Gardens, Fawley
  Hants 18 A3
Exebridge Som 27 C4
Exelby N Yorks 157 C6
Exeter Devon 13 B4
Exeter Cathedral Devon 13 B4
Exeter International
  Airport Devon 13 B4
Exford Som 26 B3
Exhall Warks 80 B4
Exley Head W Yorks 147 D4
Exminster Devon 13 C4
Exmouth Devon 13 C5
Exnaboe Shetland 285 M5
Exning Suff 86 A2
Explosion, Gosport Hants 19 A5
Exton Devon 13 C4
Exton Hants 33 C5
Exton Rutland 116 D2
Exton Som 27 B4
Exwick Devon 13 B4
Eyam Derbys 130 B2
Eydon Northants 82 B2
Eye Hereford 78 A2
Eye P'boro 100 A4
Eye Suff 104 D2
Eye Green P'boro 100 A4
Eyemouth Borders 211 D6
Eyeworth Beds 85 C4
Eyhorne Street Kent 37 A6
Eyke Suff 88 B4
Eynesbury Cambs 84 B3
Eynort Highld 246 B2
Eynsford Kent 50 C2
Eynsham Oxon 65 C5
Eype Dorset 14 B4
Eyre Highld 259 C4
Eyre Highld 248 C2
Eythorne Kent 39 A4
Eyton Hereford 78 A2
Eyton Shrops 94 C1
Eyton Wrex 110 A2
Eyton upon the Weald
  Moors Telford 111 D5

F

Faccombe Hants 46 D1
Faceby N Yorks 158 A3
Fadmoor N Yorks 159 C5
Faddiley Ches 127 D5
Faerdre Swansea 40 A1
Failand N Som 43 B4
Failford S Ayrs 193 C4
Failsworth Gtr Man 138 C1
Fain Highld 262 C3
Fair Green Norf 118 D3
Fair Hill Cumb 164 B3
Fair Oak Hants 32 D3
Fair Oak Green Hants 47 C4
Fairbourne Gwyn 90 A4
Fairburn N Yorks 140 A2
Fairfield Derbys 129 B5
Fairfield Stockton 168 D2
Fairfield Worcs 80 C3
Fairfield Worcs 96 D2
Fairford Glos 64 C2
Fairhaven Lancs 136 A2
Fairlie N Ayrs 204 C2
Fairlight E Sus 23 A6
Fairlight Cove E Sus 23 A6
Fairmile Devon 13 B5
Fairmilehead Edin 209 D5
Fairoak Staffs 111 B6
Fairseat Kent 50 C3

Fairstead Essex 70 B1
Fairstead Norf 118 D3
Fairwarp E Sus 36 D2
Fairy Cottage I o M 152 C4
Fairy Cross Devon 25 C5
Fakenham Norf 119 C6
Fakenham Magna Suff 103 D5
Fakenham Racecourse
  Norf 119 C6
Fala Midloth 210 D1
Fala Dam Midloth 210 D1
Falahill Borders 196 A2
Falcon Hereford 79 D4
Faldingworth Lincs 133 A5
Falfield S Glos 62 D2
Falkenham Suff 88 D3
Falkirk Falk 208 C1
Falkland Fife 220 D2
Falkland Palace Fife 220 D2
Falla Borders 187 B6
Fallgate Derbys 130 C3
Fallin Stirl 207 A6
Fallowfield Gtr Man 138 D1
Fallsidehill Borders 197 B5
Falmer E Sus 21 B6
Falmouth Corn 4 D3
Falsgrave N Yorks 160 C4
Falstone Northumb 177 A5
Fanagmore Highld 276 D2
Fangdale Beck N Yorks 159 B4
Fangfoss E Yorks 149 B6
Fankerton Falk 207 B5
Fanmore Argyll 224 B3
Fannich Lodge Highld 262 D4
Fans Borders 197 B5
Far Bank S Yorks 140 B4
Far Bletchley M Keynes 83 D5
Far Cotton Northants 83 B4
Far Forest Worcs 95 D5
Far Laund Derbys 114 A1
Far Sawrey Cumb 154 B2
Farcet Cambs 100 B4
Farden Shrops 94 D3
Fareham Hants 19 A4
Farewell Staffs 113 D4
Farforth Lincs 134 B3
Faringdon Oxon 64 D3
Farington Lancs 136 A4
Farlam Cumb 176 D3
Farlary Highld 273 D5
Farleigh N Som 42 C3
Farleigh Sur 49 C6
Farleigh Hungerford Som 44 D2
Farleigh Wallop Hants 33 A5
Farlesthorpe Lincs 135 B4
Farleton Cumb 154 C4
Farleton Lancs 145 A5
Farley Shrops 94 A1
Farley Staffs 113 A4
Farley Wilts 31 C6
Farley Green Sur 34 B3
Farley Hill Luton 67 A5
Farley Hill Wokingham 47 C5
Farleys End Glos 62 B3
Farlington N Yorks 149 A5
Farlow Shrops 95 C4
Farmborough Bath 43 C5
Farmcote Glos 63 A6
Farmcote Shrops 95 B5
Farmington Glos 64 B2
Farmoor Oxon 65 C5
Farmtown Moray 267 D6
Farnborough London 50 C1
Farnborough Hants 34 A1
Farnborough Warks 82 C1
Farnborough W Berks 46 A2
Farnborough Green Hants 34 A1
Farncombe Sur 34 B2
Farndish Beds 83 A6
Farndon Ches 127 D4
Farndon Notts 132 D2
Farnell Angus 233 C4
Farnham Dorset 30 D3
Farnham Essex 69 A4
Farnham N Yorks 148 A2
Farnham Suff 89 A4
Farnham Sur 34 B1
Farnham Common Bucks 48 A2
Farnham Green Essex 69 A4
Farnham Royal Bucks 48 A2
Farnhill N Yorks 147 C4
Farningham Kent 50 C2
Farnley N Yorks 147 C5
Farnley W Yorks 147 D6

Farnley Tyas W Yorks	139	B4
Farnsfield Notts	131	D6
Farnworth Gtr Man	137	C6
Farnworth Halton	127	A5
Farr Highld	252	C2
Farr Highld	241	B6
Farr Highld	278	B3
Farr House Highld	252	C2
Farringdon Devon	13	B5
Farrington Gurney Bath	43	D5
Farsley W Yorks	147	D6
Farthinghoe Northants	82	D2
Farthingloe Kent	39	A4
Farthingstone Northants	82	B3
Fartown W Yorks	139	B4
Farway Devon	14	B1
Fasag Highld	249	A5
Fascadale Highld	235	C4
Faslane Port Argyll	215	D5
Fasnacloich Argyll	227	B5
Fasnakyle Ho. Highld	251	D5
Fassfern Highld	237	B4
Fatfield T & W	179	D5
Fattahead Aberds	268	D1
Faugh Cumb	176	D3
Fauldhouse W Loth	208	D2
Faulkbourne Essex	70	B1
Faulkland Som	43	D6
Fauls Shrops	111	B4
Faversham Kent	52	C2
Favillar Moray	254	C3
Fawdington N Yorks	158	D3
Fawfieldhead Staffs	129	C5
Fawkham Green Kent	50	C2
Fawler Oxon	65	B4
Fawley Bucks	47	A5
Fawley Hants	18	A3
Fawley W Berks	46	A1
Fawley Chapel Hereford	62	A1
Faxfleet E Yorks	141	A6
Faygate W Sus	35	C5
Fazakerley Mers	136	D2
Fazeley Staffs	97	A5
Fearby N Yorks	157	C5
Fearn Highld	265	C4
Fearn Lodge Highld	264	B2
Fearn Station Highld	265	C4
Fearnan Perth	229	D6
Fearnbeg Highld	249	A4
Fearnhead Warr	137	D5
Fearnmore Highld	261	D4
Featherstone Staffs	96	A2
Featherstone W Yorks	140	A2
Featherwood Northumb	187	C7
Feckenham Worcs	80	A3
Feering Essex	70	A2
Feetham N Yorks	156	B3
Feizor N Yorks	146	A1
Felbridge Sur	35	C6
Felbrigg Norf	120	B4
Felcourt Sur	36	B1
Felden Herts	67	C5
Felin-Crai Powys	59	C5
Felindre Ceredig	75	C4
Felindre Carms	58	C2
Felindre Carms	58	B3
Felindre Carms	59	C4
Felindre Ceredig	73	C6
Felindre Powys	93	C5
Felindre Swansea	57	B6
Felindre Farchog Pembs	72	C4
Felinfach Ceredig	75	C4
Felinfach Powys	77	D4
Felinfoel Carms	57	B5
Felingwm isaf Carms	58	C2
Felingwm uchaf Carms	58	C2
Felinwynt Ceredig	73	A5
Felixkirk N Yorks	158	C3
Felixstowe Suff	88	D3
Felixstowe Ferry Suff	88	D4
Felkington Northumb	198	B3
Felkirk W Yorks	140	B1
Fell Side Cumb	163	A6
Felling T & W	179	C4
Felmersham Beds	84	B1
Felmingham Norf	120	C4
Felpham W Sus	20	C2
Felsham Suff	87	B5
Felsted Essex	69	A6
Feltham London	48	B4
Felthorpe Norf	120	D3
Felton Hereford	78	C3
Felton Northumb	189	C4
Felton N Som	43	C4
Felton Butler Shrops	110	D2
Feltwell Norf	102	B3
Fen Ditton Cambs	85	A6
Fen Drayton Cambs	85	A5
Fen End W Mid	97	D5
Fen Side Lincs	134	D3
Fenay Bridge W Yorks	139	B4
Fence Lancs	146	D2
Fence Houses T & W	179	D5
Fengate P'boro	100	B4
Fengate Norf	120	C3
Fenham Northumb	199	B4
Fenhouses Lincs	117	A5
Feniscliffe Blkburn	137	A5
Feniscowles Blkburn	137	A5
Feniton Devon	13	B6
Fenlake Beds	84	C2
Fenny Bentley Derbys	130	D6
Fenny Bridges Devon	13	B6
Fenny Compton Warks	81	B7
Fenny Drayton Leics	97	B6
Fenny Stratford M Keynes	83	D5
Fenrother Northumb	189	D4
Fenstanton Cambs	85	A5
Fenton Cambs	101	D5
Fenton Lincs	132	D3
Fenton Lincs	132	B3
Fenton Stoke	112	A2
Fenton Barns E Loth	210	B2
Fenton Town Northumb	198	C3
Fenwick E Ayrs	205	D4
Fenwick Northumb	178	B2
Fenwick Northumb	199	B4
Fenwick S Yorks	140	B3
Feochaig Argyll	190	D3
Feock Corn	4	D3
Feolin Ferry Argyll	201	B4
Ferens Art Gallery, Hull Hull	142	A2
Ferindonald Highld	247	D5
Feriniquarrie Highld	258	C1
Ferlochan Argyll	226	B4
Fern Angus	232	B2
Ferndale Rhondda	41	B5
Ferndown Dorset	17	A4
Ferness Highld	253	B5
Ferney Green Cumb	154	B3
Fernham Oxon	64	D3
Fernhill Heath Worcs	79	B6
Fernhurst W Sus	34	D1
Fernie Fife	220	C3
Ferniegair S Lnrk	194	A2
Fernilea Highld	246	A2
Fernilee Derbys	129	B5
Ferrensby N Yorks	148	A2
Ferring W Sus	20	B3
Ferry Hill Cambs	101	C5
Ferry Point Highld	264	B3
Ferrybridge W Yorks	140	A2
Ferryden Angus	233	C5
Ferryhill Aberdeen	245	B6
Ferryhill Durham	167	B5
Ferryhill Station Durham	167	B6
Ferryside Carms	56	A3
Fersfield Norf	103	C6
Fersit Highld	228	A2
Ferwig Ceredig	73	B4
Feshiebridge Highld	241	B6
Festival Park Visitor Centre, Ebbw Vale Bl Gwent	60	C3
Fetcham Sur	35	A4
Fetlar Airport Shetland	284	D8
Fetterangus Aberds	269	D4
Fettercairn Aberds	233	A4
Fettes Highld	252	A1
Fewcott Oxon	65	A6
Fewston N Yorks	147	B5
Ffair-Rhos Ceredig	75	B6
Ffairfach Carms	58	C3
Ffaldybrenin Carms	58	A3
Ffarmers Carms	58	A3
Ffawyddog Powys	60	B4
Ffestiniog Railway, Porthmadog Gwyn	107	B6
Fforest Carms	57	B5
Fforest-fach Swansea	57	C6
Ffos-y-ffin Ceredig	74	B3
Ffostrasol Ceredig	73	B6
Ffridd-Uchaf Gwyn	107	A5
Ffrith Flint	126	D2
Ffrwd Gwyn	107	A4
Ffynnon ddrain Carms	73	D7
Ffynnon-oer Ceredig	75	C4
Ffynnongroyw Flint	125	A6
Fidden Argyll	224	D2
Fiddes Aberds	245	D5
Fiddington Glos	80	D2
Fiddington Som	28	A2
Fiddleford Dorset	30	D2
Fiddlers Hamlet Essex	69	C4
Field Staffs	112	B4
Field Broughton Cumb	154	C2
Field Dalling Norf	120	B2
Field Head Leics	98	A1
Fifehead Magdalen Dorset	30	C1
Fifehead Neville Dorset	30	D1
Fifield Oxon	64	B3
Fifield Wilts	45	D5
Fifield Windsor	48	B2
Fifield Bavant Wilts	31	C4
Figheldean Wilts	31	A5
Filands Wilts	44	A3
Filby Norf	121	D6
Filey N Yorks	161	C5
Filgrave M Keynes	83	C5
Filkins Oxon	64	C3
Filleigh Devon	26	C1
Filleigh Devon	26	D2
Fillingham Lincs	133	A4
Fillongley Warks	97	C5
Filton S Glos	43	B5
Fimber E Yorks	150	A1
Finavon Angus	232	C2
Fincham Norf	102	A2
Finchampstead Wokingham	47	C5
Finchdean Hants	33	D6
Finchingfield Essex	86	D2
Finchley London	68	D2
Findern Derbys	113	B7
Findhorn Moray	265	D6
Findhorn Bridge Highld	253	D4
Findo Gask Perth	219	B5
Findochty Moray	267	C5
Findon Aberds	245	C6
Findon W Sus	21	B4
Findon Mains Highld	264	D2
Findrack Ho. Aberds	244	B3
Finedon Northants	99	D6
Fingal Street Suff	88	A3
Fingask Aberds	256	D2
Fingerpost Worcs	95	D5
Fingest Bucks	66	D2
Finghall N Yorks	157	C5
Fingland Cumb	175	C5
Fingland Dumfries	183	A5
Finglesham Kent	53	D5
Fingringhoe Essex	71	A4
Finlarig Stirl	217	A5
Finmere Oxon	82	D3
Finnart Perth	229	C4
Finningham Suff	87	A6
Finningley S Yorks	141	D4
Finnygaud Aberds	267	D6
Finsbury London	49	A6
Finstall Worcs	80	A2
Finsthwaite Cumb	154	C2
Finstock Oxon	65	B4
Finstown Orkney	282	F4
Fintry Aberds	268	D2
Fintry Dundee	220	A4
Fintry Stirl	207	B4
Finzean Aberds	244	C3
Fionnphort Argyll	224	D2
Fionnsbhagh W Isles	287	F5
Fir Tree Durham	166	B4
Firbeck S Yorks	131	A5
Firby N Yorks	157	C6
Firby N Yorks	149	A6
Firgrove Gtr Man	138	B2
Firsby Lincs	135	C4
Firsdown Wilts	31	B6
First Coast Highld	261	A6
Fishbourne I o W	19	B4
Fishbourne W Sus	20	B1
Fishbourne Palace W Sus	20	B1
Fishburn Durham	167	B6
Fishcross Clack	208	A1
Fisher Place Cumb	163	C6
Fisherford Aberds	256	C1
Fisher's Pond Hants	32	C3
Fisherstreet W Sus	34	C2
Fisherton Highld	252	A3
Fisherton S Ayrs	192	D2
Fishguard = Abergwaun Pembs	72	C2
Fishlake S Yorks	141	B4
Fishleigh Barton Devon	25	C6
Fishponds Bristol	43	B5
Fishpool Glos	62	A2
Fishtoft Lincs	117	A6
Fishtoft Drove Lincs	117	A6
Fishtown of Usan Angus	233	C5
Fishwick Borders	198	A3
Fiskavaig Highld	246	A2
Fiskerton Lincs	133	B5
Fiskerton Notts	132	D2
Fitling E Yorks	151	D5
Fittleton Wilts	31	A5
Fittleworth W Sus	20	A3
Fitton End Cambs	118	D1
Fitz Shrops	110	D3
Fitzhead Som	27	C6
Fitzwilliam W Yorks	140	B2
Fitzwilliam Museum, Cambridge Cambs	85	B6
Fiunary Highld	225	B5
Five Acres Glos	62	B1
Five Ashes E Sus	36	D3
Five Oak Green Kent	36	B4
Five Oaks Jersey	6	
Five Oaks W Sus	34	D3
Five Roads Carms	57	B4
Fivecrosses Ches	127	B5
Fivehead Som	28	C3
Flack's Green Essex	70	B1
Flackwell Heath Bucks	48	A1
Fladbury Worcs	80	C2
Fladdabister Shetland	285	K6
Flagg Derbys	129	C6
Flambards Experience, Helston Corn	3	C4
Flamborough E Yorks	161	D6
Flamingo Land, Pickering N Yorks	159	D6
Flamstead Herts	67	B5
Flamstead End Herts	68	C3
Flansham W Sus	20	B2
Flanshaw W Yorks	139	A6
Flasby N Yorks	146	B3
Flash Staffs	129	C5
Flashader Highld	258	C3
Flask Inn N Yorks	160	A3
Flaunden Herts	67	C5
Flawborough Notts	115	A5
Flawith N Yorks	148	A3
Flax Bourton N Som	43	C4
Flaxby N Yorks	148	B2
Flaxholme Derbys	114	A1
Flaxley Glos	62	B2
Flaxpool Som	27	B6
Flaxton N Yorks	149	A5
Fleckney Leics	98	B3
Flecknoe Warks	82	A2
Fledborough Notts	132	B3
Fleet Hants	47	D6
Fleet Hants	19	A6
Fleet Lincs	117	C6
Fleet Air Arm Museum, Yeovil Som	29	C5
Fleet Hargate Lincs	117	C6
Fleetham Northumb	189	A4
Fleetlands Hants	19	A4
Fleetville Herts	67	C6
Fleetwood Lancs	144	C3
Flemingston V Glam	41	D5
Flemington S Lnrk	205	C6
Flempton Suff	87	A4
Fleoideabhagh W Isles	287	F5
Fletchertown Cumb	175	D5
Fletching E Sus	36	D2
Flexbury Corn	10	A3
Flexford Sur	34	B2
Flimby Cumb	162	A3
Flimwell E Sus	37	C5
Flint = Y Fflint Flint	126	B2
Flint Mountain Flint	126	B2
Flintham Notts	115	A5
Flinton E Yorks	151	D5
Flintsham Hereford	77	B7
Flitcham Norf	119	C4
Flitton Beds	84	D2
Flitwick Beds	84	D2
Flixborough N Lincs	141	B6
Flixborough Stather N Lincs	141	B6
Flixton Gtr Man	137	D6
Flixton N Yorks	160	D4
Flixton Suff	104	C4
Flockton W Yorks	139	B5
Flodaigh W Isles	286	A4
Flodden Northumb	198	C3
Flodigarry Highld	259	A4
Flood's Ferry Cambs	101	B5
Flookburgh Cumb	154	D2
Florden Norf	104	B2
Flore Northants	82	A3
Flotterton Northumb	188	C2
Flowton Suff	88	C1
Flush House W Yorks	139	C4
Flushing Aberds	257	B5
Flushing Corn	4	D3
Flyford Flavell Worcs	80	B2
Foals Green Suff	104	D3
Fobbing Thurrock	51	A4
Fochabers Moray	266	D4
Fochriw Caerph	60	C3
Fockerby N Lincs	141	B6
Fodderletter Moray	254	D2
Fodderty Highld	251	A6
Foel Powys	109	D4
Foel-gastell Carms	57	A5
Foffarty Angus	232	D2
Foggathorpe E Yorks	149	D6
Fogo Borders	197	B6
Fogorig Borders	198	B3
Foindle Highld	276	D2
Folda Angus	231	B6
Fole Staffs	112	B4
Foleshill W Mid	97	C6
Folke Dorset	29	D6
Folkestone Kent	39	B4
Folkestone Racecourse Kent	38	B4
Folkingham Lincs	116	B3
Folkington E Sus	22	B3
Folksworth Cambs	100	C3
Folkton N Yorks	161	D4
Folla Rule Aberds	256	C2
Follifoot N Yorks	148	B2
Folly Gate Devon	11	B6
Fonthill Bishop Wilts	30	B3
Fonthill Gifford Wilts	30	B3
Fontmell Magna Dorset	30	D2
Fontwell W Sus	20	B2
Fontwell Park Racecourse W Sus	20	B3
Foolow Derbys	130	B1
Foots Cray London	50	B1
Forbestown Aberds	243	A6
Force Mills Cumb	154	B2
Forcett N Yorks	167	D4
Ford Argyll	214	B2
Ford Bucks	66	C2
Ford Devon	25	C5
Ford Glos	64	A1
Ford Northumb	198	C3
Ford Shrops	110	D3
Ford Staffs	129	D4
Ford Wilts	44	B2
Ford W Sus	20	B3
Ford End Essex	69	B6
Ford Street Som	27	D6
Fordcombe Kent	36	B3
Fordell Fife	209	B4
Forden Powys	93	A6
Forder Green Devon	8	A1
Fordham Cambs	102	D2
Fordham Essex	70	A4
Fordham Norf	102	B3
Fordhouses W Mid	96	A4
Fordingbridge Hants	31	D5
Fordon E Yorks	160	D4
Fordoun Aberds	233	A5
Ford's Green Suff	87	A6
Fordstreet Essex	70	A4
Fordwells Oxon	64	B4
Fordwich Kent	52	D3
Fordyce Aberds	267	C6
Forebridge Staffs	112	C3
Forest Durham	165	B6
Forest Becks Lancs	146	B1
Forest Gate London	49	A6
Forest Green Sur	35	B4
Forest Hall Cumb	154	A4
Forest Head Cumb	176	D3
Forest Hill Oxon	65	C6
Forest Lane Head N Yorks	148	B2
Forest Lodge Argyll	228	D2
Forest Lodge Highld	242	A4
Forest Lodge Perth	230	A4
Forest Mill Clack	208	A2
Forest Row E Sus	36	C2
Forest Town Notts	131	C5
Forestburn Gate Northumb	188	D3
Foresterseat Moray	266	D2
Forestside W Sus	33	D6
Forfar Angus	232	C2
Forgandenny Perth	219	C5
Forge Powys	91	C5
Forge Side Torf	60	C4
Forgewood N Lnrk	194	A2
Forgie Moray	267	D4
Forglen Ho. Aberds	268	D2
Formby Mers	136	C2
Forncett End Norf	104	B2
Forncett St Mary Norf	104	B2
Forncett St Peter Norf	104	B2
Forneth Perth	231	D4

Fornham All Saints Suff 87 A4
Fornham St Martin Suff 87 A4
Forres Moray 253 A6
Forrest Lodge Dumfries 182 D3
Forrestfield N Lnrk 207 D6
Forsbrook Staffs 112 A3
Forse Highld 275 A6
Forse Ho. Highld 275 A6
Forsinain Highld 279 D5
Forsinard Highld 279 D4
Forsinard Station Highld 279 D4
Forston Dorset 15 B6
Fort Augustus Highld 240 B1
Fort George Guern 6
Fort George Highld 252 A3
Fort Victoria Country Park & Marine Aquarium I o W 18 C2
Fort William Highld 237 B5
Forteviot Perth 219 C5
Forth S Lnrk 194 A4
Forth Road Bridge Fife 208 C4
Forthampton Glos 79 D6
Fortingall Perth 229 D6
Forton Hants 32 A3
Forton Lancs 145 B4
Forton Shrops 110 D3
Forton Som 14 A3
Forton Staffs 111 C6
Forton Heath Shrops 110 D3
Fortrie Aberds 256 B1
Fortrose Highld 252 A3
Fortuneswell Dorset 15 D6
Forty Green Bucks 67 D4
Forty Hill London 68 D3
Forward Green Suff 88 B1
Fosbury Wilts 45 D7
Fosdyke Lincs 117 B6
Foss Perth 230 C1
Foss Cross Glos 63 C6
Fossebridge Glos 64 B1
Foster Street Essex 69 C4
Fosterhouses S Yorks 141 B4
Foston Derbys 113 B5
Foston Lincs 115 A6
Foston N Yorks 149 A5
Foston on the Wolds E Yorks 151 B4
Fotherby Lincs 143 D5
Fotheringhay Northants 100 B2
Foubister Orkney 283 G6
Foul Mile E Sus 22 A4
Foulby W Yorks 140 B1
Foulden Borders 198 A3
Foulden Norf 102 B3
Foulis Castle Highld 264 D1
Foulridge Lancs 146 C2
Foulsham Norf 120 C2
Fountainhall Borders 196 B3
Fountains Abbey, Ripon N Yorks 147 A6
Four Ashes Staffs 95 C6
Four Ashes Suff 103 D6
Four Crosses Powys 93 A4
Four Crosses Powys 110 D1
Four Crosses Wrex 126 D2
Four Elms Kent 36 B2
Four Forks Som 28 B2
Four Gotes Cambs 118 D1
Four Lane Ends Ches 127 C5
Four Lanes Corn 3 B4
Four Marks Hants 33 B5
Four Mile Bridge Anglesey 122 C2
Four Oaks E Sus 37 D6
Four Oaks W Mid 97 C5
Four Oaks W Mid 96 B4
Four Roads Carms 57 B4
Four Roads I o M 152 E2
Four Throws Kent 37 D5
Fourlane Ends Derbys 130 D3
Fourlanes End Ches 128 D3
Fourpenny Highld 265 A4
Fourstones Northumb 177 C6
Fovant Wilts 31 C4
Foveran Aberds 257 D4
Fowey Corn 5 B6
Fowley Common Warr 137 D5
Fowlis Angus 220 A3
Fowlis Wester Perth 218 B4
Fowlmere Cambs 85 C6
Fownhope Hereford 78 D3
Fox Corner Sur 34 A2
Fox Lane Hants 34 A1
Fox Street Essex 71 A4
Foxbar Renfs 205 B4
Foxcombe Hill Oxon 65 C5
Foxdale I o M 152 D2
Foxearth Essex 87 C4
Foxfield Cumb 153 B3
Foxham Wilts 44 B3
Foxhole Corn 5 B4
Foxhole Swansea 57 C6
Foxholes N Yorks 160 D4
Foxhunt Green E Sus 22 A3
Foxley Norf 120 C2
Foxley Wilts 44 A2
Foxt Staffs 112 A4
Foxton Cambs 85 C6
Foxton Durham 167 C6
Foxton Leics 99 B4
Foxton Canal Locks Leics 98 C3
Foxup N Yorks 156 D2
Foxwist Green Ches 127 C6
Foxwood Shrops 95 D4
Foy Hereford 62 A1
Foyers Highld 251 D6
Fraddam Corn 2 B3
Fraddon Corn 4 B4
Fradley Staffs 113 D5
Fradswell Staffs 112 B3
Fraisthorpe E Yorks 151 A4
Framfield E Sus 36 D2
Framingham Earl Norf 104 A3
Framingham Pigot Norf 104 A3
Framlingham Suff 88 A3
Framlington Castle Suff 88 A3
Frampton Dorset 15 B6
Frampton Lincs 117 B6
Frampton Cotterell S Glos 43 A5
Frampton Mansell Glos 63 C5
Frampton on Severn Glos 62 C3
Frampton West End Lincs 117 A5
Framsden Suff 88 B2
Framwellgate Moor Durham 167 A5
Franche Worcs 95 D6
Frankby Mers 126 A2
Frankley Worcs 96 C2
Frank's Bridge Powys 77 B5
Frankton Warks 98 D1
Frant E Sus 36 C3
Fraserburgh Aberds 269 C4
Frating Green Essex 71 A4
Fratton Ptsmth 19 B5
Freathy Corn 6 B3
Freckenham Suff 102 D2
Freckleton Lancs 136 A3
Freeby Leics 115 C6
Freehay Staffs 112 A4
Freeland Oxon 65 B5
Freeport Hornsea Outlet Village E Yorks 151 C5
Freester Shetland 285 H6
Freethorpe Norf 105 A5
Freiston Lincs 117 A6
Fremington Devon 25 B6
Fremington N Yorks 156 B4
Frenchay S Glos 43 B5
Frenchbeer Devon 12 C1
Frenich Stirl 216 D4
Frensham Sur 34 B1
Fresgoe Highld 279 B5
Freshfield Mers 136 C1
Freshford Bath 44 C1
Freshwater I o W 18 C2
Freshwater Bay I o W 18 C2
Freshwater East Pembs 55 E6
Fressingfield Suff 104 D3
Freston Suff 88 D2
Freswick Highld 281 B5
Fretherne Glos 62 C3
Frettenham Norf 120 D4
Freuchie Fife 220 D2
Freuchies Angus 231 B6
Freystrop Pembs 55 C5
Friar's Gate E Sus 36 C2
Friarton Perth 219 B6
Friday Bridge Cambs 101 A6
Friday Street E Sus 22 B4
Fridaythorpe E Yorks 150 B1
Friern Barnet London 68 D2
Friesland Argyll 223 B4
Friesthorpe Lincs 133 A5
Frieston Lincs 116 A2
Frieth Bucks 66 D2
Frilford Oxon 65 D5
Frilsham W Berks 46 B3
Frimley Sur 34 A1
Frimley Green Sur 34 A1
Frindsbury Medway 51 B4
Fring Norf 119 B4
Fringford Oxon 65 A7
Frinsted Kent 37 A6
Frinton-on-Sea Essex 71 A6
Friockheim Angus 232 D3
Friog Gwyn 90 A4
Frisby on the Wreake Leics 115 D4
Friskney Lincs 135 D4
Friskney Eaudike Lincs 135 D4
Friskney Tofts Lincs 135 D4
Friston E Sus 22 C3
Friston Suff 89 A5
Fritchley Derbys 130 D3
Frith Bank Lincs 117 A6
Frith Common Worcs 79 A4
Fritham Hants 31 D6
Frithelstock Devon 25 D5
Frithelstock Stone Devon 25 D5
Frithville Lincs 134 D3
Frittenden Kent 37 B6
Frittiscombe Devon 8 C2
Fritton Norf 104 B3
Fritton Norf 105 A5
Fritwell Oxon 65 A6
Frizinghall W Yorks 147 D5
Frizington Cumb 162 C3
Frocester Glos 62 C3
Frodesley Shrops 94 A3
Frodingham N Lincs 141 B6
Frodsham Ches 127 B5
Frogden Borders 187 A6
Froggatt Derbys 130 B2
Froghall Staffs 112 A4
Frogmore Devon 7 C6
Frogmore Hants 34 A1
Frognall Lincs 117 D4
Frogshail Norf 121 B4
Frolesworth Leics 98 B2
Frome Som 30 A1
Frome St Quintin Dorset 15 A5
Fromes Hill Hereford 79 C4
Fron Denb 125 C5
Fron Gwyn 107 A5
Fron Gwyn 106 C3
Fron Powys 77 A4
Fron Powys 93 A6
Fron Powys 93 B5
Froncysyllte Wrex 110 A1
Frongoch Gwyn 108 B4
Frostenden Suff 105 C5
Frosterley Durham 166 B3
Frotoft Orkney 282 E5
Froxfield Wilts 45 C6
Froxfield Green Hants 33 C6
Froyle Hants 33 A6
Fryerning Essex 69 C6
Fryton N Yorks 159 D5
Fulbeck Lincs 133 D4
Fulbourn Cambs 85 B7
Fulbrook Oxon 64 B3
Fulford Som 28 C2
Fulford Staffs 112 B3
Fulford York 149 C5
Fulham London 49 B5
Fulking W Sus 21 A5
Full Sutton E Yorks 149 B6
Fullarton Glasgow 205 B6
Fullarton N Ayrs 192 B3
Fuller Street Essex 70 B1
Fuller's Moor Ches 127 D4
Fullerton Hants 32 B2
Fulletby Lincs 134 B2
Fullwood E Ayrs 205 C4
Fulmer Bucks 48 A2
Fulmodestone Norf 120 B1
Fulnetby Lincs 133 B5
Fulstow Lincs 143 D5
Fulwell T & W 179 D5
Fulwood Lancs 145 D5
Fulwood S Yorks 130 A3
Fundenhall Norf 104 B2
Fundenhall Street Norf 104 B2
Funtington W Sus 19 A6
Funtley Hants 19 A4
Funtullich Perth 218 B2
Funzie Shetland 284 D8
Furley Devon 14 A2
Furnace Argyll 214 B3
Furnace Carms 57 B5
Furnace End Warks 97 B5
Furneaux Pelham Herts 68 A4
Furness Vale Derbys 129 A5
Furze Platt Windsor 48 A1
Furzehill Devon 26 A2
Fyfett Som 28 D2
Fyfield Essex 69 C5
Fyfield Glos 64 C3
Fyfield Hants 32 A1
Fyfield Oxon 65 D5
Fyfield Wilts 45 C5
Fylingthorpe N Yorks 160 A3
Fyvie Aberds 256 C2

G

Gabhsann bho Dheas W Isles 288 B5
Gabhsann bho Thuath W Isles 288 B5
Gablon Highld 264 A3
Gabroc Hill E Ayrs 205 C4
Gaddesby Leics 115 D4
Gadebridge Herts 67 C5
Gaer Powys 60 A3
Gaerllwyd Mon 61 D6
Gaerwen Anglesey 123 C4
Gagingwell Oxon 65 A5
Gaick Lodge Highld 241 D5
Gailey Staffs 112 D3
Gainford Durham 167 D4
Gainsborough Lincs 141 D6
Gainsborough Suff 88 C2
Gainsford End Essex 86 D3
Gairloch Highld 261 C5
Gairlochy Highld 239 D5
Gairney Bank Perth 208 A4
Gairnshiel Lodge Aberds 243 B5
Gaisgill Cumb 155 A5
Gaitsgill Cumb 164 A1
Galashiels Borders 196 C3
Galgate Lancs 145 B4
Galhampton Som 29 C6
Gallaberry Dumfries 184 D2
Gallachoille Argyll 213 D5
Gallanach Argyll 226 D3
Gallanach Argyll 223 A5
Gallantry Bank Ches 127 D5
Gallatown Fife 209 A5
Galley Common Warks 97 B6
Galley Hill Cambs 85 A5
Galleyend Essex 69 C7
Galleywood Essex 69 C7
Gallin Perth 229 D4
Gallowfauld Angus 232 D2
Gallows Green Staffs 113 A4
Galltair Highld 249 D5
Galmisdale Highld 234 B3
Galmpton Devon 7 C5
Galmpton Torbay 8 B2
Galphay N Yorks 157 D6
Galston E Ayrs 193 B5
Galtrigill Highld 258 C1
Gamblesby Cumb 165 B4
Gamesley Derbys 138 D3
Gamlingay Cambs 84 B4
Gammersgill N Yorks 157 C4
Gamston Notts 132 B2
Ganarew Hereford 62 B1
Ganavan Argyll 226 C3
Gang Corn 6 A2
Ganllwyd Gwyn 108 C2
Gannochy Angus 232 A3
Gannochy Perth 219 B6
Gansclet Highld 281 D5
Ganstead E Yorks 151 D4
Ganthorpe N Yorks 159 D5
Ganton N Yorks 160 D3
Garbat Highld 263 D6
Garbhallt Argyll 214 C3
Garboldisham Norf 103 C6
Garden City Flint 126 C3
Garden Village Wrex 126 D3
Garden Village W Yorks 148 D3
Gardenstown Aberds 268 C2
Garderhouse Shetland 285 J5
Gardham E Yorks 150 C2
Gardin Shetland 284 G6
Gare Hill Som 30 A1
Garelochhead Argyll 215 C5
Garford Oxon 65 D5
Garforth W Yorks 148 D3
Gargrave N Yorks 146 B3
Gargunnock Stirl 207 A5
Garlic Street Norf 104 C3
Garlieston Dumfries 171 C6
Garlinge Green Kent 52 D3
Garlogie Aberds 245 B4
Garmond Aberds 268 D3
Garmony Argyll 225 B5
Garmouth Moray 266 C4
Garn-yr-erw Torf 60 B4
Garnant Carms 58 D3
Garndiffaith Torf 61 C4
Garndolbenmaen Gwyn 107 B4
Garnedd Conwy 124 D2
Garnett Bridge Cumb 154 B4
Garnfadryn Gwyn 106 C2
Garnkirk N Lnrk 207 D4
Garnlydan Bl Gwent 60 B3
Garnswllt Swansea 57 B6
Garrabost W Isles 288 D6
Garraron Argyll 213 B6
Garras Corn 3 C5
Garreg Gwyn 107 B6
Garrick Perth 218 C3
Garrigill Cumb 165 A5
Garriston N Yorks 157 B5
Garroch Dumfries 182 D3
Garrogie Lodge Highld 240 A3
Garros Highld 259 B4
Garrow Perth 230 D2
Garryhorn Dumfries 182 C3
Garsdale Cumb 155 C6
Garsdale Head Cumb 155 B6
Garsdon Wilts 44 A3
Garshall Green Staffs 112 B3
Garsington Oxon 65 C6
Garstang Lancs 145 C4
Garston Mers 127 A4
Garswood Mers 137 D4
Gartcosh N Lnrk 207 D4
Garth Bridgend 40 B3
Garth Gwyn 123 C5
Garth Powys 76 C3
Garth Shetland 285 H4
Garth Wrex 110 A1
Garth Row Cumb 154 B4
Garthamlock Glasgow 205 B6
Garthbrengy Powys 76 D4
Garthdee Aberdeen 245 B6
Gartheli Ceredig 75 C4
Garthmyl Powys 93 B5
Garthorpe Leics 115 C6
Garthorpe N Lincs 141 B6
Gartly Aberds 255 C6
Gartmore Stirl 206 A3
Gartnagrenach Argyll 202 C2
Gartness N Lnrk 207 D5
Gartness Stirl 206 B3
Gartocharn W Dunb 206 B2
Garton E Yorks 151 D5
Garton-on-the-Wolds E Yorks 150 B2
Gartsherrie N Lnrk 207 D5
Gartymore Highld 274 C4
Garvald E Loth 210 C2
Garvamore Highld 240 C3
Garvard Argyll 212 C1
Garvault Hotel Highld 273 A5
Garve Highld 263 D5
Garvestone Norf 103 A6
Garvock Aberds 233 A5
Garvock Invclyd 204 A2
Garway Hereford 61 A6
Garway Hill Hereford 61 A6
Gaskan Highld 236 B1
Gastard Wilts 44 C2
Gasthorpe Norf 103 C5
Gatcombe I o W 18 C3
Gate Burton Lincs 132 A3
Gate Helmsley N Yorks 149 B5
Gateacre Mers 127 A4
Gatebeck Cumb 154 C4
Gateford Notts 131 A5
Gateforth N Yorks 140 A3
Gatehead E Ayrs 192 B3
Gatehouse Northumb 177 A5
Gatehouse of Fleet Dumfries 172 C4
Gatelawbridge Dumfries 183 C7
Gateley Norf 119 C6
Gatenby N Yorks 158 C2
Gateshead T & W 179 C4
Gateshead International Stadium T & W 179 C4
Gatesheath Ches 127 C4
Gateside Aberds 244 A3
Gateside Angus 232 D2
Gateside E Renf 205 C4
Gateside Fife 219 D6
Gateside N Ayrs 204 C3
Gathurst Gtr Man 136 C4
Gatley Gtr Man 128 A3
Gattonside Borders 197 C4
Gatwick Airport W Sus 35 B5
Gaufron Powys 76 A3
Gaulby Leics 98 A3
Gauldry Fife 220 B3
Gaunt's Common Dorset 17 A4
Gautby Lincs 134 B1
Gavinton Borders 197 A6
Gawber S Yorks 139 C6
Gawcott Bucks 82 D3
Gawsworth Ches 128 C3

Gawthorpe W Yorks 139 A5
Gawthrop Cumb 155 C5
Gawthwaite Cumb 153 B3
Gay Street W Sus 34 D3
Gaydon Warks 81 B6
Gayfield Orkney 282 B5
Gayhurst M Keynes 83 C5
Gayle N Yorks 156 C2
Gayles N Yorks 157 A5
Gayton Mers 126 A2
Gayton Norf 119 D4
Gayton Northants 83 B4
Gayton Staffs 112 C3
Gayton le Marsh Lincs 135 A4
Gayton le Wold Lincs 134 A2
Gayton Thorpe Norf 119 D4
Gaywood Norf 118 C3
Gazeley Suff 86 A3
Geanies House Highld 265 C4
Gearraidh Bhailteas W Isles 286 D3
Gearraidh Bhaird W Isles 288 E4
Gearraidh na h-Aibhne W Isles 288 D3
Gearraidh na Monadh W Isles 286 E3
Geary Highld 258 B2
Geddes House Highld 253 A4
Gedding Suff 87 B5
Geddington Northants 99 C5
Gedintailor Highld 247 A4
Gedling Notts 115 A4
Gedney Lincs 117 C7
Gedney Broadgate Lincs 117 C7
Gedney Drove End Lincs 118 C1
Gedney Dyke Lincs 117 C7
Gedney Hill Lincs 117 D6
Gee Cross Gtr Man 138 D2
Geilston Argyll 206 C1
Geirinis W Isles 286 B3
Geise Highld 280 B3
Geisiadar W Isles 288 D2
Geldeston Norf 105 B4
Gell Conwy 124 C3
Gelli Pembs 55 C6
Gelli Rhondda 41 B4
Gellideg M Tydf 60 C2
Gellifor Denb 125 C6
Gelligaer Caerph 41 B6
Gellilydan Gwyn 107 C6
Gellinudd Neath 40 A2
Gellyburn Perth 219 A5
Gellywen Carms 73 D5
Gelston Dumfries 173 C5
Gelston Lincs 116 A2
Gembling E Yorks 151 B4
Gentleshaw Staffs 113 D4
Geocrab W Isles 288 H2
George Green Bucks 48 A3
George Nympton Devon 26 C2
Georgefield Dumfries 185 C5
Georgeham Devon 25 B5
Georgetown Bl Gwent 60 C3
Gerlan Gwyn 123 D6
Germansweek Devon 11 B5
Germoe Corn 2 C3
Gerrans Corn 4 D3
Gerrards Cross Bucks 48 A3
Gestingthorpe Essex 87 D4
Geuffordd Powys 109 D7
Gib Hill Ches 127 B6
Gibbet Hill Warks 98 C2
Gibbshill Dumfries 173 A5
Gidea Park London 50 A2
Gidleigh Devon 12 C1
Giffnock E Renf 205 C5
Gifford E Loth 210 D2
Giffordland N Ayrs 204 D2
Giffordtown Fife 220 C2
Giggleswick N Yorks 146 A2
Gilberdyke E Yorks 141 A6
Gilchriston E Loth 210 D1
Gilcrux Cumb 163 A4
Gildersome W Yorks 139 A5
Gildingwells S Yorks 131 A5
Gileston V Glam 41 E5
Gilfach Caerph 41 B6
Gilfach Goch Rhondda 41 C4
Gilfachrheda Ceredig 73 A7
Gillamoor N Yorks 159 C5
Gillar's Green Mers 136 D3
Gillen Highld 258 C2
Gilling East N Yorks 159 D5
Gilling West N Yorks 157 A5
Gillingham Dorset 30 C2
Gillingham Medway 51 C4
Gillingham Norf 105 B5
Gillock Highld 280 C4
Gillow Heath Staffs 128 D3
Gills Highld 281 A5
Gill's Green Kent 37 C5
Gilmanscleuch Borders 196 D2
Gilmerton Edin 209 D5
Gilmerton Perth 218 B3
Gilmonby Durham 166 D2
Gilmorton Leics 98 C2
Gilmourton S Lnrk 205 D6
Gilsland Cumb 176 C4
Gilsland Spa Cumb 176 C4
Gilston Borders 196 A3
Gilston Herts 68 B4
Gilwern Mon 60 B4
Gimingham Norf 121 B4
Giosla W Isles 288 E2
Gipping Suff 87 A6
Gipsey Bridge Lincs 117 A5
Girdle Toll N Ayrs 204 D3
Girlsta Shetland 285 H6
Girsby N Yorks 158 A2
Girtford Beds 84 B3
Girthon Dumfries 172 C4
Girton Cambs 85 A6
Girton Notts 132 C3
Girvan S Ayrs 180 B3
Gisburn Lancs 146 C2
Gisleham Suff 105 C6
Gislingham Suff 104 D1
Gissing Norf 104 C2
Gittisham Devon 13 B6
Gladestry Powys 77 B6
Gladsmuir E Loth 210 C1
Glais Swansea 40 A2
Glaisdale N Yorks 159 A6
Glame Highld 248 B2
Glamis Angus 232 D1
Glamis Castle Angus 232 D1
Glan Adda Gwyn 123 C5
Glan-Conwy Conwy 124 D3
Glan Conwy Conwy 124 B3
Glan-Duar Carms 58 A2
Glan-Dwyfach Gwyn 107 B4
Glan Gors Anglesey 123 C4
Glan-rhyd Gwyn 107 A4
Glan-traeth Anglesey 122 C2
Glan-y-don Flint 125 B6
Glan-y-nant Powys 92 C3
Glan-y-wern Gwyn 107 C6
Glan-yr-afon Anglesey 123 B6
Glan-yr-afon Gwyn 108 A4
Glan-yr-afon Gwyn 109 A5
Glanaman Carms 57 A6
Glandford Norf 120 A2
Glandwr Pembs 73 D4
Glandy Cross Carms 72 D4
Glandyfi Ceredig 91 C4
Glangrwyney Powys 60 B4
Glanmule Powys 93 B5
Glanrafon Ceredig 90 D4
Glanrhyd Gwyn 106 C2
Glanrhyd Pembs 72 B4
Glanton Northumb 188 B3
Glanton Pike Northumb 188 B3
Glanvilles Wootton Dorset 15 A6
Glapthorn Northants 100 B2
Glapwell Derbys 131 C4
Glas-allt Shiel Aberds 243 D5
Glasbury Powys 77 D5
Glaschoil Highld 253 C6
Glascoed Denb 125 B4
Glascoed Mon 61 C5
Glascoed Powys 109 D6
Glascorrie Aberds 243 C6
Glascote Staffs 97 A5
Glascwm Powys 77 B5
Glasdrum Argyll 227 B5
Glasfryn Conwy 125 D4
Glasgow Glasgow 205 B5
Glasgow Airport Renfs 205 B4
Glasgow Art Gallery & Museum Glasgow 205 B5
Glasgow Botanic Gardens Glasgow 205 B5
Glasgow Cathedral Glasgow 205 B6
Glasgow Prestwick International Airport S Ayrs 192 C3
Glashvin Highld 259 B4
Glasinfryn Gwyn 123 D5
Glasnacardoch Highld 235 A5
Glasnakille Highld 247 C4
Glasphein Highld 258 D1
Glaspwll Powys 91 C5
Glassburn Highld 251 C5
Glasserton Dumfries 171 D6
Glassford S Lnrk 194 B2
Glasshouse Hill Glos 62 A3
Glasshouses N Yorks 147 A5
Glasslie Fife 220 D2
Glasson Cumb 175 B5
Glasson Lancs 144 B4
Glassonby Cumb 164 B3
Glasterlaw Angus 232 C3
Glaston Rutland 99 A5
Glastonbury Som 29 B5
Glastonbury Abbey Som 29 B4
Glatton Cambs 100 C3
Glazebrook Warr 137 D5
Glazebury Warr 137 D5
Glazeley Shrops 95 C5
Gleadless S Yorks 130 A3
Gleadsmoss Ches 128 C3
Gleann Tholàstaidh W Isles 288 C6
Gleaston Cumb 153 C3
Gleiniant Powys 92 B3
Glemsford Suff 87 C4
Glen Dumfries 172 C3
Glen Dumfries 173 A6
Glen Auldyn I o M 152 B4
Glen Bernisdale Highld 259 D4
Glen Ho. Borders 176 A2
Glen Mona I o M 152 C4
Glen Nevis House Highld 237 B5
Glen Parva Leics 98 B2
Glen Sluain Argyll 214 C3
Glen Tanar House Aberds 244 C1
Glen Trool Lodge Dumfries 181 C6
Glen Village Falk 208 C1
Glen Vine I o M 152 D3
Glenamachrie Argyll 226 D4
Glenbarr Argyll 190 B2
Glenbeg Highld 235 D4
Glenbeg Highld 253 D6
Glenbervie Aberds 245 D4
Glenboig N Lnrk 207 D5
Glenborrodale Highld 235 D5
Glenbranter Argyll 215 C4
Glenbreck Borders 195 D5
Glenbrein Lodge Highld 240 A2
Glenbrittle House Highld 246 B3
Glenbuchat Lodge Aberds 243 A6
Glenbuck E Ayrs 194 D2
Glenburn Renfs 205 B4
Glencalvie Lodge Highld 263 B6
Glencanisp Lodge Highld 270 B4
Glencaple Dumfries 174 B2
Glencarron Lodge Highld 250 A2
Glencarse Perth 219 B6
Glencassley Castle Highld 272 D2
Glenceitlein Highld 227 B6
Glencoe Highld 237 D4
Glencraig Fife 209 A4
Glencripesdale Highld 225 A5
Glencrosh Dumfries 183 D5
Glendavan Ho. Aberds 244 B1
Glendevon Perth 219 D4
Glendoe Lodge Highld 240 B2
Glendoebeg Highld 240 B2
Glendoick Perth 220 B2
Glendoll Lodge Angus 231 A6
Glendoune S Ayrs 180 B3
Glenduckie Fife 220 C2
Glendye Lodge Aberds 244 D3
Gleneagles Hotel Perth 218 C4
Gleneagles House Perth 218 D4
Glenegedale Argyll 200 C3
Glenelg Highld 238 A2
Glenernie Moray 253 B6
Glenfarg Perth 219 C6
Glenfarquhar Lodge Aberds 245 D4
Glenferness House Highld 253 B5
Glenfeshie Lodge Highld 241 C6
Glenfiddich Distillery, Dufftown Moray 254 B4
Glenfield Leics 98 A2
Glenfinnan Highld 238 D3
Glenfoot Perth 219 C6
Glenfyne Lodge Argyll 215 A5
Glengap Dumfries 173 C4
Glengarnock N Ayrs 204 C3
Glengorm Castle Argyll 224 A3
Glengrasco Highld 259 D4
Glenhead Farm Angus 231 B6
Glenhoul Dumfries 182 D4
Glenhurich Highld 236 C2
Glenkerry Borders 185 A5
Glenkiln Dumfries 173 A6
Glenkindie Aberds 244 A1
Glenlatterach Moray 266 D2
Glenlee Dumfries 182 D4
Glenlichorn Perth 218 C2
Glenlivet Moray 254 D2
Glenlochsie Perth 231 A4
Glenloig N Ayrs 191 B5
Glenluce Dumfries 171 B4
Glenmallan Argyll 215 C5
Glenmarksie Highld 251 A5
Glenmassan Argyll 215 D4
Glenmavis N Lnrk 207 D5
Glenmaye I o M 152 D2
Glenmidge Dumfries 183 D6
Glenmore Argyll 213 A6
Glenmore Highld 259 D4
Glenmore Lodge Highld 242 B2
Glenmoy Angus 232 B2
Glenogil Angus 232 B2
Glenprosen Lodge Angus 231 B6
Glenprosen Village Angus 232 B1
Glenquiech Angus 232 B2
Glenreasdell Mains Argyll 202 C3
Glenree N Ayrs 191 C5
Glenridding Cumb 164 D1
Glenrossal Highld 272 D2
Glenrothes Fife 220 D2
Glensanda Highld 226 B3
Glensaugh Aberds 233 A4
Glenshero Lodge Highld 240 C3
Glenstockadale Dumfries 170 A2
Glenstriven Argyll 203 A5
Glentaggart S Lnrk 194 D3
Glentham Lincs 142 D2
Glentirranmuir Stirl 207 A4
Glenton Aberds 256 D1
Glentress Borders 196 C1
Glentromie Lodge Highld 241 C5
Glentrool Village Dumfries 181 D5
Glentruan I o M 152 A4
Glentruim House Highld 241 C4
Glenturret Distillery, Crieff Perth 218 B3
Glentworth Lincs 133 A4
Glenuig Highld 235 C5
Glenurquhart Highld 264 D3
Glespin S Lnrk 194 D3
Gletness Shetland 285 H6
Glewstone Hereford 62 A1
Glinton P'boro 100 A3
Glooston Leics 99 B4
Glororum Northumb 199 C5
Glossop Derbys 138 D3
Gloster Hill Northumb 189 C5
Gloucester Glos 63 B4
Gloucester Cathedral Glos 63 B4
Gloucestershire Airport Glos 63 A4
Gloup Shetland 284 C7
Glusburn N Yorks 147 C4
Glutt Lodge Highld 274 A3
Glutton Bridge Derbys 129 C5
Glympton Oxon 65 A5
Glyn-Ceiriog Wrex 109 B7
Glyn-cywarch Gwyn 107 C6
Glyn Ebwy = Ebbw Vale Bl Gwent 60 C3
Glyn-neath = Glynedd Neath 59 E5
Glynarthen Ceredig 73 B6
Glynbrochan Powys 92 C3
Glyncoch Rhondda 41 B5
Glyncorrwg Neath 40 B3
Glynde E Sus 22 B2
Glyndebourne E Sus 22 A2
Glyndyfrdwy Denb 109 A6
Glynedd = Glyn-neath Neath 59 E5
Glynogwr Bridgend 41 C4
Glyntaff Rhondda 41 C5
Glyntawe Powys 59 D5
Gnosall Staffs 112 C2
Gnosall Heath Staffs 112 C2
Goadby Leics 99 B4
Goadby Marwood Leics 115 C5
Goat Lees Kent 38 A2
Goatacre Wilts 44 B4
Goathill Dorset 29 D6
Goathland N Yorks 160 A2
Goathurst Som 28 B2
Gobernuisgach Lodge Highld 277 D5
Gobhaig W Isles 287 D5
Gobowen Shrops 110 B2
Godalming Sur 34 B
Godley Gtr Man 138 D
Godmanchester Cambs 100 D
Godmanstone Dorset 15 B
Godmersham Kent 52 D
Godney Som 29 A
Godolphin Cross Corn 3 B
Godre'r-graig Neath 59 E
Godshill Hants 31 D
Godshill I o W 18 C
Godstone Sur 35 A
Godstone Farm Sur 35 A
Godwinscroft Hants 17 B
Goetre Mon 61 C
Goferydd Anglesey 122 B
Goff's Oak Herts 68 C
Gogar Edin 209 C
Goginan Ceredig 91 D
Golan Gwyn 107 B
Golant Corn 5 B
Golberdon Corn 10 D
Golborne Gtr Man 137 D
Golcar W Yorks 139 B
Gold Hill Norf 102 B
Goldcliff Newport 42 A
Golden Cross E Sus 22 A
Golden Green Kent 36 B
Golden Grove Carms 57 A
Golden Hill Hants 17 B
Golden Pot Hants 33 A
Golden Valley Glos 63 A
Goldenhill Stoke 128 D
Golders Green London 49 A
Goldhanger Essex 70 C
Golding Shrops 94 A
Goldington Beds 84 B
Goldsborough N Yorks 148 B
Goldsborough N Yorks 169 D
Goldsithney Corn 2 B
Goldsworthy Devon 25 C
Goldthorpe S Yorks 140 C
Gollanfield Highld 253 A
Golspie Highld 274 D
Golval Highld 279 B
Gomeldon Wilts 31 B
Gomersal W Yorks 139 A
Gomshall Sur 34 B
Gonalston Notts 115 A
Gonfirth Shetland 285 G
Good Easter Essex 69 B
Gooderstone Norf 102 A
Goodleigh Devon 25 B
Goodmanham E Yorks 150 C
Goodnestone Kent 52 C
Goodnestone Kent 53 D
Goodrich Hereford 62 B
Goodrington Torbay 8 B
Goodshaw Lancs 137 A
Goodwick = Wdig Pembs 72 C
Goodwood Racecourse W Sus 20 A
Goodworth Clatford Hants 32 A
Goole E Yorks 141 A
Goonbell Corn 4 C
Goonhavern Corn 4 B
Goose Eye W Yorks 147 C
Goose Green Gtr Man 137 C
Goose Green Norf 104 C
Goose Green W Sus 21 A
Gooseham Corn 24 D
Goosey Oxon 65 D
Goosnargh Lancs 145 D
Goostrey Ches 128 B
Gorcott Hill Warks 80 A
Gord Shetland 285 L
Gordon Borders 197 B
Gordonbush Highld 274 D
Gordonsburgh Moray 267 C
Gordonstoun Moray 266 C
Gordonstown Aberds 267 D
Gordonstown Aberds 256 C
Gore Kent 53 D
Gore Cross Wilts 44 D
Gore Pit Essex 70 B
Gorebridge Midloth 209 D
Gorefield Cambs 117 D
Gorey Jersey
Gorgie Edin 209 C
Goring Oxon 47 A
Goring-by-Sea W Sus 21 B
Goring Heath Oxon 47 B
Gorleston-on-Sea Norf 105 A
Gornalwood W Mid 96 B
Gorrachie Aberds 268 D
Gorran Churchtown Corn 5 C
Gorran Haven Corn 5 C
Gorrenberry Borders 186 D

Gors Ceredig 75 A5
Gorse Hill Swindon 45 A5
Gorsedd Flint 125 B6
Gorseinon Swansea 57 C5
Gorseness Orkney 282 F5
Gorsgoch Ceredig 74 C3
Gorslas Carms 57 A5
Gorsley Glos 62 A2
Gorstan Highld 263 D5
Gorstanvorran Highld 236 B2
Gorsteyhill Staffs 128 D2
Gorsty Hill Staffs 113 C5
Gortantaoid Argyll 200 A3
Gorton Gtr Man 138 D1
Gosbeck Suff 88 B2
Gosberton Lincs 117 B5
Gosberton Clough Lincs 117 C4
Gosfield Essex 70 A1
Gosford Hereford 78 A3
Gosforth Cumb 162 D3
Gosforth T & W 179 C4
Gosmore Herts 68 A1
Gosport Hants 19 B5
Gossabrough Shetland 284 E7
Gossington Glos 62 C3
Goswick Northumb 199 B4
Gotham Notts 114 B3
Gotherington Glos 63 A5
Gott Shetland 285 J6
Goudhurst Kent 37 C5
Goulceby Lincs 134 B2
Gourdas Aberds 256 B2
Gourdon Aberds 233 A6
Gourock Inclyd 204 A2
Govan Glasgow 205 B5
Govanhill Glasgow 205 B5
Goveton Devon 7 C6
Govilon Mon 61 B4
Gowanhill Aberds 269 C5
Gowdall E Yorks 140 A4
Gowerton Swansea 57 C5
Gowkhall Fife 208 B3
Gowthorpe E Yorks 149 B6
Goxhill E Yorks 151 C4
Goxhill N Lincs 142 A3
Goxhill Haven N Lincs 142 A3
Goybre Neath 40 C2
Grabhair W Isles 288 F4
Graby Lincs 116 C3
Grade Corn 3 D5
Graffham W Sus 20 A2
Grafham Cambs 84 A3
Grafham Sur 34 B3
Grafton Hereford 78 D2
Grafton N Yorks 148 A3
Grafton Oxon 64 C3
Grafton Shrops 110 D3
Grafton Worcs 78 A3
Grafton Flyford Worcs 80 B2
Grafton Regis Northants 83 C4
Grafton Underwood Northants 99 C6
Grafty Green Kent 37 B6
Graianrhyd Denb 126 D2
Graig Conwy 124 B3
Graig Denb 125 B5
Graig-fechan Denb 125 D6
Grain Medway 51 B5
Grainsby Lincs 143 D4
Grainthorpe Lincs 143 D5
Grampound Corn 4 C4
Grampound Road Corn 4 B4
Gramsdal W Isles 286 A4
Granborough Bucks 66 A2
Granby Notts 115 B5
Grandborough Warks 82 A1
Grandtully Perth 230 C3
Grange E Ayrs 193 B4
Grange Medway 51 C4
Grange Mers 126 A2
Grange Perth 220 B2
Grange Crossroads Moray 267 D5
Grange Hall Moray 265 D6
Grange Hill Essex 68 D1
Grange Moor W Yorks 139 B5
Grange of Lindores Fife 220 C2
Grange-over-Sands Cumb 154 D3
Grange Villa Durham 179 D4
Grangemill Derbys 130 D2
Grangemouth Falk 208 B2
Grangepans Falk 208 B3
Grangetown Cardiff 41 D6
Grangetown Redcar 168 C3
Granish Highld 242 A2

Gransmoor E Yorks 151 B4
Granston Pembs 55 A4
Grantchester Cambs 85 B6
Grantham Lincs 116 B2
Grantley N Yorks 147 A6
Grantlodge Aberds 245 A4
Granton Dumfries 184 B3
Granton Edin 209 C5
Grantown-on-Spey Highld 253 D6
Grantshouse Borders 211 D5
Grappenhall Warr 127 A6
Grasby Lincs 142 C2
Grasmere Cumb 154 A2
Grasscroft Gtr Man 138 C2
Grassendale Mers 126 A3
Grassholme Durham 166 C2
Grassington N Yorks 147 A4
Grassmoor Derbys 131 C4
Grassthorpe Notts 132 C2
Grateley Hants 32 A1
Gratwich Staffs 112 B4
Graveley Cambs 84 A4
Graveley Herts 68 A2
Gravelly Hill W Mid 96 B4
Gravels Shrops 94 A1
Graven Shetland 284 F6
Graveney Kent 52 C2
Gravesend Herts 68 A4
Gravesend Kent 50 B3
Grayingham Lincs 142 D1
Grayrigg Cumb 155 B4
Grays Thurrock 50 B3
Grayshott Hants 34 C1
Grayswood Sur 34 C2
Graythorp Hrtlpl 168 C3
Grazeley Wokingham 47 C4
Greasbrough S Yorks 140 D2
Greasby Mers 126 A2
Great Abington Cambs 86 C1
Great Addington Northants 99 D6
Great Alne Warks 80 B4
Great Altcar Lancs 136 C2
Great Amwell Herts 68 B3
Great Asby Cumb 165 D4
Great Ashfield Suff 87 A5
Great Ayton N Yorks 168 D3
Great Baddow Essex 70 C1
Great Bardfield Essex 86 D2
Great Barford Beds 84 B3
Great Barr W Mid 96 B3
Great Barrington Glos 64 B3
Great Barrow Ches 127 C4
Great Barugh N Yorks 159 D6
Great Bavington Northumb 178 A1
Great Bealings Suff 88 C3
Great Bedwyn Wilts 45 C6
Great Bentley Essex 71 A5
Great Billing Northants 83 A5
Great Bircham Norf 119 B4
Great Blakenham Suff 88 B2
Great Blencow Cumb 164 B2
Great Bolas Telford 111 C5
Great Bookham Sur 35 A4
Great Bourton Oxon 82 C1
Great Bowden Leics 99 C4
Great Bradley Suff 86 B2
Great Braxted Essex 70 B2
Great Bricett Suff 87 B6
Great Brickhill Bucks 83 D6
Great Bridge W Mid 96 B2
Great Bridgeford Staffs 112 C2
Great Brington Northants 82 A3
Great Bromley Essex 71 A4
Great Broughton Cumb 162 A3
Great Broughton N Yorks 158 A4
Great Budworth Ches 127 B6
Great Burdon Darl 167 D6
Great Burgh Sur 35 A5
Great Burstead Essex 69 D6
Great Busby N Yorks 158 A4
Great Canfield Essex 69 B5
Great Carlton Lincs 135 A4
Great Casterton Rutland 100 A2
Great Chart Kent 38 A1
Great Chatwell Staffs 112 D1
Great Chesterford Essex 85 C7
Great Cheverell Wilts 44 D3
Great Chishill Cambs 85 D6
Great Clacton Essex 71 B5
Great Cliff W Yorks 139 B6
Great Clifton Cumb 162 B3
Great Coates NE Lincs 143 C4
Great Comberton Worcs 80 C2
Great Corby Cumb 176 D2

Great Cornard Suff 87 C4
Great Cowden E Yorks 151 C5
Great Coxwell Oxon 64 D3
Great Crakehall N Yorks 157 B6
Great Cransley Northants 99 D5
Great Cressingham Norf 103 A4
Great Crosby Mers 136 D2
Great Cubley Derbys 113 B5
Great Dalby Leics 115 D5
Great Denham Beds 84 C2
Great Doddington Northants 83 A5
Great Dunham Norf 119 D5
Great Dunmow Essex 69 A6
Great Durnford Wilts 31 B5
Great Easton Essex 69 A6
Great Easton Leics 99 B5
Great Eccleston Lancs 144 C4
Great Edstone N Yorks 159 C6
Great Ellingham Norf 103 B6
Great Elm Som 30 A1
Great Eversden Cambs 85 B5
Great Fencote N Yorks 157 B6
Great Finborough Suff 87 B6
Great Fransham Norf 119 D5
Great Gaddesden Herts 67 B5
Great Gidding Cambs 100 C3
Great Givendale E Yorks 149 B7
Great Glemham Suff 88 A4
Great Glen Leics 98 B3
Great Gonerby Lincs 116 B1
Great Gransden Cambs 85 B4
Great Green Norf 104 C3
Great Green Suff 87 B5
Great Habton N Yorks 159 D6
Great Hale Lincs 116 A4
Great Hallingbury Essex 69 B5
Great Hampden Bucks 66 C3
Great Harrowden Northants 99 D5
Great Harwood Lancs 146 D1
Great Haseley Oxon 66 C1
Great Hatfield E Yorks 151 C4
Great Haywood Staffs 112 C3
Great Heath W Mid 97 C6
Great Heck N Yorks 140 A3
Great Henny Essex 87 D4
Great Hockham Norf 103 B5
Great Holland Essex 71 B6
Great Horkesley Essex 87 D5
Great Hormead Herts 68 A3
Great Horton W Yorks 147 D5
Great Horwood Bucks 83 D4
Great Houghton Northants 83 B4
Great Houghton S Yorks 140 C2
Great Hucklow Derbys 130 B1
Great Kelk E Yorks 151 B4
Great Kimble Bucks 66 C3
Great Kingshill Bucks 66 D3
Great Langton N Yorks 157 B6
Great Leighs Essex 70 B1
Great Leighs Racecourse Essex 70 B1
Great Lever Gtr Man 137 C6
Great Limber Lincs 142 C3
Great Linford M Keynes 83 C5
Great Livermere Suff 103 D4
Great Longstone Derbys 130 B2
Great Lumley Durham 167 A5
Great Lyth Shrops 94 A2
Great Malvern Worcs 79 C5
Great Maplestead Essex 87 D4
Great Marton Blkpool 144 D3
Great Massingham Norf 119 C4
Great Melton Norf 104 A2
Great Milton Oxon 66 C1
Great Missenden Bucks 66 C3
Great Mitton Lancs 145 D7
Great Mongeham Kent 53 D5
Great Moulton Norf 104 B2
Great Munden Herts 68 A3
Great Musgrave Cumb 165 D5
Great Ness Shrops 110 D2
Great Notley Essex 70 A1
Great Oakley Essex 71 A5
Great Oakley Northants 99 C5
Great Offley Herts 67 A6
Great Ormside Cumb 165 D5
Great Orton Cumb 175 C6
Great Ouseburn N Yorks 148 A3
Great Oxendon Northants 99 C4
Great Oxney Green Essex 69 C6
Great Palgrave Norf 119 D5
Great Parndon Essex 68 C4

Great Paxton Cambs 84 A4
Great Plumpton Lancs 144 D3
Great Plumstead Norf 121 D5
Great Ponton Lincs 116 B2
Great Preston W Yorks 140 A2
Great Raveley Cambs 101 C4
Great Rissington Glos 64 B2
Great Rollright Oxon 81 D6
Great Ryburgh Norf 119 C6
Great Ryle Northumb 188 B3
Great Ryton Shrops 94 A2
Great Saling Essex 69 A7
Great Salkeld Cumb 164 B3
Great Sampford Essex 86 D2
Great Sankey Warr 127 A5
Great Saxham Suff 86 A3
Great Shefford W Berks 46 B1
Great Shelford Cambs 85 B6
Great Smeaton N Yorks 158 A2
Great Snoring Norf 119 B6
Great Somerford Wilts 44 A3
Great Stainton Darl 167 C6
Great Stambridge Essex 70 D2
Great Staughton Cambs 84 A3
Great Steeping Lincs 135 C4
Great Stonar Kent 53 D5
Great Strickland Cumb 164 C3
Great Stukeley Cambs 100 D4
Great Sturton Lincs 134 B2
Great Sutton Ches 126 B3
Great Sutton Shrops 94 C3
Great Swinburne Northumb 178 B1
Great Tew Oxon 65 A4
Great Tey Essex 70 A2
Great Thurkleby N Yorks 158 D3
Great Thurlow Suff 86 B2
Great Torrington Devon 25 D5
Great Tosson Northumb 188 C3
Great Totham Essex 70 B2
Great Totham Essex 70 B2
Great Tows Lincs 143 D4
Great Urswick Cumb 153 C3
Great Wakering Essex 51 A6
Great Waldingfield Suff 87 C5
Great Walsingham Norf 119 B6
Great Waltham Essex 69 B6
Great Warley Essex 69 D5
Great Washbourne Glos 80 D2
Great Weldon Northants 99 C6
Great Welnetham Suff 87 B4
Great Wenham Suff 87 D6
Great Whittington Northumb 178 B2
Great Wigborough Essex 70 B3
Great Wilbraham Cambs 86 B1
Great Wishford Wilts 31 B4
Great Witcombe Glos 63 B5
Great Witley Worcs 79 A5
Great Wolford Warks 81 D5
Great Wratting Suff 86 C2
Great Wymondley Herts 68 A2
Great Wyrley Staffs 96 A2
Great Wytheford Shrops 111 D4
Great Yarmouth Norf 105 A6
Great Yarmouth Sea Life Centre Norf 105 A6
Great Yeldham Essex 86 D3
Greater Doward Hereford 62 B1
Greatford Lincs 116 D3
Greatgate Staffs 113 A4
Greatham Hants 33 B6
Greatham Hrtlpl 168 C2
Greatham W Sus 20 A3
Greatstone on Sea Kent 38 C2
Greatworth Northants 82 C2
Greave Lancs 138 A1
Greeba I o M 152 C3
Green Denb 125 C5
Green End Beds 84 B3
Green Hammerton N Yorks 148 B3
Green Lane Powys 93 B5
Green Ore Som 43 D4
Green St Green London 50 C1
Green Street Herts 68 D1
Greenbank Shetland 284 C7
Greenburn W Loth 208 D2
Greendikes Northumb 188 A3
Greenfield Beds 84 D2
Greenfield Flint 126 B1
Greenfield Gtr Man 138 C2
Greenfield Highld 239 B6
Greenfield Oxon 66 D2
Greengairs N Lnrk 207 C5
Greenham W Berks 46 C2

Greenhaugh Northumb 177 A5
Greenhead Northumb 177 C4
Greenhill Falk 207 C6
Greenhill London 49 A4
Greenhill Kent 52 C3
Greenhill Leics 114 D2
Greenhills N Ayrs 204 C3
Greenhithe Kent 50 B2
Greenholm E Ayrs 193 B5
Greenholme Cumb 155 A4
Greenhouse Borders 187 A4
Greenhow Hill N Yorks 147 A5
Greenigoe Orkney 283 G5
Greenland Highld 280 B4
Greenlands Bucks 47 A5
Greenlaw Aberds 268 D1
Greenlaw Borders 197 B6
Greenlea Dumfries 174 A3
Greenloaning Perth 218 D3
Greenmount Community Farm, Pontnewydd Torf 61 D4
Greenmount Gtr Man 137 B6
Greenmow Shetland 285 L6
Greenock Inclyd 204 A3
Greenock West Inclyd 204 A2
Greenodd Cumb 154 C2
Greenrow Cumb 174 C4
Greens Norton Northants 82 C3
Greenside T & W 178 C3
Greensidehill Northumb 188 B2
Greenstead Green Essex 70 A2
Greensted Essex 69 C5
Greensted Church, Chipping Ongar Essex 69 C5
Greenwich London 49 B6
Greet Glos 80 D3
Greete Shrops 94 D3
Greetham Lincs 134 B3
Greetham Rutland 116 D2
Greetland W Yorks 138 A3
Gregg Hall Cumb 154 B3
Gregson Lane Lancs 137 A4
Greinetobht W Isles 287 G3
Greinton Som 28 B4
Gremista Shetland 285 J6
Grenaby I o M 152 D2
Grendon Northants 83 A5
Grendon Warks 97 A5
Grendon Common Warks 97 B5
Grendon Green Hereford 78 B3
Grendon Underwood Bucks 66 A1
Grenofen Devon 11 D5
Grenoside S Yorks 139 D6
Greosabhagh W Isles 288 H2
Gresford Wrex 126 D3
Gresham Norf 120 B3
Greshornish Highld 258 C3
Gressenhall Norf 119 D6
Gressingham Lancs 145 A5
Gresty Green Ches 128 D2
Greta Bridge Durham 166 D3
Gretna Dumfries 175 B6
Gretna Green Dumfries 175 B6
Gretton Glos 80 D3
Gretton Northants 99 B5
Gretton Shrops 94 B3
Grewelthorpe N Yorks 157 D6
Grey Green N Lincs 141 C5
Greygarth N Yorks 157 D5
Greynor Carms 57 B5
Greysouthen Cumb 162 B3
Greystoke Cumb 164 B2
Greystone Angus 232 D3
Greystone Dumfries 174 A2
Greywell Hants 47 D5
Griais W Isles 288 C5
Grianan W Isles 288 D5
Gribthorpe E Yorks 149 D6
Gridley Corner Devon 11 B4
Griff Warks 97 C6
Griffithstown Torf 61 D4
Grimbister Orkney 282 F4
Grimblethorpe Lincs 134 A2
Grimeford Village Lancs 137 B5
Grimethorpe S Yorks 140 C2
Griminis W Isles 286 A3
Grimister Shetland 284 D6
Grimley Worcs 79 A6
Grimness Orkney 283 H5
Grimoldby Lincs 134 A3
Grimpo Shrops 110 C2
Grimsargh Lancs 145 D5

Grimsbury Oxon 82 C1
Grimsby NE Lincs 143 B4
Grimscote Northants 82 B3
Grimscott Corn 10 A3
Grimsthorpe Lincs 116 C3
Grimston E Yorks 151 D5
Grimston Leics 115 C4
Grimston Norf 119 C4
Grimston York 149 B5
Grimstone Dorset 15 B6
Grinacombe Moor Devon 11 B5
Grindale E Yorks 161 D5
Grindigar Orkney 283 G6
Grindiscol Shetland 285 K6
Grindle Shrops 95 A5
Grindleford Derbys 130 B2
Grindleton Lancs 146 C1
Grindley Staffs 112 C4
Grindley Brook Shrops 111 A4
Grindlow Derbys 130 B1
Grindon Northumb 198 B3
Grindon Staffs 129 D5
Grindonmoor Gate Staffs 129 D5
Gringley on the Hill Notts 141 D5
Grinsdale Cumb 175 C6
Grinshill Shrops 111 C4
Grinton N Yorks 156 B4
Griomsidar W Isles 288 E4
Grishipoll Argyll 223 B4
Grisling Common E Sus 36 D2
Gristhorpe N Yorks 161 C4
Griston Norf 103 B5
Gritley Orkney 283 G6
Grittenham Wilts 44 A4
Grittleton Wilts 44 A2
Grizebeck Cumb 153 B3
Grizedale Cumb 154 B2
Grobister Orkney 282 E7
Groby Leics 98 A2
Groes Conwy 125 C5
Groes Neath 40 C2
Groes-faen Rhondda 41 C5
Groes-lwyd Powys 109 D7
Groesffordd Marli Denb 125 B5
Groeslon Gwyn 123 D5
Groeslon Gwyn 107 A4
Grogport Argyll 202 D3
Gromford Suff 89 B4
Gronant Flint 125 A5
Groombridge E Sus 36 C3
Grosmont Mon 61 A6
Grosmont N Yorks 160 A2
Grosvenor Museum,
Chester Ches 127 C4
Groton Suff 87 C5
Groudle Glen Railway
I o M 152 D4
Grougfoot Falk 208 C3
Grouville Jersey 6
Grove Dorset 15 D7
Grove Kent 53 C4
Grove Notts 132 B2
Grove Oxon 65 D5
Grove Park London 49 B7
Grove Vale W Mid 96 B3
Grovesend Swansea 57 B5
Grudie Highld 263 D5
Gruids Highld 272 D3
Gruinard House Highld 261 A6
Grula Highld 246 B2
Gruline Argyll 225 B4
Grunasound Shetland 285 K5
Grundisburgh Suff 88 B3
Grunsagill Lancs 146 B1
Gruting Shetland 285 J4
Grutness Shetland 285 N6
Gualachulain Highld 227 B6
Gualin Ho. Highld 276 C4
Guardbridge Fife 221 C4
Guarlford Worcs 79 C6
Guay Perth 230 D4
Guernsey Airport Guern 6
Guestling Green E Sus 23 A6
Guestling Thorn E Sus 23 A6
Guestwick Norf 120 C2
Guestwick Green Norf 120 C2
Guide Blkburn 137 A6
Guide Post Northumb 179 A4
Guilden Morden Cambs 85 C4
Guilden Sutton Ches 127 C4
Guildford Sur 34 B2
Guildtown Perth 219 A6
Guilsborough Northants 98 D3
Guilsfield Powys 109 D7

Guilton Kent 53 D4
Guineaford Devon 25 B6
Guisborough Redcar 168 D4
Guiseley W Yorks 147 C5
Guist Norf 120 C1
Guith Orkney 282 D6
Guiting Power Glos 64 A1
Gulberwick Shetland 285 K6
Gullane E Loth 210 B1
Gulval Corn 2 B2
Gulworthy Devon 11 D5
Gumfreston Pembs 55 D7
Gumley Leics 98 B3
Gummow's Shop Corn 4 B3
Gun Hill E Sus 22 A3
Gunby E Yorks 149 D6
Gunby Lincs 116 C2
Gundleton Hants 33 B5
Gunn Devon 26 B1
Gunnerside N Yorks 156 B3
Gunnerton Northumb 177 B7
Gunness N Lincs 141 B6
Gunnislake Corn 11 D5
Gunnista Shetland 285 J7
Gunthorpe Norf 120 B2
Gunthorpe Notts 115 A4
Gunthorpe P'boro 100 A3
Gunville I o W 18 C3
Gunwalloe Corn 3 C4
Gurnard I o W 18 B3
Gurnett Ches 129 B4
Gurney Slade Som 29 A6
Gurnos Powys 59 E4
Gussage All Saints Dorset 31 D4
Gussage St Michael Dorset 30 D3
Guston Kent 39 A5
Gutcher Shetland 284 D7
Guthrie Angus 232 C3
Guyhirn Cambs 101 A5
Guyhirn Gull Cambs 101 A5
Guy's Head Lincs 118 C1
Guy's Marsh Dorset 30 C2
Guyzance Northumb 189 C5
Gwaenysgor Flint 125 A5
Gwalchmai Anglesey 122 C3
Gwaun-Cae-Gurwen
Neath 59 D4
Gwaun-Leision Neath 59 D4
Gwbert Ceredig 73 B4
Gweek Corn 3 C5
Gwehelog Mon 61 C5
Gwenddwr Powys 77 C4
Gwennap Corn 4 D2
Gwenter Corn 3 D5
Gwernaffield Flint 126 C2
Gwernesney Mon 61 C6
Gwernogle Carms 58 B2
Gwernymynydd Flint 126 C2
Gwersyllt Wrex 126 D3
Gwespyr Flint 125 A6
Gwithian Corn 2 A3
Gwredog Anglesey 123 B4
Gwyddelwern Denb 109 A5
Gwyddgrug Carms 58 B1
Gwydyr Uchaf Conwy 124 C2
Gwynfryn Wrex 126 D2
Gwystre Powys 77 A4
Gwytherin Conwy 124 C3
Gyfelia Wrex 110 A2
Gyffin Conwy 124 B2
Gyre Orkney 283 G4
Gyrn-goch Gwyn 107 B4

H

Habberley Shrops 94 A1
Habergham Lancs 146 D2
Habrough NE Lincs 142 B3
Haceby Lincs 116 B3
Hacheston Suff 88 B4
Hackbridge London 49 C5
Hackenthorpe S Yorks 131 A4
Hackford Norf 103 A6
Hackforth N Yorks 157 B6
Hackland Orkney 282 E4
Hackleton Northants 83 B5
Hackness N Yorks 160 B3
Hackness Orkney 283 H4
Hackney London 49 A6
Hackthorn Lincs 133 A4
Hackthorpe Cumb 164 C3
Haconby Lincs 116 C4
Hacton London 50 A2
Hadden Borders 198 C1
Haddenham Bucks 66 C2
Haddenham Cambs 101 D6
Haddington E Loth 210 C2

Haddington Lincs 133 C4
Haddiscoe Norf 105 B5
Haddon Cambs 100 B3
Haddon Ches 129 C4
Haddon Hall Derbys 130 C2
Hade Edge W Yorks 139 C4
Hademore Staffs 97 A4
Hadfield Derbys 138 D3
Hadham Cross Herts 68 B4
Hadham Ford Herts 68 A4
Hadleigh Essex 51 A5
Hadleigh Suff 87 C6
Hadley Telford 111 D5
Hadley End Staffs 113 C5
Hadlow Kent 36 B4
Hadlow Down E Sus 36 D3
Hadnall Shrops 111 D4
Hadstock Essex 86 C1
Hady Derbys 130 B3
Hadzor Worcs 80 A2
Haffenden Quarter Kent 37 B6
Hafod-Dinbych Conwy 124 D3
Hafod-Iom Conwy 124 B3
Haggate Lancs 146 D2
Haggbeck Cumb 176 B2
Haggerston Northumb 198 B4
Haggrister Shetland 284 F5
Hagley Hereford 78 C3
Hagley Worcs 96 C2
Hagworthingham Lincs 134 C3
Haigh Gtr Man 137 C5
Haigh S Yorks 139 B5
Haigh Moor W Yorks 139 A5
Haighton Green Lancs 145 D5
Hail Weston Cambs 84 A3
Haile Cumb 162 D3
Hailes Glos 80 D3
Hailey Herts 68 B3
Hailey Oxon 65 B4
Hailsham E Sus 22 B3
Haimer Highld 280 B3
Hainault London 69 D4
Hainford Norf 120 D4
Hainton Lincs 134 A1
Hairmyres S Lnrk 205 C6
Haisthorpe E Yorks 151 A4
Hakin Pembs 55 D4
Halam Notts 132 D1
Halbeath Fife 208 B4
Halberton Devon 27 D5
Halcro Highld 280 B4
Hale Gtr Man 128 A2
Hale Halton 127 A4
Hale Hants 31 D5
Hale Bank Halton 127 A4
Hale Street Kent 37 B4
Halebarns Gtr Man 128 A2
Hales Norf 105 B4
Hales Staffs 111 B6
Hales Place Kent 52 D3
Halesfield Telford 95 A5
Halesgate Lincs 117 C6
Halesowen W Mid 96 C2
Halesworth Suff 105 D4
Halewood Mers 127 A4
Halford Shrops 94 C2
Halford Warks 81 C5
Halfpenny Furze Carms 56 A2
Halfpenny Green Staffs 95 B6
Halfway Carms 58 B3
Halfway Carms 59 B5
Halfway W Berks 46 C2
Halfway Bridge W Sus 34 D2
Halfway House Shrops 110 D2
Halfway Houses Kent 51 B6
Halifax W Yorks 138 A3
Halket E Ayrs 205 C4
Halkirk Highld 280 C3
Halkyn Flint 126 B2
Hall Dunnerdale Cumb 153 A3
Hall Green W Mid 96 C4
Hall Green W Yorks 139 B6
Hall Grove Herts 68 B2
Hall of Tankerness
Orkney 283 G6
Hall of the Forest Shrops 93 C6
Halland E Sus 22 A2
Hallaton Leics 99 B4
Hallatrow Bath 43 D5
Hallbankgate Cumb 176 D3
Hallen S Glos 43 A4
Halliburton Borders 197 B5
Hallin Highld 258 C2
Halling Medway 51 C4
Hallington Lincs 134 A3
Hallington Northumb 178 B1
Halliwell Gtr Man 137 B6

Halloughton Notts 132 D1
Hallow Worcs 79 B6
Hallrule Borders 187 B4
Halls E Loth 210 C3
Hall's Green Herts 68 A2
Hallsands Devon 8 D2
Hallthwaites Cumb 153 B2
Hallworthy Corn 10 C2
Hallyburton House Perth 220 A2
Hallyne Borders 195 B6
Halmer End Staffs 112 A1
Halmore Glos 62 C2
Halmyre Mains Borders 195 B6
Halnaker W Sus 20 B2
Halsall Lancs 136 B2
Halse Northants 82 C2
Halse Som 27 C6
Halsetown Corn 2 B3
Halsham E Yorks 143 A4
Halsinger Devon 25 B6
Halstead Essex 87 D4
Halstead Kent 50 C1
Halstead Leics 99 A4
Halstock Dorset 15 A5
Haltham Lincs 134 C2
Haltoft End Lincs 117 A6
Halton Bucks 66 B3
Halton Halton 127 A5
Halton Lancs 145 A5
Halton Northumb 178 C1
Halton Wrex 110 B2
Halton W Yorks 148 D2
Halton East N Yorks 147 B4
Halton Gill N Yorks 156 D2
Halton Holegate Lincs 135 C4
Halton Lea Gate
Northumb 176 D4
Halton West N Yorks 146 B2
Haltwhistle Northumb 177 C5
Halvergate Norf 105 A5
Halwell Devon 8 B1
Halwill Devon 11 B5
Halwill Junction Devon 11 A5
Ham Devon 14 A2
Ham Glos 62 D2
Ham London 49 B4
Ham Highld 280 A4
Ham Kent 53 D5
Ham Shetland 285 K1
Ham Wilts 46 C1
Ham Common Dorset 30 C2
Ham Green Hereford 79 C5
Ham Green Kent 37 D6
Ham Green Kent 51 C5
Ham Green N Som 43 B4
Ham Green Worcs 80 A3
Ham Street Som 29 B5
Hamble-le-Rice Hants 18 A3
Hambleden Bucks 47 A5
Hambledon Hants 33 D5
Hambledon Sur 34 C2
Hambleton Lancs 144 C3
Hambleton N Yorks 149 D4
Hambridge Som 28 C3
Hambrook S Glos 43 B5
Hambrook W Sus 19 A6
Hameringham Lincs 134 C3
Hamerton Cambs 100 D3
Hametoun Shetland 285 K1
Hamilton S Lnrk 194 A2
Hamilton Park
Racecourse S Lnrk 194 A2
Hammer W Sus 34 C1
Hammerpot W Sus 20 B3
Hammersmith London 49 B5
Hammerwich Staffs 96 A3
Hammerwood E Sus 36 C2
Hammond Street Herts 68 C3
Hammoon Dorset 30 D2
Hamnavoe Shetland 284 E4
Hamnavoe Shetland 285 K5
Hamnavoe Shetland 284 E6
Hamnavoe Shetland 284 F6
Hampden National
Stadium Glasgow 205 B5
Hampden Park E Sus 22 B4
Hamperden End Essex 86 D1
Hampnett Glos 64 B2
Hampole S Yorks 140 B3
Hampreston Dorset 17 B4
Hampstead London 49 A5
Hampstead Norreys
W Berks 46 B3
Hampsthwaite N Yorks 147 B6
Hampton London 48 C4
Hampton Shrops 95 C5
Hampton Worcs 80 C3

Hampton Bishop Hereford 78 D3
Hampton Court Palace,
Teddington London 49 C4
Hampton Heath Ches 110 A3
Hampton in Arden W Mid 97 C5
Hampton Loade Shrops 95 C5
Hampton Lovett Worcs 80 A1
Hampton Lucy Warks 81 B5
Hampton on the Hill
Warks 81 A5
Hampton Poyle Oxon 65 B6
Hamrow Norf 119 C6
Hamsey E Sus 22 A2
Hamsey Green Sur 35 A6
Hamstall Ridware Staffs 113 D5
Hamstead I o W 18 B3
Hamstead W Mid 96 B3
Hamstead Marshall
W Berks 46 C2
Hamsterley Durham 166 B4
Hamsterley Durham 178 D3
Hamstreet Kent 38 B2
Hamworthy Poole 16 B3
Hanbury Staffs 113 C5
Hanbury Worcs 80 A2
Hanbury Woodend Staffs 113 C5
Hanby Lincs 116 B3
Hanchurch Staffs 112 A2
Handbridge Ches 127 C4
Handcross W Sus 35 D5
Handforth Ches 128 A3
Handley Ches 127 D4
Handsacre Staffs 113 D4
Handsworth S Yorks 131 A4
Handsworth W Mid 96 B3
Handy Cross Devon 25 C5
Hanford Stoke 112 A2
Hanging Langford Wilts 31 B4
Hangleton W Sus 20 B3
Hanham S Glos 43 B5
Hankelow Ches 111 A5
Hankerton Wilts 63 D5
Hankham E Sus 22 B4
Hanley Stoke 112 A2
Hanley Castle Worcs 79 C6
Hanley Child Worcs 79 A4
Hanley Swan Worcs 79 C6
Hanley William Worcs 79 A4
Hanlith N Yorks 146 A3
Hanmer Wrex 110 B3
Hannah Lincs 135 B5
Hannington Hants 46 D3
Hannington Northants 99 D5
Hannington Swindon 64 D2
Hannington Wick Swindon 64 D2
Hansel Village S Ayrs 192 B3
Hanslope M Keynes 83 C5
Hanthorpe Lincs 116 C3
Hanwell London 49 A4
Hanwell Oxon 82 C1
Hanwood Shrops 94 A2
Hanworth London 48 B4
Hanworth Norf 120 B3
Happendon S Lnrk 194 C3
Happisburgh Norf 121 B5
Happisburgh Common
Norf 121 C5
Hapsford Ches 127 B4
Hapton Lancs 146 D1
Hapton Norf 104 B2
Harberton Devon 8 B1
Harbertonford Devon 8 B1
Harbledown Kent 52 D3
Harborne W Mid 96 C3
Harborough Magna Warks 98 D1
Harbottle Northumb 188 C2
Harbour Park,
Littlehampton W Sus 20 C3
Harbury Warks 81 B6
Harby Leics 115 B5
Harby Notts 132 B3
Harcombe Devon 13 B6
Harden W Mid 96 A3
Harden W Yorks 147 D4
Hardenhuish Wilts 44 B3
Hardgate Aberds 245 B4
Hardham W Sus 20 A3
Hardingham Norf 103 A6
Hardingstone Northants 83 B4
Hardington Som 43 D6
Hardington Mandeville
Som 29 D5
Hardington Marsh 15 A5
Hardley Hants 18 A3
Hardley Street Norf 105 A4
Hardmead M Keynes 83 C6
Hardrow N Yorks 156 B3

Hardstoft Derbys 131 C4
Hardway Hants 19 A5
Hardway Som 29 B7
Hardwick Bucks 66 B3
Hardwick Cambs 85 B5
Hardwick Norf 118 D3
Hardwick Norf 104 C3
Hardwick Notts 131 B6
Hardwick Northants 83 A5
Hardwick Oxon 65 C4
Hardwick Oxon 65 A6
Hardwick W Mid 96 B3
Hardwick Hall Derbys 131 C4
Hardwicke Glos 62 B3
Hardwicke Glos 63 A5
Hardwicke Hereford 77 C6
Hardy's Green Essex 70 A3
Hare Green Essex 71 A4
Hare Hatch Wokingham 47 B6
Hare Street Herts 68 A3
Hareby Lincs 134 C3
Hareden Lancs 145 B6
Harefield London 67 D5
Harehills W Yorks 148 D2
Harehope Northumb 188 A3
Harescough Cumb 165 A4
Harescombe Glos 63 B4
Haresfield Glos 63 B4
Hareshaw N Lnrk 207 D6
Hareshaw Head Northumb 177 A6
Harewood W Yorks 148 C2
Harewood End Hereford 62 A1
Harewood House, Wetherby W Yorks 148 C2
Harford Carms 58 A3
Harford Devon 7 B5
Hargate Norf 104 B2
Hargatewall Derbys 129 B6
Hargrave Ches 127 C4
Hargrave Northants 100 D2
Hargrave Suff 86 B3
Harker Cumb 175 B6
Harkland Shetland 284 E6
Harkstead Suff 88 D2
Harlaston Staffs 113 D6
Harlaw Ho. Aberds 256 D2
Harlaxton Lincs 116 B1
Harle Syke Lancs 146 D2
Harlech Gwyn 107 C5
Harlech Castle Gwyn 107 C5
Harlequin Notts 115 B4
Harlescott Shrops 111 D4
Harlesden London 49 A5
Harleston Devon 8 C1
Harleston Norf 104 C3
Harleston Suff 87 B6
Harlestone Northants 83 A4
Harley Shrops 94 A3
Harley S Yorks 139 D6
Harleyholm S Lnrk 194 C4
Harlington Beds 84 D2
Harlington London 48 B3
Harlington S Yorks 140 C2
Harlosh Highld 258 D2
Harlow Essex 69 B4
Harlow Carr RHS Garden, Harrogate N Yorks 148 B1
Harlow Hill Northumb 178 C2
Harlow Hill N Yorks 148 B1
Harlthorpe E Yorks 149 D6
Harlton Cambs 85 B5
Harman's Cross Dorset 16 C3
Harmby N Yorks 157 C5
Harmer Green Herts 68 B2
Harmer Hill Shrops 110 C3
Harmondsworth London 48 B3
Harmston Lincs 133 C4
Harnham Northumb 178 B2
Harnhill Glos 63 C6
Harold Hill London 69 D5
Harold Wood London 69 D5
Haroldston West Pembs 55 C4
Haroldswick Shetland 284 B8
Harome N Yorks 159 C5
Harpenden Herts 67 B6
Harpford Devon 13 B5
Harpham E Yorks 150 A3
Harpley Norf 119 C4
Harpley Worcs 79 A4
Harpole Northants 82 A3
Harpsdale Highld 280 C3
Harpsden Oxon 47 A5
Harpswell Lincs 133 A4
Harpur Hill Derbys 129 B5
Harpurhey Gtr Man 138 C1
Harraby Cumb 175 C7
Harrapool Highld 247 B5
Harrier Shetland 285 J1
Harrietfield Perth 219 B4
Harrietsham Kent 37 A6
Harrington Cumb 162 B2
Harrington Lincs 134 B3
Harrington Northants 99 C4
Harringworth Northants 99 B6
Harris Highld 234 A2
Harris Museum, Preston Lancs 136 A4
Harrogate N Yorks 148 B2
Harrold Beds 83 B6
Harrow London 49 A4
Harrow on the Hill London 49 A4
Harrow Street Suff 87 D5
Harrow Weald London 67 D6
Harrowbarrow Corn 6 A2
Harrowden Beds 84 C2
Harrowgate Hill Darl 167 D5
Harston Cambs 85 B6
Harston Leics 115 B6
Harswell E Yorks 150 C1
Hart Hrtlpl 168 B2
Hart Common Gtr Man 137 C5
Hart Hill Luton 67 A6
Hart Station Hrtlpl 168 B2
Hartburn Northumb 178 A2
Hartburn Stockton 168 D2
Hartest Suff 87 B4
Hartfield E Sus 36 C2
Hartford Cambs 101 D4
Hartford Ches 127 B6
Hartford End Essex 69 B6
Hartfordbridge Hants 47 D5
Hartforth N Yorks 157 A5
Harthill Ches 127 D5
Harthill N Lnrk 208 D2
Harthill S Yorks 131 A4
Hartington Derbys 129 C6
Hartland Devon 24 C3
Hartlebury Worcs 95 D6
Hartlepool Hrtlpl 168 B3
Hartlepool's Maritime Experience Hrtlpl 168 B3
Hartley Cumb 155 A6
Hartley Kent 50 C3
Hartley Kent 37 C5
Hartley Northumb 179 B5
Hartley Westpall Hants 47 D4
Hartley Wintney Hants 47 D5
Hartlip Kent 51 C5
Hartoft End N Yorks 159 B6
Harton N Yorks 149 A6
Harton Shrops 94 C2
Harton T & W 179 C5
Hartpury Glos 62 A3
Hartshead W Yorks 139 A4
Hartshill Warks 97 B6
Hartshorne Derbys 113 C7
Hartsop Cumb 164 D2
Hartwell Northants 83 B4
Hartwood N Lnrk 194 A3
Harvieston Stirl 206 B3
Harvington Worcs 80 C3
Harvington Cross Worcs 80 C3
Harwell Oxon 46 A2
Harwich Essex 88 D3
Harwood Durham 165 B6
Harwood Gtr Man 137 B6
Harwood Dale N Yorks 160 B3
Harworth Notts 140 D4
Hasbury W Mid 96 C2
Hascombe Sur 34 B2
Haselbech Northants 99 D4
Haselbury Plucknett Som 29 D4
Haseley Warks 81 A5
Haselor Warks 80 B4
Hasfield Glos 63 A4
Hasguard Pembs 55 D4
Haskayne Lancs 136 C2
Hasketon Suff 88 B3
Hasland Derbys 130 C3
Haslemere Sur 34 C2
Haslingden Lancs 137 A6
Haslingfield Cambs 85 B6
Haslington Ches 128 D2
Hassall Ches 128 D2
Hassall Green Ches 128 D2
Hassell Street Kent 38 A2
Hassendean Borders 186 A4
Hassingham Norf 105 A4
Hassocks W Sus 21 A5
Hassop Derbys 130 B2
Hastigrow Highld 281 B4
Hastingleigh Kent 38 A2
Hastings E Sus 23 B6
Hastings Castle E Sus 23 A6
Hastings Sea Life Centre E Sus 23 B6
Hastingwood Essex 69 C4
Hastoe Herts 67 C4
Haswell Durham 167 A6
Haswell Plough Durham 167 A6
Hatch Beds 84 C3
Hatch Hants 47 D4
Hatch Wilts 30 C3
Hatch Beauchamp Som 28 C3
Hatch End London 67 D6
Hatch Green Som 28 D3
Hatchet Gate Hants 18 A2
Hatching Green Herts 67 B6
Hatchmere Ches 127 B5
Hatcliffe NE Lincs 143 C4
Hatfield Hereford 78 B3
Hatfield Herts 68 C2
Hatfield S Yorks 141 C4
Hatfield Worcs 80 B1
Hatfield Broad Oak Essex 69 B5
Hatfield Garden Village Herts 68 C2
Hatfield Heath Essex 69 B5
Hatfield House Herts 68 C2
Hatfield Hyde Herts 68 B2
Hatfield Peverel Essex 70 B1
Hatfield Woodhouse S Yorks 141 C4
Hatford Oxon 64 D4
Hatherden Hants 46 D1
Hatherleigh Devon 11 A6
Hathern Leics 114 C2
Hatherop Glos 64 C2
Hathersage Derbys 130 A2
Hathershaw Gtr Man 138 C2
Hatherton Ches 111 A5
Hatherton Staffs 112 D3
Hatley St George Cambs 85 B4
Hatt Corn 6 A2
Hattingley Hants 33 B5
Hatton Aberds 257 C5
Hatton Derbys 113 C6
Hatton Lincs 134 B1
Hatton Shrops 94 B2
Hatton Warks 81 A5
Hatton Warr 127 A5
Hatton Castle Aberds 256 B2
Hatton Country World Warks 81 A5
Hatton Heath Ches 127 C4
Hatton of Fintray Aberds 245 A5
Hattoncrook Aberds 256 D3
Haugh E Ayrs 193 C4
Haugh Gtr Man 138 B2
Haugh Lincs 135 B4
Haugh Head Northumb 188 A3
Haugh of Glass Moray 255 C5
Haugh of Urr Dumfries 173 B6
Haugham Lincs 134 A3
Haughley Suff 87 A6
Haughley Green Suff 87 A6
Haughs of Clinterty Aberdeen 245 A5
Haughton Notts 132 B1
Haughton Shrops 95 B4
Haughton Shrops 110 C2
Haughton Shrops 111 D4
Haughton Shrops 95 A5
Haughton Staffs 112 C2
Haughton Castle Northumb 177 B7
Haughton Green Gtr Man 138 D2
Haughton Le Skerne Darl 167 D6
Haughton Moss Ches 127 D5
Haultwick Herts 68 A3
Haunn Argyll 224 B2
Haunn W Isles 286 E3
Haunton Staffs 113 D6
Hauxley Northumb 189 C5
Hauxton Cambs 85 B6
Havant Hants 19 A6
Haven Hereford 78 B2
Haven Bank Lincs 134 D2
Haven Side E Yorks 142 A3
Havenstreet I o W 19 B4
Havercroft W Yorks 140 B1
Haverfordwest = Hwlffordd Pembs 55 C5
Haverhill Suff 86 C2
Haverigg Cumb 153 C2
Havering-atte-Bower London 69 D5
Haveringland Norf 120 C3
Haversham M Keynes 83 C5
Haverthwaite Cumb 154 C2
Haverton Hill Stockton 168 C2
Hawarden = Penarlâg Flint 126 C3
Hawcoat Cumb 153 C3
Hawen Ceredig 73 B6
Hawes N Yorks 156 C2
Hawes Side Blkpool 144 D3
Hawes'Green Norf 104 B3
Hawford Worcs 79 A6
Hawick Borders 186 B4
Hawk Green Gtr Man 129 A4
Hawkchurch Devon 14 A3
Hawkedon Suff 86 B3
Hawkenbury Kent 37 B6
Hawkenbury Kent 36 C3
Hawkeridge Wilts 44 D2
Hawkerland Devon 13 C5
Hawkes End W Mid 97 C6
Hawkesbury S Glos 43 A6
Hawkesbury Warks 97 C6
Hawkesbury Upton S Glos 44 A1
Hawkhill Northumb 189 B5
Hawkhurst Kent 37 C5
Hawkinge Kent 39 B4
Hawkley Hants 33 C6
Hawkridge Som 26 B3
Hawkshead Cumb 154 B2
Hawkshead Hill Cumb 154 B2
Hawksland S Lnrk 194 C3
Hawkswick N Yorks 156 D3
Hawksworth Notts 115 A5
Hawksworth W Yorks 147 C5
Hawksworth W Yorks 147 D6
Hawkwell Essex 70 D2
Hawley Hants 34 A1
Hawley Kent 50 B2
Hawling Glos 63 A6
Hawnby N Yorks 158 C4
Haworth W Yorks 147 D4
Hawstead Suff 87 B4
Hawthorn Durham 168 A2
Hawthorn Rhondda 41 C6
Hawthorn Wilts 44 C2
Hawthorn Hill Brack 48 B1
Hawthorn Hill Lincs 134 D2
Hawthorpe Lincs 116 C3
Hawton Notts 132 D2
Haxby York 149 B5
Haxey N Lincs 141 C5
Hay Green Norf 118 D2
Hay-on-Wye = Y Gelli Gandryll Powys 77 C6
Hay Street Herts 68 A3
Haydock Mers 137 D4
Haydock Park Racecourse Mers 137 D4
Haydon Dorset 29 D6
Haydon Bridge Northumb 177 C6
Haydon Wick Swindon 45 A5
Haye Corn 6 A2
Hayes London 49 C7
Hayes London 48 A4
Hayfield Derbys 129 A5
Hayfield Fife 209 A5
Hayhill E Ayrs 182 A2
Hayhillock Angus 232 D3
Hayle Corn 2 B3
Haynes Beds 84 C2
Haynes Church End Beds 84 C2
Hayscastle Pembs 55 B4
Hayscastle Cross Pembs 55 B5
Hayshead Angus 233 D4
Hayton Aberdeen 245 B6
Hayton Cumb 174 D4
Hayton Cumb 176 D3
Hayton E Yorks 149 C7
Hayton Notts 132 A2
Hayton's Bent Shrops 94 C3
Haytor Vale Devon 12 D2
Haywards Heath W Sus 35 D6
Haywood S Yorks 140 B3
Haywood Oaks Notts 131 D6
Hazel Grove Gtr Man 129 A4
Hazel Street Kent 37 C4
Hazelbank S Lnrk 194 B3
Hazelbury Bryan Dorset 16 A1
Hazeley Hants 47 D5
Hazelhurst Gtr Man 138 C2
Hazelslade Staffs 112 D4
Hazelton Glos 64 B1
Hazelton Walls Fife 220 B3
Hazelwood Derbys 114 A1
Hazlemere Bucks 66 D3
Hazlerigg T & W 179 B4
Hazlewood N Yorks 147 B4
Hazon Northumb 189 C4
Heacham Norf 118 B3
Head of Muir Falk 207 B6
Headbourne Worthy Hants 32 B3
Headbrook Hereford 77 B7
Headcorn Kent 37 B6
Headingley W Yorks 148 D1
Headington Oxon 65 C6
Headlam Durham 167 D4
Headless Cross Worcs 80 A3
Headley Hants 46 C3
Headley Hants 33 B7
Headley Sur 35 A5
Headon Notts 132 B2
Heads S Lnrk 194 B2
Heads Nook Cumb 176 D2
Heage Derbys 130 D3
Healaugh N Yorks 148 C3
Healaugh N Yorks 156 B4
Heald Green Gtr Man 128 A3
Heale Devon 26 A1
Heale Som 29 A6
Healey Gtr Man 138 B1
Healey Northumb 178 D2
Healey N Yorks 157 C5
Healing NE Lincs 143 B4
Heamoor Corn 2 B2
Heanish Argyll 222 C3
Heanor Derbys 114 A2
Heanton Punchardon Devon 25 B6
Heapham Lincs 132 A3
Heart of the National Forest Leics 113 D7
Hearthstane Borders 195 D6
Heasley Mill Devon 26 B2
Heast Highld 247 C5
Heath Cardiff 41 D6
Heath Derbys 131 C4
Heath and Reach Beds 67 A4
Heath End Hants 46 C3
Heath End Sur 34 B1
Heath End Warks 81 A5
Heath Hayes Staffs 112 D4
Heath Hill Shrops 111 D6
Heath House Som 28 A4
Heath Town W Mid 96 B2
Heathcote Derbys 129 C6
Heather Leics 114 D1
Heatherfield Highld 259 D4
Heathfield Devon 12 D3
Heathfield E Sus 36 D3
Heathfield Som 27 C6
Heathhall Dumfries 174 A2
Heathrow Airport London 48 B3
Heathstock Devon 14 A2
Heathton Shrops 95 B6
Heatley Warr 128 A2
Heaton Lancs 144 A4
Heaton Staffs 129 C4
Heaton T & W 179 C4
Heaton W Yorks 147 D5
Heaton Moor Gtr Man 138 D1
Heaverham Kent 36 A3
Heaviley Gtr Man 129 A4
Heavitree Devon 13 B4
Hebburn T & W 179 C5
Hebden N Yorks 147 A4
Hebden Bridge W Yorks 138 A2
Hebron Anglesey 123 B4
Hebron Carms 73 D4
Hebron Northumb 178 A3
Heck Dumfries 184 D3
Heckfield Hants 47 C5
Heckfield Green Suff 104 D2
Heckfordbridge Essex 70 A3
Heckington Lincs 116 A4
Heckmondwike W Yorks 139 A5
Heddington Wilts 44 C3
Heddle Orkney 282 F4
Heddon-on-the-Wall Northumb 178 C3
Hedenham Norf 104 B4
Hedge End Hants 32 D3
Hedgerley Bucks 48 A2
Hedging Som 28 C3
Hedley on the Hill Northumb 178 D2
Hednesford Staffs 112 D3
Hedon E Yorks 142 A3
Hedsor Bucks 48 A2
Hedworth T & W 179 C5
Heeley City Farm, Sheffield S Yorks 130 A3
Hegdon Hill Hereford 78 B3
Heggerscales Cumb 165 D6
Heglibister Shetland 285 H5

Heighington Darl 167 C5
Heighington Lincs 133 C5
Heights of Brae Highld 263 D7
Heights of Kinlochewe
Highld 262 D2
Heilam Highld 277 B5
Heiton Borders 197 C6
Hele Devon 25 A6
Hele Devon 13 A4
Helensburgh Argyll 215 D5
Helford Corn 3 C5
Helford Passage Corn 3 C5
Helhoughton Norf 119 C5
Helions Bumpstead Essex 86 C2
Hellaby S Yorks 140 D3
Helland Corn 10 D1
Hellesdon Norf 120 D4
Hellidon Northants 82 B2
Hellifield N Yorks 146 B2
Hellingly E Sus 22 A3
Hellington Norf 104 A4
Hellister Shetland 285 J5
Helm Northumb 189 D4
Helmdon Northants 82 C2
Helmingham Suff 88 B2
Helmington Row Durham 167 B4
Helmsdale Highld 274 C4
Helmshore Lancs 137 A6
Helmsley N Yorks 159 C5
Helperby N Yorks 148 A3
Helperthorpe N Yorks 160 D3
Helpringham Lincs 116 A4
Helpston P'boro 100 A3
Helsby Ches 127 B4
Helsey Lincs 135 B5
Helston Corn 3 C4
Helstone Corn 10 C1
Helton Cumb 164 C3
Helwith Bridge N Yorks 146 A2
Hemblington Norf 121 D5
Hemel Hempstead Herts 67 C5
Hemingbrough N Yorks 149 D5
Hemingby Lincs 134 B2
Hemingford Abbots
Cambs 101 D4
Hemingford Grey Cambs 101 D4
Hemingstone Suff 88 B2
Hemington Leics 114 C2
Hemington Northants 100 C2
Hemington Som 43 D6
Hemley Suff 88 C3
Hemlington M'bro 168 D3
Hemp Green Suff 89 A4
Hempholme E Yorks 150 B3
Hempnall Norf 104 B3
Hempnall Green Norf 104 B3
Hempriggs House Highld 281 D5
Hempstead Essex 86 D2
Hempstead Medway 51 C4
Hempstead Norf 120 B3
Hempstead Norf 121 C6
Hempsted Glos 63 B4
Hempton Norf 119 C6
Hempton Oxon 82 D1
Hemsby Norf 121 D6
Hemswell Lincs 142 D1
Hemswell Cliff Lincs 133 A4
Hemsworth W Yorks 140 B2
Hemyock Devon 27 D6
Hen-feddau fawr Pembs 73 C5
Henbury Bristol 43 B4
Henbury Ches 128 B3
Hendon London 49 A5
Hendon T & W 179 D6
Hendre Flint 126 C1
Hendre-ddu Conwy 124 C3
Hendreforgan Rhondda 41 C4
Hendy Carms 57 B5
Heneglwys Anglesey 123 C4
Henfield W Sus 21 A5
Henford Devon 11 B4
Henghurst Kent 38 B1
Hengoed Caerph 41 B6
Hengoed Powys 77 B6
Hengoed Shrops 110 B1
Hengrave Suff 87 A4
Henham Essex 69 A5
Heniarth Powys 93 A5
Henlade Som 28 C2
Henley Shrops 94 D3
Henley Som 28 B4
Henley Suff 88 B2
Henley W Sus 34 D1
Henley-in-Arden Warks 81 A4

Henley-on-Thames Oxon 47 A5
Henley's Down E Sus 23 A5
Henllan Ceredig 73 B6
Henllan Denb 125 C5
Henllan Amgoed Carms 73 D4
Henllys Torf 61 D4
Henlow Beds 84 D3
Hennock Devon 12 C3
Henny Street Essex 87 D4
Henryd Conwy 124 B2
Henry's Moat Pembs 55 B6
Hensall N Yorks 140 A3
Henshaw Northumb 177 C5
Hensingham Cumb 162 C2
Henstead Suff 105 C5
Henstridge Som 30 D1
Henstridge Ash Som 29 C7
Henstridge Marsh Som 30 C1
Henton Oxon 66 C2
Henton Som 29 A4
Henwood Corn 10 D3
Heogan Shetland 285 J6
Heol-las Swansea 40 B1
Heol Senni Powys 59 C6
Heol-y-Cyw Bridgend 40 C4
Hepburn Northumb 188 A3
Hepple Northumb 188 C2
Hepscott Northumb 179 A4
Heptonstall W Yorks 138 A2
Hepworth Suff 103 D5
Hepworth W Yorks 139 C4
Herbrandston Pembs 55 D4
Hereford Hereford 78 C3
Hereford Cathedral
Hereford 78 D3
Hereford Racecourse
Hereford 78 C3
Heriot Borders 196 A2
Heritage Motor Centre,
Gaydon Warks 81 B6
Hermiston Edin 209 C4
Hermitage Borders 186 D4
Hermitage Dorset 15 A6
Hermitage W Berks 46 B3
Hermitage W Sus 19 A6
Hermon Anglesey 122 D3
Hermon Carms 73 C6
Hermon Carms 58 C3
Hermon Pembs 73 C5
Herne Kent 52 C3
Herne Bay Kent 52 C3
Herner Devon 25 C6
Hernhill Kent 52 C2
Herodsfoot Corn 5 A7
Herongate Essex 69 D6
Heronsford S Ayrs 180 C3
Herriard Hants 33 A5
Herringfleet Suff 105 B5
Herringswell Suff 102 D3
Hersden Kent 53 C4
Hersham Corn 10 A3
Hersham Sur 48 C4
Herstmonceux E Sus 22 A4
Herston Orkney 283 H5
Hertford Herts 68 B3
Hertford Heath Herts 68 B3
Hertingfordbury Herts 68 B3
Hesket Newmarket Cumb 163 A6
Hesketh Bank Lancs 136 A3
Hesketh Lane Lancs 145 C6
Heskin Green Lancs 136 B4
Hesleden Durham 168 B2
Hesleyside Northumb 177 A6
Heslington York 149 B5
Hessay York 148 B4
Hessenford Corn 6 B2
Hessett Suff 87 A5
Hessle E Yorks 142 A2
Hest Bank Lancs 145 A4
Heston London 48 B4
Hestwall Orkney 282 F3
Heswall Mers 126 A2
Hethe Oxon 65 A6
Hethersett Norf 104 A2
Hethersgill Cumb 176 C2
Hethpool Northumb 188 A1
Hett Durham 167 B5
Hetton N Yorks 146 B3
Hetton-le-Hole T & W 167 A6
Hetton Steads Northumb 198 C4
Heugh Northumb 178 B2
Heugh-head Aberds 243 A6
Heveningham Suff 104 D4
Hever Kent 36 B2
Hever Castle and
Gardens Kent 36 B2
Heversham Cumb 154 C3

Hevingham Norf 120 C3
Hewas Water Corn 5 C4
Hewelsfield Glos 62 C1
Hewish N Som 42 C3
Hewish Som 14 A4
Heworth York 149 B5
Hexham Northumb 178 C1
Hexham Abbey Northumb 178 C1
Hexham Racecourse
Northumb 177 C7
Hextable Kent 50 B2
Hexton Herts 84 D3
Hexworthy Devon 12 D1
Hey Lancs 146 C2
Heybridge Essex 69 D6
Heybridge Essex 70 C2
Heybridge Basin Essex 70 C2
Heybrook Bay Devon 7 C4
Heydon Cambs 85 C6
Heydon Norf 120 C3
Heydour Lincs 116 B3
Heylipol Argyll 222 C2
Heylor Shetland 284 E4
Heysham Lancs 144 A4
Heyshott W Sus 20 A1
Heyside Gtr Man 138 C2
Heytesbury Wilts 30 A3
Heythrop Oxon 64 A4
Heywood Gtr Man 138 B1
Heywood Wilts 44 D2
Hibaldstow N Lincs 142 C1
Hickleton S Yorks 140 C2
Hickling Norf 121 C6
Hickling Notts 115 C4
Hickling Green Norf 121 C6
Hickling Heath Norf 121 C6
Hickstead W Sus 35 D5
Hidcote Boyce Glos 81 C4
Hidcote Manor Garden,
Moreton-in-Marsh Glos 81 C4
High Ackworth W Yorks 140 B2
High Angerton Northumb 178 A2
High Bankhill Cumb 164 A3
High Barnes T & W 179 D5
High Beach Essex 68 D4
High Bentham N Yorks 145 A6
High Bickington Devon 25 C7
High Birkwith N Yorks 155 D6
High Blantyre S Lnrk 194 A1
High Bonnybridge Falk 207 C6
High Bradfield S Yorks 139 D5
High Bray Devon 26 B1
High Brooms Kent 36 B3
High Bullen Devon 25 C6
High Buston Northumb 189 C5
High Callerton Northumb 178 B3
High Catton E Yorks 149 B6
High Cogges Oxon 65 C4
High Coniscliffe Darl 167 D5
High Cross Hants 33 C6
High Cross Herts 68 B3
High Easter Essex 69 B6
High Eggborough N Yorks 140 A3
High Ellington N Yorks 157 C5
High Ercall Telford 111 D4
High Etherley Durham 167 C4
High Garrett Essex 70 A1
High Grange Durham 167 B4
High Green Norf 104 A2
High Green S Yorks 139 D6
High Green Worcs 80 C1
High Halden Kent 37 C6
High Halstow Medway 51 B4
High Ham Som 28 B4
High Harrington Cumb 162 B3
High Hatton Shrops 111 C5
High Hawsker N Yorks 160 A3
High Hesket Cumb 164 A2
High Hesleden Durham 168 B2
High Hoyland S Yorks 139 B5
High Hunsley E Yorks 150 D2
High Hurstwood E Sus 36 D2
High Hutton N Yorks 149 A6
High Ireby Cumb 163 A5
High Kelling Norf 120 A3
High Kilburn N Yorks 158 D4
High Lands Durham 166 C4
High Lane Gtr Man 129 A4
High Lane Hereford 79 A4
High Laver Essex 69 C5
High Legh Ches 128 A2
High Leven Stockton 168 D2
High Littleton Bath 43 D5
High Lorton Cumb 163 B4
High Marishes N Yorks 159 D7
High Marnham Notts 132 B3
High Melton S Yorks 140 C3

High Mickley Northumb 178 C2
High Mindork Dumfries 171 B5
High Moorland Visitor
Centre, Princetown
Devon 11 D6
High Newton Cumb 154 C3
High Newton-by-the-Sea
Northumb 189 A5
High Nibthwaite Cumb 154 C1
High Offley Staffs 112 C1
High Ongar Essex 69 C5
High Onn Staffs 112 D2
High Roding Essex 69 B6
High Row Cumb 163 A6
High Salvington W Sus 21 B4
High Shaw N Yorks 156 B2
High Spen T & W 178 D3
High Stoop Durham 166 A4
High Street Corn 5 B4
High Street Kent 37 C5
High Street Suff 89 B5
High Street Suff 105 D5
High Street Suff 87 C4
High Street Green Suff 87 B6
High Throston Hrtlpl 168 B2
High Toynton Lincs 134 C2
High Trewhitt Northumb 188 C3
High Valleyfield Fife 208 B3
High Westwood Durham 178 D3
High Wray Cumb 154 B2
High Wych Herts 69 B4
High Wycombe Bucks 66 D3
Higham Derbys 130 D3
Higham Kent 51 B4
Higham Lancs 146 D2
Higham Suff 87 D6
Higham Suff 86 A3
Higham Dykes Northumb 178 B3
Higham Ferrers Northants 83 A6
Higham Gobion Beds 84 D3
Higham on the Hill Leics 97 B6
Higham Wood Kent 36 B3
Highampton Devon 11 A5
Highbridge Highld 239 D5
Highbridge Som 28 A3
Highbrook W Sus 35 C6
Highburton W Yorks 139 B4
Highbury Som 29 A6
Highclere Hants 46 C2
Highcliffe Dorset 17 B6
Higher Ansty Dorset 16 A1
Higher Ashton Devon 12 C3
Higher Ballam Lancs 144 D3
Higher Bartle Lancs 145 D5
Higher Boscaswell Corn 2 B1
Higher Burwardsley Ches 127 D5
Higher Clovelly Devon 24 C4
Higher End Gtr Man 136 C4
Higher Kinnerton Flint 126 C3
Higher Penwortham
Lancs 136 A4
Higher Town Scilly 2 E4
Higher Walreddon Devon 11 D5
Higher Walton Lancs 137 A4
Higher Walton Warr 127 A5
Higher Wheelton Lancs 137 A5
Higher Whitley Ches 127 A6
Higher Wincham Ches 128 B1
Higher Wych Ches 110 A3
Highfield E Yorks 149 D6
Highfield Gtr Man 137 C6
Highfield N Ayrs 204 C3
Highfield Oxon 65 A6
Highfield S Yorks 130 A3
Highfield T & W 178 D3
Highfields Cambs 85 B5
Highfields Northumb 198 A3
Highgate London 49 A5
Highland Folk Museum,
Aultlairie Highld 241 C5
Highland Folk Museum,
Kingussie Highld 241 B5
Highlane Ches 128 C3
Highlane Derbys 131 A4
Highlaws Cumb 174 D4
Highleadon Glos 62 A3
Highleigh W Sus 20 C1
Highley Shrops 95 C5
Highmoor Cross Oxon 47 A5
Highmoor Hill Mon 42 A3
Highnam Glos 62 B3
Highnam Green Glos 62 A3
Highsted Kent 51 C6
Highstreet Green Essex 86 D3
Hightae Dumfries 174 A3
Hightown Ches 128 C3

Hightown Mers 136 C2
Hightown Green Suff 87 B5
Highway Wilts 44 B4
Highweek Devon 12 D3
Highworth Swindon 64 D3
Hilborough Norf 103 A4
Hilcote Derbys 131 D4
Hilcott Wilts 45 D5
Hilden Park Kent 36 B3
Hildenborough Kent 36 B3
Hildersham Cambs 86 C1
Hilderstone Staffs 112 B3
Hilderthorpe E Yorks 151 A4
Hilfield Dorset 15 A6
Hilgay Norf 102 B2
Hill Pembs 55 D7
Hill S Glos 62 D2
Hill W Mid 96 B4
Hill Brow W Sus 33 C6
Hill Dale Lancs 136 B3
Hill Dyke Lincs 117 A6
Hill End Durham 166 B3
Hill End Fife 208 A3
Hill End N Yorks 147 B4
Hill Head Hants 18 A4
Hill Head Northumb 178 C1
Hill Mountain Pembs 55 D5
Hill of Beath Fife 209 A4
Hill of Fearn Highld 265 C4
Hill of Mountblairy
Aberds 268 D1
Hill Ridware Staffs 113 D4
Hill Top Durham 166 C2
Hill Top Hants 18 A3
Hill Top W Mid 96 B2
Hill Top W Yorks 139 B6
Hill Top, Sawrey Cumb 154 B2
Hill View Dorset 16 B3
Hillam N Yorks 140 A3
Hillbeck Cumb 165 D5
Hillborough Kent 53 C4
Hillbrae Aberds 256 D2
Hillbrae Aberds 255 B7
Hillbutts Dorset 16 A3
Hillclifflane Derbys 113 A6
Hillcommon Som 27 C6
Hillend Fife 208 B4
Hillerton Devon 12 B2
Hillesden Bucks 66 A1
Hillesley Glos 43 A6
Hillfarrance Som 27 C6
Hillhead Aberds 255 C6
Hillhead Devon 8 B3
Hillhead S Ayrs 182 A2
Hillhead of Auchentumb
Aberds 269 D4
Hillhead of Cocklaw
Aberds 257 B5
Hillhouse Borders 197 A4
Hilliclay Highld 280 B3
Hillier Gardens and
Arboretum Hants 32 C2
Hillingdon London 48 A3
Hillington Glasgow 205 B5
Hillington Norf 119 C4
Hillmorton Warks 98 D2
Hillockhead Aberds 244 A1
Hillockhead Aberds 243 B6
Hills Aberds 245 C6
Hillside Angus 233 B5
Hillside Mers 136 B2
Hillside Orkney 283 H5
Hillside Shetland 285 G6
Hillswick Shetland 284 F4
Hillway I o W 19 C5
Hillwell Shetland 285 M5
Hilmarton Wilts 44 B4
Hilperton Wilts 44 D2
Hilsea Ptsmth 19 A5
Hilston E Yorks 151 D5
Hilton Aberds 257 C4
Hilton Cambs 85 A4
Hilton Cumb 165 C5
Hilton Derbys 113 B6
Hilton Dorset 16 A1
Hilton Durham 167 C4
Hilton Highld 264 B3
Hilton Shrops 95 B5
Hilton Stockton 168 D2
Hilton of Cadboll Highld 265 C4
Himbleton Worcs 80 B2
Himley Staffs 96 B1
Hincaster Cumb 154 C4
Hinckley Leics 98 B1
Hinderclay Suff 103 D6
Hinderton Ches 126 B3
Hinderwell N Yorks 169 D5

Hindford Shrops 110 B2
Hindhead Sur 34 C1
Hindley Gtr Man 137 C5
Hindley Green Gtr Man 137 C5
Hindlip Worcs 80 B1
Hindolveston Norf 120 C2
Hindon Wilts 30 B3
Hindringham Norf 120 B1
Hingham Norf 103 A6
Hinstock Shrops 111 C5
Hintlesham Suff 88 C1
Hinton Hants 17 B6
Hinton Hereford 78 D1
Hinton Northants 82 B2
Hinton Shrops 94 A2
Hinton S Glos 43 B6
Hinton Ampner Hants 33 C4
Hinton Blewett Bath 43 D4
Hinton Charterhouse Bath 43 D6
Hinton-in-the-Hedges Northants 82 D2
Hinton Martell Dorset 17 A4
Hinton on the Green Worcs 80 C3
Hinton Parva Swindon 45 A6
Hinton St George Som 28 D4
Hinton St Mary Dorset 30 D1
Hinton Waldrist Oxon 65 D4
Hints Shrops 95 D4
Hints Staffs 97 A4
Hinwick Beds 83 A6
Hinxhill Kent 38 A2
Hinxton Cambs 85 C6
Hinxworth Herts 84 C4
Hipperholme W Yorks 139 A4
Hipswell N Yorks 157 B5
Hirael Gwyn 123 C5
Hiraeth Carms 73 D4
Hirn Aberds 245 B4
Hirnant Powys 109 C5
Hirst N Lnrk 207 D6
Hirst Northumb 179 A4
Hirst Courtney N Yorks 140 A4
Hirwaen Denb 125 C6
Hirwaun Rhondda 59 E6
Hiscott Devon 25 C6
Histon Cambs 85 A6
Historic Royal Dockyard Ptsmth 19 A5
Hitcham Suff 87 B5
Hitchin Herts 68 A1
Hither Green London 49 B6
Hittisleigh Devon 12 B2
Hive E Yorks 149 D7
Hixon Staffs 112 C4
HMS Victory Ptsmth 19 A5
HMY Britannia Edin 209 C5
Hoaden Kent 53 D4
Hoaldalbert Mon 61 A5
Hoar Cross Staffs 113 C5
Hoarwithy Hereford 62 A1
Hoath Kent 53 C4
Hobarris Shrops 93 D7
Hobbister Orkney 283 G4
Hobkirk Borders 187 B4
Hobson Durham 178 D3
Hoby Leics 115 D4
Hockering Norf 120 D2
Hockerton Notts 132 D2
Hockley Essex 70 D2
Hockley Heath W Mid 97 D4
Hockliffe Beds 67 A4
Hockwold cum Wilton Norf 102 C3
Hockworthy Devon 27 D5
Hoddesdon Herts 68 C3
Hoddlesden Blkburn 137 A6
Hoddom Mains Dumfries 175 A4
Hoddomcross Dumfries 175 A4
Hodgeston Pembs 55 E6
Hodley Powys 93 B5
Hodnet Shrops 111 C5
Hodthorpe Derbys 131 B5
Hoe Hants 33 D4
Hoe Norf 120 D1
Hoe Gate Hants 33 D5
Hoff Cumb 165 D4
Hog Patch Sur 34 B1
Hoggard's Green Suff 87 B4
Hoggeston Bucks 66 A3
Hogha Gearraidh W Isles 287 G2
Hoghton Lancs 137 A5
Hognaston Derbys 130 D2
Hogsthorpe Lincs 135 B5
Holbeach Lincs 117 C6
Holbeach Bank Lincs 117 C6
Holbeach Clough Lincs 117 C6
Holbeach Drove Lincs 117 D6
Holbeach Hurn Lincs 117 C6
Holbeach St Johns Lincs 117 D6
Holbeach St Marks Lincs 117 B6
Holbeach St Matthew Lincs 117 B7
Holbeck Notts 131 B5
Holbeck W Yorks 148 D1
Holbeck Woodhouse Notts 131 B5
Holberrow Green Worcs 80 B3
Holbeton Devon 7 B5
Holborn London 49 A6
Holbrook Derbys 114 A1
Holbrook Suff 88 D2
Holbrook S Yorks 131 A4
Holburn Northumb 198 C4
Holbury Hants 18 A3
Holcombe Devon 13 D4
Holcombe Som 29 A6
Holcombe Rogus Devon 27 D5
Holcot Northants 83 A4
Holden Lancs 146 C1
Holdenby Northants 82 A3
Holdenhurst Bmouth 17 B5
Holdgate Shrops 94 C3
Holdingham Lincs 116 A3
Holditch Dorset 14 A3
Hole-in-the-Wall Hereford 62 A2
Holefield Borders 198 C2
Holehouses Ches 128 B2
Holemoor Devon 11 A5
Holestane Dumfries 183 C6
Holford Som 27 A6
Holgate York 149 B4
Holker Cumb 154 D2
Holkham Norf 119 A5
Hollacombe Devon 11 A4
Holland Orkney 282 B5
Holland Orkney 282 E7
Holland Fen Lincs 117 A5
Holland-on-Sea Essex 71 B6
Hollandstoun Orkney 282 B8
Hollee Dumfries 175 B5
Hollesley Suff 89 C4
Hollicombe Torbay 8 A2
Hollingbourne Kent 37 A6
Hollington Derbys 113 B6
Hollington E Sus 23 A5
Hollington Staffs 113 B4
Hollington Grove Derbys 113 B6
Hollingworth Gtr Man 138 D3
Hollins Gtr Man 137 C7
Hollins Green Warr 137 D5
Hollins Lane Lancs 145 B4
Hollinsclough Staffs 129 C5
Hollinwood Gtr Man 138 C2
Hollinwood Shrops 111 B4
Hollocombe Devon 26 D1
Hollow Meadows S Yorks 130 A2
Holloway Derbys 130 D3
Hollowell Northants 98 D3
Holly End Norf 101 A6
Holly Green Worcs 79 C6
Hollybush Caerph 41 A6
Hollybush E Ayrs 182 A1
Hollybush Worcs 79 D5
Hollym E Yorks 143 A5
Hollywood Worcs 96 D3
Holmbridge W Yorks 139 C4
Holmbury St Mary Sur 35 B4
Holmbush Corn 5 B5
Holmcroft Staffs 112 C3
Holme Cambs 100 C3
Holme Cumb 154 D4
Holme Notts 132 D3
Holme N Yorks 158 C2
Holme W Yorks 139 C4
Holme Chapel Lancs 138 A1
Holme Green N Yorks 149 C4
Holme Hale Norf 103 A4
Holme Lacy Hereford 78 D3
Holme Marsh Hereford 78 B1
Holme next the Sea Norf 119 A4
Holme-on-Spalding-Moor E Yorks 149 D7
Holme on the Wolds E Yorks 150 C2
Holme Pierrepont Notts 115 B4
Holme St Cuthbert Cumb 174 D4
Holme Wood W Yorks 147 D5
Holmer Hereford 78 C3
Holmer Green Bucks 67 D4
Holmes Chapel Ches 128 C2
Holmesfield Derbys 130 B3
Holmeswood Lancs 136 B3
Holmewood Derbys 131 C4
Holmfirth W Yorks 139 C4
Holmhead Dumfries 183 D5
Holmhead E Ayrs 193 C5
Holmisdale Highld 258 D1
Holmpton E Yorks 143 A5
Holmrook Cumb 153 A1
Holmsgarth Shetland 285 J6
Holmwrangle Cumb 164 A3
Holne Devon 7 A6
Holnest Dorset 15 A6
Holsworthy Devon 10 A4
Holsworthy Beacon Devon 11 A4
Holt Dorset 17 A4
Holt Norf 120 B2
Holt Wilts 44 C2
Holt Worcs 79 A6
Holt Wrex 127 D4
Holt End Hants 33 B5
Holt End Worcs 80 A3
Holt Fleet Worcs 79 A6
Holt Heath Worcs 79 A6
Holt Park W Yorks 147 C6
Holtby York 149 B5
Holton Oxon 65 C7
Holton Som 29 C6
Holton Suff 105 D4
Holton cum Beckering Lincs 133 A6
Holton Heath Dorset 16 B3
Holton le Clay Lincs 143 C4
Holton le Moor Lincs 142 D2
Holton St Mary Suff 87 D6
Holwell Dorset 29 D7
Holwell Herts 84 D3
Holwell Leics 115 C5
Holwell Oxon 64 C3
Holwick Durham 166 C2
Holworth Dorset 16 C1
Holy Cross Worcs 96 D2
Holy Island Northumb 199 B5
Holybourne Hants 33 A6
Holyhead = Caergybi Anglesey 122 B2
Holymoorside Derbys 130 C3
Holyport Windsor 48 B1
Holystone Northumb 188 C2
Holytown N Lnrk 207 D5
Holywell Cambs 101 D5
Holywell Corn 4 B2
Holywell Dorset 15 A5
Holywell E Sus 22 C3
Holywell Northumb 179 B5
Holywell = Treffynnon Flint 126 B1
Holywell Bay Fun Park, Newquay Corn 4 B2
Holywell Green W Yorks 138 B3
Holywell Lake Som 27 C6
Holywell Row Suff 102 D3
Holywood Dumfries 184 D2
Hom Green Hereford 62 A1
Homer Shrops 95 A4
Homersfield Suff 104 C3
Homington Wilts 31 C5
Honey Hill Kent 52 C3
Honey Street Wilts 45 C5
Honey Tye Suff 87 D5
Honeyborough Pembs 55 D5
Honeybourne Worcs 80 C4
Honeychurch Devon 12 A1
Honiley Warks 97 D5
Honing Norf 121 C5
Honingham Norf 120 D3
Honington Lincs 116 A2
Honington Suff 103 D5
Honington Warks 81 C5
Honiton Devon 13 A6
Honley W Yorks 139 B4
Hoo Green Ches 128 A2
Hoo St Werburgh Medway 51 B4
Hood Green S Yorks 139 C6
Hooe E Sus 23 B4
Hooe Plym 7 B4
Hooe Common E Sus 23 A4
Hook E Yorks 141 A5
Hook London 49 C4
Hook Hants 47 D5
Hook Pembs 55 C5
Hook Wilts 45 A4
Hook Green Kent 37 C4
Hook Green Kent 50 C3
Hook Norton Oxon 81 D6
Hooke Dorset 15 B5
Hookgate Staffs 111 B6
Hookway Devon 12 B3
Hookwood Sur 35 B5
Hoole Ches 127 C4
Hooley Sur 35 A5
Hoop Mon 61 C7
Hooton Ches 126 B3
Hooton Levitt S Yorks 140 D3
Hooton Pagnell S Yorks 140 C2
Hooton Roberts S Yorks 140 D2
Hop Pole Lincs 117 D4
Hope Derbys 129 A6
Hope Devon 7 D5
Hope Highld 277 C5
Hope Powys 93 A6
Hope Shrops 94 A1
Hope Staffs 129 D6
Hope = Yr Hôb Flint 126 D3
Hope Bagot Shrops 94 D3
Hope Bowdler Shrops 94 B2
Hope End Green Essex 69 A5
Hope Green Ches 129 A4
Hope Mansell Hereford 62 B2
Hope under Dinmore Hereford 78 B3
Hopeman Moray 266 C2
Hope's Green Essex 51 A4
Hopesay Shrops 94 C1
Hopley's Green Hereford 78 B1
Hopperton N Yorks 148 B3
Hopstone Shrops 95 B5
Hopton Shrops 110 C2
Hopton Shrops 111 C4
Hopton Staffs 112 C3
Hopton Suff 103 D5
Hopton Cangeford Shrops 94 C3
Hopton Castle Shrops 94 D1
Hopton on Sea Norf 105 A6
Hopton Wafers Shrops 95 D4
Hoptonheath Shrops 94 D1
Hopwas Staffs 97 A4
Hopwood Gtr Man 138 C1
Hopwood Worcs 96 D3
Horam E Sus 22 A3
Horbling Lincs 116 B4
Horbury W Yorks 139 B5
Horcott Glos 64 C2
Horden Durham 168 A2
Horderley Shrops 94 C2
Hordle Hants 17 B6
Hordley Shrops 110 B2
Horeb Ceredig 73 B6
Horeb Carms 57 B4
Horeb Carms 58 C2
Horfield Bristol 43 B5
Horham Suff 104 D3
Horkesley Heath Essex 70 A3
Horkstow N Lincs 142 B1
Horley Oxon 81 C7
Horley Sur 35 B5
Hornblotton Green Som 29 B5
Hornby Lancs 145 A5
Hornby N Yorks 157 B6
Hornby N Yorks 158 A2
Horncastle Lincs 134 C2
Hornchurch London 50 A2
Horncliffe Northumb 198 B3
Horndean Borders 198 B2
Horndean Hants 33 D6
Horndon Devon 11 D6
Horndon on the Hill Thurrock 50 A3
Horne Sur 35 B6
Horniehaugh Angus 232 B2
Horning Norf 121 D5
Horninghold Leics 99 B5
Horninglow Staffs 113 C6
Horningsea Cambs 85 A6
Horningsham Wilts 30 A2
Horningtoft Norf 119 C6
Horns Corner Kent 37 D5
Horns Cross Devon 25 C4
Horns Cross E Sus 37 D6
Hornsby Cumb 176 D3
Hornsea E Yorks 151 C5
Hornsea Bridge E Yorks 151 C5
Hornsey London 49 A6
Hornton Oxon 81 C6
Horrabridge Devon 7 A4
Horringer Suff 87 A4
Horringford I o W 18 C4
Horse Bridge Staffs 129 D4
Horsebridge Devon 11 D5
Horsebridge Hants 32 B2
Horsebrook Staffs 112 D2
Horsehay Telford 95 A4
Horseheath Cambs 86 C2
Horsehouse N Yorks 156 C4
Horsell Sur 34 A2
Horseman's Green Wrex 110 A3
Horseway Cambs 101 C6
Horsey Norf 121 C6
Horsford Norf 120 D3
Horsforth W Yorks 147 D6
Horsham Worcs 79 B5
Horsham W Sus 35 C4
Horsham St Faith Norf 120 D4
Horsington Lincs 134 C1
Horsington Som 29 C7
Horsley Derbys 114 A1
Horsley Glos 63 D4
Horsley Northumb 178 C2
Horsley Northumb 188 D1
Horsley Cross Essex 71 A5
Horsley Woodhouse Derbys 114 A1
Horsleycross Street Essex 71 A5
Horsleyhill Borders 186 B4
Horsleyhope Durham 166 A3
Horsmonden Kent 37 B4
Horspath Oxon 65 C6
Horstead Norf 121 D4
Horsted Keynes W Sus 36 D1
Horton Bucks 67 B4
Horton Dorset 17 A4
Horton Lancs 146 B2
Horton Northants 83 B5
Horton Shrops 110 C3
Horton S Glos 43 A6
Horton Som 28 D3
Horton Staffs 129 D4
Horton Swansea 57 D4
Horton Wilts 45 C4
Horton Windsor 48 B3
Horton-cum-Studley Oxon 65 B6
Horton Green Ches 110 A3
Horton Heath Hants 32 D3
Horton in Ribblesdale N Yorks 155 D7
Horton Kirby Kent 50 C2
Hortonlane Shrops 110 D3
Horwich Gtr Man 137 B5
Horwich End Derbys 129 A5
Horwood Devon 25 C6
Hose Leics 115 C5
Hoselaw Borders 198 C2
Hoses Cumb 153 A3
Hosh Perth 218 B3
Hosta W Isles 287 G2
Hoswick Shetland 285 L6
Hotham E Yorks 150 D1
Hothfield Kent 38 A1
Hoton Leics 114 C3
Houbie Shetland 284 D8
Houdston S Ayrs 181 B3
Hough Ches 128 D2
Hough Ches 128 B3
Hough Green Halton 127 A4
Hough-on-the-Hill Lincs 116 A2
Hougham Lincs 116 A1
Houghton Cambs 101 D4
Houghton Cumb 175 C7
Houghton Hants 32 B2
Houghton Pembs 55 D5
Houghton W Sus 20 A3
Houghton Conquest Beds 84 C2
Houghton Green E Sus 37 D7
Houghton Green Warr 137 D5
Houghton-le-Side Darl 167 C5
Houghton-Le-Spring T & W 167 A6
Houghton on the Hill Leics 98 A3
Houghton Regis Beds 67 A5
Houghton St Giles Norf 119 B6
Houlland Shetland 285 H5
Houlland Shetland 284 F7
Houlsyke N Yorks 159 A6
Hound Hants 18 A3
Hound Green Hants 47 D5
Houndslow Borders 197 B5
Houndwood Borders 211 D5
Hounslow London 48 B4
Hounslow Green Essex 69 B6
Housay Shetland 284 F8
House of Daviot Highld 252 B3
House of Glenmuick Aberds 243 C6
Housesteads Roman Fort Northumb 177 C5
Housetter Shetland 284 E5
Houss Shetland 285 K5
Houston Renfs 205 B4
Houstry Highld 275 A5
Houton Orkney 283 G4
Hove Brighton 21 B5

Hoveringham Notts 115 A4
Hoveton Norf 121 D5
Hovingham N Yorks 159 D5
How Cumb 176 D3
How Caple Hereford 79 D4
How End Beds 84 C2
How Green Kent 36 B2
Howbrook S Yorks 139 D6
Howden Borders 187 A5
Howden E Yorks 141 A5
Howden-le-Wear Durham 167 B4
Howe Highld 281 B5
Howe Norf 104 A3
Howe N Yorks 158 C2
Howe Bridge Gtr Man 137 C5
Howe Green Essex 70 C1
Howe of Teuchar Aberds 256 B2
Howe Street Essex 69 B6
Howe Street Essex 86 D2
Howell Lincs 116 A4
Howey Powys 77 B4
Howgate Midloth 196 A1
Howick Northumb 189 B5
Howle Durham 166 C3
Howle Telford 111 C5
Howlett End Essex 86 D1
Howley Som 14 A2
Hownam Borders 187 B6
Hownam Mains Borders 187 A6
Howpasley Borders 185 B6
Howsham N Lincs 142 C2
Howsham N Yorks 149 A6
Howslack Dumfries 184 B3
Howtel Northumb 198 C2
Howton Hereford 61 A6
Howtown Cumb 164 D2
Howwood Renfs 204 B3
Hoxne Suff 104 D2
Hoy Orkney 283 G3
Hoylake Mers 126 A2
Hoyland S Yorks 139 C6
Hoylandswaine S Yorks 139 C5
Hubberholme N Yorks 156 D3
Hubbert's Bridge Lincs 117 A5
Huby N Yorks 147 C6
Huby N Yorks 149 A4
Hucclecote Glos 63 B4
Hucking Kent 37 A6
Hucknall Notts 114 A3
Huddersfield W Yorks 139 B4
Huddington Worcs 80 B2
Hudswell N Yorks 157 A5
Huggate E Yorks 150 B1
Hugglescote Leics 114 D2
Hugh Town Scilly 2 E4
Hughenden Valley Bucks 66 D3
Hughley Shrops 94 B3
Huish Devon 25 D6
Huish Wilts 45 C5
Huish Champflower Som 27 C5
Huish Episcopi Som 28 C4
Huisinis W Isles 287 C4
Hulcott Bucks 66 B3
Hulland Derbys 113 A6
Hulland Ward Derbys 113 A6
Hullavington Wilts 44 A2
Hullbridge Essex 70 D2
Hulme Gtr Man 138 D1
Hulme End Staffs 129 D6
Hulme Walfield Ches 128 C3
Hulver Street Suff 105 C5
Hulverstone I o W 18 C2
Humber Hereford 78 B3
Humber Bridge E Yorks 142 A2
Humberside International Airport N Lincs 142 B2
Humberston NE Lincs 143 C5
Humbie E Loth 210 D1
Humbleton E Yorks 151 D5
Humbleton Northumb 188 A2
Humby Lincs 116 B3
Hume Borders 197 B6
Humshaugh Northumb 177 B7
Huna Highld 281 A5
Huncoat Lancs 146 D1
Huncote Leics 98 B2
Hundalee Borders 187 B5
Hunderthwaite Durham 166 C2
Hundle Houses Lincs 134 D2
Hundleby Lincs 134 C3
Hundleton Pembs 55 D5
Hundon Suff 86 C3
Hundred Acres Hants 33 D4

Hundred End Lancs 136 A3
Hundred House Powys 77 B5
Hungarton Leics 98 A3
Hungerford Hants 31 D5
Hungerford W Berks 46 C1
Hungerford Newtown W Berks 46 B1
Hungerton Lincs 116 C1
Hungladder Highld 258 A3
Hunmanby N Yorks 161 D4
Hunmanby Moor N Yorks 161 D5
Hunningham Warks 81 A6
Hunny Hill I o W 18 C3
Hunsdon Herts 68 B4
Hunsingore N Yorks 148 B3
Hunslet W Yorks 148 D2
Hunsonby Cumb 164 B3
Hunspow Highld 280 A4
Hunstanton Norf 118 A3
Hunstanworth Durham 166 A2
Hunsterson Ches 111 A5
Hunston Suff 87 A5
Hunston W Sus 20 B1
Hunstrete Bath 43 C5
Hunt End Worcs 80 A3
Hunter's Quay Argyll 203 A6
Hunthill Lodge Angus 232 A2
Hunting-tower Perth 219 B5
Huntingdon Cambs 100 D4
Huntingdon Racecourse Cambs 100 D4
Huntingfield Suff 104 D4
Huntingford Dorset 30 B2
Huntington E Loth 210 C1
Huntington Hereford 77 B6
Huntington Staffs 112 D3
Huntington York 149 B5
Huntley Glos 62 B3
Huntly Aberds 255 C6
Huntlywood Borders 197 B5
Hunton Kent 37 B5
Hunton N Yorks 157 B5
Hunt's Corner Norf 103 C6
Hunt's Cross Mers 127 A4
Huntsham Devon 27 C5
Huntspill Som 28 A3
Huntworth Som 28 B3
Hunwick Durham 167 B4
Hunworth Norf 120 B2
Hurdsfield Ches 129 B4
Hurley Warks 97 B5
Hurley Windsor 47 A6
Hurlford E Ayrs 193 B4
Hurliness Orkney 283 K3
Hurn Dorset 17 B5
Hurn's End Lincs 118 A1
Hursley Hants 32 C3
Hurst N Yorks 156 A4
Hurst Som 29 D4
Hurst Wokingham 47 B5
Hurst Green E Sus 37 D5
Hurst Green Lancs 145 D6
Hurst Wickham W Sus 21 A5
Hurstbourne Priors Hants 32 A3
Hurstbourne Tarrant Hants 46 D1
Hurstpierpoint W Sus 21 A5
Hurstwood Lancs 146 D2
Hurtmore Sur 34 B2
Hurworth Place Darl 157 A6
Hury Durham 166 D2
Husabost Highld 258 C2
Husbands Bosworth Leics 98 C3
Husborne Crawley Beds 83 D6
Husthwaite N Yorks 158 D4
Hutchwns Bridgend 40 D3
Huthwaite Notts 131 D4
Huttoft Lincs 135 B5
Hutton Borders 198 A3
Hutton Cumb 164 C2
Hutton E Yorks 150 B3
Hutton Essex 69 D6
Hutton Lancs 136 A3
Hutton N Som 42 D2
Hutton Buscel N Yorks 160 C3
Hutton Conyers N Yorks 158 D2
Hutton Cranswick E Yorks 150 B3
Hutton End Cumb 164 B2
Hutton Gate Redcar 168 D3
Hutton Henry Durham 168 B2
Hutton-le-Hole N Yorks 159 B6
Hutton Magna Durham 166 D4
Hutton Roof Cumb 163 A6
Hutton Roof Cumb 155 D4
Hutton Rudby N Yorks 158 A3
Hutton Sessay N Yorks 158 D3
Hutton Village Redcar 168 D3

Hutton Wandesley N Yorks 148 B4
Huxley Ches 127 C5
Huxter Shetland 285 H5
Huxter Shetland 285 G7
Huxton Borders 211 D5
Huyton Mers 136 D3
Hwlffordd = Haverfordwest Pembs 55 C5
Hycemoor Cumb 153 B1
Hyde Glos 63 C4
Hyde Gtr Man 138 D2
Hyde Hants 31 D5
Hyde Heath Bucks 67 C4
Hyde Park S Yorks 140 C3
Hydestile Sur 34 B2
Hylton Castle T & W 179 D5
Hyndford Bridge S Lnrk 194 B4
Hynish Argyll 222 D2
Hyssington Powys 93 B7
Hythe Hants 18 A3
Hythe Kent 38 B3
Hythe End Windsor 48 B3
Hythie Aberds 269 D5

I

Ibberton Dorset 16 A1
Ible Derbys 130 D2
Ibsley Hants 17 A5
Ibstock Leics 114 D2
Ibstone Bucks 66 D2
Ibthorpe Hants 46 D1
Ibworth Hants 46 D3
Ichrachan Argyll 227 C5
Ickburgh Norf 103 B4
Ickenham London 48 A3
Ickford Bucks 66 C1
Ickham Kent 53 D4
Ickleford Herts 84 D3
Icklesham E Sus 23 A6
Ickleton Cambs 85 C6
Icklingham Suff 102 D3
Ickwell Green Beds 84 C3
Ickworth House Suff 87 A4
Icomb Glos 64 A3
Idbury Oxon 64 B3
Iddesleigh Devon 11 A6
Ide Devon 12 B3
Ide Hill Kent 36 A2
Ideford Devon 12 D3
Iden E Sus 37 D7
Iden Green Kent 37 C6
Iden Green Kent 37 C5
Idle W Yorks 147 D5
Idlicote Warks 81 C5
Idmiston Wilts 31 B5
Idole Carms 57 A4
Idridgehay Derbys 113 A6
Idrigill Highld 258 B3
Idstone Oxon 45 A6
Idvies Angus 232 D3
Iffley Oxon 65 C6
Ifield W Sus 35 C5
Ifold W Sus 34 C3
Iford E Sus 22 B2
Ifton Heath Shrops 110 B2
Ightfield Shrops 111 B4
Ightham Kent 36 A3
Ightham Mote, Sevenoaks Kent 49 B6
Iken Suff 89 B5
Ilam Staffs 129 D6
Ilchester Som 29 C5
Ilderton Northumb 188 A3
Ilford London 50 A1
Ilfracombe Devon 25 A6
Ilkeston Derbys 114 A2
Ilketshall St Andrew Suff 105 C4
Ilketshall St Lawrence Suff 105 C4
Ilketshall St Margaret Suff 104 C4
Ilkley W Yorks 147 C5
Illey W Mid 96 C2
Illingworth W Yorks 138 A3
Illogan Corn 3 A4
Illston on the Hill Leics 99 B4
Ilmer Bucks 66 C2
Ilmington Warks 81 C5
Ilminster Som 28 D3
Ilsington Devon 12 D2
Ilston Swansea 57 C5
Ilton N Yorks 157 D5
Ilton Som 28 D3
Imachar N Ayrs 202 D3
Imeraval Argyll 200 D3

Immingham NE Lincs 142 B3
Imperial War Museum London 49 B6
Imperial War Museum North Gtr Man 137 D7
Impington Cambs 85 A6
Ince Ches 127 B4
Ince Blundell Mers 136 C2
Ince in Makerfield Gtr Man 137 C4
Inch of Arnhall Aberds 233 A4
Inchbare Angus 233 B4
Inchberry Moray 266 D4
Inchbraoch Angus 233 C5
Incheril Highld 262 D2
Inchgrundle Angus 232 A2
Inchina Highld 261 A6
Inchinnan Renfs 205 B4
Inchkinloch Highld 277 D6
Inchlaggan Highld 239 B5
Inchlumpie Highld 264 C1
Inchmore Highld 251 B5
Inchnacardoch Hotel Highld 240 A1
Inchnadamph Highld 271 B5
Inchree Highld 237 C4
Inchture Perth 220 B2
Inchyra Perth 219 B6
Indian Queens Corn 4 B4
Inerval Argyll 200 D3
Ingatestone Essex 69 D6
Ingbirchworth S Yorks 139 C5
Ingestre Staffs 112 C3
Ingham Lincs 133 A4
Ingham Norf 121 C5
Ingham Suff 103 D4
Ingham Corner Norf 121 C5
Ingleborough Norf 118 D1
Ingleby Derbys 114 C1
Ingleby Lincs 132 B3
Ingleby Arncliffe N Yorks 158 A3
Ingleby Barwick Stockton 168 D2
Ingleby Greenhow N Yorks 159 A4
Inglemire Hull 150 D3
Inglesbatch Bath 43 C6
Inglesham Swindon 64 D3
Ingleton Durham 167 C4
Ingleton N Yorks 155 D5
Inglewhite Lancs 145 C5
Ingliston Edin 208 C4
Ingoe Northumb 178 B2
Ingol Lancs 145 D5
Ingoldisthorpe Norf 118 B3
Ingoldmells Lincs 135 C5
Ingoldsby Lincs 116 B3
Ingon Warks 81 B5
Ingram Northumb 188 B3
Ingrave Essex 69 D6
Ingrow W Yorks 147 D4
Ings Cumb 154 B3
Ingst S Glos 43 A4
Ingworth Norf 120 C3
Inham's End Cambs 101 B4
Inkberrow Worcs 80 B3
Inkpen W Berks 46 C1
Inkstack Highld 281 A4
Inn Cumb 154 A3
Innellan Argyll 203 A6
Innerleithen Borders 196 C2
Innerleven Fife 220 D3
Innermessan Dumfries 170 A2
Innerwick E Loth 211 C4
Innerwick Perth 229 D4
Innis Chonain Argyll 227 D6
Insch Aberds 256 D1
Insh Highld 241 B6
Inshore Highld 276 B4
Inskip Lancs 145 D4
Instoneville S Yorks 140 B3
Instow Devon 25 B5
Intake S Yorks 140 C3
Inver Aberds 243 C5
Inver Highld 265 B4
Inver Perth 230 D4
Inver Mallie Highld 239 D5
Inverailort Highld 235 B6
Inveraldie Angus 220 A4
Inverallign Highld 249 A5
Inverallochy Aberds 269 C5
Inveran Highld 264 A1
Inveraray Argyll 214 B3
Inveraray Jail Argyll 214 B3
Inverarish Highld 248 C2
Inverarity Angus 232 D2
Inverarnan Stirl 215 A6
Inverasdale Highld 261 B5

Inverbeg Argyll 206 A1
Inverbervie Aberds 233 A6
Inverboyndie Aberds 268 C1
Inverbroom Highld 262 B3
Invercassley Highld 272 D2
Invercauld House Aberds 243 C4
Inverchaolain Argyll 203 A5
Invercharnan Highld 227 B6
Inverchoran Highld 251 A4
Invercreran Argyll 227 B5
Inverdruie Highld 242 A2
Inverebrie Aberds 257 C4
Invereck Argyll 215 D4
Inverenan Ho. Aberds 243 A6
Invereshie House Highld 241 B6
Inveresk E Loth 209 C6
Inverewe Gardens, Gairloch Highld 261 B5
Inverey Aberds 242 D3
Inverfarigaig Highld 251 D7
Invergarry Highld 239 B7
Invergelder Aberds 243 C5
Invergeldie Perth 218 B2
Invergordon Highld 264 D3
Invergowrie Perth 220 A3
Inverguseran Highld 247 D6
Inverhadden Perth 229 C5
Inverharroch Moray 255 C4
Inverherive Stirl 216 B3
Inverie Highld 247 E6
Inverinan Argyll 214 A2
Inverinate Highld 249 D6
Inverkeilor Angus 233 D4
Inverkeithing Fife 208 B4
Inverkeithny Aberds 256 B1
Inverkip Invclyd 204 A2
Inverkirkaig Highld 270 C3
Inverlael Highld 262 B3
Inverlochlarig Stirl 216 C4
Inverlochy Argyll 227 D6
Inverlochy Highld 237 B5
Inverlussa Argyll 213 D4
Invermark Lodge Angus 244 D1
Invermoidart Highld 235 C5
Invermoriston Highld 240 A2
Invernaver Highld 278 B3
Inverneill Argyll 213 D6
Inverness Highld 252 B2
Inverness Airport Highld 252 A3
Invernettie Aberds 257 B6
Invernoaden Argyll 215 C4
Inveroran Hotel Argyll 228 D1
Inverpolly Lodge Highld 270 C3
Inverquharity Angus 232 C2
Inverquhomery Aberds 257 B5
Inverroy Highld 239 D6
Inversanda Highld 236 D3
Invershiel Highld 238 A3
Invershin Highld 264 A1
Inversnaid Hotel Stirl 215 B6
Inverugie Aberds 257 B6
Inveruglas Argyll 215 B6
Inveruglass Highld 241 B6
Inverurie Aberds 256 D2
Invervar Perth 229 D5
Inverythan Aberds 256 B2
Inwardleigh Devon 11 B6
Inworth Essex 70 B2
Iochdar W Isles 286 B3
Iona Abbey and Cathedral Argyll 224 D1
Iping W Sus 34 D1
Ipplepen Devon 8 A2
Ipsden Oxon 47 A4
Ipsley Worcs 80 A3
Ipstones Staffs 129 D5
Ipswich Suff 88 C2
Irby Mers 126 A2
Irby in the Marsh Lincs 135 C4
Irby upon Humber NE Lincs 142 C3
Irchester Northants 83 A6
Ireby Cumb 163 A5
Ireby Lancs 155 D5
Ireland Orkney 283 G4
Ireland Shetland 285 L5
Ireland's Cross Shrops 111 A6
Ireleth Cumb 153 C3
Ireshopeburn Durham 165 B6
Irlam Gtr Man 137 D6
Irnham Lincs 116 C3
Iron Acton S Glos 43 A5
Iron Cross Warks 80 B3
Ironbridge Telford 95 A4
Ironbridge Gorge Museum, Telford Shrops 95 A4
Irongray Dumfries 173 A7

Ironmacannie Dumfries 173 A4
Ironside Aberds 268 D3
Ironville Derbys 131 D4
Irstead Norf 121 C5
Irthington Cumb 176 C2
Irthlingborough Northants 99 D6
Irton N Yorks 160 C4
Irvine N Ayrs 192 B3
Isauld Highld 279 B5
Isbister Orkney 282 E3
Isbister Orkney 282 F4
Isbister Shetland 284 D5
Isbister Shetland 285 G7
Isfield E Sus 22 A2
Isham Northants 99 D5
Islay Airport Argyll 200 C3
Isle Abbotts Som 28 C3
Isle Brewers Som 28 C3
Isle of Man Airport I o M 152 E2
Isle of Man Steam Railway I o M 152 E2
Isle of Whithorn Dumfries 171 D6
Isleham Cambs 102 D2
Isleornsay Highld 247 C6
Islesburgh Shetland 284 G5
Islesteps Dumfries 174 A2
Isleworth London 49 B4
Isley Walton Leics 114 C2
Islibhig W Isles 287 B4
Islington London 49 A6
Islip Northants 100 D1
Islip Oxon 65 B6
Istead Rise Kent 50 C3
Isycoed Wrex 127 D4
Itchen Soton 32 D3
Itchen Abbas Hants 32 B4
Itchen Stoke Hants 33 B4
Itchingfield W Sus 35 D4
Itchington S Glos 43 A5
Itteringham Norf 120 B3
Itton Devon 12 B1
Itton Common Mon 61 D6
Ivegill Cumb 164 A2
Iver Bucks 48 A3
Iver Heath Bucks 48 A3
Iveston Durham 178 D3
Ivinghoe Bucks 67 B4
Ivinghoe Aston Bucks 67 B4
Ivington Hereford 78 B2
Ivington Green Hereford 78 B2
Ivy Chimneys Essex 68 C4
Ivy Cross Dorset 30 C2
Ivy Hatch Kent 36 A3
Ivybridge Devon 7 B5
Ivychurch Kent 38 C2
Iwade Kent 51 C6
Iwerne Courtney or Shroton Dorset 30 D2
Iwerne Minster Dorset 30 D2
Ixworth Suff 103 D5
Ixworth Thorpe Suff 103 D5

J

Jack Hill N Yorks 147 B6
Jack in the Green Devon 13 A5
Jacksdale Notts 131 D4
Jackstown Aberds 256 C2
Jacobstow Corn 10 B2
Jacobstowe Devon 11 A6
Jameston Pembs 55 E6
Jamestown Dumfries 185 C6
Jamestown Highld 251 A6
Jamestown W Dunb 206 B1
Jarlshof Prehistoric Site Shetland 285 N5
Jarrow T & W 179 C5
Jarvis Brook E Sus 36 C3
Jasper's Green Essex 69 A7
Java Argyll 225 C6
Jawcraig Falk 207 C6
Jaywick Essex 71 B5
Jealott's Hill Brack 47 B6
Jedburgh Borders 187 A5
Jeffreyston Pembs 55 D6
Jellyhill E Dunb 205 A6
Jemimaville Highld 264 D3
Jersey Airport Jersey 6
Jersey Farm Herts 67 C6
Jersey Zoo & Wildlife Park Jersey 6
Jesmond T & W 179 C4
Jevington E Sus 22 B3
Jockey End Herts 67 B5
Jodrell Bank Visitor Centre, Holmes Chapel Ches 128 B2

John o'Groats Highld 281 A5
Johnby Cumb 164 B2
John's Cross E Sus 37 D5
Johnshaven Aberds 233 B5
Johnston Pembs 55 C5
Johnstone Renfs 205 B4
Johnstonebridge Dumfries 184 C3
Johnstown Carms 57 A4
Johnstown Wrex 110 A2
Joppa Edin 209 C6
Joppa S Ayrs 182 A2
Jordans Bucks 67 D4
Jordanthorpe S Yorks 130 A3
Jorvik Centre York 149 B5
Judges Lodging, Presteigne Powys 77 A7
Jump S Yorks 140 C1
Jumpers Green Dorset 17 B5
Juniper Green Edin 209 D4
Jurby East I o M 152 B3
Jurby South Motor Racing Circuit I o M 152 B3
Jurby West I o M 152 B3

K

Kaber Cumb 165 D5
Kaimend S Lnrk 195 B4
Kaimes Edin 209 D5
Kalemouth Borders 187 A6
Kames Argyll 203 A4
Kames Argyll 213 A6
Kames E Ayrs 194 D1
Kea Corn 4 C3
Keadby N Lincs 141 B6
Keal Cotes Lincs 134 C3
Kearsley Gtr Man 137 C6
Kearstwick Cumb 155 C5
Kearton N Yorks 156 B3
Kearvaig Highld 276 A3
Keasden N Yorks 145 A7
Keckwick Halton 127 A5
Keddington Lincs 134 A3
Kedington Suff 86 C3
Kedleston Derbys 113 A7
Kedleston Hall Derbys 113 A7
Keelby Lincs 142 B3
Keele Staffs 112 A2
Keeley Green Beds 84 C2
Keeston Pembs 55 C5
Keevil Wilts 44 D3
Kegworth Leics 114 C2
Kehelland Corn 3 A4
Keig Aberds 244 A3
Keighley W Yorks 147 C4
Keighley and Worth Valley Railway W Yorks 147 D4
Keil Highld 236 D3
Keilarsbrae Clack 208 A1
Keilhill Aberds 268 D2
Keillmore Argyll 213 D4
Keillour Perth 231 D6
Keills Argyll 201 B4
Keils Argyll 201 B5
Keinton Mandeville Som 29 B5
Keir Mill Dumfries 183 C6
Keisby Lincs 116 C3
Keiss Highld 281 B5
Keith Moray 267 D5
Keith Inch Aberds 257 B6
Keithock Angus 233 B4
Kelbrook Lancs 146 C3
Kelby Lincs 116 A3
Keld Cumb 164 D3
Keld N Yorks 156 A2
Keldholme N Yorks 159 C6
Kelfield N Lincs 141 C6
Kelfield N Yorks 149 D4
Kelham Notts 132 D2
Kellan Argyll 225 B4
Kellas Angus 221 A4
Kellas Moray 266 D2
Kellaton Devon 8 D2
Kelleth Cumb 155 A5
Kelleythorpe E Yorks 150 B2
Kelling Norf 120 A2
Kellingley N Yorks 140 A3
Kellington N Yorks 140 A3
Kelloe Durham 167 B6
Kelloholm Dumfries 183 A5
Kelly Devon 11 C4
Kelly Bray Corn 11 C4
Kelmarsh Northants 99 D4
Kelmscot Oxon 64 D3
Kelsale Suff 89 A4

Kelsall Ches 127 C5
Kelsall Hill Ches 127 C5
Kelshall Herts 85 D5
Kelsick Cumb 175 C4
Kelso Borders 197 C6
Kelso Racecourse Borders 197 C6
Kelstedge Derbys 130 C3
Kelstern Lincs 143 D4
Kelston Bath 43 C6
Keltneyburn Perth 229 D6
Kelton Dumfries 174 A2
Kelty Fife 208 A4
Kelvedon Essex 70 B2
Kelvedon Hatch Essex 69 D5
Kelvin S Lnrk 205 C6
Kelvinside Glasgow 205 B5
Kelynack Corn 2 B1
Kemback Fife 220 C4
Kemberton Shrops 95 A5
Kemble Glos 63 D5
Kemerton Worcs 80 D2
Kemeys Commander Mon 61 C5
Kemnay Aberds 245 A4
Kemp Town Brighton 21 B6
Kempley Glos 62 A2
Kempley Green Warks 96 D4
Kempsey Worcs 79 C6
Kempsford Glos 64 D2
Kempshott Hants 47 D4
Kempston Beds 84 C2
Kempston Hardwick Beds 84 C2
Kempton Shrops 94 C1
Kempton Park Racecourse Sur 48 B4
Kemsing Kent 36 A3
Kemsley Kent 51 C6
Kenardington Kent 38 B1
Kenchester Hereford 78 C2
Kencot Oxon 64 C3
Kendal Cumb 154 B4
Kendoon Dumfries 182 D4
Kendray S Yorks 139 C6
Kenfig Bridgend 40 C3
Kenfig Hill Bridgend 40 C3
Kenilworth Warks 97 D5
Kenilworth Castle Warks 97 D5
Kenknock Stirl 217 A4
Kenley London 35 A6
Kenley Shrops 94 A3
Kenmore Highld 249 A4
Kenmore Perth 230 D1
Kenn Devon 13 C4
Kenn N Som 42 C3
Kennacley W Isles 288 H2
Kennacraig Argyll 202 B3
Kennerleigh Devon 12 A3
Kennet Clack 208 A2
Kennethmont Aberds 255 D6
Kennett Cambs 86 A2
Kennford Devon 13 C4
Kenninghall Norf 103 C6
Kenninghall Heath Norf 103 C6
Kennington Kent 38 A2
Kennington Oxon 65 C6
Kennoway Fife 220 D3
Kenny Hill Suff 102 D2
Kennythorpe N Yorks 149 A6
Kenovay Argyll 222 C2
Kensaleyre Highld 259 C4
Kensington London 49 B5
Kensworth Beds 67 B5
Kensworth Common Beds 67 B5
Kent International Airport Kent 53 C5
Kent Street E Sus 23 A5
Kent Street Kent 37 A4
Kent Street W Sus 35 D5
Kentallen Highld 237 D4
Kentchurch Hereford 61 A6
Kentford Suff 86 A3
Kentisbeare Devon 13 A5
Kentisbury Devon 25 A7
Kentisbury Ford Devon 25 A7
Kentmere Cumb 154 A3
Kenton Devon 13 C4
Kenton Suff 88 A2
Kenton T & W 179 C4
Kenton Bankfoot T & W 179 C4
Kentra Highld 235 D5
Kents Bank Cumb 154 D2
Kent's Green Glos 62 A3
Kent's Oak Hants 32 C2
Kenwick Shrops 110 B3
Kenwyn Corn 4 C3
Keoldale Highld 277 B4
Keppanach Highld 237 C4

Keppoch Highld 249 D6
Keprigan Argyll 190 D2
Kepwick N Yorks 158 B3
Kerchesters Borders 197 C6
Keresley W Mid 97 C6
Kernborough Devon 8 C1
Kerne Bridge Hereford 62 B1
Kerris Corn 2 C2
Kerry Powys 93 C5
Kerrycroy Argyll 203 B6
Kerry's Gate Hereford 78 D1
Kerrysdale Highld 261 C5
Kersall Notts 132 C2
Kersey Suff 87 C6
Kershopefoot Cumb 176 A2
Kersoe Worcs 80 D2
Kerswell Devon 13 A5
Kerswell Green Worcs 79 C6
Kesgrave Suff 88 C3
Kessingland Suff 105 C6
Kessingland Beach Suff 105 C6
Kessington E Dunb 205 A5
Kestle Corn 5 C4
Kestle Mill Corn 4 B3
Keston London 49 C7
Keswick Cumb 163 B5
Keswick Norf 104 A3
Keswick Norf 121 B5
Ketley Telford 111 D5
Ketley Bank Telford 111 D5
Ketsby Lincs 134 B3
Kettering Northants 99 D5
Ketteringham Norf 104 A2
Kettins Perth 220 A2
Kettlebaston Suff 87 B5
Kettlebridge Fife 220 D3
Kettleburgh Suff 88 A3
Kettlehill Fife 220 D3
Kettleholm Dumfries 174 A4
Kettleness N Yorks 169 D6
Kettleshume Ches 129 B4
Kettlesing Bottom N Yorks 147 B6
Kettlesing Head N Yorks 147 B6
Kettlestone Norf 119 B6
Kettlethorpe Lincs 132 B3
Kettletoft Orkney 282 D7
Kettlewell N Yorks 156 D3
Ketton Rutland 100 A1
Kew London 49 B4
Kew Br. London 49 B4
Kew Gardens London 49 B4
Kewstoke N Som 42 C2
Kexbrough S Yorks 139 C6
Kexby Lincs 132 A3
Kexby York 149 B6
Key Green Ches 128 C3
Keyham Leics 98 A3
Keyhaven Hants 18 B2
Keyingham E Yorks 143 A4
Keymer W Sus 21 A6
Keynsham Bath 43 C5
Keysoe Beds 84 A2
Keysoe Row Beds 84 A2
Keyston Cambs 100 D2
Keyworth Notts 115 B4
Kibblesworth T & W 179 D4
Kibworth Beauchamp Leics 98 B3
Kibworth Harcourt Leics 98 B3
Kidbrooke London 49 B7
Kiddemore Green Staffs 95 A6
Kidderminster Worcs 95 D6
Kiddington Oxon 65 A5
Kidlington Oxon 65 B5
Kidmore End Oxon 47 B4
Kidsgrove Staffs 128 D3
Kidstones N Yorks 156 C3
Kidwelly = Cydweli Carms 57 B4
Kiel Crofts Argyll 226 C4
Kielder Northumb 187 D5
Kielder Castle Visitor Centre Northumb 187 D5
Kierfiold Ho. Orkney 282 F3
Kilbagie Clack 208 B2
Kilbarchan Renfs 205 B4
Kilbeg Highld 247 D5
Kilberry Argyll 202 B2
Kilbirnie N Ayrs 204 C3
Kilbride Argyll 226 D3
Kilbride Argyll 226 D3
Kilbride Highld 247 B4
Kilburn Angus 232 B1
Kilburn Derbys 114 A1
Kilburn London 49 A5
Kilburn N Yorks 158 D4
Kilby Leics 98 B3

Kilchamaig Argyll 202 B3
Kilchattan Argyll 212 C1
Kilchattan Bay Argyll 203 C6
Kilchenzie Argyll 190 C2
Kilcheran Argyll 226 C3
Kilchiaran Argyll 200 B2
Kilchoan Argyll 213 A5
Kilchoan Highld 234 D3
Kilchoman Argyll 200 B2
Kilchrenan Argyll 227 D5
Kilconquhar Fife 221 D4
Kilcot Glos 62 A2
Kilcoy Highld 252 A1
Kilcreggan Argyll 215 D5
Kildale N Yorks 159 A5
Kildalloig Argyll 190 D3
Kildary Highld 264 C3
Kildermorie Lodge Highld 263 C7
Kildonan N Ayrs 191 C6
Kildonan Lodge Highld 274 B3
Kildonnan Highld 234 B3
Kildrummy Aberds 244 A1
Kildwick N Yorks 147 C4
Kilfinan Argyll 203 A4
Kilfinnan Highld 239 C6
Kilgetty Pembs 56 B1
Kilgwrrwg Common Mon 61 D6
Kilham E Yorks 150 A3
Kilham Northumb 198 C2
Kilkenneth Argyll 222 C2
Kilkerran Argyll 190 D3
Kilkhampton Corn 24 D3
Killamarsh Derbys 131 A4
Killay Swansea 57 C6
Killbeg Argyll 225 B5
Killean Argyll 202 D1
Killearn Stirl 206 B3
Killen Highld 252 A2
Killerby Darl 167 D4
Killerton House, Exeter Devon 13 A4
Killichonan Perth 229 C4
Killiechonate Highld 239 D6
Killiecrankie Perth 225 B4
Killiecrankie Perth 230 B3
Killiemor Argyll 224 C3
Killiemore House Argyll 224 D3
Killilan Highld 249 C6
Killimster Highld 281 C5
Killin Stirl 217 A5
Killin Lodge Highld 240 B3
Killinallan Argyll 200 A3
Killinghall N Yorks 148 B1
Killington Cumb 155 C5
Killingworth T & W 179 B4
Killmahumaig Argyll 213 C5
Killochyett Borders 196 B3
Killocraw Argyll 190 B2
Killundine Highld 225 B4
Kilmacolm Inclyd 204 B3
Kilmaha Argyll 214 B2
Kilmahog Stirl 217 D6
Kilmalieu Highld 236 D2
Kilmaluag Highld 259 A4
Kilmany Fife 220 B3
Kilmarie Highld 247 C4
Kilmarnock E Ayrs 193 B4
Kilmaron Castle Fife 220 C3
Kilmartin Argyll 213 C6
Kilmaurs E Ayrs 205 D4
Kilmelford Argyll 213 A6
Kilmeny Argyll 200 B3
Kilmersdon Som 43 D5
Kilmeston Hants 33 C4
Kilmichael Argyll 190 C2
Kilmichael Glassary Argyll 214 C2
Kilmichael of Inverlussa Argyll 213 D5
Kilmington Devon 14 B2
Kilmington Wilts 30 B1
Kilmonivaig Highld 239 D5
Kilmorack Highld 251 B6
Kilmore Argyll 226 D3
Kilmore Highld 247 D5
Kilmory Argyll 202 A2
Kilmory Argyll 235 C4
Kilmory Highld 246 D2
Kilmory N Ayrs 191 C5
Kilmuir Highld 258 D2
Kilmuir Highld 252 B2
Kilmuir Highld 264 C3
Kilmuir Highld 258 A3
Kilmun Argyll 215 D4

Kilmun Argyll 214 A2
Kiln Pit Hill Northumb 178 D2
Kilncadzow S Lnrk 194 B3
Kildown Kent 37 C5
Kilnhurst S Yorks 140 D2
Kilninian Argyll 224 B2
Kilninver Argyll 226 D3
Kilnsea E Yorks 143 B6
Kilnsey N Yorks 146 A3
Kilnwick E Yorks 150 C2
Kilnwick Percy E Yorks 149 B1
Kiloran Argyll 212 C1
Kilpatrick N Ayrs 191 C5
Kilpeck Hereford 78 D2
Kilphedir Highld 274 C3
Kilpin E Yorks 141 A5
Kilpin Pike E Yorks 141 A5
Kilrenny Fife 221 D5
Kilsby Northants 98 D2
Kilspindie Perth 220 B2
Kilsyth N Lnrk 207 C5
Kiltarlity Highld 251 B7
Kilton Notts 131 B5
Kilton Som 27 A6
Kilton Thorpe Redcar 169 D4
Kilvaxter Highld 258 B3
Kilve Som 27 A6
Kilvington Notts 115 A5
Kilwinning N Ayrs 204 D3
Kimber worth S Yorks 140 D2
Kimberley Norf 103 A6
Kimberley Notts 114 A3
Kimble Wick Bucks 66 C3
Kimblesworth Durham 167 A5
Kimbolton Cambs 84 A2
Kimbolton Hereford 78 A3
Kimcote Leics 98 C2
Kimmeridge Dorset 16 D3
Kimmerston Northumb 198 C3
Kimpton Hants 32 A1
Kimpton Herts 68 B1
Kinbrace Highld 274 A2
Kinbuck Stirl 218 D2
Kincaple Fife 221 C4
Kincardine Fife 208 B2
Kincardine Highld 264 B2
Kincardine Bridge Fife 208 B2
Kincardine O'Neil Aberds 244 C2
Kinclaven Perth 219 A6
Kincorth Aberdeen 245 B6
Kincorth Ho. Moray 265 D6
Kincraig Highld 241 B6
Kincraigie Perth 230 D3
Kindallachan Perth 230 D3
Kinderland, Scarborough
  N Yorks 160 B4
Kineton Glos 64 A1
Kineton Warks 81 B6
Kinfauns Perth 219 B6
King Edward Aberds 268 D2
King Sterndale Derbys 129 B5
Kingairloch Highld 236 D2
Kingarth Argyll 203 C5
Kingcoed Mon 61 C6
Kingerby Lincs 142 D2
Kingham Oxon 64 A3
Kingholm Quay Dumfries 174 A2
Kinghorn Fife 209 B5
Kingie Highld 239 B5
Kinglassie Fife 209 A5
Kingoodie Perth 220 B3
King's Acre Hereford 78 C2
King's Bromley Staffs 113 D5
King's Caple Hereford 62 A1
King's Cliffe Northants 100 B2
Kings College Chapel,
  Cambridge Cambs 85 B6
King's Coughton Warks 80 B3
King's Heath W Mid 96 C3
Kings Hedges Cambs 85 A6
Kings Langley Herts 67 C5
King's Lynn Norf 118 C3
King's Meaburn Cumb 165 C4
Kings Muir Borders 196 C1
King's Newnham Warks 98 D1
King's Newton Derbys 114 C1
King's Norton Leics 98 A3
King's Norton W Mid 96 D3
King's Nympton Devon 26 D1
King's Pyon Hereford 78 B2
King's Ripton Cambs 101 D4
King's Somborne Hants 32 B2
King's Stag Dorset 30 D1

King's Stanley Glos 63 C4
King's Sutton Northants 82 D1
King's Thorn Hereford 78 D3
King's Walden Herts 67 A6
Kings Worthy Hants 32 B3
Kingsand Corn 6 B3
Kingsbarns Fife 221 C5
Kingsbridge Devon 7 C6
Kingsbridge Som 27 B4
Kingsburgh Highld 258 C3
Kingsbury London 49 A5
Kingsbury Warks 97 B5
Kingsbury Episcopi Som 28 C4
Kingsclere Hants 46 D3
Kingscote Glos 63 D4
Kingscott Devon 25 D6
Kingscross N Ayrs 191 C6
Kingsdon Som 29 C5
Kingsdown Kent 39 A5
Kingseat Fife 208 A4
Kingsey Bucks 66 C2
Kingsfold W Sus 35 C4
Kingsford E Ayrs 205 D4
Kingsford Worcs 95 C6
Kingsforth N Lincs 142 B2
Kingsgate Kent 53 B5
Kingsheanton Devon 25 B6
Kingshouse Hotel Highld 237 D6
Kingside Hill Cumb 175 C4
Kingskerswell Devon 8 A2
Kingskettle Fife 220 D3
Kingsland Anglesey 122 B2
Kingsland Hereford 78 A2
Kingsley Ches 127 B5
Kingsley Hants 33 B6
Kingsley Staffs 112 A4
Kingsley Green W Sus 34 C1
Kingsley Holt Staffs 112 A4
Kingsley Park Northants 83 A4
Kingsmuir Angus 232 D2
Kingsmuir Fife 221 D5
Kingsnorth Kent 38 B2
Kingstanding W Mid 96 B3
Kingsteignton Devon 12 D3
Kingsthorpe Northants 83 A4
Kingston Cambs 85 B5
Kingston Devon 7 C5
Kingston Dorset 16 A1
Kingston Dorset 16 D3
Kingston E Loth 210 B2
Kingston Hants 17 A5
Kingston I o W 18 C3
Kingston Kent 52 D3
Kingston Moray 266 C4
Kingston Bagpuize Oxon 65 D5
Kingston Blount Oxon 66 D2
Kingston by Sea W Sus 21 B5
Kingston Deverill Wilts 30 B2
Kingston Gorse W Sus 20 B3
Kingston Lacy,
  Wimborne Minster
  Dorset 16 A3
Kingston Lisle Oxon 45 A7
Kingston Maurward Dorset 15 B7
Kingston near Lewes E Sus 22 B1
Kingston on Soar Notts 114 C3
Kingston Russell Dorset 15 B5
Kingston St Mary Som 28 C2
Kingston Seymour N Som 42 C3
Kingston Upon Hull Hull 142 A2
Kingston upon Thames
  London 49 C4
Kingston Vale London 49 B5
Kingstone Hereford 78 D2
Kingstone Som 28 D3
Kingstone Staffs 113 C4
Kingstown Cumb 175 C6
Kingswear Devon 8 B2
Kingswells Aberdeen 245 B5
Kingswinford W Mid 96 C1
Kington Hereford 77 B6
Kington Worcs 80 B2
Kington Langley Wilts 44 B3
Kington Magna Dorset 30 C1
Kington St Michael Wilts 44 B3
Kingussie Highld 241 B5
Kingweston Som 29 B5
Kininvie Ho. Moray 254 B4

Kinkell Bridge Perth 218 C4
Kinknockie Aberds 257 B5
Kinlet Shrops 95 C5
Kinloch Fife 220 C2
Kinloch Highld 234 A2
Kinloch Highld 271 A6
Kinloch Highld 247 C5
Kinloch Perth 231 D5
Kinloch Perth 231 D6
Kinloch Hourn Highld 238 B3
Kinloch Laggan Highld 240 D3
Kinloch Lodge Highld 277 C6
Kinloch Rannoch Perth 229 C5
Kinlochan Highld 236 C2
Kinlochard Stirl 217 D4
Kinlochbeoraid Highld 238 D2
Kinlochbervie Highld 276 C3
Kinlocheil Highld 236 B3
Kinlochewe Highld 262 D2
Kinlochleven Highld 237 C5
Kinlochmoidart Highld 235 C6
Kinlochmorar Highld 238 C2
Kinlochmore Highld 237 C5
Kinlochspelve Argyll 225 D5
Kinloid Highld 235 B5
Kinloss Moray 265 D6
Kinmel Bay Conwy 125 A4
Kinmuck Aberds 256 E3
Kinmundy Aberds 245 A5
Kinnadie Aberds 257 B4
Kinnaird Perth 220 B2
Kinnaird Castle Angus 233 C4
Kinneff Aberds 233 A6
Kinnelhead Dumfries 184 B3
Kinnell Angus 233 C4
Kinnerley Shrops 110 C2
Kinnersley Hereford 78 C1
Kinnersley Worcs 79 C6
Kinnerton Powys 77 A6
Kinnesswood Perth 219 D6
Kinninvie Durham 166 C3
Kinnordy Angus 232 C1
Kinoulton Notts 115 B4
Kinross Perth 219 D6
Kinrossie Perth 219 A6
Kinsbourne Green Herts 67 B6
Kinsey Heath Ches 111 A5
Kinsham Hereford 78 A1
Kinsham Worcs 80 D2
Kinsley W Yorks 140 B2
Kinson Bmouth 17 B4
Kintbury W Berks 46 C1
Kintessack Moray 265 D5
Kintillo Perth 219 C6
Kintocher Aberds 244 B2
Kinton Hereford 94 D2
Kinton Shrops 110 D2
Kintore Aberds 245 A4
Kintour Argyll 201 C4
Kintra Argyll 224 D2
Kintra Argyll 200 D3
Kintraw Argyll 213 B6
Kinuachdrachd Argyll 213 C5
Kinveachy Highld 242 A2
Kinver Staffs 95 C6
Kippax W Yorks 148 D3
Kippen Stirl 207 A4
Kippford or Scaur
  Dumfries 173 C6
Kirbister Orkney 283 G4
Kirbister Orkney 282 E7
Kirbuster Orkney 282 E3
Kirby Bedon Norf 104 A3
Kirby Bellars Leics 115 D5
Kirby Cane Norf 105 B4
Kirby Cross Essex 71 A6
Kirby Grindalythe N Yorks 150 A2
Kirby Hill N Yorks 148 A2
Kirby Hill N Yorks 157 A5
Kirby Knowle N Yorks 158 C3
Kirby-le-Soken Essex 71 A6
Kirby Misperton N Yorks 159 D6
Kirby Muxloe Leics 98 A2
Kirby Row Norf 105 B4
Kirby Sigston N Yorks 158 B3
Kirby Underdale E Yorks 149 B7
Kirby Wiske N Yorks 158 C2
Kirdford W Sus 34 D3
Kirk Highld 281 C4
Kirk Bramwith S Yorks 140 B4
Kirk Deighton N Yorks 148 B2
Kirk Ella E Yorks 142 A2
Kirk Hallam Derbys 114 A2
Kirk Hammerton N Yorks 148 B3
Kirk Ireton Derbys 130 D2
Kirk Langley Derbys 113 B6
Kirk Merrington Durham 167 B5

Kirk Michael I o M 152 B3
Kirk of Shotts N Lnrk 207 D6
Kirk Sandall S Yorks 140 C4
Kirk Smeaton N Yorks 140 B3
Kirk Yetholm Borders 188 A1
Kirkabister Shetland 285 K6
Kirkandrews Dumfries 172 D4
Kirkandrews upon Eden
  Cumb 175 C6
Kirkbampton Cumb 175 C6
Kirkbean Dumfries 174 C2
Kirkbride Cumb 175 C5
Kirkbuddo Angus 232 D3
Kirkburn Borders 196 C1
Kirkburn E Yorks 150 B2
Kirkburton W Yorks 139 B4
Kirkby Lincs 142 D2
Kirkby Mers 136 D3
Kirkby N Yorks 158 A4
Kirkby Fleetham N Yorks 157 B6
Kirkby Green Lincs 133 D5
Kirkby In Ashfield Notts 131 D5
Kirkby-in-Furness Cumb 153 B3
Kirkby la Thorpe Lincs 116 A4
Kirkby Lonsdale Cumb 155 D5
Kirkby Malham N Yorks 146 A2
Kirkby Mallory Leics 98 A1
Kirkby Malzeard N Yorks 157 D6
Kirkby Mills N Yorks 159 C6
Kirkby on Bain Lincs 134 C2
Kirkby Overblow N Yorks 148 C2
Kirkby Stephen Cumb 155 A6
Kirkby Thore Cumb 165 C4
Kirkby Underwood Lincs 116 C3
Kirkby Wharfe N Yorks 148 C4
Kirkbymoorside N Yorks 159 C5
Kirkcaldy Fife 209 A5
Kirkcambeck Cumb 176 C3
Kirkcarswell Dumfries 173 D5
Kirkcolm Dumfries 170 A2
Kirkconnel Dumfries 183 A5
Kirkconnell Dumfries 174 B2
Kirkcowan Dumfries 171 A5
Kirkcudbright Dumfries 173 C4
Kirkdale Mers 136 D2
Kirkfieldbank S Lnrk 194 B3
Kirkgunzeon Dumfries 173 B6
Kirkham Lancs 144 D4
Kirkham N Yorks 149 A6
Kirkhamgate W Yorks 139 A5
Kirkharle Northumb 178 A2
Kirkheaton Northumb 178 B2
Kirkheaton W Yorks 139 B4
Kirkhill Angus 233 B4
Kirkhill Highld 252 B1
Kirkhill Midloth 209 D5
Kirkhill Moray 254 C3
Kirkhope Borders 186 A2
Kirkhouse Borders 196 C2
Kirkiboll Highld 277 C6
Kirkibost Highld 247 C4
Kirkinch Angus 231 D7
Kirkinner Dumfries 171 B6
Kirkintilloch E Dunb 205 A6
Kirkland Cumb 162 C3
Kirkland Cumb 165 B4
Kirkland Dumfries 183 C6
Kirkland Dumfries 183 A5
Kirkleatham Redcar 168 C3
Kirklevington Stockton 158 A3
Kirkley Suff 105 B6
Kirklington Notts 132 C1
Kirklington N Yorks 157 C7
Kirklinton Cumb 176 C2
Kirkliston Edin 208 C4
Kirkmaiden Dumfries 170 D3
Kirkmichael Perth 231 C4
Kirkmichael S Ayrs 192 E3
Kirkmuirhill S Lnrk 194 B2
Kirknewton Northumb 198 C3
Kirknewton W Loth 208 D4
Kirkney Aberds 255 C6
Kirkoswald Cumb 164 A3
Kirkoswald S Ayrs 192 E2
Kirkpatrick Durham
  Dumfries 173 A5
Kirkpatrick-Fleming
  Dumfries 175 A5
Kirksanton Cumb 153 B2
Kirkstall W Yorks 147 D6
Kirkstead Lincs 134 C1
Kirkstile Aberds 255 C6
Kirkstyle Highld 281 A5
Kirkton Aberds 256 D1
Kirkton Aberds 268 E1
Kirkton Angus 232 D2
Kirkton Angus 220 A4

Kirkton Borders 186 B4
Kirkton Dumfries 184 D2
Kirkton Fife 220 B3
Kirkton Highld 249 D5
Kirkton Highld 249 B6
Kirkton Highld 265 A4
Kirkton Highld 252 A3
Kirkton Perth 219 C4
Kirkton S Lnrk 194 D4
Kirkton Stirl 217 D5
Kirkton Manor Borders 195 C7
Kirkton of Airlie Angus 231 C7
Kirkton of Auchterhouse
  Angus 220 A3
Kirkton of Auchterless
  Aberds 256 B2
Kirkton of Barevan Highld 253 B4
Kirkton of Bourtie Aberds 256 D3
Kirkton of Collace Perth 219 A6
Kirkton of Craig Angus 233 C5
Kirkton of Culsalmond
  Aberds 256 C1
Kirkton of Durris Aberds 245 C4
Kirkton of Glenbuchat
  Aberds 243 A6
Kirkton of Glenisla Angus 231 B6
Kirkton of Kingoldrum
  Angus 232 C1
Kirkton of Largo Fife 220 D4
Kirkton of Lethendy
  Perth 231 D5
Kirkton of Logie Buchan
  Aberds 257 D4
Kirkton of Maryculter
  Aberds 245 C5
Kirkton of Menmuir
  Angus 232 B3
Kirkton of Monikie Angus 221 A5
Kirkton of Oyne Aberds 256 D1
Kirkton of Rayne Aberds 256 D1
Kirkton of Skene Aberds 245 B5
Kirkton of Tough Aberds 244 A3
Kirktonhill Borders 196 A3
Kirktown Aberds 269 D5
Kirktown of Alvah Aberds 268 C1
Kirktown of Deskford
  Moray 267 C6
Kirktown of Fetteresso
  Aberds 245 D5
Kirktown of Mortlach
  Moray 254 C4
Kirktown of Slains
  Aberds 257 D5
Kirkurd Borders 195 B6
Kirkwall Orkney 282 F5
Kirkwall Airport Orkney 283 G5
Kirkwhelpington
  Northumb 178 A1
Kirmington N Lincs 142 B3
Kirmond le Mire Lincs 142 D3
Kirn Argyll 203 A6
Kirriemuir Angus 232 C1
Kirstead Green Norf 104 B3
Kirtlebridge Dumfries 175 A5
Kirtleton Dumfries 185 D5
Kirtling Cambs 86 B2
Kirtling Green Cambs 86 B2
Kirtlington Oxon 65 B5
Kirtomy Highld 278 B3
Kirton Lincs 117 B6
Kirton Notts 132 C1
Kirton Suff 88 D3
Kirton End Lincs 117 A5
Kirton Holme Lincs 117 A5
Kirton in Lindsey N Lincs 142 D1
Kislingbury Northants 82 B3
Kites Hardwick Warks 82 A1
Kittisford Som 27 C5
Kittle Swansea 57 D5
Kitt's Green W Mid 97 C4
Kitt's Moss Gtr Man 128 A3
Kittybrewster Aberdeen 245 B6
Kitwood Hants 33 B5
Kivernoll Hereford 78 D2
Kiveton Park S Yorks 131 A4
Knaith Lincs 132 A3
Knaith Park Lincs 132 A3
Knap Corner Dorset 30 C2
Knaphill Sur 34 A2
Knapp Perth 220 A2
Knapp Som 28 C3
Knapthorpe Notts 132 D2
Knapton Norf 121 B5
Knapton York 149 B4
Knapton Green Hereford 78 B2
Knapwell Cambs 85 A5
Knaresborough N Yorks 148 B2

Knarsdale Northumb 177 D4
Knauchland Moray 267 D6
Knaven Aberds 256 B3
Knayton N Yorks 158 C3
Knebworth Herts 68 A2
Knebworth House, Stevenage Herts 68 A2
Knedlington E Yorks 141 A5
Kneesall Notts 132 C2
Kneesworth Cambs 85 C5
Kneeton Notts 115 A5
Knelston Swansea 57 D4
Knenhall Staffs 112 B3
Knettishall Suff 103 C5
Knightacott Devon 26 B1
Knightcote Warks 81 B6
Knightley Dale Staffs 112 C2
Knighton Devon 7 C4
Knighton Leicester 98 A2
Knighton Staffs 111 C6
Knighton Staffs 111 A6
Knighton = Tref-y-Clawdd Powys 93 D6
Knightshayes Court Devon 27 D4
Knightswood Glasgow 205 B5
Knightwick Worcs 79 B5
Knill Hereford 77 A6
Knipton Leics 115 B6
Knitsley Durham 166 A4
Kniveton Derbys 130 D2
Knock Argyll 225 C4
Knock Cumb 165 C4
Knock Moray 267 D6
Knockally Highld 275 B5
Knockan Highld 271 C5
Knockandhu Moray 254 D3
Knockando Moray 254 B2
Knockando Ho. Moray 254 B3
Knockbain Highld 252 A2
Knockbreck Highld 258 B2
Knockbrex Dumfries 172 D3
Knockdee Highld 280 B3
Knockdolian S Ayrs 180 C3
Knockenkelly N Ayrs 191 C6
Knockentiber E Ayrs 192 B3
Knockespock Ho. Aberds 255 D6
Knockfarrel Highld 251 A7
Knockglass Dumfries 170 B2
Knockhill Motor Racing Circuit Fife 208 A3
Knockholt Kent 36 A2
Knockholt Pound Kent 36 A2
Knockie Lodge Highld 240 A2
Knockin Shrops 110 C2
Knockinlaw E Ayrs 193 B4
Knocklearn Dumfries 173 A5
Knocknaha Argyll 190 D2
Knocknain Dumfries 170 A1
Knockrome Argyll 201 A5
Knocksharry I o M 152 C2
Knodishall Suff 89 A5
Knole House & Gardens Kent 36 A3
Knolls Green Ches 128 B3
Knolton Wrex 110 B2
Knolton Bryn Wrex 110 B2
Knook Wilts 30 A3
Knossington Leics 99 A5
Knott End-on-Sea Lancs 144 C3
Knotting Beds 84 A2
Knotting Green Beds 84 A2
Knottingley W Yorks 140 A3
Knotts Cumb 164 C2
Knotts Lancs 146 B1
Knotty Ash Mers 136 D3
Knotty Green Bucks 67 D4
Knowbury Shrops 94 D3
Knowe Dumfries 181 D5
Knowehead Dumfries 182 C4
Knowes of Elrick Aberds 267 D7
Knowesgate Northumb 178 A1
Knoweton N Lnrk 194 A2
Knowhead Aberds 269 D4
Knowl Hill Windsor 47 B6
Knowle Bristol 43 B5
Knowle Devon 12 A2
Knowle Devon 13 C5
Knowle Devon 25 B5
Knowle Shrops 94 D3
Knowle W Mid 97 D4
Knowle Green Lancs 145 D6
Knowle Park W Yorks 147 C4
Knowlton Dorset 31 D4
Knowlton Kent 53 D4
Knowsley Mers 136 D3
Knowsley Safari Park Mers 136 D3
Knowstone Devon 26 C3
Knox Bridge Kent 37 B5
Knucklas Powys 93 D6
Knuston Northants 83 A6
Knutsford Ches 128 B2
Knutton Staffs 112 A2
Knypersley Staffs 128 D3
Kuggar Corn 3 D5
Kyle of Lochalsh Highld 249 D4
Kyleakin Highld 247 B6
Kylerhea Highld 247 B6
Kylesknoydart Highld 238 C2
Kylesku Highld 271 A5
Kylesmorar Highld 238 C2
Kylestrome Highld 271 A5
Kyllachy House Highld 252 D3
Kynaston Shrops 110 C2
Kynnersley Telford 111 D5
Kyre Magna Worcs 79 A4

L

La Fontenelle Guern 6
La Planque Guern 6
Labost W Isles 288 C3
Lacasaidh W Isles 288 E4
Lacasdal W Isles 288 D5
Laceby NE Lincs 143 C4
Lacey Green Bucks 66 D3
Lach Dennis Ches 128 B2
Lackford Suff 102 D3
Lacock Wilts 44 C3
Ladbroke Warks 81 B7
Laddingford Kent 37 B4
Lade Bank Lincs 134 D3
Ladock Corn 4 B3
Lady Orkney 282 C7
Ladybank Fife 220 C3
Ladykirk Borders 198 B2
Ladysford Aberds 269 C4
Laga Highld 235 D5
Lagalochan Argyll 214 A1
Lagavulin Argyll 201 D4
Lagg Argyll 201 A5
Lagg N Ayrs 191 C5
Laggan Argyll 200 C2
Laggan Highld 239 C6
Laggan Highld 241 C4
Laggan Highld 235 C6
Laggan S Ayrs 181 C4
Lagganulva Argyll 224 B3
Laide Highld 261 A5
Laigh Fenwick E Ayrs 205 D4
Laigh Glengall S Ayrs 192 D3
Laighmuir E Ayrs 205 D4
Laindon Essex 50 A3
Lair Highld 250 B2
Lairg Highld 272 D3
Lairg Lodge Highld 272 D3
Lairg Muir Highld 272 D3
Lairgmore Highld 252 C1
Laisterdyke W Yorks 147 D5
Laithes Cumb 164 B2
Lake I o W 19 C4
Lake Wilts 31 B5
Lakenham Norf 104 A3
Lakenheath Suff 102 C3
Lakesend Norf 101 B7
Lakeside Cumb 154 C2
Lakeside and Haverthwaite Railway Cumb 153 B2
Laleham Sur 48 C3
Laleston Bridgend 40 D3
Lamarsh Essex 87 D4
Lamas Norf 120 C4
Lambden Borders 197 B6
Lamberhurst Kent 37 C4
Lamberhurst Quarter Kent 37 C4
Lamberton Borders 198 A3
Lambeth London 49 B6
Lambhill Glasgow 205 B5
Lambley Notts 115 A4
Lambley Northumb 177 D4
Lamborough Hill Oxon 65 C5
Lambourn W Berks 46 B1
Lambourne End Essex 69 D4
Lambs Green W Sus 35 C5
Lambston Pembs 55 C5
Lambton T & W 179 D4
Lamerton Devon 11 D5
Lamesley T & W 179 D4
Laminess Orkney 282 D7
Lamington Highld 264 C3
Lamington S Lnrk 195 C4
Lamlash N Ayrs 191 B6
Lamloch Dumfries 182 C3
Lamonby Cumb 164 B2
Lamorna Corn 2 C2
Lamorran Corn 4 C3
Lampardbrook Suff 88 A3
Lampeter = Llanbedr Pont Steffan Ceredig 75 D4
Lampeter Velfrey Pembs 56 A1
Lamphey Pembs 55 D6
Lamplugh Cumb 162 B3
Lamport Northants 99 D4
Lamyatt Som 29 B6
Lana Devon 10 B4
Lanark S Lnrk 194 B3
Lancaster Lancs 145 A4
Lancaster Leisure Park Lancs 145 A4
Lanchester Durham 167 A4
Lancing W Sus 21 B4
Landbeach Cambs 85 A6
Landcross Devon 25 C5
Landerberry Aberds 245 B4
Landford Wilts 31 D6
Landford Manor Wilts 31 C6
Landimore Swansea 57 C4
Landkey Devon 25 B6
Landore Swansea 57 C6
Landrake Corn 6 A2
Land's End Corn 2 C1
Land's End Airport Corn 2 C1
Landscove Devon 8 A1
Landshipping Pembs 55 C6
Landshipping Quay Pembs 55 C6
Landulph Corn 6 A3
Landwade Suff 86 A2
Lane Corn 4 A3
Lane End Bucks 66 D3
Lane End Cumb 153 A2
Lane End Dorset 16 B2
Lane End Hants 33 C4
Lane End I o W 19 C5
Lane End Lancs 146 C2
Lane Ends Lancs 146 D1
Lane Ends Lancs 146 B1
Lane Ends N Yorks 146 C3
Lane Head Derbys 129 B6
Lane Head Durham 166 D4
Lane Head Gtr Man 137 D5
Lane Head W Yorks 139 C4
Lane Side Lancs 137 A6
Laneast Corn 10 C3
Laneham Notts 132 B3
Lanehead Durham 165 A6
Lanehead Northumb 177 A5
Lanercost Cumb 176 C3
Laneshaw Bridge Lancs 146 C3
Lanfach Caerph 41 B7
Langar Notts 115 B5
Langbank Renfs 204 A3
Langbar N Yorks 147 B4
Langburnshiels Borders 186 C4
Langcliffe N Yorks 146 A2
Langdale Highld 278 D2
Langdale End N Yorks 160 B3
Langdon Corn 10 C4
Langdon Beck Durham 165 B6
Langdon Hills Essex 50 A3
Langdyke Fife 220 D3
Langenhoe Essex 71 B4
Langford Beds 84 C3
Langford Devon 13 A5
Langford Essex 70 C2
Langford Notts 132 D3
Langford Oxon 64 C3
Langford Budville Som 27 C6
Langham Essex 87 D6
Langham Norf 120 A2
Langham Rutland 115 D6
Langham Suff 103 E5
Langhaugh Borders 195 C7
Langho Lancs 145 D7
Langholm Dumfries 185 D6
Langleeford Northumb 188 A2
Langley Ches 129 B4
Langley Hants 18 A3
Langley Herts 68 A2
Langley Kent 37 A6
Langley Northumb 177 C6
Langley Slough 48 B3
Langley Warks 81 A4
Langley W Sus 33 C7
Langley Burrell Wilts 44 B3
Langley Common Derbys 113 B6
Langley Heath Kent 37 A6
Langley Lower Green Essex 85 D6
Langley Marsh Som 27 C5
Langley Park Durham 167 A5
Langley Street Norf 105 A4
Langley Upper Green Essex 85 D6
Langney E Sus 22 B4
Langold Notts 131 A5
Langore Corn 10 C4
Langport Som 28 C4
Langrick Lincs 117 A5
Langridge Bath 43 C6
Langridge Ford Devon 25 C6
Langrigg Cumb 175 D4
Langrish Hants 33 C6
Langsett S Yorks 139 C5
Langshaw Borders 197 C4
Langside Perth 218 C2
Langskaill Orkney 282 C5
Langstone Hants 19 A6
Langstone Newport 61 D5
Langthorne N Yorks 157 B6
Langthorpe N Yorks 148 A2
Langthwaite N Yorks 156 A4
Langtoft E Yorks 150 A3
Langtoft Lincs 116 D4
Langton Durham 167 D4
Langton Lincs 134 C2
Langton Lincs 134 B3
Langton N Yorks 149 A6
Langton by Wragby Lincs 133 B6
Langton Green Kent 36 C3
Langton Green Suff 104 D2
Langton Herring Dorset 15 C6
Langton Matravers Dorset 17 D4
Langtree Devon 25 D5
Langwathby Cumb 164 B3
Langwell Ho. Highld 275 B5
Langwell Lodge Highld 271 D4
Langwith Derbys 131 C5
Langwith Junction Derbys 131 C5
Langworth Lincs 133 B5
Lanhydrock House, Bodmin Corn 5 A5
Lanivet Corn 5 A5
Lanlivery Corn 5 B5
Lanner Corn 4 D2
Lanreath Corn 5 B6
Lansallos Corn 5 B6
Lansdown Glos 63 A5
Lanteglos Highway Corn 5 B6
Lanton Borders 187 A5
Lanton Northumb 198 C3
Lapford Devon 12 A2
Laphroaig Argyll 200 D3
Lapley Staffs 112 D2
Lapworth Warks 97 D4
Larachbeg Highld 225 B5
Larbert Falk 207 B6
Larden Green Ches 127 D5
Largie Aberds 255 C7
Largiemore Argyll 214 D2
Largoward Fife 221 D4
Largs N Ayrs 204 C2
Largybeg N Ayrs 191 C6
Largymore N Ayrs 191 C6
Larkfield Invclyd 204 A2
Larkhall S Lnrk 194 A2
Larkhill Wilts 31 A5
Larling Norf 103 C5
Larriston Borders 186 D4
Lartington Durham 166 D3
Lary Aberds 243 B6
Lasham Hants 33 A5
Lashenden Kent 37 B6
Lassington Glos 62 A3
Lassodie Fife 208 A4
Lastingham N Yorks 159 B6
Latcham Som 29 A4
Latchford Herts 68 A3
Latchford Warr 127 A6
Latchingdon Essex 70 C2
Latchley Corn 11 D5
Lately Common Warr 137 D5
Lathbury M Keynes 83 C5
Latheron Highld 275 A5
Latheronwheel Highld 275 A5
Latheronwheel Ho. Highld 275 A5
Lathones Fife 221 D4
Latimer Bucks 67 D5
Latteridge S Glos 43 A5
Lattiford Som 29 C6
Latton Wilts 64 D1
Latton Bush Essex 69 C4
Lauchintilly Aberds 245 A4
Lauder Borders 197 B4
Laugharne Carms 56 A3
Laughterton Lincs 132 B3
Laughton E Sus 22 A3
Laughton Leics 98 C3
Laughton Lincs 116 B3
Laughton Lincs 141 D6
Laughton Common S Yorks 131 A5
Laughton en le Morthen S Yorks 131 A5
Launcells Corn 10 A3
Launceston Corn 10 C4
Launton Oxon 65 A7
Laurencekirk Aberds 233 A5
Laurieston Dumfries 173 B4
Laurieston Falk 208 C2
Lavendon M Keynes 83 B6
Lavenham Suff 87 C5
Laverhay Dumfries 185 C4
Laversdale Cumb 176 C2
Laverstock Wilts 31 B5
Laverstoke Hants 32 A3
Laverton Glos 80 D3
Laverton N Yorks 157 D6
Laverton Som 44 D1
Lavister Wrex 126 D3
Law S Lnrk 194 A3
Lawers Perth 217 A6
Lawers Perth 218 B2
Lawford Essex 88 D1
Lawhitton Corn 11 C4
Lawkland N Yorks 146 A1
Lawley Telford 95 A4
Lawnhead Staffs 112 C2
Lawrenny Pembs 55 D6
Lawshall Suff 87 B4
Lawton Hereford 78 B2
Laxey I o M 152 C4
Laxey Wheel and Mines I o M 152 C4
Laxfield Suff 104 D3
Laxfirth Shetland 285 J6
Laxfirth Shetland 285 H6
Laxford Bridge Highld 276 D3
Laxo Shetland 285 G6
Laxobigging Shetland 284 F6
Laxton E Yorks 141 A5
Laxton Notts 132 C2
Laxton Northants 99 B6
Laycock W Yorks 147 C4
Layer Breton Essex 70 B3
Layer de la Haye Essex 70 B3
Layer Marney Essex 70 B3
Layham Suff 87 C6
Laylands Green W Berks 46 C1
Laytham E Yorks 149 D6
Layton Blkpool 144 D3
Lazenby Redcar 168 C3
Lazonby Cumb 164 B3
Le Planel Guern 6
Le Villocq Guern 6
Lea Derbys 130 D3
Lea Hereford 62 A2
Lea Lincs 132 A3
Lea Shrops 94 C1
Lea Shrops 94 A2
Lea Wilts 44 A3
Lea Marston Warks 97 B5
Lea Town Lancs 145 D4
Leabrooks Derbys 131 D4
Leac a Li W Isles 288 H2
Leachkin Highld 252 B2
Leadburn Midloth 196 A1
Leaden Roding Essex 69 B5
Leadenham Lincs 133 D4
Leadgate Cumb 165 A5
Leadgate Durham 178 D3
Leadgate Northumb 178 D3
Leadhills S Lnrk 183 A6
Leafield Oxon 64 B4
Leagrave Luton 67 A5
Leake N Yorks 158 B3
Leake Commonside Lincs 134 D3
Lealholm N Yorks 159 A6
Lealt Argyll 213 C4
Lealt Highld 259 B5
Leamington Hastings Warks 82 A1
Leamonsley Staffs 96 A4
Leamside Durham 167 A6
Leanaig Highld 252 A1
Leargybreck Argyll 201 A5
Leasgill Cumb 154 C3
Leasingham Lincs 116 A3
Leasingthorne Durham 167 C5
Leasowe Mers 136 D1

Leatherhead Sur 35 A4
Leatherhead Common Sur 35 A4
Leathley N Yorks 147 C6
Leaton Shrops 110 D3
Leaveland Kent 52 D2
Leavening N Yorks 149 A6
Leaves Green London 49 C7
Leazes Durham 178 D3
Lebberston N Yorks 161 C4
Lechlade-on-Thames Glos 64 D3
Leck Lancs 155 D5
Leckford Hants 32 B2
Leckfurin Highld 278 C3
Leckgruinart Argyll 200 B2
Leckhampstead Bucks 83 D4
Leckhampstead W Berks 46 B2
Leckhampstead Thicket
　W Berks 46 B2
Leckhampton Glos 63 B5
Leckie Highld 262 D2
Leckmelm Highld 262 A3
Leckwith V Glam 41 D6
Leconfield E Yorks 150 C3
Ledaig Argyll 226 C4
Ledburn Bucks 67 A4
Ledbury Hereford 79 D5
Ledcharrie Stirl 217 B5
Ledgemoor Hereford 78 B2
Ledicot Hereford 78 A2
Ledmore Highld 271 C5
Lednagullin Highld 278 B3
Ledsham Ches 126 B3
Ledsham W Yorks 140 A2
Ledston W Yorks 140 A2
Ledston Luck W Yorks 148 D3
Ledwell Oxon 65 A5
Lee Argyll 224 D3
Lee Devon 25 A5
Lee Hants 32 D2
Lee Lancs 145 B5
Lee Shrops 110 B3
Lee Brockhurst Shrops 111 C4
Lee Clump Bucks 67 C4
Lee Mill Devon 7 B5
Lee Moor Devon 7 A4
Lee-on-the-Solent Hants 19 A4
Leeans Shetland 285 J5
Leebotten Shetland 285 L6
Leebotwood Shrops 94 B2
Leece Cumb 153 D3
Leechpool Pembs 55 C5
Leeds Kent 37 A6
Leeds W Yorks 148 D1
Leeds Bradford
　International Airport
　W Yorks 147 C6
Leeds Castle Kent 37 A6
Leeds City Art Gallery
　W Yorks 148 D1
Leedstown Corn 3 B4
Leek Staffs 129 D4
Leek Wootton Warks 81 A5
Leekbrook Staffs 129 D4
Leeming N Yorks 157 C6
Leeming Bar N Yorks 157 B6
Lees Derbys 113 B6
Lees Gtr Man 138 C2
Lees W Yorks 147 D4
Leeswood Flint 126 C2
Legbourne Lincs 134 A3
Legerwood Borders 197 B4
Legoland Windsor 48 B2
Legsby Lincs 133 A6
Leicester Leicester 98 A2
Leicester Forest East Leics 98 A2
Leicester Racecourse
　Leics 98 A3
Leigh Dorset 15 A6
Leigh Glos 63 A4
Leigh Gtr Man 137 C5
Leigh Kent 36 B3
Leigh Shrops 94 A1
Leigh Sur 35 B5
Leigh Wilts 63 D6
Leigh Worcs 79 B5
Leigh Beck Essex 51 A5
Leigh Common Som 30 C1
Leigh Delamere Wilts 44 B2
Leigh Green Kent 37 C7
Leigh on Sea Sthend 51 A5
Leigh Park Hants 19 A6
Leigh Sinton Worcs 79 B5
Leigh upon Mendip Som 29 A6
Leigh Woods N Som 43 B4

Leighswood W Mid 96 A3
Leighterton Glos 63 D4
Leighton N Yorks 157 D5
Leighton Powys 93 A6
Leighton Shrops 95 A4
Leighton Som 29 A7
Leighton Bromswold
　Cambs 100 D3
Leighton Buzzard Beds 67 A4
Leinthall Earls Hereford 78 A2
Leinthall Starkes Hereford 78 A2
Leintwardine Hereford 94 D2
Leire Leics 98 B2
Leirinmore Highld 277 B5
Leiston Suff 89 A5
Leitfie Perth 231 D6
Leith Edin 209 C5
Leitholm Borders 198 B1
Lelant Corn 2 B3
Lelley E Yorks 151 D5
Lem Hill Worcs 95 D5
Lemmington Hall
　Northumb 189 B4
Lempitlaw Borders 198 C1
Lenchwick Worcs 80 C3
Lendalfoot S Ayrs 180 C3
Lendrick Lodge Stirl 217 D5
Lenham Kent 37 A6
Lenham Heath Kent 37 B7
Lennel Borders 198 B2
Lennoxtown E Dunb 205 A6
Lenton Lincs 116 B3
Lenton Nottingham 114 B3
Lentran Highld 252 B1
Lenwade Norf 120 D2
Leny Ho. Stirl 217 D6
Lenzie E Dunb 205 A6
Leoch Angus 220 A3
Leochel-Cushnie Aberds 244 A2
Leominster Hereford 78 B2
Leonard Stanley Glos 63 C4
Leonardslee Gardens
　W Sus 35 D5
Leorin Argyll 200 D3
Lepe Hants 18 B3
Lephin Highld 258 D1
Lephinchapel Argyll 214 C2
Lephinmore Argyll 214 C2
Leppington N Yorks 149 A6
Lepton W Yorks 139 B5
Lerryn Corn 5 B6
Lerwick Shetland 285 J6
Lerwick (Tingwall)
　Airport Shetland 285 J6
Lesbury Northumb 189 B5
Leslie Aberds 255 D6
Leslie Fife 220 D2
Lesmahagow S Lnrk 194 C3
Lesnewth Corn 10 B2
Lessendrum Aberds 255 B6
Lessingham Norf 121 C5
Lessonhall Cumb 175 C5
Leswalt Dumfries 170 A2
Letchmore Heath Herts 67 D6
Letchworth Herts 84 D4
Letcombe Bassett Oxon 46 A1
Letcombe Regis Oxon 46 A1
Letham Angus 232 D3
Letham Falk 208 B1
Letham Fife 220 C3
Letham Perth 219 B5
Letham Grange Angus 233 D4
Lethenty Aberds 256 B3
Letheringham Suff 88 B3
Letheringsett Norf 120 B2
Lettaford Devon 12 C2
Lettan Orkney 282 C8
Letterewe Highld 261 C6
Letterfearn Highld 249 D5
Letterfinlay Highld 239 C6
Lettermorar Highld 235 B6
Lettermore Argyll 224 B3
Letters Highld 262 B3
Letterston Pembs 55 B5
Lettoch Highld 242 A3
Lettoch Highld 254 C1
Letton Hereford 78 C1
Letton Hereford 94 D1
Letton Green Norf 103 A5
Letty Green Herts 68 B2
Letwell S Yorks 131 A5
Leuchars Fife 221 B4
Leuchars Ho. Moray 266 C3
Leumrabhagh W Isles 288 F4
Levan Invclyd 204 A2
Levaneag Shetland 285 G6
Levedale Staffs 112 D2

Leven E Yorks 151 C4
Leven Fife 220 D3
Levencorroch N Ayrs 191 C6
Levens Cumb 154 C3
Levens Green Herts 68 A3
Levenshulme Gtr Man 138 D1
Levenwick Shetland 285 L6
Leverburgh = An t-Ob
　W Isles 287 F5
Leverington Cambs 118 D1
Leverton Lincs 117 A7
Leverton Highgate Lincs 117 A7
Leverton Lucasgate Lincs 117 A7
Leverton Outgate Lincs 117 A7
Levington Suff 88 D3
Levisham N Yorks 160 B2
Levishie Highld 240 A2
Lew Oxon 64 C4
Lewannick Corn 10 C3
Lewdown Devon 11 C5
Lewes E Sus 22 A2
Leweston Pembs 55 B5
Lewisham London 49 B6
Lewiston Highld 251 D7
Lewistown Bridgend 40 C4
Lewknor Oxon 66 D2
Leworthy Devon 10 A4
Leworthy Devon 26 B1
Lewtrenchard Devon 11 C5
Lexden Essex 70 A3
Ley Aberds 244 A2
Ley Corn 5 A6
Leybourne Kent 37 A4
Leyburn N Yorks 157 B5
Leyfields Staffs 97 A5
Leyhill Bucks 67 C4
Leyland Lancs 136 A4
Leylodge Aberds 245 A4
Leymoor W Yorks 139 B4
Leys Aberds 269 D5
Leys Perth 220 A2
Leys Castle Highld 252 B2
Leys of Cossans Angus 232 D1
Leysdown-on-Sea Kent 52 B2
Leysmill Angus 233 D4
Leysters Pole Hereford 78 A3
Leyton London 49 A6
Leytonstone London 49 A6
Lezant Corn 10 D4
Leziate Norf 118 D3
Lhanbryde Moray 266 C3
Liatrie Highld 250 C4
Libanus Powys 60 A1
Libberton S Lnrk 195 B4
Liberton Edin 209 D5
Liceasto W Isles 288 H2
Lichfield Staffs 96 A4
Lichfield Cathedral Staffs 113 D5
Lickey Worcs 96 D2
Lickey End Worcs 96 D2
Lickfold W Sus 34 D2
Liddel Orkney 283 K5
Liddesdale Highld 236 D1
Liddington Swindon 45 A6
Lidgate Suff 86 B3
Lidget S Yorks 141 C4
Lidget Green W Yorks 147 D5
Lidgett Notts 131 C6
Lidlington Beds 84 D1
Lidstone Oxon 65 A4
Lieurary Highld 279 B6
Liff Angus 220 A3
Lifton Devon 11 C4
Liftondown Devon 11 C4
Lighthorne Warks 81 B6
Lightwater Sur 48 C2
Lightwater Valley N Yorks 157 D6
Lightwood Stoke 112 A3
Lightwood Green Ches 111 A5
Lightwood Green Wrex 110 A2
Lilbourne Northants 98 D2
Lilburn Tower Northumb 188 A3
Lilleshall Telford 111 D6
Lilley Herts 67 A6
Lilley W Berks 46 B2
Lilliesleaf Borders 186 A4
Lillingstone Dayrell Bucks 83 D4
Lillingstone Lovell Bucks 83 C4
Lillington Dorset 29 D6
Lillington Warks 81 A6
Lilliput Poole 17 B4
Lilstock Som 27 A6
Lilyhurst Shrops 111 D6
Limbury Luton 67 A5
Limebrook Hereford 78 A1
Limefield Gtr Man 137 B7
Limekilnburn S Lnrk 194 A2

Limekilns Fife 208 B3
Limerigg Falk 207 C6
Limerstone I o W 18 C3
Limington Som 29 C5
Limpenhoe Norf 105 A4
Limpley Stoke Wilts 44 C1
Limpsfield Sur 36 A2
Limpsfield Chart Sur 36 A2
Linby Notts 131 D5
Linchmere W Sus 34 C1
Lincluden Dumfries 174 A2
Lincoln Lincs 133 B4
Lincoln Castle Lincs 133 B4
Lincoln Cathedral Lincs 133 B4
Lincomb Worcs 79 A6
Lincombe Devon 7 B6
Lindal in Furness Cumb 153 C3
Lindale Cumb 154 C3
Lindean Borders 196 C3
Lindfield W Sus 35 D6
Lindford Hants 33 B7
Lindifferon Fife 220 C3
Lindisfarne Priory, Holy
　Island Northumb 199 B5
Lindley W Yorks 139 B4
Lindley Green N Yorks 147 C6
Lindores Fife 220 C2
Lindridge Worcs 79 A4
Lindsell Essex 69 A6
Lindsey Suff 87 C5
Linford Hants 17 A5
Linford Thurrock 50 B3
Lingague I o M 152 D2
Lingards Wood W Yorks 138 B3
Lingbob W Yorks 147 D4
Lingdale Redcar 169 D4
Lingen Hereford 78 A1
Lingfield Sur 36 B1
Lingfield Park
　Racecourse Sur 36 B1
Lingreabhagh W Isles 287 F5
Lingwood Norf 105 A4
Linicro Highld 258 B3
Linkenholt Hants 46 D1
Linkhill Kent 37 D6
Linkinhorne Corn 10 D4
Linklater Orkney 283 K5
Linksness Orkney 283 G3
Linktown Fife 209 A5
Linley Shrops 94 B1
Linley Green Hereford 79 B4
Linlithgow W Loth 208 C3
Linlithgow Bridge W Loth 208 C2
Linshiels Northumb 188 C1
Linsiadar W Isles 288 D3
Linsidemore Highld 264 A1
Linslade Beds 67 A4
Linstead Parva Suff 104 D4
Linstock Cumb 176 D2
Linthwaite W Yorks 139 B4
Lintlaw Borders 198 A2
Lintmill Moray 267 C6
Linton Borders 187 A6
Linton Cambs 86 C1
Linton Derbys 113 D6
Linton Hereford 62 A2
Linton Kent 37 B5
Linton Northumb 189 D5
Linton N Yorks 146 A3
Linton W Yorks 148 C2
Linton-on-Ouse N Yorks 148 A3
Linwood Hants 17 A5
Linwood Lincs 133 A6
Linwood Renfs 205 B4
Lionacleit W Isles 286 B3
Lional W Isles 288 A6
Liphook Hants 34 C1
Liscard Mers 136 D2
Liscombe Som 26 B3
Liskeard Corn 6 A1
L'Islet Guern 6
Liss Hants 33 C6
Liss Forest Hants 33 C6
Lissett E Yorks 151 B4
Lissington Lincs 133 A6
Lisvane Cardiff 41 C6
Liswerry Newport 42 A2
Litcham Norf 119 D5
Litchborough Northants 82 B3
Litchfield Hants 46 D2
Litherland Mers 136 D2
Litlington Cambs 85 C5
Litlington E Sus 22 B3
Little Abington Cambs 86 C1
Little Addington Northants 99 D6
Little Alne Warks 80 A4
Little Altcar Mers 136 C2

Little Asby Cumb 155 A5
Little Assynt Highld 271 B4
Little Aston Staffs 96 A3
Little Atherfield I o W 18 C3
Little Ayre Orkney 283 H4
Little-ayre Shetland 285 G5
Little Ayton N Yorks 168 D3
Little Baddow Essex 70 C1
Little Badminton S Glos 44 A2
Little Ballinluig Perth 230 C3
Little Bampton Cumb 175 C5
Little Bardfield Essex 86 D2
Little Barford Beds 84 B3
Little Barningham Norf 120 B3
Little Barrington Glos 64 B3
Little Barrow Ches 127 B4
Little Barugh N Yorks 159 D6
Little Bavington Northumb 178 B1
Little Bealings Suff 88 C3
Little Bedwyn Wilts 45 C6
Little Bentley Essex 71 A5
Little Berkhamsted Herts 68 C2
Little Billing Northants 83 A5
Little Birch Hereford 78 D3
Little Blakenham Suff 88 C2
Little Blencow Cumb 164 B2
Little Bollington Ches 128 A2
Little Bookham Sur 35 A4
Little Bowden Leics 99 C4
Little Bradley Suff 86 B2
Little Brampton Shrops 94 C1
Little Brechin Angus 232 B3
Little Brickhill M Keynes 83 D6
Little Brington Northants 82 A3
Little Bromley Essex 71 A4
Little Broughton Cumb 162 A3
Little Budworth Ches 127 C5
Little Burstead Essex 69 D6
Little Bytham Lincs 116 D3
Little Carlton Lincs 134 A3
Little Carlton Notts 132 D2
Little Casterton Rutland 100 A3
Little Cawthorpe Lincs 134 A3
Little Chalfont Bucks 67 D4
Little Chart Kent 38 A1
Little Chesterford Essex 85 C7
Little Cheverell Wilts 44 D3
Little Chishill Cambs 85 D6
Little Clacton Essex 71 B5
Little Clifton Cumb 162 B3
Little Colp Aberds 256 B2
Little Comberton Worcs 80 C2
Little Common E Sus 23 B5
Little Compton Warks 81 D5
Little Cornard Suff 87 D4
Little Cowarne Hereford 79 B4
Little Coxwell Oxon 64 D3
Little Crakehall N Yorks 157 B6
Little Cressingham Norf 103 A4
Little Crosby Mers 136 C2
Little Dalby Leics 115 D5
Little Dawley Telford 95 A4
Little Dens Aberds 257 B5
Little Dewchurch Hereford 78 D3
Little Downham Cambs 101 C7
Little Driffield E Yorks 150 B3
Little Dunham Norf 119 D5
Little Dunkeld Perth 230 D4
Little Dunmow Essex 69 A6
Little Easton Essex 69 A6
Little Eaton Derbys 114 A1
Little Eccleston Lancs 144 C4
Little Ellingham Norf 103 B6
Little End Essex 69 C5
Little Eversden Cambs 85 B5
Little Faringdon Oxon 64 C3
Little Fencote N Yorks 157 B6
Little Fenton N Yorks 148 D4
Little Finborough Suff 87 B6
Little Fransham Norf 119 D6
Little Gaddesden Herts 67 B4
Little Gidding Cambs 100 C3
Little Glemham Suff 88 B4
Little Glenshee Perth 219 A4
Little Green Som 29 A7
Little Gransden Cambs 85 B4
Little Grimsby Lincs 143 D5
Little Gruinard Highld 261 B6
Little Habton N Yorks 159 D6
Little Hadham Herts 68 A4
Little Hale Lincs 116 A4
Little Hallingbury Essex 69 B4
Little Hampden Bucks 66 C3
Little Harrowden Northants 99 D5
Little Haseley Oxon 66 C1
Little Hatfield E Yorks 151 C4
Little Hautbois Norf 121 C4

Little Haven Pembs 55 C4
Little Hay Staffs 96 A4
Little Hayfield Derbys 129 A5
Little Haywood Staffs 112 C4
Little Heath W Mid 97 C6
Little Hereford Hereford 78 A3
Little Horkesley Essex 87 D5
Little Horsted E Sus 22 A2
Little Horton W Yorks 147 D5
Little Horwood Bucks 83 D4
Little Houghton Northants 83 B5
Little Houghton S Yorks 140 C2
Little Hucklow Derbys 129 B6
Little Hulton Gtr Man 137 C6
Little Humber E Yorks 142 A3
Little Hungerford W Berks 46 B3
Little Irchester Northants 83 A6
Little Kimble Bucks 66 C3
Little Kineton Warks 81 B6
Little Kingshill Bucks 66 D3
Little Langdale Cumb 154 A2
Little Langford Wilts 31 B4
Little Laver Essex 69 C5
Little Leigh Ches 127 B6
Little Leighs Essex 69 B7
Little Lever Gtr Man 137 C6
Little London Bucks 66 B1
Little London E Sus 22 A3
Little London Hants 32 A2
Little London Hants 47 D4
Little London Lincs 117 C5
Little London Lincs 118 C1
Little London Lincs 120 C3
Little London Norf 92 C4
Little Longstone Derbys 130 B1
Little Lynturk Aberds 244 A2
Little Malvern Worcs 79 C5
Little Maplestead Essex 87 D4
Little Marcle Hereford 79 D4
Little Marlow Bucks 47 A6
Little Marsden Lancs 146 D2
Little Massingham Norf 119 C4
Little Melton Norf 104 A2
Little Mill Mon 61 C5
Little Milton Oxon 65 C7
Little Missenden Bucks 67 D4
Little Musgrave Cumb 165 D5
Little Ness Shrops 110 D3
Little Neston Ches 126 B2
Little Newcastle Pembs 55 B5
Little Newsham Durham 166 D4
Little Oakley Essex 71 A6
Little Oakley Northants 99 C5
Little Orton Cumb 175 C6
Little Ouseburn N Yorks 148 A3
Little Paxton Cambs 84 A3
Little Petherick Corn 9 D5
Little Pitlurg Moray 255 B5
Little Plumpton Lancs 144 D3
Little Plumstead Norf 121 D5
Little Ponton Lincs 116 B2
Little Raveley Cambs 101 D4
Little Reedness E Yorks 141 A6
Little Ribston N Yorks 148 B2
Little Rissington Glos 64 B2
Little Ryburgh Norf 119 C6
Little Ryle Northumb 188 B3
Little Salkeld Cumb 164 B3
Little Sampford Essex 86 D2
Little Sandhurst Brack 47 C6
Little Saxham Suff 86 A3
Little Scatwell Highld 251 A5
Little Sessay N Yorks 158 D3
Little Shelford Cambs 85 B6
Little Singleton Lancs 144 D3
Little Skillymarno Aberds 269 D4
Little Smeaton N Yorks 140 B3
Little Snoring Norf 119 B6
Little Sodbury S Glos 43 A6
Little Somborne Hants 32 B2
Little Somerford Wilts 44 A3
Little Stainforth N Yorks 146 A2
Little Stainton Darl 167 C6
Little Stanney Ches 127 B4
Little Staughton Beds 84 A3
Little Steeping Lincs 135 C4
Little Stoke Staffs 112 B3
Little Stonham Suff 88 A2
Little Stretton Leics 98 A3
Little Stretton Shrops 94 B2
Little Strickland Cumb 164 D3
Little Stukeley Cambs 100 D4
Little Sutton Ches 126 B3
Little Tew Oxon 65 A4
Little Thetford Cambs 102 D1
Little Thirkleby N Yorks 158 D3
Little Thurlow Suff 86 B2

Little Thurrock Thurrock 50 B3
Little Torboll Highld 264 A3
Little Torrington Devon 25 D5
Little Totham Essex 70 B2
Little Toux Aberds 267 D6
Little Town Cumb 163 C5
Little Town Lancs 145 D6
Little Urswick Cumb 153 C3
Little Wakering Essex 51 A6
Little Walden Essex 86 D1
Little Waldingfield Suff 87 C5
Little Walsingham Norf 119 B6
Little Waltham Essex 69 B7
Little Warley Essex 69 D6
Little Weighton E Yorks 150 D2
Little Weldon Northants 99 C6
Little Welnetham Suff 87 A4
Little Wenlock Telford 95 A4
Little Whittingham Green Suff 104 D3
Little Wilbraham Cambs 86 B1
Little Wishford Wilts 31 B4
Little Witley Worcs 79 A5
Little Wittenham Oxon 65 D6
Little Wolford Warks 81 D5
Little Wratting Suff 86 C2
Little Wymington Beds 83 A6
Little Wymondley Herts 68 A2
Little Wyrley Staffs 96 A3
Little Yeldham Essex 86 D3
Littlebeck N Yorks 160 A2
Littleborough Gtr Man 138 B2
Littleborough Notts 132 A3
Littlebourne Kent 53 D4
Littlebredy Dorset 15 C5
Littlebury Essex 85 D7
Littlebury Green Essex 85 D6
Littledean Glos 62 B2
Littleferry Highld 265 A4
Littleham Devon 13 C5
Littleham Devon 25 C5
Littlehampton W Sus 20 B3
Littlehempston Devon 8 A2
Littlehoughton Northumb 189 B5
Littlemill Aberds 243 C6
Littlemill E Ayrs 182 A2
Littlemill Highld 253 A5
Littlemill Northumb 189 B5
Littlemoor Dorset 15 C6
Littlemore Oxon 65 C6
Littleover Derby 114 B1
Littleport Cambs 102 C1
Littlestone on Sea Kent 38 C2
Littlethorpe Leics 98 B2
Littlethorpe N Yorks 148 A2
Littleton Ches 127 C4
Littleton Hants 32 B3
Littleton Perth 220 A2
Littleton Som 29 B4
Littleton Sur 48 C3
Littleton Sur 34 B2
Littleton Drew Wilts 44 A2
Littleton-on-Severn S Glos 43 A4
Littleton Pannell Wilts 44 D4
Littletown Durham 167 A6
Littlewick Green Windsor 47 B6
Littleworth Beds 84 C2
Littleworth Glos 63 C4
Littleworth Oxon 64 D4
Littleworth Staffs 112 D4
Littleworth Worcs 80 B1
Litton Derbys 129 B6
Litton N Yorks 156 D3
Litton Som 43 D4
Litton Cheney Dorset 15 B5
Liurbost W Isles 288 E4
Liverpool Mers 136 D2
Liverpool Airport Mers 127 A4
Liverpool Cathedral (C of E) Mers 126 A3
Liverpool Cathedral (RC) Mers 136 D2
Liverpool John Lennon Airport Mers 127 A4
Liversedge W Yorks 139 A5
Liverton Devon 12 D3
Liverton Redcar 169 D5
Livingston W Loth 208 D3
Livingston Village W Loth 208 D3
Lixwm Flint 125 B6
Lizard Corn 3 D5
Llaingoch Anglesey 122 B2
Llaithddu Powys 93 C4
Llan Powys 91 B6
Llanaber Gwyn 90 A4

Llanaelhaearn Gwyn 106 B3
Llanafan Ceredig 75 A5
Llanafan-fawr Powys 76 B3
Llanallgo Anglesey 123 B4
Llanandras = Presteigne Powys 77 A7
Llanarmon Gwyn 107 C4
Llanarmon Dyffryn Ceiriog Wrex 109 B6
Llanarmon-yn-Ial Denb 126 D1
Llanarth Mon 61 B5
Llanarth Ceredig 73 A7
Llanarthne Carms 58 C2
Llanasa Flint 125 A6
Llanbabo Anglesey 122 B3
Llanbadarn Fawr Ceredig 90 D4
Llanbadarn Fynydd Powys 93 D5
Llanbadarn-y-Garreg Powys 77 C5
Llanbadoc Mon 61 C5
Llanbadrig Anglesey 122 A3
Llanbeder Newport 61 D5
Llanbedr Gwyn 107 D5
Llanbedr Powys 77 C5
Llanbedr Powys 60 A4
Llanbedr-Dyffryn-Clwyd Denb 125 D6
Llanbedr Pont Steffan = Lampeter Ceredig 75 D4
Llanbedr-y-cennin Conwy 124 C2
Llanbedrgoch Anglesey 123 B5
Llanbedrog Gwyn 106 C3
Llanberis Gwyn 123 D5
Llanbethêry V Glam 41 E5
Llanbister Powys 93 D5
Llanblethian V Glam 41 D4
Llanboidy Carms 73 D5
Llanbradach Caerph 41 B6
Llanbrynmair Powys 91 B6
Llancarfan V Glam 41 D5
Llancayo Mon 61 C5
Llancloudy Hereford 61 A6
Llancynfelyn Ceredig 90 C4
Llandaff Cardiff 41 D6
Llandanwg Gwyn 107 D5
Llandarcy Neath 40 B2
Llandawke Carms 56 A2
Llanddaniel Fab Anglesey 123 C4
Llanddarog Carms 57 A5
Llanddeiniol Ceredig 75 A4
Llanddeiniolen Gwyn 123 D5
Llandderfel Gwyn 109 B4
Llanddeusant Anglesey 122 B3
Llanddeusant Carms 59 C4
Llanddew Powys 77 D4
Llanddewi Swansea 57 D4
Llanddewi-Brefi Ceredig 75 C5
Llanddewi Rhydderch Mon 61 B5
Llanddewi Velfrey Pembs 56 A1
Llanddewi'r Cwm Powys 76 C4
Llanddoged Conwy 124 C3
Llanddona Anglesey 123 C5
Llanddowror Carms 56 A2
Llanddulas Conwy 125 B4
Llanddwywe Gwyn 107 D5
Llanddyfnan Anglesey 123 C5
Llandefaelog Fach Powys 76 D4
Llandefaelog-tre'r-graig Powys 77 E5
Llandefalle Powys 77 D5
Llandegai Gwyn 123 C5
Llandegfan Anglesey 123 C5
Llandegla Denb 126 D1
Llandegley Powys 77 A5
Llandegveth Mon 61 D5
Llandegwning Gwyn 106 C2
Llandeilo Carms 58 C3
Llandeilo Graban Powys 77 C4
Llandeilo'r Fan Powys 59 B5
Llandeloy Pembs 55 B4
Llandenny Mon 61 C6
Llandevenny Mon 42 A3
Llandewednock Corn 3 D5
Llandewi Ystradenny Powys 77 A5
Llandinabo Hereford 61 A7
Llandinam Powys 92 C4
Llandissilio Pembs 55 B7
Llandogo Mon 62 C1
Llandough V Glam 41 D5
Llandough V Glam 41 D6
Llandovery = Llanymddyfri Carms 59 B4
Llandow V Glam 40 D4
Llandre Ceredig 90 D4
Llandre Carms 58 A3

Llandrillo Denb 109 B5
Llandrillo-yn-Rhos Conwy 124 A3
Llandrindod = Llandrindod Wells Powys 77 A4
Llandrindod Wells = Llandrindod Powys 77 A4
Llandrinio Powys 110 D1
Llandudno Conwy 124 A2
Llandudno Junction = Cyffordd Llandudno Conwy 124 B2
Llandwrog Gwyn 107 A4
Llandybie Carms 57 A6
Llandyfaelog Carms 57 A4
Llandyfan Carms 57 A6
Llandyfriog Ceredig 73 B6
Llandyfrydog Anglesey 123 B4
Llandygwydd Ceredig 73 B5
Llandynan Denb 109 A6
Llandyrnog Denb 125 C6
Llandysilio Powys 110 D1
Llandyssil Powys 93 B5
Llandysul Ceredig 73 B7
Llanedeyrn Cardiff 41 C7
Llanedi Carms 57 B5
Llaneglwys Powys 77 D4
Llanegryn Gwyn 90 B3
Llanegwad Carms 58 C2
Llaneilian Anglesey 123 A4
Llanelian-yn-Rhos Conwy 124 B3
Llanelidan Denb 125 D6
Llanelieu Powys 77 D5
Llanellen Mon 61 B5
Llanelli Carms 57 C5
Llanelltyd Gwyn 91 A5
Llanelly Mon 60 B4
Llanelly Hill Mon 60 B4
Llanelwedd Powys 76 B4
Llanelwy = St Asaph Denb 125 B5
Llanenddwyn Gwyn 107 D5
Llanengan Gwyn 106 D2
Llanerchymedd Anglesey 123 B4
Llanerfyl Powys 92 A4
Llanfachraeth Anglesey 122 B3
Llanfachreth Gwyn 108 C2
Llanfaelog Anglesey 122 C3
Llanfaelrhys Powys 106 D2
Llanfaenor Mon 61 B6
Llanfaes Anglesey 123 C6
Llanfaes Powys 60 A2
Llanfaethlu Anglesey 122 B3
Llanfaglan Gwyn 123 D4
Llanfair Gwyn 107 D5
Llanfair-ar-y-bryn Carms 59 B5
Llanfair Caereinion Powys 93 A5
Llanfair Clydogau Ceredig 75 C5
Llanfair-Dyffryn-Clwyd Denb 125 D6
Llanfair Kilgheddin Mon 61 C5
Llanfair-Nant-Gwyn Pembs 73 C4
Llanfair Talhaiarn Conwy 125 B4
Llanfair Waterdine Shrops 93 D6
Llanfair-ym-Muallt = Builth Wells Powys 76 B4
Llanfairfechan Conwy 124 B1
Llanfairpwll-gwyngyll Anglesey 123 C5
Llanfairyneubwll Anglesey 122 C3
Llanfairynghornwy Anglesey 122 A3
Llanfallteg Carms 56 A1
Llanfaredd Powys 77 B4
Llanfarian Ceredig 75 A4
Llanfechain Powys 109 C6
Llanfechan Powys 76 B3
Llanfechell Anglesey 122 A3
Llanfendigaid Gwyn 90 B3
Llanferres Denb 126 C1
Llanfflewyn Anglesey 122 B3
Llanfihangel-ar-arth Carms 58 B1
Llanfihangel-Crucorney Mon 61 A5
Llanfihangel Glyn Myfyr Conwy 109 A4
Llanfihangel Nant Bran Powys 59 B6
Llanfihangel-nant-Melan Powys 77 B5
Llanfihangel Rhydithon Powys 77 A5
Llanfihangel Rogiet Mon 42 A3
Llanfihangel Tal-y-llyn Powys 60 A3

Llanfihangel-uwch-Gwili Carms 58 C1
Llanfihangel-y-Creuddyn Ceredig 75 A5
Llanfihangel-y-pennant Gwyn 107 B5
Llanfihangel-y-pennant Gwyn 91 B4
Llanfihangel-y-traethau Gwyn 107 C5
Llanfihangel-yn-Ngwynfa Powys 109 D5
Llanfihangel yn Nhowyn Anglesey 122 C3
Llanfilo Powys 77 D5
Llanfoist Powys 61 B4
Llanfor Gwyn 108 B4
Llanfrechfa Torf 61 D5
Llanfrothen Gwyn 107 B6
Llanfrynach Powys 60 A2
Llanfwrog Anglesey 122 B3
Llanfwrog Denb 125 D6
Llanfyllin Powys 109 D6
Llanfynydd Carms 58 C2
Llanfynydd Flint 126 D2
Llanfyrnach Pembs 73 C5
Llangadfan Powys 109 D5
Llangadog Carms 59 C4
Llangadwaladr Anglesey 122 D3
Llangadwaladr Powys 109 B6
Llangaffo Anglesey 123 D4
Llangain Carms 56 A3
Llangammarch Wells Powys 76 C3
Llangan V Glam 41 D4
Llangarron Hereford 62 A1
Llangasty Talyllyn Powys 60 A3
Llangathen Carms 58 C2
Llangattock Powys 60 B4
Llangattock Lingoed Mon 61 A5
Llangattock nigh Usk Mon 61 C5
Llangattock-Vibon-Avel Mon 61 B6
Llangedwyn Powys 109 C6
Llangefni Anglesey 123 C4
Llangeinor Bridgend 40 C4
Llangeitho Ceredig 75 C5
Llangeler Carms 73 C6
Llangelynin Gwyn 90 B3
Llangendeirne Carms 57 A4
Llangennech Carms 57 B5
Llangennith Swansea 57 C4
Llangenny Powys 60 B4
Llangernyw Conwy 124 C3
Llangian Gwyn 106 D2
Llanglydwen Carms 73 D4
Llangoed Anglesey 123 C6
Llangoedmor Ceredig 73 B4
Llangollen Denb 109 A7
Llangolman Powys 55 B7
Llangors Powys 60 A3
Llangovan Mon 61 C6
Llangower Gwyn 108 B4
Llangrannog Ceredig 73 A6
Llangristiolus Anglesey 123 C4
Llangrove Hereford 62 B1
Llangua Mon 61 A5
Llangunllo Powys 93 D6
Llangunnor Carms 57 A4
Llangurig Powys 92 D3
Llangwm Conwy 109 A4
Llangwm Mon 61 C6
Llangwm Pembs 55 D5
Llangwnnadl Gwyn 106 C2
Llangwyfan Denb 125 C6
Llangwyfan-isaf Anglesey 122 D3
Llangwyllog Anglesey 123 C4
Llangwyryfon Ceredig 75 A4
Llangybi Gwyn 107 B4
Llangybi Mon 61 D5
Llangybi Ceredig 75 C5
Llangyfelach Swansea 57 C6
Llangynhafal Denb 125 C6
Llangynidr Powys 60 B3
Llangynin Carms 56 A2
Llangynog Carms 56 A3
Llangynog Powys 109 C5
Llangynwyd Bridgend 40 C3
Llanhamlach Powys 60 A2
Llanharan Rhondda 41 C5
Llanharry Rhondda 41 C5
Llanhilleth = Llanhilleth Bl Gwent 41 A7

Llanhilleth = Llanhiledd
Bl Gwent 41 A7
Llanidloes Powys 92 C3
Llaniestyn Gwyn 106 C2
Llanifyny Powys 91 D6
Llanigon Powys 77 D6
Llanilar Ceredig 75 A5
Llanilid Rhondda 41 C4
Llanilltud Fawr =
Llantwit Major V Glam 41 E4
Llanishen Cardiff 41 C6
Llanishen Mon 61 C6
Llanllawddog Carms 58 C1
Llanllechid Gwyn 123 D6
Llanllowell Mon 61 D5
Llanllugan Powys 93 A4
Llanllwch Carms 56 A3
Llanllwchaiarn Powys 93 B5
Llanllwni Carms 58 B1
Llanllyfni Gwyn 107 A4
Llanmadoc Swansea 57 C4
Llanmaes V Glam 41 E4
Llanmartin Newport 42 A2
Llanmihangel V Glam 41 D4
Llanmorlais Swansea 57 C5
Llannefydd Conwy 125 B4
Llannon Carms 57 B5
Llannor Gwyn 106 C3
Llanon Ceredig 75 B4
Llanover Mon 61 C5
Llanpumsaint Carms 73 D7
Llanreithan Pembs 55 B4
Llanrhaeadr Denb 125 C5
Llanrhaeadr-ym-
Mochnant Powys 109 C6
Llanrhian Pembs 54 A4
Llanrhidian Swansea 57 C4
Llanrhos Conwy 124 A2
Llanrhyddlad Anglesey 122 B3
Llanrhystud Ceredig 75 B4
Llanrosser Hereford 77 D6
Llanrothal Hereford 61 B6
Llanrug Gwyn 123 D5
Llanrumney Cardiff 41 C7
Llanrwst Conwy 124 C3
Llansadurnen Carms 56 A2
Llansadwrn Anglesey 123 C5
Llansadwrn Carms 58 B3
Llansaint Carms 56 B3
Llansamlet Swansea 40 B1
Llansannan Conwy 125 C4
Llansannor V Glam 41 D4
Llansantffraed Ceredig 75 B4
Llansantffraed Powys 60 A3
Llansantffraed
Cwmdeuddwr Powys 76 A3
Llansantffraed-in-Elvel
Powys 77 B4
Llansantffraid-ym-
Mechain Powys 109 C7
Llansawel Carms 58 B3
Llansilin Powys 109 C7
Llansoy Mon 61 C6
Llanspyddid Powys 60 A2
Llanstadwell Pembs 55 D5
Llansteffan Carms 56 A3
Llanstephan Powys 77 C5
Llantarnam Torf 61 D5
Llanteg Pembs 56 A1
Llanthony Mon 61 A4
Llantilio Crossenny Mon 61 B5
Llantilio Pertholey Mon 61 B5
Llantood Pembs 73 B4
Llantrisant Anglesey 122 B3
Llantrisant Mon 61 D5
Llantrisant Rhondda 41 C5
Llantrithyd V Glam 41 D5
Llantwit Fardre Rhondda 41 C5
Llantwit Major =
Llanilltud Fawr V Glam 41 E4
Llanuwchllyn Gwyn 108 B3
Llanvaches Newport 61 D6
Llanvair Discoed Mon 61 D6
Llanvapley Mon 61 B5
Llanvetherine Mon 61 B5
Llanveynoe Hereford 77 D7
Llanvihangel Gobion Mon 61 C5
Llanvihangel-Ystern-
Llewern Mon 61 B6
Llanwarne Hereford 61 A7
Llanwddyn Powys 109 D5
Llanwenog Ceredig 74 D3
Llanwern Newport 42 A2
Llanwinio Carms 73 D5

Llanwnda Gwyn 107 A4
Llanwnda Pembs 72 C2
Llanwnnen Ceredig 75 D4
Llanwnog Powys 92 B4
Llanwrda Carms 59 B4
Llanwrin Powys 91 B5
Llanwrthwl Powys 76 A3
Llanwrtud = Llanwrtyd
Wells Powys 76 C2
Llanwrtyd Powys 76 C2
Llanwrtyd Wells =
Llanwrtud Powys 76 C2
Llanwyddelan Powys 93 A4
Llanyblodwel Shrops 110 C1
Llanybri Carms 56 A3
Llanybydder Carms 58 A2
Llanycefn Pembs 55 B6
Llanychaer Pembs 72 C2
Llanycil Gwyn 108 B4
Llanycrwys Carms 75 D5
Llanymawddwy Gwyn 91 A7
Llanymddyfri =
Llandovery Carms 59 B4
Llanymynech Powys 110 C1
Llanynghenedl Anglesey 122 B3
Llanynys Denb 125 C6
Llanyre Powys 76 A4
Llanystumdwy Gwyn 107 C4
Llanywern Powys 60 A3
Llawhaden Pembs 55 C6
Llawnt Shrops 110 B1
Llawr Dref Gwyn 106 D2
Llawryglyn Powys 92 B3
Llay Wrex 126 D3
Llechcynfarwy Anglesey 122 B3
Llecheiddior Gwyn 107 B4
Llechfaen Powys 60 A2
Llechryd Caerph 60 C3
Llechryd Ceredig 73 B5
Llechrydau Powys 110 B1
Llechwedd Slate
Caverns, Blaenau
Ffestiniog Gwyn 108 A2
Lledrod Ceredig 75 A5
Llenmerewig Powys 93 B5
Llethrid Swansea 57 C5
Llidiad Nenog Carms 58 B2
Llidiardau Powys 108 B3
Llidiart-y-parc Denb 109 A6
Llithfaen Gwyn 106 B3
Llong Flint 126 C2
Llowes Powys 77 C5
Llundain-fach Ceredig 75 C4
Llwydcoed Rhondda 41 A4
Llwyn Shrops 93 C6
Llwyn-du Mon 61 B4
Llwyn-hendy Carms 57 C5
Llwyn-têg Carms 57 B5
Llwyn-y-brain Carms 56 A1
Llwyn-y-groes Ceredig 75 C4
Llwyncelyn Ceredig 74 C3
Llwyndafydd Ceredig 73 A6
Llwynderw Powys 93 A6
Llwyndyrys Gwyn 106 B3
Llwyngwril Gwyn 90 B3
Llwynmawr Wrex 110 B1
Llwynypia Rhondda 41 B4
Llynclys Shrops 110 C1
Llynfaes Anglesey 123 C4
Llys-y-frân Pembs 55 B6
Llysfaen Conwy 124 B3
Llyswen Powys 77 D5
Llysworney V Glam 41 D4
Llywel Powys 59 B5
Loan Falk 208 C2
Loanend Northumb 198 A3
Loanhead Midloth 209 D5
Loans S Ayrs 192 B3
Loans of Tullich Highld 265 C4
Lobb Devon 25 B5
Loch a Charnain W Isles 286 B4
Loch a'Ghainmhich
W Isles 288 E3
Loch Baghasdail =
Lochboisdale W Isles 286 E3
Loch Choire Lodge Highld 273 A4
Loch Euphoirt W Isles 287 H3
Loch Head Dumfries 171 C5
Loch Loyal Lodge Highld 277 D7
Loch nam Madadh =
Lochmaddy W Isles 287 H4
Loch Ness Monster
Exhibition,
Drumnadrochit Highld 252 C1
Loch Sgioport W Isles 286 C4
Lochailort Highld 235 B6
Lochaline Highld 225 B5

Lochanhully Highld 253 D5
Lochans Dumfries 170 B2
Locharbriggs Dumfries 184 D2
Lochassynt Lodge Highld 271 B4
Lochavich Ho. Argyll 214 A2
Lochawe Argyll 227 D6
Lochboisdail = Loch
Baghasdail W Isles 286 E3
Lochbuie Argyll 225 D5
Lochcarron Highld 249 C5
Lochdhu Highld 279 D6
Lochdochart House Stirl 216 B4
Lochdon Argyll 225 C6
Lochdrum Highld 263 C4
Lochead Argyll 202 A2
Lochearnhead Stirl 217 B5
Lochee Dundee 220 A3
Lochend Highld 252 C1
Lochend Highld 281 B4
Locherben Dumfries 184 C2
Lochfoot Dumfries 173 A6
Lochgair Argyll 214 C2
Lochgarthside Highld 240 A3
Lochgelly Fife 209 A4
Lochgilphead Argyll 214 D1
Lochgoilhead Argyll 215 B5
Lochhill Moray 266 C3
Lochindorb Lodge Highld 253 C5
Lochinver Highld 270 B3
Lochlane Perth 218 B3
Lochluichart Highld 263 D5
Lochmaben Dumfries 184 D3
Lochmaddy = Loch nam
Madadh W Isles 287 H4
Lochmore Cottage Highld 280 D2
Lochmore Lodge Highld 271 A5
Lochore Fife 209 A4
Lochportain W Isles 287 G4
Lochranza N Ayrs 203 C4
Lochs Crofts Moray 266 C4
Lochside Aberds 233 B5
Lochside Highld 277 C5
Lochside Highld 274 A2
Lochside Highld 253 A4
Lochslin Highld 265 B4
Lochstack Lodge Highld 276 D3
Lochton Aberds 245 C4
Lochty Angus 232 B3
Lochty Fife 221 D5
Lochty Perth 219 B5
Lochuisge Highld 236 D1
Lochurr Dumfries 183 D5
Lochwinnoch Renfs 204 C3
Lochwood Dumfries 184 C3
Lochyside Highld 237 B5
Lockengate Corn 5 A5
Lockerbie Dumfries 185 D4
Lockeridge Wilts 45 C5
Lockerley Hants 32 C1
Locking N Som 42 D2
Lockinge Oxon 46 A2
Lockington E Yorks 150 C2
Lockington Leics 114 C2
Locklywood Shrops 111 C5
Locks Heath Hants 18 A4
Lockton N Yorks 160 B2
Lockwood W Yorks 139 B4
Locomotion Museum,
Shildon Durham 167 C5
Loddington Leics 99 A4
Loddington Northants 99 D5
Loddiswell Devon 7 C6
Loddon Norf 105 B4
Lode Cambs 86 A1
Loders Dorset 15 B4
Lodsworth W Sus 34 D2
Lofthouse N Yorks 157 D5
Lofthouse W Yorks 139 A6
Loftus Redcar 169 D5
Logan E Ayrs 193 C5
Logan Mains Dumfries 170 C2
Loganlea W Loth 208 D2
Loggerheads Staffs 111 B6
Logie Angus 233 B4
Logie Fife 220 B4
Logie Moray 253 A6
Logie Coldstone Aberds 244 B1
Logie Hill Highld 264 C3
Logie Newton Aberds 256 C1
Logie Pert Angus 233 B4
Logiealmond Lodge
Perth 219 A4
Logierait Perth 230 C3
Login Carms 73 D4
Lolworth Cambs 85 A5
Lonbain Highld 248 A3
Londesborough E Yorks 150 C1

London = City of = City of
London London 49 A6
London City Airport
London 50 A1
London Colney Herts 68 C1
London Gatwick Airport 35 B5
London Heathrow Airport
London 48 B3
London Luton Airport
Luton 67 A6
London Stansted Airport
Essex 69 A5
London Zoo London 49 A5
Londonderry N Yorks 157 C7
Londonthorpe Lincs 116 B2
Londubh Highld 261 B5
Lonemore Highld 264 B3
Long Ashton N Som 43 B4
Long Bennington Lincs 115 A6
Long Bredy Dorset 15 B5
Long Buckby Northants 82 A3
Long Clawson Leics 115 C5
Long Common Hants 32 D4
Long Compton Staffs 112 C2
Long Compton Warks 81 D5
Long Crendon Bucks 66 C1
Long Crichel Dorset 30 D3
Long Ditton Sur 49 C4
Long Drax N Yorks 141 A4
Long Duckmanton Derbys 131 B4
Long Eaton Derbys 114 B2
Long Green Worcs 79 D6
Long Hanborough Oxon 65 B5
Long Itchington Warks 81 A7
Long Lawford Warks 98 D1
Long Load Som 29 C4
Long Marston Herts 66 B3
Long Marston N Yorks 148 B4
Long Marston Warks 81 C4
Long Marton Cumb 165 C4
Long Melford Suff 87 C4
Long Newnton Glos 63 D5
Long Newton E Loth 210 D2
Long Preston N Yorks 146 B2
Long Riston E Yorks 151 C4
Long Sight Gtr Man 138 C2
Long Stratton Norf 104 B2
Long Street M Keynes 83 C4
Long Sutton Hants 33 A6
Long Sutton Lincs 118 C1
Long Sutton Som 29 C4
Long Thurlow Suff 87 A6
Long Whatton Leics 114 C2
Long Wittenham Oxon 65 D6
Longbar N Ayrs 204 C3
Longbenton T & W 179 C4
Longborough Glos 64 A2
Longbridge Warks 81 A5
Longbridge W Mid 96 D3
Longbridge Deverill Wilts 30 A2
Longburton Dorset 29 D6
Longcliffe Derbys 130 D2
Longcot Oxon 64 D3
Longcroft Falk 207 C5
Longden Shrops 94 A2
Longdon Staffs 113 D4
Longdon Worcs 79 D6
Longdon Green Staffs 113 D4
Longdon on Tern Telford 111 D5
Longdown Devon 12 B3
Longdowns Corn 4 D2
Longfield Kent 50 C3
Longfield Shetland 285 M5
Longford Derbys 113 B6
Longford Glos 63 A4
Longford London 48 B3
Longford Shrops 111 B5
Longford Telford 111 D6
Longford W Mid 97 C6
Longfordlane Derbys 113 B6
Longforgan Perth 220 B3
Longformacus Borders 197 A5
Longframlington
Northumb 189 C4
Longham Dorset 17 B4
Longham Norf 119 D6
Longhaven Aberds 257 C6
Longhill Aberds 269 D4
Longhirst Northumb 179 A4
Longhope Glos 62 B2
Longhope Orkney 283 H4
Longhorsley Northumb 189 D4
Longhoughton Northumb 189 B5
Longlane Derbys 113 B6
Longlane W Berks 46 B2
Longleat, Warminster
Wilts 30 A2

Longlevens Glos 63 A4
Longley W Yorks 139 C4
Longley Green Worcs 79 B5
Longmanhill Aberds 268 C2
Longmoor Camp Hants 33 B6
Longmorn Moray 266 D3
Longnewton Borders 187 A4
Longnewton Stockton 167 D6
Longney Glos 62 B3
Longniddry E Loth 210 C1
Longnor Shrops 94 A2
Longnor Staffs 129 C5
Longparish Hants 32 A3
Longport Stoke 112 A2
Longridge Lancs 145 D6
Longridge Staffs 112 D3
Longridge W Loth 208 D2
Longriggend N Lnrk 207 C6
Longsdon Staffs 129 D4
Longshaw Gtr Man 136 C4
Longside Aberds 257 B5
Longstanton Cambs 85 A5
Longstock Hants 32 B2
Longstone Pembs 56 B1
Longstowe Cambs 85 B5
Longthorpe P'boro 100 B3
Longthwaite Cumb 164 C2
Longton Lancs 136 A3
Longton Stoke 112 A3
Longtown Cumb 175 B6
Longtown Hereford 61 A5
Longview Mers 136 D3
Longville in the Dale
Shrops 94 B3
Longwick Bucks 66 C2
Longwitton Northumb 178 A2
Longwood Shrops 95 A4
Longworth Oxon 65 D4
Longyester E Loth 210 D2
Lonmay Aberds 269 D5
Lonmore Highld 258 D2
Looe Corn 6 B1
Loose Kent 37 A5
Loosley Row Bucks 66 C3
Lopcombe Corner Wilts 31 B6
Lopen Som 28 D4
Loppington Shrops 110 C3
Lopwell Devon 6 A3
Lorbottle Northumb 188 C3
Lorbottle Hall Northumb 188 C3
Lord's Cricket Ground
London 49 A5
Lornty Perth 231 D5
Loscoe Derbys 114 A2
Losgaintir W Isles 287 E5
Lossiemouth Moray 266 B3
Lossit Argyll 200 C1
Lostford Shrops 111 B5
Lostock Gralam Ches 128 B1
Lostock Green Ches 128 B1
Lostock Hall Lancs 136 A4
Lostock Junction Gtr Man 137 C5
Lostwithiel Corn 5 B6
Loth Orkney 282 D7
Lothbeg Highld 274 C3
Lothersdale N Yorks 146 C3
Lothmore Highld 274 C3
Loudwater Bucks 67 D4
Loughborough Leics 114 D3
Loughor Swansea 57 C5
Loughton Essex 68 D4
Loughton M Keynes 83 D5
Loughton Shrops 95 C4
Louis Tussaud's
Waxworks Blkpool 144 D3
Lound Lincs 116 D3
Lound Notts 132 A1
Lound Suff 105 B6
Lount Leics 114 D7
Louth Lincs 134 A3
Love Clough Lancs 137 A7
Lovedean Hants 33 D5
Lover Wilts 31 C6
Loversall S Yorks 140 D3
Loves Green Essex 69 C6
Lovesome Hill N Yorks 158 B2
Loveston Pembs 55 D6
Lovington Som 29 B5
Low Ackworth W Yorks 140 B2
Low Barlings Lincs 133 B5
Low Bentham N Yorks 145 A6
Low Bradfield S Yorks 139 D5
Low Bradley N Yorks 147 C4
Low Braithwaite Cumb 164 A2
Low Brunton Northumb 177 B2
Low Burnham N Lincs 141 C5
Low Burton N Yorks 157 C6

Low – Mal 341

Low Buston Northumb 189 C5
Low Catton E Yorks 149 B6
Low Clanyard Dumfries 170 D3
Low Coniscliffe Darl 167 D5
Low Crosby Cumb 176 D2
Low Dalby N Yorks 160 C2
Low Dinsdale Darl 167 D6
Low Ellington N Yorks 157 C6
Low Etherley Durham 167 C4
Low Fell T & W 179 D4
Low Fulney Lincs 117 C5
Low Garth N Yorks 159 A6
Low Gate Northumb 177 C7
Low Grantley N Yorks 157 D6
Low Habberley Worcs 95 D6
Low Ham Som 28 C4
Low Hesket Cumb 164 A2
Low Hesleyhurst Northumb 188 D3
Low Hutton N Yorks 149 A6
Low Laithe N Yorks 147 A5
Low Leighton Derbys 129 A5
Low Lorton Cumb 163 B4
Low Marishes N Yorks 159 D7
Low Marnham Notts 132 C3
Low Mill N Yorks 159 B5
Low Moor Lancs 146 C1
Low Moor W Yorks 139 A4
Low Moorsley T & W 167 A6
Low Newton Cumb 154 C3
Low Newton-by-the-Sea Northumb 189 A5
Low Row Cumb 163 A6
Low Row Cumb 176 C3
Low Row N Yorks 156 B3
Low Salchrie Dumfries 170 A2
Low Smerby Argyll 190 C3
Low Torry Fife 208 B3
Low Worsall N Yorks 158 A2
Low Wray Cumb 154 A2
Lowbridge House Cumb 154 A4
Lowca Cumb 162 B2
Lowdham Notts 115 A4
Lowe Shrops 111 B4
Lowe Hill Staffs 129 D4
Lower Aisholt Som 28 B2
Lower Arncott Oxon 65 B7
Lower Ashton Devon 12 C3
Lower Assendon Oxon 47 A5
Lower Badcall Highld 276 D2
Lower Bartle Lancs 145 D4
Lower Basildon W Berks 47 B4
Lower Beeding W Sus 35 D5
Lower Benefield Northants 100 C1
Lower Boddington Northants 82 B1
Lower Brailes Warks 81 D6
Lower Breakish Highld 247 B5
Lower Broadheath Worcs 79 B6
Lower Bullingham Hereford 78 D3
Lower Cam Glos 62 C3
Lower Chapel Powys 76 D4
Lower Chute Wilts 45 D7
Lower Cragabus Argyll 200 D3
Lower Crossings Derbys 129 A5
Lower Cumberworth W Yorks 139 C5
Lower Cwm-twrch Powys 59 D4
Lower Darwen Blkburn 137 A5
Lower Dean Beds 84 A2
Lower Diabaig Highld 261 D4
Lower Dicker E Sus 22 A3
Lower Dinchope Shrops 94 C2
Lower Down Shrops 94 C1
Lower Drift Corn 2 C2
Lower Dunsforth N Yorks 148 A3
Lower Egleton Hereford 79 C4
Lower Elkstone Staffs 129 D5
Lower End Beds 67 A4
Lower Everleigh Wilts 45 D5
Lower Farringdon Hants 33 B6
Lower Foxdale I o M 152 D2
Lower Frankton Shrops 110 B2
Lower Froyle Hants 33 A6
Lower Gledfield Highld 264 A1
Lower Green Norf 120 B1
Lower Hacheston Suff 88 B4
Lower Halistra Highld 258 C2
Lower Halstow Kent 51 C5
Lower Hardres Kent 52 D3
Lower Hawthwaite Cumb 153 B3
Lower Heath Ches 128 C3
Lower Hempriggs Moray 266 C2
Lower Hergest Hereford 77 B6
Lower Heyford Oxon 65 A5
Lower Higham Kent 51 B4
Lower Holbrook Suff 88 D2
Lower Hordley Shrops 110 C2
Lower Horsebridge E Sus 22 A3
Lower Killeyan Argyll 200 D2
Lower Kingswood Sur 35 A5
Lower Kinnerton Ches 126 C3
Lower Langford N Som 42 C3
Lower Largo Fife 220 D4
Lower Leigh Staffs 112 B4
Lower Lemington Glos 81 D5
Lower Lenie Highld 251 D7
Lower Lydbrook Glos 62 B1
Lower Lye Hereford 78 A2
Lower Machen Newport 42 A1
Lower Maes-coed Hereford 78 D1
Lower Mayland Essex 70 C3
Lower Midway Derbys 113 C7
Lower Milovaig Highld 258 C1
Lower Moor Worcs 80 C2
Lower Nazeing Essex 68 C3
Lower Netchwood Shrops 95 B4
Lower Ollach Highld 247 A4
Lower Penarth V Glam 41 D6
Lower Penn Staffs 95 B6
Lower Pennington Hants 18 B2
Lower Peover Ches 128 B2
Lower Pexhill Ches 128 B3
Lower Place Gtr Man 138 B2
Lower Quinton Warks 81 C4
Lower Rochford Worcs 79 A4
Lower Seagry Wilts 44 A3
Lower Shelton Beds 84 C1
Lower Shiplake Oxon 47 B5
Lower Shuckburgh Warks 82 A1
Lower Slaughter Glos 64 A2
Lower Stanton St Quintin Wilts 44 A3
Lower Stoke Medway 51 B5
Lower Stondon Beds 84 D3
Lower Stow Bedon Norf 103 B5
Lower Street Norf 121 B4
Lower Street Norf 121 D5
Lower Strensham Worcs 80 C2
Lower Stretton Warr 127 A6
Lower Sundon Beds 67 A5
Lower Swanwick Hants 18 A3
Lower Swell Glos 64 A2
Lower Tean Staffs 112 B4
Lower Thurlton Norf 105 B5
Lower Tote Highld 259 B5
Lower Town Pembs 72 C2
Lower Tysoe Warks 81 C6
Lower Upham Hants 32 D4
Lower Vexford Som 27 B6
Lower Weare Som 42 D3
Lower Welson Hereford 77 B6
Lower Whitley Ches 127 B6
Lower Wield Hants 33 A5
Lower Winchendon Bucks 66 B2
Lower Withington Ches 128 C3
Lower Woodend Bucks 47 A6
Lower Woodford Wilts 31 B5
Lower Wyche Worcs 79 C5
Lowesby Leics 99 A4
Lowestoft Suff 105 B6
Loweswater Cumb 163 B4
Lowford Hants 32 D3
Lowgill Cumb 155 B5
Lowgill Lancs 145 A6
Lowick Northants 100 C1
Lowick Northumb 198 C4
Lowick Bridge Cumb 154 C1
Lowick Green Cumb 154 C1
Lowlands Torf 61 D4
Lowmoor Row Cumb 165 C4
Lownie Moor Angus 232 D2
Lowsonford Warks 81 A4
Lowther Cumb 164 C3
Lowthorpe E Yorks 150 A3
Lowton Gtr Man 137 D5
Lowton Common Gtr Man 137 D5
Loxbeare Devon 27 D4
Loxhill Sur 34 C3
Loxhore Devon 25 B7
Loxley Warks 81 B5
Loxton N Som 42 D2
Loxwood W Sus 34 C3
Lubcroy Highld 271 D6
Lubenham Leics 99 C4
Luccombe Som 27 A4
Luccombe Village I o W 19 D4
Lucker Northumb 199 C5
Luckett Corn 11 D4
Luckington Wilts 44 A2
Lucklawhill Fife 220 B4
Luckwell Bridge Som 27 B4
Lucton Hereford 78 A2
Ludag W Isles 286 E3
Ludborough Lincs 143 D4
Ludchurch Pembs 56 A1
Luddenden W Yorks 138 A3
Luddenden Foot W Yorks 138 A3
Luddesdown Kent 50 C3
Luddington N Lincs 141 B6
Luddington Warks 81 B4
Luddington in the Brook Northants 100 C3
Lude House Perth 230 B2
Ludford Lincs 134 A2
Ludford Shrops 94 D3
Ludgershall Bucks 66 B1
Ludgershall Wilts 45 D6
Ludgvan Corn 2 B3
Ludham Norf 121 D5
Ludlow Shrops 94 D3
Ludlow Racecourse Shrops 94 D2
Ludwell Wilts 30 C3
Ludworth Durham 167 A6
Luffincott Devon 10 B4
Lugar E Ayrs 193 C5
Lugg Green Hereford 78 A2
Luggate Burn E Loth 210 C3
Luggiebank N Lnrk 207 C5
Lugton E Ayrs 205 C4
Lugwardine Hereford 78 C3
Luib Highld 247 B4
Lulham Hereford 78 C2
Lullenden Sur 36 B2
Lullington Derbys 113 D6
Lullington Som 44 D1
Lulsgate Bottom N Som 43 C4
Lulsley Worcs 79 B5
Lulworth Castle Dorset 16 C2
Lumb W Yorks 138 A3
Lumby N Yorks 148 D3
Lumloch E Dunb 205 B6
Lumphanan Aberds 244 B2
Lumphinnans Fife 209 A4
Lumsdaine Borders 211 D5
Lumsden Aberds 255 D5
Lunan Angus 233 C4
Lunanhead Angus 232 C2
Luncarty Perth 219 B5
Lund E Yorks 150 C2
Lund N Yorks 149 D5
Lund Shetland 284 C7
Lunderton Aberds 269 E6
Lundie Angus 220 A2
Lundie Highld 239 A5
Lundin Links Fife 220 D4
Lunga Argyll 213 B5
Lunna Shetland 284 G6
Lunning Shetland 284 G7
Lunnon Swansea 57 D5
Lunsford's Cross E Sus 23 A5
Lunt Mers 136 C2
Luntley Hereford 78 B1
Luppitt Devon 13 A6
Lupset W Yorks 139 B6
Lupton Cumb 155 C4
Lurgashall W Sus 34 D2
Lusby Lincs 134 C3
Luson Devon 7 C5
Luss Argyll 206 A1
Lussagiven Argyll 213 D4
Lusta Highld 258 C2
Lustleigh Devon 12 C2
Luston Hereford 78 A2
Luthermuir Aberds 233 B4
Luthrie Fife 220 C3
Luton Devon 13 D4
Luton Luton 67 A5
Luton Medway 51 C4
Lutterworth Leics 98 C2
Lutton Devon 7 B4
Lutton Lincs 118 C1
Lutton Northants 100 C3
Lutworthy Devon 26 D2
Luxborough Som 27 B4
Luxulyan Corn 5 B5
Lybster Highld 275 A6
Lydbury North Shrops 94 C1
Lydcott Devon 26 B1
Lydd Kent 38 C2
Lydd on Sea Kent 38 C2
Lydden Kent 39 A4
Lydden Motor Racing Circuit Kent 39 A4
Lyddington Rutland 99 B5
Lyde Green Hants 47 D5
Lydeard St Lawrence Som 27 B6
Lydford Devon 11 C6
Lydford-on-Fosse Som 29 B5
Lydgate W Yorks 138 A2
Lydham Shrops 94 B1
Lydiard Green Wilts 45 A4
Lydiard Millicent Wilts 45 A4
Lydiate Mers 136 C2
Lydlinch Dorset 30 D1
Lydney Glos 62 C2
Lydstep Pembs 55 E6
Lye W Mid 96 C2
Lye Green Bucks 67 C4
Lye Green E Sus 36 C3
Lyford Oxon 65 D4
Lymbridge Green Kent 38 A3
Lyme Park, Disley Ches 129 A4
Lyme Regis Dorset 14 B3
Lyminge Kent 38 A3
Lymington Hants 18 B2
Lyminster W Sus 20 B3
Lymm Warr 128 A1
Lymore Hants 18 B1
Lympne Kent 38 B3
Lympsham Som 42 D2
Lympstone Devon 13 C4
Lynchat Highld 241 B5
Lyndale Ho. Highld 258 C3
Lyndhurst Hants 18 A2
Lyndon Rutland 99 A6
Lyne Sur 48 C3
Lyne Down Hereford 79 D4
Lyne of Gorthleck Highld 252 D1
Lyne of Skene Aberds 245 A4
Lyneal Shrops 110 B3
Lyneham Oxon 64 A3
Lyneham Wilts 44 B4
Lynemore Highld 253 D6
Lynemouth Northumb 189 D5
Lyness Orkney 283 H4
Lyng Norf 120 D2
Lyng Som 28 C3
Lynmouth Devon 26 A2
Lynsted Kent 51 C6
Lynton Devon 26 A2
Lynton & Lynmouth Cliff Railway Devon 26 A2
Lyon's Gate Dorset 15 A6
Lyonshall Hereford 78 B1
Lytchett Matravers Dorset 16 B3
Lytchett Minster Dorset 16 B3
Lyth Highld 281 B4
Lytham Lancs 136 A2
Lytham St Anne's Lancs 136 A2
Lythe N Yorks 169 D6
Lythes Orkney 283 K5

M

Mabe Burnthouse Corn 4 D2
Mabie Dumfries 174 A2
Mablethorpe Lincs 135 A5
Macclesfield Ches 129 B4
Macclesfield Forest Ches 129 B4
Macduff Aberds 268 C2
Mace Green Suff 88 C2
Macharioch Argyll 190 E3
Machen Caerph 41 C7
Machrihanish Argyll 190 C2
Machynlleth Powys 91 B5
Machynys Carms 57 C5
Mackerel's Common W Sus 34 D3
Mackworth Derbys 113 B7
Macmerry E Loth 210 C1
Madame Tussaud's London 49 A5
Madderty Perth 219 B4
Maddiston Falk 208 C2
Madehurst W Sus 20 A2
Madeley Staffs 111 A6
Madeley Telford 95 A4
Madeley Heath Staffs 112 A1
Madeley Park Staffs 112 A1
Madingley Cambs 85 A5
Madley Hereford 78 D2
Madresfield Worcs 79 C6
Madron Corn 2 B2
Maen-y-groes Ceredig 73 A6
Maenaddwyn Anglesey 123 B4
Maenclochog Pembs 55 B6
Maendy V Glam 41 D5
Maentwrog Gwyn 107 B6
Maer Staffs 112 B1
Maerdy Conwy 109 A5
Maerdy Rhondda 41 B4
Maes-Treylow Powys 77 A6
Maesbrook Shrops 110 C1
Maesbury Shrops 110 C2
Maesbury Marsh Shrops 110 C2
Maesgwyn-Isaf Powys 109 D6
Maesgwynne Carms 73 D5
Maeshafn Denb 126 C2
Maesllyn Ceredig 73 B6
Maesmynis Powys 76 C4
Maesteg Bridgend 40 B3
Maestir Ceredig 75 D4
Maesy cwmmer Caerph 41 B6
Maesybont Carms 57 A5
Maesycrugiau Carms 58 A1
Maesymeillion Ceredig 73 B7
Magdalen Laver Essex 69 C5
Maggieknockater Moray 254 B4
Magham Down E Sus 22 A4
Maghull Mers 136 C2
Magna Science Adventure Centre, Rotherham S Yorks 140 D2
Magor Mon 42 A3
Magpie Green Suff 104 D1
Maiden Bradley Wilts 30 B2
Maiden Law Durham 167 A4
Maiden Newton Dorset 15 B5
Maiden Wells Pembs 55 E5
Maidencombe Torbay 8 A3
Maidenhall Suff 88 C2
Maidenhead Windsor 48 A1
Maidens S Ayrs 192 E2
Maiden's Green Brack 48 B1
Maidensgrave Suff 88 C3
Maidenwell Corn 10 D2
Maidenwell Lincs 134 B3
Maidford Northants 82 B3
Maids Moreton Bucks 83 D4
Maidstone Kent 37 A5
Maidwell Northants 99 D4
Mail Shetland 285 L6
Main Powys 109 D6
Maindee Newport 42 A2
Mains of Airies Dumfries 170 A1
Mains of Allardice Aberds 233 A6
Mains of Annochie Aberds 257 B4
Mains of Ardestie Angus 221 A5
Mains of Balhall Angus 232 B3
Mains of Ballindarg Angus 232 C2
Mains of Balnakettle Aberds 233 A4
Mains of Birness Aberds 257 C4
Mains of Burgie Moray 266 D1
Mains of Clunas Highld 253 B4
Mains of Crichie Aberds 257 B4
Mains of Dalvey Highld 254 C2
Mains of Dellavaird Aberds 245 D4
Mains of Drum Aberds 245 C5
Mains of Edingight Moray 267 D6
Mains of Fedderate Aberds 268 E3
Mains of Inkhorn Aberds 257 C4
Mains of Mayen Moray 255 B6
Mains of Melgund Angus 232 C3
Mains of Thornton Aberds 233 A4
Mains of Watten Highld 281 C4
Mainsforth Durham 167 B6
Mainsriddle Dumfries 174 C2
Mainstone Shrops 93 C6
Maisemore Glos 63 A4
Malacleit W Isles 287 G2
Malborough Devon 7 D6
Malcoff Derbys 129 A5
Maldon Essex 70 C2
Malham N Yorks 146 A3
Maligar Highld 259 B4
Mallaig Highld 235 A5
Malleny Mills Edin 209 D4
Malling Stirl 217 D5
Mallory Park Motor Racing Circuit Leics 98 A1
Malltraeth Anglesey 123 D4
Mallwyd Gwyn 91 A6
Malmesbury Wilts 44 A3
Malmsmead Devon 26 A2
Malpas Ches 110 A3
Malpas Corn 4 C3
Malpas Newport 61 D5
Malswick Glos 62 A3
Maltby Stockton 168 D2
Maltby S Yorks 140 D3
Maltby le Marsh Lincs 135 A4
Malting Green Essex 70 A3

Maltman's Hill Kent 37 B7
Malton N Yorks 159 D6
Malvern Link Worcs 79 C5
Malvern Wells Worcs 79 C5
Mamble Worcs 95 D4
Man-moel Caerph 41 A6
Manaccan Corn 3 C5
Manafon Powys 93 A5
Manais W Isles 287 F6
Manar Ho. Aberds 256 D2
Manaton Devon 12 C2
Manby Lincs 134 A3
Mancetter Warks 97 B6
Manchester Gtr Man 138 D1
Manchester Airport Gtr Man 128 A3
Manchester National Velodrome Gtr Man 138 D1
Mancot Flint 126 C3
Mandally Highld 239 B6
Manea Cambs 101 C6
Manfield N Yorks 167 D5
Mangaster Shetland 284 F5
Mangotsfield S Glos 43 B5
Mangurstadh W Isles 287 A5
Mankinholes W Yorks 138 A2
Manley Ches 127 B5
Mannal Argyll 222 C2
Mannerston W Loth 208 C3
Manningford Bohune Wilts 45 D5
Manningford Bruce Wilts 45 D5
Manningham W Yorks 147 D5
Mannings Heath W Sus 35 D5
Mannington Dorset 17 A4
Manningtree Essex 88 D1
Mannofield Aberdeen 245 B6
Manor Estate S Yorks 130 A3
Manor Park London 50 A1
Manorbier Pembs 55 E6
Manordeilo Carms 58 C3
Manorhill Borders 197 C5
Manorowen Pembs 72 C2
Mansel Lacy Hereford 78 C2
Manselfield Swansea 57 D5
Mansell Gamage Hereford 78 C1
Mansergh Cumb 155 C5
Mansfield E Ayrs 182 A4
Mansfield Notts 131 C5
Mansfield Woodhouse Notts 131 C5
Mansriggs Cumb 154 C1
Manston Dorset 30 D2
Manston Kent 53 C5
Manston W Yorks 148 D2
Manswood Dorset 16 A3
Manthorpe Lincs 116 D3
Manthorpe Lincs 116 B2
Manton N Lincs 142 C1
Manton Notts 131 B5
Manton Rutland 99 A5
Manton Wilts 45 C5
Manuden Essex 69 A4
Manx Electric Railway I o M 152 B4
Maperton Som 29 C6
Maple Cross Herts 67 D5
Maplebeck Notts 132 C2
Mapledurham Oxon 47 B4
Mapledurwell Hants 47 D4
Maplehurst W Sus 35 D4
Maplescombe Kent 50 C2
Mapleton Derbys 113 A5
Mapleton E Yorks 151 C5
Mapperley Derbys 114 A2
Mapperley Park Nottingham 114 A3
Mapperton Dorset 15 B5
Mappleborough Green Warks 80 A3
Mappowder Dorset 16 A1
Mar Lodge Aberds 242 C3
Maraig W Isles 288 G2
Marazanvose Corn 4 B3
Marazion Corn 2 B3
Marbhig W Isles 288 F5
Marbury Ches 111 A4
March Cambs 101 B6
March S Lnrk 184 A2
Marcham Oxon 65 D5
Marchamley Shrops 111 C4
Marchington Staffs 113 B5
Marchington Woodlands Staffs 113 C5
Marchroes Gwyn 106 D3
Marchwiel Wrex 110 A2
Marchwood Hants 32 D2
Marcross V Glam 40 E4
Marden Hereford 78 C3
Marden Kent 37 B5
Marden T & W 179 B5
Marden Wilts 45 D4
Marden Beech Kent 37 B5
Marden Thorn Kent 37 B5
Mardy Mon 61 B5
Marefield Leics 99 A4
Mareham le Fen Lincs 134 C2
Mareham on the Hill Lincs 134 C2
Marehay Derbys 114 A1
Marehill W Sus 20 A3
Maresfield E Sus 36 D2
Marfleet Hull 142 A3
Marford Wrex 126 D3
Margam Neath 40 C2
Margaret Marsh Dorset 30 D2
Margaret Roding Essex 69 B5
Margaretting Essex 69 C6
Margate Kent 53 B5
Margnaheglish N Ayrs 191 B6
Margrove Park Redcar 169 D4
Marham Norf 119 D4
Marhamchurch Corn 10 A3
Marholm P'boro 100 A3
Mariandyrys Anglesey 123 B6
Marianglas Anglesey 123 B5
Mariansleigh Devon 26 C2
Marionburgh Aberds 245 B4
Marishader Highld 259 B4
Maritime and Industrial Museum Swansea 57 C6
Marjoriebanks Dumfries 184 D3
Mark Dumfries 170 B3
Mark S Ayrs 180 D2
Mark Som 28 A3
Mark Causeway Som 28 A3
Mark Cross E Sus 22 A2
Mark Cross E Sus 36 C3
Markbeech Kent 36 B2
Markby Lincs 135 B4
Market Bosworth Leics 97 A7
Market Deeping Lincs 116 E4
Market Drayton Shrops 111 B5
Market Harborough Leics 99 C4
Market Lavington Wilts 44 D4
Market Overton Rutland 116 D1
Market Rasen Lincs 133 A6
Market Rasen Racecourse Lincs 133 A6
Market Stainton Lincs 134 B2
Market Warsop Notts 131 C5
Market Weighton E Yorks 150 C1
Market Weston Suff 103 D5
Markethill Perth 220 A2
Markfield Leics 114 D2
Markham Caerph 41 A6
Markham Moor Notts 132 B2
Markinch Fife 220 D2
Markington N Yorks 148 A1
Marks Tey Essex 70 A3
Marksbury Bath 43 C5
Markyate Herts 67 B5
Marland Gtr Man 138 B1
Marlborough Wilts 45 C5
Marlbrook Hereford 78 B3
Marlbrook Worcs 96 D2
Marlcliff Warks 80 B3
Marldon Devon 8 A2
Marlesford Suff 88 B4
Marley Green Ches 111 A4
Marley Hill T & W 179 D4
Marley Mount Hants 17 B6
Marlingford Norf 104 A2
Marloes Pembs 54 D3
Marlow Bucks 47 A6
Marlow Hereford 94 D2
Marlow Bottom Bucks 47 A6
Marlpit Hill Kent 36 B2
Marlpool Derbys 114 A2
Marnhull Dorset 30 D1
Marnoch Aberds 267 D6
Marnock N Lnrk 207 D5
Marple Gtr Man 129 A4
Marple Bridge Gtr Man 129 A4
Marr S Yorks 140 C3
Marrel Highld 274 C4
Marrick N Yorks 157 B4
Marrister Shetland 285 G7
Marros Carms 56 B2
Marsden T & W 179 C5
Marsden W Yorks 138 B3
Marsett N Yorks 156 C3
Marsh Devon 28 D2
Marsh W Yorks 147 D4
Marsh Baldon Oxon 65 D6
Marsh Gibbon Bucks 66 A1
Marsh Green Devon 13 B5
Marsh Green Kent 36 B2
Marsh Green Staffs 128 D3
Marsh Lane Derbys 131 B4
Marsh Street Som 27 A4
Marshall's Heath Herts 67 B6
Marshalsea Dorset 14 A3
Marshalswick Herts 67 C6
Marsham Norf 120 C3
Marshaw Lancs 145 B5
Marshborough Kent 53 D5
Marshbrook Shrops 94 C2
Marshchapel Lincs 143 D5
Marshfield Newport 42 A1
Marshfield S Glos 44 B1
Marshgate Corn 10 B2
Marshland St James Norf 101 A7
Marshside Mers 136 B2
Marshwood Dorset 14 B3
Marske N Yorks 157 A5
Marske-by-the-Sea Redcar 168 C4
Marston Ches 127 B6
Marston Hereford 78 B1
Marston Lincs 116 A1
Marston Oxon 65 C6
Marston Staffs 112 D2
Marston Staffs 112 C3
Marston Warks 97 B5
Marston Wilts 44 D3
Marston Doles Warks 82 B1
Marston Green W Mid 97 C4
Marston Magna Som 29 C5
Marston Meysey Wilts 64 D2
Marston Montgomery Derbys 113 B5
Marston Moretaine Beds 84 C1
Marston on Dove Derbys 113 C6
Marston St Lawrence Northants 82 C2
Marston Stannett Hereford 78 B3
Marston Trussell Northants 98 C3
Marstow Hereford 62 B1
Marsworth Bucks 67 B4
Marten Wilts 45 D6
Marthall Ches 128 B3
Martham Norf 121 D6
Martin Hants 31 D4
Martin Kent 39 A5
Martin Lincs 133 D6
Martin Lincs 134 C2
Martin Dales Lincs 134 C1
Martin Drove End Hants 31 C4
Martin Hussingtree Worcs 80 A1
Martin Mill Kent 39 A5
Martinhoe Devon 26 A1
Martinhoe Cross Devon 26 A1
Martinscroft Warr 127 A6
Martinstown Dorset 15 C6
Martlesham Suff 88 C3
Martlesham Heath Suff 88 C3
Martletwy Pembs 55 C6
Martley Worcs 79 B5
Martock Som 29 D4
Marton Ches 128 C3
Marton E Yorks 151 D4
Marton Lincs 132 A3
Marton M'bro 168 D3
Marton N Yorks 148 A3
Marton N Yorks 159 C6
Marton Shrops 93 A6
Marton Shrops 110 C3
Marton Warks 81 A7
Marton-le-Moor N Yorks 158 D2
Martyr Worthy Hants 32 B4
Martyr's Green Sur 34 A3
Marwell Zoo, Bishop's Waltham Hants 32 C4
Marwick Orkney 282 E3
Marwood Devon 25 B6
Mary Arden's House, Stratford-upon-Avon Warks 81 B4
Mary Rose Ptsmth 19 A5
Mary Tavy Devon 11 D6
Marybank Highld 251 A6
Maryburgh Highld 252 A1
Maryhill Glasgow 205 B5
Marykirk Aberds 233 B4
Marylebone Gtr Man 137 C4
Marypark Moray 254 C2
Maryport Cumb 162 A3
Maryport Dumfries 170 D3
Maryton Angus 233 C4
Marywell Aberds 244 C2
Marywell Aberds 245 C6
Marywell Angus 233 D4
Masham N Yorks 157 C6
Mashbury Essex 69 B6
Masongill N Yorks 155 D5
Masonhill S Ayrs 192 C3
Mastin Moor Derbys 131 B4
Mastrick Aberdeen 245 B5
Matching Essex 69 B5
Matching Green Essex 69 B5
Matching Tye Essex 69 B5
Matfen Northumb 178 B2
Matfield Kent 37 B4
Mathern Mon 62 D1
Mathon Hereford 79 C5
Mathry Pembs 55 A4
Matlaske Norf 120 B3
Matlock Derbys 130 C2
Matlock Bath Derbys 130 D2
Matson Glos 63 B4
Matterdale End Cumb 164 C1
Mattersey Notts 132 A1
Mattersey Thorpe Notts 132 A1
Mattingley Hants 47 D5
Mattishall Norf 120 D2
Mattishall Burgh Norf 120 D2
Mauchline E Ayrs 193 C4
Maud Aberds 257 B4
Maugersbury Glos 64 A3
Maughold I o M 152 B4
Mauld Highld 251 C6
Maulden Beds 84 D2
Maulds Meaburn Cumb 165 D4
Maunby N Yorks 158 C2
Maund Bryan Hereford 78 B3
Maundown Som 27 C5
Mautby Norf 121 D6
Mavis Enderby Lincs 134 C3
Maw Green Ches 128 D2
Mawbray Cumb 174 D3
Mawdesley Lancs 136 B3
Mawdlam Bridgend 40 C3
Mawgan Corn 3 C5
Mawla Corn 4 C2
Mawnan Corn 3 C5
Mawnan Smith Corn 3 C5
Mawsley Northants 99 D5
Maxey P'boro 100 A3
Maxstoke Warks 97 C5
Maxton Borders 197 C5
Maxton Kent 39 A5
Maxwellheugh Borders 197 C6
Maxwelltown Dumfries 174 A2
Maxworthy Corn 10 B3
May Bank Staffs 112 A2
Mayals Swansea 57 C6
Maybole S Ayrs 192 E3
Mayfield E Sus 36 D3
Mayfield Midloth 209 D6
Mayfield Staffs 113 A5
Mayfield W Loth 208 D2
Mayford Sur 34 A2
Mayland Essex 70 C3
Maynard's Green E Sus 22 A3
Maypole Mon 61 B6
Maypole Scilly 2 E4
Maypole Green Essex 70 A3
Maypole Green Norf 105 B5
Maypole Green Suff 88 A3
Maywick Shetland 285 L5
Meadle Bucks 66 C3
Meadowtown Shrops 93 A7
Meaford Staffs 112 B2
Meal Bank Cumb 154 B4
Mealabost W Isles 288 D5
Mealabost Bhuirgh W Isles 288 B5
Mealsgate Cumb 175 D5
Meanwood W Yorks 148 D1
Mearbeck N Yorks 146 A2
Meare Som 29 A4
Meare Green Som 28 C3
Mears Ashby Northants 83 A5
Measham Leics 114 D1
Meath Green Sur 35 B5
Meathop Cumb 154 C3
Meaux E Yorks 150 D3
Meavy Devon 7 A4
Medbourne Leics 99 B4
Medburn Northumb 178 B3
Meddon Devon 24 D3
Meden Vale Notts 131 C5
Medlam Lincs 134 D3
Medmenham Bucks 47 A6
Medomsley Durham 178 D3
Medstead Hants 33 B5
Meer End W Mid 97 D5
Meerbrook Staffs 129 C4
Meers Bridge Lincs 135 A4
Meesden Herts 85 D6
Meeth Devon 11 A6
Meggethead Borders 195 D6
Meidrim Carms 73 D5
Meifod Denb 125 D5
Meifod Powys 109 D6
Meigle N Ayrs 204 B1
Meigle Perth 231 D6
Meikle Earnock S Lnrk 194 A2
Meikle Ferry Highld 264 B3
Meikle Forter Angus 231 B5
Meikle Gluich Highld 264 B2
Meikle Pinkerton E Loth 211 C4
Meikle Strath Aberds 233 A4
Meikle Tarty Aberds 257 D4
Meikle Wartle Aberds 256 C2
Meikleour Perth 219 A6
Meinciau Carms 57 A4
Meir Stoke 112 A3
Meir Heath Staffs 112 A3
Melbourn Cambs 85 C5
Melbourne Derbys 114 C1
Melbourne E Yorks 149 C6
Melbourne S Lnrk 195 B5
Melbury Abbas Dorset 30 C2
Melbury Bubb Dorset 15 A5
Melbury Osmond Dorset 15 A5
Melbury Sampford Dorset 15 A5
Melby Shetland 285 H3
Melchbourne Beds 84 A2
Melcombe Bingham Dorset 16 A1
Melcombe Regis Dorset 15 C6
Meldon Devon 11 B6
Meldon Northumb 178 A3
Meldreth Cambs 85 C5
Meldrum Ho. Aberds 256 D3
Melfort Argyll 213 A6
Melgarve Highld 240 C2
Meliden Denb 125 A5
Melin-y-coed Conwy 124 C3
Melin-y-ddôl Powys 93 A4
Melin-y-grug Powys 93 A4
Melin-y-Wig Denb 109 A5
Melinbyrhedyn Powys 91 C6
Melincourt Neath 40 A3
Melkinthorpe Cumb 164 C3
Melkridge Northumb 177 C5
Melksham Wilts 44 C3
Melldalloch Argyll 203 A4
Melling Lancs 155 D4
Melling Mers 136 C2
Melling Mount Mers 136 C3
Mellis Suff 104 D2
Mellon Charles Highld 261 A5
Mellon Udrigle Highld 261 A5
Mellor Gtr Man 129 A4
Mellor Lancs 145 D6
Mellor Brook Lancs 145 D6
Mells Som 30 A1
Melmerby Cumb 165 B4
Melmerby N Yorks 158 D2
Melmerby N Yorks 157 C4
Melplash Dorset 15 B4
Melrose Borders 197 C4
Melsetter Orkney 283 K3
Melsonby N Yorks 157 A5
Meltham W Yorks 138 B4
Melton Suff 88 B3
Melton Constable Norf 120 B2
Melton Mowbray Leics 115 D5
Melton Ross N Lincs 142 B2
Meltonby E Yorks 149 B6
Melvaig Highld 261 B4
Melverley Shrops 110 D2
Melverley Green Shrops 110 D2
Melvich Highld 279 B4
Membury Devon 14 A2
Memsie Aberds 269 C4
Memus Angus 232 C2
Menabilly Corn 5 B5
Menai Bridge = Porthaethwy Anglesey 123 C
Mendham Suff 104 C
Mendlesham Suff 88 A
Mendlesham Green Suff 88 A
Menheniot Corn 6 A
Mennock Dumfries 183 B
Menston W Yorks 147 C
Menstrie Clack 207 A
Menthorpe N Yorks 149 D5
Mentmore Bucks 67 B4

Meoble Highld 238 D1
Meole Brace Shrops 110 D3
Meols Mers 136 D1
Meonstoke Hants 33 D5
Meopham Kent 50 C3
Meopham Station Kent 50 C3
Mepal Cambs 101 C6
Meppershall Beds 84 D3
Merbach Hereford 77 C7
Mere Ches 128 A2
Mere Wilts 30 B2
Mere Brow Lancs 136 B3
Mere Green W Mid 96 B4
Mereclough Lancs 146 D2
Mereside Blkpool 144 D3
Mereworth Kent 37 A4
Mergie Aberds 245 D4
Meriden W Mid 97 C5
Merkadale Highld 246 A2
Merkland Dumfries 173 A5
Merkland S Ayrs 181 B4
Merkland Lodge Highld 271 B7
Merley Poole 17 B4
Merlin's Bridge Pembs 55 C5
Merrington Shrops 110 C3
Merrion Pembs 55 E5
Merriott Som 28 D4
Merrivale Devon 11 D6
Merrow Sur 34 A3
Merrymeet Corn 6 A1
Merseyside Maritime Museum Mers 136 D2
Mersham Kent 38 B2
Merstham Sur 35 A5
Merston W Sus 20 B1
Merstone I o W 18 C4
Merther Corn 4 C3
Merthyr Carms 73 D6
Merthyr Cynog Powys 76 D3
Merthyr-Dyfan V Glam 41 E6
Merthyr Mawr Bridgend 40 D3
Merthyr Tudful = Merthyr Tydfil M Tydf 60 C2
Merthyr Tydfil = Merthyr Tudful M Tydf 60 C2
Merthyr Vale M Tydf 41 B5
Merton Devon 25 D6
Merton London 49 B5
Merton Norf 103 B5
Merton Oxon 65 B6
Mervinslaw Borders 187 B5
Meshaw Devon 26 D2
Messing Essex 70 B2
Messingham N Lincs 141 C6
Metfield Suff 104 C3
Metheringham Lincs 133 C5
Methil Fife 209 A6
Methlem Gwyn 106 C1
Methley W Yorks 140 A1
Methlick Aberds 256 C3
Methven Perth 219 B5
Methwold Norf 102 B3
Methwold Hythe Norf 102 B3
Metroland, Gateshead T & W 179 C4
Mettingham Suff 105 C4
Mevagissey Corn 5 C5
Mewith Head N Yorks 145 A2
Mexborough S Yorks 140 C2
Mey Highld 281 A4
Meysey Hampton Glos 64 D2
Miabhag W Isles 288 H2
Miabhag W Isles 287 E5
Miabhig W Isles 287 A5
Michaelchurch Hereford 61 A7
Michaelchurch Escley Hereford 77 D7
Michaelchurch on Arrow Powys 77 B6
Michaelston-le-Pit V Glam 41 E6
Michaelston-y-Fedw Newport 42 A1
Michaelstow Corn 10 D1
Micheldever Hants 32 B4
Michelmersh Hants 32 C2
Mickfield Suff 88 A2
Mickle Trafford Ches 127 C4
Micklebring S Yorks 140 D3
Mickleby N Yorks 169 D6
Mickleham Sur 35 A4
Mickleover Derby 113 B7
Micklethwaite W Yorks 147 C5
Mickleton Durham 166 C2
Mickleton Glos 81 C4
Mickletown W Yorks 140 A1

Mickley N Yorks 157 D6
Mickley Square Northumb 178 C2
Mid Ardlaw Aberds 269 C4
Mid Auchinleck Invclyd 204 A3
Mid Beltie Aberds 244 B3
Mid Calder W Loth 208 D3
Mid Cloch Forbie Aberds 268 D2
Mid Clyth Highld 275 A6
Mid-Hants Railway (Watercress Line), New Alresford Hants 33 B4
Mid Lavant W Sus 20 B1
Mid Main Highld 251 C6
Mid Urchany Highld 253 B4
Mid Walls Shetland 285 H4
Mid Yell Shetland 284 D7
Midbea Orkney 282 C5
Middle Assendon Oxon 47 A5
Middle Aston Oxon 65 A5
Middle Barton Oxon 65 A5
Middle Cairncake Aberds 256 B3
Middle Claydon Bucks 66 A2
Middle Drums Angus 232 C3
Middle Handley Derbys 131 B4
Middle Littleton Worcs 80 C3
Middle Maes-coed Hereford 78 D1
Middle Mill Pembs 54 B4
Middle Rasen Lincs 133 A5
Middle Rigg Perth 219 D5
Middle Tysoe Warks 81 C6
Middle Wallop Hants 32 B1
Middle Winterslow Wilts 31 B5
Middle Woodford Wilts 31 B5
Middlebie Dumfries 175 A5
Middleforth Green Lancs 136 A4
Middleham N Yorks 157 C5
Middlehope Shrops 94 C2
Middlemarsh Dorset 15 A6
Middlemuir Aberds 257 D4
Middlesbrough M'bro 168 C2
Middleshaw Cumb 155 C4
Middleshaw Dumfries 174 A4
Middlesmoor N Yorks 157 D4
Middlestone Durham 167 B5
Middlestone Moor Durham 167 B5
Middlestown W Yorks 139 B5
Middlethird Borders 197 B5
Middleton Aberds 245 A5
Middleton Argyll 222 C2
Middleton Cumb 155 C5
Middleton Derbys 130 C2
Middleton Derbys 130 C1
Middleton Essex 87 D4
Middleton Gtr Man 138 C1
Middleton Hants 32 A3
Middleton Hereford 78 A3
Middleton Lancs 144 B4
Middleton Midloth 196 A2
Middleton Norf 118 D3
Middleton Northants 99 C5
Middleton Northumb 178 A2
Middleton Northumb 199 C5
Middleton N Yorks 159 C6
Middleton Perth 219 D6
Middleton Perth 231 D5
Middleton Shrops 94 D3
Middleton Shrops 93 B6
Middleton Shrops 110 C2
Middleton Suff 89 A5
Middleton Swansea 57 D4
Middleton Warks 97 B4
Middleton W Yorks 139 A5
Middleton W Yorks 147 C5
Middleton Cheney Northants 82 C1
Middleton Green Staffs 112 B3
Middleton Hall Northumb 188 A2
Middleton-in-Teesdale Durham 166 C2
Middleton Moor Suff 89 A5
Middleton-on-Leven N Yorks 158 A3
Middleton-on-Sea W Sus 20 B2
Middleton on the Hill Hereford 78 A3
Middleton-on-the-Wolds E Yorks 150 C2
Middleton One Row Darl 167 D6
Middleton Priors Shrops 95 B4
Middleton Quernham N Yorks 158 D2
Middleton Railway, Hunslet W Yorks 139 A6
Middleton St George Darl 167 D6

Middleton Scriven Shrops 95 C4
Middleton Stoney Oxon 65 A6
Middleton Tyas N Yorks 157 A6
Middletown Cumb 162 D2
Middletown Powys 110 D2
Middlewich Ches 128 C1
Middlewood Green Suff 88 A1
Middlezoy Som 28 B3
Middridge Durham 167 C5
Midfield Highld 277 B6
Midge Hall Lancs 136 A4
Midgeholme Cumb 176 D4
Midgham W Berks 46 C3
Midgley W Yorks 138 A3
Midgley W Yorks 139 B5
Midhopestones S Yorks 139 D5
Midhurst W Sus 34 D1
Midlem Borders 186 A4
Midmar Aberds 244 B3
Midsomer Norton Bath 43 D5
Midton Invclyd 204 A2
Midtown Highld 277 B6
Midtown Highld 261 B5
Midtown of Buchromb Moray 254 B4
Midville Lincs 134 D3
Midway Ches 129 A4
Migdale Highld 264 A2
Migvie Aberds 244 B1
Milarrochy Stirl 206 A2
Milborne Port Som 29 D6
Milborne St Andrew Dorset 16 B2
Milborne Wick Som 29 C6
Milbourne Northumb 178 B3
Milburn Cumb 165 C4
Milbury Heath S Glos 62 D2
Milcombe Oxon 81 D7
Milden Suff 87 C5
Mildenhall Suff 102 D3
Mildenhall Wilts 45 C6
Mile Cross Norf 120 D4
Mile Elm Wilts 44 C3
Mile End Essex 70 A3
Mile End Glos 62 B1
Mile Oak Brighton 21 B5
Milebrook Powys 93 D7
Milebush Kent 37 B5
Mileham Norf 119 D6
Milesmark Fife 208 B3
Milestones, Basingstoke Hants 47 D4
Milfield Northumb 198 C3
Milford Derbys 114 A1
Milford Devon 24 C3
Milford Powys 93 B4
Milford Staffs 112 C3
Milford Sur 34 B2
Milford Wilts 31 C5
Milford Haven = Aberdaugleddau Pembs 55 D5
Milford on Sea Hants 18 B1
Milkwall Glos 62 C1
Milkwell Wilts 30 C3
Mill Bank W Yorks 138 A3
Mill Common Suff 105 C5
Mill End Bucks 47 A5
Mill End Herts 85 D5
Mill Green Essex 69 C6
Mill Green Norf 104 C2
Mill Green Suff 87 C5
Mill Hill London 68 D2
Mill Lane Hants 47 D5
Mill of Kingoodie Aberds 256 D3
Mill of Muiresk Aberds 256 B1
Mill of Sterin Aberds 243 C6
Mill of Uras Aberds 245 D5
Mill Place N Lincs 142 C1
Mill Side Cumb 154 C3
Mill Street Norf 120 D2
Milland W Sus 34 D1
Millarston Renfs 205 B4
Millbank Aberds 257 B6
Millbank Highld 280 B3
Millbeck Cumb 163 B5
Millbounds Orkney 282 D6
Millbreck Aberds 257 B5
Millbridge Sur 34 B1
Millbrook Beds 84 D2
Millbrook Corn 6 B3
Millbrook Soton 32 D2
Millburn S Ayrs 193 C4
Millcombe Devon 8 C2
Millcorner E Sus 37 D6
Milldale Staffs 129 D6
Millden Lodge Angus 232 A3
Milldens Angus 232 C3

Millennium Stadium Cardiff 41 D6
Millerhill Midloth 209 D6
Miller's Dale Derbys 129 B6
Miller's Green Derbys 130 D2
Millgreen Shrops 111 C5
Millhalf Hereford 77 C6
Millhayes Devon 14 A2
Millhead Lancs 154 D3
Millheugh S Lnrk 194 A2
Millholme Cumb 155 B4
Millhouse Argyll 203 A4
Millhouse Cumb 163 A6
Millhouse Green S Yorks 139 C5
Millhousebridge Dumfries 185 D4
Millhouses S Yorks 130 A3
Millikenpark Renfs 205 B4
Millin Cross Pembs 55 C5
Millington E Yorks 150 B1
Millmeece Staffs 112 B2
Millom Cumb 153 B2
Millook Corn 10 B2
Millpool Corn 10 D2
Millport N Ayrs 204 C1
Millquarter Dumfries 182 D4
Millthorpe Lincs 116 B4
Millthrop Cumb 155 B5
Milltimber Aberdeen 245 B5
Milltown Corn 5 B6
Milltown Derbys 130 C3
Milltown Devon 25 B6
Milltown Dumfries 175 A6
Milltown of Aberdalgie Perth 219 B5
Milltown of Auchindoun Moray 255 B4
Milltown of Craigston Aberds 268 D2
Milltown of Edinvillie Moray 254 B3
Milltown of Kildrummy Aberds 244 A1
Milltown of Rothiemay Moray 255 B6
Milltown of Towie Aberds 244 A1
Milnathort Perth 219 D6
Milner's Heath Ches 127 C4
Milngavie E Dunb 205 A5
Milnrow Gtr Man 138 B2
Milnshaw Lancs 137 A6
Milnthorpe Cumb 154 C3
Milo Carms 57 A5
Milson Shrops 95 D4
Milstead Kent 37 A7
Milston Wilts 31 A5
Milton Angus 232 D1
Milton Cambs 85 A6
Milton Cumb 176 C3
Milton Derbys 113 C7
Milton Dumfries 171 B4
Milton Dumfries 173 A6
Milton Dumfries 183 D6
Milton Highld 251 A5
Milton Highld 251 C6
Milton Highld 252 B1
Milton Highld 281 C5
Milton Highld 264 C3
Milton Moray 267 C6
Milton Notts 132 B2
Milton N Som 42 C2
Milton Oxon 82 D1
Milton Oxon 65 D5
Milton Pembs 55 D6
Milton Perth 219 C4
Milton Ptsmth 19 B5
Milton Stirl 217 D5
Milton Stoke 129 D4
Milton W Dunb 205 A4
Milton Abbas Dorset 16 A2
Milton Abbot Devon 11 D5
Milton Bridge Midloth 209 D5
Milton Bryan Beds 83 D6
Milton Clevedon Som 29 B6
Milton Coldwells Aberds 257 C4
Milton Combe Devon 6 A3
Milton Damerel Devon 25 D4
Milton End Glos 64 C2
Milton Ernest Beds 84 B2
Milton Green Ches 127 D4
Milton Hill Oxon 65 D5
Milton Keynes M Keynes 83 D5
Milton Keynes Village M Keynes 83 D5
Milton Lilbourne Wilts 45 C5
Milton Malsor Northants 83 B4
Milton Morenish Perth 217 A6
Milton of Auchinhove Aberds 244 B2

Milton of Balgonie Fife 220 D3
Milton of Buchanan Stirl 206 A2
Milton of Campfield Aberds 244 B3
Milton of Campsie E Dunb 205 A6
Milton of Corsindae Aberds 244 B3
Milton of Cushnie Aberds 244 A2
Milton of Dalcapon Perth 230 C3
Milton of Edradour Perth 230 C3
Milton of Gollanfield Highld 252 A3
Milton of Lesmore Aberds 255 D5
Milton of Logie Aberds 244 B1
Milton of Murtle Aberdeen 245 B5
Milton of Noth Aberds 255 D6
Milton of Tullich Aberds 243 C6
Milton on Stour Dorset 30 C1
Milton Regis Kent 51 C6
Milton under Wychwood Oxon 64 B3
Miltonduff Moray 266 C2
Miltonhill Moray 266 C1
Miltonise Dumfries 180 D3
Milverton Som 27 C6
Milverton Warks 81 A6
Milwich Staffs 112 B3
Minard Argyll 214 C2
Minchinhampton Glos 63 C4
Mindrum Northumb 198 C2
Minehead Som 27 A4
Minera Wrex 126 D2
Minesmere RSPB Nature Reserve Suff 89 A5
Minety Wilts 63 D6
Minffordd Gwyn 107 C5
Minffordd Gwyn 91 A5
Minffordd Gwyn 123 C5
Miningsby Lincs 134 C3
Minions Corn 10 D3
Minishant S Ayrs 192 D3
Minllyn Gwyn 91 A6
Minnes Aberds 257 D4
Minngearraidh W Isles 286 D3
Minnigaff Dumfries 171 A6
Minnonie Aberds 268 C2
Minskip N Yorks 148 A2
Minstead Hants 32 D1
Minsted W Sus 34 D1
Minster Kent 51 B6
Minster Kent 53 C5
Minster Lovell Oxon 64 B4
Minsterley Shrops 94 A1
Minsterworth Glos 62 B3
Minterne Magna Dorset 15 A6
Minting Lincs 134 B1
Mintlaw Aberds 257 B5
Minto Borders 187 A4
Minton Shrops 94 B2
Minwear Pembs 55 C6
Minworth W Mid 97 B4
Mirbister Orkney 282 E4
Mirehouse Cumb 162 C2
Mireland Highld 281 B5
Mirfield W Yorks 139 B5
Miserden Glos 63 C5
Miskin Rhondda 41 C5
Misson Notts 141 D4
Misterton Leics 98 C2
Misterton Notts 141 D5
Misterton Som 15 A4
Mistley Essex 88 D2
Mitcham London 49 C5
Mitchel Troy Mon 61 B6
Mitcheldean Glos 62 B2
Mitchell Corn 4 B3
Mitcheltroy Common Mon 61 C6
Mitford Northumb 178 A3
Mithian Corn 4 B2
Mitton Staffs 112 D2
Mixbury Oxon 82 D3
Moats Tye Suff 87 B6
Mobberley Ches 128 B2
Mobberley Staffs 112 A4
Moccas Hereford 78 C1
Mochdre Conwy 124 B3
Mochdre Powys 93 C4
Mochrum Dumfries 171 C5
Mockbeggar Hants 17 A5
Mockerkin Cumb 162 B3
Modbury Devon 7 B5

Moddershall Staffs 112 B3
Model Village,
  Babbacombe Devon 8 A3
Moelfre Anglesey 123 B5
Moelfre Powys 109 C6
Moffat Dumfries 184 B3
Moggerhanger Beds 84 C3
Moira Leics 113 D7
Mol-chlach Highld 246 C3
Molash Kent 52 D2
Mold = Yr Wyddgrug
  Flint 126 C2
Moldgreen W Yorks 139 B4
Molehill Green Essex 69 A5
Molescroft E Yorks 150 C3
Molesden Northumb 178 A3
Molesworth Cambs 100 D2
Moll Highld 247 A4
Molland Devon 26 C3
Mollington Ches 126 B3
Mollington Oxon 82 C1
Mollinsburn N Lnrk 207 C5
Monachty Ceredig 75 B4
Monachylemore Stirl 217 C4
Monar Lodge Highld 250 B4
Monaughty Powys 77 A6
Monbodde House Aberds 233 A5
Mondynes Aberds 233 A5
Monevechadan Argyll 215 B4
Monewden Suff 88 B3
Moneydie Perth 219 B5
Moniaive Dumfries 183 C5
Monifieth Angus 221 A4
Monikie Angus 221 A4
Monimail Fife 220 C2
Monington Pembs 72 B4
Monk Bretton S Yorks 139 C6
Monk Fryston N Yorks 140 A3
Monk Sherborne Hants 47 D4
Monk Soham Suff 88 A3
Monk Street Essex 69 A6
Monken Hadley London 68 D2
Monkhopton Shrops 95 B4
Monkland Hereford 78 B2
Monkleigh Devon 25 C5
Monknash V Glam 40 D4
Monkokehampton Devon 11 A6
Monks Eleigh Suff 87 C5
Monk's Gate W Sus 35 D5
Monks Heath Ches 128 B3
Monks Kirby Warks 98 C1
Monks Risborough Bucks 66 C3
Monkseaton T & W 179 B5
Monkshill Aberds 256 B2
Monksilver Som 27 B5
Monkspath W Mid 96 D4
Monkswood Mon 61 C5
Monkton Devon 14 A1
Monkton Kent 53 C4
Monkton Pembs 55 D5
Monkton S Ayrs 192 C3
Monkton Combe Bath 44 C1
Monkton Deverill Wilts 30 B2
Monkton Farleigh Wilts 44 C2
Monkton Heathfield Som 28 C2
Monkton Up Wimborne
  Dorset 31 D4
Monkwearmouth T & W 179 D5
Monkwood Hants 33 B5
Monmouth = Trefynwy
  Mon 61 B7
Monmouth Cap Mon 61 A5
Monnington on Wye
  Hereford 78 C1
Monreith Dumfries 171 C5
Monreith Mains Dumfries 171 C5
Mont Saint Guern 6
Montacute Som 29 D4
Montacute House Som 29 D5
Montcoffer Ho. Aberds 268 C1
Montford Argyll 203 B6
Montford Shrops 110 D3
Montford Bridge Shrops 110 D3
Montgarrie Aberds 244 A2
Montgomery =
  Trefaldwyn Powys 93 B6
Montrave Fife 220 D3
Montrose Angus 233 C5
Montsale Essex 71 D4
Monxton Hants 32 A2
Monyash Derbys 129 C6
Monymusk Aberds 244 A3
Monzie Perth 218 B3
Monzie Castle Perth 218 B3

Moodiesburn N Lnrk 207 C4
Moonzie Fife 220 C3
Moor Allerton W Yorks 148 D1
Moor Crichel Dorset 16 A3
Moor End E Yorks 149 D7
Moor End York 149 B5
Moor Monkton N Yorks 148 B4
Moor of Granary Moray 253 A6
Moor of Ravenstone
  Dumfries 171 C5
Moor Row Cumb 162 C3
Moor Street Kent 51 C5
Moorby Lincs 134 C2
Moordown Bmouth 17 B4
Moore Halton 127 A5
Moorend Glos 62 C3
Moorends S Yorks 141 B4
Moorgate S Yorks 140 D2
Moorgreen Notts 114 A2
Moorhall Derbys 130 B3
Moorhampton Hereford 78 C1
Moorhead W Yorks 147 D5
Moorhouse Cumb 175 C6
Moorhouse Notts 132 C2
Moorlinch Som 28 B3
Moorsholm Redcar 169 D4
Moorside Gtr Man 138 C2
Moorthorpe W Yorks 140 B2
Moortown Hants 17 A5
Moortown I o W 18 C3
Moortown Lincs 142 D2
Morangie Highld 264 B3
Morar Highld 235 A5
Morborne Cambs 100 B3
Morchard Bishop Devon 12 A2
Morcombelake Dorset 14 B4
Morcott Rutland 99 A6
Morda Shrops 110 C1
Morden Dorset 16 B3
Morden London 49 C5
Mordiford Hereford 78 D3
Mordon Durham 167 C6
More Shrops 94 B1
Morebath Devon 27 C4
Morebattle Borders 187 A6
Morecambe Lancs 144 A4
Morefield Highld 262 A3
Moreleigh Devon 7 B6
Morenish Perth 217 A5
Moresby Cumb 162 B2
Moresby Parks Cumb 162 C2
Morestead Hants 32 C4
Moreton Dorset 16 C2
Moreton Essex 69 C5
Moreton Mers 136 D1
Moreton Oxon 66 C1
Moreton Staffs 112 D1
Moreton Corbet Shrops 111 C4
Moreton-in-Marsh Glos 81 D5
Moreton Jeffries Hereford 79 C4
Moreton Morrell Warks 81 B6
Moreton on Lugg Hereford 78 C3
Moreton Pinkney Northants 82 C2
Moreton Say Shrops 111 B5
Moreton Valence Glos 62 C3
Moretonhampstead Devon 12 C2
Morfa Carms 57 A5
Morfa Carms 57 C5
Morfa Bach Carms 56 A3
Morfa Bychan Gwyn 107 A4
Morfa Glas Neath 59 E5
Morfa Nefyn Gwyn 106 B2
Morfydd Denb 109 A6
Morgan's Vale Wilts 31 C5
Moriah Ceredig 75 A5
Morland Cumb 164 C3
Morley Derbys 114 A1
Morley Durham 166 C4
Morley W Yorks 139 A5
Morley Green Ches 128 A3
Morley St Botolph Norf 104 B1
Morningside Edin 209 C5
Morningside N Lnrk 194 A3
Morningthorpe Norf 104 B3
Morpeth Northumb 179 A4
Morphie Aberds 233 B5
Morrey Staffs 113 D5
Morris Green Essex 86 D3
Morriston Swansea 57 C6
Morston Norf 120 A2
Mortehoe Devon 25 A5
Mortimer W Berks 47 C4
Mortimer West End Hants 47 C4
Mortimer's Cross Hereford 78 A2
Mortlake London 49 B5
Morton Cumb 175 C6

Morton Derbys 131 C4
Morton Lincs 116 C3
Morton Lincs 141 D6
Morton Lincs 132 C3
Morton Norf 120 D3
Morton Notts 132 D2
Morton Shrops 110 C1
Morton S Glos 62 D2
Morton Bagot Warks 80 A4
Morton-on-Swale
  N Yorks 157 B7
Morvah Corn 2 B2
Morval Corn 6 B1
Morvich Highld 249 D6
Morvich Highld 273 D5
Morville Shrops 95 B4
Morville Heath Shrops 95 B4
Morwenstow Corn 24 D3
Mosborough S Yorks 131 A4
Moscow E Ayrs 205 D4
Mosedale Cumb 163 A6
Moseley W Mid 96 C3
Moseley W Mid 96 B2
Moseley Worcs 79 B6
Mosquito Aircraft
  Museum, London
  Colney Herts 68 C1
Moss Argyll 222 C2
Moss Highld 235 D5
Moss S Yorks 140 B3
Moss Wrex 126 D3
Moss Bank Mers 136 D4
Moss Edge Lancs 144 C4
Moss End Brack 47 B6
Moss of Barmuckity
  Moray 266 C3
Moss Pit Staffs 112 C3
Moss-side Highld 253 A4
Moss Side Lancs 144 D3
Mossat Aberds 244 A1
Mossbank Shetland 284 F6
Mossbay Cumb 162 B2
Mossblown S Ayrs 193 C4
Mossbrow Gtr Man 128 A2
Mossburnford Borders 187 B5
Mossdale Dumfries 173 A4
Mossend N Lnrk 207 D5
Mosser Cumb 163 B4
Mossfield Highld 264 C2
Mossgiel E Ayrs 193 C4
Mosside Angus 232 C2
Mossley Ches 128 C3
Mossley Gtr Man 138 C2
Mossley Hill Mers 126 A3
Mosstodloch Moray 266 D4
Mosston Angus 232 D3
Mossy Lea Lancs 136 B4
Mosterton Dorset 15 A4
Moston Gtr Man 138 C1
Moston Shrops 111 C4
Moston Green Ches 128 C2
Mostyn Flint 125 A6
Mostyn Quay Flint 125 A6
Motcombe Dorset 30 C2
Mothecombe Devon 7 C5
Motherby Cumb 164 C2
Motherwell N Lnrk 194 A2
Mottingham London 49 B7
Mottisfont Hants 32 C2
Mottisfont Abbey Garden
  Hants 32 C2
Mottistone I o W 18 C3
Mottram in Longdendale
  Gtr Man 138 D2
Mottram St Andrew Ches 128 B3
Mouldsworth Ches 127 B5
Moulin Perth 230 C3
Moulsecoomb Brighton 21 B6
Moulsford Oxon 46 A3
Moulsoe M Keynes 83 C6
Moulton Ches 127 C6
Moulton Lincs 117 C6
Moulton Northants 83 A4
Moulton N Yorks 157 A6
Moulton Suff 86 A2
Moulton V Glam 41 D5
Moulton Chapel Lincs 117 D5
Moulton Eaugate Lincs 117 D6
Moulton St Mary Norf 105 A4
Moulton Seas End Lincs 117 C6
Mounie Castle Aberds 256 D2
Mount Corn 4 B2
Mount Corn 5 A6
Mount Highld 253 B5
Mount Bures Essex 87 D5
Mount Canisp Highld 264 C3

Mount Hawke Corn 4 C2
Mount Pleasant Ches 128 D3
Mount Pleasant Derbys 114 A1
Mount Pleasant Derbys 113 D6
Mount Pleasant Flint 126 B2
Mount Pleasant Hants 18 B1
Mount Pleasant W Yorks 139 A5
Mount Sorrel Wilts 31 C4
Mount Tabor W Yorks 138 A3
Mountain W Yorks 147 D4
Mountain Ash =
  Aberpennar Rhondda 41 B5
Mountain Cross Borders 195 B6
Mountain Water Pembs 55 B5
Mountbenger Borders 196 D2
Mountfield E Sus 37 D5
Mountgerald Highld 264 D1
Mountjoy Corn 4 A3
Mountnessing Essex 69 D6
Mounton Mon 61 D7
Mountsorrel Leics 114 D3
Mousehole Corn 2 C2
Mousen Northumb 199 C5
Mouswald Dumfries 174 A3
Mow Cop Ches 128 D3
Mowhaugh Borders 187 A7
Mowsley Leics 98 C3
Moxley W Mid 96 B2
Moy Highld 240 D2
Moy Highld 252 C3
Moy Hall Highld 252 C3
Moy Ho. Moray 265 D6
Moy Lodge Highld 240 D2
Moyles Court Hants 17 A5
Moylgrove Pembs 72 B4
Muasdale Argyll 202 D1
Much Birch Hereford 78 D3
Much Cowarne Hereford 79 C4
Much Dewchurch Hereford 78 D2
Much Hadham Herts 68 B4
Much Hoole Lancs 136 A3
Much Marcle Hereford 79 D4
Much Wenlock Shrops 95 A4
Muchalls Aberds 245 C6
Muchelney Som 28 C4
Muchlarnick Corn 5 B7
Muchrachd Highld 251 C4
Muckernich Highld 252 A1
Mucking Thurrock 50 A3
Muckleford Dorset 15 B6
Muckleton Staffs 111 B6
Muckleton Shrops 111 C4
Muckletown Aberds 255 D6
Muckton Lincs 134 A3
Mudale Highld 272 A3
Muddiford Devon 25 B6
Mudeford Dorset 17 B5
Mudford Som 29 D5
Mudgley Som 28 A4
Mugdock Stirl 205 A5
Mugeary Highld 246 A3
Mugginton Derbys 113 A6
Muggleswick Durham 166 A3
Muie Highld 273 D4
Muir Aberds 242 D3
Muir of Fairburn Highld 251 A6
Muir of Fowlis Aberds 244 A2
Muir of Ord Highld 252 A1
Muir of Pert Angus 220 A4
Muirden Aberds 268 D2
Muirdrum Angus 221 A5
Muirhead Angus 220 A3
Muirhead Fife 220 D2
Muirhead N Lnrk 207 D4
Muirhead S Ayrs 192 B3
Muirhouselaw Borders 187 A5
Muirhouses Falk 208 B3
Muirkirk E Ayrs 194 D1
Muirmill Stirl 207 B5
Muirshearlich Highld 239 D5
Muirskie Aberds 245 C5
Muirtack Aberds 257 C4
Muirton Highld 264 D3
Muirton Perth 219 B6
Muirton Perth 218 C4
Muirton Mains Highld 251 A6
Muirton of Ardblair Perth 231 D5
Muirton of Ballochy
  Angus 233 B4
Muiryfold Aberds 268 D2
Muker N Yorks 156 B3
Mulbarton Norf 104 A2
Mulben Moray 267 D4
Mulindry Argyll 200 C3
Mullardoch House Highld 250 C4
Mullion Corn 3 D4

Mullion Cove Corn 3 D
Mumby Lincs 135 B
Muncaster Owl Trust
  World HQ Cumb 153 A
Munderfield Row Hereford 79 B
Munderfield Stocks
  Hereford 79 B
Mundesley Norf 121 B
Mundford Norf 103 B
Mundham Norf 104 B
Mundon Essex 70 C
Mundurno Aberdeen 245 A
Munerigie Highld 239 B
Muness Shetland 284 C
Mungasdale Highld 261 A
Mungrisdale Cumb 163 A
Munlochy Highld 252 A
Munsley Hereford 79 C
Munslow Shrops 94 C
Murchington Devon 12 C
Murcott Oxon 65 B
Murkle Highld 280 B
Murlaggan Highld 238 C
Murlaggan Highld 239 D
Murra Orkney 283 G
Murrayfield Edin 209 C
Murrayfield Stadium Edin 209 C
Murrays Motorcycle
  Museum I o M 152 C
Murrow Cambs 101 A
Mursley Bucks 66 A
Murthill Angus 232 C
Murthly Perth 219 A
Murton Cumb 165 C
Murton Durham 167 A
Murton Northumb 198 B
Murton York 149 B
Musbury Devon 14 B
Muscoates N Yorks 159 C
Musdale Argyll 226 D
Museum of Childhood,
  Bethnal Green London 49 A
Museum of the Broads,
  Sutton Norf 121 C
Musselburgh E Loth 209 C
Musselburgh Racecourse
  E Loth 209 C
Muston Leics 115 B
Muston N Yorks 161 D
Mustow Green Worcs 95 D
Mutehill Dumfries 173 D
Mutford Suff 105 C
Muthill Perth 218 C
Mutterton Devon 13 A
Muxton Telford 111 D
Mybster Highld 280 C
Myddfai Carms 59 C
Myddle Shrops 110 C
Mydroilyn Ceredig 74 C
Myerscough Lancs 145 D
Mylor Bridge Corn 4 D
Mynachlog-ddu Pembs 72 C
Myndtown Shrops 94 C
Mynydd Bach Ceredig 75 A
Mynydd-bach Mon 61 D
Mynydd Bodafon Anglesey 123 B
Mynydd-isa Flint 126 C
Mynyddygarreg Carms 57 B
Mynytho Gwyn 106 C
Myrebird Aberds 245 C
Myrelandhorn Highld 281 C
Myreside Perth 220 B
Myrtle Hill Carms 59 B
Mytchett Sur 34 A
Mytholm W Yorks 138 A
Mytholmroyd W Yorks 138 A
Myton-on-Swale N Yorks 148 A
Mytton Shrops 110 D

N

Na Gearrannan W Isles 288 C
Naast Highld 261 B
Nackington Kent 52 D
Nacton Suff 88 C
Nafferton E Yorks 150 B
Nailbridge Glos 62 B
Nailsbourne Som 28 C
Nailsea N Som 42 B
Nailstone Leics 97 A
Nailsworth Glos 63 D
Nairn Highld 253 A
Nalderswood Sur 35 B
Nancegollan Corn 3 B
Nancledra Corn 2 B
Nanhoron Gwyn 106 C

Nannau Gwyn	108	C2
Nannerch Flint	125	C6
Nanpantan Leics	114	D3
Nanpean Corn	5	B4
Nanstallon Corn	5	A5
Nant-ddu Powys	60	B2
Nant-glas Powys	76	A3
Nant Peris Gwyn	107	A6
Nant Uchaf Denb	125	D5
Nant-y-Bai Carms	59	A4
Nant-y-cafn Neath	59	E5
Nant-y-derry Mon	61	C5
Nant-y-ffin Carms	58	B2
Nant-y-moel Bridgend	40	B4
Nant-y-pandy Conwy	124	B1
Nanternis Ceredig	73	A6
Nantgaredig Carms	58	C1
Nantgarw Rhondda	41	C6
Nantglyn Denb	125	C5
Nantgwyn Powys	92	D3
Nantlle Gwyn	107	A5
Nantmawr Shrops	110	C1
Nantmel Powys	76	A4
Nantmor Gwyn	107	B6
Nantwich Ches	127	D6
Nantycaws Carms	57	A4
Nantyffyllon Bridgend	40	B3
Nantyglo Bl Gwent	60	B3
Naphill Bucks	66	D3
Nappa N Yorks	146	B2
Napton on the Hill Warks	82	A1
Narberth = Arberth Pembs	55	C7
Narborough Leics	98	B2
Narborough Norf	119	D4
Nasareth Gwyn	107	A4
Naseby Northants	98	D3
Nash Bucks	83	D4
Nash Hereford	77	A7
Nash Newport	42	A2
Nash Shrops	95	D4
Nash Lee Bucks	66	C3
Nassington Northants	100	B2
Nasty Herts	68	A3
Nateby Cumb	155	A6
Nateby Lancs	145	C4
National Agricultural Centre, Stoneleigh Warks	97	D6
National Botanic Garden of Wales Carms	57	A5
National Cycle Collection, Llandrindod Wells Powys	77	A4
National Exhibition Centre, Birmingham W Mid	97	C4
National Fishing Heritage Centre, Grimsby NE Lincs	143	C4
National Gallery London	49	B5
National Hockey Stadium M Keynes	83	D5
National Ice Centre Nottingham	114	B3
National Maritime Museum London	49	B6
National Maritime Museum, Falmouth Corn	4	D3
National Motor Museum, Beaulieu Hants	18	A2
National Museum of Photography, Bradford W Yorks	147	D5
National Museum of Wales Cardiff	41	D6
National Portrait Gallery (See National Gallery) London	49	A5
National Railway Museum York	149	B4
National Seal Sanctuary, Gweek Corn	3	C5
National Space Science Centre Leics	98	A2
National Squash Centre Gtr Man	138	D1
Natland Cumb	154	C4
Natural History Museum London	49	B5
Natureland Seal Sanctuary, Skegness Lincs	135	C5
Naughton Suff	87	C6
Naunton Glos	64	A2
Naunton Worcs	80	D1
Naunton Beauchamp Worcs	80	B2
Navenby Lincs	133	D4
Navestock Heath Essex	69	D5
Navestock Side Essex	69	D5
Navidale Highld	274	C4
Nawton N Yorks	159	C5
Nayland Suff	87	D5
Nazeing Essex	68	C4
Neacroft Hants	17	B5
Neal's Green Warks	97	C6
Neap Shetland	285	H7
Near Sawrey Cumb	154	B2
Neasham Darl	167	D6
Neath = Castell-Nedd Neath	40	B2
Neath Abbey Neath	40	B2
Neatishead Norf	121	C5
Nebo Anglesey	123	A4
Nebo Ceredig	75	B4
Nebo Conwy	124	D3
Nebo Gwyn	107	A4
Necton Norf	103	A4
Nedd Highld	270	A4
Nedderton Northumb	179	A4
Nedging Tye Suff	87	C6
Needham Norf	104	C3
Needham Market Suff	88	B1
Needingworth Cambs	101	D5
Needwood Staffs	113	C5
Neen Savage Shrops	95	D4
Neen Sollars Shrops	95	D4
Neenton Shrops	95	C4
Nefyn Gwyn	106	B3
Neilston E Renf	205	C4
Neinthirion Powys	92	A3
Neithrop Oxon	82	C1
Nelly Andrews Green Powys	93	A6
Nelson Caerph	41	B6
Nelson Lancs	146	D2
Nelson Village Northumb	179	B4
Nemphlar S Lnrk	194	B3
Nempnett Thrubwell Bath	43	C4
Nene Terrace Lincs	101	A4
Nenthall Cumb	165	A5
Nenthead Cumb	165	A5
Nenthorn Borders	197	C5
Nerabus Argyll	200	C2
Nercwys Flint	126	C2
Nerston S Lnrk	205	C6
Nesbit Northumb	198	C3
Ness Ches	126	B3
Ness Gardens, Connah's Quay Ches	126	B3
Nesscliffe Shrops	110	D2
Neston Ches	126	B2
Neston Wilts	44	C2
Nether Alderley Ches	128	B3
Nether Blainslie Borders	197	B4
Nether Booth Derbys	129	A6
Nether Broughton Leics	115	C4
Nether Burrow Lancs	155	D5
Nether Cerne Dorset	15	B6
Nether Compton Dorset	29	D5
Nether Crimond Aberds	256	D3
Nether Dalgliesh Borders	185	B5
Nether Dallachy Moray	267	C4
Nether Exe Devon	13	A4
Nether Glasslaw Aberds	268	D3
Nether Handwick Angus	232	D1
Nether Haugh S Yorks	140	D2
Nether Heage Derbys	130	D3
Nether Heyford Northants	82	B3
Nether Hindhope Borders	187	B6
Nether Howecleuch S Lnrk	184	A3
Nether Kellet Lancs	145	A5
Nether Kinmundy Aberds	257	B5
Nether Langwith Notts	131	B5
Nether Leask Aberds	257	C5
Nether Lenshie Aberds	256	B1
Nether Monynut Borders	211	D4
Nether Padley Derbys	130	B2
Nether Park Aberds	269	D5
Nether Poppleton York	149	B4
Nether Silton N Yorks	158	B3
Nether Stowey Som	28	B1
Nether Urquhart Fife	219	D6
Nether Wallop Hants	32	B2
Nether Wasdale Cumb	163	D4
Nether Whitacre Warks	97	B5
Nether Worton Oxon	82	D1
Netheravon Wilts	31	A5
Netherbrough Orkney	282	F4
Netherburn S Lnrk	194	B3
Netherbury Dorset	15	B4
Netherby Cumb	175	A6
Netherby N Yorks	148	C2
Nethercote Warks	82	A2
Nethercott Devon	25	B5
Netherend Glos	62	C1
Netherfield E Sus	23	A5
Netherhampton Wilts	31	C5
Netherlaw Dumfries	173	D5
Netherley Aberds	245	C5
Netherley Mers	127	A4
Nethermill Dumfries	184	D3
Nethermuir Aberds	257	B4
Netherplace E Renf	205	C5
Netherseal Derbys	113	D6
Netherthird E Ayrs	182	A3
Netherthong W Yorks	139	C4
Netherthorpe S Yorks	131	A5
Netherton Angus	232	C3
Netherton Devon	12	D3
Netherton Hants	46	D1
Netherton Mers	136	C2
Netherton Northumb	188	C2
Netherton Oxon	65	D5
Netherton Perth	231	C5
Netherton Stirl	205	A5
Netherton W Mid	96	C2
Netherton Worcs	80	C2
Netherton N Yorks	139	B4
Netherton W Yorks	139	B5
Nethertown Cumb	162	D2
Nethertown Highld	281	A5
Netherwitton Northumb	189	D4
Netherwood E Ayrs	193	C6
Nethy Bridge Highld	253	D6
Netley Hants	18	A3
Netley Marsh Hants	32	D2
Netteswell Essex	69	B4
Nettlebed Oxon	47	A5
Nettlebridge Som	29	A6
Nettlecombe Dorset	15	B5
Nettleden Herts	67	B5
Nettleham Lincs	133	B5
Nettlestead Kent	37	A4
Nettlestead Green Kent	37	A4
Nettlestone I o W	19	B5
Nettlesworth Durham	167	A5
Nettleton Lincs	142	C3
Nettleton Wilts	44	B2
Neuadd Carms	58	C3
Nevendon Essex	70	D1
Nevern Pembs	72	B3
Nevis Range Ski Centre, Torlundy Highld	237	B5
New Abbey Dumfries	174	B2
New Aberdour Aberds	268	C3
New Addington London	49	C6
New Alresford Hants	33	B4
New Alyth Perth	231	D6
New Arley Warks	97	C5
New Ash Green Kent	50	C3
New Barn Kent	50	C3
New Barnetby N Lincs	142	B2
New Barton Northants	83	A5
New Bewick Northumb	188	A3
New-bigging Angus	231	D6
New Bilton Warks	98	D1
New Bolingbroke Lincs	134	D3
New Boultham Lincs	133	B4
New Bradwell M Keynes	83	C5
New Brancepeth Durham	167	A5
New Bridge Wrex	110	A1
New Brighton Flint	126	C2
New Brighton Mers	136	D2
New Brinsley Notts	131	D4
New Broughton Wrex	126	D3
New Buckenham Norf	104	B1
New Byth Aberds	268	D3
New Catton Norf	120	D4
New Cheriton Hants	33	C4
New Costessey Norf	120	D3
New Cowper Cumb	174	D4
New Cross Ceredig	75	A5
New Cross London	49	B6
New Cumnock E Ayrs	182	A4
New Deer Aberds	256	B3
New Delaval Northumb	179	B4
New Duston Northants	83	A4
New Earswick York	149	B5
New Edlington S Yorks	140	D3
New Elgin Moray	266	C3
New Ellerby E Yorks	151	D4
New Eltham London	50	B1
New End Worcs	80	B3
New Farnley W Yorks	147	D6
New Ferry Mers	126	A3
New Fryston W Yorks	140	A2
New Galloway Dumfries	172	A4
New Gilston Fife	220	D4
New Grimsby Scilly	2	E3
New Hainford Norf	120	D4
New Hartley Northumb	179	B5
New Haw Sur	48	C3
New Hedges Pembs	56	B1
New Herrington T & W	179	D5
New Hinksey Oxon	65	C6
New Holkham Norf	119	B5
New Holland N Lincs	142	A2
New Houghton Derbys	131	C4
New Houghton Norf	119	C4
New Houses N Yorks	155	D7
New Humberstone Leicester	98	A3
New Hutton Cumb	155	B4
New Hythe Kent	37	A5
New Inn Carms	58	B1
New Inn Mon	61	C6
New Inn Pembs	55	A6
New Inn Torf	61	D5
New Invention Shrops	93	D6
New Invention W Mid	96	A2
New Kelso Highld	249	B6
New Kingston Notts	114	C3
New Lanark S Lnrk	194	B3
New Lanark Village & Visitor Centre, Lanark S Lnrk	194	B3
New Lane Lancs	136	B3
New Lane End Warr	137	D5
New Leake Lincs	135	D4
New Leeds Aberds	269	D4
New Longton Lancs	136	A4
New Luce Dumfries	170	A3
New Malden London	49	C5
New Marske Redcar	168	C4
New Marton Shrops	110	B2
New Micklefield W Yorks	148	D3
New Mill Aberds	245	D4
New Mill Herts	67	B4
New Mill Wilts	45	C5
New Mill W Yorks	139	C4
New Mills Corn	4	B3
New Mills Derbys	129	A4
New Mills Powys	93	A4
New Milton Hants	17	B6
New Moat Pembs	55	B6
New Ollerton Notts	131	C6
New Oscott W Mid	96	B3
New Park N Yorks	148	B1
New Pitsligo Aberds	268	D3
New Pleasurewood Hills Leisure Park, Lowestoft Suff	105	B6
New Polzeath Corn	9	D5
New Quay = Ceinewydd Ceredig	73	A6
New Rackheath Norf	121	D4
New Radnor Powys	77	A6
New Rent Cumb	164	B2
New Ridley Northumb	178	D2
New Road Side N Yorks	146	C3
New Romney Kent	38	C2
New Rossington S Yorks	140	D4
New Row Ceredig	75	A6
New Row Lancs	145	D6
New Row N Yorks	168	D4
New Sarum Wilts	31	B5
New Silksworth T & W	179	D5
New Stevenston N Lnrk	194	A2
New Street Staffs	129	D5
New Street Lane Shrops	111	B5
New Swanage Dorset	17	C4
New Totley S Yorks	130	B3
New Town E Loth	210	C1
New Tredegar = Tredegar Newydd Caerph	41	A6
New Trows S Lnrk	194	C3
New Ulva Argyll	213	D5
New Walsoken Cambs	101	A6
New Waltham NE Lincs	143	C4
New Whittington Derbys	130	B3
New Wimpole Cambs	85	C5
New Winton E Loth	210	C1
New Yatt Oxon	65	B4
New York Lincs	134	D2
New York N Yorks	147	A5
Newall W Yorks	147	C5
Newark Orkney	282	C8
Newark P'boro	100	A4
Newark Castle Notts	132	D2
Newark-on-Trent Notts	132	D2
Newarthill N Lnrk	194	A2
Newbarns Cumb	153	C3
Newbattle Midloth	209	D6
Newbiggin Cumb	153	A1
Newbiggin Cumb	153	D3
Newbiggin Cumb	164	C2
Newbiggin Cumb	164	A3
Newbiggin Cumb	165	C4
Newbiggin Durham	166	C2
Newbiggin N Yorks	156	B3
Newbiggin N Yorks	156	C3
Newbiggin-by-the-Sea Northumb	179	A5
Newbiggin-on-Lune Cumb	155	A6
Newbigging Angus	220	A4
Newbigging Angus	221	A4
Newbigging S Lnrk	195	B5
Newbold Derbys	130	B3
Newbold Leics	114	D2
Newbold on Avon Warks	98	D1
Newbold on Stour Warks	81	C5
Newbold Pacey Warks	81	B5
Newbold Verdon Leics	98	A1
Newborough Anglesey	123	D4
Newborough P'boro	100	A4
Newborough Staffs	113	C5
Newbottle Northants	82	D2
Newbottle T & W	179	D5
Newbourne Suff	88	C3
Newbridge Caerph	41	B7
Newbridge Ceredig	75	C4
Newbridge Corn	2	B2
Newbridge Corn	6	A2
Newbridge Dumfries	174	A2
Newbridge Edin	208	C4
Newbridge Hants	32	D1
Newbridge I o W	18	C3
Newbridge Pembs	55	A5
Newbridge Green Worcs	79	D6
Newbridge-on-Usk Mon	61	D5
Newbridge on Wye Powys	76	B4
Newbrough Northumb	177	C6
Newbuildings Devon	12	A2
Newburgh Aberds	257	D4
Newburgh Aberds	269	D4
Newburgh Borders	185	A6
Newburgh Fife	220	C2
Newburgh Lancs	136	B3
Newburn T & W	178	C3
Newbury W Berks	46	C2
Newbury Park London	50	A1
Newbury Racecourse W Berks	46	C2
Newby Cumb	164	C3
Newby Lancs	146	C2
Newby N Yorks	155	D6
Newby N Yorks	168	D3
Newby N Yorks	160	B4
Newby Bridge Cumb	154	C2
Newby East Cumb	176	D2
Newby Hall, Ripon N Yorks	148	A2
Newby West Cumb	175	C6
Newby Wiske N Yorks	158	C2
Newcastle Mon	61	B6
Newcastle Shrops	93	C6
Newcastle Discovery T & W	179	C4
Newcastle Emlyn = Castell Newydd Emlyn Carms	73	B6
Newcastle International Airport T & W	178	B3
Newcastle Racecourse T & W	179	B4
Newcastle-under-Lyme Staffs	112	A2
Newcastle Upon Tyne T & W	179	C4
Newcastleton = Copshaw Holm Borders	176	A2
Newchapel Pembs	73	C5
Newchapel Powys	92	C3
Newchapel Staffs	128	D3
Newchapel Sur	35	B6
Newchurch Carms	73	D6
Newchurch I o W	19	C4
Newchurch Kent	38	B2
Newchurch Lancs	146	D2
Newchurch Mon	61	D6
Newchurch Powys	77	B6
Newchurch Staffs	113	C5
Newcott Devon	14	A2
Newcraighall Edin	209	C6
Newdigate Sur	35	B4
Newell Green Brack	48	B1

Newenden Kent 37 D6
Newent Glos 62 A3
Newerne Glos 62 C2
Newfield Durham 167 B5
Newfield Highld 264 C3
Newford Scilly 2 E4
Newfound Hants 46 D3
Newgale Pembs 54 B4
Newgate Norf 120 A2
Newgate Street Herts 68 C3
Newhall Ches 111 A5
Newhall Derbys 113 C6
Newhall House Highld 264 D2
Newhall Point Highld 264 D3
Newham Northumb 189 A4
Newham Hall Northumb 189 A4
Newhaven Derbys 129 D6
Newhaven Edin 209 C5
Newhaven E Sus 22 B2
Newhey Gtr Man 138 B2
Newholm N Yorks 169 D6
Newhouse N Lnrk 207 D5
Newick E Sus 36 D2
Newingreen Kent 38 B3
Newington Kent 51 C5
Newington Kent 38 B3
Newington Kent 53 C5
Newington Notts 141 D4
Newington Oxon 65 D7
Newington Shrops 94 C2
Newland Glos 62 C1
Newland Hull 150 D3
Newland N Yorks 141 A4
Newland Worcs 79 C5
Newlandrig Midloth 209 D6
Newlands Borders 186 D4
Newlands Highld 252 B3
Newlands Moray 266 D4
Newlands Northumb 178 D2
Newland's Corner Sur 34 B3
Newlands of Geise Highld 280 B2
Newlands of Tynet Moray 267 C4
Newlands Park Anglesey 122 B2
Newlandsmuir S Lnrk 205 C6
Newlot Orkney 282 F6
Newlyn Corn 2 C2
Newmachar Aberds 245 A5
Newmains N Lnrk 194 A3
Newmarket Suff 86 A2
Newmarket W Isles 288 D5
Newmarket Racecourse
    Suff 86 A2
Newmill Borders 186 B3
Newmill Corn 2 B2
Newmill Moray 267 D5
Newmill of Inshewan
    Angus 232 B2
Newmills of Boyne
    Aberds 267 D6
Newmiln Perth 219 A6
Newmilns E Ayrs 193 B5
Newnham Cambs 85 B6
Newnham Glos 62 B2
Newnham Hants 47 D5
Newnham Herts 84 D4
Newnham Kent 51 D6
Newnham Northants 82 B2
Newnham Bridge Worcs 79 A4
Newpark Fife 221 C4
Newport Devon 25 B6
Newport E Yorks 150 D1
Newport Essex 85 D7
Newport Highld 275 B5
Newport I o W 18 C4
Newport Norf 121 D7
Newport Telford 111 D6
Newport = Casnewydd
    Newport 42 A2
Newport = Trefdraeth
    Pembs 72 C3
Newport Museum & Art
    Gallery Newport 42 A2
Newport-on-Tay Fife 220 B4
Newport Pagnell M Keynes 83 C5
Newpound Common
    W Sus 34 D3
Newquay Corn 4 A3
Newquay Airport Corn 4 A3
Newquay Sea Life Centre
    Corn 4 A2
Newsbank Ches 128 C3
Newseat Aberds 256 C2
Newseat Aberds 257 B5
Newsham Northumb 179 B5

Newsham N Yorks 166 D4
Newsham N Yorks 158 C2
Newsholme E Yorks 141 A5
Newsholme Lancs 146 B2
Newsome W Yorks 139 B4
Newstead Borders 197 C4
Newstead Notts 131 D5
Newstead Northumb 189 A4
Newstead Abbey, Kirkby
    in Ashfield Notts 131 D5
Newthorpe N Yorks 148 D3
Newton Argyll 214 C3
Newton Borders 187 A5
Newton Bridgend 40 D3
Newton Cambs 85 C6
Newton Cambs 118 D1
Newton Cardiff 42 B1
Newton Ches 127 D5
Newton Ches 127 C4
Newton Ches 127 B5
Newton Cumb 153 C3
Newton Derbys 131 D4
Newton Dorset 30 D1
Newton Dumfries 185 C4
Newton Dumfries 175 A5
Newton Gtr Man 138 D2
Newton Hereford 78 D1
Newton Hereford 78 B3
Newton Highld 264 D3
Newton Highld 271 A5
Newton Highld 281 D5
Newton Highld 252 B3
Newton Lancs 144 D4
Newton Lancs 145 B6
Newton Lancs 155 D4
Newton Lincs 116 B3
Newton Moray 266 C2
Newton Norf 119 D5
Newton Notts 115 A4
Newton Northants 99 C5
Newton Northumb 178 C2
Newton Perth 218 A3
Newton S Lnrk 205 B6
Newton S Lnrk 194 C4
Newton Staffs 112 C4
Newton Suff 87 C5
Newton Swansea 57 D6
Newton S Yorks 140 C3
Newton Warks 98 D2
Newton Wilts 31 C6
Newton W Loth 208 C3
Newton Abbot Devon 12 D3
Newton Abbot
    Racecourse Devon 12 D3
Newton Arlosh Cumb 175 C4
Newton Aycliffe Durham 167 C5
Newton Bewley Hrtlpl 168 C2
Newton Blossomville
    M Keynes 83 B6
Newton Bromswold
    Northants 84 A1
Newton Burgoland Leics 97 A6
Newton by Toft Lincs 133 A5
Newton Ferrers Devon 7 C4
Newton Flotman Norf 104 B3
Newton Hall Northumb 178 C2
Newton Harcourt Leics 98 B3
Newton Heath Gtr Man 138 C1
Newton Ho. Aberds 256 D1
Newton Kyme N Yorks 148 C3
Newton-le-Willows Mers 137 D4
Newton-le-Willows
    N Yorks 157 C6
Newton Longville Bucks 83 D5
Newton Mearns E Renf 205 C5
Newton Morrell N Yorks 157 A6
Newton Mulgrave
    N Yorks 169 D5
Newton-on-Rawcliffe
    N Yorks 159 B7
Newton-on-the-Moor
    Northumb 189 C4
Newton on Trent Lincs 132 B3
Newton Park Argyll 203 B6
Newton Poppleford Devon 13 C5
Newton Purcell Oxon 82 D3
Newton Regis Warks 97 A5
Newton Reigny Cumb 164 B2
Newton St Cyres Devon 12 B3
Newton St Faith Norf 120 D4
Newton St Loe Bath 43 C6

Newton St Petrock Devon 25 D5
Newton Solney Derbys 113 C6
Newton Stacey Hants 32 A3
Newton Stewart Dumfries 171 A6
Newton Tony Wilts 31 A6
Newton Tracey Devon 25 C6
Newton under Roseberry
    Redcar 168 D3
Newton upon Derwent
    E Yorks 149 C6
Newton Valence Hants 33 B6
Newtonairds Dumfries 183 D6
Newtongrange Midloth 209 D6
Newtonhill Aberds 245 C6
Newtonhill Highld 252 B1
Newtonmill Angus 233 B4
Newtonmore Highld 241 C5
Newtown Argyll 214 B3
Newtown Ches 127 B5
Newtown Corn 3 C5
Newtown Cumb 174 D3
Newtown Cumb 176 C3
Newtown Derbys 129 A4
Newtown Devon 26 C2
Newtown Glos 62 C2
Newtown Glos 80 D2
Newtown Hants 31 D6
Newtown Hants 32 C2
Newtown Hants 33 D5
Newtown Hants 46 C2
Newtown Hants 32 D4
Newtown Hants 18 A3
Newtown Hereford 79 C4
Newtown Highld 240 B1
Newtown I o M 152 D3
Newtown I o W 18 B3
Newtown Northumb 188 C3
Newtown Northumb 188 A3
Newtown Northumb 198 C3
Newtown Poole 17 B4
Newtown Shrops 110 B3
Newtown Staffs 129 C4
Newtown Staffs 129 C5
Newtown Wilts 30 C3
Newtown = Y
    Drenewydd Powys 93 B5
Newtown Linford Leics 98 A2
Newtown St Boswells
    Borders 197 C4
Newtown Unthank Leics 98 A1
Newtyle Angus 231 D6
Neyland Pembs 55 D5
Niarbyl I o M 152 D2
Nibley S Glos 43 A5
Nibley Green Glos 62 D3
Nibon Shetland 284 F5
Nicholashayne Devon 27 D6
Nicholaston Swansea 57 D5
Nidd N Yorks 148 A2
Nigg Aberdeen 245 B6
Nigg Highld 265 C4
Nigg Ferry Highld 264 D3
Nightcott Som 26 C3
Nilig Denb 125 D5
Nine Ashes Essex 69 C5
Nine Mile Burn Midloth 195 A6
Nine Wells Pembs 54 B3
Ninebanks Northumb 177 D5
Ninfield E Sus 23 A5
Ningwood I o W 18 C2
Nisbet Borders 187 A5
Nisthouse Orkney 282 F4
Nisthouse Shetland 285 G7
Niton I o W 18 D4
Nitshill Glasgow 205 B5
No Man's Heath Ches 111 A4
No Man's Heath Warks 97 A5
Noak Hill London 69 D5
Noblethorpe S Yorks 139 C5
Nobottle Northants 82 A3
Nocton Lincs 133 C5
Noke Oxon 65 B6
Nolton Pembs 55 C4
Nolton Haven Pembs 55 C4
Nomansland Devon 26 D3
Nomansland Wilts 31 D6
Noneley Shrops 110 C3
Nonikiln Highld 264 C2
Nonington Kent 53 D4
Noonsbrough Shetland 285 H4
Norbreck Blkpool 144 C3
Norbridge Hereford 79 C5
Norbury Ches 111 A4
Norbury Derbys 113 A5
Norbury Shrops 94 B1
Norbury Staffs 112 C1
Nordelph Norf 102 A1

Norden Gtr Man 138 B1
Norden Heath Dorset 16 C3
Nordley Shrops 95 B4
Norham Northumb 198 B3
Norley Ches 127 B5
Norleywood Hants 18 B2
Norman Cross Cambs 100 B3
Normanby N Lincs 141 B6
Normanby N Yorks 159 C6
Normanby Redcar 168 D3
Normanby-by-Spital
    Lincs 133 A5
Normanby by Stow Lincs 132 A3
Normanby le Wold Lincs 142 D3
Normandy Sur 34 A2
Norman's Bay E Sus 23 B4
Norman's Green Devon 13 A5
Normanstone Suff 105 B6
Normanton Derby 114 B1
Normanton Leics 115 A6
Normanton Lincs 116 A2
Normanton Notts 132 D2
Normanton Rutland 99 A6
Normanton W Yorks 140 A1
Normanton le Heath
    Leics 114 D1
Normanton on Soar
    Notts 114 C3
Normanton-on-the-
    Wolds Notts 115 B4
Normanton on Trent
    Notts 132 C2
Normoss Lancs 144 D3
Norney Sur 34 B2
Norrington Common Wilts 44 C2
Norris Green Mers 136 D2
Norris Hill Leics 114 D1
North Anston S Yorks 131 A5
North Aston Oxon 65 A5
North Baddesley Hants 32 D2
North Ballachulish Highld 237 C4
North Barrow Som 29 C6
North Barsham Norf 119 B6
North Benfleet Essex 51 A4
North Bersted W Sus 20 B2
North Berwick E Loth 210 B2
North Boarhunt Hants 33 D5
North Bovey Devon 12 C2
North Bradley Wilts 44 D2
North Brentor Devon 11 C5
North Brewham Som 29 B7
North Buckland Devon 25 A5
North Burlingham Norf 121 D5
North Cadbury Som 29 C6
North Cairn Dumfries 180 C1
North Carlton Lincs 133 B4
North Carrine Argyll 190 E2
North Cave E Yorks 150 D1
North Cerney Glos 63 C6
North Charford Wilts 31 D5
North Charlton Northumb 189 A4
North Cheriton Som 29 C6
North Cliff E Yorks 151 C5
North Cliffe E Yorks 150 D1
North Clifton Notts 132 B3
North Cockerington Lincs 143 D5
North Coker Som 29 D5
North Collafirth Shetland 284 E5
North Common E Sus 36 D1
North Connel Argyll 226 C4
North Cornelly Bridgend 40 C3
North Cotes Lincs 143 C5
North Cove Suff 105 C5
North Cowton N Yorks 157 A6
North Crawley M Keynes 83 C6
North Cray London 50 B1
North Creake Norf 119 B5
North Curry Som 28 C3
North Dalton E Yorks 150 B2
North Dawn Orkney 283 G5
North Deighton N Yorks 148 B2
North Duffield N Yorks 149 D5
North Elkington Lincs 143 D4
North Elmham Norf 120 C1
North Elmsall W Yorks 140 B2
North End Bucks 66 A3
North End E Yorks 151 D5
North End Essex 69 B6
North End Hants 46 C2
North End Lincs 117 A5
North End Norf 103 B6
North End N Som 42 C3
North End Ptsmth 19 A5
North End Som 28 C2
North End W Sus 21 B4

North Featherstone
    W Yorks 140 A2
North Ferriby E Yorks 142 A1
North Frodingham
    E Yorks 151 B4
North Gluss Shetland 284 F5
North Gorley Hants 31 D5
North Green Norf 104 C3
North Green Suff 89 A4
North Greetwell Lincs 133 B5
North Grimston N Yorks 150 A1
North Halley Orkney 283 G6
North Halling Medway 51 C4
North Hayling Hants 19 A6
North Hazelrigg Northumb 199 C4
North Heasley Devon 26 B2
North Heath W Sus 34 D3
North Hill Cambs 101 D6
North Hill Corn 10 D3
North Hinksey Oxon 65 C5
North Holmwood Sur 35 B4
North Howden E Yorks 149 D6
North Huish Devon 7 B6
North Hykeham Lincs 133 C4
North Johnston Pembs 55 C5
North Kelsey Lincs 142 C2
North Kelsey Moor Lincs 142 C2
North Kessock Highld 252 B2
North Killingholme
    N Lincs 142 B3
North Kilvington N Yorks 158 C3
North Kilworth Leics 98 C3
North Kirkton Aberds 269 D6
North Kiscadale N Ayrs 191 C6
North Kyme Lincs 133 D6
North Lancing W Sus 21 B4
North Lee Bucks 66 C3
North Leigh Oxon 65 B4
North Leverton with
    Habblesthorpe Notts 132 A2
North Littleton Worcs 80 C3
North Lopham Norf 103 C6
North Luffenham Rutland 99 A6
North Marden W Sus 33 D7
North Marston Bucks 66 A2
North Middleton Midloth 196 A2
North Middleton
    Northumb 188 A3
North Molton Devon 26 C2
North Moreton Oxon 46 A3
North Mundham W Sus 20 B1
North Muskham Notts 132 D2
North Newbald E Yorks 150 D2
North Newington Oxon 81 D7
North Newnton Wilts 45 D5
North Newton Som 28 B2
North Nibley Glos 62 D3
North Norfolk Railway,
    Sheringham Norf 120 A3
North Oakley Hants 46 D3
North Ockendon London 50 A2
North Ormesby M'bro 168 C3
North Ormsby Lincs 143 D4
North Otterington
    N Yorks 158 C2
North Owersby Lincs 142 D2
North Perrott Som 15 A4
North Petherton Som 28 B2
North Petherwin Corn 10 C3
North Pickenham Norf 103 A4
North Piddle Worcs 80 B2
North Poorton Dorset 15 B5
North Port Argyll 227 D5
North Queensferry Fife 208 B4
North Radworthy Devon 26 B2
North Rauceby Lincs 116 A3
North Reston Lincs 134 A3
North Rigton N Yorks 148 C1
North Rode Ches 128 C3
North Roe Shetland 284 E5
North Ronaldsay Airport
    Orkney 282 B8
North Runcton Norf 118 D3
North Sandwick Shetland 284 D7
North Scale Cumb 153 D2
North Scarle Lincs 132 C3
North Seaton Northumb 179 A4
North Shian Argyll 226 B4
North Shields T & W 179 C5
North Shoebury Sthend 51 A6
North Shore Blkpool 144 D3
North Side Cumb 162 B3
North Side P'boro 101 B4
North Skelton Redcar 169 D4
North Somercotes Lincs 143 D6
North Stainley N Yorks 157 D6
North Stainmore Cumb 165 D6

North Stifford Thurrock 50 A3
North Stoke Bath 43 C6
North Stoke Oxon 47 A4
North Stoke W Sus 20 A3
North Street Hants 33 B5
North Street Kent 52 D2
North Street Medway 51 B5
North Street W Berks 47 B4
North Sunderland
　Northumb 199 C6
North Tamerton Corn 10 B4
North Tawton Devon 12 A1
North Thoresby Lincs 143 D4
North Tidworth Wilts 31 A6
North Togston Northumb 189 C5
North Tuddenham Norf 120 D2
North Walbottle T & W 178 C3
North Walsham Norf 121 B4
North Waltham Hants 33 A5
North Warnborough Hants 47 D5
North Water Bridge
　Angus 233 B4
North Watten Highld 280 C4
North Weald Bassett Essex 69 C4
North Wheatley Notts 132 A2
North Whilborough Devon 8 A2
North Wick Bath 43 C4
North Willingham Lincs 133 A6
North Wingfield Derbys 131 C4
North Witham Lincs 116 C2
North Woolwich London 50 B1
North Wootton Dorset 29 D6
North Wootton Norf 118 C3
North Wootton Som 29 A5
North Wraxall Wilts 44 B2
North Wroughton Swindon 45 A5
North Yorkshire Moors
　Railway, Pickering
　N Yorks 160 C2
Northacre Norf 103 B5
Northallerton N Yorks 158 B2
Northam Devon 25 C5
Northam Soton 32 D3
Northampton Northants 83 A4
Northaw Herts 68 C2
Northbeck Lincs 116 A3
Northborough P'boro 100 A3
Northbourne Kent 53 D5
Northbridge Street E Sus 37 D5
Northchapel W Sus 34 D2
Northchurch Herts 67 C4
Northcott Devon 10 B4
Northdown Kent 53 B5
Northdyke Orkney 282 E3
Northend Bath 44 C1
Northend Bucks 66 D2
Northend Warks 81 B6
Northenden Gtr Man 137 D7
Northfield Aberdeen 245 B6
Northfield Borders 211 D6
Northfield E Yorks 142 A2
Northfield W Mid 96 D3
Northfields Lincs 100 A2
Northfleet Kent 50 B3
Northgate Lincs 117 C4
Northhouse Borders 186 C3
Northiam E Sus 37 D6
Northill Beds 84 C3
Northington Hants 33 B4
Northlands Lincs 134 D3
Northlea Durham 179 D6
Northleach Glos 64 B2
Northleigh Devon 14 B1
Northlew Devon 11 B6
Northmoor Oxon 65 C5
Northmoor Green or
　Moorland Som 28 B3
Northmuir Angus 232 C1
Northney Hants 19 A6
Northolt London 48 A4
Northop Flint 126 C2
Northop Hall Flint 126 C2
Northorpe Lincs 116 D3
Northorpe Lincs 117 B5
Northorpe Lincs 141 D6
Northover Som 29 B4
Northover Som 29 C5
Northowram W Yorks 139 A4
Northport Dorset 16 C3
Northpunds Shetland 285 L6
Northrepps Norf 120 B4
Northtown Orkney 283 H5
Northumbria Craft
　Centre, Morpeth
　Northumb 178 A3
Northway Glos 80 D2
Northwich Ches 127 B6

Northwick S Glos 43 A4
Northwold Norf 102 B3
Northwood Derbys 130 C2
Northwood London 67 D5
Northwood I o W 18 B3
Northwood Kent 53 C5
Northwood Shrops 110 B3
Northwood Green Glos 62 B3
Norton E Sus 22 B2
Norton Glos 63 A4
Norton Halton 127 A5
Norton Herts 84 D4
Norton I o W 18 C2
Norton Mon 61 B6
Norton Notts 131 B5
Norton Northants 82 A3
Norton Powys 77 A7
Norton Shrops 94 C2
Norton Shrops 94 A3
Norton Shrops 95 A5
Norton Stockton 168 C2
Norton Suff 87 A5
Norton S Yorks 140 B3
Norton Wilts 44 A2
Norton Worcs 80 B1
Norton Worcs 80 C3
Norton W Sus 20 C1
Norton W Sus 20 B2
Norton Bavant Wilts 30 A3
Norton Bridge Staffs 112 B2
Norton Canes Staffs 96 A3
Norton Canon Hereford 78 C1
Norton Corner Norf 120 C2
Norton Disney Lincs 132 D3
Norton East Staffs 96 A3
Norton Ferris Wilts 30 B1
Norton Fitzwarren Som 28 C1
Norton Green I o W 18 C2
Norton Hawkfield Bath 43 C4
Norton Heath Essex 69 C6
Norton in Hales Shrops 111 B6
Norton-in-the-Moors
　Stoke 128 D3
Norton-Juxta-Twycross
　Leics 97 A6
Norton-le-Clay N Yorks 158 D3
Norton Lindsey Warks 81 A5
Norton Malreward Bath 43 C5
Norton Mandeville Essex 69 C5
Norton-on-Derwent
　N Yorks 159 D6
Norton St Philip Som 43 D6
Norton sub Hamdon Som 29 D4
Norton Woodseats
　S Yorks 130 A3
Norwell Notts 132 C2
Norwell Woodhouse
　Notts 132 C2
Norwich Norf 104 A3
Norwich Castle Museum
　Norf 104 A3
Norwich Cathedral Norf 104 A3
Norwich International
　Airport Norf 120 D4
Norwick Shetland 284 B8
Norwood Derbys 131 A4
Norwood Hill Sur 35 B5
Norwoodside Cambs 101 B6
Noseley Leics 99 B4
Noss Shetland 285 M5
Noss Mayo Devon 7 C4
Nosterfield N Yorks 157 C6
Nostie Highld 249 D5
Notgrove Glos 64 A2
Nothe Fort, Weymouth
　Dorset 15 D6
Nottage Bridgend 40 D3
Nottingham Nottingham 114 B3
Nottingham Castle
　Museum Nottingham 114 B3
Nottingham East
　Midlands Airport Leics 114 C2
Nottingham Racecourse
　Nottingham 114 B3
Nottington Dorset 15 C6
Notton Wilts 44 C3
Notton W Yorks 139 B6
Nounsley Essex 70 B1
Noutard's Green Worcs 79 A5
Novar House Highld 264 D2
Nox Shrops 110 D3
Nuffield Oxon 47 A4
Nun Hills Lancs 138 A1
Nun Monkton N Yorks 148 B4
Nunburnholme E Yorks 150 C1
Nuncargate Notts 131 D5
Nuneaton Warks 97 B6

Nuneham Courtenay Oxon 65 D6
Nunney Som 30 A1
Nunnington N Yorks 159 D5
Nunnykirk Northumb 188 D3
Nunsthorpe NE Lincs 143 C4
Nunthorpe M'bro 168 D3
Nunthorpe York 149 B5
Nunton Wilts 31 C5
Nunwick N Yorks 157 D7
Nupend Glos 62 C3
Nursling Hants 32 D2
Nursted Hants 33 C6
Nutbourne W Sus 20 A3
Nutbourne W Sus 19 A6
Nutfield Sur 35 A6
Nuthall Notts 114 A3
Nuthampstead Herts 85 D6
Nuthurst W Sus 35 D4
Nutley E Sus 36 D2
Nutley Hants 33 A5
Nutwell S Yorks 140 C4
Nybster Highld 281 B5
Nyetimber W Sus 20 C1
Nyewood W Sus 33 C7
Nymans Garden, Crawley
　W Sus 35 D5
Nymet Rowland Devon 12 A2
Nymet Tracey Devon 12 A2
Nympsfield Glos 63 C4
Nynehead Som 27 C6
Nyton W Sus 20 B2

O

Oad Street Kent 51 C5
Oadby Leics 98 A3
Oak Cross Devon 11 B6
Oakamoor Staffs 113 A4
Oakbank W Loth 208 D3
Oakdale Caerph 41 B6
Oake Som 27 C6
Oaken Staffs 95 A6
Oakenclough Lancs 145 C5
Oakengates Telford 111 D6
Oakenholt Flint 126 B2
Oakenshaw Durham 167 B5
Oakenshaw W Yorks 139 A4
Oakerthorpe Derbys 130 D3
Oakes W Yorks 139 B4
Oakfield Torf 61 D5
Oakford Ceredig 74 C3
Oakford Devon 27 C4
Oakfordbridge Devon 27 C4
Oakgrove Ches 129 C4
Oakham Rutland 99 A5
Oakhanger Hants 33 B6
Oakhill Som 29 A6
Oakhurst Kent 36 A3
Oakington Cambs 85 A6
Oaklands Herts 68 B2
Oaklands Powys 76 B4
Oakle Street Glos 62 B3
Oakley Beds 84 B2
Oakley Bucks 66 B1
Oakley Fife 208 B3
Oakley Hants 46 D3
Oakley Oxon 66 C2
Oakley Poole 17 B4
Oakley Suff 104 D2
Oakley Green Windsor 48 B2
Oakley Park Powys 92 C3
Oakmere Ches 127 C5
Oakridge Glos 63 C5
Oakridge Hants 47 D4
Oaks Shrops 94 A2
Oaks Green Derbys 113 B5
Oaksey Wilts 63 D5
Oakthorpe Leics 113 D7
Oakwood Adventure
　Park, Narberth Pembs 55 C6
Oakwoodhill Sur 35 C4
Oakworth W Yorks 147 D4
Oape Highld 272 D2
Oare Kent 52 C2
Oare Som 26 A3
Oare W Berks 46 B3
Oare Wilts 45 C5
Oasby Lincs 116 B3
Oathlaw Angus 232 C2
Oatlands N Yorks 148 B2
Oban Argyll 226 D3
Oban Highld 238 D2
Oborne Dorset 29 D6
Obthorpe Lincs 116 D3
Occlestone Green Ches 128 C1
Occold Suff 104 D2
Ochiltree E Ayrs 193 C5
Ochtermuthill Perth 218 C3

Ochtertyre Perth 218 B3
Ockbrook Derbys 114 B2
Ockham Sur 34 A3
Ockle Highld 235 C4
Ockley Sur 35 C4
Ocle Pychard Hereford 78 C3
Octon E Yorks 150 A3
Octon Cross Roads
　E Yorks 150 A3
Odcombe Som 29 D5
Odd Down Bath 43 C6
Oddendale Cumb 164 D3
Odder Lincs 133 B4
Oddingley Worcs 80 B2
Oddington Glos 64 A3
Oddington Oxon 65 B6
Odell Beds 83 B6
Odie Orkney 282 E7
Odiham Hants 47 D5
Odstock Wilts 31 C5
Odstone Leics 97 A6
Offchurch Warks 81 A6
Offenham Worcs 80 C3
Offham E Sus 22 A1
Offham Kent 37 A4
Offham W Sus 20 B3
Offord Cluny Cambs 84 A4
Offord Darcy Cambs 84 A4
Offton Suff 87 C6
Offwell Devon 14 B1
Ogbourne Maizey Wilts 45 B5
Ogbourne St Andrew Wilts 45 B5
Ogbourne St George Wilts 45 B6
Ogil Angus 232 B2
Ogle Northumb 178 B3
Ogmore V Glam 40 D3
Ogmore-by-Sea V Glam 40 D3
Ogmore Vale Bridgend 40 B4
Okeford Fitzpaine Dorset 30 D2
Okehampton Devon 11 B6
Okehampton Camp Devon 11 B6
Okraquoy Shetland 285 K6
Old Northants 99 D4
Old Aberdeen Aberdeen 245 B6
Old Alresford Hants 33 B4
Old Arley Warks 97 B5
Old Basford Nottingham 114 A3
Old Basing Hants 47 D4
Old Bewick Northumb 188 A3
Old Blacksmith's Shop
　Centre, Gretna Green
　Dumfries 175 B6
Old Bolingbroke Lincs 134 C3
Old Bramhope W Yorks 147 C6
Old Brampton Derbys 130 B3
Old Bridge of Tilt Perth 230 B2
Old Bridge of Urr
　Dumfries 173 B5
Old Buckenham Norf 103 B6
Old Burghclere Hants 46 D2
Old Byland N Yorks 159 C4
Old Cassop Durham 167 B6
Old Castleton Borders 186 D4
Old Catton Norf 120 D4
Old Clee NE Lincs 143 C4
Old Cleeve Som 27 A5
Old Clipstone Notts 131 C6
Old Colwyn Conwy 124 B3
Old Coulsdon London 35 A6
Old Crombie Aberds 267 D6
Old Dailly S Ayrs 181 B4
Old Dalby Leics 115 C4
Old Deer Aberds 257 B4
Old Denaby S Yorks 140 D2
Old Edlington S Yorks 140 D3
Old Eldon Durham 167 C5
Old Ellerby E Yorks 151 D4
Old Felixstowe Suff 88 D4
Old Fletton P'boro 100 B3
Old Glossop Derbys 138 D3
Old Goole E Yorks 141 A5
Old Hall Powys 91 D7
Old Heath Essex 71 A4
Old Heathfield E Sus 36 D3
Old Hill W Mid 96 C2
Old House, Rochford
　Essex 70 D2
Old Hunstanton Norf 118 A3
Old Hurst Cambs 101 D4
Old Hutton Cumb 155 C4
Old Kea Corn 4 C3
Old Kilpatrick W Dunb 205 A4
Old Kinnernie Aberds 245 B4
Old Knebworth Herts 68 A2
Old Langho Lancs 145 D7
Old Laxey I o M 152 C4
Old Leake Lincs 135 D4
Old Malton N Yorks 159 D6

Old Micklefield W Yorks 148 D3
Old Milton Hants 17 B6
Old Milverton Warks 81 A5
Old Monkland N Lnrk 207 D5
Old Netley Hants 18 A3
Old Philpstoun W Loth 208 C3
Old Quarrington Durham 167 B6
Old Radnor Powys 77 B6
Old Rattray Aberds 269 D5
Old Rayne Aberds 256 D1
Old Romney Kent 38 C2
Old Sarum, Salisbury Wilts 31 B5
Old Sodbury S Glos 43 A6
Old Somerby Lincs 116 B2
Old Stratford Northants 83 C4
Old Thirsk N Yorks 158 C3
Old Town Cumb 164 A2
Old Town Cumb 155 C4
Old Town Northumb 188 D1
Old Town Scilly 2 E4
Old Trafford Gtr Man 137 D7
Old Tupton Derbys 130 C3
Old Warden Beds 84 C3
Old Weston Cambs 100 D2
Old Whittington Derbys 130 B3
Old Wick Highld 281 C5
Old Windsor Windsor 48 B2
Old Wives Lees Kent 52 D2
Old Woking Sur 34 A3
Old Woodhall Lincs 134 C2
Oldany Highld 270 A4
Oldberrow Warks 80 A4
Oldborough Devon 12 A2
Oldbury Shrops 95 B5
Oldbury Warks 97 B6
Oldbury W Mid 96 C2
Oldbury-on-Severn S Glos 62 D2
Oldbury on the Hill Glos 44 A2
Oldcastle Bridgend 40 D4
Oldcastle Mon 61 A5
Oldcotes Notts 131 A5
Oldfallow Staffs 112 D3
Oldford Som 44 D1
Oldham Gtr Man 138 C2
Oldhamstocks E Loth 211 C4
Oldland S Glos 43 B5
Oldmeldrum Aberds 256 D3
Oldshore Beg Highld 276 C2
Oldshoremore Highld 276 C3
Oldstead N Yorks 158 C4
Oldtown Aberds 255 D6
Oldtown of Ord Aberds 267 D7
Oldway Swansea 57 D5
Oldways End Devon 26 C3
Oldwhat Aberds 268 D3
Olgrinmore Highld 280 C2
Oliver's Battery Hants 32 C3
Ollaberry Shetland 284 E5
Ollerton Ches 128 B2
Ollerton Notts 131 C6
Ollerton Shrops 111 C5
Olmarch Ceredig 75 C5
Olney M Keynes 83 B5
Olrig Ho. Highld 280 B3
Olton W Mid 96 C4
Olveston S Glos 43 A5
Olwen Ceredig 75 D4
Ombersley Worcs 79 A6
Ompton Notts 132 C1
Onchan I o M 152 D3
Onecote Staffs 129 D5
Onen Mon 61 B6
Ongar Hill Norf 118 C2
Ongar Street Hereford 78 A1
Onibury Shrops 94 D2
Onich Highld 237 C4
Onllwyn Neath 59 D5
Onneley Staffs 111 A6
Onslow Village Sur 34 B2
Onthank E Ayrs 205 D4
Openwoodgate Derbys 114 A1
Opinan Highld 261 A5
Opinan Highld 261 C4
Orange Lane Borders 198 B1
Orange Row Norf 118 C2
Orasaigh W Isles 288 F4
Orbliston Moray 266 D4
Orbost Highld 258 D2
Orby Lincs 135 C4
Orchard Hill Devon 25 C5
Orchard Portman Som 28 C2
Orcheston Wilts 31 A4
Orcop Hereford 61 A6
Orcop Hill Hereford 61 A6

Ord Highld 247 C5
Ordhead Aberds 244 A3
Ordie Aberds 244 B1
Ordiequish Moray 266 D4
Ordsall Notts 132 A1
Ore E Sus 23 A6
Oreton Shrops 95 C4
Orford Suff 89 C5
Orford Warr 137 D5
Orgreave Staffs 113 D5
Orlestone Kent 38 B1
Orleton Hereford 78 A2
Orleton Worcs 79 A4
Orlingbury Northants 99 D5
Ormesby Redcar 168 D3
Ormesby St Margaret Norf 121 D6
Ormesby St Michael Norf 121 D6
Ormiclate Castle W Isles 286 C3
Ormiscaig Highld 261 A5
Ormiston E Loth 209 D7
Ormsaigbeg Highld 234 D3
Ormsaigmore Highld 234 D3
Ormsary Argyll 202 A2
Ormsgill Cumb 153 C2
Ormskirk Lancs 136 C3
Orpington London 50 C1
Orrell Gtr Man 136 C4
Orrell Mers 136 D2
Orrisdale I o M 152 B3
Orroland Dumfries 173 D5
Orsett Thurrock 50 A3
Orslow Staffs 112 D2
Orston Notts 115 A5
Orthwaite Cumb 163 A5
Ortner Lancs 145 B5
Orton Cumb 155 A5
Orton Northants 99 D5
Orton Longueville P'boro 100 B3
Orton-on-the-Hill Leics 97 A6
Orton Waterville P'boro 100 B3
Orwell Cambs 85 B5
Osbaldeston Lancs 145 D6
Osbaldwick York 149 B5
Osbaston Shrops 110 C2
Osborne House I o W 18 B4
Osbournby Lincs 116 B3
Oscroft Ches 127 C5
Ose Highld 258 D3
Osgathorpe Leics 114 D2
Osgodby Lincs 142 D2
Osgodby N Yorks 149 D5
Osgodby N Yorks 161 C4
Oskaig Highld 248 C2
Oskamull Argyll 224 B3
Osmaston Derbys 113 A6
Osmaston Derby 114 B1
Osmington Dorset 16 C1
Osmington Mills Dorset 16 C1
Osmotherley N Yorks 158 B3
Ospisdale Highld 264 B3
Ospringe Kent 52 C2
Ossett W Yorks 139 A5
Ossington Notts 132 C2
Ostend Essex 70 D3
Oswaldkirk N Yorks 159 D5
Oswaldtwistle Lancs 137 A6
Oswestry Shrops 110 C1
Otford Kent 36 A3
Otham Kent 37 A5
Othery Som 28 B3
Otley Suff 88 B3
Otley W Yorks 147 C6
Otter Ferry Argyll 214 D2
Otterbourne Hants 32 C3
Otterburn Northumb 188 D1
Otterburn N Yorks 146 B2
Otterburn Camp Northumb 188 D1
Otterham Corn 10 B2
Otterhampton Som 28 A2
Ottershaw Sur 48 C3
Otterswick Shetland 284 E7
Otterton Devon 13 C5
Ottery St Mary Devon 13 C5
Ottinge Kent 38 A3
Ottringham E Yorks 143 A4
Oughterby Cumb 175 C5
Oughtershaw N Yorks 156 C2
Oughterside Cumb 174 D4
Oughtibridge S Yorks 139 D6
Oughtrington Warr 128 A1
Oulston N Yorks 158 D4
Oulton Cumb 175 C5
Oulton Norf 120 C3

Oulton Staffs 112 B3
Oulton Suff 105 B6
Oulton W Yorks 139 A6
Oulton Broad Suff 105 B6
Oulton Park Motor Racing Circuit Ches 127 C5
Oulton Street Norf 120 C3
Oundle Northants 100 C2
Ousby Cumb 165 B4
Ousdale Highld 275 B4
Ousden Suff 86 B3
Ousefleet E Yorks 141 A6
Ouston Durham 179 D4
Ouston Northumb 178 B2
Out Newton E Yorks 143 A5
Out Rawcliffe Lancs 144 C4
Outertown Orkney 282 F3
Outgate Cumb 154 B2
Outhgill Cumb 155 A6
Outlane W Yorks 138 B3
Outwell Norf 101 A7
Outwick Hants 31 D5
Outwood Sur 35 B6
Outwood W Yorks 139 A6
Outwoods Staffs 112 D1
Ovenden W Yorks 138 A3
Ovenscloss Borders 196 C3
Over Cambs 101 D5
Over Ches 127 C6
Over S Glos 43 A4
Over Compton Dorset 29 D5
Over Green W Mid 97 B4
Over Haddon Derbys 130 C2
Over Hulton Gtr Man 137 C5
Over Kellet Lancs 154 D4
Over Kiddington Oxon 65 A5
Over Knutsford Ches 128 B2
Over Monnow Mon 61 B7
Over Norton Oxon 64 A4
Over Peover Ches 128 B2
Over Silton N Yorks 158 B3
Over Stowey Som 28 B1
Over Stratton Som 28 D4
Over Tabley Ches 128 A2
Over Wallop Hants 32 B1
Over Whitacre Warks 97 B5
Over Worton Oxon 65 A5
Overbister Orkney 282 C7
Overbury Worcs 80 D2
Overcombe Dorset 15 C6
Overgreen Derbys 130 B3
Overleigh Som 29 B4
Overley Green Warks 80 B3
Overpool Ches 126 B3
Overscaig Hotel Highld 271 B7
Overseal Derbys 113 D6
Oversland Kent 52 D2
Overstone Northants 83 A5
Overstrand Norf 120 A4
Overthorpe Northants 82 C1
Overton Aberdeen 245 A5
Overton Ches 127 B5
Overton Dumfries 174 B2
Overton Hants 32 A4
Overton Lancs 144 B4
Overton N Yorks 149 B4
Overton Shrops 94 D3
Overton Swansea 57 D4
Overton W Yorks 139 B5
Overton = Owrtyn Wrex 110 A2
Overton Bridge Wrex 110 A2
Overtown N Lnrk 194 A3
Oving Bucks 66 A2
Oving W Sus 20 B2
Ovingdean Brighton 21 B6
Ovingham Northumb 178 C2
Ovington Durham 166 D4
Ovington Essex 86 C3
Ovington Hants 33 B4
Ovington Norf 103 A5
Ovington Northumb 178 C2
Ower Hants 32 D2
Owermoigne Dorset 16 C1
Owlbury Shrops 93 B7
Owler Bar Derbys 130 B2
Owlerton S Yorks 130 A3
Owl's Green Suff 88 A3
Owlswick Bucks 66 C2
Owmby Lincs 142 C2
Owmby-by-Spital Lincs 133 A5
Owrtyn = Overton Wrex 110 A2
Owslebury Hants 32 C4
Owston Leics 99 A4
Owston S Yorks 140 B3
Owston Ferry N Lincs 141 C6
Owstwick E Yorks 151 D5
Owthorne E Yorks 143 A5
Owthorpe Notts 115 B4

Oxborough Norf 102 A3
Oxburgh Hall Norf 102 A3
Oxcombe Lincs 134 B3
Oxen Park Cumb 154 C2
Oxenholme Cumb 154 C4
Oxenhope W Yorks 147 D4
Oxenton Glos 80 D2
Oxenwood Wilts 45 D7
Oxford Oxon 65 C6
Oxford University Botanic Garden Oxon 65 C6
Oxhey Herts 67 D6
Oxhill Warks 81 C6
Oxley W Mid 96 A2
Oxley Green Essex 70 B3
Oxley's Green E Sus 37 D4
Oxnam Borders 187 B6
Oxshott Sur 48 C4
Oxspring S Yorks 139 C5
Oxted Sur 36 A1
Oxton Borders 196 A3
Oxton Notts 131 D6
Oxwich Swansea 57 D4
Oxwick Norf 119 C6
Oykel Bridge Highld 271 D6
Oyne Aberds 256 D1

P

Pabail Iarach W Isles 288 D6
Pabail Uarach W Isles 288 D6
Pace Gate N Yorks 147 B5
Packington Leics 114 D1
Padanaram Angus 232 C2
Padbury Bucks 83 D4
Paddington London 49 A5
Paddlesworth Kent 38 B3
Paddock Wood Kent 37 B4
Paddockhaugh Moray 266 D3
Paddockhole Dumfries 185 D5
Padfield Derbys 138 D3
Padiham Lancs 146 D1
Padog Conwy 124 D3
Padside N Yorks 147 B5
Padstow Corn 9 D5
Padworth W Berks 47 C4
Page Bank Durham 167 B5
Pagham W Sus 20 C1
Paglesham Eastend Essex 70 D3
Paglesham Churchend Essex 70 D3
Paibeil W Isles 287 H2
Paible W Isles 287 E5
Paignton Torbay 8 A2
Paignton & Dartmouth Steam Railway Devon 8 A2
Paignton Zoo Torbay 8 B2
Pailton Warks 98 C1
Painscastle Powys 77 C5
Painshawfield Northumb 178 C2
Painsthorpe E Yorks 149 B7
Painswick Glos 63 C4
Pairc Shiaboist W Isles 288 C3
Paisley Renfs 205 B4
Pakefield Suff 105 B6
Pakenham Suff 87 A5
Palace House, Beaulieu Hants 18 A2
Palace of Holyroodhouse Edin 209 C6
Pale Gwyn 109 B4
Palestine Hants 31 A6
Paley Street Windsor 47 B6
Palfrey W Mid 96 B3
Palgowan Dumfries 181 C5
Palgrave Suff 104 D2
Pallion T & W 179 D5
Palmarsh Kent 38 B3
Palnackie Dumfries 173 C6
Palnure Dumfries 171 A6
Palterton Derbys 131 C4
Pamber End Hants 47 D4
Pamber Green Hants 47 D4
Pamber Heath Hants 47 C4
Pamphill Dorset 16 A3
Pampisford Cambs 85 C6
Pan Orkney 283 H4
Panbride Angus 221 A5
Pancrasweek Devon 10 A3
Pandy Gwyn 90 B4
Pandy Mon 61 A5
Pandy Powys 91 B7
Pandy Wrex 109 B6
Pandy Tudur Conwy 124 C3
Panfield Essex 70 A1
Pangbourne W Berks 47 B4
Pannal N Yorks 148 B2
Panshanger Herts 68 B2

Pant Shrops 110 C1
Pant-glas Carms 58 C2
Pant-glas Gwyn 107 B4
Pant-glâs Powys 91 C5
Pant-glas Shrops 110 B1
Pant-teg Carms 58 C1
Pant Mawr Powys 91 D6
Pant-y-Caws Carms 73 D4
Pant-y-dwr Powys 92 D3
Pant-y-ffridd Powys 93 A5
Pant-y-Wacco Flint 125 B6
Pant-yr-awel Bridgend 40 C4
Pantgwyn Ceredig 73 B5
Pantgwyn Carms 58 C2
Pantlasau Swansea 57 C6
Panton Lincs 134 B1
Pantperthog Gwyn 91 B5
Pantyffynnon Carms 57 A6
Pantymwyn Flint 126 C1
Panxworth Norf 121 D5
Papa Westray Airport Orkney 282 B5
Papcastle Cumb 163 A4
Papigoe Highld 281 C5
Papil Shetland 285 K5
Papley Orkney 283 H5
Papple E Loth 210 C2
Papplewick Notts 131 D5
Papworth Everard Cambs 85 A4
Papworth St Agnes Cambs 85 A4
Par Corn 5 B5
Paradise Wildlife Park, Broxbourne Herts 68 C3
Parbold Lancs 136 B3
Parbrook Som 29 B5
Parbrook W Sus 34 D3
Parc Gwyn 108 B3
Parc-Seymour Newport 61 D6
Parc-y-rhôs Carms 75 D4
Parcllyn Ceredig 73 A5
Pardshaw Cumb 162 B3
Parham Suff 88 A4
Park Dumfries 183 C7
Park Corner Oxon 47 A4
Park Corner Windsor 47 A6
Park End M'boro 168 D3
Park End Northumb 177 B6
Park Gate Hants 18 A4
Park Hill Notts 132 D1
Park Hill N Yorks 148 A2
Park Rose Pottery and Leisure Park, Bridlington E Yorks 151 A4
Park Street W Sus 35 C4
Parkend Glos 62 C2
Parkeston Essex 88 D3
Parkgate Ches 126 B2
Parkgate Dumfries 184 D3
Parkgate Kent 37 C6
Parkgate Sur 35 B5
Parkham Devon 25 C4
Parkham Ash Devon 25 C4
Parkhill Ho. Aberds 245 A5
Parkhouse Mon 61 C6
Parkhouse Green Derbys 131 C4
Parkhurst I o W 18 B3
Parkmill Swansea 57 D5
Parkneuk Aberds 233 A5
Parkstone Poole 17 B4
Parley Cross Dorset 17 B4
Parracombe Devon 26 A1
Parrog Pembs 72 C3
Parsley Hay Derbys 129 C6
Parson Cross S Yorks 139 D6
Parson Drove Cambs 101 A5
Parsonage Green Essex 69 C7
Parsonby Cumb 163 A4
Parson's Heath Essex 71 A4
Partick Glasgow 205 B5
Partington Gtr Man 137 D6
Partney Lincs 135 C4
Parton Cumb 162 B2
Parton Dumfries 173 A4
Parton Glos 63 A4
Partridge Green W Sus 21 A4
Parwich Derbys 130 D1
Passenham Northants 83 D4
Paston Norf 121 B5
Patchacott Devon 11 B5
Patcham Brighton 21 B6
Patching W Sus 20 B3
Patchole Devon 25 A7
Patchway S Glos 43 A5
Pateley Bridge N Yorks 147 A5
Paternoster Heath Essex 70 B3
Path of Condie Perth 219 C5
Pathe Som 28 B3
Pathead Aberds 233 B5

Pathhead E Ayrs 182 A4
Pathhead Fife 209 A5
Pathhead Midloth 209 D6
Pathstruie Perth 219 C5
Patna E Ayrs 182 A2
Patney Wilts 45 D4
Patrick I o M 152 C2
Patrick Brompton N Yorks 157 B6
Patrington E Yorks 143 A5
Patrixbourne Kent 52 D3
Patterdale Cumb 164 D1
Pattingham Staffs 95 B6
Pattishall Northants 82 B3
Pattiswick Green Essex 70 A2
Patton Bridge Cumb 155 B4
Paul Corn 2 C2
Paulerspury Northants 83 C4
Paull E Yorks 142 A3
Paulton Bath 43 D5
Paultons Park, Totton Hants 32 D2
Pavenham Beds 84 B1
Pawlett Som 28 A3
Pawston Northumb 198 C2
Paxford Glos 81 D4
Paxton Borders 198 A3
Payhembury Devon 13 A5
Paythorne Lancs 146 B2
Peacehaven E Sus 22 B2
Peak Dale Derbys 129 B5
Peak Forest Derbys 129 B6
Peakirk P'boro 100 A3
Pearsie Angus 232 C1
Pease Pottage W Sus 35 C5
Peasedown St John Bath 43 D6
Peasemore W Berks 46 B2
Peasenhall Suff 89 A4
Peaslake Sur 34 B3
Peasley Cross Mers 136 D4
Peasmarsh E Sus 37 D6
Peaston E Loth 210 D1
Peastonbank E Loth 210 D1
Peat Inn Fife 221 D4
Peathill Aberds 269 C4
Peatling Magna Leics 98 B2
Peatling Parva Leics 98 C2
Peaton Shrops 94 C3
Peats Corner Suff 88 A2
Pebmarsh Essex 87 D4
Pebworth Worcs 80 C4
Pecket Well N Yorks 138 A2
Peckforton Ches 127 D5
Peckham London 49 B6
Peckleton Leics 98 A1
Pedlinge Kent 38 B3
Pedmore W Mid 96 C2
Pedwell Som 28 B4
Peebles Borders 196 B1
Peel I o M 152 C2
Peel Common Hants 19 A4
Peel Park S Lnrk 205 C6
Peening Quarter Kent 37 D6
Pegsdon Beds 84 D3
Pegswood Northumb 179 A4
Pegwell Kent 53 C5
Peinchorran Highld 247 A4
Peinlich Highld 259 C4
Pelaw T & W 179 C4
Pelcomb Bridge Pembs 55 C5
Pelcomb Cross Pembs 55 C5
Peldon Essex 70 B3
Pellon W Yorks 138 A3
Pelsall W Mid 96 A3
Pelton Durham 179 D4
Pelutho Cumb 174 D4
Pelynt Corn 5 B7
Pemberton Gtr Man 137 C4
Pembrey Carms 57 B4
Pembrey Motor Racing Circuit Carms 57 B4
Pembridge Hereford 78 B1
Pembroke = Penfro Pembs 55 D5
Pembroke Castle Pembs 55 D5
Pembroke Dock = Doc Penfro Pembs 55 D5
Pembury Kent 36 B4
Pen-bont Rhydybeddau Ceredig 91 D4
Pen-clawdd Swansea 57 C5
Pen-ffordd Pembs 55 B6
Pen-groes-oped Mon 61 C5
Pen-llyn Anglesey 122 B3
Pen-lon Anglesey 123 D4
Pen-sarn Gwyn 107 B4
Pen-sarn Gwyn 107 D5
Pen-twyn Mon 61 C7
Pen-y-banc Carms 58 C3

Pen-y-bont Carms 73 D6
Pen-y-bont Gwyn 91 B5
Pen-y-bont Gwyn 107 D6
Pen-y-bont Powys 109 C7
Pen-y-bont ar Ogwr =
Bridgend Bridgend 40 D4
Pen-y-bryn Gwyn 91 A4
Pen-y-bryn Pembs 73 B4
Pen-y-cae Powys 59 D5
Pen-y-cae-mawr Mon 61 D6
Pen-y-cefn Flint 125 B6
Pen-y-clawdd Mon 61 C6
Pen-y-coedcae Rhondda 41 C5
Pen-y-fai Bridgend 40 C3
Pen-y-garn Ceredig 90 D4
Pen-y-garn Carms 58 B2
Pen-y-garnedd Anglesey 123 C5
Pen-y-gop Conwy 108 A4
Pen-y-graig Gwyn 106 C1
Pen-y-groes Carms 57 A5
Pen-y-groeslon Gwyn 106 C2
Pen-y-Gwryd Hotel Gwyn 107 A6
Pen-y-stryt Denb 126 D1
Pen-yr-heol Mon 61 B6
Pen-yr-Heolgerrig M Tydf 60 C2
Penallt Mon 61 B7
Penally Pembs 55 E7
Penalt Hereford 62 A1
Penare Corn 5 C4
Penarlâg = Hawarden
Flint 126 C3
Penarth V Glam 41 D6
Penbryn Ceredig 73 A5
Pencader Carms 58 B1
Pencaenewydd Gwyn 107 B4
Pencaitland E Loth 210 D1
Pencarnisiog Anglesey 122 C3
Pencarreg Carms 75 D4
Pencelli Powys 60 A2
Pencoed Bridgend 41 C5
Pencombe Hereford 78 B3
Pencoyd Hereford 61 A7
Pencraig Hereford 62 A1
Pencraig Powys 109 C5
Pendeen Corn 2 B1
Pendennis Castle Corn 4 D3
Penderyn Rhondda 59 E6
Pendine Carms 56 B2
Pendlebury Gtr Man 137 C6
Pendleton Lancs 146 D1
Pendock Worcs 79 D5
Pendoggett Corn 9 D6
Pendomer Som 29 D5
Pendoylan V Glam 41 D5
Pendre Bridgend 40 C4
Penegoes Powys 91 B5
Penfro = Pembroke
Pembs 55 D5
Pengam Caerph 41 B6
Penge London 49 B6
Pengenffordd Powys 77 D5
Pengorffwysfa Anglesey 123 A4
Pengover Green Corn 6 A1
Penhale Corn 3 D4
Penhale Corn 4 B4
Penhalvaen Corn 4 D2
Penhill Swindon 45 A5
Penhow Newport 61 D6
Penhurst E Sus 23 A4
Peniarth Gwyn 90 B4
Penicuik Midloth 209 D5
Peniel Carms 58 C1
Peniel Denb 125 C5
Penifiler Highld 259 D4
Peninver Argyll 190 C3
Penisarwaun Gwyn 123 D5
Penistone S Yorks 139 C5
Penjerrick Corn 4 D2
Penketh Warr 127 A5
Penkill S Ayrs 181 B4
Penkridge Staffs 112 D3
Penley Wrex 110 B3
Penllergaer Swansea 57 C6
Penllyn V Glam 41 D4
Penmachno Conwy 124 D2
Penmaen Swansea 57 D5
Penmaenan Conwy 124 B2
Penmaenmawr Conwy 124 B2
Penmaenpool Gwyn 91 A4
Penmark V Glam 41 E5
Penmarth Corn 4 D2
Penmon Anglesey 123 B6
Penmore Mill Argyll 224 A3
Penmorfa Ceredig 73 A6
Penmorfa Gwyn 107 B5
Penmynydd Anglesey 123 C5
Penn Bucks 67 D4
Penn W Mid 96 B1

Penn Street Bucks 67 D4
Pennal Gwyn 91 B5
Pennan Aberds 268 C3
Pennant Ceredig 75 B4
Pennant Denb 109 B5
Pennant Denb 125 D5
Pennant Powys 91 C6
Pennant Melangell
Powys 109 C5
Pennar Pembs 55 D5
Pennard Swansea 57 D5
Pennerley Shrops 94 B1
Pennington Cumb 153 C3
Pennington Gtr Man 137 D5
Pennington Hants 18 B2
Penny Bridge Cumb 154 C2
Pennycross Argyll 225 D4
Pennygate Norf 121 C5
Pennygown Argyll 225 B4
Pennymoor Devon 26 D3
Pennywell T & W 179 D5
Penparc Ceredig 73 B5
Penparc Pembs 55 A4
Penparcau Ceredig 90 D3
Penperlleni Mon 61 C5
Penpillick Corn 5 B5
Penpol Corn 4 D3
Penpoll Corn 5 B6
Penpont Dumfries 183 C6
Penpont Powys 59 C6
Penrherber Carms 73 C5
Penrhiw goch Carms 57 A5
Penrhiw-llan Ceredig 73 B6
Penrhiw-pâl Ceredig 73 B6
Penrhiwceiber Rhondda 41 B5
Penrhôs Gwyn 106 C3
Penrhos Mon 61 B6
Penrhos Gwyn 59 D4
Penrhosfeilw Anglesey 122 B2
Penrhyn Bay Conwy 124 A3
Penrhyn Castle Gwyn 123 C6
Penrhyn-coch Ceredig 90 D4
Penrhyndeudraeth Gwyn 107 C6
Penrhynside Conwy 124 A3
Penrice Swansea 57 D4
Penrith Cumb 164 B3
Penrose Corn 9 D4
Penruddock Cumb 164 C2
Penryn Corn 4 D2
Pensarn Carms 57 A4
Pensarn Conwy 125 B4
Pensax Worcs 79 A5
Pensby Mers 126 A2
Penselwood Som 30 B1
Pensford Bath 43 C5
Penshaw T & W 179 D5
Penshurst Kent 36 B3
Pensilva Corn 6 A1
Penston E Loth 210 C1
Pentewan Corn 5 C5
Pentir Gwyn 123 D5
Pentire Corn 4 A2
Pentlow Essex 87 C4
Pentney Norf 119 D4
Penton Mewsey Hants 32 A2
Pentraeth Anglesey 123 C5
Pentre Carms 57 A5
Pentre Powys 93 C4
Pentre Powys 93 B6
Pentre Rhondda 41 B4
Pentre Shrops 110 D2
Pentre Wrex 110 A1
Pentre Wrex 109 B6
Pentre-bâch Ceredig 75 D4
Pentre-bach Powys 59 B6
Pentre Berw Anglesey 123 C4
Pentre-bont Conwy 124 D2
Pentre-celyn Denb 125 D6
Pentre-Celyn Powys 91 B6
Pentre-chwyth Swansea 57 C6
Pentre-cwrt Carms 73 C6
Pentre Dolau-Honddu
Powys 76 C3
Pentre-dwr Swansea 40 B1
Pentre-galar Pembs 73 C4
Pentre-Gwenlais Carms 57 A6
Pentre Gwynfryn Gwyn 107 D5
Pentre Halkyn Flint 126 B2
Pentre-Isaf Conwy 124 C3
Pentre Llanrhaeadr Denb 125 C5
Pentre-llwyn-llŵyd Powys 76 B3
Pentre-llyn Ceredig 75 A5
Pentre-llyn cymmer
Conwy 125 D4
Pentre Meyrick V Glam 41 D4
Pentre-poeth Newport 42 A1
Pentre-rhew Ceredig 75 C5

Pentre-tafarn-y-fedw
Conwy 124 C3
Pentre-ty-gwyn Carms 59 B5
Pentrebach M Tydf 41 A5
Pentrebach Swansea 57 B6
Pentrebeirdd Powys 109 D6
Pentrecagal Carms 73 B6
Pentredwr Denb 109 A6
Pentrefelin Ceredig 75 D5
Pentrefelin Carms 58 C2
Pentrefelin Conwy 124 B3
Pentrefelin Gwyn 107 C5
Pentrefoelas Conwy 124 D3
Pentregat Ceredig 73 A6
Pentreheyling Shrops 93 B6
Pentre'r Felin Conwy 124 C3
Pentre'r-felin Powys 59 B6
Pentrich Derbys 130 D3
Pentridge Dorset 31 D4
Pentyrch Cardiff 41 C6
Penuchadre V Glam 40 D3
Penuwch Ceredig 75 B4
Penwithick Corn 5 B5
Penwyllt Powys 59 D5
Penybanc Carms 57 A6
Penybont Powys 77 A5
Penybontfawr Powys 109 C5
Penycae Wrex 110 A1
Penycwm Pembs 54 B4
Penyffordd Flint 126 C3
Penyffridd Gwyn 107 A5
Penygarnedd Powys 109 C6
Penygraig Rhondda 41 B4
Penygroes Gwyn 107 A4
Penygroes Pembs 73 C4
Penyrheol Caerph 41 C6
Penysarn Anglesey 123 A4
Penywaun Rhondda 41 A4
Penzance Corn 2 B2
Penzance Heliport Corn 2 B2
People's Palace Glasgow 205 B6
Peopleton Worcs 80 B2
Peover Heath Ches 128 B2
Peper Harow Sur 34 B2
Perceton N Ayrs 204 D3
Percie Aberds 244 C2
Percyhorner Aberds 269 C4
Periton Som 27 A4
Perivale London 49 A4
Perkinsville Durham 179 D4
Perlethorpe Notts 131 B6
Perranarworthal Corn 4 D2
Perranporth Corn 4 B2
Perranuthnoe Corn 2 C3
Perranzabuloe Corn 4 B2
Perry Barr W Mid 96 B3
Perry Green Herts 68 B4
Perry Green Wilts 44 A3
Perry Street Kent 50 B3
Perryfoot Derbys 129 A6
Pershall Staffs 112 B2
Pershore Worcs 80 C2
Pert Angus 233 B4
Pertenhall Beds 84 A2
Perth Perth 219 B6
Perth Racecourse Perth 219 B6
Perthy Shrops 110 B2
Perton Staffs 95 B6
Pertwood Wilts 30 B2
Peter Tavy Devon 11 D6
Peterborough P'boro 100 B3
Peterborough Cathedral
P'boro 100 B3
Peterburn Highld 261 B4
Peterchurch Hereford 78 D1
Peterculter Aberdeen 245 B5
Peterhead Aberds 257 B6
Peterlee Durham 168 A2
Peter's Green Herts 67 B6
Peters Marland Devon 25 D5
Petersfield Hants 33 C6
Peterston super-Ely
V Glam 41 D5
Peterstone Wentlooge
Newport 42 A1
Peterstow Hereford 62 A1
Petertown Orkney 283 G4
Petham Kent 52 D3
Petrockstow Devon 11 A6
Pett E Sus 23 A6
Pettaugh Suff 88 B2
Petteridge Kent 37 B4
Pettinain S Lnrk 195 B4
Pettistree Suff 88 B3
Petton Devon 27 C5
Petton Shrops 110 C3
Petts Wood London 50 C1
Petty Aberds 256 C2

Pettycur Fife 209 B5
Pettymuick Aberds 257 D4
Petworth W Sus 34 D2
Petworth House W Sus 34 D2
Pevensey E Sus 22 B4
Pevensey Bay E Sus 23 B4
Pewsey Wilts 45 C5
Philham Devon 24 C3
Philiphaugh Borders 186 A3
Phillack Corn 2 B3
Philleigh Corn 4 D3
Philpstoun W Loth 208 C3
Phocle Green Hereford 62 A2
Phoenix Green Hants 47 D5
Pica Cumb 162 B3
Piccotts End Herts 67 C5
Pickering N Yorks 159 C6
Picket Piece Hants 32 A2
Picket Post Hants 17 A5
Pickhill N Yorks 158 C2
Picklescott Shrops 94 B2
Pickletillem Fife 220 B4
Pickmere Ches 128 B1
Pickney Som 28 C1
Pickstock Telford 111 C6
Pickwell Devon 25 A5
Pickwell Leics 115 D5
Pickworth Lincs 116 B3
Pickworth Rutland 116 D2
Picton Ches 127 B4
Picton Flint 125 A6
Picton N Yorks 158 A3
Piddinghoe E Sus 22 B2
Piddington Northants 83 B5
Piddington Oxon 66 B1
Piddlehinton Dorset 15 B7
Piddletrenthide Dorset 15 B7
Pidley Cambs 101 D5
Piece Hall Art Gallery,
Halifax W Yorks 138 A3
Piercebridge Darl 167 D5
Pierowall Orkney 282 C5
Pigdon Northumb 178 A3
Pikehall Derbys 130 D1
Pilgrims Hatch Essex 69 D5
Pilham Lincs 141 D6
Pill N Som 43 B4
Pillaton Corn 6 A2
Pillerton Hersey Warks 81 C6
Pillerton Priors Warks 81 C5
Pilleth Powys 77 A6
Pilley Hants 18 B2
Pilley S Yorks 139 C6
Pilling Lancs 144 C4
Pilling Lane Lancs 144 C3
Pillowell Glos 62 C2
Pillwell Dorset 30 D1
Pilning S Glos 43 A4
Pilsbury Derbys 129 C6
Pilsdon Dorset 14 B4
Pilsgate P'boro 100 A2
Pilsley Derbys 130 B2
Pilsley Derbys 131 C4
Pilton Devon 25 B6
Pilton Northants 100 C2
Pilton Rutland 99 A6
Pilton Som 29 A5
Pilton Green Swansea 57 D4
Pimperne Dorset 16 A3
Pin Mill Suff 88 D3
Pinchbeck Lincs 117 C5
Pinchbeck Bars Lincs 117 C4
Pinchbeck West Lincs 117 C5
Pincheon Green S Yorks 141 B4
Pinehurst Swindon 45 A5
Pinfold Lancs 136 B2
Pinged Carms 57 B4
Pinhoe Devon 13 B4
Pinkneys Green Windsor 47 A6
Pinley W Mid 97 D6
Pinminnoch S Ayrs 180 B3
Pinmore S Ayrs 181 B4
Pinmore Mains S Ayrs 181 B4
Pinner London 48 A4
Pinvin Worcs 80 C2
Pinwherry S Ayrs 180 C3
Pinxton Derbys 131 D4
Pipe and Lyde Hereford 78 C3
Pipe Gate Shrops 111 A6
Piperhill Highld 253 A4
Piper's Pool Corn 10 C3
Pipewell Northants 99 C5
Pippacott Devon 25 B6
Pipton Powys 77 D5
Pirbright Sur 34 A2
Pirnmill N Ayrs 202 D3
Pirton Herts 84 D3
Pirton Worcs 80 C1

Pisgah Ceredig 75 A5
Pisgah Stirl 218 D2
Pishill Oxon 47 A5
Pistyll Gwyn 106 B3
Pitagowan Perth 230 B2
Pitblae Aberds 269 C4
Pitblado Aberds 219 B5
Pitcairngreen Perth 219 B5
Pitcalnie Highld 265 C4
Pitcaple Aberds 256 D2
Pitch Green Bucks 66 C2
Pitch Place Sur 34 A2
Pitchcombe Glos 63 C4
Pitchcott Bucks 66 A2
Pitchford Shrops 94 A3
Pitcombe Som 29 B6
Pitcorthie Fife 221 D5
Pitcox E Loth 210 C3
Pitcur Perth 220 A2
Pitfichie Aberds 244 A3
Pitforthie Aberds 233 A6
Pitgrudy Highld 264 A3
Pitkennedy Angus 232 C3
Pitkevy Fife 220 D2
Pitkierie Fife 221 D5
Pitlessie Fife 220 D3
Pitlochry Perth 230 C3
Pitmachie Aberds 256 D1
Pitmain Highld 241 B5
Pitmedden Aberds 256 D3
Pitminster Som 28 D2
Pitmuies Angus 232 D3
Pitmunie Aberds 244 A3
Pitney Som 29 C4
Pitscottie Fife 220 C4
Pitsea Essex 51 A4
Pitsford Northants 83 A4
Pitsmoor S Yorks 130 A3
Pitstone Bucks 67 B4
Pitstone Green Bucks 67 B4
Pitt Rivers Museum (See
University Museum)
Oxon 65 C6
Pittendreich Moray 266 C2
Pittentrail Highld 273 D5
Pittenweem Fife 221 D5
Pittington Durham 167 A6
Pittodrie Aberds 256 D1
Pitton Wilts 31 B6
Pittswood Kent 36 B4
Pittulie Aberds 269 C4
Pity Me Durham 167 A5
Pityme Corn 9 D5
Pityoulish Highld 242 A2
Pixey Green Suff 104 D3
Pixham Sur 35 A4
Pixley Hereford 79 D4
Place Newton N Yorks 160 D2
Plaidy Aberds 268 D2
Plains N Lnrk 207 D5
Plaish Shrops 94 B3
Plaistow W Sus 34 C3
Plaitford Hants 32 D1
Plank Lane Gtr Man 137 D5
Plas-canol Gwyn 90 A3
Plas Gogerddan Ceredig 90 D4
Plas Llwyngwern Powys 91 B5
Plas Mawr, Conwy Conwy 124 B2
Plas Nantyr Wrex 109 B6
Plas-yn-Cefn Denb 125 B5
Plastow Green Hants 46 C3
Platt Kent 36 A4
Platt Bridge Gtr Man 137 C5
Platts Common S Yorks 139 C6
Plawsworth Durham 167 A5
Plaxtol Kent 36 A4
Play Hatch Oxon 47 B5
Playden E Sus 37 D7
Playford Suff 88 C3
Playing Place Corn 4 C3
Playley Green Glos 79 D5
Plealey Shrops 94 A2
Plean Stirl 207 B6
Pleasington Blkburn 137 A5
Pleasley Derbys 131 C5
Pleasure Island Theme
Park NE Lincs 143 C5
Pleckgate Blkburn 145 D6
Plenmeller Northumb 177 C5
Pleshey Essex 69 B6
Plockton Highld 249 C5
Plocrapol W Isles 288 H2
Ploughfield Hereford 78 C1
Plowden Shrops 94 C1
Ploxgreen Shrops 94 A1
Pluckley Kent 38 A1

Pluckley Thorne Kent 37 B7
Plumbland Cumb 163 A4
Plumley Ches 128 B2
Plumpton Cumb 164 B2
Plumpton E Sus 21 A6
Plumpton Green E Sus 21 A6
Plumpton Head Cumb 164 B3
Plumpton Racecourse E Sus 21 A6
Plumstead London 50 B1
Plumstead Norf 120 B3
Plumtree Notts 115 B4
Plungar Leics 115 B5
Plush Dorset 15 A7
Plwmp Ceredig 73 A6
Plymouth Plym 6 B3
Plymouth City Airport Plym 7 A4
Plympton Plym 7 B4
Plymstock Plym 7 B4
Plymtree Devon 13 A5
Pockley N Yorks 159 C5
Pocklington E Yorks 149 C7
Pode Hole Lincs 117 C5
Podimore Som 29 C5
Podington Beds 83 A6
Podmore Staffs 112 B1
Point Clear Essex 71 B4
Pointon Lincs 116 B4
Pokesdown Bmouth 17 B5
Pol a Charra W Isles 286 E3
Polbae Dumfries 181 D4
Polbain Highld 270 C2
Polbathic Corn 6 B2
Polbeth W Loth 208 D3
Polchar Highld 242 B1
Pole Elm Worcs 79 C6
Polebrook Northants 100 C2
Polegate E Sus 22 B3
Poles Highld 264 A3
Polesden Lacey, Dorking Sur 35 A4
Polesworth Warks 97 A5
Polgigga Corn 2 C1
Polglass Highld 270 D3
Polgooth Corn 5 B4
Poling W Sus 20 B3
Polkerris Corn 5 B5
Polla Highld 277 C4
Pollington E Yorks 140 B4
Polloch Highld 236 C1
Pollok Glasgow 205 B5
Pollok House Glasgow 205 B5
Pollokshields Glasgow 205 B5
Polmassick Corn 5 C4
Polmont Falk 208 C2
Polnessan E Ayrs 182 A2
Polnish Highld 235 B6
Polperro Corn 5 B7
Polruan Corn 5 B6
Polsham Som 29 A5
Polstead Suff 87 D5
Poltalloch Argyll 213 C6
Poltimore Devon 13 B4
Polton Midloth 209 D5
Polwarth Borders 197 A6
Polyphant Corn 10 C3
Polzeath Corn 9 D5
Ponders End London 68 D3
Pondersbridge Cambs 101 B4
Pondtail Hants 34 A1
Ponsanooth Corn 4 D2
Ponsworthy Devon 12 D2
Pont Aber Carms 59 C4
Pont Aber-Geirw Gwyn 108 C2
Pont-ar-gothi Carms 58 C2
Pont ar Hydfer Powys 59 C5
Pont-ar-llechau Carms 59 C4
Pont Cwm Pydew Denb 109 B5
Pont Cyfyng Conwy 124 D2
Pont Cysyllte Wrex 110 A1
Pont Dolydd Prysor Gwyn 108 B2
Pont-faen Powys 76 D3
Pont Fronwydd Gwyn 108 C3
Pont-gareg Pembs 72 B4
Pont-Henri Carms 57 B4
Pont-Llogel Powys 109 D5
Pont Pen-y-benglog Gwyn 123 D6
Pont Rhyd-goch Conwy 124 C1
Pont-Rhyd-sarn Gwyn 108 C3
Pont Rhyd-y-cyff Bridgend 40 C3
Pont-rhyd-y-groes Ceredig 75 A6
Pont-rug Gwyn 123 D5

Pont Senni = Sennybridge Powys 59 C6
Pont-siân Ceredig 74 D3
Pont-y-gwaith Rhondda 41 B5
Pont-y-pant Conwy 124 D2
Pont y Pennant Gwyn 108 C4
Pont-y-Pŵl = Pontypool Torf 61 C4
Pont yclun Rhondda 41 C5
Pont yr Afon-Gam Gwyn 108 A2
Pont-yr-hafod Pembs 55 B5
Pontamman Carms 57 A6
Pontantwn Carms 57 A4
Pontardawe Neath 40 A2
Pontarddulais Swansea 57 B5
Pontarsais Carms 58 C1
Pontblyddyn Flint 126 C2
Pontbren Araeth Carms 58 C3
Pontbren Llwyd Rhondda 59 E6
Pontefract W Yorks 140 A2
Pontefract Racecourse W Yorks 140 A2
Ponteland Northumb 178 B3
Ponterwyd Ceredig 91 D5
Pontesbury Shrops 94 A1
Pontfadog Wrex 110 B1
Pontfaen Pembs 55 A6
Pontgarreg Ceredig 73 A6
Ponthir Torf 61 D5
Ponthirwaun Ceredig 73 B5
Pontllanfraith Caerph 41 B6
Pontlliw Swansea 57 B6
Pontllyfni Gwyn 107 A4
Pontlottyn Caerph 60 C3
Pontneddfechan Powys 59 E6
Pontnewydd Torf 61 D4
Pontrhydfendigaid Ceredig 75 B6
Pontrhydyfen Neath 40 B2
Pontrilas Hereford 61 A5
Pontrobert Powys 109 D6
Ponts Green E Sus 23 A4
Pontshill Hereford 62 A2
Pontsticill M Tydf 60 B3
Pontwgan Conwy 124 B2
Pontyates Carms 57 B4
Pontyberem Carms 57 A5
Pontycymer Bridgend 40 B4
Pontyglasier Pembs 72 C4
Pontypool = Pont-y-Pŵl Torf 61 C4
Pontypridd Rhondda 41 C5
Pontywaun Caerph 41 B7
Pooksgreen Hants 32 D2
Pool Corn 3 A4
Pool W Yorks 147 C6
Pool o'Muckhart Clack 219 D5
Pool Quay Powys 110 D1
Poole Poole 17 B4
Poole Keynes Glos 63 D5
Poolend Staffs 129 D4
Poolewe Highld 261 B5
Pooley Bridge Cumb 164 C2
Poolfold Staffs 128 D3
Poolhill Glos 62 A3
Poolsbrook Derbys 131 B4
Pootings Kent 36 B2
Pope Hill Pembs 55 C5
Popeswood Brack 47 C6
Popham Hants 33 A4
Poplar London 49 A6
Popley Hants 47 D4
Porchester Notts 114 A3
Porchfield I o W 18 B3
Porin Highld 251 A5
Poringland Norf 104 A3
Porkellis Corn 3 B4
Porlock Som 26 A3
Porlock Weir Som 26 A3
Port Ann Argyll 214 D2
Port Appin Argyll 226 B4
Port Arthur Shetland 285 K5
Port Askaig Argyll 201 B4
Port Bannatyne Argyll 203 B5
Port Carlisle Cumb 175 B5
Port Charlotte Argyll 200 C2
Port Clarence Stockton 168 C2
Port Driseach Argyll 203 A4
Port e Vullen I o M 152 B4
Port Ellen Argyll 200 D3
Port Elphinstone Aberds 256 E2
Port Erin I o M 152 E1
Port Erroll Aberds 257 C5
Port-Eynon Swansea 57 D4
Port Gaverne Corn 9 C6
Port Glasgow Inverclyd 204 A3
Port Henderson Highld 261 C4
Port Isaac Corn 9 C5
Port Lamont Argyll 203 A5

Port Lion Pembs 55 D5
Port Logan Dumfries 170 C2
Port Mholair W Isles 288 D6
Port Mor Highld 234 C3
Port Mulgrave N Yorks 169 D5
Port Nan Giùran W Isles 288 D6
Port nan Long W Isles 287 G3
Port Nis W Isles 288 A6
Port of Menteith Stirl 217 D5
Port Quin Corn 9 C5
Port Ramsay Argyll 226 B3
Port St Mary I o M 152 E2
Port Sunlight Mers 126 A3
Port Talbot Neath 40 B2
Port Tennant Swansea 57 C6
Port Wemyss Argyll 200 C1
Port William Dumfries 171 C5
Portachoillan Argyll 202 C2
Portavadie Argyll 203 B4
Portbury N Som 43 B4
Portchester Hants 19 A5
Portclair Highld 240 A2
Portencalzie Dumfries 180 D2
Portencross N Ayrs 204 D1
Portesham Dorset 15 C6
Portessie Moray 267 C5
Portfield Gate Pembs 55 C5
Portgate Devon 11 C5
Portgordon Moray 267 C4
Portgower Highld 274 C4
Porth Corn 4 A3
Porth Rhondda 41 B5
Porth Navas Corn 3 C5
Porth Tywyn = Burry Port Carms 57 B4
Porth-y-waen Shrops 110 C1
Porthaethwy = Menai Bridge Anglesey 123 C5
Porthallow Corn 3 C5
Porthallow Corn 6 B1
Porthcawl Bridgend 40 D3
Porthcothan Corn 9 D4
Porthcurno Corn 2 C1
Porthgain Pembs 54 A4
Porthill Shrops 110 D3
Porthkerry V Glam 41 E5
Porthleven Corn 3 C4
Porthllechog Anglesey 123 A4
Porthmadog Gwyn 107 C5
Porthmeor Corn 2 B2
Portholland Corn 5 C4
Porthoustock Corn 3 C6
Porthpean Corn 5 B5
Porthtowan Corn 3 A4
Porthyrhyd Carms 57 A5
Porthyrhyd Carms 59 B4
Portincaple Argyll 215 C5
Portington E Yorks 149 D6
Portinnisherrich Argyll 214 A2
Portinscale Cumb 163 B5
Portishead N Som 42 B3
Portkil Argyll 215 D5
Portknockie Moray 267 C5
Portlethen Aberds 245 C6
Portling Dumfries 173 C6
Portloe Corn 4 D4
Portmahomack Highld 265 B5
Portmeirion Gwyn 107 C5
Portmeirion Village Gwyn 107 C5
Portmellon Corn 5 C5
Portmore Hants 18 B2
Portnacroish Argyll 226 B4
Portnahaven Argyll 200 C1
Portnalong Highld 246 A2
Portnaluchaig Highld 235 B5
Portnancon Highld 277 B5
Portnellan Stirl 216 B4
Portobello Edin 209 C6
Porton Wilts 31 B5
Portpatrick Dumfries 170 B2
Portreath Corn 3 A4
Portree Highld 259 D4
Portscatho Corn 4 D3
Portsea Ptsmth 19 A5
Portskerra Highld 279 B4
Portskewett Mon 43 A4
Portslade Brighton 21 B5
Portslade-by-Sea Brighton 21 B5
Portsmouth Ptsmth 19 A5
Portsmouth W Yorks 138 A2
Portsmouth Sea Life Centre Ptsmth 19 B5
Portsonachan Argyll 227 D5
Portsoy Aberds 267 C6
Portswood Soton 32 D3
Porttanachy Moray 267 C4
Portuairk Highld 234 D3

Portway Hereford 78 D2
Portway Worcs 96 D3
Portwrinkle Corn 6 B2
Poslingford Suff 86 C3
Postbridge Devon 12 D1
Postcombe Oxon 66 D2
Postling Kent 38 B3
Postwick Norf 104 A3
Potholm Dumfries 185 D6
Potsgrove Beds 67 A4
Pott Row Norf 119 C4
Pott Shrigley Ches 129 B4
Potten End Herts 67 C5
Potter Brompton N Yorks 160 D3
Potter Heigham Norf 121 D6
Potter Street Essex 69 C4
Potterhanworth Lincs 133 C5
Potterhanworth Booths Lincs 133 C5
Potteries Museum & Art Gallery, Stoke-on-Trent Stoke 112 A2
Potterne Wilts 44 D3
Potterne Wick Wilts 44 D4
Potternewton W Yorks 148 D2
Potterspury Northants 83 C4
Potter's Cross Staffs 95 C6
Potterspury Northants 83 C4
Potterton Aberds 245 A6
Potterton W Yorks 148 D3
Potto N Yorks 158 A3
Potton Beds 84 C4
Poughill Corn 10 A3
Poughill Devon 12 A3
Poulshot Wilts 44 D3
Poulton Glos 64 C2
Poulton Mers 136 D2
Poulton-le-Fylde Lancs 144 D3
Pound Bank Worcs 95 D5
Pound Green E Sus 36 D3
Pound Green I o W 18 C2
Pound Green Worcs 95 D5
Pound Hill W Sus 35 C5
Poundfield E Sus 36 C3
Poundland S Ayrs 180 C3
Poundon Bucks 66 A1
Poundsgate Devon 12 D2
Poundstock Corn 10 B3
Powburn Northumb 188 B3
Powderham Devon 13 C4
Powderham Castle Devon 13 C4
Powerstock Dorset 15 B5
Powfoot Dumfries 174 B4
Powick Worcs 79 B6
Powis Castle, Welshpool Powys 93 A6
Powmill Perth 208 A3
Poxwell Dorset 16 C1
Poyle Slough 48 B3
Poynings W Sus 21 A5
Poyntington Dorset 29 D6
Poynton Ches 129 A4
Poynton Green Telford 111 D4
Poystreet Green Suff 87 B5
Praa Sands Corn 2 C3
Pratt's Bottom London 50 C1
Praze Corn 2 B3
Praze-an-Beeble Corn 3 B4
Predannack Wollas Corn 3 D4
Prees Shrops 111 B4
Prees Green Shrops 111 B4
Prees Heath Shrops 111 B4
Prees Higher Heath Shrops 111 B4
Prees Lower Heath Shrops 111 B4
Preesall Lancs 144 C3
Preesgweene Shrops 110 B1
Prenderguest Borders 198 A3
Prendwick Northumb 188 B3
Prengwyn Ceredig 73 B7
Prenteg Gwyn 107 B5
Prenton Mers 126 A3
Prescot Mers 136 D3
Prescott Shrops 110 C3
Pressen Northumb 198 C2
Prestatyn Denb 125 A6
Prestbury Ches 129 B4
Prestbury Glos 63 A5
Presteigne = Llanandras Powys 77 A7
Presthope Shrops 94 B3
Prestleigh Som 29 A6
Preston Borders 198 A1
Preston Brighton 21 B6
Preston Devon 12 D3
Preston Dorset 15 C7
Preston E Loth 210 C2

Preston E Yorks 151 D4
Preston Glos 63 C6
Preston Glos 79 D4
Preston Herts 68 A1
Preston Kent 52 C2
Preston Kent 53 C4
Preston Lancs 136 A4
Preston Northumb 189 A4
Preston Rutland 99 A5
Preston Shrops 111 D4
Preston Wilts 44 B4
Preston Wilts 45 B6
Preston Bagot Warks 81 A4
Preston Bissett Bucks 66 A1
Preston Bowyer Som 27 C6
Preston Brockhurst Shrops 111 C4
Preston Brook Halton 127 A5
Preston Candover Hants 33 A5
Preston Capes Northants 82 B2
Preston Crowmarsh Oxon 65 D7
Preston Gubbals Shrops 110 D3
Preston Hall Museum, Stockton-on-Tees Stockton 168 D2
Preston on Stour Warks 81 C5
Preston on the Hill Halton 127 A5
Preston on Wye Hereford 78 C1
Preston Plucknett Som 29 D5
Preston St Mary Suff 87 B5
Preston-under-Scar N Yorks 157 B4
Preston upon the Weald Moors Telford 111 D5
Preston Wynne Hereford 78 C3
Prestonmill Dumfries 174 C2
Prestonpans E Loth 209 C6
Prestwich Gtr Man 137 C7
Prestwick Northumb 178 B3
Prestwick S Ayrs 192 C3
Prestwood Bucks 66 C3
Price Town Bridgend 40 B4
Prickwillow Cambs 102 C1
Priddy Som 43 D4
Priest Hutton Lancs 154 D4
Priest Weston Shrops 93 B6
Priesthaugh Borders 186 C3
Primethorpe Leics 98 B2
Primrose Green Norf 120 D2
Primrose Valley N Yorks 161 D5
Primrosehill Herts 67 C5
Princes Gate Pembs 56 A1
Princes Risborough Bucks 66 C3
Princethorpe Warks 97 D7
Princetown Caerph 60 B3
Princetown Devon 11 D6
Prinknash Abbey, Gloucester Glos 63 B4
Prion Denb 125 C5
Prior Muir Fife 221 C5
Prior Park Northumb 198 A3
Priors Frome Hereford 78 D3
Priors Hardwick Warks 82 B1
Priors Marston Warks 82 B1
Priorslee Telford 111 D6
Priory Church, Lancaster Lancs 145 A4
Priory Wood Hereford 77 C6
Priston Bath 43 C5
Pristow Green Norf 104 C2
Prittlewell Sthend 51 A5
Privett Hants 33 C5
Prixford Devon 25 B6
Probus Corn 4 D3
Proncy Highld 264 A3
Prospect Cumb 174 D4
Prudhoe Northumb 178 C2
Ptarmigan Lodge Stirl 215 B6
Pubil Perth 228 D3
Puckeridge Herts 68 A3
Puckington Som 28 D3
Pucklechurch S Glos 43 B5
Pucknall Hants 32 C2
Puckrup Glos 80 D1
Puddinglake Ches 128 C2
Puddington Ches 126 B3
Puddington Devon 26 D3
Puddledock Norf 103 B6
Puddletown Dorset 16 B1
Pudleston Hereford 78 B3
Pudsey W Yorks 147 D6
Pulborough W Sus 20 A3
Puleston Telford 111 C6
Pulford Ches 126 D3
Pulham Dorset 15 A7
Pulham Market Norf 104 C2
Pulham St Mary Norf 104 C3

Pulloxhill Beds 84 D2
Pumpherston W Loth 208 D3
Pumsaint Carms 58 A3
Puncheston Pembs 55 B6
Puncknowle Dorset 15 C5
Punnett's Town E Sus 36 D4
Purbrook Hants 19 A5
Purewell Dorset 17 B5
Purfleet Thurrock 50 B2
Puriton Som 28 A3
Purleigh Essex 70 C2
Purley London 49 C6
Purley W Berks 47 B4
Purlogue Shrops 93 D6
Purls Bridge Cambs 101 C6
Purse Caundle Dorset 29 D6
Purslow Shrops 94 C1
Purston Jaglin W Yorks 140 B2
Purton Glos 62 C2
Purton Glos 62 C2
Purton Wilts 45 A4
Purton Stoke Wilts 64 D1
Pury End Northants 83 C4
Pusey Oxon 65 D4
Putley Hereford 79 D4
Putney London 49 B5
Putsborough Devon 25 A5
Puttenham Herts 66 B3
Puttenham Sur 34 B2
Puxton N Som 42 C3
Pwll Carms 57 B4
Pwll-glas Denb 125 D6
Pwll-trap Carms 56 A2
Pwll-y-glaw Neath 40 B2
Pwllcrochan Pembs 55 D5
Pwllgloyw Powys 76 D4
Pwllheli Gwyn 106 C3
Pwllmeyric Mon 61 D7
Pye Corner Newport 42 A2
Pye Green Staffs 112 D3
Pyecombe W Sus 21 A5
Pyewipe NE Lincs 143 B4
Pyle I o W 18 D3
Pyle = Y Pîl Bridgend 40 C3
Pylle Som 29 B6
Pymoor Cambs 101 C6
Pyrford Sur 34 A3
Pyrton Oxon 66 D1
Pytchley Northants 99 D5
Pyworthy Devon 10 A4

Q
Quabbs Shrops 93 C6
Quadring Lincs 117 B5
Quainton Bucks 66 B2
Quarley Hants 31 A6
Quarndon Derbys 114 A1
Quarrier's Homes Invclyd 204 B3
Quarrington Lincs 116 A3
Quarrington Hill Durham 167 B6
Quarry Bank W Mid 96 C2
Quarry Bank Mill,
  Wilmslow Ches 128 A3
Quarryford E Loth 210 D2
Quarryhill Highld 264 B3
Quarrywood Moray 266 C2
Quarter S Lnrk 194 A2
Quatford Shrops 95 B5
Quatt Shrops 95 C5
Quebec Durham 167 A4
Quedgeley Glos 63 B4
Queen Adelaide Cambs 102 C1
Queen Camel Som 29 C5
Queen Charlton Bath 43 C5
Queen Dart Devon 26 D3
Queen Oak Dorset 30 B1
Queen Street Kent 37 B4
Queen Street Wilts 44 A4
Queenborough Kent 51 B6
Queenhill Worcs 79 D6
Queen's Head Shrops 110 C2
Queen's Park Beds 84 C2
Queen's Park Northants 83 A4
Queen's View Centre,
  Loch Tummel Perth 230 C2
Queensbury W Yorks 147 D5
Queensferry Edin 208 C4
Queensferry Flint 126 C3
Queenstown Blkpool 144 D3
Queenzieburn N Lnrk 207 C4
Quemerford Wilts 44 C4
Quendale Shetland 285 M5
Quendon Essex 85 D7
Queniborough Leics 115 D4
Quenington Glos 64 C2
Quernmore Lancs 145 B5
Quethiock Corn 6 A2

Quholm Orkney 282 F3
Quicks Green W Berks 46 B3
Quidenham Norf 103 C6
Quidhampton Hants 46 D3
Quidhampton Wilts 31 B5
Quilquox Aberds 257 C4
Quina Brook Shrops 111 B4
Quindry Orkney 283 H5
Quinton Northants 83 B4
Quinton W Mid 96 C2
Quintrell Downs Corn 4 A3
Quixhill Staffs 113 A5
Quoditch Devon 11 B5
Quoig Perth 218 B3
Quorndon Leics 114 D3
Quothquan S Lnrk 195 C4
Quoyloo Orkney 282 E3
Quoyness Orkney 283 G3
Quoys Shetland 284 B8
Quoys Shetland 285 G6

R
Raasay Ho. Highld 248 C2
Rabbit's Cross Kent 37 B5
Raby Mers 126 B3
Rachan Mill Borders 195 C6
Rachub Gwyn 123 D6
Rackenford Devon 26 D3
Rackham W Sus 20 A3
Rackheath Norf 121 D4
Racks Dumfries 174 A3
Rackwick Orkney 283 H3
Rackwick Orkney 282 C5
Radbourne Derbys 113 B6
Radcliffe Gtr Man 137 C6
Radcliffe Northumb 189 C5
Radcliffe on Trent Notts 115 B4
Radclive Bucks 82 D3
Radcot Oxon 64 D3
Raddery Highld 252 A3
Radernie Fife 221 D4
Radford Semele Warks 81 A6
Radipole Dorset 15 C6
Radlett Herts 67 D6
Radley Oxon 65 D6
Radmanthwaite Notts 131 C5
Radmoor Shrops 111 C5
Radmore Green Ches 127 D5
Radnage Bucks 66 D2
Radstock Bath 43 D5
Radstone Northants 82 C2
Radway Warks 81 C6
Radway Green Ches 128 D2
Radwell Beds 84 B2
Radwell Herts 84 D4
Radwinter Essex 86 D2
Radyr Cardiff 41 C6
RAF Museum, Cosford
  Shrops 95 A5
RAF Museum, Hendon
  London 49 A5
Rafford Moray 253 A6
Ragdale Leics 115 D4
Raglan Mon 61 C6
Ragley Hall Warks 80 B3
Ragnall Notts 132 B3
Rahane Argyll 215 D5
Rainford Mers 136 C3
Rainford Junction Mers 136 C3
Rainham London 50 A2
Rainham Medway 51 C5
Rainhill Mers 136 D3
Rainhill Stoops Mers 136 D4
Rainow Ches 129 B4
Rainton N Yorks 158 D2
Rainworth Notts 131 D5
Raisbeck Cumb 155 A5
Raise Cumb 165 A5
Rait Perth 220 B2
Raithby Lincs 134 A3
Raithby Lincs 134 C3
Rake W Sus 33 C7
Rakewood Gtr Man 138 B2
Ram Carms 75 D4
Ram Lane Kent 38 A1
Ramasaig Highld 258 D1
Rame Corn 4 D2
Rame Corn 6 C3
Rameldry Mill Bank Fife 220 D3
Ramnageo Shetland 284 C8
Rampisham Dorset 15 A5
Rampside Cumb 153 D3
Rampton Cambs 85 A6
Rampton Notts 132 B2
Ramsbottom Gtr Man 137 B6
Ramsbury Wilts 45 B6
Ramscraigs Highld 275 B5

Ramsdean Hants 33 C6
Ramsdell Hants 46 D3
Ramsden Oxon 65 B4
Ramsden Bellhouse Essex 69 D7
Ramsden Heath Essex 69 D7
Ramsey Cambs 101 C4
Ramsey Essex 88 D3
Ramsey I o M 152 B4
Ramsey Forty Foot
  Cambs 101 C5
Ramsey Heights Cambs 101 C4
Ramsey Island Essex 70 C3
Ramsey Mereside Cambs 101 C4
Ramsey St Mary's Cambs 101 C4
Ramseycleuch Borders 185 A5
Ramsgate Kent 53 C5
Ramsgill N Yorks 157 D5
Ramshorn Staffs 113 A4
Ramsnest Common Sur 34 C2
Ranais W Isles 288 E5
Ranby Lincs 134 B2
Ranby Notts 131 A6
Rand Lincs 133 B6
Randwick Glos 63 C4
Ranfurly Renfs 204 B3
Rangag Highld 280 D3
Rangemore Staffs 113 C5
Rangeworthy S Glos 43 A5
Rankinston E Ayrs 182 A2
Ranmoor S Yorks 130 A3
Ranmore Common Sur 35 A4
Rannerdale Cumb 163 C4
Rannoch Station Perth 228 C3
Ranochan Highld 238 D2
Ranskill Notts 131 A6
Ranton Staffs 112 C2
Ranworth Norf 121 D5
Raploch Stirl 207 A5
Rapness Orkney 282 C6
Rascal Moor E Yorks 149 D7
Rascarrel Dumfries 173 D5
Rashierreive Aberds 257 D4
Raskelf N Yorks 158 D3
Rassau Bl Gwent 60 B3
Rastrick W Yorks 139 A4
Ratagan Highld 238 A3
Ratby Leics 98 A2
Ratcliffe Culey Leics 97 B6
Ratcliffe on Soar Leics 114 C2
Ratcliffe on the Wreake
  Leics 115 D4
Rathen Aberds 269 C5
Rathillet Fife 220 B3
Rathmell N Yorks 146 B2
Ratho Edin 208 C4
Ratho Station Edin 208 C4
Rathven Moray 267 C5
Ratley Warks 81 C6
Ratlinghope Shrops 94 B2
Rattar Highld 281 A4
Ratten Row Lancs 144 C4
Rattery Devon 7 A6
Rattlesden Suff 87 B5
Rattray Perth 231 D5
Raughton Head Cumb 164 A1
Raunds Northants 100 D1
Ravenfield S Yorks 140 D2
Ravenglass Cumb 153 A1
Ravenglass and Eskdale
  Railway & Museum
  Cumb 153 A1
Raveningham Norf 105 B4
Ravenscar N Yorks 160 A3
Ravenscraig Invclyd 204 A2
Ravensdale I o M 152 B3
Ravensden Beds 84 B2
Ravenseat N Yorks 156 A2
Ravenshead Notts 131 D5
Ravensmoor Ches 127 D6
Ravensthorpe Northants 98 D3
Ravensthorpe W Yorks 139 A5
Ravenstone Leics 114 D2
Ravenstone M Keynes 83 B5
Ravenstonedale Cumb 155 A6
Ravenstown Cumb 154 D2
Ravenstruther S Lnrk 194 B4
Ravensworth N Yorks 157 A5
Raw N Yorks 160 A3
Rawcliffe E Yorks 141 A4
Rawcliffe York 149 B4
Rawcliffe Bridge E Yorks 141 A4
Rawdon W Yorks 147 D6
Rawmarsh S Yorks 140 D2
Rawreth Essex 70 D1
Rawridge Devon 14 A2
Rawtenstall Lancs 137 A7
Raxton Aberds 256 C3
Raydon Suff 87 D6

Raylees Northumb 188 D2
Rayleigh Essex 70 D2
Rayne Essex 70 A1
Rayners Lane London 48 A4
Raynes Park London 49 C5
Reach Cambs 86 A1
Read Lancs 146 D1
Reading Reading 47 B5
Reading Street Kent 37 C7
Reagill Cumb 165 D4
Rearquhar Highld 264 A3
Rearsby Leics 115 D4
Reaster Highld 281 B4
Reawick Shetland 285 J5
Reay Highld 279 B5
Rechullin Highld 249 A5
Reculver Kent 53 C4
Red Dial Cumb 175 D5
Red House Glass Cone,
  Wordsley W Mid 96 C1
Red Houses Jersey 6
Red Lodge Suff 102 D2
Red Rail Hereford 62 A1
Red Rock Gtr Man 137 C4
Red Roses Carms 56 A2
Red Row Northumb 189 D5
Red Street Staffs 128 D3
Red Wharf Bay Anglesey 123 B5
Redberth Pembs 55 D6
Redbourn Herts 67 B6
Redbourne N Lincs 142 D1
Redbrook Glos 62 B1
Redbrook Wrex 111 A4
Redburn Highld 264 D1
Redburn Highld 253 B5
Redburn Northumb 177 C5
Redcar Redcar 168 C4
Redcar Racecourse
  Redcar 168 C4
Redcastle Angus 233 C4
Redcastle Highld 252 B1
Redcliff Bay N Som 42 B3
Redding Falk 208 C2
Reddingmuirhead Falk 208 C2
Reddish Gtr Man 138 D1
Redditch Worcs 80 A3
Rede Suff 87 B4
Redenhall Norf 104 C3
Redesdale Camp
  Northumb 187 D7
Redesmouth Northumb 177 A6
Redford Aberds 233 A5
Redford Angus 232 D3
Redford Durham 166 B3
Redfordgreen Borders 185 A6
Redgorton Perth 219 B5
Redgrave Suff 103 D6
Redhill Aberds 256 C1
Redhill Aberds 245 B4
Redhill N Som 42 C3
Redhill Sur 35 A5
Redhouse Argyll 202 B3
Redhouses Argyll 200 B3
Redisham Suff 105 C5
Redland Bristol 43 B4
Redland Orkney 282 E4
Redlingfield Suff 104 D2
Redlynch Som 29 B7
Redlynch Wilts 31 C6
Redmarley D'Abitot Glos 79 D5
Redmarshall Stockton 167 C6
Redmile Leics 115 B5
Redmire N Yorks 156 B4
Redmoor Corn 5 A5
Rednal Shrops 110 C2
Redpath Borders 197 C4
Redpoint Highld 261 D4
Redruth Corn 3 A4
Redvales Gtr Man 137 C7
Redwick Newport 42 A3
Redwick S Glos 43 A4
Redworth Darl 167 C5
Reed Herts 85 D5
Reedham Norf 105 A5
Reedness E Yorks 141 A5
Reeds Beck Lincs 134 C2
Reepham Lincs 133 B5
Reepham Norf 120 C2
Reeth N Yorks 156 B4
Regaby I o M 152 B4
Regoul Highld 253 A4
Reiff Highld 270 C2
Reigate Sur 35 A5
Reighton N Yorks 161 D5
Reighton Gap N Yorks 161 D5
Reinigeadal W Isles 288 G3
Reiss Highld 281 C5

Rejerrah Corn 4 B2
Releath Corn 3 B4
Relubbus Corn 2 B3
Relugas Moray 253 B5
Remenham Wokingham 47 A5
Remenham Hill Wokingham 47 A5
Remony Perth 229 D6
Rempstone Notts 114 C3
Rendcomb Glos 63 C6
Rendham Suff 88 A4
Rendlesham Suff 88 B4
Renfrew Renfs 205 B5
Renhold Beds 84 B2
Renishaw Derbys 131 B4
Rennington Northumb 189 B5
Renton W Dunb 206 C1
Renwick Cumb 164 A3
Repps Norf 121 D6
Repton Derbys 113 C7
Reraig Highld 249 D5
Rescobie Angus 232 C3
Resipole Highld 235 D6
Resolis Highld 264 D2
Resolven Neath 40 A3
Reston Borders 211 D5
Reswallie Angus 232 C3
Retew Corn 4 B4
Retford Notts 132 A2
Rettendon Essex 70 D1
Rettendon Place Essex 70 D1
Revesby Lincs 134 C2
Revesby Bridge Lincs 134 C3
Rew Street I o W 18 B3
Rewe Devon 13 B4
Reydon Suff 105 D5
Reydon Smear Suff 105 D5
Reymerston Norf 103 A6
Reynalton Pembs 55 D6
Reynoldston Swansea 57 C4
Rezare Corn 11 D4
Rhaeadr Gwy =
  Rhayader Powys 76 A3
Rhandirmwyn Carms 59 A4
Rhayader = Rhaeadr
  Gwy Powys 76 A3
Rhedyn Gwyn 106 C2
Rhemore Highld 225 A4
Rhencullen I o M 152 B3
Rhes-y-cae Flint 126 B1
Rhewl Denb 125 C6
Rhewl Denb 109 A6
Rhian Highld 272 C3
Rhicarn Highld 270 B3
Rhiconich Highld 276 C3
Rhicullen Highld 264 C2
Rhidorroch Ho. Highld 262 A3
Rhifail Highld 278 D3
Rhigos Rhondda 59 E6
Rhilochan Highld 273 D5
Rhiroy Highld 262 B3
Rhisga = Risca Caerph 60 D4
Rhiw Gwyn 106 D2
Rhiwabon = Ruabon
  Wrex 110 A2
Rhiwbina Cardiff 41 C6
Rhiwbryfdir Gwyn 107 B6
Rhiwderin Newport 42 A1
Rhiwlas Gwyn 123 D5
Rhiwlas Gwyn 108 B4
Rhiwlas Gwyn 109 B6
Rhiwlas Powys 109 B6
Rhodes Gtr Man 138 C1
Rhodes Minnis Kent 38 A3
Rhodesia Notts 131 B5
Rhodiad Pembs 54 B3
Rhondda Rhondda 41 B4
Rhonehouse or Kelton
  Hill Dumfries 173 C5
Rhoose = Y Rhws V Glam 41 E5
Rhôs Carms 73 C6
Rhôs Neath 40 A2
Rhos-fawr Gwyn 106 C3
Rhos-goch Powys 77 C5
Rhos-hill Pembs 73 B4
Rhos-on-Sea Conwy 124 A3
Rhos-y-brithdir Powys 109 C6
Rhos-y-garth Ceredig 75 A5
Rhos-y-gwaliau Gwyn 108 B4
Rhos-y-llan Gwyn 106 C2
Rhos-y-Madoc Wrex 110 A2
Rhos-y-meirch Powys 77 A6
Rhosaman Carms 59 D4
Rhosbeirio Anglesey 122 A3
Rhoscefnhir Anglesey 123 C5
Rhoscolyn Anglesey 122 C2
Rhoscrowther Pembs 55 D5

Rhosesmor Flint 126 C2
Rhosgadfan Gwyn 107 A5
Rhosgoch Anglesey 123 B4
Rhoshirwaun Gwyn 106 D1
Rhoslan Gwyn 107 B4
Rhoslefain Gwyn 90 B3
Rhosllanerchrugog Wrex 110 A1
Rhosmaen Carms 58 C3
Rhosmeirch Anglesey 123 C4
Rhosneigr Anglesey 122 C3
Rhosnesni Wrex 126 D3
Rhosrobin Wrex 126 D3
Rhossili Swansea 57 D4
Rhosson Pembs 54 B3
Rhostryfan Gwyn 107 A4
Rhostyllen Wrex 110 A2
Rhosybol Anglesey 123 B4
RHS Garden, Wisley Sur 34 A3
Rhu Argyll 202 B3
Rhu Argyll 215 D5
Rhuallt Denb 125 B5
Rhuddall Heath Ches 127 C5
Rhuddlan Ceredig 58 A1
Rhuddlan Denb 125 B5
Rhue Highld 262 A2
Rhulen Powys 77 B5
Rhunahaorine Argyll 202 D2
Rhuthun = Ruthin Denb 125 D6
Rhyd Gwyn 107 B6
Rhyd Powys 92 A3
Rhyd-Ddu Gwyn 107 B6
Rhyd-moel-ddu Powys 93 D4
Rhyd-Rosser Ceredig 75 B4
Rhyd-uchaf Gwyn 108 B4
Rhyd-wen Gwyn 91 A5
Rhyd-y-clafdy Gwyn 106 C3
Rhyd-y-foel Conwy 125 B4
Rhyd-y-fro Neath 59 E4
Rhyd-y-gwin Swansea 57 B6
Rhyd-y-meirch Mon 61 C5
Rhyd-y-meudwy Denb 125 D6
Rhyd-y-pandy Swansea 57 B6
Rhyd-y-sarn Gwyn 107 B6
Rhyd-yr-onen Gwyn 90 B4
Rhydaman = Ammanford
  Carms 57 A6
Rhydargaeau Carms 58 C1
Rhydcymerau Carms 58 B2
Rhydd Worcs 79 C6
Rhydding Neath 40 B2
Rhydfudr Ceredig 75 B4
Rhydlewis Ceredig 73 B6
Rhydlios Gwyn 106 C1
Rhydlydan Conwy 124 D3
Rhydness Powys 77 C5
Rhydowen Ceredig 74 D3
Rhydspence Hereford 77 C6
Rhydtalog Flint 126 D2
Rhydwyn Anglesey 122 B3
Rhydycroesau Shrops 110 B1
Rhydyfelin Ceredig 75 A4
Rhydyfelin Rhondda 41 C5
Rhydymain Gwyn 108 C3
Rhydymwyn Flint 126 C2
Rhyl = Y Rhyl Denb 125 A5
Rhymney = Rhymni
  Caerph 60 C3
Rhymni = Rhymney
  Caerph 60 C3
Rhynd Fife 221 B4
Rhynd Perth 219 B6
Rhynie Aberds 255 D5
Rhynie Highld 265 C4
Ribbesford Worcs 95 D5
Ribblehead N Yorks 155 D6
Ribbleton Lancs 145 D6
Ribchester Lancs 145 D6
Ribigill Highld 277 C6
Riby Lincs 142 C3
Riby Cross Roads Lincs 142 C3
Riccall N Yorks 149 D5
Riccarton E Ayrs 193 B4
Richards Castle Hereford 78 A2
Richings Park Bucks 48 B3
Richmond London 49 B4
Richmond N Yorks 157 A5
Rickarton Aberds 245 D5
Rickinghall Suff 103 D6
Rickleton T & W 179 D4
Rickling Essex 85 D6
Rickmansworth Herts 67 D5
Riddings Cumb 175 A7
Riddings Derbys 131 D4
Riddlecombe Devon 25 D7
Riddlesden W Yorks 147 C4

Riddrie Glasgow 205 B6
Ridge Dorset 16 C3
Ridge Hants 32 D2
Ridge Wilts 30 B3
Ridge Green Sur 35 B6
Ridge Lane Warks 97 B5
Ridgebourne Powys 77 A4
Ridgehill N Som 43 C4
Ridgeway Cross Hereford 79 C5
Ridgewell Essex 86 C3
Ridgewood E Sus 22 A2
Ridgmont Beds 84 D1
Riding Mill Northumb 178 C2
Ridleywood Wrex 127 D4
Ridlington Norf 121 B5
Ridlington Rutland 99 A5
Ridsdale Northumb 177 A7
Riechip Perth 231 D4
Riemore Perth 230 D4
Rienachait Highld 270 A3
Rievaulx N Yorks 159 C4
Rievaulx Abbey N Yorks 159 C4
Rift House Hrtlpl 168 B2
Rigg Dumfries 175 B5
Riggend N Lnrk 207 C5
Rigsby Lincs 135 B4
Rigside S Lnrk 194 C3
Riley Green Lancs 137 A5
Rileyhill Staffs 113 D5
Rilla Mill Corn 10 D3
Rillington N Yorks 160 D2
Rimington Lancs 146 C2
Rimpton Som 29 C6
Rimswell E Yorks 143 A5
Rinaston Pembs 55 B5
Ringasta Shetland 285 M5
Ringford Dumfries 173 C4
Ringinglow S Yorks 130 A2
Ringland Norf 120 D3
Ringles Cross E Sus 36 D2
Ringmer E Sus 22 A2
Ringmore Devon 7 C5
Ringorm Moray 254 B3
Ring's End Cambs 101 A5
Ringsfield Suff 105 C5
Ringsfield Corner Suff 105 C5
Ringshall Herts 67 B4
Ringshall Suff 87 B6
Ringshall Stocks Suff 87 B6
Ringstead Norf 119 A4
Ringstead Northants 100 D1
Ringwood Hants 17 A5
Ringwould Kent 39 A5
Rinmore Aberds 243 A7
Rinnigill Orkney 283 H4
Rinsey Corn 2 C3
Riof W Isles 288 D2
Ripe E Sus 22 A3
Ripley Derbys 130 D3
Ripley Hants 17 B5
Ripley N Yorks 148 A1
Ripley Sur 34 A3
Riplingham E Yorks 150 D2
Ripon N Yorks 157 D7
Ripon Cathedral N Yorks 157 D7
Ripon Racecourse
  N Yorks 148 A2
Rippingale Lincs 116 C3
Ripple Kent 39 A5
Ripple Worcs 79 D6
Ripponden W Yorks 138 B3
Rireavach Highld 262 A2
Risabus Argyll 200 D3
Risbury Hereford 78 B3
Risby Suff 86 A3
Risca = Rhisga Caerph 60 D4
Rise E Yorks 151 C4
Riseden E Sus 36 C4
Risegate Lincs 117 C5
Riseholme Lincs 133 B4
Riseley Beds 84 A2
Riseley Wokingham 47 C5
Rishangles Suff 88 A2
Rishton Lancs 146 D1
Rishworth W Yorks 138 B3
Rising Bridge Lancs 137 A6
Risley Derbys 114 B2
Risley Warr 137 D5
Risplith N Yorks 147 A6
Rispond Highld 277 B5
Rivar Wilts 45 C7
Rivenhall End Essex 70 B2
River Bank Cambs 86 A1
Riverhead Kent 36 A3
Rivington Lancs 137 B5
Roa Island Cumb 153 D3
Roachill Devon 26 C3
Road Green Norf 104 B3

Roade Northants 83 B4
Roadhead Cumb 176 B3
Roadmeetings S Lnrk 194 B3
Roadside Highld 280 B3
Roadside of Catterline
  Aberds 233 A6
Roadside of Kinneff
  Aberds 233 A6
Roadwater Som 27 B5
Roag Highld 258 D2
Roath Cardiff 41 D6
Rob Roy and Trossachs
  Visitor Centre,
  Callander Stirl 217 D6
Robert Burns Centre,
  Dumfries Dumfries 174 A2
Roberton Borders 186 B3
Roberton S Lnrk 194 D4
Robertsbridge E Sus 37 D5
Roberttown W Yorks 139 A4
Robeston Cross Pembs 55 C4
Robeston Wathen Pembs 55 C6
Robin Hood W Yorks 139 A6
Robin Hood Doncaster
  Sheffield International
  Airport S Yorks 141 D4
Robin Hood's Bay N Yorks 160 A3
Roborough Devon 25 D6
Roborough Devon 7 A4
Roby Mers 136 D3
Roby Mill Lancs 136 C4
Rocester Staffs 113 B5
Roch Pembs 55 B4
Roch Gate Pembs 55 B4
Rochdale Gtr Man 138 B1
Roche Corn 5 A4
Rochester Medway 51 C4
Rochester Northumb 188 D1
Rochester Castle Medway 51 C4
Rochester Cathedral
  Medway 51 C4
Rochford Essex 70 D2
Rock Corn 9 D5
Rock Northumb 189 A5
Rock W Sus 21 A4
Rock Ferry Mers 126 A3
Rockbeare Devon 13 B5
Rockbourne Hants 31 D5
Rockcliffe Cumb 175 B6
Rockcliffe Dumfries 173 C6
Rockfield Highld 265 B5
Rockfield Mon 61 B6
Rockford Hants 17 A5
Rockhampton S Glos 62 D2
Rockingham Northants 99 B5
Rockingham Motor
  Speedway Northants 99 B6
Rockland All Saints Norf 103 B5
Rockland St Mary Norf 104 A4
Rockland St Peter Norf 103 B5
Rockley Wilts 45 B5
Rockwell End Bucks 47 A5
Rockwell Green Som 27 C6
Rodborough Glos 63 C4
Rodbourne Swindon 45 A5
Rodbourne Wilts 44 A3
Rodbourne Cheney
  Swindon 45 A5
Rodd Hereford 77 A7
Roddam Northumb 188 A3
Rodden Dorset 15 C6
Rode Som 44 D2
Rode Heath Ches 128 D3
Rodeheath Ches 128 C3
Roden Telford 111 D4
Rodhuish Som 27 B5
Rodington Telford 111 D4
Rodley Glos 62 B3
Rodley W Yorks 147 D6
Rodmarton Glos 63 D5
Rodmell E Sus 22 B2
Rodmersham Kent 51 C6
Rodney Stoke Som 42 D3
Rodsley Derbys 113 A6
Rodway Som 28 B2
Rodwell Dorset 15 D6
Roe Green Herts 85 D5
Roecliffe N Yorks 148 A2
Roehampton London 49 B5
Roesound Shetland 284 G5
Roffey W Sus 35 C4
Rogart Highld 273 D5
Rogart Station Highld 273 D5
Rogate W Sus 33 C7
Rogerstone Newport 42 A1
Roghadal W Isles 287 F5
Rogiet Mon 42 A3

Rogue's Alley Cambs 101 A5
Roke Oxon 66 D1
Roker T & W 179 D6
Rolleston Leics 99 A4
Rolleston Notts 132 D2
Rolleston-on-Dove Staffs 113 C6
Rolston E Yorks 151 C5
Rolvenden Kent 37 C6
Rolvenden Layne Kent 37 C6
Romaldkirk Durham 166 C2
Roman Baths & Pump
  Room, Bath Bath 43 C6
Romanby N Yorks 158 B2
Romannobridge Borders 195 B6
Romansleigh Devon 26 C2
Romford London 50 A2
Romiley Gtr Man 138 D2
Romney, Hythe and
  Dymchurch Light
  Railway Kent 38 B3
Romsey Hants 32 C2
Romsey Town Cambs 85 B6
Romsley Shrops 95 C5
Romsley Worcs 96 D2
Ronague I o M 152 D2
Rookhope Durham 166 A2
Rookley I o W 18 C4
Rooks Bridge Som 42 D2
Roos E Yorks 151 D5
Roosebeck Cumb 153 D3
Rootham's Green Beds 84 B3
Rootpark S Lnrk 195 A4
Ropley Hants 33 B5
Ropley Dean Hants 33 B5
Ropsley Lincs 116 B2
Rora Aberds 269 D5
Rorandle Aberds 244 A3
Rorrington Shrops 93 A7
Roscroggan Corn 3 A4
Rose Corn 4 B2
Rose Ash Devon 26 C2
Rose Green W Sus 20 C2
Rose Grove Lancs 146 D2
Rose Hill E Sus 22 A2
Rose Hill Lancs 146 D2
Rose Hill Suff 88 C2
Roseacre Kent 37 A5
Roseacre Lancs 144 D4
Rosebank S Lnrk 194 B3
Rosebrough Northumb 189 A4
Rosebush Pembs 55 B6
Rosecare Corn 10 B2
Rosedale Abbey N Yorks 159 B6
Roseden Northumb 188 A3
Rosefield Highld 253 A4
Rosehall Highld 272 D2
Rosehaugh Mains Highld 252 A2
Rosehearty Aberds 269 C4
Rosehill Shrops 111 B5
Roseisle Moray 266 C2
Roselands E Sus 22 B4
Rosemarket Pembs 55 D5
Rosemarkie Highld 252 A3
Rosemary Lane Devon 27 D6
Rosemount Perth 231 D5
Rosenannon Corn 5 A4
Rosewell Midloth 209 D5
Roseworth Stockton 168 C2
Roseworthy Corn 3 B4
Rosgill Cumb 164 D3
Roshven Highld 235 C6
Roskhill Highld 258 D2
Roskill House Highld 252 A2
Rosley Cumb 175 D6
Rosliston Derbys 113 D6
Rosneath Argyll 215 D5
Ross Dumfries 172 D4
Ross Northumb 199 C5
Ross Perth 218 B2
Ross-on-Wye Hereford 62 A2
Rossett Wrex 126 D3
Rossett Green N Yorks 148 B2
Rossie Ochill Perth 219 C5
Rossie Priory Perth 220 A2
Rossington S Yorks 140 D4
Rosskeen Highld 264 D2
Rossland Renfs 205 A4
Roster Highld 281 E4
Rostherne Ches 128 A2
Rosthwaite Cumb 163 C5
Roston Derbys 113 A5
Rosyth Fife 208 B4
Rothbury Northumb 188 C3
Rotherby Leics 115 D4
Rotherfield E Sus 36 D3
Rotherfield Greys Oxon 47 A5

Rotherfield Peppard Oxon 47 A5
Rotherham S Yorks 140 D2
Rothersthorpe Northants 83 B4
Rotherwick Hants 47 D5
Rothes Moray 254 B3
Rothesay Argyll 203 B5
Rothiebrisbane Aberds 256 C2
Rothiemurchus Estate
  Visitor Centre Highld 242 A2
Rothienorman Aberds 256 C2
Rothiesholm Orkney 282 E7
Rothley Leics 114 D3
Rothley Northumb 178 A2
Rothley Shield East
  Northumb 188 D3
Rothmaise Aberds 256 C1
Rothwell Lincs 142 D3
Rothwell Northants 99 C5
Rothwell W Yorks 139 A6
Rothwell Haigh W Yorks 139 A6
Rotsea E Yorks 150 B3
Rottal Angus 232 B1
Rotten End Suff 89 A4
Rottingdean Brighton 21 B6
Rottington Cumb 162 C2
Rotunda, Folkestone Kent 39 B4
Roud I o W 18 C4
Rough Close Staffs 112 B3
Rough Common Kent 52 D3
Rougham Norf 119 C5
Rougham Suff 87 A5
Rougham Green Suff 87 A5
Roughburn Highld 240 D1
Roughlee Lancs 146 C2
Roughley W Mid 96 B4
Roughsike Cumb 176 B3
Roughton Lincs 134 C2
Roughton Norf 120 B4
Roughton Shrops 95 B5
Roughton Moor Lincs 134 C2
Roundhay W Yorks 148 D2
Roundstonefoot Dumfries 185 B4
Roundstreet Common
  W Sus 34 D3
Roundway Wilts 44 C4
Rous Lench Worcs 80 B3
Rousdon Devon 14 B2
Routenburn N Ayrs 204 B1
Routh E Yorks 150 C3
Row Corn 10 D1
Row Cumb 154 C3
Row Heath Essex 71 B5
Rowanburn Dumfries 175 A7
Rowardennan Stirl 206 A1
Rowde Wilts 44 C3
Rowen Conwy 124 B2
Rowfoot Northumb 177 C4
Rowhedge Essex 71 A4
Rowhook W Sus 35 C4
Rowington Warks 81 A5
Rowland Derbys 130 B2
Rowlands Castle Hants 33 D6
Rowlands Gill T & W 178 D3
Rowledge Sur 33 A7
Rowlestone Hereford 61 A5
Rowley E Yorks 150 D2
Rowley Shrops 93 A7
Rowley Hill W Yorks 139 B4
Rowley Regis W Mid 96 C2
Rowly Sur 34 B3
Rowney Green Worcs 96 D3
Rownhams Hants 32 D2
Rowrah Cumb 162 C3
Rowsham Bucks 66 B3
Rowsley Derbys 130 C2
Rowstock Oxon 46 A2
Rowston Lincs 133 D5
Rowton Ches 127 C4
Rowton Shrops 110 D2
Rowton Telford 111 D5
Roxburgh Borders 197 C6
Roxby N Lincs 141 B7
Roxby N Yorks 169 D5
Roxton Beds 84 B3
Roxwell Essex 69 C6
Royal Botanic Gardens
  Edin 209 C5
Royal Leamington Spa
  Warks 81 A6
Royal Museum of
  Scotland Edin 209 C5
Royal Oak Darl 167 C5
Royal Oak Lancs 136 C3
Royal Pavilion, Brighton
  Brighton 21 B6
Royal Tunbridge Wells
  Kent 36 C3

Royal Welch Fusiliers Regimental Museum (See Caernarfon Castle) Gwyn 123 D4
Royal Worcester Porcelain, Worcester Worcs 79 B6
Roybridge Highld 239 D6
Roydhouse W Yorks 139 B5
Roydon Essex 68 C4
Roydon Norf 119 C4
Roydon Norf 104 C1
Roydon Hamlet Essex 68 C4
Royston Herts 85 C5
Royston S Yorks 139 B6
Royton Gtr Man 138 C2
Rozel Jersey 6
Ruabon = Rhiwabon Wrex 110 A2
Ruaig Argyll 222 C3
Ruan Lanihorne Corn 4 C3
Ruan Minor Corn 3 D5
Ruarach Highld 249 D6
Ruardean Glos 62 B2
Ruardean Woodside Glos 62 B2
Rubery Worcs 96 D2
Ruckcroft Cumb 164 A3
Ruckhall Hereford 78 D2
Ruckinge Kent 38 B2
Ruckland Lincs 134 B3
Ruckley Shrops 94 A3
Rudbaxton Pembs 55 B5
Rudby N Yorks 158 A3
Ruddington Notts 114 B3
Rudford Glos 62 A3
Rudge Shrops 95 B6
Rudge Som 44 D2
Rudgeway S Glos 43 A5
Rudgwick W Sus 34 C3
Rudhall Hereford 62 A2
Rudheath Ches 128 B1
Rudley Green Essex 70 C2
Rudry Caerph 41 C6
Rudston E Yorks 150 A3
Rudyard Staffs 129 D4
Rufford Lancs 136 B3
Rufforth York 148 B4
Rugby Warks 98 D2
Rugeley Staffs 112 D4
Ruglen S Ayrs 181 A4
Ruilick Highld 251 B7
Ruishton Som 28 C2
Ruisigearraidh W Isles 287 F4
Ruislip London 48 A3
Ruislip Common London 48 A3
Rumbling Bridge Perth 208 A3
Rumburgh Suff 104 C4
Rumford Corn 9 D4
Rumney Cardiff 41 D7
Runcorn Halton 127 A5
Runcton W Sus 20 B1
Runcton Holme Norf 102 A2
Rundlestone Devon 11 D6
Runfold Sur 34 B1
Runhall Norf 103 A6
Runham Norf 105 A6
Runham Norf 121 D6
Runnington Som 27 C6
Runsell Green Essex 70 C1
Runswick Bay N Yorks 169 D6
Runwell Essex 70 D1
Ruscombe Wokingham 47 B5
Rush Green London 50 A2
Rush-head Aberds 256 B3
Rushall Hereford 79 D4
Rushall Norf 104 C2
Rushall Wilts 45 D5
Rushall W Mid 96 A3
Rushbrooke Suff 87 A4
Rushbury Shrops 94 B3
Rushden Herts 85 D5
Rushden Northants 83 A6
Rushenden Kent 51 B6
Rushford Norf 103 C5
Rushlake Green E Sus 22 A4
Rushmere Suff 105 C5
Rushmere St Andrew Suff 88 C3
Rushmoor Sur 34 B1
Rushock Worcs 96 D1
Rusholme Gtr Man 138 D1
Rushton Ches 127 C5
Rushton Northants 99 C5
Rushton Shrops 95 A4
Rushton Spencer Staffs 129 C4
Rushwick Worcs 79 B6
Rushyford Durham 167 C5
Ruskie Stirl 217 D6
Ruskington Lincs 133 D5

Rusland Cumb 154 C2
Rusper W Sus 35 C5
Ruspidge Glos 62 B2
Russell's Water Oxon 47 A5
Russel's Green Suff 104 D3
Rusthall Kent 36 C3
Rustington W Sus 20 B3
Ruston N Yorks 160 C3
Ruston Parva E Yorks 150 A3
Ruswarp N Yorks 160 A2
Rutherford Borders 197 C5
Rutherglen S Lnrk 205 B6
Ruthernbridge Corn 5 A5
Ruthin = Rhuthun Denb 125 D6
Ruthin Craft Centre Denb 125 D6
Ruthrieston Aberdeen 245 B6
Ruthven Aberds 255 B6
Ruthven Angus 231 D6
Ruthven Highld 253 C4
Ruthven Highld 241 C5
Ruthven House Angus 231 D7
Ruthvoes Corn 4 A4
Ruthwell Dumfries 174 B3
Ruyton-XI-Towns Shrops 110 C2
Ryal Northumb 178 B2
Ryal Fold Blkburn 137 A5
Ryall Dorset 14 B4
Ryarsh Kent 37 A4
Rydal Cumb 154 A2
Ryde I o W 19 B4
Rye E Sus 37 D7
Rye Foreign E Sus 37 D6
Rye Harbour E Sus 38 D1
Rye Park Herts 68 B3
Rye Street Worcs 79 D5
Ryecroft Gate Staffs 129 C4
Ryehill E Yorks 143 A4
Ryhall Rutland 116 D3
Ryhill W Yorks 140 B1
Ryhope T & W 179 D6
Rylstone N Yorks 146 B3
Ryme Intrinseca Dorset 29 D5
Ryther N Yorks 149 D4
Ryton Glos 79 D5
Ryton N Yorks 159 D6
Ryton Shrops 95 A5
Ryton T & W 178 C3
Ryton-on-Dunsmore Warks 97 D6

S
Sabden Lancs 146 D1
Sacombe Herts 68 B3
Sacriston Durham 167 A5
Sadberge Darl 167 D6
Saddell Argyll 190 B3
Saddington Leics 98 B3
Saddle Bow Norf 118 D3
Saddlescombe W Sus 21 A5
Sadgill Cumb 154 A3
Saffron Walden Essex 86 D1
Sageston Pembs 55 D6
Saham Hills Norf 103 A5
Saham Toney Norf 103 A5
Saighdinis W Isles 287 H3
Saighton Ches 127 C4
St Abbs Borders 211 D6
St Abb's Haven Borders 211 D6
St Agnes Corn 4 B2
St Agnes Scilly 2 F3
St Albans Herts 67 C6
St Alban's Abbey Herts 67 C6
St Allen Corn 4 B3
St Andrews Fife 221 C5
St Andrew's Major V Glam 41 D6
St Anne Ald 7
St Annes Lancs 136 A2
St Ann's Dumfries 184 C3
St Ann's Chapel Corn 11 D5
St Ann's Chapel Devon 7 C5
St Anthony Corn 3 C5
St Anthony's Hill E Sus 22 B4
St Arvans Mon 61 D7
St Asaph = Llanelwy Denb 125 B5
St Athan V Glam 41 E5
St Aubin Jersey 6
St Austell Corn 5 B5
St Bees Cumb 162 C2
St Blazey Corn 5 B5
St Boswells Borders 197 C4
St Brelade Jersey 6
St Breock Corn 9 D5
St Breward Corn 10 D1
St Briavels Glos 62 C1
St Bride's Pembs 54 C4
St Brides Major V Glam 40 D3

St Bride's Netherwent Mon 42 A3
St Brides super Ely V Glam 41 D5
St Brides Wentlooge Newport 42 A1
St Budeaux Plym 6 B3
St Buryan Corn 2 C2
St Catherine Bath 44 B1
St Catherine's Argyll 215 B4
St Clears = Sanclêr Carms 56 A2
St Cleer Corn 6 A1
St Clement Corn 4 C3
St Clements Jersey 6
St Clement's Caves, Hastings E Sus 23 A6
St Clether Corn 10 C3
St Colmac Argyll 203 B5
St Columb Major Corn 4 A4
St Columb Minor Corn 4 A3
St Columb Road Corn 4 B4
St Combs Aberds 269 C5
St Cross South Elmham Suff 104 C3
St Cyrus Aberds 233 B5
St David's Perth 218 B4
St David's = Tyddewi Pembs 54 B3
St Day Corn 4 C2
St Dennis Corn 4 B4
St Devereux Hereford 78 D2
St Dogmaels Pembs 73 B4
St Dogwells Pembs 55 B5
St Dominick Corn 6 A3
St Donat's V Glam 40 E4
St Edith's Wilts 44 C3
St Endellion Corn 9 D5
St Enoder Corn 4 B3
St Erme Corn 4 B3
St Erney Corn 6 B2
St Erth Corn 2 B3
St Ervan Corn 9 D4
St Eval Corn 4 A3
St Ewe Corn 5 C4
St Fagans Cardiff 41 D6
St Fagans Museum of Welsh Life Cardiff 41 D6
St Fergus Aberds 269 D5
St Fillans Perth 217 B6
St Florence Pembs 55 D6
St Genny's Corn 10 B2
St George Conwy 125 B4
St George's V Glam 41 D5
St Germans Corn 6 B2
St Giles Lincs 133 B4
St Giles Cathedral Edin 209 C5
St Giles in the Wood Devon 25 D6
St Giles on the Heath Devon 11 B4
St Harmon Powys 92 D3
St Helen Auckland Durham 167 C4
St Helena Warks 97 A5
St Helen's E Sus 23 A6
St Helens I o W 19 C5
St Helens Mers 136 D4
St Helier London 49 C5
St Helier Jersey 6
St Hilary Corn 2 B3
St Hilary V Glam 41 D5
Saint Hill W Sus 36 C1
St Illtyd Bl Gwent 41 A7
St Ippollitts Herts 68 A1
St Ishmael's Pembs 54 D4
St Issey Corn 9 D5
St Ive Corn 6 A2
St Ives Cambs 101 D5
St Ives Corn 2 A3
St Ives Dorset 17 A5
St James South Elmham Suff 104 C4
St Jidgey Corn 9 E5
St John Corn 6 B3
St John's I o M 152 C2
St John's Jersey 6
St John's Sur 34 A2
St John's Worcs 79 B6
St John's Chapel Durham 166 B1
St John's Fen End Norf 118 D2
St John's Highway Norf 118 D2
St John's Town of Dalry Dumfries 182 D3
St Judes I o M 152 B3
St Just Corn 2 B1
St Just in Roseland Corn 4 D3
St Just in Roseland Corn 4 D3
St Katherine's Aberds 256 C2
St Keverne Corn 3 C5

St Kew Corn 9 D6
St Kew Highway Corn 9 D6
St Keyne Corn 6 A1
St Lawrence Corn 5 A5
St Lawrence Essex 70 C3
St Lawrence I o W 18 D4
St Leonard's Bucks 67 C4
St Leonards Dorset 17 A5
St Leonards E Sus 23 B5
Saint Leonards S Lnrk 205 C6
St Levan Corn 2 C1
St Lythans V Glam 41 D6
St Mabyn Corn 9 D6
St Madoes Perth 219 B6
St Margaret South Elmham Suff 104 C4
St Margaret's Hereford 78 D1
St Margarets Herts 68 B3
St Margaret's at Cliffe Kent 39 A5
St Margaret's Hope Orkney 283 H5
St Mark's I o M 152 D2
St Martin Corn 6
St Martins Corn 3 C5
St Martin's Jersey 6
St Martins Perth 219 A6
St Martin's Shrops 110 B2
St Mary Bourne Hants 46 D2
St Mary Church V Glam 41 D5
St Mary Cray London 50 C1
St Mary Hill V Glam 41 D4
St Mary Hoo Medway 51 B5
St Mary in the Marsh Kent 38 C2
St Mary's Jersey 6
St Mary's Orkney 283 G5
St Mary's Bay Kent 38 C2
St Mary's Church Warks 81 A5
St Maughans Mon 61 B6
St Mawes Corn 4 D3
St Mawgan Corn 4 A3
St Mellion Corn 6 A2
St Mellons Cardiff 42 A1
St Merryn Corn 9 D4
St Mewan Corn 5 B4
St Michael Caerhays Corn 5 C4
St Michael Penkevil Corn 4 C3
St Michael South Elmham Suff 104 C4
St Michael's Kent 37 C6
St Michaels Worcs 78 A3
St Michael's Mount, Penzance Corn 2 C3
St Michael's on Wyre Lancs 145 C4
St Minver Corn 9 D5
St Monans Fife 221 D5
St Neot Corn 5 A6
St Neots Cambs 84 A3
St Newlyn East Corn 4 B3
St Nicholas Pembs 72 C1
St Nicholas V Glam 41 D5
St Nicholas at Wade Kent 53 C4
St Ninians Stirl 207 A5
St Osyth Essex 71 B5
St Osyth Heath Essex 71 B5
St Ouens Jersey 6
St Owens Cross Hereford 62 A1
St Paul's Cathedral London 49 A6
St Paul's Cray London 50 C1
St Paul's Walden Herts 68 A1
St Peter Port Guern 6
St Peter's Jersey 6
St Peter's Kent 53 C5
St Petrox Pembs 55 E5
St Pinnock Corn 5 A7
St Quivox S Ayrs 192 C3
St Ruan Corn 3 D5
St Sampson Guern 6
St Stephen Corn 4 B4
St Stephen's Corn 10 C4
St Stephens Corn 6 B3
St Stephens Herts 67 C6
St Teath Corn 9 C6
St Thomas Devon 13 B4
St Tudy Corn 9 D6
St Twynnells Pembs 55 E5
St Veep Corn 5 B6
St Vigeans Angus 233 D4
St Wenn Corn 4 A4
St Weonards Hereford 61 A6
Saintbury Glos 80 D4
Salcombe Devon 7 D6
Salcombe Regis Devon 13 C6
Salcott Essex 70 B3
Sale Gtr Man 137 D6
Sale Green Worcs 80 B2
Saleby Lincs 135 B4

Salehurst E Sus 37 D5
Salem Ceredig 91 D4
Salem Carms 58 C3
Salen Argyll 225 B4
Salen Highld 235 D5
Salesbury Lancs 145 D6
Salford Beds 83 D6
Salford Gtr Man 137 D7
Salford Oxon 64 A3
Salford Priors Warks 80 B3
Salfords Sur 35 B5
Salhouse Norf 121 D5
Saline Fife 208 A3
Salisbury Wilts 31 C5
Salisbury Cathedral Wilts 31 C5
Salisbury Racecourse Wilts 31 C5
Sallachan Highld 236 C3
Sallachy Highld 249 C6
Sallachy Highld 272 D3
Salle Norf 120 C3
Salmonby Lincs 134 B3
Salmond's Muir Angus 221 A5
Salperton Glos 64 A1
Salph End Beds 84 B2
Salsburgh N Lnrk 207 D6
Salt Staffs 112 C3
Salt End E Yorks 142 A3
Saltaire W Yorks 147 D5
Saltaire 1853 Gallery W Yorks 147 D5
Saltash Corn 6 B3
Saltburn Highld 264 D3
Saltburn-by-the-Sea Redcar 169 C4
Saltby Leics 115 C6
Saltcoats Cumb 153 A1
Saltcoats N Ayrs 204 D2
Saltdean Brighton 22 B1
Salter Lancs 145 A6
Salterforth Lancs 146 C2
Salterswall Ches 127 C6
Saltfleet Lincs 143 D6
Saltfleetby All Saints Lincs 143 D6
Saltfleetby St Clements Lincs 143 D6
Saltfleetby St Peter Lincs 143 D6
Saltford Bath 43 C5
Salthouse Norf 120 A2
Saltmarshe E Yorks 141 A5
Saltney Flint 126 C3
Salton N Yorks 159 D6
Saltwick Northumb 178 B3
Saltwood Kent 38 B3
Salum Argyll 222 C3
Salvington W Sus 21 B4
Salwarpe Worcs 80 A1
Salwayash Dorset 15 B4
Sambourne Warks 80 A3
Sambrook Telford 111 C6
Samhla W Isles 287 H2
Samlesbury Lancs 145 D5
Samlesbury Bottoms Lancs 137 A5
Sammy Miller's Motorcycle Museum Hants 17 B6
Sampford Arundel Som 27 D6
Sampford Brett Som 27 A5
Sampford Courtenay Devon 12 A1
Sampford Peverell Devon 27 D5
Sampford Spiney Devon 11 D6
Sampool Bridge Cumb 154 C3
Samuelston E Loth 210 C1
Sanachan Highld 249 B5
Sanaigmore Argyll 200 A2
Sanclêr = St Clears Carms 56 A2
Sancreed Corn 2 C2
Sancton E Yorks 150 D2
Sand Highld 261 A6
Sand Shetland 285 J5
Sand Hole E Yorks 149 D7
Sand Hutton N Yorks 149 B5
Sandaig Highld 247 D6
Sandal Magna W Yorks 139 B6
Sandale Cumb 175 D5
Sanday Airport Orkney 282 C7
Sandbach Ches 128 C2
Sandbank Argyll 215 D4
Sandbanks Poole 17 C4
Sandend Aberds 267 C6
Sanderstead London 49 C6
Sandfields Glos 63 A5

Sandford Cumb 165 D5
Sandford Devon 12 A3
Sandford Dorset 16 C3
Sandford I o W 18 C4
Sandford N Som 42 D3
Sandford Shrops 111 B4
Sandford S Lnrk 194 B2
Sandford on Thames Oxon 65 C6
Sandford Orcas Dorset 29 C6
Sandford St Martin Oxon 65 A5
Sandfordhill Aberds 257 B6
Sandgate Kent 38 B3
Sandgreen Dumfries 172 C3
Sandhaven Aberds 269 C4
Sandhead Dumfries 170 C2
Sandhills Sur 34 C2
Sandhoe Northumb 178 C1
Sandholme E Yorks 150 D1
Sandholme Lincs 117 B6
Sandhurst Brack 47 C6
Sandhurst Glos 63 A4
Sandhurst Kent 37 D5
Sandhurst Cross Kent 37 D5
Sandhutton N Yorks 158 C2
Sandiacre Derbys 114 B2
Sandilands Lincs 135 A5
Sandilands S Lnrk 194 C3
Sandiway Ches 127 B6
Sandleheath Hants 31 D5
Sandling Kent 37 A5
Sandlow Green Ches 128 C2
Sandness Shetland 285 H3
Sandon Essex 70 C1
Sandon Herts 85 D5
Sandon Staffs 112 B3
Sandown I o W 19 C4
Sandown Park Racecourse Sur 48 C4
Sandplace Corn 6 B1
Sandridge Herts 67 B6
Sandridge Wilts 44 C3
Sandringham Norf 118 C3
Sandsend N Yorks 169 D6
Sandside Ho. Highld 279 B5
Sandsound Shetland 285 J5
Sandtoft N Lincs 141 C5
Sandway Kent 37 A6
Sandwell W Mid 96 C3
Sandwich Kent 53 D5
Sandwick Cumb 164 D2
Sandwick Orkney 283 K5
Sandwick Shetland 285 L6
Sandwith Cumb 162 C2
Sandy Beds 84 C3
Sandy Carms 57 B4
Sandy Bank Lincs 134 D2
Sandy Haven Pembs 55 D4
Sandy Lane Wilts 44 C3
Sandy Lane Wrex 110 A2
Sandycroft Flint 126 C3
Sandyford Dumfries 185 C5
Sandyford Stoke 128 D3
Sandygate I o M 152 B3
Sandyhills Dumfries 173 C6
Sandylands Lancs 144 A4
Sandypark Devon 12 C2
Sandysike Cumb 175 B6
Sangobeg Highld 277 B5
Sangomore Highld 277 B5
Sanna Highld 234 D3
Sanndabhaig W Isles 288 D5
Sanndabhaig W Isles 286 B4
Sannox N Ayrs 203 D5
Sanquhar Dumfries 183 B5
Santa Pod Raceway Beds 83 A6
Santon N Lincs 142 B1
Santon Bridge Cumb 163 D4
Santon Downham Suff 103 C4
Sapcote Leics 98 B1
Sapey Common Hereford 79 A5
Sapiston Suff 103 D5
Sapley Cambs 100 D4
Sapperton Glos 63 C5
Sapperton Lincs 116 B3
Saracen's Head Lincs 117 C6
Sarclet Highld 281 D5
Sardis Carms 57 B5
Sarn Bridgend 40 C4
Sarn Powys 93 B6
Sarn Bach Gwyn 106 D3
Sarn Meyllteyrn Gwyn 106 C2
Sarnau Ceredig 73 A6
Sarnau Carms 56 A3
Sarnau Gwyn 109 B4
Sarnau Powys 76 D3

Sarnau Powys 110 D1
Sarnesfield Hereford 78 B1
Saron Carms 73 C6
Saron Carms 57 A6
Saron Denb 125 C5
Saron Gwyn 107 A4
Saron Gwyn 123 D5
Sarratt Herts 67 D5
Sarre Kent 53 C4
Sarsden Oxon 64 A3
Sarsgrum Highld 277 B4
Satley Durham 166 A4
Satron N Yorks 156 B3
Satterleigh Devon 26 C1
Satterthwaite Cumb 154 B2
Satwell Oxon 47 A5
Sauchen Aberds 244 A3
Saucher Perth 219 A6
Sauchie Clack 208 A1
Sauchieburn Aberds 233 B4
Saughall Ches 126 B3
Saughtree Borders 187 D4
Saul Glos 62 C3
Saundby Notts 132 A2
Saundersfoot Pembs 56 B1
Saunderton Bucks 66 C2
Saunton Devon 25 B5
Sausthorpe Lincs 134 C3
Saval Highld 272 D3
Savary Highld 225 B5
Savile Park W Yorks 138 A3
Sawbridge Warks 82 A2
Sawbridgeworth Herts 69 B4
Sawdon N Yorks 160 C3
Sawley Derbys 114 B2
Sawley Lancs 146 C1
Sawley N Yorks 147 A6
Sawston Cambs 85 C6
Sawtry Cambs 100 C3
Saxby Leics 115 D6
Saxby Lincs 133 A5
Saxby All Saints N Lincs 142 B1
Saxelbye Leics 115 C5
Saxham Street Suff 88 A1
Saxilby Lincs 132 B3
Saxlingham Norf 120 B2
Saxlingham Green Norf 104 B3
Saxlingham Nethergate Norf 104 B3
Saxlingham Thorpe Norf 104 B3
Saxmundham Suff 89 A4
Saxon Street Cambs 86 B2
Saxondale Notts 115 B4
Saxtead Suff 88 A3
Saxtead Green Suff 88 A3
Saxthorpe Norf 120 B3
Saxton N Yorks 148 D3
Sayers Common W Sus 21 A5
Scackleton N Yorks 159 D5
Scadabhagh W Isles 288 H2
Scaftworth Notts 141 D4
Scagglethorpe N Yorks 160 D2
Scaitcliffe Lancs 137 A6
Scalasaig Argyll 212 C1
Scalby E Yorks 141 A6
Scalby N Yorks 160 B4
Scaldwell Northants 99 D4
Scale Houses Cumb 164 A3
Scaleby Cumb 176 C2
Scaleby Hill Cumb 176 C2
Scales Cumb 153 C3
Scales Cumb 163 B6
Scales Cumb 145 D4
Scalford Leics 115 C5
Scaling N Yorks 169 D5
Scallastle Argyll 225 C5
Scalloway Shetland 285 K6
Scalpay W Isles 288 H3
Scalpay Ho. Highld 247 B5
Scalpsie Argyll 203 C5
Scamadale Highld 235 A6
Scamblesby Lincs 134 B2
Scamodale Highld 236 B2
Scampston N Yorks 160 D2
Scampton Lincs 133 B4
Scapa Orkney 283 G5
Scapegoat Hill W Yorks 138 B3
Scar Orkney 282 C7
Scarborough N Yorks 160 C4
Scarborough Sea Life Centre N Yorks 160 B4
Scarcliffe Derbys 131 C4
Scarcroft W Yorks 148 C2
Scarcroft Hill W Yorks 148 C2
Scardroy Highld 250 A4
Scarff Shetland 284 E4
Scarfskerry Highld 281 A4
Scargill Durham 166 D3

Scarinish Argyll 222 C3
Scarisbrick Lancs 136 B2
Scarning Norf 119 D6
Scarrington Notts 115 A5
Scartho NE Lincs 143 C4
Scarwell Orkney 282 E3
Scatness Shetland 285 M5
Scatraig Highld 252 C3
Scawby N Lincs 142 C1
Scawsby S Yorks 140 C3
Scawton N Yorks 158 C4
Scayne's Hill W Sus 35 D6
Scethrog Powys 60 A3
Scholar Green Ches 128 D3
Scholes W Yorks 139 C4
Scholes W Yorks 139 A4
Scholes W Yorks 148 D2
School Green Ches 127 C6
Science & Industry Museum, Manchester Gtr Man 138 D1
Science Centre Glasgow 205 B5
Science Museum London 49 B5
Scleddau Pembs 55 A5
Sco Ruston Norf 121 C4
Scofton Notts 131 A6
Scole Norf 104 D2
Scolpaig W Isles 287 G2
Scone Perth 219 B6
Scone Palace, Perth Perth 219 B6
Sconser Highld 247 A4
Scoonie Fife 220 D3
Scoor Argyll 224 E3
Scopwick Lincs 133 D5
Scoraig Highld 262 A2
Scorborough E Yorks 150 C3
Scorrier Corn 4 C2
Scorton Lancs 145 C5
Scorton N Yorks 157 A6
Scotbheinn W Isles 286 A4
Scotby Cumb 176 D2
Scotch Corner N Yorks 157 A6
Scotforth Lancs 145 B4
Scothern Lincs 133 B5
Scotland Gate Northumb 179 A4
Scotlandwell Perth 219 D6
Scotney Castle Garden Kent 37 C4
Scotsburn Highld 264 C3
Scotscalder Station Highld 280 C2
Scotscraig Fife 220 B4
Scots'Gap Northumb 178 A2
Scotston Aberds 233 A5
Scotston Perth 230 D3
Scotstoun Glasgow 205 B5
Scotstown Highld 236 C2
Scotswood T & W 178 C3
Scottas Highld 247 D6
Scotter Lincs 141 C6
Scotterthorpe Lincs 141 C6
Scottlethorpe Lincs 116 C3
Scotton Lincs 141 D6
Scotton N Yorks 157 B5
Scotton N Yorks 148 B2
Scottow Norf 121 C4
Scoughall E Loth 210 B3
Scoulag Argyll 203 C6
Scoulton Norf 103 A5
Scourie Highld 276 D2
Scourie More Highld 276 D2
Scousburgh Shetland 285 M5
Scrabster Highld 280 B2
Scrafield Lincs 134 C3
Scrainwood Northumb 188 C2
Scrane End Lincs 117 A6
Scraptoft Leics 98 A3
Scratby Norf 121 D7
Scrayingham N Yorks 149 A6
Scredington Lincs 116 A3
Scremby Lincs 135 C4
Scremerston Northumb 198 B4
Screveton Notts 115 A5
Scrivelsby Lincs 134 C2
Scriven N Yorks 148 B2
Scrooby Notts 141 D4
Scropton Derbys 113 B5
Scrub Hill Lincs 134 D2
Scruton N Yorks 157 B6
Sculcoates Hull 150 D3
Sculthorpe Norf 119 B5
Scunthorpe N Lincs 141 B6
Scurlage Swansea 57 D4
Sea Palling Norf 121 C6
Sea Zoo Anglesey 123 D4
Seaborough Dorset 14 A4
Seacombe Mers 136 D2

Seacroft Lincs 135 C5
Seacroft W Yorks 148 D2
Seadyke Lincs 117 B6
Seafield S Ayrs 192 C3
Seafield W Loth 208 D3
Seaford E Sus 22 C2
Seaforth Mers 136 D2
Seagrave Leics 115 D4
Seaham Durham 168 A2
Seahouses Northumb 199 C6
Seal Kent 36 A3
Sealand Flint 126 C3
Seale Sur 34 B1
Seamer N Yorks 168 D2
Seamer N Yorks 160 C4
Seamill N Ayrs 204 D2
Searby Lincs 142 C2
Seasalter Kent 52 C2
Seascale Cumb 162 D3
Seathorne Lincs 135 C5
Seathwaite Cumb 153 A3
Seathwaite Cumb 163 C5
Seatoller Cumb 163 C5
Seaton Corn 6 B2
Seaton Cumb 162 A3
Seaton Devon 14 C2
Seaton Durham 179 D5
Seaton E Yorks 151 C4
Seaton Northumb 179 B5
Seaton Rutland 99 B6
Seaton Burn T & W 179 B4
Seaton Carew Hrtlpl 168 C3
Seaton Delaval Northumb 179 B5
Seaton Ross E Yorks 149 C6
Seaton Sluice Northumb 179 B5
Seatown Aberds 267 C6
Seatown Dorset 14 B4
Seave Green N Yorks 159 A4
Seaview I o W 19 B5
Seaville Cumb 175 C4
Seavington St Mary Som 28 D3
Seavington St Michael Som 28 D4
Sebergham Cumb 164 A1
Seckington Warks 97 A5
Second Coast Highld 261 A6
Sedbergh Cumb 155 B5
Sedbury Glos 62 D1
Sedbusk N Yorks 156 B2
Sedgeberrow Worcs 80 D3
Sedgebrook Lincs 115 B6
Sedgefield Durham 167 C6
Sedgefield Racecourse Durham 167 C6
Sedgeford Norf 119 B4
Sedgehill Wilts 30 C2
Sedgley W Mid 96 B2
Sedgwick Cumb 154 C4
Sedlescombe E Sus 23 A5
Sedlescombe Street E Sus 23 A5
Seend Wilts 44 C3
Seend Cleeve Wilts 44 C3
Seer Green Bucks 67 D4
Seething Norf 104 B4
Sefton Mers 136 C2
Seghill Northumb 179 B4
Seifton Shrops 94 C2
Seighford Staffs 112 C2
Seilebost W Isles 287 E5
Seion Gwyn 123 D5
Seisdon Staffs 95 B6
Seisiadar W Isles 288 D6
Selattyn Shrops 110 B1
Selborne Hants 33 B6
Selby N Yorks 149 D5
Selham W Sus 34 D2
Selhurst London 49 C6
Selkirk Borders 186 A3
Selkirk Glass Borders 186 A3
Sellack Hereford 62 A1
Sellafirth Shetland 284 D7
Sellibister Orkney 282 C8
Sellindge Kent 38 B2
Sellindge Lees Kent 38 B3
Selling Kent 52 D2
Sells Green Wilts 44 C3
Selly Oak W Mid 96 C3
Selmeston E Sus 22 B3
Selsdon London 49 C6
Selsey W Sus 20 C1
Selsfield Common W Sus 35 C6
Selside Cumb 39 A4
Selside N Yorks 155 D7
Selsley Glos 63 C4
Selsted Kent 39 A4
Selston Notts 131 D4
Selworthy Som 27 A4
Semblister Shetland 285 H5
Semer Suff 87 C5
Semington Wilts 44 C2
Semley Wilts 30 C2

Send Sur 34 A3
Send Marsh Sur 34 A3
Senghenydd Caerph 41 B6
Sennen Corn 2 C1
Sennen Cove Corn 2 C1
Sennybridge = Pont Senni Powys 59 C6
Serlby Notts 131 A6
Sessay N Yorks 158 D3
Setchey Norf 118 D3
Setley Hants 18 A2
Setter Shetland 285 H5
Setter Shetland 284 E6
Setter Shetland 285 J7
Settiscarth Orkney 282 F4
Settle N Yorks 146 A2
Settrington N Yorks 160 D2
Seven Kings London 50 A1
Seven Sisters Neath 59 E5
Sevenhampton Glos 63 A6
Sevenoaks Kent 36 A3
Sevenoaks Weald Kent 36 A3
Severn Beach S Glos 43 A4
Severn Bridges Visitor Centre S Glos 43 A4
Severn Stoke Worcs 79 C6
Severn Valley Railway Worcs 95 D5
Severnhampton Swindon 64 D3
Sevington Kent 38 A2
Sewards End Essex 86 D1
Sewardstone Essex 68 D3
Sewardstonebury Essex 68 D3
Sewerby E Yorks 151 A4
Seworgan Corn 4 D2
Sewstern Leics 116 C1
Sezincote Glos 81 D4
Sgarasta Mhor W Isles 287 E5
Sgiogarstaigh W Isles 288 A6
Shabbington Bucks 66 C1
Shackerstone Leics 97 A6
Shackleford Sur 34 B2
Shade W Yorks 138 A2
Shadforth Durham 167 A6
Shadingfield Suff 105 C5
Shadoxhurst Kent 38 B1
Shadsworth Blkburn 137 A6
Shadwell Norf 103 C5
Shadwell W Yorks 148 D2
Shaftesbury Dorset 30 C2
Shafton S Yorks 140 B1
Shakespeare's Birthplace, Stratford-upon-Avon Warks 81 B5
Shalbourne Wilts 45 C7
Shalcombe I o W 18 C2
Shalden Hants 33 A5
Shaldon Devon 13 D4
Shalfleet I o W 18 C3
Shalford Essex 69 A7
Shalford Sur 34 B3
Shalford Green Essex 69 A7
Shallowford Devon 26 A2
Shalmsford Street Kent 52 D2
Shalstone Bucks 82 D3
Shamley Green Sur 34 B3
Shandon Argyll 215 D5
Shandwick Highld 265 C4
Shangton Leics 99 B4
Shankhouse Northumb 179 B4
Shanklin I o W 19 C4
Shanklin Chine I o W 19 C4
Shanquhar Aberds 255 C6
Shanzie Perth 231 C6
Shap Cumb 164 D3
Shapwick Dorset 16 A3
Shapwick Som 28 B4
Shardlow Derbys 114 B2
Shareshill Staffs 96 A2
Sharlston W Yorks 140 B1
Sharlston Common W Yorks 140 B1
Sharnbrook Beds 84 B1
Sharnford Leics 98 B1
Sharoe Green Lancs 145 D5
Sharow N Yorks 158 D2
Sharp Street Norf 121 C5
Sharpenhoe Beds 84 D2
Sharperton Northumb 188 C2
Sharpness Glos 62 C2
Sharpthorne W Sus 35 C6
Sharrington Norf 120 B2
Shatterford Worcs 95 C5
Shaugh Prior Devon 7 A4
Shavington Ches 128 D2

Shaw Gtr Man 138 C2
Shaw W Berks 46 C2
Shaw Wilts 44 C2
Shaw Green Lancs 136 B4
Shaw Mills N Yorks 147 A6
Shawbury Shrops 111 C4
Shawdon Hall Northumb 188 B3
Shawell Leics 98 C2
Shawford Hants 32 C3
Shawforth Lancs 138 A1
Shawhead Dumfries 173 A6
Shawhill Dumfries 175 B5
Shawton S Lnrk 194 B1
Shawtonhill S Lnrk 194 B1
Shear Cross Wilts 30 A2
Shearington Dumfries 174 B3
Shearsby Leics 98 B3
Shebbear Devon 11 A5
Shebdon Staffs 111 C6
Shebster Highld 279 B6
Sheddens E Renf 205 C5
Shedfield Hants 33 D4
Sheen Staffs 129 C6
Sheepscar W Yorks 148 D2
Sheepscombe Glos 63 B4
Sheepstor Devon 7 A4
Sheepwash Devon 11 A5
Sheepway N Som 42 B3
Sheepy Magna Leics 97 A6
Sheepy Parva Leics 97 A6
Sheering Essex 69 B5
Sheerness Kent 51 B6
Sheet Hants 33 C6
Sheffield S Yorks 130 A3
Sheffield Bottom W Berks 47 C4
Sheffield Green E Sus 36 D2
Sheffield Park, Uckfield
  E Sus 36 D2
Shefford Beds 84 D3
Shefford Woodlands
  W Berks 46 B1
Sheigra Highld 276 B2
Sheinton Shrops 95 A4
Shelderton Shrops 94 D2
Sheldon Derbys 129 C6
Sheldon Devon 13 A6
Sheldon W Mid 97 C4
Sheldwich Kent 52 D2
Shelf W Yorks 139 A4
Shelfanger Norf 104 C2
Shelfield Warks 80 A4
Shelfield W Mid 96 A3
Shelford Notts 115 A4
Shellacres Northumb 198 B2
Shelley Essex 69 C5
Shelley Suff 87 D6
Shelley W Yorks 139 B5
Shellingford Oxon 64 D4
Shellow Bowells Essex 69 C6
Shelsley Beauchamp
  Worcs 79 A5
Shelsley Walsh Worcs 79 A5
Shelthorpe Leics 114 D3
Shelton Beds 84 A2
Shelton Norf 104 B3
Shelton Notts 115 A5
Shelton Shrops 110 D3
Shelton Green Norf 104 B3
Shelve Shrops 94 B1
Shelwick Hereford 78 C3
Shenfield Essex 69 D6
Shenington Oxon 81 C6
Shenley Herts 68 C1
Shenley Brook End
  M Keynes 83 D5
Shenley Church End
  M Keynes 83 D5
Shenleybury Herts 68 C1
Shenmore Hereford 78 D1
Shennanton Dumfries 171 A5
Shenstone Staffs 96 A4
Shenstone Worcs 95 D6
Shenton Leics 97 A6
Shenval Highld 251 D6
Shenval Moray 254 D3
Shepeau Stow Lincs 117 D6
Shephall Herts 68 A2
Shepherd's Green Oxon 47 A5
Shepherd's Port Norf 118 B3
Shepherdswell Kent 39 A4
Shepley W Yorks 139 C4
Shepperdine S Glos 62 D2
Shepperton Sur 48 C3
Shepreth Cambs 85 C5
Shepshed Leics 114 D2
Shepton Beauchamp Som 28 D4
Shepton Mallet Som 29 A6
Shepton Montague Som 29 B6

Shepway Kent 37 A5
Sheraton Durham 168 B2
Sherborne Dorset 29 D6
Sherborne Glos 64 B2
Sherborne St John Hants 47 D4
Sherbourne Warks 81 A5
Sherburn Durham 167 A6
Sherburn N Yorks 160 D3
Sherburn Hill Durham 167 A6
Sherburn in Elmet
  N Yorks 148 D3
Shere Sur 34 B3
Shereford Norf 119 C5
Sherfield English Hants 32 C1
Sherfield on Loddon Hants 47 D4
Sherford Devon 8 C1
Sheriff Hutton N Yorks 149 A5
Sheriffhales Shrops 111 D6
Sheringham Norf 120 A3
Sherington M Keynes 83 C5
Shernal Green Worcs 80 A2
Shernborne Norf 119 B4
Sherrington Wilts 30 B3
Sherston Wilts 44 A2
Sherwood Green Devon 25 C6
Shettleston Glasgow 205 B6
Shevington Gtr Man 136 C4
Shevington Moor Gtr Man 136 B4
Shevington Vale Gtr Man 136 C4
Sheviock Corn 6 B2
Shide I o W 18 C3
Shiel Bridge Highld 238 A3
Shieldaig Highld 249 A5
Shieldaig Highld 261 C5
Shieldhill Dumfries 184 D3
Shieldhill Falk 208 C1
Shieldhill S Lnrk 195 B5
Shielfoot Highld 235 D5
Shielhill Angus 232 C2
Shielhill Invclyd 204 A2
Shifford Oxon 65 C4
Shifnal Shrops 95 A5
Shilbottle Northumb 189 C4
Shildon Durham 167 C5
Shillingford Devon 27 C4
Shillingford Oxon 65 D6
Shillingford St George
  Devon 13 C4
Shillingstone Dorset 30 D2
Shillington Beds 84 D3
Shillmoor Northumb 188 C1
Shilton Oxon 64 C3
Shilton Warks 97 C7
Shilvington Northumb 178 A3
Shimpling Norf 104 C2
Shimpling Suff 87 B4
Shimpling Street Suff 87 B4
Shincliffe Durham 167 A5
Shiney Row T & W 179 D5
Shinfield Wokingham 47 C5
Shingham Norf 102 A3
Shingle Street Suff 89 C4
Shinner's Bridge Devon 8 A1
Shinness Highld 272 C3
Shipbourne Kent 36 A3
Shipdham Norf 103 A5
Shipham Som 42 D3
Shiphay Torbay 8 A2
Shiplake Oxon 47 B5
Shipley Derbys 114 A2
Shipley Northumb 189 B4
Shipley Shrops 95 B6
Shipley W Sus 35 D4
Shipley W Yorks 147 D5
Shipley Shiels Northumb 187 D6
Shipmeadow Suff 105 C4
Shippea Hill Station
  Cambs 102 C2
Shippon Oxon 65 D5
Shipston-on-Stour Warks 81 C5
Shipton Glos 63 B6
Shipton N Yorks 149 B4
Shipton Shrops 94 B3
Shipton Bellinger Hants 31 A6
Shipton Gorge Dorset 15 B4
Shipton Green W Sus 19 A7
Shipton Moyne Glos 44 A2
Shipton on Cherwell Oxon 65 B5
Shipton Solers Glos 63 B6
Shipton-under-
  Wychwood Oxon 64 B3
Shiptonthorpe E Yorks 150 C1
Shirburn Oxon 66 D1
Shirdley Hill Lancs 136 B2
Shire Horse Centre,
  Stratford-upon-Avon
  Warks 81 B5
Shirebrook Derbys 131 C5

Shiregreen S Yorks 139 D6
Shirehampton Bristol 43 B4
Shiremoor T & W 179 B5
Shirenewton Mon 61 D6
Shireoaks Notts 131 A5
Shirkoak Kent 38 B1
Shirl Heath Hereford 78 B2
Shirland Derbys 130 D3
Shirley Derbys 113 A6
Shirley London 49 C6
Shirley Soton 32 D3
Shirley W Mid 96 D4
Shirrell Heath Hants 33 D4
Shirwell Devon 25 B6
Shirwell Cross Devon 25 B6
Shiskine N Ayrs 191 C5
Shobdon Hereford 78 A2
Shobnall Staffs 113 C6
Shobrooke Devon 12 A3
Shoby Leics 115 D4
Shocklach Ches 110 A3
Shoeburyness Sthend 51 A6
Sholden Kent 53 D5
Sholing Soton 32 D3
Shoot Hill Shrops 110 D3
Shop Corn 24 D3
Shop Corn 9 D4
Shop Corner Suff 88 D3
Shore Mill Highld 264 D3
Shoreditch London 49 A6
Shoreham Kent 50 C2
Shoreham Airport W Sus 21 B5
Shoreham-By-Sea W Sus 21 B5
Shoresdean Northumb 198 B3
Shoreswood Northumb 198 B3
Shoreton Highld 264 D2
Shorncote Glos 63 D6
Shorne Kent 50 B3
Short Heath W Mid 96 A2
Shortacombe Devon 11 C6
Shortgate E Sus 22 A2
Shortlanesend Corn 4 C3
Shortlees E Ayrs 193 B4
Shortstown Beds 84 C2
Shorwell I o W 18 C3
Shoscombe Bath 43 D6
Shotatton Shrops 110 C2
Shotesham Norf 104 B3
Shotgate Essex 70 D1
Shotley Suff 88 D3
Shotley Bridge Durham 178 D2
Shotley Gate Suff 88 D3
Shotleyfield Northumb 178 D2
Shottenden Kent 52 D2
Shottermill Sur 34 C1
Shottery Warks 81 B4
Shotteswell Warks 81 C7
Shottisham Suff 88 C4
Shottle Derbys 113 A7
Shottlegate Derbys 113 A7
Shotton Durham 168 B2
Shotton Flint 126 C3
Shotton Northumb 198 C2
Shotton Colliery Durham 167 A6
Shotts N Lnrk 207 D6
Shotwick Ches 126 B3
Shouldham Norf 102 A2
Shouldham Thorpe Norf 102 A2
Shoulton Worcs 79 B6
Shover's Green E Sus 37 C4
Shrawardine Shrops 110 D3
Shrawley Worcs 79 A6
Shrewley Common Warks 81 A5
Shrewsbury Shrops 110 D3
Shrewton Wilts 31 A4
Shripney W Sus 20 B2
Shrivenham Oxon 45 A6
Shropham Norf 103 B5
Shrub End Essex 70 A3
Shucknall Hereford 78 C3
Shudy Camps Cambs 86 C2
Shulishadermor Highld 259 D4
Shurdington Glos 63 B5
Shurlock Row Windsor 47 B6
Shurrery Highld 279 C6
Shurrery Lodge Highld 279 C6
Shurton Som 28 A2
Shustoke Warks 97 B5
Shute Devon 14 B2
Shute Devon 12 A3
Shutford Oxon 81 C6
Shuthonger Glos 80 D1
Shutlanger Northants 83 B4
Shuttington Warks 97 A5
Shuttlewood Derbys 131 B4
Siabost bho Dheas
  W Isles 288 C3

Siabost bho Thuath
  W Isles 288 C3
Siadar W Isles 288 B4
Siadar Iarach W Isles 288 B4
Siadar Uarach W Isles 288 B4
Sibbaldbie Dumfries 185 D4
Sibbertoft Northants 98 C3
Sibdon Carwood Shrops 94 C2
Sibford Ferris Oxon 81 D6
Sibford Gower Oxon 81 D6
Sible Hedingham Essex 86 D3
Sibsey Lincs 134 D3
Sibson Cambs 100 B2
Sibson Leics 97 A6
Sibthorpe Notts 115 A5
Sibton Suff 89 A4
Sibton Green Suff 105 D4
Sicklesmere Suff 87 A4
Sicklinghall N Yorks 148 C2
Sid Devon 13 C6
Sidbury Devon 13 B6
Sidbury Shrops 95 C4
Sidcot N Som 42 D3
Sidcup London 50 B1
Siddick Cumb 162 A3
Siddington Ches 128 B3
Siddington Glos 63 D6
Sidemoor Worcs 96 D2
Sidestrand Norf 121 B4
Sidford Devon 13 B6
Sidlesham W Sus 20 C1
Sidley E Sus 23 B5
Sidlow Sur 35 B5
Sidmouth Devon 13 C6
Sigford Devon 12 D2
Sigglesthorne E Yorks 151 C4
Sighthill Edin 209 C4
Sigingstone V Glam 41 D4
Signet Oxon 64 B3
Silchester Hants 47 C4
Sildinis W Isles 288 F3
Sileby Leics 114 D3
Silecroft Cumb 153 B2
Silfield Norf 104 B2
Silian Ceredig 75 C4
Silk Willoughby Lincs 116 A3
Silkstone S Yorks 139 C5
Silkstone Common
  S Yorks 139 C5
Silloth Cumb 174 C4
Sills Northumb 188 C1
Sillyearn Moray 267 D6
Siloh Carms 59 B4
Silpho N Yorks 160 B3
Silsden W Yorks 147 C4
Silsoe Beds 84 D2
Silver End Essex 70 B2
Silverburn Midloth 209 D5
Silverdale Lancs 154 D3
Silverdale Staffs 112 A2
Silvergate Norf 120 C3
Silverhill E Sus 23 A5
Silverley's Green Suff 104 D3
Silverstone Northants 82 C3
Silverstone Motor Racing
  Circuit Northants 82 C3
Silverton Devon 13 A4
Silvington Shrops 95 D4
Silwick Shetland 285 J4
Simmondley Derbys 138 D3
Simonburn Northumb 177 B6
Simonsbath Som 26 B2
Simonstone Lancs 146 D1
Simprim Borders 198 B2
Simpson M Keynes 83 D5
Simpson Cross Pembs 55 C4
Sinclair's Hill Borders 198 A2
Sinclairston E Ayrs 182 A2
Sinderby N Yorks 158 C2
Sinderhope Northumb 177 D6
Sindlesham Wokingham 47 C5
Singdean Borders 187 C4
Singleborough Bucks 83 D4
Singleton Lancs 144 D3
Singleton W Sus 20 A1
Singlewell Kent 50 B3
Sinkhurst Green Kent 37 B6
Sinnahard Aberds 244 A1
Sinnington N Yorks 159 C6
Sinton Green Worcs 79 A6
Sipson London 48 B3
Sirhowy Bl Gwent 60 B3
Sisland Norf 104 B4
Sissinghurst Kent 37 C5
Sissinghurst, Cranbrook
  Kent 37 C6
Sisterpath Borders 197 B6
Siston S Glos 43 B5

Sithney Corn 3 C4
Sittingbourne Kent 51 C5
Six Ashes Staffs 95 C5
Six Hills Leics 115 C4
Six Mile Bottom Cambs 86 B1
Sixhills Lincs 133 A6
Sixpenny Handley Dorset 30 D3
Sizewell Suff 89 A5
Skail Highld 278 D3
Skaill Orkney 282 B5
Skaill Orkney 282 D5
Skaill Orkney 283 G6
Skara Brae Orkney 282 F3
Skares E Ayrs 182 A3
Skateraw E Loth 211 C4
Skaw Shetland 284 G7
Skeabost Highld 259 D4
Skeabrae Orkney 282 E3
Skeeby N Yorks 157 A6
Skeffington Leics 99 A4
Skeffling E Yorks 143 B5
Skegby Notts 131 C4
Skegness Lincs 135 C5
Skelberry Shetland 285 M5
Skelbo Highld 264 A3
Skelbrooke S Yorks 140 B3
Skeldyke Lincs 117 B6
Skellingthorpe Lincs 133 B4
Skellister Shetland 285 H6
Skellow S Yorks 140 B3
Skelmanthorpe W Yorks 139 B5
Skelmersdale Lancs 136 C3
Skelmonae Aberds 256 C3
Skelmorlie N Ayrs 204 B1
Skelmuir Aberds 257 B4
Skelpick Highld 278 C3
Skelton Cumb 164 B2
Skelton E Yorks 141 A5
Skelton N Yorks 157 A4
Skelton Redcar 169 D4
Skelton York 149 B4
Skelton-on-Ure N Yorks 148 A2
Skelwick Orkney 282 C5
Skelwith Bridge Cumb 154 A2
Skendleby Lincs 135 C4
Skene Ho. Aberds 245 B4
Skenfrith Mon 61 A6
Skerne E Yorks 150 B3
Skeroblingarry Argyll 190 C3
Skerray Highld 278 B2
Skerton Lancs 145 A4
Sketchley Leics 98 B1
Sketty Swansea 57 C6
Skewen Neath 40 B2
Skewsby N Yorks 159 D5
Skeyton Norf 120 C4
Skiag Bridge Highld 271 B5
Skibo Castle Highld 264 B3
Skidbrooke Lincs 143 D6
Skidbrooke North End
  Lincs 143 D6
Skidby E Yorks 150 D3
Skilgate Som 27 C4
Skillington Lincs 116 C1
Skinburness Cumb 174 C4
Skinflats Falk 208 B2
Skinidin Highld 258 D2
Skinnet Highld 277 B6
Skinningrove Redcar 169 C5
Skipness Argyll 202 C3
Skippool Lancs 144 C3
Skipsea E Yorks 151 B4
Skipsea Brough E Yorks 151 B4
Skipton N Yorks 146 B3
Skipton-on-Swale
  N Yorks 158 D2
Skipwith N Yorks 149 D5
Skirbeck Lincs 117 A6
Skirbeck Quarter Lincs 117 A6
Skirlaugh E Yorks 151 D4
Skirling Borders 195 C5
Skirmett Bucks 47 A5
Skirpenbeck E Yorks 149 B6
Skirwith Cumb 165 B4
Skirza Highld 281 B5
Skulamus Highld 247 B5
Skullomie Highld 277 B7
Skyborry Green Shrops 93 D6
Skye of Curr Highld 253 D5
Skyreholme N Yorks 147 A4
Slackhall Derbys 129 A5
Slackhead Moray 267 C5
Slad Glos 63 C4
Slade Devon 25 A6
Slade Pembs 55 C5

Slade Green London 50 B2
Slaggyford Northumb 177 D4
Slaidburn Lancs 145 B7
Slaithwaite W Yorks 138 B3
Slaley Northumb 178 D1
Slamannan Falk 207 C6
Slapton Bucks 67 A4
Slapton Devon 8 C2
Slapton Northants 82 C3
Slatepit Dale Derbys 130 C3
Slattocks Gtr Man 138 C1
Slaugham W Sus 35 D5
Slaughterford Wilts 44 B2
Slawston Leics 99 B4
Sleaford Hants 33 B7
Sleaford Lincs 116 A3
Sleagill Cumb 164 D3
Sleapford Telford 111 D5
Sledge Green Worcs 79 D6
Sledmere E Yorks 150 A2
Sleightholme Durham 166 D2
Sleights N Yorks 160 A2
Slepe Dorset 16 B3
Slickly Highld 281 B4
Sliddery N Ayrs 191 C5
Sligachan Hotel Highld 246 B3
Slimbridge Glos 62 C3
Slimbridge Wildfowl & Wetlands Centre, Frampton on Severn Glos 62 C3
Slindon Staffs 112 B2
Slindon W Sus 20 B2
Slinfold W Sus 35 C4
Sling Gwyn 123 D6
Slingsby N Yorks 159 D5
Slioch Aberds 255 C6
Slip End Beds 67 B5
Slip End Herts 85 D4
Slipton Northants 99 D6
Slitting Mill Staffs 112 A4
Slochd Highld 253 D4
Slockavullin Argyll 213 C6
Sloley Norf 121 C4
Sloothby Lincs 135 B4
Slough Slough 48 B2
Slough Green W Sus 35 D5
Sluggan Highld 253 D4
Slumbay Highld 249 C5
Slyfield Sur 34 A2
Slyne Lancs 145 A4
Smailholm Borders 197 C5
Small Dole W Sus 21 A5
Small Hythe Kent 37 C6
Smallbridge Gtr Man 138 B2
Smallburgh Norf 121 C5
Smallburn Aberds 257 B5
Smallburn E Ayrs 194 D1
Smalley Derbys 114 A2
Smallfield Sur 35 B6
Smallridge Devon 14 A3
Smannell Hants 32 A2
Smardale Cumb 155 A6
Smarden Kent 37 B6
Smarden Bell Kent 37 B6
Smeatharpe Devon 28 D1
Smeeth Kent 38 B2
Smeeton Westerby Leics 98 B3
Smercleit W Isles 286 E3
Smerral Highld 275 A5
Smethwick W Mid 96 C3
Smirisary Highld 235 C5
Smisby Derbys 114 D1
Smith Green Lancs 145 B4
Smithfield Cumb 176 C2
Smithincott Devon 27 D5
Smith's Green Essex 69 A5
Smithstown Highld 261 C4
Smithton Highld 252 B3
Smithy Green Ches 128 B2
Smockington Leics 98 C1
Smoogro Orkney 283 G4
Smythe's Green Essex 70 B3
Snaefell Mountain Railway I o M 152 C4
Snaigow House Perth 231 D4
Snailbeach Shrops 94 A1
Snailwell Cambs 86 A2
Snainton N Yorks 160 C3
Snaith E Yorks 140 A4
Snape N Yorks 157 C6
Snape Suff 89 B4
Snape Green Lancs 136 B2
Snarestone Leics 97 A6
Snarford Lincs 133 A5

Snargate Kent 38 C1
Snave Kent 38 C2
Snead Powys 93 B7
Sneath Common Norf 104 C2
Sneaton N Yorks 160 A2
Sneatonthorpe N Yorks 160 A3
Snelland Lincs 133 A5
Snelston Derbys 113 A5
Snetterton Motor Racing Circuit Norf 103 C6
Snettisham Norf 118 B3
Snibston Discovery Park, Coalville Leics 114 D2
Sniseabhal W Isles 286 C3
Snitter Northumb 188 C3
Snitterby Lincs 142 D1
Snitterfield Warks 81 B5
Snitton Shrops 94 D3
Snodhill Hereford 77 C7
Snodland Kent 51 C3
Snowden Hill S Yorks 139 C5
Snowdon Mountain Railway, Llanberis Gwyn 107 A6
Snowdown Kent 53 D4
Snowshill Glos 80 D3
Snowshill Manor Glos 80 D3
Snydale W Yorks 140 B2
Soar Anglesey 122 C3
Soar Carms 58 C3
Soar Devon 7 D6
Soar-y-Mynydd Ceredig 76 B1
Soberton Hants 33 D5
Soberton Heath Hants 33 D5
Sockbridge Cumb 164 C3
Sockburn Darl 158 A2
Soham Cambs 102 D1
Soham Cotes Cambs 102 D1
Solas W Isles 287 G3
Soldon Cross Devon 24 D4
Soldridge Hants 33 B5
Sole Street Kent 50 C3
Sole Street Kent 38 A2
Solihull W Mid 97 C4
Sollers Dilwyn Hereford 78 B2
Sollers Hope Hereford 79 D4
Sollom Lancs 136 B3
Solva Pembs 54 B3
Somerby Leics 115 D5
Somerby Lincs 142 C2
Somercotes Derbys 131 D4
Somerford Dorset 17 B5
Somerford Keynes Glos 63 D6
Somerley W Sus 19 B7
Somerleyton Suff 105 B5
Somersal Herbert Derbys 113 B5
Somersby Lincs 134 B3
Somersham Cambs 101 D5
Somersham Suff 88 C1
Somerton Oxon 65 A5
Somerton Som 29 C4
Sompting W Sus 21 B4
Sonning Wokingham 47 B5
Sonning Common Oxon 47 A5
Sonning Eye Oxon 47 B5
Sontley Wrex 110 A2
Sopley Hants 17 B5
Sopwell Herts 67 C6
Sopworth Wilts 44 A2
Sorbie Dumfries 171 C6
Sordale Highld 280 B3
Sorisdale Argyll 223 A5
Sorn E Ayrs 193 C5
Sornhill E Ayrs 193 B5
Sortat Highld 281 B4
Sotby Lincs 134 B2
Sots Hole Lincs 133 C6
Sotterley Suff 105 C5
Soudley Shrops 111 C6
Soughton Flint 126 C2
Soulbury Bucks 66 A3
Soulby Cumb 165 D5
Souldern Oxon 82 D2
Souldrop Beds 84 A1
Sound Ches 111 A5
Sound Shetland 285 H5
Sound Shetland 285 J6
Sound Heath Ches 111 A5
Soundwell S Glos 43 B5
Sourhope Borders 188 A1
Sourin Orkney 282 D5
Sourton Devon 11 B6
Soutergate Cumb 153 B3
South Acre Norf 119 D5
South Allington Devon 8 D1
South Alloa Falk 208 A1
South Ambersham W Sus 34 D2
South Anston S Yorks 131 A5

South Ascot Windsor 48 C2
South Ballachulish Highld 237 D4
South Balloch S Ayrs 181 B5
South Bank Redcar 168 C3
South Barrow Som 29 C6
South Beach Gwyn 106 C3
South Benfleet Essex 51 A4
South Bersted W Sus 20 B2
South Brent Devon 7 F2
South Brewham Som 29 B7
South Broomhill Northumb 189 D5
South Burlingham Norf 105 A4
South Cadbury Som 29 C6
South Cairn Dumfries 170 A1
South Carlton Lincs 133 B4
South Cave E Yorks 150 D2
South Cerney Glos 63 D6
South Chard Som 14 A3
South Charlton Northumb 189 A4
South Cheriton Som 29 C6
South Cliffe E Yorks 150 D1
South Clifton Notts 132 B3
South Cockerington Lincs 134 A3
South Cornelly Bridgend 40 C3
South Cove Suff 105 C5
South Creagan Argyll 227 B4
South Creake Norf 119 B5
South Croxton Leics 115 D4
South Croydon London 49 C6
South Dalton E Yorks 150 C2
South Darenth Kent 50 C2
South Duffield N Yorks 149 D5
South Elkington Lincs 134 A2
South Elmsall W Yorks 140 B2
South End Bucks 66 A3
South End Cumb 153 D3
South End N Lincs 142 A3
South Erradale Highld 261 C4
South Fambridge Essex 70 D2
South Fawley W Berks 46 A1
South Ferriby N Lincs 142 A1
South Garth Shetland 284 D7
South Garvan Highld 236 B3
South Glendale W Isles 286 E3
South Godstone Sur 35 B6
South Gorley Hants 31 D5
South Green Essex 69 D6
South Green Kent 51 C5
South-haa Shetland 284 E5
South Ham Hants 47 D4
South Hanningfield Essex 70 D1
South Harting W Sus 33 D6
South Hatfield Herts 68 C2
South Hayling Hants 19 B6
South Hazelrigg Northumb 199 C4
South Heath Bucks 67 C4
South Heighton E Sus 22 B2
South Hetton Durham 167 A6
South Hiendley W Yorks 140 B1
South Hill Corn 10 D4
South Hinksey Oxon 65 C6
South Hole Devon 24 C3
South Holme N Yorks 159 D5
South Holmwood Sur 35 B4
South Hornchurch London 50 A2
South Hykeham Lincs 133 C4
South Hylton T & W 179 D5
South Kelsey Lincs 142 D2
South Kessock Highld 252 B2
South Killingholme N Lincs 142 B3
South Kilvington N Yorks 158 C3
South Kilworth Leics 98 C3
South Kirkby W Yorks 140 B2
South Kirkton Aberds 245 B4
South Kiscadale N Ayrs 191 C6
South Kyme Lincs 117 A4
South Lancing W Sus 21 B4
South Leigh Oxon 65 C4
South Leverton Notts 132 A2
South Littleton Worcs 80 C3
South Lopham Norf 103 C6
South Luffenham Rutland 99 A6
South Malling E Sus 22 A2
South Marston Swindon 45 A5
South Middleton Northumb 188 A2
South Milford N Yorks 148 D3
South Millbrex Aberds 256 B3
South Milton Devon 7 C6
South Mimms Herts 68 C2
South Molton Devon 26 C2
South Moreton Oxon 46 A3
South Mundham W Sus 20 B1
South Muskham Notts 132 D2

South Newbald E Yorks 150 D2
South Newington Oxon 81 D7
South Newton Wilts 31 B4
South Normanton Derbys 131 D4
South Norwood London 49 C6
South Nutfield Sur 35 B6
South Ockendon Thurrock 50 A2
South Ormsby Lincs 134 B3
South Otterington N Yorks 158 C2
South Owersby Lincs 142 D2
South Oxhey Herts 67 D6
South Perrott Dorset 15 A4
South Petherton Som 28 D4
South Petherwin Corn 10 C4
South Pickenham Norf 103 A4
South Pool Devon 7 C6
South Port Argyll 227 D5
South Radworthy Devon 26 B2
South Rauceby Lincs 116 A3
South Raynham Norf 119 C5
South Reston Lincs 135 A4
South Runcton Norf 102 A2
South Scarle Notts 132 C3
South Shian Argyll 226 B4
South Shields T & W 179 C5
South Shields Museum T & W 179 C5
South Shore Blkpool 144 D3
South Somercotes Lincs 143 D6
South Stainley N Yorks 148 A2
South Stainmore Cumb 165 D6
South Stoke Oxon 46 A3
South Stoke W Sus 20 B3
South Street E Sus 22 A1
South Street London 36 A2
South Street Kent 52 C3
South Street Kent 52 D2
South Tawton Devon 12 B1
South Thoresby Lincs 135 B4
South Tidworth Wilts 31 A6
South Town Hants 33 B5
South View Hants 47 D4
South Walsham Norf 121 D5
South Warnborough Hants 33 A6
South Weald Essex 69 D5
South Weston Oxon 66 D2
South Wheatley Corn 10 B3
South Wheatley Notts 132 A2
South Whiteness Shetland 285 J5
South Widcombe Bath 43 D4
South Wigston Leics 98 B2
South Willingham Lincs 134 A1
South Wingfield Derbys 130 D3
South Witham Lincs 116 D2
South Wonston Hants 32 B3
South Woodham Ferrers Essex 70 D2
South Wootton Norf 118 C3
South Wraxall Wilts 44 C2
South Zeal Devon 12 B1
Southall London 48 A4
Southam Glos 63 A5
Southam Warks 81 A7
Southampton Soton 32 D3
Southampton International Airport Hants 32 D3
Southborough Kent 36 B3
Southbourne Bmouth 17 B5
Southbourne W Sus 19 A6
Southburgh Norf 103 A5
Southburn E Yorks 150 B2
Southchurch Sthend 51 A6
Southcott Wilts 45 D5
Southcourt Bucks 66 B3
Southdean Borders 187 C5
Southdene Mers 136 D3
Southease E Sus 22 B2
Southend Argyll 190 E2
Southend W Berks 46 B3
Southend Wilts 45 B5
Southend Airport Essex 51 A5
Southend-on-Sea Sthend 51 A5
Southend Sea Life Centre Essex 51 A5
Southerndown V Glam 40 D3
Southerness Dumfries 174 C2
Southery Norf 102 B2
Southfield Highld 179 B4
Southfleet Kent 50 B3
Southgate Ceredig 75 A4
Southgate London 68 D2
Southgate Norf 120 C3
Southgate Swansea 57 D5
Southill Beds 84 C3

Southleigh Devon 14 B2
Southminster Essex 70 D3
Southmoor Oxon 65 D4
Southoe Cambs 84 A3
Southolt Suff 88 A2
Southorpe P'boro 100 A2
Southowram W Yorks 139 A4
Southport Mers 136 B2
Southpunds Shetland 285 M5
Southrepps Norf 121 B4
Southrey Lincs 133 C6
Southrop Glos 64 C2
Southrope Hants 33 A5
Southsea Ptsmth 19 B5
Southstoke Bath 43 C6
Southtown Norf 105 A6
Southtown Orkney 283 H5
Southwaite Cumb 164 A2
Southwark London 49 B6
Southwater W Sus 35 D4
Southwater Street W Sus 35 D4
Southway Som 29 A5
Southwell Dorset 15 D6
Southwell Notts 132 D1
Southwell Minster Notts 132 D2
Southwell Racecourse Notts 132 D2
Southwick Hants 19 A5
Southwick Northants 100 B2
Southwick T & W 179 D5
Southwick Wilts 44 D2
Southwick W Sus 21 B5
Southwold Suff 105 C6
Southwood Norf 105 A4
Southwood Som 29 B5
Soval Lodge W Isles 288 E4
Sowber Gate N Yorks 158 C2
Sowerby N Yorks 158 C3
Sowerby W Yorks 138 A3
Sowerby Bridge W Yorks 138 A3
Sowerby Row Cumb 164 B1
Sowood W Yorks 138 B3
Sowton Devon 13 B4
Soyal Highld 264 A1
Spa Common Norf 121 B4
Spacey Houses N Yorks 148 B2
Spadeadam Farm Cumb 176 B3
Spalding Lincs 117 C5
Spaldington E Yorks 149 D6
Spaldwick Cambs 100 D3
Spalford Notts 132 C3
Spanby Lincs 116 B3
Sparham Norf 120 D2
Spark Bridge Cumb 154 C2
Sparkford Som 29 C6
Sparkhill W Mid 96 C3
Sparkwell Devon 7 B4
Sparrow Green Norf 119 D6
Sparrowpit Derbys 129 A5
Sparsholt Hants 32 B3
Sparsholt Oxon 46 A1
Spartylea Northumb 165 A6
Spaunton N Yorks 159 C6
Spaxton Som 28 B2
Spean Bridge Highld 239 D6
Spear Hill W Sus 21 A4
Speen Bucks 66 D3
Speen W Berks 46 C2
Speeton N Yorks 161 D5
Speke Mers 127 A4
Speke Hall Mers 127 A4
Speldhurst Kent 36 B3
Spellbrook Herts 69 B4
Spelsbury Oxon 64 A4
Spelter Bridgend 40 B3
Spencers Wood Wokingham 47 C5
Spennithorne N Yorks 157 C5
Spennymoor Durham 167 B5
Spetchley Worcs 80 B1
Spetisbury Dorset 16 A3
Spexhall Suff 105 C4
Spey Bay Moray 267 C4
Speybridge Highld 253 D6
Speyview Moray 254 B3
Spilsby Lincs 135 C4
Spindlestone Northumb 199 C5
Spinkhill Derbys 131 B4
Spinningdale Highld 264 B2
Spirit of the West, St Columb Major Corn 4 A4
Spirthill Wilts 44 B3
Spital Hill S Yorks 140 D4
Spital in the Street Lincs 133 A4
Spitfire and Hurricane Memorial, Manston Kent 53 C5
Spithurst E Sus 22 A2

Spittal Dumfries 171 B5
Spittal E Loth 210 C1
Spittal Highld 280 C3
Spittal Northumb 198 A4
Spittal Pembs 55 B5
Spittal Stirl 206 B3
Spittal of Glenmuick Aberds 243 D6
Spittal of Glenshee Perth 231 A5
Spittalfield Perth 231 D5
Spixworth Norf 120 D4
Splayne's Green E Sus 36 D2
Spofforth N Yorks 148 B2
Spon End W Mid 97 D6
Spon Green Flint 126 C2
Spondon Derby 114 B2
Spooner Row Norf 104 B1
Sporle Norf 119 D5
Spott E Loth 210 C3
Spratton Northants 99 D4
Spreakley Sur 34 B1
Spreyton Devon 12 B2
Spridlington Lincs 133 A5
Spring Vale S Yorks 139 C5
Spring Valley I o M 152 D3
Springburn Glasgow 205 B6
Springfield Dumfries 175 B6
Springfield Essex 69 C7
Springfield Fife 220 C3
Springfield Moray 253 A6
Springfield W Mid 96 C3
Springhill Staffs 96 A2
Springholm Dumfries 173 B6
Springkell Dumfries 175 A5
Springside N Ayrs 192 B3
Springthorpe Lincs 132 A3
Springwell T & W 179 D4
Sproatley E Yorks 151 D4
Sproston Green Ches 128 C2
Sprotbrough S Yorks 140 C3
Sproughton Suff 88 C2
Sprouston Borders 197 C6
Sprowston Norf 120 D4
Sproxton Leics 115 C6
Sproxton N Yorks 159 C5
Spurstow Ches 127 D5
Spynie Moray 266 C3
Squires Gate Blkpool 144 D3
Srannda W Isles 287 F5
Sronphadruig Lodge Perth 229 A6
SS Great Britain Bristol 43 B4
Stableford Shrops 95 B5
Stableford Staffs 112 B2
Stacey Bank S Yorks 139 D5
Stackhouse N Yorks 146 A2
Stackpole Pembs 55 E5
Staddiscombe Devon 7 B4
Staddlethorpe E Yorks 141 A6
Stadhampton Oxon 65 D7
Stadhlaigearraidh W Isles 286 C3
Staffield Cumb 164 A3
Staffin Highld 259 B4
Stafford Staffs 112 C3
Stagsden Beds 84 C1
Stainburn Cumb 162 B3
Stainburn N Yorks 147 C6
Stainby Lincs 116 C2
Staincross S Yorks 139 B6
Staindrop Durham 166 C4
Staines Sur 48 B3
Stainfield Lincs 116 C3
Stainfield Lincs 133 B6
Stainforth N Yorks 146 A2
Stainforth S Yorks 140 B4
Staining Lancs 144 D3
Stainland W Yorks 138 B3
Stainsacre N Yorks 160 A3
Stainsby Derbys 131 C4
Stainton Cumb 154 C4
Stainton Cumb 164 C2
Stainton Durham 166 D3
Stainton M'bro 168 D2
Stainton N Yorks 157 B5
Stainton S Yorks 140 D3
Stainton by Langworth Lincs 133 B5
Stainton le Vale Lincs 142 D3
Stainton with Adgarley Cumb 153 C3
Staintondale N Yorks 160 B3
Stair Cumb 163 B5
Stair E Ayrs 193 C4
Stairhaven Dumfries 171 B4
Staithes N Yorks 169 D5
Stake Pool Lancs 144 C4
Stakeford Northumb 179 A4
Stalbridge Dorset 30 D1
Stalbridge Weston Dorset 29 D7
Stalham Norf 121 C5
Stalham Green Norf 121 C5
Stalisfield Green Kent 51 D6
Stalling Busk N Yorks 156 C3
Stallingborough NE Lincs 142 B3
Stalmine Lancs 144 C3
Stalybridge Gtr Man 138 D2
Stambourne Essex 86 D3
Stambourne Green Essex 86 D3
Stamford Lincs 100 A2
Stamford Bridge Ches 127 C4
Stamford Bridge E Yorks 149 B6
Stamfordham Northumb 178 B2
Stanah Cumb 163 C6
Stanborough Herts 68 B2
Stanbridge Beds 67 A4
Stanbridge Dorset 17 A4
Stanbrook Worcs 79 C6
Stanbury W Yorks 147 D4
Stand Gtr Man 137 C6
Stand N Lnrk 207 D5
Standburn Falk 208 C2
Standeford Staffs 96 A2
Standen Kent 37 B6
Standen, East Grinstead W Sus 36 C1
Standford Hants 33 B7
Standingstone Cumb 162 A3
Standish Gtr Man 137 B4
Standlake Oxon 65 C4
Standon Hants 32 C3
Standon Herts 68 A3
Standon Staffs 112 B2
Stane N Lnrk 194 A3
Stanfield Norf 119 C6
Stanford Beds 84 C3
Stanford Kent 38 B3
Stanford Bishop Hereford 79 B4
Stanford Bridge Worcs 79 A5
Stanford Dingley W Berks 46 B3
Stanford in the Vale Oxon 64 D4
Stanford-le-Hope Thurrock 50 A3
Stanford on Avon Northants 98 D2
Stanford on Soar Notts 114 C3
Stanford on Teme Worcs 79 A5
Stanford Rivers Essex 69 C5
Stanfree Derbys 131 B4
Stanghow Redcar 169 D4
Stanground P'boro 100 B4
Stanhoe Norf 119 B5
Stanhope Borders 195 D6
Stanhope Durham 166 B2
Stanion Northants 99 C6
Stanley Derbys 114 A2
Stanley Durham 178 D3
Stanley Lancs 136 C3
Stanley Perth 219 A6
Stanley Staffs 129 D4
Stanley W Yorks 139 A6
Stanley Common Derbys 114 A2
Stanley Gate Lancs 136 C3
Stanley Hill Hereford 79 C4
Stanlow Ches 127 B4
Stanmer Brighton 21 B6
Stanmore London 67 D6
Stanmore Hants 32 C3
Stanmore W Berks 46 B2
Stannergate Dundee 220 A4
Stanningley W Yorks 147 D6
Stannington Northumb 179 B4
Stannington S Yorks 130 A3
Stansbatch Hereford 78 A1
Stansfield Suff 86 B3
Stanstead Suff 87 C4
Stanstead Abbotts Herts 68 B3
Stansted Kent 50 C3
Stansted Airport Essex 69 A5
Stansted Mountfitchet Essex 69 A5
Stanton Glos 80 D3
Stanton Mon 61 A5
Stanton Northumb 178 A3
Stanton Staffs 113 A5
Stanton Suff 103 D5
Stanton by Bridge Derbys 114 C1
Stanton-by-Dale Derbys 114 B2
Stanton Drew Bath 43 C4
Stanton Fitzwarren Swindon 64 D2
Stanton Harcourt Oxon 65 C5
Stanton Hill Notts 131 C4
Stanton in Peak Derbys 130 C2
Stanton Lacy Shrops 94 D2
Stanton Long Shrops 94 B3
Stanton-on-the-Wolds Notts 115 B4
Stanton Prior Bath 43 C5
Stanton St Bernard Wilts 45 C4
Stanton St John Oxon 65 C6
Stanton St Quintin Wilts 44 B3
Stanton Street Suff 87 A5
Stanton under Bardon Leics 114 D2
Stanton upon Hine Heath Shrops 111 C4
Stanton Wick Bath 43 C5
Stanwardine in the Fields Shrops 110 C3
Stanwardine in the Wood Shrops 110 C3
Stanway Essex 70 A3
Stanway Glos 80 D3
Stanway Green Suff 104 D3
Stanwell Sur 48 B3
Stanwell Moor Sur 48 B3
Stanwick Northants 100 D1
Stanwick-St-John N Yorks 167 D4
Stanwix Cumb 175 C7
Stanydale Shetland 285 H4
Staoinebrig W Isles 286 C3
Stape N Yorks 159 B6
Stapehill Dorset 17 A4
Stapeley Ches 111 A5
Stapeley Water Gardens, Nantwich Ches 127 D6
Stapenhill Staffs 113 C6
Staple Kent 53 D4
Staple Som 27 A6
Staple Cross E Sus 37 D5
Staple Fitzpaine Som 28 D2
Staplefield W Sus 35 D5
Stapleford Cambs 85 B6
Stapleford Herts 68 B3
Stapleford Leics 115 D6
Stapleford Lincs 132 D3
Stapleford Notts 114 B2
Stapleford Wilts 31 B4
Stapleford Abbotts Essex 69 D5
Stapleford Tawney Essex 69 D5
Staplegrove Som 28 C2
Staplehay Som 28 C2
Staplehurst Kent 37 B5
Staplers I o W 18 C4
Stapleton Bristol 43 B5
Stapleton Cumb 176 B3
Stapleton Hereford 78 A1
Stapleton Leics 98 B1
Stapleton N Yorks 167 D5
Stapleton Shrops 94 A2
Stapleton Som 29 C4
Stapley Som 28 D1
Staploe Beds 84 A3
Staplow Hereford 79 C4
Star Fife 220 D3
Star Pembs 73 C5
Star Som 42 D3
Stara Orkney 282 E3
Starbeck N Yorks 148 B2
Starbotton N Yorks 156 D3
Starcross Devon 13 C4
Stareton Warks 97 D6
Starkholmes Derbys 130 D3
Starlings Green Essex 85 D6
Starston Norf 104 C3
Startforth Durham 166 D3
Startley Wilts 44 A3
Stathe Som 28 C3
Stathern Leics 115 B5
Station Town Durham 168 B2
Staughton Green Cambs 84 A3
Staughton Highway Cambs 84 A3
Staunton Glos 62 B1
Staunton Glos 62 A3
Staunton in the Vale Notts 115 A6
Staunton on Arrow Hereford 78 A1
Staunton on Wye Hereford 78 C1
Staveley Cumb 154 C2
Staveley Cumb 154 B3
Staveley Derbys 131 B4
Staveley N Yorks 148 A2
Staverton Devon 8 A1
Staverton Glos 63 A4
Staverton Northants 82 A2
Staverton Wilts 44 C2
Staverton Bridge Glos 63 A4
Stawell Som 28 B3
Staxigoe Highld 281 C5
Staxton N Yorks 160 D4
Staylittle Powys 91 C6
Staynall Lancs 144 C3
Staythorpe Notts 132 D2
Stean N Yorks 157 D4
Stearsby N Yorks 159 D5
Steart Som 28 A2
Stebbing Essex 69 A6
Stebbing Green Essex 69 A6
Stedham W Sus 34 D1
Steele Road Borders 186 D4
Steen's Bridge Hereford 78 B3
Steep Hants 33 C6
Steep Marsh Hants 33 C6
Steeple Dorset 16 C3
Steeple Essex 70 C3
Steeple Ashton Wilts 44 D3
Steeple Aston Oxon 65 A5
Steeple Barton Oxon 65 A5
Steeple Bumpstead Essex 86 C2
Steeple Claydon Bucks 66 A1
Steeple Gidding Cambs 100 C3
Steeple Langford Wilts 31 B4
Steeple Morden Cambs 85 C4
Steeton W Yorks 147 C4
Stein Highld 258 C2
Steinmanhill Aberds 256 B2
Stelling Minnis Kent 38 A3
Stemster Highld 280 B3
Stemster Ho. Highld 280 B3
Stenalees Corn 5 B5
Stenhousemuir Falk 207 B6
Stenigot Lincs 134 A2
Stenness Shetland 284 F4
Stenscholl Highld 259 B4
Stenso Orkney 282 E4
Stenson Derbys 114 C1
Stenton E Loth 210 C3
Stenton Fife 209 A5
Stenwith Lincs 115 B6
Stepaside Pembs 56 B1
Stepping Hill Gtr Man 129 A4
Steppingley Beds 84 D2
Stepps N Lnrk 205 B6
Sterndale Moor Derbys 129 C6
Sternfield Suff 89 A4
Sterridge Devon 25 A6
Stert Wilts 44 D4
Stetchworth Cambs 86 B2
Stevenage Herts 68 A2
Stevenston N Ayrs 204 D2
Steventon Hants 32 A4
Steventon Oxon 65 D5
Stevington Beds 84 B1
Stewartby Beds 84 C2
Stewarton Argyll 190 D2
Stewarton E Ayrs 205 D4
Stewkley Bucks 66 A3
Stewton Lincs 134 A3
Steyne Cross I o W 19 C5
Steyning W Sus 21 A4
Steynton Pembs 55 D5
Stibb Corn 24 D3
Stibb Cross Devon 25 D5
Stibb Green Wilts 45 C6
Stibbard Norf 120 C1
Stibbington Cambs 100 B2
Stichill Borders 197 C6
Sticker Corn 5 B4
Stickford Lincs 134 D3
Sticklepath Devon 12 B1
Stickney Lincs 134 D3
Stiffkey Norf 119 A6
Stifford's Bridge Hereford 79 C5
Stillingfleet N Yorks 149 C4
Stillington N Yorks 149 A4
Stillington Stockton 167 C6
Stilton Cambs 100 C3
Stinchcombe Glos 62 D3
Stinsford Dorset 15 B7
Stirchley Telford 95 A5
Stirkoke Ho. Highld 281 C5
Stirling Aberds 257 B6
Stirling Stirl 207 A5
Stirling Castle Stirl 207 A5
Stisted Essex 70 A1
Stithians Corn 4 D2
Stittenham Highld 264 C2
Stivichall W Mid 97 D6
Stixwould Lincs 134 C1
Stoak Ches 127 B4
Stobieside S Lnrk 193 B6
Stobo Borders 195 C6
Stoborough Dorset 16 C3
Stoborough Green Dorset 16 C3
Stobshiel E Loth 210 D1
Stobswood Northumb 189 D5
Stock Essex 69 D6
Stock Green Worcs 80 B2
Stock Wood Worcs 80 B3
Stockbridge Hants 32 B2
Stockbury Kent 51 C5
Stockcross W Berks 46 C2
Stockdalewath Cumb 164 A1
Stockerston Leics 99 B5
Stockheath Hants 19 A6
Stockiemuir Stirl 206 B3
Stocking Pelham Herts 69 A4
Stockingford Warks 97 B6
Stockland Devon 14 A2
Stockland Bristol Som 28 A2
Stockleigh English Devon 12 A3
Stockleigh Pomeroy Devon 12 A3
Stockley Wilts 44 C4
Stocklinch Som 28 D3
Stockport Gtr Man 138 D1
Stocksbridge S Yorks 139 D5
Stocksfield Northumb 178 C2
Stockton Hereford 78 A3
Stockton Norf 105 B4
Stockton Shrops 93 A6
Stockton Shrops 95 B5
Stockton Warks 82 A1
Stockton Wilts 30 B3
Stockton Heath Warr 127 A6
Stockton-on-Tees Stockton 168 D2
Stockton on Teme Worcs 79 A5
Stockton on the Forest York 149 B5
Stockwood Park Museum, Luton Luton 67 B5
Stodmarsh Kent 53 C4
Stody Norf 120 B2
Stoer Highld 270 B3
Stoford Som 29 D5
Stoford Wilts 31 B4
Stogumber Som 27 B5
Stogursey Som 28 A2
Stoke Devon 24 C3
Stoke Hants 46 D2
Stoke Hants 19 A6
Stoke Medway 51 B5
Stoke Suff 88 C2
Stoke Abbott Dorset 15 A4
Stoke Albany Northants 99 C5
Stoke Ash Suff 104 D2
Stoke Bardolph Notts 115 A4
Stoke Bliss Worcs 79 A4
Stoke Bruerne Northants 83 C4
Stoke by Clare Suff 86 C3
Stoke-by-Nayland Suff 87 D5
Stoke Canon Devon 13 B4
Stoke Charity Hants 32 B3
Stoke Climsland Corn 11 D4
Stoke D'Abernon Sur 35 A4
Stoke Doyle Northants 100 C2
Stoke Dry Rutland 99 B5
Stoke Farthing Wilts 31 C4
Stoke Ferry Norf 102 B3
Stoke Fleming Devon 8 C2
Stoke Gabriel Devon 8 B2
Stoke Gifford S Glos 43 B5
Stoke Golding Leics 97 B6
Stoke Goldington M Keynes 83 C5
Stoke Green Bucks 48 A2
Stoke Hammond Bucks 66 A3
Stoke Heath Shrops 111 C5
Stoke Holy Cross Norf 104 A3
Stoke Lacy Hereford 79 C4
Stoke Lyne Oxon 65 A6
Stoke Mandeville Bucks 66 B3
Stoke Newington London 49 A6
Stoke on Tern Shrops 111 C5
Stoke-on-Trent Stoke 112 A2
Stoke Orchard Glos 63 A5
Stoke Poges Bucks 48 A2
Stoke Prior Hereford 78 B3
Stoke Prior Worcs 80 A2
Stoke Rivers Devon 26 B1
Stoke Rochford Lincs 116 C2
Stoke Row Oxon 47 A4
Stoke St Gregory Som 28 C3
Stoke St Mary Som 28 C2
Stoke St Michael Som 29 A6
Stoke St Milborough Shrops 94 C3
Stoke sub Hamdon Som 29 D4
Stoke Talmage Oxon 66 D1
Stoke Trister Som 30 C1
Stoke Wake Dorset 16 A1
Stokeford Dorset 16 C2
Stokeham Notts 132 B2
Stokeinteignhead Devon 13 D4

Stokenchurch Bucks 66 D2
Stokenham Devon 8 C2
Stokesay Shrops 94 C2
Stokesby Norf 121 D6
Stokesley N Yorks 158 A4
Stolford Som 28 A2
Ston Easton Som 43 D5
Stondon Massey Essex 69 C5
Stone Bucks 66 B2
Stone Glos 62 D2
Stone Kent 38 C1
Stone Kent 50 B2
Stone Staffs 112 B3
Stone S Yorks 131 A5
Stone Worcs 95 D6
Stone Allerton Som 42 D3
Stone Bridge Corner
  P'boro 101 A4
Stone Chair W Yorks 139 A4
Stone Cross E Sus 22 B4
Stone Cross Kent 53 D5
Stone-edge Batch N Som 42 B3
Stone House Cumb 155 C6
Stoneferry Hull 151 D4
Stonefield S Lnrk 194 A1
Stonegate E Sus 37 D4
Stonegate N Yorks 159 A6
Stonegrave N Yorks 159 D5
Stonehaugh Northumb 177 B5
Stonehaven Aberds 245 D5
Stonehenge, Amesbury
  Wilts 31 A5
Stonehouse Glos 63 C4
Stonehouse Northumb 177 D4
Stonehouse S Lnrk 194 B2
Stoneleigh Warks 97 D6
Stonely Cambs 84 A3
Stoner Hill Hants 33 C6
Stone's Green Essex 71 A5
Stonesby Leics 115 C6
Stonesfield Oxon 65 B4
Stonethwaite Cumb 163 C5
Stoney Cross Hants 31 D6
Stoney Middleton Derbys 130 B2
Stoney Stanton Leics 98 B1
Stoney Stoke Som 29 B7
Stoney Stratton Som 29 B6
Stoney Stretton Shrops 94 A1
Stoneybreck Shetland 285 L3
Stoneyburn W Loth 208 D2
Stoneygate Aberds 257 C5
Stoneygate Leicester 98 A3
Stoneyhills Essex 70 D3
Stoneykirk Dumfries 170 B2
Stoneywood Aberdeen 245 A5
Stoneywood Falk 207 B5
Stonganess Shetland 284 C7
Stonham Aspal Suff 88 B2
Stonnall Staffs 96 A3
Stonor Oxon 47 A5
Stonton Wyville Leics 99 B4
Stony Cross Hereford 79 C5
Stony Stratford M Keynes 83 C4
Stonyfield Highld 264 C2
Stoodleigh Devon 27 D4
Stopes S Yorks 130 A2
Stopham W Sus 20 A3
Stopsley Luton 67 A6
Stores Corner Suff 89 C4
Storeton Mers 126 A3
Stornoway W Isles 288 D5
Stornoway Airport
  W Isles 288 D5
Storridge Hereford 79 C5
Storrington W Sus 20 A3
Storrs Cumb 154 B2
Storth Cumb 154 C3
Storwood E Yorks 149 C6
Stotfield Moray 266 B3
Stotfold Beds 84 D4
Stottesdon Shrops 95 C4
Stoughton Leics 98 A3
Stoughton Sur 34 A2
Stoughton W Sus 33 D7
Stoul Highld 235 A6
Stoulton Worcs 80 C2
Stour Provost Dorset 30 C1
Stour Row Dorset 30 C2
Stourbridge W Mid 96 C2
Stourhead Garden Wilts 30 B1
Stourpaine Dorset 16 A2

Stourport on Severn
  Worcs 95 D6
Stourton Staffs 95 C6
Stourton Warks 81 D5
Stourton Wilts 30 B1
Stourton Caundle Dorset 29 D7
Stove Orkney 282 D7
Stove Shetland 285 L6
Stoven Suff 105 C5
Stow Borders 196 B3
Stow Lincs 132 A3
Stow Lincs 116 B3
Stow Bardolph Norf 102 A2
Stow Bedon Norf 103 B5
Stow cum Quy Cambs 85 A7
Stow Longa Cambs 100 D3
Stow Maries Essex 70 D2
Stow-on-the-Wold Glos 64 A2
Stowbridge Norf 102 A2
Stowe Shrops 93 D7
Stowe-by-Chartley Staffs 112 C4
Stowe Green Glos 62 C1
Stowe House and
  Gardens, Buckingham
  Bucks 82 D3
Stowell Som 29 C6
Stowford Devon 11 C5
Stowlangtoft Suff 87 A5
Stowmarket Suff 87 B6
Stowting Kent 38 A3
Stowupland Suff 87 B6
Straad Argyll 203 B5
Strachan Aberds 244 C3
Stradbroke Suff 104 D3
Stradishall Suff 86 B3
Stradsett Norf 102 A2
Stragglethorpe Lincs 133 D4
Straid S Ayrs 180 B3
Straith Dumfries 183 D6
Straiton Edin 209 D5
Straiton S Ayrs 181 A5
Straloch Aberds 256 D3
Straloch Perth 230 B4
Stramshall Staffs 113 B4
Strang I o M 152 D3
Stranraer Dumfries 170 A2
Stratfield Mortimer
  W Berks 47 C4
Stratfield Saye Hants 47 C4
Stratfield Turgis Hants 47 C4
Stratford London 49 A6
Stratford Racecourse
  Warks 81 B4
Stratford St Andrew Suff 89 A4
Stratford St Mary Suff 87 D6
Stratford Sub Castle Wilts 31 B5
Stratford Tony Wilts 31 C4
Stratford-upon-Avon
  Warks 81 B4
Strath Highld 281 C4
Strath Highld 261 C4
Strathan Highld 238 C3
Strathan Highld 277 B6
Strathan Highld 270 B3
Strathaven S Lnrk 194 B2
Strathblane Stirl 205 A5
Strathcanaird Highld 271 D4
Strathcarron Highld 249 B6
Strathcoil Argyll 225 C5
Strathdon Aberds 243 A6
Strathellie Aberds 269 C5
Strathkinness Fife 221 C4
Strathmashie House
  Highld 240 C3
Strathmiglo Fife 220 C2
Strathmore Lodge Highld 280 D3
Strathpeffer Highld 251 A6
Strathrannoch Highld 263 C5
Strathtay Perth 230 C3
Strathvaich Lodge Highld 263 C5
Strathwhillan N Ayrs 191 B6
Strathy Highld 279 B4
Strathyre Stirl 217 C5
Stratton Corn 10 A3
Stratton Dorset 15 B6
Stratton Glos 63 C6
Stratton Audley Oxon 65 A7
Stratton on the Fosse Som 43 D5
Stratton St Margaret
  Swindon 45 A5
Stratton St Michael Norf 104 B3
Stratton Strawless Norf 120 C4
Stravithie Fife 221 C5
Streat E Sus 21 A6
Streatham London 49 B6
Streatley Beds 67 A5
Streatley W Berks 46 A3
Street Lancs 145 B5

Street N Yorks 159 A6
Street Som 29 B4
Street Dinas Shrops 110 B2
Street End Kent 52 D3
Street End W Sus 20 C1
Street Gate T & W 179 D4
Street Lydan Wrex 110 B3
Streethay Staffs 113 D5
Streetlam N Yorks 157 B7
Streetly W Mid 96 B3
Streetly End Cambs 86 C2
Strefford Shrops 94 C2
Strelley Notts 114 A3
Strensall York 149 A5
Stretcholt Som 28 A2
Strete Devon 8 C2
Stretford Gtr Man 137 D7
Strethall Essex 85 D6
Stretham Cambs 101 D7
Strettington W Sus 20 B1
Stretton Ches 127 D4
Stretton Derbys 130 C3
Stretton Rutland 116 D2
Stretton Staffs 112 D2
Stretton Staffs 113 C6
Stretton Warr 127 A6
Stretton Grandison
  Hereford 79 C4
Stretton-on-Dunsmore
  Warks 97 D7
Stretton-on-Fosse Warks 81 D5
Stretton Sugwas Hereford 78 C2
Stretton under Fosse
  Warks 98 C1
Stretton Westwood Shrops 94 B3
Strichen Aberds 269 D4
Strines Gtr Man 129 A4
Stringston Som 28 A1
Strixton Northants 83 A6
Stroat Glos 62 D1
Stromeferry Highld 249 C5
Stromemore Highld 249 C5
Stromness Orkney 283 G3
Stronaba Highld 239 D6
Stronachlachar Stirl 216 C4
Stronchreggan Highld 237 B4
Stronchrubie Highld 271 C5
Strone Argyll 215 D4
Strone Highld 252 D1
Strone Highld 239 D5
Strone Inverclyd 204 A2
Stronmilchan Argyll 227 D6
Stronsay Airport Orkney 282 E7
Strontian Highld 236 C2
Strood Medway 51 C4
Strood Green Sur 35 B5
Strood Green W Sus 34 D3
Strood Green W Sus 35 C4
Stroud Glos 63 C4
Stroud Hants 33 C6
Stroud Green Essex 70 D2
Stroxton Lincs 116 B2
Struan Highld 246 A2
Struan Perth 230 B2
Strubby Lincs 135 A4
Strumpshaw Norf 104 A4
Strutherhill S Lnrk 194 B2
Struy Highld 251 C5
Stryt-issa Wrex 110 A1
Stuartfield Aberds 257 B4
Stub Place Cumb 153 A1
Stubbington Hants 19 A4
Stubbins Lancs 137 B6
Stubbs Cross Kent 38 B1
Stubb's Green Norf 104 B3
Stubbs Green Norf 105 B4
Stubhampton Dorset 30 D3
Stubton Lincs 115 A6
Stuckgowan Argyll 215 B6
Stuckton Hants 31 D5
Stud Green Windsor 48 B1
Studham Beds 67 B5
Studland Dorset 17 C4
Studley Warks 80 A3
Studley Wilts 44 B3
Studley Roger N Yorks 157 D6
Stump Cross Essex 85 C7
Stuntney Cambs 102 D1
Sturbridge Staffs 112 B2
Sturmer Essex 86 C2
Sturminster Marshall
  Dorset 16 A3
Sturminster Newton
  Dorset 30 D1
Sturry Kent 52 C3
Sturton N Lincs 142 C1
Sturton by Stow Lincs 132 A3
Sturton le Steeple Notts 132 A2

Stuston Suff 104 D2
Stutton N Yorks 148 C3
Stutton Suff 88 D2
Styal Ches 128 A3
Styrrup Notts 140 D4
Suainebost W Isles 288 A6
Suardail W Isles 288 D5
Succoth Aberds 255 C5
Succoth Argyll 215 B5
Suckley Worcs 79 B5
Suckquoy Orkney 283 K5
Sudborough Northants 99 C6
Sudbourne Suff 89 B5
Sudbrook Lincs 116 A2
Sudbrook Mon 43 A4
Sudbrooke Lincs 133 B5
Sudbury Derbys 113 B5
Sudbury London 49 A4
Sudbury Suff 87 C4
Suddie Highld 252 A2
Sudeley Castle and
  Gardens Glos 63 A6
Sudgrove Glos 63 C5
Suffield Norf 120 B4
Suffield N Yorks 160 B3
Sugnall Staffs 112 B1
Suladale Highld 258 C3
Sulaisiadar W Isles 288 D6
Sulby I o M 152 B3
Sulgrave Northants 82 C2
Sulham W Berks 47 B4
Sulhamstead W Berks 47 C4
Sulland Orkney 282 C6
Sullington W Sus 20 A3
Sullom Shetland 284 F5
Sullom Voe Oil Terminal
  Shetland 284 F5
Sully V Glam 41 E6
Sumburgh Shetland 285 N6
Sumburgh Airport
  Shetland 285 M5
Summer Bridge N Yorks 147 A6
Summer-house Darl 167 D5
Summercourt Corn 4 B3
Summerfield Norf 119 B4
Summergangs Hull 151 D4
Summerleaze Mon 42 A3
Summerlee Heritage
  Centre, Coatbridge
  N Lnrk 207 D5
Summersdale W Sus 20 B1
Summerseat Gtr Man 137 B6
Summertown Oxon 65 C6
Summit Gtr Man 138 C2
Sunbury-on-Thames Sur 48 C4
Sundaywell Dumfries 183 D6
Sunderland Argyll 200 B2
Sunderland Cumb 163 A4
Sunderland T & W 179 D5
Sunderland Bridge
  Durham 167 B5
Sundhope Borders 196 D2
Sundon Park Luton 67 A5
Sundown Adventure
  Land, Rampton Notts 132 B2
Sundridge Kent 36 A2
Sunipol Argyll 224 A2
Sunk Island E Yorks 143 B4
Sunningdale Windsor 48 C2
Sunninghill Windsor 48 C2
Sunningwell Oxon 65 C5
Sunniside Durham 166 B4
Sunniside T & W 179 D4
Sunnyhurst Blkburn 137 A5
Sunnylaw Stirl 207 A5
Sunnyside W Sus 36 C1
Sunton Wilts 45 D6
Surbiton London 49 C4
Surby I o M 152 D2
Surfleet Lincs 117 C5
Surfleet Seas End Lincs 117 C5
Surlingham Norf 104 A4
Sustead Norf 120 B3
Susworth Lincs 141 C6
Sutcombe Devon 24 D4
Suton Norf 104 B1
Sutors of Cromarty
  Highld 265 D4
Sutterby Lincs 134 B3
Sutterton Lincs 117 B5
Sutton Beds 84 C4
Sutton Cambs 101 D6
Sutton London 49 C5
Sutton Kent 39 A5
Sutton Mers 136 D4
Sutton Norf 121 C5
Sutton Notts 115 B5
Sutton Notts 132 A1

Sutton N Yorks 140 A2
Sutton Oxon 65 C5
Sutton P'boro 100 B2
Sutton Shrops 95 C5
Sutton Shrops 111 B5
Sutton Som 29 B6
Sutton Staffs 111 C6
Sutton Suff 88 C4
Sutton Sur 34 B4
Sutton S Yorks 140 B3
Sutton W Sus 20 A2
Sutton at Hone Kent 50 B2
Sutton Bassett Northants 99 B4
Sutton Benger Wilts 44 B3
Sutton Bonington Notts 114 C3
Sutton Bridge Lincs 118 C1
Sutton Cheney Leics 97 A7
Sutton Coldfield W Mid 96 B4
Sutton Courtenay Oxon 65 D6
Sutton Crosses Lincs 118 C1
Sutton Grange N Yorks 157 D6
Sutton Green Sur 34 A3
Sutton Howgrave N Yorks 157 D7
Sutton In Ashfield Notts 131 D4
Sutton-in-Craven
  N Yorks 147 C4
Sutton in the Elms Leics 98 B2
Sutton Ings Hull 151 D4
Sutton Lane Ends Ches 129 B4
Sutton Leach Mers 136 D4
Sutton Maddock Shrops 95 A5
Sutton Mallet Som 28 B3
Sutton Mandeville Wilts 30 C3
Sutton Manor Mers 136 D4
Sutton Montis Som 29 C6
Sutton on Hull Hull 151 D4
Sutton on Sea Lincs 135 A5
Sutton-on-the-Forest
  N Yorks 149 A4
Sutton on the Hill Derbys 113 B6
Sutton on Trent Notts 132 C2
Sutton St Edmund Lincs 117 D6
Sutton St James Lincs 117 D6
Sutton St Nicholas
  Hereford 78 C3
Sutton Scarsdale Derbys 131 C4
Sutton Scotney Hants 32 B3
Sutton under Brailes
  Warks 81 D6
Sutton-under-
  Whitestonecliffe
  N Yorks 158 C3
Sutton upon Derwent
  E Yorks 149 C6
Sutton Valence Kent 37 B6
Sutton Veny Wilts 30 A3
Sutton Waldron Dorset 30 D2
Sutton Weaver Ches 127 B5
Sutton Wick Bath 43 D4
Swaby Lincs 134 B3
Swadlincote Derbys 113 D7
Swaffham Norf 103 A4
Swaffham Bulbeck Cambs 86 A1
Swaffham Prior Cambs 86 A1
Swafield Norf 121 B4
Swainby N Yorks 158 A3
Swainshill Hereford 78 C2
Swainsthorpe Norf 104 A3
Swainswick Bath 43 C6
Swalcliffe Oxon 81 D6
Swalecliffe Kent 52 C3
Swallow Lincs 142 C3
Swallowcliffe Wilts 30 C3
Swallowfield Wokingham 47 C5
Swallownest S Yorks 131 A4
Swallows Cross Essex 69 D6
Swan Green Ches 128 B2
Swan Green Suff 104 D3
Swanage Dorset 17 D4
Swanage Railway Dorset 17 D4
Swanbister Orkney 283 G4
Swanbourne Bucks 66 A3
Swanland E Yorks 142 A1
Swanley Kent 50 C2
Swanley Village Kent 50 C2
Swanmore Hants 33 D4
Swannery, Abbotsbury
  Dorset 15 C5
Swannington Leics 114 D2
Swannington Norf 120 D3
Swanscombe Kent 50 B3
Swansea = Abertawe
  Swansea 57 C6
Swanton Abbott Norf 121 C4
Swanton Morley Norf 120 D2
Swanton Novers Norf 120 B2
Swanton Street Kent 37 A6
Swanwick Derbys 131 D4

Swanwick Hants 18 A4
Swarby Lincs 116 A3
Swardeston Norf 104 A3
Swarister Shetland 284 E7
Swarkestone Derbys 114 C1
Swarland Northumb 189 C4
Swarland Estate
Northumb 189 C4
Swarthmoor Cumb 153 C3
Swathwick Derbys 130 C3
Swaton Lincs 116 B4
Swavesey Cambs 85 A5
Sway Hants 18 B1
Swayfield Lincs 116 C2
Swaythling Soton 32 D3
Sweet Green Worcs 79 A4
Sweetham Devon 12 B3
Sweethouse Corn 5 A5
Swefling Suff 88 A4
Swepstone Leics 114 D1
Swerford Oxon 81 D6
Swettenham Ches 128 C3
Swetton N Yorks 157 D5
Swffryd Bl Gwent 60 D4
Swiftsden E Sus 37 D5
Swilland Suff 88 B2
Swillington W Yorks 148 D2
Swimbridge Devon 25 C7
Swimbridge Newland
Devon 25 B7
Swinbrook Oxon 64 B3
Swinderby Lincs 132 C3
Swindon Glos 63 A5
Swindon Staffs 95 B6
Swindon Swindon 45 A5
Swine E Yorks 151 D4
Swinefleet E Yorks 141 A5
Swineshead Beds 84 A2
Swineshead Lincs 117 A5
Swineshead Bridge Lincs 117 A5
Swiney Highld 275 A6
Swinford Leics 98 D2
Swinford Oxon 65 C5
Swingate Notts 114 A3
Swingfield Minnis Kent 39 A4
Swingfield St Kent 39 A4
Swinhoe Northumb 189 A5
Swinhope Lincs 143 D4
Swining Shetland 284 G6
Swinithwaite N Yorks 156 C4
Swinnow Moor W Yorks 147 D6
Swinscoe Staffs 113 A5
Swinside Hall Borders 187 B6
Swinstead Lincs 116 C3
Swinton Borders 198 B2
Swinton Gtr Man 137 C6
Swinton N Yorks 157 D6
Swinton N Yorks 159 D6
Swinton S Yorks 140 D2
Swintonmill Borders 198 B2
Swithland Leics 114 D3
Swordale Highld 264 D1
Swordland Highld 238 C1
Swordly Highld 278 B3
Sworton Heath Ches 128 A1
Swydd-ffynnon Ceredig 75 B5
Swynnerton Staffs 112 B2
Swyre Dorset 15 C5
Sychtyn Powys 92 A3
Syde Glos 63 B5
Sydenham London 49 B6
Sydenham Oxon 66 C2
Sydenham Damerel Devon 11 D5
Syderstone Norf 119 B5
Sydling St Nicholas Dorset 15 B6
Sydmonton Hants 46 D2
Syerston Notts 115 A5
Syke Gtr Man 138 B1
Sykehouse S Yorks 140 B4
Sykes Lancs 145 B6
Syleham Suff 104 D3
Sylen Carms 57 B5
Symbister Shetland 285 G7
Symington S Ayrs 192 B3
Symington S Lnrk 195 C4
Symonds Yat Hereford 62 B1
Symondsbury Dorset 14 B4
Synod Inn Ceredig 73 A7
Syon Park & House London 49 B4
Syre Highld 278 D2
Syreford Glos 63 A6
Syresham Northants 82 C3
Syston Leics 115 D4
Syston Lincs 116 A2
Sytchampton Worcs 79 A6
Sywell Northants 83 A5

T

Taagan Highld 262 D2
Tàbost W Isles 288 A6
Tàbost W Isles 288 F4
Tackley Oxon 65 A5
Tacleit W Isles 288 D2
Tacolneston Norf 104 B2
Taddington Derbys 129 B6
Taddiport Devon 25 D5
Tadley Hants 47 C4
Tadlow Beds 85 C4
Tadmarton Oxon 81 D6
Tadworth Sur 35 A5
Tafarn-y-gelyn Denb 126 C1
Tafarnau-bach Bl Gwent 60 B3
Taff's Well Rhondda 41 C6
Tafolwern Powys 91 B6
Tai Conwy 124 C2
Tai-bach Powys 109 C6
Tai-mawr Conwy 109 A4
Tai-Ucha Denb 125 D5
Taibach Neath 40 C2
Taigh a Ghearraidh
W Isles 287 G2
Tain Highld 264 B3
Tain Highld 280 B4
Tainant Wrex 110 A1
Tainlon Gwyn 107 A4
Tai'r-Bull Powys 60 A1
Tairbeart = Tarbert
W Isles 288 G2
Tairgwaith Neath 59 D4
Takeley Essex 69 A5
Takeley Street Essex 69 A5
Tal-sarn Ceredig 75 C4
Tal-y-bont Ceredig 91 D4
Tal-y-bont Conwy 124 C2
Tal-y-bont Gwyn 123 C6
Tal-y-bont Gwyn 107 D5
Tal-y-cafn Conwy 124 B2
Tal-y-llyn Gwyn 91 B5
Tal-y-wern Powys 91 B6
Talachddu Powys 77 D4
Talacre Flint 125 A6
Talardd Gwyn 108 C3
Talaton Devon 13 B5
Talbenny Pembs 54 C4
Talbot Green Rhondda 41 C5
Talbot Village Poole 17 B4
Tale Devon 13 A5
Talerddig Powys 92 A3
Talgarreg Ceredig 74 C3
Talgarth Powys 77 D5
Talisker Highld 246 A2
Talke Staffs 128 D3
Talkin Cumb 176 D3
Talla Linnfoots Borders 195 D6
Talladale Highld 261 C6
Tallarn Green Wrex 110 A3
Tallentire Cumb 163 A4
Talley Carms 58 B3
Tallington Lincs 100 A2
Talmine Highld 277 B6
Talog Carms 73 D6
Talsarn Carms 59 C4
Talsarnau Gwyn 107 C6
Talskiddy Corn 4 A4
Talwrn Anglesey 123 C4
Talwrn Wrex 110 A1
Talybont-on-Usk Powys 60 A3
Talygarn Rhondda 41 C5
Talyllyn Powys 60 A3
Talysarn Gwyn 107 A4
Talywain Torf 61 C4
Tame Bridge N Yorks 158 A4
Tamerton Foliot Plym 6 A3
Tamworth Staffs 97 A5
Tan Hinon Powys 91 D6
Tan-lan Conwy 124 C2
Tan-lan Gwyn 107 B6
Tan-y-bwlch Gwyn 107 B6
Tan-y-fron Conwy 125 C4
Tan-y-graig Anglesey 123 C5
Tan-y-graig Gwyn 106 C3
Tan-y-groes Ceredig 73 B5
Tan-y-pistyll Powys 109 C5
Tan-yr-allt Gwyn 107 A4
Tandem W Yorks 139 B4
Tanden Kent 37 C7
Tandridge Sur 35 A6
Tanerdy Carms 73 D7
Tanfield Durham 178 D3
Tanfield Lea Durham 178 D3
Tangasdal W Isles 286 G2
Tangiers Pembs 55 C5
Tangley Hants 46 D1

Tanglwst Carms 73 C6
Tangmere W Sus 20 B2
Tangwick Shetland 284 F4
Tank Museum, Bovington
Dorset 16 C2
Tankersley S Yorks 139 C6
Tankerton Kent 52 C3
Tannach Highld 281 D5
Tannachie Aberds 245 D4
Tannadice Angus 232 C2
Tannington Suff 88 A3
Tansley Derbys 130 D3
Tansley Knoll Derbys 130 C3
Tansor Northants 100 B2
Tantobie Durham 178 D3
Tanton N Yorks 168 D3
Tanworth-in-Arden Warks 96 D4
Tanygrisiau Gwyn 107 B6
Tanyrhydiau Ceredig 75 B6
Taobh a Chaolais W Isles 286 E3
Taobh a Thuath Loch
Aineort W Isles 286 D3
Taobh a Tuath Loch
Baghasdail W Isles 286 D3
Taobh a'Ghlinne W Isles 288 F4
Taobh Tuath W Isles 287 F4
Taplow Bucks 48 A2
Tapton Derbys 130 B3
Tarbat Ho. Highld 264 C3
Tarbert Argyll 213 D4
Tarbert Argyll 202 B3
Tarbert Argyll 202 C1
Tarbert = Tairbeart
W Isles 288 G2
Tarbet Argyll 215 B6
Tarbet Highld 276 D2
Tarbet Highld 238 C1
Tarbock Green Mers 127 A4
Tarbolton S Ayrs 193 C4
Tarbrax S Lnrk 195 A5
Tardebigge Worcs 80 A3
Tarfside Angus 232 A2
Tarland Aberds 244 B1
Tarleton Lancs 136 A3
Tarlogie Highld 264 B3
Tarlscough Lancs 136 B3
Tarlton Glos 63 D5
Tarnbrook Lancs 145 B5
Tarporley Ches 127 C5
Tarr Som 27 B6
Tarrant Crawford Dorset 16 A3
Tarrant Gunville Dorset 30 D3
Tarrant Hinton Dorset 30 D3
Tarrant Keyneston Dorset 16 A3
Tarrant Launceston Dorset 16 A3
Tarrant Monkton Dorset 16 A3
Tarrant Rawston Dorset 16 A3
Tarrant Rushton Dorset 16 A3
Tarrel Highld 265 B4
Tarring Neville E Sus 22 B2
Tarrington Hereford 79 C4
Tarsappie Perth 219 B6
Tarskavaig Highld 247 D4
Tarves Aberds 256 C3
Tarvie Highld 251 A6
Tarvie Perth 230 B4
Tarvin Ches 127 C4
Tasburgh Norf 104 B3
Tasley Shrops 95 B4
Taston Oxon 65 A4
Tate Gallery London 49 B5
Tate Gallery, Albert Dock
Mers 126 A3
Tate Modern London 49 B6
Tate St Ives Corn 2 A3
Tatenhill Staffs 113 C6
Tathall End M Keynes 83 C5
Tatham Lancs 145 A6
Tathwell Lincs 134 A3
Tatling End Bucks 48 A3
Tatsfield Sur 36 A2
Tattenhall Ches 127 D4
Tattenhoe M Keynes 83 D5
Tatterford Norf 119 C5
Tattersett Norf 119 B5
Tattershall Lincs 134 D2
Tattershall Bridge Lincs 134 D1
Tattershall Thorpe Lincs 134 D2
Tattingstone Suff 88 D2
Tatton House, Knutsford
Ches 128 A2
Tatworth Som 14 A3
Taunton Som 28 C2
Taunton Racecourse Som 28 C2
Taverham Norf 120 D3
Tavernspite Pembs 56 A1
Tavistock Devon 11 D5
Taw Green Devon 12 B1

Tawstock Devon 25 C6
Taxal Derbys 129 B5
Tay Bridge Dundee 220 B4
Tayinloan Argyll 202 D1
Taymouth Castle Perth 230 D1
Taynish Argyll 213 D5
Taynton Glos 62 A3
Taynton Oxon 64 B3
Taynuilt Argyll 227 C5
Tayport Fife 221 B4
Tayvallich Argyll 213 D5
Tealby Lincs 142 D3
Tealing Angus 220 A4
Teangue Highld 247 D5
Teanna Mhachair W Isles 287 H2
Tebay Cumb 155 A5
Tebworth Beds 67 A4
Tedburn St Mary Devon 12 B3
Teddington Glos 80 D2
Teddington London 49 B4
Tedstone Delamere
Hereford 79 B4
Tedstone Wafre Hereford 79 B4
Teeton Northants 98 D3
Teffont Evias Wilts 30 B3
Teffont Magna Wilts 30 B3
Tegryn Pembs 73 C5
Teigh Rutland 115 D6
Teigncombe Devon 12 C1
Teigngrace Devon 12 D3
Teignmouth Devon 13 D4
Telford Telford 95 A4
Telham E Sus 23 A5
Tellisford Som 44 D2
Telscombe E Sus 22 B2
Telscombe Cliffs E Sus 22 B1
Templand Dumfries 184 D3
Temple Corn 10 D2
Temple Glasgow 205 B5
Temple Midloth 196 A2
Temple Balsall W Mid 97 D5
Temple Bar Ceredig 75 C4
Temple Bar Carms 57 A5
Temple Cloud Bath 43 D5
Temple Combe Som 29 C7
Temple Ewell Kent 39 A4
Temple Grafton Warks 80 B4
Temple Guiting Glos 64 A1
Temple Herdewyke Warks 81 B6
Temple Hirst N Yorks 140 A4
Temple Normanton
Derbys 131 C4
Temple Sowerby Cumb 165 C4
Templehall Fife 209 A5
Templeton Devon 26 D3
Templeton Pembs 55 C7
Templeton Bridge Devon 26 D3
Templetown Durham 178 D3
Tempsford Beds 84 B3
Ten Mile Bank Norf 102 B2
Tenbury Wells Worcs 78 A3
Tenby = Dinbych-y-
Pysgod Pembs 56 B1
Tendring Essex 71 A5
Tendring Green Essex 71 A5
Tenston Orkney 282 F3
Tenterden Kent 37 C6
Terling Essex 70 B1
Ternhill Shrops 111 B5
Terregles Banks Dumfries 174 A2
Terrick Bucks 66 C3
Terrington N Yorks 159 D5
Terrington St Clement
Norf 118 D2
Terrington St John Norf 118 D2
Teston Kent 37 A5
Testwood Hants 32 D2
Tetbury Glos 63 D4
Tetbury Upton Glos 63 C4
Tetchill Shrops 110 B2
Tetcott Devon 10 B4
Tetford Lincs 134 B3
Tetney Lincs 143 C5
Tetney Lock Lincs 143 C5
Tetsworth Oxon 66 C1
Tettenhall W Mid 96 A1
Teuchan Aberds 257 C5
Teversal Notts 131 C4
Teversham Cambs 85 B6
Teviothead Borders 186 C3
Tewel Aberds 245 D5
Tewin Herts 68 B2
Tewkesbury Glos 80 D1
Tewkesbury Abbey Glos 80 D1
Teynham Kent 51 C6
Thackthwaite Cumb 163 B4
Thainston Aberds 233 A4
Thakeham W Sus 21 A4

Thame Oxon 66 C2
Thames Ditton Sur 49 C4
Thames Haven Thurrock 51 A4
Thamesmead London 50 A1
Thanington Kent 52 D3
Thankerton S Lnrk 195 C4
Tharston Norf 104 B2
Thatcham W Berks 46 C3
Thatto Heath Mers 136 D4
Thaxted Essex 86 D2
The Aird Highld 259 C4
The All England Jumping
Course, Hickstead
W Sus 21 A5
The Arms Norf 103 B4
The Bage Hereford 77 C6
The Balloch Perth 218 C3
The Barony Orkney 282 E3
The Bluebell Railway,
Sheffield Park E Sus 36 D2
The Bog Shrops 94 B1
The Bourne Sur 33 A7
The Braes Highld 247 A4
The Broad Hereford 78 A2
The Burrell Collection
Glasgow 205 B5
The Butts Som 30 A1
The Camp Glos 63 C5
The Camp Herts 67 C6
The Chequer Wrex 110 A3
The City Bucks 66 D2
The Common Wilts 31 B6
The Craigs Highld 263 A6
The Cronk I o M 152 B3
The Dell Suff 105 B5
The Den N Ayrs 204 C3
The Dinosaur Museum,
Dorchester Dorset 15 B7
The Eals Northumb 177 A5
The Eaves Glos 62 C2
The Flatt Cumb 176 B3
The Four Alls Shrops 111 B5
The Friars, Aylesford Kent 37 A5
The Garths Shetland 284 B8
The Green Cumb 153 B2
The Green Wilts 30 B2
The Grove Dumfries 174 A2
The Hall Shetland 284 D8
The Haven W Sus 34 C3
The Heath Norf 120 C3
The Heath Suff 88 D2
The Hill Cumb 153 B2
The Howe Cumb 154 C3
The Howe I o M 152 E1
The Hundred Hereford 78 A3
The Lee Bucks 67 C4
The Lhen I o M 152 A3
The Living RainForest
W Berks 46 B3
The Long Man of
Wilmington E Sus 22 B3
The Lost Gardens of
Heligan, Mevagissey Corn 5 C4
The Lowry, Salford
Gtr Man 137 D7
The Marsh Powys 93 B7
The Marsh Wilts 45 A4
The Middles Durham 179 D4
The Moor Kent 37 D5
The Moors Centre, Danby
N Yorks 159 A6
The Mumbles = Y
Mwmbwls Swansea 57 D6
The Murray S Lnrk 205 C6
The National Archives,
Kew London 49 B4
The National Tramway
Museum, Crich Derbys 130 D3
The Needles Old Battery
I o W 18 C1
The Neuk Aberds 245 C4
The Oval Bath 43 C6
The Oval Cricket Ground
London 49 B6
The Oxford Story, Oxford
Oxon 65 C6
The Pole of Itlaw Aberds 268 D1
The Quarry Glos 62 D3
The Rhos Pembs 55 C6
The Rock Telford 95 A4
The Ryde Herts 68 C2
The Sands Sur 34 B1
The Stocks Kent 37 D7
The Tales of Robin Hood
Nottingham 114 B3

The Throat Wokingham	47	C6
The Tutankhamun Exhibition, Dorchester Dorset	15	B6
The Vauld Hereford	78	C3
The Vyne Hants	47	D4
The World of Beatrix Potter, Bowness-on-Windermere Cumb	154	B3
The Wyke Shrops	95	A5
Theakston N Yorks	157	C7
Thealby N Lincs	141	B6
Theale Som	29	A4
Theale W Berks	47	B4
Thearne E Yorks	150	D3
Theberton Suff	89	A5
Theddingworth Leics	98	C3
Theddlethorpe All Saints Lincs	135	A4
Theddlethorpe St Helen Lincs	135	A4
Thelbridge Barton Devon	26	D2
Thelnetham Suff	103	D6
Thelveton Norf	104	C2
Thelwall Warr	127	A6
Themelthorpe Norf	120	C2
Thenford Northants	82	C2
Therfield Herts	85	D5
Thetford Lincs	116	D4
Thetford Norf	103	C4
Theydon Bois Essex	68	D4
Thickwood Wilts	44	B2
Thimbleby Lincs	134	C2
Thimbleby N Yorks	158	B3
Thingwall Mers	126	A2
Thirdpart N Ayrs	204	D1
Thirlby N Yorks	158	C3
Thirlestane Borders	197	B4
Thirn N Yorks	157	C6
Thirsk N Yorks	158	C3
Thirsk Racecourse N Yorks	158	C3
Thirtleby E Yorks	151	D4
Thistleton Lancs	144	D4
Thistleton Rutland	116	D2
Thistley Green Suff	102	D2
Thixendale N Yorks	150	A1
Thockrington Northumb	178	B1
Tholomas Drove Cambs	101	A5
Tholthorpe N Yorks	148	A3
Thomas Chapel Pembs	55	D7
Thomas Close Cumb	164	A2
Thomastown Aberds	255	C6
Thompson Norf	103	B5
Thomshill Moray	266	D3
Thong Kent	50	B3
Thongsbridge W Yorks	139	C4
Thoralby N Yorks	156	C4
Thoresway Lincs	142	D3
Thorganby Lincs	143	D4
Thorganby N Yorks	149	C5
Thorgill N Yorks	159	B6
Thorington Suff	105	D5
Thorington Street Suff	87	D6
Thorlby N Yorks	146	B3
Thorley Herts	69	B4
Thorley Street Herts	69	B4
Thorley Street I o W	18	C2
Thormanby N Yorks	158	D3
Thornaby on Tees Stockton	168	D2
Thornage Norf	120	B2
Thornborough Bucks	83	D4
Thornborough N Yorks	157	D6
Thornbury Devon	11	A5
Thornbury Hereford	79	B4
Thornbury S Glos	62	D2
Thornbury W Yorks	147	D5
Thornby Northants	98	D3
Thorncliffe Staffs	129	D5
Thorncombe Dorset	14	A3
Thorncombe Dorset	16	A2
Thorncombe Street Sur	34	B3
Thorncote Green Beds	84	C3
Thorncross I o W	18	C3
Thorndon Suff	88	A2
Thorndon Cross Devon	11	B6
Thorne S Yorks	141	B4
Thorne St Margaret Som	27	C5
Thorner W Yorks	148	C2
Thorney Notts	132	B3
Thorney P'boro	101	A4
Thorney Crofts E Yorks	143	A4
Thorney Green Suff	87	A6
Thorney Hill Hants	17	B5
Thorney Toll Cambs	101	A5
Thornfalcon Som	28	C2
Thornford Dorset	29	D6
Thorngumbald E Yorks	143	A4
Thornham Norf	119	A4
Thornham Magna Suff	104	D2
Thornham Parva Suff	104	D2
Thornhaugh P'boro	100	A2
Thornhill Caerph	41	C6
Thornhill Cumb	162	D3
Thornhill Derbys	130	A1
Thornhill Dumfries	183	C6
Thornhill Soton	32	D3
Thornhill Stirl	207	A4
Thornhill W Yorks	139	B5
Thornhill Edge W Yorks	139	B5
Thornhill Lees W Yorks	139	B5
Thornholme E Yorks	151	A4
Thornley Durham	166	B4
Thornley Durham	167	B6
Thornliebank E Renf	205	C5
Thorns Suff	86	B3
Thorns Green Ches	128	A2
Thornsett Derbys	129	A5
Thornthwaite Cumb	163	B5
Thornthwaite N Yorks	147	B5
Thornton Angus	232	D1
Thornton Bucks	83	D4
Thornton E Yorks	149	C6
Thornton Fife	209	A5
Thornton Lancs	144	C3
Thornton Leics	98	A1
Thornton Lincs	134	C2
Thornton Mers	136	C2
Thornton M'bro	168	D2
Thornton Northumb	198	B3
Thornton Pembs	55	D5
Thornton W Yorks	147	D5
Thornton Curtis N Lincs	142	B2
Thornton Heath London	49	C6
Thornton Hough Mers	126	A3
Thornton in Craven N Yorks	146	C3
Thornton-le-Beans N Yorks	158	B2
Thornton-le-Clay N Yorks	149	A5
Thornton-le-Dale N Yorks	160	C2
Thornton le Moor Lincs	142	D2
Thornton-le-Moor N Yorks	158	C2
Thornton-le-Moors Ches	127	B4
Thornton-le-Street N Yorks	158	C3
Thornton Rust N Yorks	156	C3
Thornton Steward N Yorks	157	C5
Thornton Watlass N Yorks	157	C6
Thorntonhall S Lnrk	205	C5
Thorntonloch E Loth	211	C4
Thorntonpark Northumb	198	B3
Thornwood Common Essex	69	C4
Thornydykes Borders	197	B5
Thoroton Notts	115	A5
Thorp Arch W Yorks	148	C3
Thorpe Derbys	129	D6
Thorpe E Yorks	150	C2
Thorpe Lincs	135	A4
Thorpe Norf	105	B5
Thorpe Notts	115	A5
Thorpe N Yorks	147	A4
Thorpe Sur	48	C3
Thorpe Abbotts Norf	104	D2
Thorpe Acre Leics	114	C3
Thorpe Arnold Leics	115	C5
Thorpe Audlin W Yorks	140	B2
Thorpe Bassett N Yorks	160	D2
Thorpe Bay Sthend	51	A6
Thorpe by Water Rutland	99	B5
Thorpe Common Suff	88	D3
Thorpe Constantine Staffs	97	A5
Thorpe Culvert Lincs	135	C4
Thorpe End Norf	121	D4
Thorpe Fendykes Lincs	135	C4
Thorpe Green Essex	71	A5
Thorpe Green Suff	87	B5
Thorpe Hesley S Yorks	140	D1
Thorpe in Balne S Yorks	140	B3
Thorpe in the Fallows Lincs	133	A4
Thorpe Langton Leics	99	B4
Thorpe Larches Durham	167	C6
Thorpe-le-Soken Essex	71	A5
Thorpe le Street E Yorks	150	C1
Thorpe Malsor Northants	99	D5
Thorpe Mandeville Northants	82	C2
Thorpe Market Norf	120	B4
Thorpe Marriot Norf	120	D3
Thorpe Morieux Suff	87	B5
Thorpe on the Hill Lincs	133	C4
Thorpe Park, Chertsey Sur	48	C3
Thorpe St Andrew Norf	104	A3
Thorpe St Peter Lincs	135	C4
Thorpe Salvin S Yorks	131	A5
Thorpe Satchville Leics	115	D5
Thorpe Thewles Stockton	168	C2
Thorpe Tilney Lincs	133	D6
Thorpe Underwood N Yorks	148	B3
Thorpe Waterville Northants	100	C2
Thorpe Willoughby N Yorks	149	D4
Thorpeness Suff	89	B5
Thorrington Essex	71	A4
Thorverton Devon	13	A4
Thrandeston Suff	104	D2
Thrapston Northants	100	D1
Thrashbush N Lnrk	207	D5
Threapland Cumb	163	A4
Threapland N Yorks	146	A3
Threapwood Ches	110	A3
Threapwood Staffs	112	A4
Threave Gardens Dumfries	173	B5
Three Ashes Hereford	61	A7
Three Bridges W Sus	35	C5
Three Burrows Corn	4	C2
Three Chimneys Kent	37	C6
Three Cocks Powys	77	D5
Three Counties Showground, Malvern Worcs	79	C5
Three Crosses Swansea	57	C5
Three Cups Corner E Sus	36	D4
Three Holes Norf	101	A7
Three Leg Cross E Sus	37	C4
Three Legged Cross Dorset	17	A4
Three Oaks E Sus	23	A6
Threehammer Common Norf	121	D5
Threekingham Lincs	116	B3
Threemile Cross Wokingham	47	C5
Threemilestone Corn	4	C2
Threemiletown W Loth	208	C3
Threlkeld Cumb	163	B6
Threshfield N Yorks	146	A3
Thrigby Norf	121	D6
Thringarth Durham	166	C2
Thringstone Leics	114	D2
Thrintoft N Yorks	157	B7
Thriplow Cambs	85	C6
Throckenholt Lincs	101	A5
Throcking Herts	85	D5
Throckley T & W	178	C3
Throckmorton Worcs	80	C2
Throphill Northumb	178	A3
Thropton Northumb	188	C3
Throsk Stirl	207	A6
Throwleigh Devon	12	B1
Throwley Kent	52	D1
Thrumpton Notts	114	B3
Thrumster Highld	281	D5
Thrunton Northumb	188	B3
Thrupp Glos	63	C4
Thrupp Oxon	65	B5
Thrushelton Devon	11	C5
Thrussington Leics	115	D4
Thruxton Hants	32	A1
Thruxton Hereford	78	D2
Thruxton Motor Racing Circuit Hants	32	A1
Thrybergh S Yorks	140	D2
Thulston Derbys	114	B2
Thundergay N Ayrs	202	D3
Thundersley Essex	51	A4
Thundridge Herts	68	B3
Thurcaston Leics	114	D3
Thurcroft S Yorks	131	A4
Thurgarton Norf	120	B3
Thurgarton Notts	115	A4
Thurgoland S Yorks	139	C5
Thurlaston Leics	98	B2
Thurlaston Warks	98	D1
Thurlbear Som	28	C2
Thurlby Lincs	116	D4
Thurlby Lincs	133	C4
Thurleigh Beds	84	B2
Thurlestone Devon	7	C5
Thurloxton Som	28	B2
Thurlstone S Yorks	139	C5
Thurlton Norf	105	B5
Thurlwood Ches	128	D3
Thurmaston Leics	98	A3
Thurnby Leics	98	A3
Thurne Norf	121	D6
Thurnham Kent	37	A6
Thurnham Lancs	145	B4
Thurning Norf	120	C2
Thurning Northants	100	C2
Thurnscoe S Yorks	140	C2
Thurnscoe East S Yorks	140	C2
Thursby Cumb	175	C6
Thursford Norf	120	B1
Thursford Collection, Fakenham Norf	120	B1
Thursley Sur	34	C2
Thurso Highld	280	B3
Thurso East Highld	280	B3
Thurstaston Mers	126	A2
Thurston Suff	87	A5
Thurstonfield Cumb	175	C6
Thurstonland W Yorks	139	B4
Thurton Norf	104	A4
Thurvaston Derbys	113	B6
Thuxton Norf	103	A6
Thwaite N Yorks	156	B2
Thwaite Suff	88	A2
Thwaite St Mary Norf	104	B4
Thwaites W Yorks	147	C4
Thwaites Brow W Yorks	147	C4
Thwing E Yorks	160	D4
Tibbermore Perth	219	B5
Tibberton Glos	62	A3
Tibberton Telford	111	C5
Tibberton Worcs	80	B2
Tibenham Norf	104	C2
Tibshelf Derbys	131	C4
Tibthorpe E Yorks	150	B2
Ticehurst E Sus	37	C4
Tichborne Hants	33	B4
Tickencote Rutland	100	A1
Tickenham N Som	42	B3
Tickhill S Yorks	140	D3
Ticklerton Shrops	94	B2
Ticknall Derbys	114	C1
Tickton E Yorks	150	C3
Tidcombe Wilts	45	D6
Tiddington Oxon	66	C1
Tiddington Warks	81	B5
Tidebrook E Sus	36	D4
Tideford Corn	6	B2
Tideford Cross Corn	6	A2
Tidenham Glos	62	D1
Tideswell Derbys	129	B6
Tidmarsh W Berks	47	B4
Tidmington Warks	81	D5
Tidpit Hants	31	D4
Tidworth Wilts	31	A6
Tiers Cross Pembs	55	C5
Tiffield Northants	82	B3
Tifty Aberds	256	B2
Tigerton Angus	232	B3
Tigh-na-Blair Perth	218	C2
Tighnabruaich Argyll	203	A4
Tighnafiline Highld	261	B5
Tigley Devon	7	A6
Tilbrook Cambs	84	A2
Tilbury Thurrock	50	B3
Tilbury Juxta Clare Essex	86	C3
Tile Cross W Mid	97	C4
Tile Hill W Mid	97	D5
Tilehurst Reading	47	B4
Tilford Sur	34	B1
Tilgate W Sus	35	C5
Tilgate Forest Row W Sus	35	C5
Tillathrowie Aberds	255	C5
Tilley Shrops	111	C4
Tillicoultry Clack	208	A2
Tillingham Essex	70	C3
Tillington Hereford	78	C2
Tillington W Sus	34	D2
Tillington Common Hereford	78	C2
Tillyarblet Angus	232	B3
Tillybirloch Aberds	244	B3
Tillycorthie Aberds	257	D4
Tillydrine Aberds	244	C3
Tillyfour Aberds	244	A2
Tillyfourie Aberds	244	A3
Tillygarmond Aberds	244	C3
Tillygreig Aberds	256	D3
Tillykerrie Aberds	256	D3
Tilmanstone Kent	53	D5
Tilney All Saints Norf	118	D2
Tilney High End Norf	118	D2
Tilney St Lawrence Norf	118	D2
Tilshead Wilts	31	A4
Tilstock Shrops	111	B4
Tilston Ches	127	D4
Tilstone Fearnall Ches	127	C5
Tilsworth Beds	67	A4
Tilton on the Hill Leics	99	A4
Timberland Lincs	133	D6
Timbersbrook Ches	128	C3
Timberscombe Som	27	A4
Timble N Yorks	147	B5
Timperley Gtr Man	128	A2
Timsbury Bath	43	D5
Timsbury Hants	32	C2
Timsgearraidh W Isles	287	A5
Timworth Green Suff	87	A4
Tincleton Dorset	16	B1
Tindale Cumb	176	D4
Tingewick Bucks	82	D3
Tingley W Yorks	139	A5
Tingrith Beds	84	D2
Tingwall Orkney	282	E4
Tinhay Devon	11	C4
Tinshill W Yorks	147	D6
Tinsley S Yorks	140	D2
Tintagel Corn	9	C6
Tintagel Castle Corn	9	C6
Tintern Abbey Mon	62	C1
Tintern Parva Mon	62	C1
Tintinhull Som	29	D5
Tintwistle Derbys	138	D3
Tinwald Dumfries	184	D3
Tinwell Rutland	100	A2
Tipperty Aberds	257	D4
Tipsend Norf	101	B7
Tipton W Mid	96	B2
Tipton St John Devon	13	B5
Tiptree Essex	70	B2
Tir-y-dail Carms	57	A6
Tirabad Powys	59	A5
Tiraghoil Argyll	224	D2
Tiree Airport Argyll	222	C2
Tirley Glos	63	A4
Tirphil Caerph	41	A6
Tirril Cumb	164	C3
Tisbury Wilts	30	C3
Tisman's Common W Sus	34	C3
Tissington Derbys	130	D1
Titchberry Devon	24	C3
Titchfield Hants	18	A4
Titchmarsh Northants	100	D2
Titchwell Norf	119	A4
Tithby Notts	115	B4
Titley Hereford	78	A1
Titlington Northumb	189	B4
Titsey Sur	36	A2
Tittensor Staffs	112	B2
Tittleshall Norf	119	C5
Tiverton Ches	127	C5
Tiverton Devon	27	D4
Tivetshall St Margaret Norf	104	C2
Tivetshall St Mary Norf	104	C2
Tividale W Mid	96	B2
Tivy Dale S Yorks	139	C5
Tixall Staffs	112	C3
Tixover Rutland	99	A6
Toab Orkney	283	G6
Toab Shetland	285	M5
Toadmoor Derbys	130	D3
Tobermory Argyll	225	A4
Toberonochy Argyll	213	B5
Tobha Mor W Isles	286	C3
Tobhtarol W Isles	288	D2
Tobson W Isles	288	D2
Tocher Aberds	256	C1
Tockenham Wilts	44	B4
Tockenham Wick Wilts	44	A4
Tockholes Blkburn	137	A5
Tockington S Glos	43	A5
Tockwith N Yorks	148	B3
Todber Dorset	30	C2
Todding Hereford	94	D2
Toddington Beds	67	A5
Toddington Glos	80	D3
Todenham Glos	81	D5
Todhills Cumb	175	B6
Todlachie Aberds	244	A3
Todmorden W Yorks	138	A2
Todrig Borders	186	B3
Todwick S Yorks	131	A4
Toft Cambs	85	B5
Toft Lincs	116	D3
Toft Hill Durham	167	C4
Toft Hill Lincs	134	C2
Toft Monks Norf	105	B5
Toft next Newton Lincs	133	A5
Toftrees Norf	119	C5
Tofts Highld	281	B5
Toftwood Norf	120	D1
Togston Northumb	189	C5
Tokavaig Highld	247	C5

Tokers Green Oxon	47 B5	Torrish Highld	274 C3
Tolastadh a Chaolais W Isles	288 D2	Torrisholme Lancs	145 A4
Tolastadh bho Thuath W Isles	288 C6	Torroble Highld	272 D3
Toll Bar S Yorks	140 C3	Torry Aberdeen	245 B6
Toll End W Mid	96 B2	Torry Aberds	255 C5
Toll of Birness Aberds	257 C5	Torryburn Fife	208 B3
Tolland Som	27 B6	Torterston Aberds	257 B5
Tollard Royal Wilts	30 D3	Torthorwald Dumfries	174 A3
Tollbar End W Mid	97 D6	Tortington W Sus	20 B3
Toller Fratrum Dorset	15 B5	Tortworth S Glos	62 D3
Toller Porcorum Dorset	15 B5	Torvaig Highld	259 D4
Tollerton Notts	115 B4	Torver Cumb	154 B1
Tollerton N Yorks	148 A4	Torwood Falk	207 B6
Tollesbury Essex	70 B3	Torworth Notts	131 A6
Tolleshunt D'Arcy Essex	70 B3	Tosberry Devon	24 C3
Tolleshunt Major Essex	70 B3	Toscaig Highld	249 C4
Tolm W Isles	288 D5	Toseland Cambs	84 A4
Tolpuddle Dorset	16 B1	Tosside N Yorks	146 B1
Tolvah Highld	241 C6	Tostock Suff	87 A5
Tolworth London	49 C4	Totaig Highld	258 C2
Tomatin Highld	253 D4	Totaig Highld	249 D5
Tombreck Highld	252 C2	Tote Highld	259 D4
Tomchrasky Highld	239 A6	Totegan Highld	279 B4
Tomdoun Highld	239 B5	Tothill Lincs	135 A4
Tomich Highld	251 D5	Totland I o W	18 C2
Tomich Highld	264 C2	Totnes Devon	8 A2
Tomich House Highld	252 B1	Toton Notts	114 B3
Tomintoul Aberds	242 C4	Totronald Argyll	223 B4
Tomintoul Moray	243 A4	Totscore Highld	258 B3
Tomnaven Moray	255 C5	Tottenham London	68 D3
Tomnavoulin Moray	254 D3	Tottenhill Norf	118 D3
Ton-Pentre Rhondda	41 B4	Tottenhill Row Norf	118 D3
Tonbridge Kent	36 B3	Totteridge London	68 D2
Tondu Bridgend	40 C3	Totternhoe Beds	67 A4
Tonfanau Gwyn	90 B3	Tottington Gtr Man	137 B6
Tong Shrops	95 A5	Totton Hants	32 D2
Tong W Yorks	147 D6	Touchen End Windsor	48 B1
Tong Norton Shrops	95 A5	Tournaig Highld	261 B5
Tonge Leics	114 C2	Toux Aberds	269 D4
Tongham Sur	34 B1	Tovil Kent	37 A5
Tongland Dumfries	173 C4	Tow Law Durham	166 B4
Tongue Highld	277 C6	Toward Argyll	203 B6
Tongue End Lincs	117 D4	Towcester Northants	82 C3
Tongwynlais Cardiff	41 C6	Towcester Racecourse Northants	83 C4
Tonna Neath	40 B2	Towednack Corn	2 B2
Tonwell Herts	68 B3	Tower End Norf	118 D3
Tonypandy Rhondda	41 B4	Tower Knowe Visitor Centre, Kielder Water Northumb	177 A4
Tonyrefail Rhondda	41 C5	Tower of London London	49 A6
Toot Baldon Oxon	65 C6	Towersey Oxon	66 C2
Toot Hill Essex	69 C5	Towie Aberds	244 A1
Toothill Hants	32 D2	Towie Aberds	268 C3
Top of Hebers Gtr Man	138 C1	Towiemore Moray	255 B4
Topcliffe N Yorks	158 D3	Town End Cambs	101 B6
Topcroft Norf	104 B3	Town End Cumb	154 C3
Topcroft Street Norf	104 B3	Town Row E Sus	36 C3
Toppesfield Essex	86 D3	Town Yetholm Borders	187 A7
Toppings Gtr Man	137 B6	Townend W Dunb	205 A4
Topsham Devon	13 C4	Towngate Lincs	116 D4
Torbay Torbay	8 B3	Townhead Cumb	164 B3
Torbeg N Ayrs	191 C5	Townhead Dumfries	173 D4
Torboll Farm Highld	264 A3	Townhead S Ayrs	181 A4
Torbrex Stirl	207 A5	Townhead S Yorks	139 C4
Torbryan Devon	8 A2	Townhead of Greenlaw Dumfries	173 B5
Torcross Devon	8 C2	Townhill Fife	208 B4
Tore Highld	252 A2	Townsend Bucks	66 C2
Torinturk Argyll	202 B3	Townsend Herts	67 C6
Torksey Lincs	132 B3	Townshend Corn	2 B3
Torlum W Isles	286 A3	Towthorpe York	149 B5
Torlundy Highld	237 B5	Towton N Yorks	148 D3
Tormarton S Glos	43 B6	Towyn Conwy	125 B4
Tormisdale Argyll	200 C1	Toxteth Mers	126 A3
Tormitchell S Ayrs	181 B4	Toynton All Saints Lincs	134 C3
Tormore N Ayrs	191 B4	Toynton Fen Side Lincs	134 C3
Tornagrain Highld	252 B3	Toynton St Peter Lincs	135 C4
Tornahaish Aberds	243 B5	Toy's Hill Kent	36 A2
Tornaveen Aberds	244 B3	Trabboch E Ayrs	193 C4
Torness Highld	252 D1	Traboe Corn	3 C5
Toronto Durham	167 B4	Tradespark Highld	253 A4
Torpenhow Cumb	163 A5	Tradespark Orkney	283 G5
Torphichen W Loth	208 C2	Trafford Park Gtr Man	137 D6
Torphins Aberds	244 B3	Trago Mills, Newton Abbot Devon	12 D3
Torpoint Corn	6 B3	Trallong Powys	59 C6
Torquay Torbay	8 A3	Tranent E Loth	209 C7
Torquhan Borders	196 B3	Tranmere Mers	126 A3
Torran Argyll	214 B1	Trantlebeg Highld	279 C4
Torran Highld	248 B2	Trantlemore Highld	279 C4
Torran Highld	264 C3	Tranwell Northumb	178 A3
Torrance E Dunb	205 A6	Trapp Carms	57 A6
Torrans Argyll	224 D3	Traprain E Loth	210 C2
Torranyard N Ayrs	204 D3	Traquair Borders	196 C2
Torre Torbay	8 A3	Trawden Lancs	146 D3
Torridon Highld	249 A6	Trawsfynydd Gwyn	108 B2
Torridon Ho. Highld	249 A5		
Torrin Highld	247 B4		
Torrisdale Highld	278 B2		
Torrisdale-Square Argyll	190 B3		

Tre-Taliesin Ceredig	91 C4	Trelill Corn	9 D6
Tre-vaughan Carms	73 D7	Trelissick Corn	4 D3
Tre-wyn Mon	61 A5	Trelissick Garden, Feock Corn	4 D3
Trealaw Rhondda	41 B5	Trellech Mon	61 C7
Treales Lancs	144 D4	Trellech Grange Mon	61 C6
Trearddur Anglesey	122 C2	Trelogan Flint	125 A6
Treaslane Highld	258 C3	Trelystan Powys	93 A6
Trebah Garden, Mawnan Smith Corn	3 C5	Tremadog Gwyn	107 B5
Trebanog Rhondda	41 B5	Tremail Corn	10 C2
Trebanos Neath	40 A2	Tremain Ceredig	73 B5
Trebartha Corn	10 D3	Tremaine Corn	10 C3
Trebarwith Corn	9 C6	Tremar Corn	6 A1
Trebetherick Corn	9 D5	Trematon Corn	6 B2
Treborough Som	27 B5	Tremeirchion Denb	125 B5
Trebudannon Corn	4 A3	Trenance Corn	4 A3
Trebullett Corn	10 D4	Trenarren Corn	5 C5
Treburley Corn	10 D4	Trench Telford	111 D5
Trebyan Corn	5 A5	Treneglos Corn	10 C3
Trecastle Powys	59 C5	Trenewan Corn	5 B6
Trecenydd Caerph	41 C6	Trent Dorset	29 D5
Trecwn Pembs	55 A5	Trent Vale Stoke	112 A2
Trecynon Rhondda	41 A4	Trentham Stoke	112 A2
Tredavoe Corn	2 C2	Trentishoe Devon	26 A1
Treddiog Pembs	55 B4	Treoes V Glam	40 D4
Tredegar Bl Gwent	60 C3	Treorchy = Treorci Rhondda	41 B4
Tredegar Newydd = New Tredegar Caerph	41 A6	Treorci = Treorchy Rhondda	41 B4
Tredington Glos	63 A5	Tre'r-ddôl Ceredig	91 C4
Tredington Warks	81 C5	Trerule Foot Corn	6 B2
Tredinnick Corn	9 D5	Tresaith Ceredig	73 A5
Tredomen Powys	77 D5	Tresawle Corn	4 C3
Tredunnock Mon	61 D5	Trescott Staffs	95 B6
Tredustan Powys	77 D5	Trescowe Corn	2 B3
Treen Corn	2 C1	Tresham Glos	62 D3
Treeton S Yorks	131 A4	Tresillian Corn	4 C3
Tref-y-Clawdd = Knighton Powys	93 D6	Tresinwen Pembs	72 B1
Trefaldwyn = Montgomery Powys	93 B6	Treskinnick Cross Corn	10 B3
Trefasser Pembs	72 C1	Tresmeer Corn	10 C3
Trefdraeth Anglesey	123 C4	Tresparrett Corn	10 B2
Trefdraeth = Newport Pembs	72 C3	Tresparrett Posts Corn	10 B2
Trefecca Ceredig	77 D5	Tressait Perth	230 B2
Trefechan Ceredig	90 D3	Tresta Shetland	285 H5
Trefeglwys Powys	92 B3	Tresta Shetland	284 D8
Trefenter Ceredig	75 B5	Treswell Notts	132 B2
Treffgarne Pembs	55 B5	Trethosa Corn	4 B4
Treffynnon Pembs	54 B4	Trethurgy Corn	5 B5
Treffynnon = Holywell Flint	126 B1	Tretio Pembs	54 B3
Trefgarn Owen Pembs	55 B4	Tretire Hereford	62 A1
Trefil Bl Gwent	60 B3	Tretower Powys	60 A3
Trefilan Ceredig	75 C4	Treuddyn Flint	126 D2
Trefin Pembs	54 A4	Trevalga Corn	10 C1
Treflach Shrops	110 C1	Trevalyn Wrex	126 D3
Trefnanney Powys	109 D7	Trevanson Corn	9 D5
Trefnant Denb	125 B5	Trevarren Corn	4 A4
Trefonen Shrops	110 C1	Trevarrian Corn	4 A3
Trefor Anglesey	122 B3	Trevarrick Corn	5 C4
Trefor Gwyn	106 B3	Trevaughan Carms	56 A1
Treforest Rhondda	41 C5	Treveighan Corn	9 D6
Trefriw Conwy	124 C2	Trevellas Corn	4 B2
Trefynwy = Monmouth Mon	61 B7	Treverva Corn	4 D2
Tregadillett Corn	10 C3	Trevethin Torf	61 C4
Tregaian Anglesey	123 C4	Trevigro Corn	6 A2
Tregare Mon	61 B6	Treviscoe Corn	4 B4
Tregaron Ceredig	75 C5	Trevone Corn	9 D4
Tregarth Gwyn	123 D6	Trewarmett Corn	10 C1
Tregeare Corn	10 C3	Trewassa Corn	10 C2
Tregeiriog Wrex	109 B6	Trewellard Corn	2 B1
Tregele Anglesey	122 A3	Trewen Corn	10 C3
Tregidden Corn	3 C5	Trewennack Corn	3 C4
Treglemais Pembs	54 B4	Trewern Powys	110 D1
Tregole Corn	10 B2	Trewethern Corn	9 D6
Tregonetha Corn	5 A4	Trewidland Corn	6 B1
Tregony Corn	4 C4	Trewint Corn	10 C3
Tregoss Corn	5 A4	Trewint Corn	10 B2
Tregoyd Powys	77 D6	Trewithian Corn	4 D3
Tregroes Ceredig	73 B7	Trewoofe Corn	2 C2
Tregurrian Corn	4 A3	Trewoon Corn	5 B4
Tregynon Powys	93 B4	Treworga Corn	4 C3
Trehafod Rhondda	41 B5	Treworlas Corn	4 D3
Treharris M Tydf	41 B5	Treyarnon Corn	9 D4
Treherbert Rhondda	40 B4	Treyford W Sus	33 D7
Trekenner Corn	10 D4	Trezaise Corn	5 B4
Treknow Corn	9 C6	Triangle W Yorks	138 A3
Trelan Corn	3 D5	Trickett's Cross Dorset	17 A4
Trelash Corn	10 B2	Triffleton Pembs	55 B5
Trelassick Corn	4 B3	Trimdon Durham	167 B6
Trelawnyd Flint	125 B5	Trimdon Colliery Durham	167 B6
Trelech Carms	73 C5	Trimdon Grange Durham	167 B6
Treleddyd-fawr Pembs	54 B3	Trimingham Norf	121 B4
Trelewis M Tydf	41 B6	Trimley Lower Street Suff	88 D3
Treligga Corn	9 C6	Trimley St Martin Suff	88 D3
Trelights Corn	9 D5	Trimley St Mary Suff	88 D3

Trimpley Worcs	95 D5
Trimsaran Carms	57 B4
Trimstone Devon	25 A5
Trinafour Perth	229 B6
Trinant Caerph	41 A7
Tring Herts	67 B4
Tring Wharf Herts	67 B4
Trinity Angus	233 B4
Trinity Jersey	6
Trisant Ceredig	75 A6
Trislaig Highld	237 B4
Trispen Corn	4 B3
Tritlington Northumb	189 D5
Trochry Perth	230 D3
Trodigal Argyll	190 C2
Troed-rhiwdalar Powys	76 B3
Troedyraur Ceredig	73 B6
Troedyrhiw M Tydf	41 A5
Tromode I o M	152 D3
Trondavoe Shetland	284 F5
Troon Corn	3 B4
Troon S Ayrs	192 B3
Trosaraidh W Isles	286 E3
Trossachs Hotel Stirl	217 D5
Troston Suff	103 D4
Trottiscliffe Kent	50 C3
Trotton W Sus	34 D1
Troutbeck Cumb	154 A3
Troutbeck Cumb	164 C1
Troutbeck Bridge Cumb	154 A3
Trow Green Glos	62 C1
Trowbridge Wilts	44 D2
Trowell Notts	114 B2
Trowle Common Wilts	44 D2
Trowley Bottom Herts	67 B5
Trows Borders	197 C5
Trowse Newton Norf	104 A3
Trudoxhill Som	30 A1
Trull Som	28 C2
Trumaisgearraidh W Isles	287 G3
Trumpan Highld	258 B2
Trumpet Hereford	79 D4
Trumpington Cambs	85 B6
Trunch Norf	121 B4
Trunnah Lancs	144 C3
Truro Corn	4 C3
Truro Cathedral Corn	4 C3
Trusham Devon	12 C3
Trusley Derbys	113 B6
Trusthorpe Lincs	135 A5
Trysull Staffs	95 B6
Tubney Oxon	65 D5
Tuckenhay Devon	8 B2
Tuckhill Shrops	95 C5
Tuckingmill Corn	3 A4
Tuddenham Suff	102 D3
Tuddenham St Martin Suff	88 C2
Tudeley Kent	36 B4
Tudhoe Durham	167 B5
Tudorville Hereford	62 A1
Tudweiliog Gwyn	106 C2
Tuesley Sur	34 B2
Tuffley Glos	63 B4
Tufton Hants	32 A3
Tufton Pembs	55 B6
Tugby Leics	99 A4
Tugford Shrops	94 C3
Tullibardine Perth	218 C4
Tullibody Clack	207 A6
Tullich Argyll	214 A3
Tullich Highld	252 D2
Tullich Muir Highld	264 C3
Tullie House, Carlisle Cumb	175 C6
Tulliemet Perth	230 C3
Tulloch Aberds	233 A5
Tulloch Aberds	256 C3
Tulloch Perth	219 B5
Tulloch Castle Highld	264 D1
Tullochgorm Argyll	214 C2
Tulloes Angus	232 D3
Tullybannocher Perth	218 B2
Tullybelton Perth	219 A5
Tullyfergus Perth	231 D6
Tullymurdoch Perth	231 C5
Tullynessle Aberds	244 A2
Tumble Carms	57 A5
Tumby Woodside Lincs	134 D2
Tummel Bridge Perth	229 C6
Tunga W Isles	288 D5
Tunstall E Yorks	151 D6
Tunstall Kent	51 C5
Tunstall Lancs	155 D5

Tunstall Norf 105 A5
Tunstall N Yorks 157 B6
Tunstall Stoke 128 D3
Tunstall Suff 89 B4
Tunstall T & W 179 D5
Tunstead Derbys 129 B6
Tunstead Gtr Man 138 C3
Tunstead Norf 121 C4
Tunworth Hants 33 A5
Tupsley Hereford 78 C3
Tupton Derbys 130 C3
Tur Langton Leics 99 B4
Turgis Green Hants 47 D4
Turin Angus 232 C3
Turkdean Glos 64 B2
Turleigh Wilts 44 C2
Turn Lancs 137 B7
Turnastone Hereford 78 D1
Turnberry S Ayrs 192 E2
Turnditch Derbys 113 A6
Turners Hill W Sus 35 C6
Turners Puddle Dorset 16 B2
Turnford Herts 68 C3
Turnhouse Edin 209 C4
Turnworth Dorset 16 A2
Turriff Aberds 268 D2
Turton Bottoms Blkburn 137 B6
Turves Cambs 101 B5
Turvey Beds 83 B6
Turville Bucks 66 D2
Turville Heath Bucks 66 D2
Turweston Bucks 82 D3
Tushielaw Borders 185 A6
Tutbury Staffs 113 C6
Tutnall Worcs 96 D2
Tutshill Glos 62 D1
Tuttington Norf 120 C4
Tutts Clump W Berks 46 B3
Tuxford Notts 132 B2
Twatt Orkney 282 E3
Twatt Shetland 285 H5
Twechar E Dunb 207 C4
Tweedmouth Northumb 198 A3
Tweedsmuir Borders 195 D5
Twelve Heads Corn 4 C2
Twemlow Green Ches 128 C2
Twenty Lincs 117 C4
Twerton Bath 43 C6
Twickenham London 49 B4
Twickenham Stadium London 48 B4
Twigworth Glos 63 A4
Twineham W Sus 21 A5
Twinhoe Bath 43 D6
Twinstead Essex 87 D4
Twinstead Green Essex 87 D4
Twiss Green Warr 137 D5
Twiston Lancs 146 C2
Twitchen Devon 26 B2
Twitchen Shrops 94 D1
Two Bridges Devon 11 D7
Two Dales Derbys 130 C2
Two Mills Ches 126 B3
Twycross Leics 97 A6
Twycross Zoo, Ashby-de-la-Zouch Leics 97 A6
Twyford Bucks 66 A1
Twyford Derbys 114 C1
Twyford Hants 32 C3
Twyford Leics 115 D5
Twyford Lincs 116 C2
Twyford Norf 120 C2
Twyford Wokingham 47 B5
Twyford Common Hereford 78 D3
Twyn-y-Sheriff Mon 61 C6
Twynholm Dumfries 173 C4
Twynning Glos 80 D1
Twyning Green Glos 80 D2
Twynllanan Carms 59 C4
Twynmynydd Carms 57 A6
Twywell Northants 99 D6
Ty-draw Conwy 124 D3
Ty-hen Carms 73 D6
Ty-hen Gwyn 106 C1
Ty-mawr Anglesey 123 B4
Ty Mawr Carms 58 A2
Ty Mawr Cwm Conwy 108 A4
Ty-nant Conwy 109 A4
Ty-nant Gwyn 108 C4
Ty-uchaf Powys 109 C5
Tyberton Hereford 78 D1
Tyburn W Mid 96 B4
Tycroes Carms 57 A6
Tycrwyn Powys 109 D6

Tydd Gote Lincs 118 D1
Tydd St Giles Cambs 118 D1
Tydd St Mary Lincs 118 D1
Tyddewi = St David's Pembs 54 B3
Tyddyn-mawr Gwyn 107 B5
Tye Green Essex 86 D1
Tye Green Essex 70 A1
Tye Green Essex 69 C4
Tyldesley Gtr Man 137 C5
Tyler Hill Kent 52 C3
Tylers Green Bucks 67 D4
Tylorstown Rhondda 41 B5
Tylwch Powys 92 C3
Tyn-y-celyn Wrex 109 B6
Tyn-y-coed Shrops 110 C1
Tyn-y-fedwen Powys 109 B6
Tyn-y-ffridd Powys 109 B6
Tyn-y-graig Powys 76 B4
Ty'n-y-groes Conwy 124 B2
Ty'n-y-maes Gwyn 123 D6
Tyn-y-pwll Anglesey 123 B4
Ty'n-yr-eithin Ceredig 75 B5
Tyncelyn Ceredig 75 B5
Tyndrum Stirl 216 A3
Tyne Tunnel T & W 179 C5
Tyneham Dorset 16 C2
Tynehead Midloth 196 A2
Tynemouth T & W 179 C5
Tynemouth Sea Life Centre T & W 179 B5
Tynewydd Rhondda 40 B4
Tyninghame E Loth 210 C3
Tynron Dumfries 183 C6
Tynygongl Anglesey 123 B5
Tynygraig Ceredig 75 B5
Ty'r-felin-isaf Conwy 124 C3
Tyrie Aberds 269 C4
Tythecott Devon 25 D5
Tythegston Bridgend 40 D3
Tytherington Ches 129 B4
Tytherington S Glos 43 A5
Tytherington Som 30 A1
Tytherington Wilts 30 A3
Tytherleigh Devon 14 A3
Tywardreath Corn 5 B5
Tywyn Conwy 124 B2
Tywyn Gwyn 90 B3

U

Uachdar W Isles 286 A3
Uags Highld 249 C4
Ubbeston Green Suff 104 D4
Ubley Bath 43 D4
Uckerby N Yorks 157 A6
Uckfield E Sus 36 D2
Uckington Glos 63 A5
Uddingston S Lnrk 207 D4
Uddington S Lnrk 194 C3
Udimore E Sus 23 A6
Udny Green Aberds 256 D3
Udny Station Aberds 257 D4
Udston S Lnrk 194 A1
Udstonhead S Lnrk 194 B2
Uffcott Wilts 45 B5
Uffculme Devon 27 D5
Uffington Lincs 100 A2
Uffington Oxon 45 A7
Uffington Shrops 111 D4
Ufford P'boro 100 A2
Ufford Suff 88 B3
Ufton Warks 81 A6
Ufton Nervet W Berks 47 C4
Ugadale Argyll 190 C3
Ugborough Devon 7 B5
Uggeshall Suff 105 C5
Ugglebarnby N Yorks 160 A2
Ughill S Yorks 139 D5
Ugley Essex 69 A5
Ugley Green Essex 69 A5
Ugthorpe N Yorks 169 D5
Uidh W Isles 286 G2
Uig Argyll 215 D4
Uig Highld 258 B3
Uig Highld 258 C1
Uigen W Isles 287 A5
Uigshader Highld 259 D4
Uisken Argyll 224 E2
Ulbster Highld 281 D5
Ulceby Lincs 135 B4
Ulceby N Lincs 142 B3
Ulceby Skitter N Lincs 142 B3
Ulcombe Kent 37 B6
Uldale Cumb 163 A5
Uley Glos 62 D3

Ulgham Northumb 189 D5
Ullapool Highld 262 A3
Ullenhall Warks 80 A4
Ullenwood Glos 63 B5
Ulleskelf N Yorks 148 C4
Ullesthorpe Leics 98 C2
Ulley S Yorks 131 A4
Ullingswick Hereford 78 C3
Ullinish Highld 246 A2
Ullock Cumb 162 B3
Ulnes Walton Lancs 136 B4
Ulpha Cumb 153 A2
Ulrome E Yorks 151 B4
Ulsta Shetland 284 E6
Ulva House Argyll 224 C3
Ulverston Cumb 154 D1
Ulwell Dorset 17 C4
Umberleigh Devon 25 C7
Unapool Highld 271 A5
Unasary W Isles 286 D3
Underbarrow Cumb 154 B3
Undercliffe W Yorks 147 D5
Underhoull Shetland 284 C7
Underriver Kent 36 A3
Underwood Notts 131 D4
Undy Mon 42 A3
Unifirth Shetland 285 H4
Union Cottage Aberds 245 C5
Union Mills I o M 152 D3
Union Street E Sus 37 C5
University Museum, Oxford Oxon 65 C6
Unst Airport Shetland 284 C8
Unstone Derbys 130 B3
Unstone Green Derbys 130 B3
Unthank Cumb 164 B2
Unthank Cumb 165 A4
Unthank End Cumb 164 B2
Up Cerne Dorset 15 A6
Up Exe Devon 13 A4
Up Hatherley Glos 63 A5
Up Holland Lancs 136 C4
Up Marden W Sus 33 D6
Up Nately Hants 47 D4
Up Somborne Hants 32 B2
Up Sydling Dorset 15 A6
Upavon Wilts 45 D5
Upchurch Kent 51 C5
Upcott Hereford 78 B1
Upend Cambs 86 B2
Upgate Norf 120 D3
Uphall W Loth 208 C3
Uphall Station W Loth 208 C3
Upham Devon 12 A3
Upham Hants 32 C4
Uphampton Worcs 79 A6
Uphill N Som 42 D2
Uplawmoor E Renf 205 C4
Upleadon Glos 62 A3
Upleatham Redcar 168 D4
Uplees Kent 52 C1
Uploders Dorset 15 B5
Uplowman Devon 27 D5
Uplyme Devon 14 B3
Upminster London 50 A2
Upnor Medway 51 B4
Upottery Devon 14 A2
Uppark, Petersfield Hants 33 D6
Upper Affcot Shrops 94 C2
Upper Ardchronie Highld 264 B2
Upper Arley Worcs 95 C5
Upper Arncott Oxon 65 B7
Upper Astrop Northants 82 D2
Upper Badcall Highld 276 D2
Upper Beeding W Sus 21 A4
Upper Benefield Northants 100 C1
Upper Bighouse Highld 279 C4
Upper Boddington Northants 82 B1
Upper Borth Ceredig 90 D4
Upper Boyndlie Aberds 269 C4
Upper Brailes Warks 81 D6
Upper Breinton Hereford 78 C2
Upper Broadheath Worcs 79 B6
Upper Broughton Notts 115 C4
Upper Bucklebury W Berks 46 C3
Upper Burnhaugh Aberds 245 C5
Upper Caldecote Beds 84 C3
Upper Catesby Northants 82 B2
Upper Chapel Powys 76 C4
Upper Church Village Rhondda 41 C5
Upper Chute Wilts 45 D7
Upper Clatford Hants 32 A2

Upper Clynnog Gwyn 107 B4
Upper Cumberworth W Yorks 139 C5
Upper Cwm-twrch Powys 59 D4
Upper Cwmbran Torf 61 D4
Upper Dallachy Moray 267 C4
Upper Dean Beds 84 A2
Upper Denby W Yorks 139 C5
Upper Denton Cumb 176 C4
Upper Derraid Highld 253 C6
Upper Dicker E Sus 22 B3
Upper Dovercourt Essex 88 D3
Upper Druimfin Argyll 225 A4
Upper Dunsforth N Yorks 148 A3
Upper Eathie Highld 264 D3
Upper Elkstone Staffs 129 D5
Upper End Derbys 129 B5
Upper Farringdon Hants 33 B6
Upper Framilode Glos 62 B3
Upper Glenfintaig Highld 239 D6
Upper Gornal W Mid 96 B2
Upper Gravenhurst Beds 84 D3
Upper Green Mon 61 B5
Upper Green W Berks 46 C1
Upper Grove Common Hereford 62 A1
Upper Hackney Derbys 130 C2
Upper Hale Sur 34 B1
Upper Halistra Highld 258 C2
Upper Halling Medway 50 C3
Upper Hambleton Rutland 99 A5
Upper Hardres Court Kent 52 D3
Upper Hartfield E Sus 36 C2
Upper Haugh S Yorks 140 D2
Upper Heath Shrops 94 C3
Upper Hellesdon Norf 120 D4
Upper Helmsley N Yorks 149 B5
Upper Hergest Hereford 77 B6
Upper Heyford Northants 82 B3
Upper Heyford Oxon 65 A5
Upper Hill Hereford 78 B2
Upper Hopton W Yorks 139 B4
Upper Horsebridge E Sus 22 A3
Upper Hulme Staffs 129 C5
Upper Inglesham Swindon 64 D3
Upper Inverbrough Highld 253 C4
Upper Killay Swansea 57 C5
Upper Knockando Moray 254 B2
Upper Lambourn W Berks 45 A7
Upper Leigh Staffs 112 B4
Upper Lenie Highld 251 D7
Upper Lochton Aberds 244 C3
Upper Longdon Staffs 113 D4
Upper Lybster Highld 275 A6
Upper Lydbrook Glos 62 B2
Upper Maes-coed Hereford 78 D1
Upper Midway Derbys 113 C6
Upper Milovaig Highld 258 D1
Upper Minety Wilts 63 D6
Upper Mitton Worcs 95 D6
Upper North Dean Bucks 66 D3
Upper Obney Perth 219 A5
Upper Ollach Highld 247 A4
Upper Padley Derbys 130 B2
Upper Pollicott Bucks 66 B2
Upper Poppleton York 149 B4
Upper Quinton Warks 81 C4
Upper Ratley Hants 32 C2
Upper Rissington Glos 64 B3
Upper Rochford Worcs 79 A4
Upper Sandaig Highld 238 A1
Upper Sanday Orkney 283 G6
Upper Sapey Hereford 79 A4
Upper Seagry Wilts 44 A3
Upper Shelton Beds 84 C1
Upper Sheringham Norf 120 A3
Upper Skelmorlie N Ayrs 204 B2
Upper Slaughter Glos 64 A2
Upper Soudley Glos 62 B2
Upper Stondon Beds 84 D3
Upper Stowe Northants 82 B3
Upper Stratton Swindon 45 A5
Upper Street Hants 31 D5
Upper Street Norf 121 D5
Upper Street Norf 121 D5
Upper Street Suff 88 D2
Upper Strensham Worcs 80 D2
Upper Sundon Beds 67 A5
Upper Swell Glos 64 A2
Upper Tean Staffs 112 B4
Upper Tillyrie Perth 219 D6
Upper Tooting London 49 B5
Upper Tote Highld 259 C5
Upper Town N Som 43 C4
Upper Treverward Shrops 93 D6
Upper Tysoe Warks 81 C6

Upper Upham Wilts 45 B6
Upper Wardington Oxon 82 C1
Upper Weald M Keynes 83 D4
Upper Weedon Northants 82 B3
Upper Wield Hants 33 B5
Upper Winchendon Bucks 66 B2
Upper Witton W Mid 96 B3
Upper Woodend Aberds 244 A3
Upper Woodford Wilts 31 B5
Upper Wootton Hants 46 D3
Upper Wyche Worcs 79 C5
Upperby Cumb 175 C7
Uppermill Gtr Man 138 C2
Uppersound Shetland 285 J6
Upperthong W Yorks 139 C4
Upperthorpe N Lincs 141 C5
Upperton W Sus 34 D2
Uppertown Derbys 130 C3
Uppertown Highld 281 A5
Uppertown Orkney 283 H5
Uppingham Rutland 99 B5
Uppington Shrops 95 A4
Upsall N Yorks 158 C3
Upshire Essex 68 C4
Upstreet Kent 53 C4
Upthorpe Suff 103 D5
Upton Cambs 100 D3
Upton Ches 127 C4
Upton Corn 10 A3
Upton Dorset 16 C1
Upton Dorset 16 B3
Upton Hants 32 D2
Upton Hants 46 D1
Upton Leics 97 B6
Upton Lincs 132 A3
Upton Mers 126 A2
Upton Norf 121 D5
Upton Notts 132 D2
Upton Notts 132 B2
Upton Northants 83 A4
Upton Oxon 46 A3
Upton P'boro 100 A3
Upton Slough 48 B2
Upton Som 27 C4
Upton W Yorks 140 B2
Upton Bishop Hereford 62 A2
Upton Cheyney S Glos 43 C5
Upton Cressett Shrops 95 B4
Upton Cross Corn 10 D3
Upton Grey Hants 33 A5
Upton Hellions Devon 12 A3
Upton House Warks 81 C6
Upton Lovell Wilts 30 A3
Upton Magna Shrops 111 D4
Upton Noble Som 29 B7
Upton Pyne Devon 13 B4
Upton St Leonard's Glos 30 A2
Upton Scudamore Wilts 30 A2
Upton Snodsbury Worcs 80 B2
Upton upon Severn Worcs 79 C6
Upton Warren Worcs 80 A2
Upwaltham W Sus 20 A2
Upware Cambs 102 D1
Upwell Norf 101 A6
Upwey Dorset 15 C6
Upwood Cambs 101 C4
Uradale Shetland 285 K6
Urafirth Shetland 284 F5
Urchfont Wilts 44 D4
Urdimarsh Hereford 78 C3
Ure Shetland 284 F4
Ure Bank N Yorks 157 D7
Urgha W Isles 288 H2
Urishay Common Hereford 77 D7
Urlay Nook Stockton 167 D6
Urmston Gtr Man 137 D6
Urpeth Durham 179 D4
Urquhart Highld 252 A1
Urquhart Moray 266 C3
Urquhart Castle, Drumnadrochit Highld 252 D1
Urra N Yorks 159 A4
Urray Highld 251 A7
Ushaw Moor Durham 167 A5
Usk = Brynbuga Mon 61 C5
Usselby Lincs 142 D2
Usworth T & W 179 D5
Utkinton Ches 127 C5
Utley W Yorks 147 C4
Uton Devon 12 B3
Uttoxeter Staffs 113 D5
Uttoxeter Racecourse Staffs 113 B4

Uwchmynydd Gwyn 106 D1
Uxbridge London 48 A3
Uyeasound Shetland 284 C7
Uzmaston Pembs 55 C5

V

Valley Anglesey	122	C2
Valley Truckle Corn	10	C1
Valleyfield Dumfries	173	C4
Valsgarth Shetland	284	B8
Valtos Highld	259	B5
Van Powys	92	C3
Vange Essex	51	A4
Varteg Torf	61	C4
Vatten Highld	258	D2
Vaul Argyll	222	C3
Vaynor M Tydf	60	B2
Veensgarth Shetland	285	J6
Velindre Powys	77	D5
Vellow Som	27	B5
Veness Orkney	282	E6
Venn Green Devon	25	D4
Venn Ottery Devon	13	B5
Vennington Shrops	94	A1
Venny Tedburn Devon	12	B3
Ventnor I o W	19	D4
Ventnor Botanic Garden I o W	19	D4
Vernham Dean Hants	46	D1
Vernham Street Hants	46	D1
Vernolds Common Shrops	94	C2
Verwood Dorset	17	A4
Veryan Corn	4	D4
Vicarage Devon	14	C2
Vickerstown Cumb	153	D2
Victoria Corn	5	A4
Victoria S Yorks	139	C4
Victoria and Albert Museum London	49	B5
Vidlin Shetland	284	G6
Viewpark N Lnrk	207	D5
Vigo Village Kent	50	C3
Vinehall Street E Sus	37	D5
Vine's Cross E Sus	22	A3
Viney Hill Glos	62	C2
Virginia Water Sur	48	C3
Virginstow Devon	11	B4
Vobster Som	29	A7
Voe Shetland	285	G6
Voe Shetland	284	E5
Vowchurch Hereford	78	D1
Voxter Shetland	284	F5
Voy Orkney	282	F3

W

Wackerfield Durham	167	C4
Wacton Norf	104	B2
Wadbister Shetland	285	J6
Wadborough Worcs	80	C2
Waddesdon Bucks	66	B2
Waddesdon Manor, Aylesbury Bucks	66	B2
Waddingham Lincs	142	D1
Waddington Lancs	146	C1
Waddington Lincs	133	C4
Wadebridge Corn	9	D5
Wadeford Som	28	D3
Wadenhoe Northants	100	C2
Wadesmill Herts	68	B3
Wadhurst E Sus	36	C4
Wadshelf Derbys	130	B3
Wadsley S Yorks	139	D6
Wadsley Bridge S Yorks	139	D6
Wadworth S Yorks	140	D3
Waen Denb	125	C6
Waen Denb	125	C4
Waen Fach Powys	109	D7
Waen Goleugoed Denb	125	B5
Wag Highld	274	B4
Wainfleet All Saints Lincs	135	D4
Wainfleet Bank Lincs	135	D4
Wainfleet St Mary Lincs	135	D5
Wainfleet Tofts Lincs	135	D4
Wainhouse Corner Corn	10	B2
Wainscott Medway	51	B4
Wainstalls W Yorks	138	A3
Waitby Cumb	155	A6
Waithe Lincs	143	C4
Wake Lady Green N Yorks	159	B5
Wakefield W Yorks	139	A6
Wakehurst Place Garden, Crawley W Sus	35	C6
Wakerley Northants	99	B6
Wakes Colne Essex	70	A2
Walberswick Suff	105	D5
Walberton W Sus	20	B2
Walbottle T & W	178	C3
Walcot Lincs	116	B3
Walcot N Lincs	141	A6
Walcot Shrops	94	C1
Walcot Telford	111	D4
Walcot Swindon	45	A5
Walcot Green Norf	104	C2
Walcote Leics	98	C2
Walcote Warks	80	B4
Walcott Lincs	133	D6
Walcott Norf	121	B5
Walden N Yorks	156	C4
Walden Head N Yorks	156	C3
Walden Stubbs N Yorks	140	B3
Waldersey Cambs	101	A6
Walderslade Medway	51	C4
Walderton W Sus	33	D6
Walditch Dorset	15	B4
Waldley Derbys	113	B5
Waldridge Durham	179	D4
Waldringfield Suff	88	C3
Waldringfield Heath Suff	88	C3
Waldron E Sus	22	A3
Wales S Yorks	131	A4
Walesby Lincs	142	D3
Walesby Notts	132	B1
Walford Hereford	94	D1
Walford Hereford	62	A1
Walford Shrops	110	C3
Walford Heath Shrops	110	D3
Walgherton Ches	111	A5
Walgrave Northants	99	D5
Walhampton Hants	18	B2
Walk Mill Lancs	146	D2
Walkden Gtr Man	137	C6
Walker T & W	179	C4
Walker Art Gallery Mers	136	D2
Walker Barn Ches	129	B4
Walker Fold Lancs	145	C6
Walkerburn Borders	196	C2
Walkeringham Notts	141	D5
Walkerith Lincs	141	D5
Walkern Herts	68	A2
Walker's Green Hereford	78	C3
Walkerville N Yorks	157	B6
Walkford Dorset	17	B6
Walkhampton Devon	7	A4
Walkington E Yorks	150	D2
Walkley S Yorks	130	A3
Walkley Clogs, Hebden Bridge W Yorks	138	A3
Wall Northumb	177	C7
Wall Staffs	96	A4
Wall Bank Shrops	94	B3
Wall Heath W Mid	96	C1
Wall under Heywood Shrops	94	B3
Wallaceton Dumfries	183	D6
Wallacetown S Ayrs	181	A4
Wallacetown S Ayrs	192	C3
Wallands Park E Sus	22	A2
Wallasey Mers	136	D2
Wallcrouch E Sus	37	C4
Wallingford Oxon	47	A4
Wallington London	49	C5
Wallington Hants	19	A4
Wallington Herts	85	D4
Wallington House, Ponteland Northumb	178	A2
Wallis Pembs	55	B6
Walliswood Sur	35	C4
Walls Shetland	285	J4
Wallsend T & W	179	C4
Wallston V Glam	41	D6
Wallyford E Loth	209	C6
Walmer Kent	53	D5
Walmer Bridge Lancs	136	A3
Walmersley Gtr Man	137	B7
Walmley W Mid	96	B4
Walney Island Airport Cumb	153	C2
Walpole Suff	105	D4
Walpole Cross Keys Norf	118	D2
Walpole Highway Norf	118	D2
Walpole Marsh Norf	118	D1
Walpole St Andrew Norf	118	D2
Walpole St Peter Norf	118	D2
Walsall W Mid	96	B3
Walsall Arboretum W Mid	96	B3
Walsall Wood W Mid	96	A3
Walsden W Yorks	138	A2
Walsgrave on Sowe W Mid	97	C6
Walsham le Willows Suff	103	D5
Walshaw Gtr Man	137	B6
Walshford N Yorks	148	B3
Walsoken Cambs	118	D1
Walston S Lnrk	195	B5
Walsworth Herts	84	D4
Walters Ash Bucks	66	D3
Walterston V Glam	41	D5
Walterstone Hereford	61	A5
Waltham Kent	38	A3
Waltham NE Lincs	143	C4
Waltham Abbey Essex	68	C3
Waltham Chase Hants	33	D4
Waltham Cross Herts	68	C3
Waltham on the Wolds Leics	115	C6
Waltham St Lawrence Windsor	47	B6
Walthamstow London	49	A6
Walton Cumb	176	C3
Walton Derbys	130	C3
Walton Leics	98	C2
Walton Mers	136	D2
Walton M Keynes	83	D5
Walton P'boro	100	A3
Walton Powys	77	B6
Walton Som	29	B4
Walton Staffs	112	B2
Walton Suff	88	D3
Walton Telford	111	D4
Walton Warks	81	B5
Walton W Yorks	139	B6
Walton W Yorks	148	C3
Walton Cardiff Glos	80	D2
Walton East Pembs	55	B6
Walton Hall Warr	127	A6
Walton-in-Gordano N Som	42	B3
Walton-le-Dale Lancs	137	A4
Walton-on-Thames Sur	48	C4
Walton on the Hill Staffs	112	C3
Walton on the Hill Sur	35	A5
Walton-on-the-Naze Essex	71	A6
Walton on the Wolds Leics	114	D3
Walton-on-Trent Derbys	113	D6
Walton West Pembs	55	C4
Walwen Flint	126	B2
Walwick Northumb	177	B7
Walworth Darl	167	D5
Walworth Gate Darl	167	C5
Walwyn's Castle Pembs	55	C4
Wambrook Som	14	A2
Wanborough Sur	34	B2
Wanborough Swindon	45	A6
Wandsworth London	49	B5
Wangford Suff	105	D5
Wanlockhead Dumfries	183	A6
Wansford E Yorks	150	B3
Wansford P'boro	100	B2
Wanstead London	49	A7
Wanstrow Som	29	A7
Wanswell Glos	62	C2
Wantage Oxon	46	A1
Wapley S Glos	43	B6
Wappenbury Warks	81	A6
Wappenham Northants	82	C3
Warbleton E Sus	22	A4
Warblington Hants	19	A6
Warborough Oxon	65	D6
Warboys Cambs	101	C5
Warbreck Blkpool	144	D3
Warbstow Corn	10	B3
Warburton Gtr Man	128	A2
Warcop Cumb	165	D5
Ward End W Mid	96	C4
Ward Green Suff	87	A6
Warden Kent	52	B2
Warden Northumb	177	C7
Wardhill Orkney	282	E7
Wardington Oxon	82	C1
Wardlaw Borders	185	A5
Wardle Ches	127	D6
Wardle Gtr Man	138	B2
Wardley Rutland	99	A5
Wardlow Derbys	130	B1
Wardy Hill Cambs	101	C6
Ware Herts	68	B3
Ware Kent	53	C4
Wareham Dorset	16	C3
Warehorne Kent	38	B1
Waren Mill Northumb	199	C5
Warenford Northumb	189	A4
Warenton Northumb	199	C5
Wareside Herts	68	B3
Waresley Cambs	84	B4
Waresley Worcs	95	D6
Warfield Brack	48	B1
Warfleet Devon	8	B2
Wargrave Wokingham	47	B5
Warham Norf	119	A6
Warhill Gtr Man	138	D2
Wark Northumb	177	B6
Wark Northumb	198	C2
Warkleigh Devon	26	C1
Warkton Northants	99	D5
Warkworth Northants	82	C1
Warkworth Northumb	189	C5
Warlaby N Yorks	158	B2
Warland W Yorks	138	A2
Warleggan Corn	5	A6
Warlingham Sur	35	A6
Warmfield W Yorks	140	A1
Warmingham Ches	128	C2
Warmington Northants	100	B2
Warmington Warks	81	C7
Warminster Wilts	30	A2
Warmlake Kent	37	A6
Warmley S Glos	43	B5
Warmley Tower S Glos	43	B5
Warmonds Hill Northants	83	A6
Warmsworth S Yorks	140	C3
Warmwell Dorset	16	C1
Warndon Worcs	80	B1
Warnford Hants	33	C5
Warnham W Sus	35	C4
Warninglid W Sus	35	D5
Warren Ches	128	B3
Warren Pembs	55	E5
Warren Heath Suff	88	C3
Warren Row Windsor	47	A6
Warren Street Kent	51	D6
Warrington M Keynes	83	B5
Warrington Warr	127	A6
Warsash Hants	18	A3
Warslow Staffs	129	D5
Warter E Yorks	150	B1
Warthermarske N Yorks	157	D6
Warthill N Yorks	149	B5
Wartling E Sus	23	B4
Wartnaby Leics	115	C5
Warton Lancs	136	A3
Warton Lancs	154	D3
Warton Northumb	188	C3
Warton Warks	97	A5
Warwick Warks	81	A5
Warwick Bridge Cumb	176	D2
Warwick Castle Warks	81	A5
Warwick on Eden Cumb	176	D2
Warwick Racecourse Warks	81	A5
Wasbister Orkney	282	D4
Wasdale Head Cumb	163	D4
Wash Common W Berks	46	C2
Washaway Corn	5	A5
Washbourne Devon	8	B1
Washfield Devon	27	D4
Washfold N Yorks	157	A4
Washford Som	27	A5
Washford Pyne Devon	26	D3
Washingborough Lincs	133	B5
Washington T & W	179	D5
Washington W Sus	21	A4
Wasing W Berks	46	C3
Waskerley Durham	166	A3
Wasperton Warks	81	B5
Wasps Nest Lincs	133	C5
Wass N Yorks	159	D4
Watchet Som	27	A5
Watchfield Oxon	64	D3
Watchfield Som	28	A3
Watchgate Cumb	154	B4
Watchhill Cumb	175	D4
Watcombe Torbay	8	A3
Watendlath Cumb	163	C5
Water Devon	12	C2
Water Lancs	138	A1
Water End E Yorks	149	D6
Water End Herts	67	B5
Water End Herts	68	C2
Water Newton Cambs	100	B3
Water Orton Warks	97	B4
Water Stratford Bucks	82	D3
Water Yeat Cumb	154	C1
Waterbeach Cambs	85	A6
Waterbeck Dumfries	175	A5
Watercress Line (Mid Hants Railway), Alton Hants	33	B5
Waterden Norf	119	B5
Waterfall Staffs	129	D5
Waterfoot E Renf	205	C5
Waterfoot Lancs	138	A1
Waterford Hants	18	B2
Waterford Herts	68	B3
Waterhead Cumb	154	A2
Waterheads Borders	196	A1
Waterhouses Durham	167	A4
Waterhouses Staffs	129	D5
Wateringbury Kent	37	A4
Waterloo Gtr Man	138	C2
Waterloo Highld	247	B5
Waterloo Mers	136	D2
Waterloo N Lnrk	194	A3
Waterloo Norf	120	D4
Waterloo Perth	219	A5
Waterloo Poole	17	B4
Waterloo Shrops	111	B4
Waterloo Port Gwyn	123	D4
Waterlooville Hants	19	A5
Watermeetings S Lnrk	184	A2
Watermillock Cumb	164	C2
Watermouth Castle, Ilfracombe Devon	25	A6
Waterperry Oxon	66	C1
Waterrow Som	27	C5
Water's Nook Gtr Man	137	C5
Waters Upton Telford	111	D5
Watersfield W Sus	20	A3
Watershed Mill Visitor Centre, Settle N Yorks	146	A2
Waterside Aberds	257	D5
Waterside Blkburn	137	A6
Waterside Cumb	175	D5
Waterside E Ayrs	182	B2
Waterside E Ayrs	205	D4
Waterside E Dunb	207	C4
Waterside E Renf	205	C5
Waterstock Oxon	66	C1
Waterston Pembs	55	D5
Watford Herts	67	D6
Watford Northants	82	A3
Watford Gap W Mid	96	A4
Wath N Yorks	147	A5
Wath N Yorks	157	D7
Wath N Yorks	159	D5
Wath Brow Cumb	162	C3
Wath upon Dearne S Yorks	140	C2
Watley's End S Glos	43	A5
Watlington Norf	118	D3
Watlington Oxon	66	D1
Watnall Notts	114	A3
Watten Highld	280	C4
Wattisfield Suff	103	D6
Wattisham Suff	87	B6
Wattlesborough Heath Shrops	110	D2
Watton E Yorks	150	B3
Watton Norf	103	A5
Watton at Stone Herts	68	B3
Wattston N Lnrk	207	C5
Wattstown Rhondda	41	B5
Wauchan Highld	238	D3
Waulkmill Lodge Orkney	283	G4
Waun Powys	91	B6
Waun-y-clyn Carms	57	B4
Waunarlwydd Swansea	57	C6
Waunclunda Carms	58	B3
Waunfawr Gwyn	107	A5
Waungron Swansea	57	B5
Waunlwyd Bl Gwent	60	C3
Wavendon M Keynes	83	D6
Waverbridge Cumb	175	D5
Waverton Ches	127	C4
Waverton Cumb	175	D5
Wawne E Yorks	150	D3
Waxham Norf	121	C6
Waxholme E Yorks	143	A5
Way Kent	53	C5
Way Village Devon	26	D3
Wayfield Medway	51	C4
Wayford Som	14	A4
Waymills Shrops	111	A4
Wayne Green Mon	61	B6
Wdig = Goodwick Pembs	72	C2
Weachyparn Aberds	268	D1
Weald Oxon	64	C4
Weald and Downland Open Air Museum, Chichester W Sus	20	A1
Wealdstone London	49	A4
Weardley W Yorks	148	C1
Weare Som	42	D3
Weare Giffard Devon	25	C5
Wearhead Durham	165	B6
Weasdale Cumb	155	A5
Weasenham All Saints Norf	119	C5
Weasenham St Peter Norf	119	C5
Weatherhill Sur	35	B6
Weaverham Ches	127	B6
Weaverthorpe N Yorks	160	D3
Webheath Worcs	80	A3
Wedderlairs Aberds	256	C3
Wedderlie Borders	197	A5
Weddington Warks	97	B6

Wedgwood Visitor Centre, Barlaston Staffs 112 B2
Wedhampton Wilts 45 D4
Wedmore Som 28 A4
Wednesbury W Mid 96 B2
Wednesfield W Mid 96 A2
Weedon Bucks 66 B3
Weedon Bec Northants 82 B3
Weedon Lois Northants 82 C3
Weeford Staffs 96 A4
Week Devon 26 D2
Week St Mary Corn 10 B3
Weeke Hants 32 B3
Weekley Northants 99 C5
Weel E Yorks 150 D3
Weeley Essex 71 A5
Weeley Heath Essex 71 A5
Weem Perth 230 D2
Weeping Cross Staffs 112 C3
Weethley Gate Warks 80 B3
Weeting Norf 102 C3
Weeting Heath NNR Norf 102 C3
Weeton E Yorks 143 A5
Weeton Lancs 144 D3
Weeton N Yorks 148 C1
Weetwood Hall Northumb 188 A3
Weir Lancs 138 A1
Weir Quay Devon 6 A3
Welborne Norf 120 E2
Welbourn Lincs 133 D4
Welburn N Yorks 149 A6
Welburn N Yorks 159 C5
Welbury N Yorks 158 A2
Welby Lincs 116 B2
Welches Dam Cambs 101 C6
Welcombe Devon 24 D3
Weld Bank Lancs 137 B4
Weldon Northumb 189 D4
Welford Northants 98 C3
Welford W Berks 46 B2
Welford-on-Avon Warks 81 B4
Welham Leics 99 B4
Welham Notts 132 A2
Welham Green Herts 68 C2
Well Hants 33 A6
Well Lincs 135 B4
Well N Yorks 157 C6
Well End Bucks 48 A1
Well Heads W Yorks 147 D4
Well Hill Kent 50 C1
Well Town Devon 13 A4
Welland Worcs 79 C5
Wellbank Angus 221 A4
Welldale Dumfries 175 B4
Wellesbourne Warks 81 B5
Welling London 50 B1
Wellingborough Northants 83 A5
Wellingham Norf 119 C5
Wellingore Lincs 133 D4
Wellington Cumb 162 D3
Wellington Hereford 78 C2
Wellington Som 27 C6
Wellington Telford 111 D5
Wellington Heath Hereford 79 C5
Wellington Hill W Yorks 148 D2
Wellow Bath 43 D6
Wellow I o W 18 C2
Wellow Notts 131 C6
Wellpond Green Herts 68 A4
Wells Som 29 A5
Wells Cathedral Som 29 A5
Wells Green Ches 128 D1
Wells-Next-The-Sea Norf 119 A6
Wellsborough Leics 97 A6
Wellswood Torbay 8 A3
Wellwood Fife 208 B3
Welney Norf 102 B1
Welsh Bicknor Hereford 62 B1
Welsh End Shrops 111 B4
Welsh Frankton Shrops 110 B2
Welsh Highland Railway, Caernarfon Gwyn 123 D4
Welsh Highland Railway, Porthmadog Gwyn 107 C5
Welsh Hook Pembs 55 B5
Welsh National Velodrome Newport 42 A2
Welsh Newton Hereford 61 B6
Welsh St Donats V Glam 41 D5
Welshampton Shrops 110 B3
Welshpool = Y Trallwng Powys 93 A6
Welton Cumb 164 A1

Welton E Yorks 142 A1
Welton Lincs 133 B5
Welton Northants 82 A2
Welton Hill Lincs 133 A5
Welton le Marsh Lincs 135 C4
Welton le Wold Lincs 134 A2
Welwick E Yorks 143 A5
Welwyn Herts 68 B2
Welwyn Garden City Herts 68 B2
Wem Shrops 111 C4
Wembdon Som 28 B2
Wembley London 49 A4
Wembley Stadium London 49 A4
Wembury Devon 7 C4
Wembworthy Devon 12 A1
Wemyss Bay Invclyd 204 B1
Wenallt Ceredig 75 A5
Wenallt Gwyn 109 A4
Wendens Ambo Essex 85 D7
Wendlebury Oxon 65 B6
Wendling Norf 119 D6
Wendover Bucks 66 C3
Wendron Corn 3 B4
Wendy Cambs 85 C5
Wenfordbridge Corn 10 D1
Wenhaston Suff 105 D5
Wennington Cambs 100 D4
Wennington London 50 A2
Wennington Lancs 155 D5
Wensley Derbys 130 C2
Wensley N Yorks 157 C4
Wentbridge W Yorks 140 B2
Wentnor Shrops 94 B1
Wentworth Cambs 101 D6
Wentworth S Yorks 140 D1
Wenvoe V Glam 41 D6
Weobley Hereford 78 B2
Weobley Marsh Hereford 78 B2
Wereham Norf 102 A2
Wergs W Mid 95 A6
Wern Powys 109 D4
Wern Powys 110 D1
Wernffrwd Swansea 57 C5
Wernyrheolydd Mon 61 B5
Werrington Corn 10 C4
Werrington P'boro 100 A3
Werrington Staffs 112 A3
Wervin Ches 127 B4
Wesham Lancs 144 D4
Wessington Derbys 130 D3
West Acre Norf 119 D4
West Adderbury Oxon 82 D1
West Allerdean Northumb 198 B3
West Alvington Devon 7 C6
West Amesbury Wilts 31 A5
West Anstey Devon 26 C3
West Ashby Lincs 134 B2
West Ashling W Sus 19 A7
West Ashton Wilts 44 D2
West Auckland Durham 167 C4
West Ayton N Yorks 160 C3
West Bagborough Som 27 B6
West Barkwith Lincs 133 A6
West Barnby N Yorks 169 D6
West Barns E Loth 210 C3
West Barsham Norf 119 B6
West Bay Dorset 15 B4
West Beckham Norf 120 B3
West Bedfont Sur 48 B3
West Benhar N Lnrk 208 D1
West Bergholt Essex 70 A3
West Bexington Dorset 15 C5
West Bilney Norf 119 D4
West Blatchington Brighton 21 B5
West Bowling W Yorks 147 D5
West Bradford Lancs 146 C1
West Bradley Som 29 B5
West Bretton W Yorks 139 B5
West Bridgford Notts 114 B3
West Bromwich W Mid 96 B3
West Buckland Devon 26 B1
West Buckland Som 28 C1
West Burrafirth Shetland 285 H4
West Burton N Yorks 156 C4
West Burton W Sus 20 A2
West Butterwick N Lincs 141 C6
West Byfleet Sur 48 C3
West Caister Norf 121 D7
West Calder W Loth 208 D3
West Camel Som 29 C5
West Challow Oxon 46 A1
West Chelborough Dorset 15 A5
West Chevington Northumb 189 D5
West Chiltington W Sus 20 A3
West Chiltington Common W Sus 20 A3
West Chinnock Som 29 D4

West Chisenbury Wilts 45 D5
West Clandon Sur 34 A3
West Cliffe Kent 39 A5
West Clyne Highld 274 D2
West Clyth Highld 275 A6
West Coker Som 29 D5
West Compton Dorset 15 B5
West Compton Som 29 A5
West Cowick E Yorks 140 A4
West Cranmore Som 29 A6
West Cross Swansea 57 D6
West Cullery Aberds 245 B4
West Curry Corn 10 B3
West Curthwaite Cumb 175 D6
West Darlochan Argyll 190 C2
West Dean Wilts 31 C6
West Dean W Sus 20 A1
West Deeping Lincs 100 A3
West Derby Mers 136 D2
West Dereham Norf 102 A2
West Didsbury Gtr Man 138 D1
West Ditchburn Northumb 189 A4
West Down Devon 25 A6
West Drayton London 48 B3
West Drayton Notts 132 B2
West Ella E Yorks 142 A2
West End Beds 84 B1
West End E Yorks 150 D2
West End E Yorks 151 D4
West End Hants 32 D3
West End Lancs 137 A6
West End Norf 103 A5
West End Norf 121 D7
West End N Som 42 C3
West End N Yorks 147 B5
West End Oxon 65 C5
West End S Lnrk 195 B4
West End Suff 105 C5
West End Sur 48 C2
West End S Yorks 141 C4
West End Wilts 30 C3
West End Wilts 44 B3
West End W Sus 21 A5
West End Green Hants 47 C4
West Farleigh Kent 37 A5
West Felton Shrops 110 C2
West Fenton E Loth 210 B1
West Ferry Dundee 221 A4
West Firle E Sus 22 B2
West Ginge Oxon 46 A2
West Grafton Wilts 45 C6
West Green Hants 47 D5
West Greenskares Aberds 268 C2
West Grimstead Wilts 31 C6
West Grinstead W Sus 35 D4
West Haddlesey N Yorks 140 A3
West Haddon Northants 98 D3
West Hagbourne Oxon 46 A3
West Hagley Worcs 96 C2
West Hall Cumb 176 C3
West Hallam Derbys 114 A2
West Halton N Lincs 141 A7
West Ham London 49 A7
West Handley Derbys 130 B3
West Hanney Oxon 65 D5
West Hanningfield Essex 70 D1
West Hardwick W Yorks 140 B2
West Harnham Wilts 31 C5
West Harptree Bath 43 D4
West Hatch Som 28 C2
West Head Norf 102 A1
West Heath Ches 128 C3
West Heath Hants 34 A1
West Heath Hants 46 D3
West Helmsdale Highld 274 C4
West Hendred Oxon 46 A2
West Heslerton N Yorks 160 D3
West Hill Devon 13 B5
West Hill E Yorks 151 A4
West Hill N Som 42 B3
West Hoathly W Sus 35 C6
West Holme Dorset 16 C2
West Horndon Essex 50 A3
West Horrington Som 29 A5
West Horsley Sur 34 A3
West Horton Northumb 198 C4
West Hougham Kent 39 A4
West Houlland Shetland 285 H4
West-houses Derbys 131 D4
West Huntington York 149 B5
West Hythe Kent 38 B3
West Ilsley W Berks 46 A2
West Itchenor W Sus 19 A6
West Keal Lincs 134 C3
West Kennett Wilts 45 C5
West Kilbride N Ayrs 204 D2
West Kingsdown Kent 50 C2
West Kington Wilts 44 B2

West Kinharrachie Aberds 257 C4
West Kirby Mers 126 A2
West Knapton N Yorks 160 D2
West Knighton Dorset 16 C1
West Knoyle Wilts 30 B2
West Kyloe Northumb 199 B4
West Lambrook Som 28 D4
West Langdon Kent 39 A5
West Langwell Highld 273 D4
West Lavington Wilts 44 D4
West Lavington W Sus 34 D1
West Layton N Yorks 157 A5
West Lea Durham 168 A2
West Leake Notts 114 C3
West Learmouth Northumb 198 C2
West Leigh Devon 12 A1
West Lexham Norf 119 D5
West Lilling N Yorks 149 A5
West Linton Borders 195 A6
West Liss Hants 33 C6
West Littleton S Glos 43 B6
West Looe Corn 6 B1
West Luccombe Som 26 A3
West Lulworth Dorset 16 C2
West Lutton N Yorks 150 A2
West Lydford Som 29 B5
West Lyng Som 28 C3
West Lynn Norf 118 C3
West Malling Kent 37 A4
West Malvern Worcs 79 C5
West Marden W Sus 33 D6
West Marina E Sus 23 B5
West Markham Notts 132 B2
West Marsh NE Lincs 143 B4
West Marton N Yorks 146 B2
West Meon Hants 33 C5
West Mersea Essex 71 B4
West Midlands Safari Park, Kidderminster Worcs 95 D6
West Milton Dorset 15 B5
West Minster Kent 51 B6
West Molesey Sur 48 C4
West Monkton Som 28 C2
West Moors Dorset 17 A4
West Morriston Borders 197 B5
West Muir Angus 232 B3
West Ness N Yorks 159 D5
West Newham Northumb 178 B2
West Newton E Yorks 151 D4
West Newton Norf 118 C3
West Norwood London 49 B6
West Ogwell Devon 12 D3
West Orchard Dorset 30 D2
West Overton Wilts 45 C5
West Park Hrtlpl 168 B2
West Parley Dorset 17 B4
West Peckham Kent 36 A4
West Pelton Durham 179 D4
West Pennard Som 29 B5
West Pentire Corn 4 A2
West Perry Cambs 84 A3
West Putford Devon 25 D4
West Quantoxhead Som 27 A6
West Rainton Durham 167 A6
West Rasen Lincs 133 A5
West Raynham Norf 119 C5
West Retford Notts 132 A1
West Rounton N Yorks 158 A3
West Row Suff 102 D2
West Rudham Norf 119 C5
West Runton Norf 120 A3
West Saltoun E Loth 210 D1
West Sandwick Shetland 284 E6
West Scrafton N Yorks 157 C4
West Sleekburn Northumb 179 A4
West Somerset Railway, Minehead Som 27 A4
West Somerton Norf 121 D6
West Stafford Dorset 16 C1
West Stockwith Notts 141 D5
West Stoke W Sus 20 B1
West Stonesdale N Yorks 156 A2
West Stoughton Som 28 A4
West Stour Dorset 30 C1
West Stourmouth Kent 53 C4
West Stow Suff 103 D4
West Stowell Wilts 45 C5
West Strathan Highld 277 B6
West Stratton Hants 32 A4
West Street Kent 37 A7
West Tanfield N Yorks 157 D6
West Taphouse Corn 5 A6
West Tarbert Argyll 202 B3
West Thirston Northumb 189 D4
West Thorney W Sus 19 A6

West Thurrock Thurrock 50 B2
West Tilbury Thurrock 50 B3
West Tisted Hants 33 C5
West Tofts Norf 103 B4
West Tofts Perth 219 A6
West Torrington Lincs 133 A6
West Town Hants 19 B6
West Town N Som 42 C3
West Tytherley Hants 32 C1
West Tytherton Wilts 44 B3
West Walton Norf 118 D1
West Walton Highway Norf 118 D1
West Wellow Hants 32 D1
West Wemyss Fife 209 A6
West Wick N Som 42 C2
West Wickham Cambs 86 C2
West Wickham London 49 C6
West Williamston Pembs 55 D6
West Willoughby Lincs 116 A2
West Winch Norf 118 D3
West Winterslow Wilts 31 B6
West Wittering W Sus 19 B6
West Witton N Yorks 157 C4
West Woodburn Northumb 177 A6
West Woodhay W Berks 46 C1
West Woodlands Som 30 A1
West Worldham Hants 33 B6
West Worlington Devon 26 D2
West Worthing W Sus 21 B4
West Wratting Cambs 86 B2
West Wycombe Bucks 66 D3
West Wylam Northumb 178 C3
West Yell Shetland 284 E6
Westacott Devon 25 B6
Westbere Kent 52 C3
Westborough Lincs 115 A6
Westbourne Bmouth 17 B4
Westbourne Suff 88 C2
Westbourne W Berks 19 A6
Westbrook W Berks 46 B2
Westbury Bucks 82 D3
Westbury Shrops 94 A1
Westbury Wilts 44 D2
Westbury Leigh Wilts 44 D2
Westbury-on-Severn Glos 62 B3
Westbury on Trym Bristol 43 B4
Westbury-sub-Mendip Som 29 A5
Westby Lancs 144 D3
Westcliff-on-Sea Sthend 51 A5
Westcombe Som 29 B6
Westcote Glos 64 A3
Westcott Bucks 66 B2
Westcott Devon 13 A5
Westcott Sur 35 B4
Westcott Barton Oxon 65 A5
Westdean E Sus 22 C3
Westdene Brighton 21 B5
Wester Aberchalder Highld 252 D1
Wester Balgedie Perth 219 D6
Wester Culbeuchly Aberds 268 C1
Wester Dechmont W Loth 208 D3
Wester Denoon Angus 232 D1
Wester Fintray Aberds 245 A5
Wester Gruinards Highld 263 A7
Wester Lealty Highld 264 C2
Wester Milton Highld 253 A5
Wester Newburn Fife 220 D4
Wester Quarff Shetland 285 K6
Wester Skeld Shetland 285 J4
Westerdale Highld 280 C3
Westerdale N Yorks 159 A5
Westerfield Suff 88 C2
Westergate W Sus 20 B2
Westerham Kent 36 A2
Westerhope T & W 178 C3
Westerleigh S Glos 43 B6
Westerton Angus 233 C4
Westerton Durham 167 B5
Westerton W Sus 20 B1
Westerwick Shetland 285 J4
Westfield Cumb 162 B2
Westfield E Sus 23 A6
Westfield Hereford 79 C5
Westfield Highld 279 B6
Westfield N Lnrk 207 C5
Westfield Norf 103 A5
Westfield W Loth 208 C2
Westfields Dorset 15 A7
Westfields of Rattray Perth 231 D5
Westgate Durham 166 B2
Westgate N Lincs 141 C5

Westgate Norf 119 A5
Westgate Norf 119 A6
Westgate on Sea Kent 53 B5
Westhall Aberds 256 D1
Westhall Suff 105 C5
Westham Dorset 15 D6
Westham E Sus 22 B4
Westham Som 28 A4
Westhampnett W Sus 20 B1
Westhay Som 28 A4
Westhead Lancs 136 C3
Westhide Hereford 78 C3
Westhill Aberds 245 B5
Westhill Highld 252 B3
Westhope Hereford 78 B2
Westhope Shrops 94 C2
Westhorpe Lincs 117 B5
Westhorpe Suff 87 A6
Westhoughton Gtr Man 137 C5
Westhouse N Yorks 155 D5
Westhumble Sur 35 A4
Westing Shetland 284 C7
Westlake Devon 7 B5
Westleigh Devon 25 C5
Westleigh Devon 27 D5
Westleigh Gtr Man 137 C5
Westleton Suff 89 A5
Westley Shrops 94 A1
Westley Suff 87 A4
Westley Waterless Cambs 86 B2
Westlington Bucks 66 B2
Westlinton Cumb 175 B6
Westmarsh Kent 53 C4
Westmeston E Sus 21 A6
Westmill Herts 68 A3
Westminster London 49 B6
Westminster Cathedral
London 49 B5
Westmuir Angus 232 C1
Westness Orkney 282 E4
Westnewton Cumb 174 D4
Westnewton Northumb 198 C3
Westoe T & W 179 C5
Weston Bath 43 C6
Weston Ches 128 D2
Weston Devon 13 C6
Weston Dorset 15 D6
Weston Halton 127 A5
Weston Hants 33 C6
Weston Herts 85 D4
Weston Lincs 117 C5
Weston Notts 132 C2
Weston Northants 82 C2
Weston N Yorks 147 C5
Weston Shrops 94 B3
Weston Shrops 111 C4
Weston W Berks 46 B1
Weston Beggard Hereford 78 C3
Weston by Welland
Northants 99 B4
Weston Colville Cambs 86 B2
Weston Coyney Stoke 112 A3
Weston Favell Northants 83 A4
Weston Green Cambs 86 B2
Weston Green Norf 120 D3
Weston Heath Shrops 112 D1
Weston Hills Lincs 117 C5
Weston-in-Gordano
N Som 42 B3
Weston Jones Staffs 111 C6
Weston Longville Norf 120 D3
Weston Lullingfields
Shrops 110 C3
Weston-on-the-Green
Oxon 65 B6
Weston-on-Trent Derbys 114 C2
Weston Park Staffs 112 D2
Weston Patrick Hants 33 A5
Weston Rhyn Shrops 110 B1
Weston-Sub-Edge Glos 80 C4
Weston-super-Mare
N Som 42 C2
Weston Turville Bucks 66 B3
Weston under Lizard
Staffs 112 D2
Weston under Penyard
Hereford 62 A2
Weston under Wetherley
Warks 81 A6
Weston Underwood
Derbys 113 A6
Weston Underwood
M Keynes 83 B5
Westonbirt Glos 44 A2
Westonbirt Arboretum,
Tetbury Glos 44 A2

Westoncommon Shrops 110 C3
Westoning Beds 84 D2
Westonzoyland Som 28 B3
Westow N Yorks 149 A6
Westport Argyll 190 C2
Westport Som 28 D3
Westray Airport Orkney 282 B5
Westrigg W Loth 208 D2
Westruther Borders 197 B5
Westry Cambs 101 B5
Westville Notts 114 A3
Westward Cumb 175 D5
Westward Ho! Devon 25 C5
Westwell Kent 38 A1
Westwell Oxon 64 C3
Westwell Leacon Kent 38 A1
Westwick Cambs 85 A6
Westwick Durham 166 D3
Westwick Norf 121 C4
Westwood Devon 13 B5
Westwood Wilts 44 D2
Westwoodside N Lincs 141 C5
Wetheral Cumb 176 D2
Wetherby W Yorks 148 C3
Wetherby Racecourse
W Yorks 148 C3
Wetherden Suff 87 A6
Wetheringsett Suff 88 A2
Wethersfield Essex 86 D3
Wethersta Shetland 284 G5
Wetherup Street Suff 88 A2
Wetley Rocks Staffs 112 A3
Wettenhall Ches 127 C6
Wetton Staffs 129 D6
Wetwang E Yorks 150 B2
Wetwood Staffs 111 B6
Wexcombe Wilts 45 D6
Wexham Street Bucks 48 A2
Weybourne Norf 120 A3
Weybread Suff 104 C3
Weybridge Sur 48 C3
Weycroft Devon 14 B3
Weydale Highld 280 B3
Weyhill Hants 32 A2
Weymouth Dorset 15 D6
Weymouth Sea Life Park
Dorset 15 C6
Whaddon Bucks 83 D5
Whaddon Cambs 85 C5
Whaddon Glos 63 B4
Whaddon Wilts 31 C5
Whale Cumb 164 C3
Whaley Derbys 131 B5
Whaley Bridge Derbys 129 A5
Whaley Thorns Derbys 131 B5
Whaligoe Highld 281 D5
Whalley Lancs 146 D1
Whalsay Airport Shetland 284 G7
Whalton Northumb 178 A3
Wham N Yorks 146 A1
Whaplode Lincs 117 C6
Whaplode Drove Lincs 117 D6
Whaplode St Catherine
Lincs 117 C6
Wharfe N Yorks 146 A1
Wharles Lancs 144 D4
Wharncliffe Side S Yorks 139 D5
Wharram le Street
N Yorks 150 A1
Wharton Ches 127 C6
Wharton Green Ches 127 C6
Whashton N Yorks 157 A5
Whatcombe Dorset 16 A2
Whatcote Warks 81 C6
Whatfield Suff 87 C6
Whatley Som 14 A3
Whatley Som 30 A1
Whatlington E Sus 23 A5
Whatstandwell Derbys 130 D3
Whatton Notts 115 B5
Whauphill Dumfries 171 C6
Whaw N Yorks 156 A3
Wheatacre Norf 105 B5
Wheatcroft Derbys 131 D4
Wheathampstead Herts 68 B1
Wheathill Shrops 95 C4
Wheatley Devon 13 B4
Wheatley Hants 33 A6
Wheatley Oxon 65 C6
Wheatley S Yorks 140 C3
Wheatley W Yorks 138 A3
Wheatley Hill Durham 167 B6
Wheaton Aston Staffs 112 D2
Wheddon Cross Som 27 B4
Wheedlemont Aberds 255 D5
Wheelerstreet Sur 34 B2
Wheelock Ches 128 D2

Wheelock Heath Ches 128 D2
Wheelton Lancs 137 A5
Wheen Angus 232 A1
Wheldrake York 149 C5
Whelford Glos 64 D2
Whelpley Hill Bucks 67 C4
Whempstead Herts 68 A3
Whenby N Yorks 149 A5
Whepstead Suff 87 B4
Wherstead Suff 88 C2
Wherwell Hants 32 A2
Wheston Derbys 129 B6
Whetsted Kent 37 B4
Whetstone Leics 98 B2
Whicham Cumb 153 B2
Whichford Warks 81 D6
Whickham T & W 179 C4
Whiddon Down Devon 12 B1
Whigstreet Angus 232 D2
Whilton Northants 82 A3
Whim Farm Borders 195 A7
Whimble Devon 11 A4
Whimple Devon 13 B5
Whimpwell Green Norf 121 C5
Whinburgh Norf 103 A6
Whinnieliggate Dumfries 173 C5
Whinnyfold Aberds 257 C5
Whippingham I o W 18 B4
Whipsnade Beds 67 B5
Whipsnade Wild Animal
Park, Dunstable Beds 67 B5
Whipton Devon 13 B4
Whirlow S Yorks 130 A3
Whisby Lincs 133 C4
Whissendine Rutland 115 D6
Whissonsett Norf 119 C6
Whistlefield Argyll 215 C4
Whistlefield Argyll 215 C5
Whistley Green Wokingham 47 B5
Whiston Mers 136 D3
Whiston Northants 83 A5
Whiston Staffs 112 D2
Whiston Staffs 112 A4
Whiston S Yorks 131 A4
Whitbeck Cumb 153 B2
Whitbourne Hereford 79 B5
Whitbread Hop Farm,
Beltring Kent 37 B4
Whitburn T & W 179 C6
Whitburn W Loth 208 D2
Whitburn Colliery T & W 179 C6
Whitby Ches 126 B3
Whitby N Yorks 169 D6
Whitby Abbey N Yorks 169 D7
Whitbyheath Ches 126 B3
Whitchurch Bath 43 C5
Whitchurch Bucks 66 A2
Whitchurch Cardiff 41 C6
Whitchurch Devon 11 D5
Whitchurch Hants 32 A3
Whitchurch Hereford 62 B1
Whitchurch Oxon 47 B4
Whitchurch Pembs 54 B3
Whitchurch Shrops 111 A4
Whitchurch
Canonicorum Dorset 14 B3
Whitchurch Hill Oxon 47 B4
Whitcombe Dorset 15 C7
Whitcott Keysett Shrops 93 C6
White Coppice Lancs 137 B5
White Lackington Dorset 15 B7
White Ladies Aston Worcs 80 B2
White Lund Lancs 144 A4
White Mill Carms 58 C1
White Ness Shetland 285 J5
White Notley Essex 70 B1
White Pit Lincs 134 B3
White Post Notts 131 D6
White Post Farm Centre,
Farnsfield Notts 131 D6
White Rocks Hereford 61 A6
White Roding Essex 69 B5
White Waltham Windsor 47 B6
Whiteacen Moray 254 B3
Whiteacre Heath Warks 97 B5
Whitebridge Highld 240 A2
Whitebrook Mon 62 C1
Whiteburn Borders 197 B4
Whitecairn Dumfries 171 B4
Whitecairns Aberds 245 A6
Whitecastle S Lnrk 195 B5
Whitechapel Lancs 145 C5
Whitecleat Orkney 283 G6
Whitecraig E Loth 209 C6
Whitecroft Glos 62 C2
Whitecross Corn 9 D5
Whitecross Falk 208 C2

Whitecross Staffs 112 C2
Whiteface Highld 264 B3
Whitefarland N Ayrs 202 D3
Whitefaulds S Ayrs 192 E2
Whitefield Gtr Man 137 C7
Whitefield Perth 219 A6
Whiteford Aberds 256 D2
Whitegate Ches 127 C6
Whitehall Blkburn 137 A5
Whitehall W Sus 35 D4
Whitehall Village Orkney 282 E7
Whitehaven Cumb 162 C2
Whitehill Hants 33 B6
Whitehills Aberds 268 C1
Whitehills S Lnrk 205 C6
Whitehough Derbys 129 A5
Whitehouse Aberds 244 A3
Whitehouse Argyll 202 B3
Whiteinch Glasgow 205 B5
Whitekirk E Loth 210 B2
Whitelaw S Lnrk 205 D6
Whiteleas T & W 179 C5
Whiteley Bank I o W 19 C4
Whiteley Green Ches 129 B4
Whiteley Village Sur 48 C3
Whitemans Green W Sus 35 D6
Whitemire Moray 253 A5
Whitemoor Corn 5 B4
Whitemore Staffs 128 C3
Whitenap Hants 32 C2
Whiteoak Green Oxon 64 B4
Whiteparish Wilts 31 C6
Whiterashes Aberds 256 D3
Whiterow Highld 281 D5
Whiteshill Glos 63 C4
Whiteside Northumb 177 C5
Whiteside W Loth 208 D2
Whitesmith E Sus 22 A3
Whitestaunton Som 28 D2
Whitestone Devon 12 B3
Whitestone Devon 25 A5
Whitestone Warks 97 C6
Whitestones Aberds 268 D3
Whitestreet Green Suff 87 D5
Whitewall Corner N Yorks 159 D6
Whiteway Glos 63 B5
Whiteway Glos 63 B5
Whitewell Aberds 269 C4
Whitewell Lancs 145 C6
Whitewell Bottom Lancs 138 A1
Whiteworks Devon 11 D7
Whitfield Kent 39 A5
Whitfield Northants 82 D3
Whitfield Northumb 177 D5
Whitfield S Glos 62 D2
Whitford Devon 14 B2
Whitford Flint 125 B6
Whitgift E Yorks 141 A6
Whitgreave Staffs 112 C2
Whithorn Dumfries 171 C6
Whiting Bay N Ayrs 191 C6
Whitkirk W Yorks 148 D2
Whitland Carms 56 A1
Whitletts S Ayrs 192 C3
Whitley N Yorks 140 A3
Whitley Reading 47 B5
Whitley Wilts 44 C2
Whitley Bay T & W 179 B5
Whitley Chapel Northumb 178 D1
Whitley Lower W Yorks 139 B5
Whitley Row Kent 36 A2
Whitlock's End W Mid 96 D4
Whitminster Glos 62 C3
Whitmore Staffs 112 A2
Whitnage Devon 27 D5
Whitnash Warks 81 A6
Whitney-on-Wye Hereford 77 C6
Whitrigg Cumb 163 A5
Whitrigg Cumb 175 C5
Whitsbury Hants 31 D5
Whitsome Borders 198 A2
Whitson Newport 42 A2
Whitstable Kent 52 C3
Whitstone Corn 10 B3
Whittingham Northumb 188 B3
Whittingslow Shrops 94 C2
Whittington Derbys 131 B4
Whittington Glos 63 A6
Whittington Lancs 155 D5
Whittington Norf 102 B3
Whittington Shrops 110 B2
Whittington Staffs 95 C6
Whittington Staffs 97 A4
Whittington Worcs 80 B1
Whittle-le-Woods Lancs 137 A4
Whittlebury Northants 82 C3
Whittlesey Cambs 101 B4
Whittlesford Cambs 85 C6

Whittlestone Head
Blkburn 137 B6
Whitton Borders 187 A6
Whitton N Lincs 141 A7
Whitton Northumb 188 C3
Whitton Powys 77 A6
Whitton Shrops 94 D3
Whitton Stockton 167 C6
Whitton Suff 88 C2
Whittonditch Wilts 45 B6
Whittonstall Northumb 178 D2
Whitway Hants 46 D2
Whitwell Derbys 131 B5
Whitwell Herts 68 A1
Whitwell I o W 18 D4
Whitwell N Yorks 157 B6
Whitwell Rutland 99 A6
Whitwell-on-the-Hill
N Yorks 149 A6
Whitwell Street Norf 120 C3
Whitwick Leics 114 D2
Whitwood W Yorks 140 A2
Whitworth Lancs 138 B1
Whixall Shrops 111 B4
Whixley N Yorks 148 B3
Whoberley W Mid 97 D6
Whorlton Durham 166 D4
Whorlton N Yorks 158 A3
Whygate Northumb 177 B5
Whyle Hereford 78 A3
Whyteleafe Sur 35 A6
Wibdon Glos 62 D1
Wibsey W Yorks 147 D5
Wibtoft Leics 98 C1
Wichenford Worcs 79 A5
Wichling Kent 37 A7
Wick Bmouth 17 B5
Wick Devon 13 A6
Wick Highld 281 C5
Wick S Glos 43 B6
Wick Shetland 285 K6
Wick V Glam 40 D4
Wick Wilts 31 C5
Wick Worcs 80 C2
Wick Airport Highld 281 C5
Wick Hill Wokingham 47 C5
Wick St Lawrence N Som 42 C2
Wicken Cambs 102 D1
Wicken Northants 83 D4
Wicken Bonhunt Essex 85 D6
Wicken Green Village
Norf 119 B5
Wickenby Lincs 133 A5
Wickersley S Yorks 140 D2
Wickford Essex 70 D1
Wickham Hants 33 D4
Wickham W Berks 46 B1
Wickham Bishops Essex 70 B2
Wickham Market Suff 88 B4
Wickham St Paul Essex 87 D4
Wickham Skeith Suff 88 A1
Wickham Street Suff 86 B3
Wickham Street Suff 88 A1
Wickhambreux Kent 53 D4
Wickhambrook Suff 86 B3
Wickhamford Worcs 80 C3
Wickhampton Norf 105 A5
Wicklewood Norf 104 A1
Wickmere Norf 120 B3
Wicksteed Park,
Kettering Northants 99 D5
Wickwar S Glos 43 A6
Widdington Essex 86 D1
Widdrington Northumb 189 D5
Widdrington Station
Northumb 189 D5
Wide Open T & W 179 B4
Widecombe in the Moor
Devon 12 D2
Widegates Corn 6 B1
Widemouth Bay Corn 10 A3
Widewall Orkney 283 H5
Widford Essex 69 C6
Widford Herts 68 B4
Widham Wilts 45 A4
Widmer End Bucks 66 D3
Widmerpool Notts 115 C4
Widnes Halton 127 A5
Wigan Gtr Man 137 C4
Wigan Pier Gtr Man 137 C4
Wiggaton Devon 13 B6
Wiggenhall St Germans
Norf 118 D2

Wiggenhall St Mary Magdalen Norf 118 D2
Wiggenhall St Mary the Virgin Norf 118 D2
Wigginton Herts 67 B4
Wigginton Oxon 81 D6
Wigginton Staffs 97 A5
Wigginton York 149 B4
Wigglesworth N Yorks 146 B2
Wiggonby Cumb 175 C5
Wiggonholt W Sus 20 A3
Wighill N Yorks 148 C3
Wighton Norf 119 B6
Wigley Hants 32 D2
Wigmore Hereford 78 A2
Wigmore Medway 51 C5
Wigsley Notts 132 B3
Wigsthorpe Northants 100 C2
Wigston Leics 98 B3
Wigthorpe Notts 131 A5
Wigtoft Lincs 117 B5
Wigton Cumb 175 D5
Wigtown Dumfries 171 B6
Wigtwizzle S Yorks 139 D5
Wike W Yorks 148 C2
Wike Well End S Yorks 141 B4
Wilbarston Northants 99 C5
Wilberfoss E Yorks 149 B6
Wilberlee W Yorks 138 B3
Wilburton Cambs 101 D6
Wilby Norf 103 C6
Wilby Northants 83 A5
Wilby Suff 104 D3
Wilcot Wilts 45 C5
Wilcott Shrops 110 D2
Wilday Green Derbys 130 B3
Wildboarclough Ches 129 C4
Wilden Beds 84 B2
Wilden Worcs 95 D6
Wildfowl and Wetland Centre, Martin Mere Lancs 136 B3
Wildhern Hants 46 D1
Wildhill Herts 68 C2
Wildlife & Dinosaur Park, Combe Martin Devon 25 A6
Wildmoor Worcs 96 D2
Wildsworth Lincs 141 D6
Wilford Notts 114 B3
Wilkesley Ches 111 A5
Wilkhaven Highld 265 B5
Wilkieston W Loth 208 D4
Willand Devon 27 D5
Willaston Ches 126 B3
Willaston Ches 128 D1
Willen M Keynes 83 C5
Willenhall W Mid 97 D6
Willenhall W Mid 96 B2
Willerby E Yorks 150 D3
Willerby N Yorks 160 D4
Willersey Glos 80 D4
Willersley Hereford 77 C7
Willesborough Kent 38 A2
Willesborough Lees Kent 38 A2
Willesden London 49 A5
Willett Som 27 B6
Willey Shrops 95 B4
Willey Warks 98 C1
Willey Green Sur 34 A2
Williamscott Oxon 82 C1
Willian Herts 84 D4
Willingale Essex 69 C5
Willingdon E Sus 22 B3
Willingham Cambs 101 D6
Willingham by Stow Lincs 132 A3
Willington Beds 84 C3
Willington Derbys 113 C6
Willington Durham 167 B4
Willington T & W 179 C5
Willington Warks 81 D5
Willington Corner Ches 127 C5
Willisham Tye Suff 87 B6
Willitoft E Yorks 149 D6
Williton Som 27 A5
Willoughbridge Staffs 111 A6
Willoughby Lincs 135 B4
Willoughby Warks 82 A2
Willoughby-on-the-Wolds Notts 115 C4
Willoughby Waterleys Leics 98 B2
Willoughton Lincs 142 D1

Willows Green Essex 69 B7
Willsbridge S Glos 43 B5
Willsworthy Devon 11 C6
Wilmcote Warks 81 B4
Wilmington Devon 14 B2
Wilmington E Sus 22 B3
Wilmington Kent 50 B2
Wilminstone Devon 11 D5
Wilmslow Ches 128 A3
Wilnecote Staffs 97 A5
Wilpshire Lancs 145 D6
Wilsden W Yorks 147 D4
Wilsford Lincs 116 A3
Wilsford Wilts 45 D5
Wilsford Wilts 31 B5
Wilsill N Yorks 147 A5
Wilsley Pound Kent 37 C5
Wilsom Hants 33 B6
Wilson Leics 114 C2
Wilsontown S Lnrk 195 A4
Wilstead Beds 84 C2
Wilsthorpe Lincs 116 D3
Wilstone Herts 67 B4
Wilton Borders 186 B3
Wilton Cumb 162 C3
Wilton N Yorks 160 C2
Wilton Redcar 168 D3
Wilton Wilts 31 B4
Wilton Wilts 45 C6
Wilton House, Salisbury Wilts 31 B5
Wimbish Essex 86 D1
Wimbish Green Essex 86 D2
Wimblebury Staffs 112 D4
Wimbledon London 49 B5
Wimbledon All England Tennis Club London 49 B5
Wimblington Cambs 101 B6
Wimborne Minster Dorset 17 B4
Wimborne Minster Dorset 17 B4
Wimborne St Giles Dorset 31 D4
Wimbotsham Norf 102 A2
Wimpole Hall and Home Farm, Royston Cambs 85 B5
Wimpson Soton 32 D2
Wimpstone Warks 81 C5
Wincanton Som 29 C7
Wincanton Racecourse Som 29 C7
Wincham Ches 128 B1
Winchburgh W Loth 208 C3
Winchcombe Glos 63 A6
Winchelsea E Sus 23 A7
Winchelsea Beach E Sus 23 A7
Winchester Hants 32 C3
Winchester Cathedral Hants 32 C3
Winchet Hill Kent 37 B5
Winchfield Hants 47 D5
Winchmore Hill Bucks 67 D4
Winchmore Hill London 68 D3
Wincle Ches 129 C4
Wincobank S Yorks 140 D1
Windermere Cumb 154 B3
Winderton Warks 81 C6
Windhill Highld 252 B1
Windhouse Shetland 284 D6
Windlehurst Gtr Man 129 A4
Windlesham Sur 48 C2
Windley Derbys 113 A7
Windmill Hill E Sus 22 A4
Windmill Hill Som 28 D3
Windrush Glos 64 B2
Windsor N Lincs 141 B5
Windsor Windsor 48 B2
Windsor Castle Windsor 48 B2
Windsor Racecourse Windsor 48 B2
Windsoredge Glos 63 C4
Windygates Fife 220 D3
Windyknowe W Loth 208 D2
Windywalls Borders 197 C6
Wineham W Sus 35 D5
Winestead E Yorks 143 A4
Winewall Lancs 146 C3
Winfarthing Norf 104 C2
Winford I o W 19 C4
Winford N Som 43 C4
Winforton Hereford 77 C6
Winfrith Newburgh Dorset 16 C2
Wing Bucks 66 A3
Wing Rutland 99 A5
Wingate Durham 168 B2
Wingates Gtr Man 137 C5
Wingates Northumb 189 D4
Wingerworth Derbys 130 C3
Wingfield Beds 67 A5

Wingfield Suff 104 D3
Wingfield Wilts 44 D2
Wingham Kent 53 D4
Wingmore Kent 38 A3
Wingrave Bucks 66 B3
Winkburn Notts 132 D2
Winkfield Brack 48 B2
Winkfield Row Brack 48 B1
Winkhill Staffs 129 D5
Winklebury Hants 47 D4
Winkleigh Devon 12 A1
Winksley N Yorks 157 D6
Winkton Dorset 17 B5
Winlaton T & W 178 C3
Winless Highld 281 C5
Winmarleigh Lancs 145 C4
Winnal Hereford 78 D2
Winnall Hants 32 C3
Winnersh Wokingham 47 B5
Winscales Cumb 162 B3
Winscombe N Som 42 D3
Winsford Ches 127 C6
Winsford Som 27 B4
Winsham Som 14 A3
Winshill Staffs 113 C6
Winskill Cumb 164 B3
Winslade Hants 33 A5
Winsley Wilts 44 C2
Winslow Bucks 66 A2
Winson Glos 64 C1
Winson Green W Mid 96 C3
Winsor Hants 32 D2
Winster Cumb 154 B3
Winster Derbys 130 C2
Winston Durham 166 D4
Winston Suff 88 A2
Winston Green Suff 88 A2
Winstone Glos 63 C5
Winswell Devon 25 D5
Winter Gardens Essex 51 A4
Winterborne Clenston Dorset 16 A2
Winterborne Herringston Dorset 15 C6
Winterborne Houghton Dorset 16 A2
Winterborne Kingston Dorset 16 B2
Winterborne Monkton Dorset 15 C6
Winterborne Monkton Wilts 45 B5
Winterborne Stickland Dorset 16 A2
Winterborne Whitechurch Dorset 16 A2
Winterborne Zelston Dorset 16 B2
Winterbourne S Glos 43 A5
Winterbourne W Berks 46 B2
Winterbourne Abbas Dorset 15 B6
Winterbourne Dauntsey Wilts 31 B5
Winterbourne Down S Glos 43 B5
Winterbourne Earls Wilts 31 B5
Winterbourne Gunner Wilts 31 B5
Winterbourne Steepleton Dorset 15 C6
Winterbourne Stoke Wilts 31 A4
Winterburn N Yorks 146 B3
Winteringham N Lincs 142 A1
Winterley Ches 128 D2
Wintersett W Yorks 140 B1
Wintershill Hants 32 D4
Winterton N Lincs 142 B1
Winterton-on-Sea Norf 121 D6
Winthorpe Lincs 135 C5
Winthorpe Notts 132 D3
Winton Bmouth 17 B4
Winton Cumb 165 D5
Winton N Yorks 158 B3
Wintringham N Yorks 160 D2
Winwick Cambs 100 C3
Winwick Northants 98 D3
Winwick Warr 137 D5
Wirksworth Derbys 130 D2
Wirksworth Moor Derbys 130 D3
Wirswall Ches 111 A4
Wisbech Cambs 101 A6
Wisbech St Mary Cambs 101 A6
Wisborough Green W Sus 34 D3
Wiseton Notts 132 A2
Wishaw N Lnrk 194 A2
Wishaw Warks 97 B4

Wisley Sur 34 A3
Wispington Lincs 134 B2
Wissenden Kent 37 B7
Wissett Suff 105 D4
Wistanstow Shrops 94 C2
Wistanswick Shrops 111 C5
Wistaston Ches 128 D1
Wistaston Green Ches 128 D1
Wiston Pembs 55 C6
Wiston S Lnrk 195 C4
Wiston W Sus 21 A4
Wistow Cambs 101 C4
Wistow N Yorks 149 D4
Wiswell Lancs 146 D1
Witcham Cambs 101 C6
Witchampton Dorset 16 A3
Witchford Cambs 101 D7
Witham Essex 70 B2
Witham Friary Som 30 A1
Witham on the Hill Lincs 116 D3
Withcall Lincs 134 A2
Withdean Brighton 21 B6
Witherenden Hill E Sus 36 D4
Witheridge Devon 26 D3
Witherley Leics 97 B6
Withern Lincs 135 A4
Withernsea E Yorks 143 A5
Withernwick E Yorks 151 C4
Withersdale Street Suff 104 C3
Withersfield Suff 86 C2
Witherslack Cumb 154 C3
Withiel Corn 5 A4
Withiel Florey Som 27 B4
Withington Glos 63 B6
Withington Gtr Man 138 D1
Withington Hereford 78 C3
Withington Shrops 111 D4
Withington Staffs 112 B4
Withington Green Ches 128 B3
Withleigh Devon 27 D4
Withnell Lancs 137 A5
Withybrook Warks 98 C1
Withycombe Som 27 A5
Withycombe Raleigh Devon 13 C5
Withyham E Sus 36 C2
Withypool Som 26 B3
Witley Sur 34 C2
Witnesham Suff 88 B2
Witney Oxon 65 B4
Wittering P'boro 100 A2
Wittersham Kent 37 D6
Witton Angus 232 A3
Witton Worcs 80 A1
Witton Bridge Norf 121 B5
Witton Gilbert Durham 167 A5
Witton-le-Wear Durham 167 B4
Witton Park Durham 167 B4
Wiveliscombe Som 27 C5
Wivelrod Hants 33 B5
Wivelsfield E Sus 35 D6
Wivelsfield Green E Sus 35 D6
Wivenhoe Essex 71 A4
Wivenhoe Cross Essex 71 A4
Wiveton Norf 120 A2
Wix Essex 71 A5
Wixford Warks 80 B3
Wixhill Shrops 111 C4
Wixoe Suff 86 C3
Woburn Beds 83 D6
Woburn Abbey, Woburn Beds 83 D6
Woburn Sands M Keynes 83 D6
Woburn Wild Animal Kingdom Beds 83 D6
Wokefield Park W Berks 47 C4
Woking Sur 34 A3
Wokingham Wokingham 47 C6
Wolborough Devon 12 D3
Wold Newton E Yorks 160 D4
Wold Newton NE Lincs 143 D4
Woldingham Sur 35 A6
Wolfclyde S Lnrk 195 C5
Wolferton Norf 118 C3
Wolfhill Perth 219 A6
Wolf's Castle Pembs 55 B5
Wolfsdale Pembs 55 B5
Woll Borders 186 A3
Wollaston Northants 83 A6
Wollaston Shrops 110 D2
Wollaton Nottingham 114 B3
Wollaton Hall Nottingham 114 B3
Wollerton Shrops 111 B5
Wollescote W Mid 96 C2
Wolsingham Durham 166 B3
Wolstanton Staffs 112 A2
Wolston Warks 97 D7

Wolvercote Oxon 65 C5
Wolverhampton W Mid 96 B2
Wolverhampton Racecourse W Mid 96 A2
Wolverley Shrops 110 B3
Wolverley Worcs 95 D6
Wolverton Hants 46 D3
Wolverton M Keynes 83 C5
Wolverton Warks 81 A5
Wolverton Common Hants 46 D3
Wolvesnewton Mon 61 D6
Wolvey Warks 98 C1
Wolviston Stockton 168 C2
Wombleton N Yorks 159 C5
Wombourne Staffs 95 B6
Wombwell S Yorks 140 C1
Womenswold Kent 53 D4
Womersley N Yorks 140 B3
Wonastow Mon 61 B6
Wonersh Sur 34 B3
Wonson Devon 12 C1
Wonston Hants 32 B3
Wooburn Bucks 48 A2
Wooburn Green Bucks 48 A2
Wood Dalling Norf 120 C2
Wood End Herts 68 A3
Wood End Warks 96 D4
Wood End Warks 97 B5
Wood Enderby Lincs 134 C2
Wood Field Sur 35 A4
Wood Green London 68 D3
Wood Green Animal Shelter, Godmanchester Cambs 85 A4
Wood Hayes W Mid 96 A2
Wood Lanes Ches 129 A4
Wood Norton Norf 120 C2
Wood Street Norf 121 C5
Wood Street Sur 34 A2
Wood Walton Cambs 100 C4
Woodacott Devon 11 A4
Woodale N Yorks 156 D4
Woodbank Argyll 190 D2
Woodbastwick Norf 121 D5
Woodbeck Notts 132 B2
Woodborough Notts 115 A4
Woodborough Wilts 45 D5
Woodbridge Dorset 29 D7
Woodbridge Suff 88 C3
Woodbury Devon 13 C5
Woodbury Salterton Devon 13 C5
Woodchester Glos 63 C4
Woodchurch Kent 38 B1
Woodchurch Mers 126 A2
Woodcombe Som 27 A4
Woodcote Oxon 47 A4
Woodcott Hants 46 D2
Woodcroft Glos 62 D1
Woodcutts Dorset 30 D3
Woodditton Cambs 86 B2
Woodeaton Oxon 65 B6
Woodend Cumb 153 A2
Woodend Northants 82 C3
Woodend W Sus 19 A7
Woodend Green Northants 82 C3
Woodfalls Wilts 31 C5
Woodfield Oxon 65 A6
Woodfield S Ayrs 192 C3
Woodford Corn 24 D3
Woodford Devon 8 B1
Woodford Glos 62 D2
Woodford London 68 D4
Woodford Gtr Man 128 A3
Woodford Northants 99 D6
Woodford Bridge London 68 D4
Woodford Halse Northants 82 B2
Woodgate Norf 120 D2
Woodgate W Mid 96 C2
Woodgate Worcs 80 A2
Woodgate W Sus 20 B2
Woodgreen Hants 31 D5
Woodhall Herts 68 B2
Woodhall Inclyd 204 A3
Woodhall N Yorks 156 B3
Woodhall Spa Lincs 134 C1
Woodham Sur 48 C3
Woodham Ferrers Essex 70 D1
Woodham Mortimer Essex 70 C2
Woodham Walter Essex 70 C2
Woodhaven Fife 220 B4
Woodhead Aberds 256 C2
Woodhey Gtr Man 137 B6
Woodhill Shrops 95 C5
Woodhorn Northumb 179 A4
Woodhouse Leics 114 D3
Woodhouse N Lincs 141 C5
Woodhouse S Yorks 131 A4
Woodhouse W Yorks 148 D1

Woodhouse W Yorks 140 A1
Woodhouse Eaves Leics 114 D3
Woodhouse Park Gtr Man 128 A3
Woodhouselee Midloth 209 D5
Woodhouselees Dumfries 175 A6
Woodhouses Staffs 113 D5
Woodhurst Cambs 101 D5
Woodingdean Brighton 21 B6
Woodkirk W Yorks 139 A5
Woodland Devon 8 A1
Woodland Durham 166 C3
Woodland Leisure Park, Dartmouth Devon 8 B2
Woodlands Aberds 245 C4
Woodlands Dorset 17 A4
Woodlands Hants 32 D2
Woodlands Highld 264 D1
Woodlands N Yorks 148 B2
Woodlands S Yorks 140 C3
Woodlands Park Windsor 47 B6
Woodlands St Mary W Berks 46 B1
Woodlane Staffs 113 C5
Woodleigh Devon 7 C6
Woodlesford W Yorks 139 A6
Woodley Gtr Man 138 D2
Woodley Wokingham 47 B5
Woodmancote Glos 62 D3
Woodmancote Glos 63 C6
Woodmancote Glos 63 A5
Woodmancote W Sus 19 A6
Woodmancote W Sus 21 A5
Woodmancott Hants 33 A4
Woodmansey E Yorks 150 D3
Woodmansterne Sur 35 A5
Woodminton Wilts 31 C4
Woodnesborough Kent 53 D5
Woodnewton Northants 100 B2
Woodplumpton Lancs 145 D5
Woodrising Norf 103 A5
Wood's Green E Sus 36 C4
Woodseaves Shrops 111 B5
Woodseaves Staffs 112 C1
Woodsend Wilts 45 B6
Woodsetts S Yorks 131 A5
Woodsford Dorset 16 B1
Woodside Aberdeen 245 B6
Woodside Aberds 257 B5
Woodside Brack 48 B2
Woodside Fife 220 D4
Woodside Hants 18 B2
Woodside Herts 68 C2
Woodside Perth 220 A2
Woodside Farm and Wildfowl Park, Luton Beds 67 B5
Woodside of Arbeadie Aberds 245 C4
Woodstock Oxon 65 B5
Woodstock Pembs 55 B6
Woodthorpe Derbys 131 B4
Woodthorpe Leics 114 D3
Woodthorpe Lincs 135 A4
Woodthorpe York 149 C4
Woodton Norf 104 B3
Woodtown Devon 25 C5
Woodtown Devon 25 C5
Woodvale Mers 136 B2
Woodville Derbys 113 D7
Woodyates Dorset 31 D4
Woofferton Shrops 78 A3
Wookey Som 29 A5
Wookey Hole Som 29 A5
Wookey Hole Caves & Papermill, Wells Som 29 A5
Wool Dorset 16 C2
Woolacombe Devon 25 A5
Woolage Green Kent 39 A4
Woolaston Glos 62 D1
Woolavington Som 28 A3
Woolbeding W Sus 34 D1
Wooldale W Yorks 139 C4
Wooler Northumb 188 A2
Woolfardisworthy Devon 24 C4
Woolfardisworthy Devon 12 A3
Woolfords Cottages S Lnrk 195 A5
Woolhampton W Berks 46 C3
Woolhope Hereford 79 D4
Woolhope Cockshoot Hereford 79 D4
Woolland Dorset 16 A1
Woollaton Devon 25 D5
Woolley Bath 43 C6
Woolley Cambs 100 D3
Woolley Corn 24 D3
Woolley Derbys 130 C3
Woolley W Yorks 139 B6
Woolmer Green Herts 68 B2
Woolmere Green Worcs 80 A2
Woolpit Suff 87 A5
Woolscott Warks 82 A1
Woolsington T & W 178 C3
Woolstanwood Ches 128 D1
Woolstaston Shrops 94 B2
Woolsthorpe Lincs 115 B6
Woolsthorpe Lincs 116 C2
Woolston Devon 7 C6
Woolston Shrops 94 C2
Woolston Shrops 110 C2
Woolston Soton 32 D3
Woolston Warr 127 A6
Woolstone M Keynes 83 D5
Woolstone Oxon 45 A6
Woolton Mers 127 A4
Woolton Hill Hants 46 C2
Woolverstone Suff 88 D2
Woolverton Som 44 D1
Woolwich London 50 B1
Woolwich Ferry London 50 B1
Woonton Hereford 78 B1
Wooperton Northumb 188 A3
Woore Shrops 111 A6
Wootten Green Suff 104 D3
Wootton Beds 84 C2
Wootton Hants 17 B6
Wootton Hereford 78 B1
Wootton Kent 39 A4
Wootton N Lincs 142 B2
Wootton Northants 83 B4
Wootton Oxon 65 B5
Wootton Oxon 65 C5
Wootton Shrops 94 D2
Wootton Shrops 110 C2
Wootton Staffs 112 C2
Wootton Staffs 113 A5
Wootton Bassett Wilts 45 A4
Wootton Bridge I o W 18 B4
Wootton Common I o W 18 B4
Wootton Courtenay Som 27 A4
Wootton Fitzpaine Dorset 14 B3
Wootton Rivers Wilts 45 C5
Wootton St Lawrence Hants 46 D3
Wootton Wawen Warks 81 A4
Worcester Worcs 79 B6
Worcester Cathedral Worcs 79 B6
Worcester Park London 49 C5
Worcester Racecourse Worcs 79 B6
Wordsley W Mid 96 C1
Worfield Shrops 95 B5
Work Orkney 282 F5
Workington Cumb 162 B2
Worksop Notts 131 B5
Worlaby N Lincs 142 B2
World of James Herriot N Yorks 158 C3
World's End W Berks 46 B2
Worle N Som 42 C2
Worleston Ches 127 D6
Worlingham Suff 105 C5
Worlington Suff 102 D2
Worlingworth Suff 88 A3
Wormald Green N Yorks 148 A2
Wormbridge Hereford 78 D2
Wormegay Norf 118 D3
Wormelow Tump Hereford 78 D2
Wormhill Derbys 129 B6
Wormingford Essex 87 D5
Worminghall Bucks 66 C1
Wormington Glos 80 D3
Worminster Som 29 A5
Wormit Fife 220 B3
Wormleighton Warks 82 B1
Wormley Herts 68 C3
Wormley Sur 34 C2
Wormley West End Herts 68 C3
Wormshill Kent 37 A6
Wormsley Hereford 78 C2
Worplesdon Sur 34 A2
Worrall S Yorks 139 D6
Worsbrough S Yorks 139 C6
Worsbrough Common S Yorks 139 C6
Worsley Gtr Man 137 C6
Worstead Norf 121 C5
Worsthorne Lancs 146 D2
Worston Lancs 146 C1
Worswell Devon 7 C4
Worth Kent 53 D5
Worth W Sus 35 C6
Worth Matravers Dorset 16 D3
Wortham Suff 104 D1
Worthen Shrops 94 A1
Worthenbury Wrex 110 A3
Worthing Norf 120 D1
Worthing W Sus 21 B4
Worthington Leics 114 C2
Worting Hants 47 D4
Wortley S Yorks 139 D6
Wortley W Yorks 147 D6
Worton N Yorks 156 B3
Worton Wilts 44 D3
Wortwell Norf 104 C3
Wotherton Shrops 93 A6
Wotter Devon 7 A4
Wotton Sur 35 B4
Wotton-under-Edge Glos 62 D3
Wotton Underwood Bucks 66 B1
Woughton on the Green M Keynes 83 D5
Wouldham Kent 51 C4
Wrabness Essex 88 D2
Wrafton Devon 25 B5
Wragby Lincs 133 B6
Wragby W Yorks 140 B2
Wragholme Lincs 143 D5
Wramplingham Norf 104 A2
Wrangbrook W Yorks 140 B2
Wrangham Aberds 256 C1
Wrangle Lincs 135 D4
Wrangle Bank Lincs 135 D4
Wrangle Lowgate Lincs 135 D4
Wrangway Som 27 D6
Wrantage Som 28 C3
Wrawby N Lincs 142 C2
Wraxall Dorset 15 A5
Wraxall N Som 42 B3
Wraxall Som 29 B6
Wray Lancs 145 A6
Wraysbury Windsor 48 B3
Wrayton Lancs 155 D5
Wrea Green Lancs 144 D3
Wreay Cumb 164 C2
Wreay Cumb 164 A2
Wrecclesham Sur 34 B1
Wrecsam = Wrexham Wrex 126 D3
Wrekenton T & W 179 D4
Wrelton N Yorks 159 C6
Wrenbury Ches 111 A4
Wrench Green N Yorks 160 C3
Wreningham Norf 104 B2
Wrentham Suff 105 C5
Wrenthorpe W Yorks 139 A6
Wrentnall Shrops 94 A2
Wressle E Yorks 149 D6
Wressle N Lincs 142 C1
Wrestlingworth Beds 85 C4
Wretham Norf 103 C5
Wretton Norf 102 B2
Wrexham = Wrecsam Wrex 126 D3
Wrexham Industrial Estate Wrex 110 A2
Wribbenhall Worcs 95 D5
Wrightington Bar Lancs 136 B4
Wrinehill Staffs 111 A6
Wrington N Som 42 C3
Writhlington Bath 43 D6
Writtle Essex 69 C6
Wrockwardine Telford 111 D5
Wroot N Lincs 141 C5
Wrotham Kent 36 A4
Wrotham Heath Kent 36 A4
Wroughton Swindon 45 A5
Wroxall I o W 19 D4
Wroxall Warks 97 D5
Wroxeter Shrops 94 A3
Wroxham Norf 121 D5
Wroxham Barns, Hoveton Norf 121 C5
Wroxton Oxon 81 C7
Wyaston Derbys 113 A5
Wyberton Lincs 117 A6
Wyboston Beds 84 B3
Wybunbury Ches 111 A6
Wych Cross E Sus 36 C2
Wychbold Worcs 80 A2
Wyck Hants 33 B6
Wyck Rissington Glos 64 A2
Wycoller Lancs 146 D3
Wycomb Leics 115 C5
Wycombe Marsh Bucks 66 D3
Wyddial Herts 85 D5
Wye Kent 38 A2
Wyesham Mon 61 B7
Wyfordby Leics 115 D5
Wyke Dorset 30 C1
Wyke Shrops 95 A4
Wyke Sur 34 A2
Wyke W Yorks 139 A4
Wyke Regis Dorset 15 D6
Wykeham N Yorks 160 C3
Wykeham N Yorks 159 D7
Wyken W Mid 97 C6
Wykey Shrops 110 C2
Wylam Northumb 178 C3
Wylde Green W Mid 96 B4
Wyllie Caerph 41 B6
Wylye Wilts 31 B4
Wymering Ptsmth 19 A5
Wymeswold Leics 115 C4
Wymington Beds 83 A6
Wymondham Leics 115 D6
Wymondham Norf 104 A2
Wyndham Bridgend 40 B4
Wynford Eagle Dorset 15 B5
Wyng Orkney 283 H4
Wynyard Village Stockton 168 C2
Wyre Piddle Worcs 80 C2
Wysall Notts 115 C4
Wythall Worcs 96 D3
Wytham Oxon 65 C5
Wythburn Cumb 163 C6
Wythenshawe Gtr Man 128 A3
Wythop Mill Cumb 163 B4
Wyton Cambs 101 D4
Wyverstone Suff 87 A6
Wyverstone Street Suff 87 A6
Wyville Lincs 116 C1
Wyvis Lodge Highld 263 C6

Y

Y Bala = Bala Gwyn 108 B4
Y Barri = Barry V Glam 41 E6
Y Bont-Faen = Cowbridge V Glam 41 D4
Y Drenewydd = Newtown Powys 93 B5
Y Felinheli Gwyn 123 D5
Y Fenni = Abergavenny Mon 61 B4
Y Fflint = Flint Flint 126 B2
Y Ffôr Gwyn 106 C3
Y-Ffrith Denb 125 A5
Y Gelli Gandryll = Hay-on-Wye Powys 77 C6
Y Mwmbwls = The Mumbles Swansea 57 D6
Y Pîl = Pyle Bridgend 40 C3
Y Rhws = Rhoose V Glam 41 E5
Y Rhyl = Rhyl Denb 125 A5
Y Trallwng = Welshpool Powys 93 A6
Y Waun = Chirk Wrex 110 B1
Yaddlethorpe N Lincs 141 C6
Yafford I o W 18 C3
Yafforth N Yorks 158 B2
Yalding Kent 37 A4
Yanworth Glos 63 B6
Yapham E Yorks 149 B6
Yapton W Sus 20 B2
Yarburgh Lincs 143 D5
Yarcombe Devon 14 A2
Yard Som 27 B5
Yardley W Mid 96 C4
Yardley Gobion Northants 83 C4
Yardley Hastings Northants 83 B5
Yardro Powys 77 B6
Yarkhill Hereford 79 C4
Yarlet Staffs 112 C3
Yarlington Som 29 C6
Yarlside Cumb 153 D3
Yarm Stockton 168 D2
Yarmouth I o W 18 C2
Yarmouth Racecourse Norf 121 D7
Yarnbrook Wilts 44 D2
Yarnfield Staffs 112 B2
Yarnscombe Devon 25 C6
Yarnton Oxon 65 B5
Yarpole Hereford 78 A2
Yarrow Borders 196 D2
Yarrow Feus Borders 196 D2
Yarsop Hereford 78 C2
Yarwell Northants 100 B2
Yate S Glos 43 A6
Yateley Hants 47 C6
Yatesbury Wilts 45 B4
Yattendon W Berks 46 B3
Yatton Hereford 78 A2
Yatton N Som 42 C3
Yatton Keynell Wilts 44 B2
Yaverland I o W 19 C5
Yaxham Norf 120 D2
Yaxley Cambs 100 B3
Yaxley Suff 104 D2
Yazor Hereford 78 C2
Yeading London 48 A4
Yeadon W Yorks 147 C6
Yealand Conyers Lancs 154 D4
Yealand Redmayne Lancs 154 D4
Yealmpton Devon 7 B4
Yearby Redcar 168 C4
Yearsley N Yorks 159 D4
Yeaton Shrops 110 D3
Yeaveley Derbys 113 A5
Yedingham N Yorks 160 D2
Yeldon Beds 84 A2
Yelford Oxon 65 C4
Yelland Devon 25 B5
Yelling Cambs 85 A4
Yelvertoft Northants 98 D2
Yelverton Devon 7 A4
Yelverton Norf 104 A3
Yenston Som 29 C7
Yeo Mill Devon 26 C3
Yeoford Devon 12 B2
Yeolmbridge Corn 10 C4
Yeovil Som 29 D5
Yeovil Marsh Som 29 D5
Yeovilton Som 29 C5
Yerbeston Pembs 55 D6
Yesnaby Orkney 282 F3
Yetlington Northumb 188 C3
Yetminster Dorset 29 D5
Yettington Devon 13 C5
Yetts o'Muckhart Clack 219 D5
Yieldshields S Lnrk 194 A3
Yiewsley London 48 A3
Ynys-meudwy Neath 59 E4
Ynysboeth Rhondda 41 B5
Ynysddu Caerph 41 B6
Ynysgyfflog Gwyn 90 A4
Ynyshir Rhondda 41 B5
Ynyslas Ceredig 90 C4
Ynystawe Swansea 40 A1
Ynysybwl Rhondda 41 B5
Yockenthwaite N Yorks 156 D3
Yockleton Shrops 110 D2
Yokefleet E Yorks 141 A6
Yoker Glasgow 205 B5
Yonder Bognie Aberds 255 B6
York York 149 B4
York Castle Museum York 149 B5
York Minster York 149 B5
York Racecourse York 149 C4
York Town Sur 47 C6
Yorkletts Kent 52 C2
Yorkley Glos 62 C2
Yorkshire Museum York 149 B4
Yorkshire Sculpture Park, Wakefield W Yorks 139 B5
Yorton Shrops 111 C4
Youlgreave Derbys 130 C2
Youlstone Devon 24 D3
Youlthorpe E Yorks 149 B6
Youlton N Yorks 148 A3
Young Wood Lincs 133 B6
Young's End Essex 70 B1
Yoxall Staffs 113 D5
Yoxford Suff 89 A4
Yr Hôb = Hope Flint 126 D3
Yr Wyddgrug = Mold Flint 126 C2
Ysbyty-Cynfyn Ceredig 75 A6
Ysbyty Ifan Conwy 108 A3
Ysbyty Ystwyth Ceredig 75 A6
Ysceifiog Flint 125 B6
Yspitty Carms 57 C5
Ystalyfera Neath 59 E4
Ystrad Rhondda 41 B4
Ystrad Aeron Ceredig 75 C4
Ystrad-mynach Caerph 41 B6
Ystradfellte Powys 59 D6
Ystradffin Carms 76 C1
Ystradgynlais Powys 59 D4
Ystradmeurig Ceredig 75 B6
Ystradowen Carms 59 D4
Ystradowen V Glam 41 D5
Ystumtuen Ceredig 75 A6
Ythanbank Aberds 257 C4
Ythanwells Aberds 256 C1
Ythsie Aberds 256 C3

Z

Zeal Monachorum Devon 12 A2
Zeals Wilts 30 B1
Zelah Corn 4 B3
Zennor Corn 2 B2

Notes

Notes

Notes

Notes